D1551244

Greenwich Readers : 6

The Sociology of Crime and Deviance: Selected Issues

The Sociology of Crime and Deviance: Selected Issues

edited by

SUSAN CAFFREY

SENIOR LECTURER IN SOCIOLOGY
UNIVERSITY OF GREENWICH

with
GARY MUNDY

Greenwich University Press

First published in 1995 by
Greenwich University Press
Unit 42
Dartford Trade Park
Hawley Road
Dartford
Kent DA1 1PF
United Kingdom

British Library Cataloguing-in-Publication Data
A CIP catalogue record for this book is available from the British Library

ISBN 1 874529 52 3

Designed and produced for Greenwich University Press by
Angela Allwright and Kirsten Brown.

Printed in Great Britain by The Bath Press, Avon.

Contents

Introduction

This anthology is intended to give the reader an insight into a variety of the theoretical approaches to crime and deviance in contemporary society, addressing some common-sense assumptions and critically analysing them. The collection focuses attention upon important but selected themes within the area of the Sociology of Crime and Deviance. These are divided into four broad areas: the social construction of crime and the production and reproduction of criminal statistics; crime and gender, with particular attention focused upon women as offenders and victims; a critical examination of the criminal justice system, in particular police methods and courtroom procedures; and the place of the mass media in the social construction of crime and deviance. Attention is given to the various explanations that focus upon why crimes are differentiated between gender, age and ethnicity; the role which the media play in representing criminal and deviant behaviour in a variety of forms; the problems involved in using statistics in any analysis of crime; and the institutional structure of the criminal justice system and how it processes offenders from their initial apprehension to the punishments which it subsequently delivers.

The social construction of crime

Realist criminology[1] sees the value of the interactionist approach to criminal statistics; that is, the collection of criminal statistics is a social process and because of this they must be regarded as subject to interpretation. Nonetheless, realist criminologists argue that for those who wish to theorise about crime it is necessary to obtain a detailed knowledge about the 'facts' of crime. It is not possible to ignore the criminal statistics that have been produced; they may not reflect reality but they do give us a partial view of it.

The extracts by Mike Maguire, Malcolm Young and the article by Antonia Cretney *et al.* all examine the various problems of a statistical analysis of crime. All give a good example of how certain crimes, in this case violence against the person, can often go unrecorded by the police and thus disappear from the official statistics. These pieces should alert one to the problems of using official statistics in any analysis of crime, although they do not discount the use of statistics *per se*. The realist trend in criminology has emphasised the essential nature of empirical work and statistical analysis in understanding patterns of criminality. The use of methods such as victimisation studies is a way of obtaining information which is truer to the object of criminological study, although even these are shown to have their own problems and limitations.

Mike Maguire's *Crime Statistics, Patterns and Trends* demonstrates the relationship between the way in which criminological research is done and the theory which emerges from this. Maguire gives an account of the recent developments within criminological methodology and how this, in turn, has shaped the types of concerns which criminological theory has taken on. In doing so, he shows the importance attached to the way in which facts and figures are collected and recorded and how this affects the way in which the problem of crime is perceived. Malcolm Young's *Crime or Offence? A Structuring Principle* is particularly interesting in this respect as the author is himself an ex-member of the police force. Young displays the various strategies which the police force have employed in constructing clear up rates. For example, he highlights the way in which 'clear-up' squads often visited persons already convicted of crimes in order to attribute other unsolved offences to them. As he points out, these crimes are often 'solved' falsely as the admission of further offences, particularly when not especially severe, rarely result in further charges being brought. Again, this demonstrates the problems involved in using 'official' statistics in criminological research.

Crime, gender and gender relations

When looking at gender and crime we need to pay attention to the way in which gender is singled out as an important variable in any analysis of criminal and deviant activity. Within this reader focus is given to the relationship between gender and crime, in particular to the way in which women are seen as both perpetrators and victims of criminal and deviant activity. The criminality of women and how criminology has traditionally explained this is discussed in Frances Heidensohn's *Understanding Female Criminality*. She highlights the way in which the early positivist criminology, as expressed by criminologists like Lombroso, treated women as though they were a race apart. When dealing with women's criminality Heidensohn shows how similar assumptions operated within other theoretical positions to that which emerged from the physiological explanations for criminality. She also highlights how similar assumptions operate within the theory which emerged when physiological explanations for criminality had been all but discredited. The work of Pollak for example, which at a time when criminological theory was dominated by various shades of social positivism, still tended to treat women as being determined by their physiological make-up.

Although primary focus is given to women and crime, in Paul Willis' extract attention is focused upon the way in which young men give symbolic meanings to activities such as fighting, etc. This social group has been singled out by criminological theory, the general public and policy-makers. Willis examines the everyday life of a group of young men in the West Midlands and attempts to understand their behaviour through the meaning which it has for them. He portrays a world in which excessive drinking and football hooliganism are not the meaningless peculiarities which they are often portrayed as being, but are in fact part of a much larger symbolic world from which they gain a sense of that world. We see from Paul Willis' work that although young men have been singled out as a social group by criminologists and policy-makers as characterising the typical delinquent, a different perspective can be given to this group.

The second set of readings addresses the social context in which women become the victims of crime. Tony Eardley's *Violence and Sexuality* rejects the idea that there is something in the physiological make-up of men which makes them prone to violent behaviour. Eardley argues that an understanding of male aggression can only be made through an understanding of the masculine identity and how this is culturally reproduced. Whilst asserting that this does not excuse men from responsibility for such behaviour, he argues that any successful strategy which is aimed at protecting women cannot merely revolve around the idea that men must be discouraged from such behaviour through harsher sentencing or through an increase in the legal recognition of violence within domestic settings. He argues that it can only be done through a revolution in the way in which male identity is constructed and reproduced through the practices of child care, employment, etc.

Lorenne Clark and Debra Lewis's *Women, Property and Rape* directs our attention to the legal and cultural forces which perpetuate violence by men upon women. The extract focuses upon the way in which women are constructed as being either 'legitimate' or 'illegitimate' victims of rape. This distinction is one which the authors trace to the rationale behind the emergence of rape laws, which they see as being not to protect the rights of women, but rather to protect the rights of men and the threat from other men over what was considered as men's legitimate property. They argue that women become seen as more available in relation to the autonomy which they have from ties to men.

We see the way in which cultural forces are maintained in the social relations between young women and men in Sue Lees' work. In the *Structure of Sexual Relations* there is an investigation of the vocabulary and attitudes of a group of young men and women. Lees argues that the way in which female sexuality is referred to, both by males and females, is instrumental in controlling the behaviour of young women. She argues that the derogatory vocabulary used to represent young women is instrumental in constructing the boundaries of acceptable and non-acceptable behaviour. Like Clark and Lewis, Lees sees that the only option for young women who want to avoid such abuse is to enter into 'dependant' relations with men. Rebecca Morley and Audrey Mullender's report for the Police Research Group provides a discussion of the methods which state agencies can take in limiting domestic violence against women. Whereas the readings by Clark and Lewis, Lees and Eardley focus upon the cultural context which encourages such behaviour, Morley and Mullender examine the possibilities for reducing the problem through improvements in police practices and agencies which operate to support the victims of domestic violence, such as refuges, Women's Aid groups, etc.

Social institutions and the construction of crime and deviance

The way in which we come to have an understanding of crime and deviance is affected and moulded by both the criminal justice system and the mass media. In Robert Reiner's recent article on *Policing and the Police*, he draws our attention to the different ways in which the concept of social control has been used. First, the functionalist sociologists, headed by Parsons, who saw social control as a means of underpinning the social order. This underpinning was maintained by the social institutions which made up the criminal justice system. Alternative positions, which challenged that held by Parsons, were initially led by the labelling 'theorists'. They did not see the necessity of these institutions to maintain social order, rather they argued that these institutions helped to create categories of crime and deviance. Later, various Marxist and critical criminologists have maintained this position, drawing attention to the way other social institutions have performed a similar but ideological means of social control. In this last section attention is given to these social institutions. It is necessary when looking at the media not only to address its role as an ideological means of social control but also to assess its limitations. When looking at the criminal justice system, it is viewed both as a system which is ostensibly ensuring that justice is delivered to the members of a given society and also as a means of exercising a tighter grip upon the potential criminals in Western society. In order to assess the achievement of this institution it is necessary to look at the ways in which this endeavour is undermined by particular social practices within its constituent parts.

The media and the construction of crime and deviance

The four pieces which relate to issues of the media and crime come from varying perspectives and reflect the particular times in which they were written. Stanley Cohen's *Deviance and Moral Panics* is the classic text on moral panics and marks out the original idea of how the media is involved in turning the public's attention towards particular types of crime. It looks at the way in which the media have constructed the meaning of particular behaviour and in turn served to make it a focus for widespread social concern. Cohen argues that the fear of crime people have is one that is constructed through the way in which the media concentrate on certain types of deviance and subsequently turn these into issues which appear to threaten the values which hold society together.

Cohen's work looks primarily at conflicts between youth subcultures and how this came to represent a whole set of issues about conflict between class and generations. However, the extract can also be seen as being constructive in understanding later media concerns in the 1990s with single mothers, child violence, etc., which might be seen as representing a similar phenomenon to that which Cohen provides an analysis of.

Philip Schlesinger's *The Interpretation of Violence* highlights the way in which the media not only report violence but also play a large role in constructing the meaning which it has for those who receive these reports; for example, the difference between legitimate and illegitimate acts of violence. This in turn can be seen as being relevant to the debates about the extent to which the media merely reflect the violence within society or, alternatively, how they exaggerate its presence. Schlesinger argues that it is not only a question of the amount of violence which the media transmits but, just as importantly, the meaning which violence is given through its representations.

Such approaches to the media, however, are not without their critics and P.A.J. Waddington's *Mugging as a Moral Panic* examines some of the problems which approaches like that of Cohen's poses. Waddington argues that the use of such terms as 'moral panic' to describe the fear of crime which the public has does not do justice to the differences which exist between imagined fears and those fears which have a basis in the reality of people's day-to-day lives. Whilst not arguing against the role of the media in constructing the ideas which we have about crime, he nonetheless argues for an analysis which is able to differentiate between 'rational' and 'irrational' concerns.

Angela McRobbie's *Folk Devils Fight Back* also provides a view of the role of the media which goes beyond the one-sided analysis of 'Moral Panics'. She looks at how the media can serve as a creator of moral panics but can also be used by those sections of society around whom such fears have been constructed to resist the way in which they have been represented by engaging in active self-representation. This can be seen as showing the problems involved in seeing the media merely in terms of producing stereotypical images. McRobbie argues that it can also be used by the victims of such representations in resisting these stereotypes.

The institutions of the criminal justice system

The readings which relate to the institutions of the criminal justice system examine the various stages and procedures within this system. They focus particularly on the methods which the police employ in solving crime, the procedure of the courts, through to the way in which punishment itself is carried out. John Lea and Jock Young's *The Drift Towards Military Policing* highlights the fundamental changes which have taken place in police methods in post-war Britain and examines the effects of this in terms of the relationship which the police have with the public. Lea and Young argue that this relationship is essential to any successful crime prevention strategy as it is the public who provide the information for the resolution of the vast majority of crimes. They argue, though, that in the last thirty years the police have increasingly relied on methods which alienate those whom they need to use. They highlight how this is particularly true with regard to the ethnic minorities in Britain's inner cities.

The drift to what they refer to as 'military policing' is one in which the police increasingly operate by stopping people in the hope of finding them guilty of doing something wrong as opposed to acting on any firm information. As they point out, this results in an increase in the stopping of members of the public who are innocent of any offence with the result that they alienate possible future sources of information. This situation is a cycle in which lack of information from the public leads to an increase in reliance by the police on such methods and the perpetual worsening of police/public relations. Lea and Young argue that the only way around this is to radically restructure the way in which policing is controlled. They argue for a democratically controlled police force whose methods are accountable to the people and localities whom they serve.

John Solomos' *Black Youth, Crime and the Ghetto*, when read in conjunction with the article by Lea and Young, displays what Solomos sees as being the guiding principles behind police methods in Britain's inner cities and how this leads to the situation which Lea and Young describe. Solomos argues that police methods have been structured around fundamentally racist concepts of who offenders are and, working with these assumptions, have proceeded to bring in such measures as the 'stop and search' regulations which were eventually seen as being instrumental in the violence which flared in Britain's inner cities in the early to mid 1980s.

The section included from the Islington Crime Survey, itself a good example of the strength of victimisation studies, also demonstrates the way in which some of the above theories relate to the reality of how police methods are perceived by sections of the public in inner city London. By breaking down the data into ethnic group, age, sex, etc., it is able to pinpoint more precisely those sections of the population who feel most aggrieved by the way in which they have been dealt with by the police and how, in turn, this affects the way in which they are likely to conduct their dealings with the police in the future. It also displays how many of the assumptions which policing in inner cities has been predicated upon, i.e. that ethnic minorities bring with them a different set of values which disrupts the previous uniform nature of values and behaviour, are fundamentally mistaken. It shows how ethnic minority groups, as much as the ethnic majority, are not against the idea of policing in principle, and how these two different communities display a marked similarity in the types of offences which they feel the police should be focusing upon.

Turning to the next way in which the criminal is processed, Stephen Hester and Peter Eglin focus upon courtroom procedures. They look at the way in which the courtroom functions from the perspective of symbolic interactionism. They show that much of courtroom procedure is geared more towards expedience and the smooth running of the court than it is towards administering justice. They argue that contrary to the view that lawyers are servants of their clients, the way in which they behave in court and the advice that they give their clients, for example around issues of plea bargaining, etc., are geared towards ensuring that the court continues to function in an unproblematic way. Consequently, this functioning has more to do with the needs and requirements of those professionals who run it than it has to do with serving the interests of the public and the deliverance of justice.

With regard to the way in which society deals with offenders once found guilty, the anthology includes a look at the changes that have taken place in the ideas which lie behind the role of institutions dealing with this and, subsequently, how these ideas have been put into practice. Dario Melossi and Massimo Pavarini's *The Creation of the Modern Prison in England and Europe* describes the historical and social context of the emergence of the prison as the dominant form of punishment in European and later North American society. They argue that the ideas which underpin this form of punishment are ones which arise from the emergence of capitalist relations and the ethic of work and discipline which accompanied this. The pieces by Nils Christie highlight the way in which the trend towards imprisonment has spiralled out of control, mostly in America, but also in Europe. Christie argues that all previous attempts to reduce crime through efforts to improve those conditions which most commonly produce criminals have been gradually dispensed with. In their place has emerged what he refers to as the Western 'Gulag', that is, vast numbers of citizens spending larger parts of their life removed from society. Christie argues that ideas of rehabilitation etc., have also been dispensed with and replaced by the idea that criminals should be temporarily or permanently incapacitated.

Christie focuses upon the disturbing reasons for this trend, which he sees as lying not in the fact that increasing amounts of crime are being committed but rather through the way in which crime control has become big business, spawning a vast industry which has the potential to include more and more people within its control mechanisms. We can see this trend exemplified in the article by Douglas McDonald, *Public Imprisonment by Private Means*, which looks at the recent trends towards the privatisation of prisons in the USA, Australia and Great Britain. It examines some of the reasons why state withdrawal from the incarceration end of social control is becoming an increasingly attractive option to Western governments. McDonald, though, addresses the ethical issues which accompany this trend and examines some of the questions which arise from it.

Lastly, Stanley Cohen gives us another theoretical overview when he traces the way in which methods of control and the theories behind these are closely related to the way in which modern society has conceptualised the problem of order. He argues that it is the concept of urban environments as essentially 'disordered' sites which has provided the motivation behind policies which seek to rectify this. Cohen also stresses that methods of control can only be understood in the context of the wider issues of political ideologies, the nature of professional control, the concept of human nature, and what he refers to as the crisis in welfare liberalism.

Susan Caffrey
Gary Mundy
1995

Reference

1.   Realist criminology is a term that relates to a distinct approach to crime which emerged in the 1980s. A concise explanation of its basic tenets is contained in Jock Young's 'Ten Points of Realism' in *Rethinking Criminology. The Realist Debate*, J. Young & R. Matthews (eds.), Sage Publications, London, 1992.

Publisher's note

The contents of the readings in this anthology have been reproduced as they appear in the publications from which they are taken. In the majority of cases footnotes and bibliographic material are included, the exceptions being where they are of excessive length. Photographs have not been reproduced.

THE SOCIAL CONSTRUCTION OF CRIME

1.
Criminalizing Assault: The Failure of the 'Offence Against Society' Model

Antonia Cretney, Gwynn Davis, Chris Clarkson,*
and Jon Shepherd†

The authors undertook a study of assault, starting outside the justice system with 93 assault victims admitted to the Accident and Emergency Department of a city-centre hospital. They found that in relation to this type of offence the police do not respond to 'crime'; they respond to 'complaints' from an 'aggrieved'. If the victim is too fearful or for some other reason is reluctant to co-operate with the prosecution effort, matters proceed no further. This does not conform to the 'offence against society' model of criminal justice advanced by academic commentators. In fact this model is applied at the court stage of the criminal process, when the victim interest may be neglected entirely, but not at the vitally important stage of police/victim interaction.

Many commentators upon our criminal justice processes have lamented the disappearance of the victim and the appropriation of the conflict by agents of the state (most notably, Christie 1977). Having recently conducted a study of the criminalization of assault in which we took the victim as our starting point, we can confirm the degree to which victims of assault, once they have made a statement of complaint, may be minimally involved thereafter. If the defendant pleads guilty they are, in effect, rendered redundant. If, on the other hand, the alleged assailant contests the charge, the victim may be subjected to a gruelling examination of his or her own character and behaviour, all in the interests of a process which has largely public, or symbolic, purposes. There is a paradox here in that if we consider the initial police response to reports of violence, this is almost entirely dependent upon the victim's commitment to criminalization. We observed time and time again that the police do not respond to 'crime', they respond to 'complaints' from an 'aggrieved'. If there is no complaint the police will generally take no action — even in respect of very serious assaults. They might find themselves chatting to an assault victim in the Bristol Royal

* The first three named co-authors are members of the Faculty of Law, University of Bristol. The research upon which this article is based was funded by the Economic and Social Research Council. The authors are indebted to the Avon and Somerset Constabulary for their exemplary co-operation in putting us in touch with individual police officers, and to the staff of the Accident and Emergency Department of the Bristol Royal Infirmary for facilitating access to patients. We should like to express our thanks to our colleague Stephen Jones for his contribution to the project, and to Pat Hammond, Research Secretary, for her invaluable assistance throughout. We are also grateful to Professor Andrew Ashworth for his comments on an earlier draft of the article.

† University of Wales College of Medicine

Infirmary, or they might pick up an assault victim in the street at 3 a.m. and give her a lift, but they will seldom take the matter further unless the victim demonstrates a firm commitment to the prosecution process. So the police, apparently, are not responding to harm done to 'the fabric of society'. This of course might be a pragmatic decision (no 'complaint', no successful prosecution), but it is inconsistent with a view of crime as an offence against the sovereign authority; it is also inconsistent with the marginalization of the victim interest thereafter. One might have thought, if an 'offence against society' model were in operation, that this would apply to every stage of the proceedings (in which case the police would respond to *offences* rather than to *complaints);* but it doesn't seem to do so. In fact there are two models, complainant-orientated at the police end and 'offence against society' orientated at the court end. Or to put this another way, there appears to be a striking inconsistency between the initial stages of the criminalization process and its later development.

We are interested in this disjunction because it appears to be insufficiently recognized. An article by Ashworth (1986), bearing on this theme, provides a useful counterpoint to the argument which we shall try to develop. For example, on the theory of criminal liability, Ashworth asserts that the predominant purpose of criminal proceedings is to declare public disapproval of the offender's conduct by means of public trial and conviction and the imposition of a penal sanction. Ashworth endorses the principle of offender compensation to the victim as one element in criminal proceedings, but he also argues that the processes of prosecution, conviction, and sentence are matters for the state, acting in the public interest. 'It must remain open', Ashworth suggests, 'whether the particular victim's interests should count for more than those of any other member of the community.' This tentativeness regarding the victim's proper place in the justice process reflects the prevailing ideology, but it serves to disguise the divergence between the interests of victims and those of the police, the CPS and the courts. We shall examine the way in which the burden of registering a 'complaint', and then of sustaining commitment to the prosecution process, bears heavily upon those who seek, for a variety of reasons, to invoke the criminal law.

If a theoretical model departs too far from empirical reality, that model should be abandoned, or at least substantially modified. Ashworth at one point addresses himself to the question of what should happen when the police and CPS wish to press criminal charges but the victim demurs. Ashworth argues, as he must, given his adherence to the offence against society model, that the wishes of the individual victim should not be determinative. He concedes that 'there are classes of case where the victim's wish not to have a prosecution is sometimes allowed to prevail', but implies that this is a departure from the norm. (He refers specifically to 'domestic' violence and suggests that in this group of cases non-prosecution at the victim's behest may be rationalized on public interest grounds on the basis that it is desirable, where possible, to maintain the family unit.) We are being offered a theoretical model rather than an account of police/ victim interaction on the ground, but this inevitably carries with it an implication that the model bears (or is capable of bearing) some approximation to reality. We would argue that it is, to that extent, misleading. For example, it is not that the victim's wish (that the assailant not be prosecuted) is 'sometimes' allowed to prevail. It is *invariably* allowed to prevail. When it comes to determining the police response to reported assaults, victim attitude is the *first* consideration, largely overriding that of offence seriousness. Ashworth acknowledges that the central role of victims in providing evidence gives them *de facto* power to frustrate some prosecutions, but he argues that in principle the victim's wishes should be subordinated to the public interest in matters of prosecution policy. But, as we shall demonstrate, that is not what happens. The model needs to be revised.

The research background

We gained access to 93 assault victims in Autumn 1990 and Spring 1991 through the Accident and Emergency Department of the Bristol Royal Infirmary. We approached patients either during their initial attendance at the Department, or whilst they received in-patient treatment, or when they returned for subsequent out-patient treatment, or by letter. Following our initial contact, and usually within a few days or weeks of the assault, we spent approximately an hour with each victim, discussing as fully as possible the circumstances of their assault, their attitude towards criminalization, and their reflections on what had happened to them and its implications in the longer term. Where the assault *had* been reported to the police (and recorded by them) we interviewed the officer principally concerned and, where prosecution followed, we observed all court proceedings. Our study enabled us to gain a full picture of victims, of their 'story', and of any subsequent engagement between this story and the justice process.

'Assault' has a technical, legal definition as well as a lay meaning, but we did not take the various legal definitions as our starting point. Rather, we began with the hospital definition, based on the patient's own account, and approached patients who had suffered varying degrees of injury in a great variety of circumstances. Access to hospital patients freed us from dependence upon victims' perceptions that the injury done to them merited police involvement. We did not assume any close correspondence between a victim's account of his or her experience and the legal definition of that particular 'assault'. On the contrary, one of our objectives was to study the relationship between (a) a certain type of behaviour, resulting in injury; (b) definition of that behaviour — first by victims, and secondly by the police and courts; and (c) the response to that behaviour, either within the framework of criminal prosecution or independently of it. We were able to examine the motives of those who reported violence, their expectations in reporting, and the manner in which the justice system fulfilled those expectations.

Of the 93 cases in our sample, 22 led to a conviction. The main 'drop-out' points were: (i) through failure to inform the police in the first instance (19 cases); (ii) through there being no formal 'complaint' in cases where the assault was brought to police attention (20 cases); and (iii) through the police being unable to identify the assailant or amass sufficient evidence against him (16 cases). There was also a significant failure rate later in the process, at the point when cases were brought to court. This arose principally through victims' failure to sustain a commitment to the prosecution process (six cases).

Reasons for reporting and non-reporting

Some victims of assault choose to report the incident purely as an act of citizenship, a reflection of their adherence to the rule of law. But most will feel that they have some personal stake in what follows. Some nurture an animus against their assailant: they want him to suffer in his turn for the hurt which he has inflicted on them. Others wish the assailant to be made to answer publicly for his violence. Most victims attach greater importance to denunciation in a public forum than they do to the imposition of a specific penalty. Another very important motivation is the desire to tell one's story and, through doing this, to secure vindication. This appears to be a stronger motivation, for most victims, than their wish to secure financial compensation. In many instances they do not consider compensation to be a realistic possibility, although that is not to say that they would turn it down if it were offered.

Although assault victims may have several good reasons for reporting the matter to the police, the fact is that many choose not to do so. Successive British Crime Surveys as well as other victim surveys (e.g. Sparks *et al.* 1977) have revealed this to be the case. Our own contact with victims, many of them living in conditions of severe deprivation, taught us that there are some people for whom exposure to violence and the threat of violence is part of everyday life. Many incidents of assault, taking place in the open, on the street, in underpasses or outside pubs, go unrecorded. Heavy drinkers, especially, may become involved in an altercation and perhaps collapse as the result of blows they receive, unaware that they might lay claim to being an assault victim and certainly with no intention of reporting the incident to the police.

Those assault victims who do go to the police may be loath to commit themselves to the arrest and charge of their assailant. This is notoriously true of 'domestic' violence and we found ample reason why this should be so. Where the police were called, the woman's most pressing need was usually for an immediate show of strength, either to remove the assailant from the scene or to deter him from further violence. A woman driven to seek police help may well be unable to see beyond her immediate need.

Seriousness of injury is not of itself sufficient to ensure that an assault is reported. Some very serious assaults in our sample were not reported, or were reported in a manner which made it highly unlikely that the police would pursue an investigation. One young man, who suffered heavy bruising to his face and body, the loss of two teeth, a broken nose, and possible kidney damage as the result of a prolonged beating in a pub lavatory, did visit a police station immediately after the attack. However, his ambivalence was apparent in that, for reasons connected with the character of his assailant and the fact that he was bound to encounter him again, he chose not to give that person's name to the police.

Serious assault is a grim business at the best of times, but there is a significant difference between, say, a blow struck in the course of a dispute between two motorists and violence in the context of an on-going relationship. In the one case the victim's course of action is straightforward — report the matter to the police and assist in any way possible with the prosecution process. But where there is some power relationship — as in 'domestic' violence, or where a drug baron rules his particular fiefdom by means of his ruthless commitment to violence — there may be no effective remedy.

Fear of reprisals was acknowledged by approximately 14 per cent of the assault victims whom we interviewed — a much higher proportion than is reported in most crime surveys.[1] Such fears were especially prominent in those cases where victim and assailant had an on-going relationship, whether as sexual partners, family members, habitués of a common social environment such as a pub, or as members of the drugs underworld. In these disparate circumstances many assault victims believed that neither the police nor the courts would be able to prevent further attacks were the assailant so minded.

The importance of the distinction between reporting and 'complaining'

The victim of an assault, reporting the incident to the police, may understand himself to be complaining about the harm suffered and to be asking for police assistance in bringing the assailant to book. In police parlance, however, he or she will not be 'making a complaint'. The act of reporting violence does not constitute a complaint. Without a formal complaint on the part of the victim the police are unlikely, in all but the most serious cases, to investigate an assault. They may even fail to record the 'crime' at all. The police response to assault might be characterized as 'no complaint, no investigation'. The initial stages of the criminalization process depend heavily upon the victim's commitment to 'making a complaint' and, as a necessary corollary, upon his or her acceptance of the burdens which may follow.

Even where the injuries to the victim merit a charge under section 18 or section 20,[2] the importance of the victim's 'complaint' is paramount. In one of our cases the police arrived at a public house to find the licensee on the point of being taken to hospital for treatment to a severely lacerated hand. His assailant, about whose identity there was no dispute, was still at the scene. The offender was not arrested, however, until some days after the incident, when the police had satisfied themselves that the victim wished to 'complain'.

The distinction between reporting and complaining is, not surprisingly, unclear to many victims. They suppose that in telling the police the circumstances of their victimization they are co-operating in the criminalization process. The police do not explain to them that reporting an assault is one thing, 'complaining' quite another. It is this second stage in the process which commits the victim (and the police) to an investigation of the offence and, where possible, to prosecution of the offender. 'Making a complaint' is a police term of art which means *you are prepared to take this all the way to court and, if necessary, to give evidence*. Only when they have this assurance will the police act. Quite often they will prefer to deflect the victim from this course, but it is characteristic of victim/police interaction that the fact that he or she has *been* deflected will not be made plain to the victim.

The reasons for this dependence upon the victim in the initial stages of criminalization (in contrast to the 'disappearance' of the victim during the prosecution stage) are both ideological and practical. One officer justified the police insistence upon obtaining a complaint from the victim on the grounds that it was up to the victim whether or not he or she wished to define what had been done as a crime:

> If you give me your permission to hit you, then that's perfectly all right.
> The fact that someone else doesn't like it, it's nothing to do with them.
> You're your own person and you have to make your own complaints.

This argument, which equates 'not complaining' with 'giving permission', ignores the many reasons why a person may feel unable to initiate criminal proceedings. But more importantly it demonstrates the attitudes which inform police practice on the ground. One case in our sample, the assault on Amanda Britton,[3] provides a good example of the operation of the 'no complaint, no investigation' principle: a passing police car picked up Britton as she stood by a phone box, bleeding and with a broken nose following an attack by her boyfriend. They gave her a lift to a friend's flat but, according to Britton, made no suggestion that she might wish to initiate criminal proceedings against the boyfriend. From these officers' point of view there may have been no indication that Britton wished to 'complain'. She, on the other hand, may have assumed that her status as complainant went without saying — it was reflected in her obvious victimization.

Victims who report an assault with the initial intention of pressing criminal charges may have their resolve tested by delays in the handling of their case. On occasion we were led to suspect that such delays were deliberate. In Britton's case the delay (of some weeks) in arresting her boyfriend, coupled with the police emphasis upon the importance of her role as complainant, led to a weakening in Britton's resolve. So in this instance the apparently dilatory and sceptical police response induced the lack of commitment to the prosecution process with which officers sometimes stereotype women complainants. Reflecting upon her experience, Britton commented: 'It should be the police that press charges as opposed to me.' This, then, was a classic case of the police and victim having different purposes, the result being that each felt dissatisfied at what they took to be the other's lack of resolution. This in turn could be traced back to the divergence of interests inherent in two models of criminal justice which we identify — the one applied early in the case; the other superimposed at the court stage.

The gap which exists between reporting and 'complaining' has consequences which are functional for some of the actors in these dramas, dysfunctional for others. First, there is the possibility of misunderstanding — victims may not appreciate that more is required of them. Secondly, the distinction is helpful to the police in that it reflects their operational distinction between being a victim and being a victim who will 'stand up'; they are likely to be interested only in the latter. Thirdly, it enables the police to weed out unmeritorious or otherwise dubious victims without their realizing that they *are* being weeded out. Where the focus of police effort is so firmly upon achieving successful prosecution, the need for a victim able to bear the burden of this process becomes paramount. It is unlikely that many victims who turn to the police following an attack are in a position to appreciate police priorities or are aware of the distinction between reporting and complaining. A victim who is uncertain about his wish to see his assailant prosecuted may find his uncertainty compounded by an apparent lack of encouragement on the part of the police. The police for their part may see this as a judicious weeding out of potentially weak complainants. None of this squares with the offence against society model.

Occasional attempts to implement the model: testing to destruction

The striking common element in many of the assault cases whose progress we followed, and a particular feature of domestic violence cases and of assaults perpetrated within the drugs underworld, was the extent to which a focus upon prosecution, and the evidential requirements which go along with prosecution, failed to meet the victim's need for security in his or her person for the future. This is counter-productive to the extent that these people are inadequately supported in their fragile commitment to the prosecution process. We did however observe five assault cases, amongst the most serious in our sample, in which the police either persuaded an obviously reluctant victim to make a statement identifying his assailant, or else charged the alleged assailant before determining whether the victim (who was very seriously injured and in hospital) was prepared to make a written statement. In these atypical cases the police were influenced, it seemed to us, by the horrific nature of the injuries sustained, by the high profile which was afforded to these assaults in the local press, and, in at least three instances, by their wish to 'nail' powerful local villains. Three of the assaults were drugs related; another was a drunken stabbing; and the fifth was 'domestic'. Four of the five victims were at obvious risk of intimidation and further reprisals.

The one case in which the police put together a case file without an initial statement from the victim had to be dropped when they failed to persuade the victim to 'make a complaint'. In this instance the victim, Howard Henderson, had sustained a severe beating in the course of an attack by a drugs dealer who suspected Henderson of trespassing on his domain. In the course of the attack Henderson's jaw was broken in several places. It was Henderson's girlfriend who reported the assault to the police and she later endorsed the police attempts to persuade Henderson to co-operate in bringing his assailant to book. The alleged offender was arrested and charged. However, the case had to be dropped when the police failed to persuade Henderson to 'make a complaint'. An officer, giving vent to his frustrations at the failure of this case, described the experience as:

> . . . a lot of hard work, a lot of paperwork, and to sum it up quite frankly — for bog-all. And it even goes a stage further than that. That is why some of them think it is safe to go on committing offences out there, because there aren't going to be any witnesses. They can get away with the fact that there's a good chance that the aggrieved party won't go to court.

The 'domestic' assault to which we referred foundered at committal when the victim refused to testify against her partner. Louise Purnell had been held captive and beaten severely, suffering internal injuries. Initially she had agreed to make a complaint against her assailant and was supported in this by her aunt. The police were anxious for a prosecution in view of the severity of Purnell's injuries. They attempted to support Purnell, even engineering an offer of alternative housing for her — which she refused. After some time, however, Purnell told the police that she did not want her assailant prosecuted. Summonsed to appear at the committal proceedings, Purnell refused to answer questions and the assault charges against her partner were dropped.

Timothy Paxman, whose face was slashed with a Stanley knife and his arms broken in an attack with a baseball bat, refused to identify his assailant in court and the prosecution offered no further evidence. Paxman, a heroin addict, was set upon by a dealer to whom he owed £50. Although he identified his assailant to the police he was reluctant to testify and only agreed to make a statement under some pressure from the officer in the case. In a pre-trial 'confrontation' engineered by the police, Paxman claimed that he could not identify his assailant. His failure in court therefore came as no surprise.

Of the other cases amongst this group, one victim, Steven Barker, failed to attend the trial, while the other, David Freeman, failed to attend the *second* hearing in his case, there having previously been an aborted trial in the course of which Freeman had endured the rigours of cross-examination. All these victims had suffered very serious injuries. All, apart from Purnell, were themselves offenders. Neither Paxman nor Barker were committed to the prosecution process from the outset: their defaulting came as no surprise to the police officers involved. Freeman, partly because he had managed to break his drug dependency, partly because his middle-class parents offered him accommodation away from the drugs milieu, did display considerable commitment, although even he fell at the final hurdle as, one might argue, few would not have done.

Although it is in relation to domestic violence that the wavering complainant is most often discussed, it is clear that the problem is not confined to assaults in that context. Assaults which take place in the criminal underworld, not least where drug dealing is concerned, often produce victims who cannot meet the standard of a committed and 'innocent' complainant. The failure of the prosecution effort in the above cases (indeed, in *any* case in which the victim withdraws co-operation) suggests that police insistence on having a 'complaint' and, if at all possible, a sound complainant, is justified *in practical terms*.

The victim in court

Having identified the centrality of the 'complaint', and of the victim's willingness to sustain a commitment to the process, we now turn to a consideration of the assault victim's experience in court. In fact only 29 of the 93 assaults in our sample were prosecuted (31 per cent). Of these, nine (31 per cent) were the subject of an immediate guilty plea; nine (31 per cent) were the subject of a not guilty plea but the defendant pleaded in due course to a lesser charge; six (21 per cent) were aborted when the prosecution offered no evidence (or, in mid-trial, offered no *further* evidence); four defendants (14 per cent) were tried and found guilty; and one defendant was tried and found not guilty. These figures reflect the significance of the plea-bargain and this, of course, is one aspect of the proceedings from which victims are totally excluded. Having initiated the process, the victim loses all effective decision-making power beyond the decision to withdraw his or her co-operation.

Other researchers in this field have observed that the prosecution process offers the victim few rewards (see, in particular, Shapland *et al.* 1985, *passim;* and Rock 1991). Our experience accords with theirs. The justice system exposes victims to inconvenience at best, humiliation at worst. This may not be apparent to those who have no direct experience of it. A police officer told us without apparent irony of the faith which members of the Asian community exhibited in the 'system', a faith which made them untypically reliable complainants:

> To some extent a lot of the foreign people tend to not back out because they don't know the system. They've put the complaint in and therefore that's the complaint and it sees its natural course.

His unspoken assumption was that anyone who did 'know the system' would appreciate that persisting in a complaint was likely to provide a small return on much investment.

The harassment endured by some assault victims at court has been commented upon by Rock (1991) and was a feature of several of the cases which we followed. Fundamental to this, Rock suggests, is the dubious status of the victim arising from the evidential requirements of the court. The demand for 'uncontaminated' evidence leads to the segregation of prosecution witnesses from professional court users, exposing them to threats from defence witnesses and other supporters of the defendant. Rock refers to the 'pariah-like' status of the victim in his role as witness for the prosecution. So whilst the victim may come to court seeking vindication and redress, he is likely in fact to experience a long and lonely wait in a public place, in fear of being further abused. Indeed, he may have to endure this several times. Adjournments are frequent. Victims who steel themselves to give evidence may be required to screw their courage to the sticking point all over again. This is trying even for those with great respect for the law and its procedures. Where a victim is more ambivalent in attitude, and where his lifestyle is not well ordered, he may find the demands made upon him as a witness unsustainable.

Whatever it is that the victim hopes to get out of his attendance at court, he is likely to be disappointed. He may hope, for example, to secure 'symbolic' denunciation of the offender's bad conduct. Many victims seek public recognition of the harm which they have suffered. Denunciation may be of greater importance to them than the imposition of a specific penalty. As one victim of a 'domestic' assault explained her motivation to us:

> Perhaps it just makes it more real — it happened and it's sort of proved
> to have happened because it's in court being discussed.

Given this aspiration, it might be thought that public and private interests at this point coalesce, so that both might be satisfied. Unfortunately, this is seldom the case. While courts provide a public forum for determining guilt or innocence in relation to indictments, they do not enable participants to arrive at 'the truth', or to feel confident that the stories told in court have in reality anatomized the events which gave rise to the charge (on this theme, see Pannick 1987: 53; Rock 1991; and McConville et al. 1991). A victim who seeks emotional catharsis is likely to find the experience very frustrating. Having been told by the police that 'a court is only a place where you can tell your story' (to quote from one police handbook designed for victims of domestic violence), she is likely to find herself treated as unclean and untruthful by defence counsel whose job it is to discredit her evidence. She has only limited redress against the misrepresentations (or change of emphasis) likely to be reflected in the defence plea in mitigation, and no control either over the presentation of the prosecution story, tacitly assumed to be her own. To take one example, Annie Cresswell had a history of victimization at the hands of her partner, from whom she had recently separated. On this occasion she was attacked in front of her seven-year-old son and threatened with a knife. In due course her assailant pleaded guilty to a section 47 charge. He alleged that the incident had been a 'one-off', caused by Cresswell's 'drink problem', and that the two of them were 'getting back together'. No mention was made of the knife threat which had triggered the report to the police. Such misrepresentations or omissions contribute to an inadequate account of the victim's 'story', this, no doubt mistakenly, being what Cresswell had understood the proceedings to be about.

Another factor which militates against truth-telling in court is the tendency for court processes to exclude contextual behaviour in their narrow focus upon proving the charge. As a result, an assault which takes place within a long-term relationship will be presented as an isolated incident. The court is unlikely to be given much insight into the causes of the assault, the motivations of the participants, or the balance of culpability. By excluding material which is deemed to have no legal relevance, the trial becomes 'irrelevant' to the victim.

Apart from the story which is told in court, the other things that matter to victims are the charge and sentence. Assault victims will not understand the technical distinctions between various levels of assault charge, but they are likely to interpret a *reduction* in the level of charge as an indication that a less serious view is now being taken of the incident. The sentence imposed is likewise regarded by victims as a yardstick of their own worth in the eyes of the court. Press accounts of high profile trials commonly feature victims' dismay in the face of supposedly inadequate sentences. It struck us very forcibly that sentencers are pursuing primarily 'public' purposes. A judge in the Crown Court may take care to justify his sentence, but this justification is offered to the wider public and not specifically to the victim of the offence. The court's attempt to balance the various 'public' interests carries little resonance with victims. They resist having *their* interests subsumed within the wider 'public' interest. One example may suffice. Ronald Price, a probationer police officer, had his nose broken by a man whom he had just arrested. The blow took Price by surprise and knocked him unconscious. His assailant ran off but was arrested soon afterwards and charged with a section 18 offence. It transpired that he had been released only two weeks previously from a prison sentence imposed in respect of another assault. When the case came to court the defendant pleaded guilty to a reduced section 47 charge. Price, who had needed a second operation to alleviate breathing problems resulting from the blow, was in court and heard the defendant sentenced to 15 months imprisonment, suspended for two years. The judge explained that he wanted the defendant to continue to have the benefit of probation supervision, something which he had enjoyed for only a few weeks prior to his imprisonment on the earlier assault charge. He made no reference to the severity of Price's injury. As the defendant was said to be without means, there was no order for compensation. The victim, unsurprisingly, was mortified.

Compensation orders are the principal means by which the victim's private interest finds expression within criminal proceedings. Of the 19 non-custodial sentences which we saw imposed, ten (53 per cent) were accompanied by an order that the defendant pay compensation. The ordering of compensation appeared to us to be unpredictable, even random. A defendant's claim that he had no means was generally accepted without any attempt to check the truth of this statement. Widely differing awards were made in apparently similar circumstances. Sometimes the award seemed to represent a genuine attempt to require the offender to pay a sum commensurate with the harm inflicted; in other cases it was little more than token (Miers 1992). We would agree with Miers that compensation awards, at present, are a poorly assimilated postscript to a procedure which retains its quintessentially 'public' character. But we should be careful not to give the impression that greater emphasis upon this form of order would in itself achieve an equivalence between the early stages of criminalization and its later development. To think this would be a mistake for two reasons. First, even if greater emphasis were given to compensation, the sentencing process might retain its essentially public character. Secondly, victims are interested in compensation, but many of those who go to the police have entirely non-pecuniary motives. These too are legitimate and, under the present arrangements, even less likely to be satisfied.

We would conclude, as others have done, that the criminalization process exposes victims to further distress whilst failing to meet the needs which underlay their original commitment to the process. The adversarial trial is not designed to promote truth-finding. The hearing may fail to address what the victim regards as the key issues, partly because it excises an incident from its context. The penalty imposed may not reflect the harm suffered. In summary, the victim's experience of the courtroom is likely to alienate, and to offer little in return for the further pains inflicted.

The coherence of the model

Miers has observed that it is 'a matter of mundane note that the interests of crime victims have traditionally been subordinated to powerful and persisting objectives of the criminal justice system' (Miers 1992). Our own research confirmed that victims' perception of the harm suffered is frequently not matched by legal definitions, while conduct of the case by the police and the presentation of these matters in court often fails to reflect the victim's own account. We can conclude that the relationship between victim needs, victims' intentions in reporting acts of violence, and the actual outcome via the justice system is a complex one in which the legal process frequently and for a variety of reasons fails the individual victim.

If we accept, as most academic commentators and practitioners do accept, that the main purpose of criminal proceedings is to enable the state to respond to a wrong done to itself, then neglect of the victim interest may be seen as regrettable, but understandable and, perhaps, inevitable. If however we recognize the system's absolute reliance upon victims — not only as reporters, but as staunch 'complainants' and witnesses — we begin to perceive a remarkable disjunction between this absolute reliance upon victims as the 'trigger' of criminalization and the subsequent rigorous adherence to an offence against society model. This is not simply an academic point: one might suggest that there is something morally disreputable about a system which relies so heavily upon individual crime victims as the fuel to drive an engine which has only public, or symbolic, purposes.

The nub of our argument follows from the finding that successful prosecution of assaults depends absolutely upon victims' commitment to the process; that victims have, in effect, a power of veto; and that the police, recognizing the central importance of staunch victims to what they would regard as 'good process', operate their own filter whereby the hesitant complainant, the drunk, the verbally unskilled, the 'domestic', and the morally dubious are deflected from assuming full 'complainant' status. Of course we understand the reasons for this: such victims are unlikely to withstand the rigours of the criminal process or to convince the trier of fact.

This picture — what we take to be the day to day reality of the processing of assaults — does not accord with the offence against society model as this is advanced by academic commentators. For example, Ashworth declares that the victim

> has no right to consent to the infliction of most serious injuries and some other acts; no right to veto a prosecution, to demand a prosecution or to commute or demand a sentence; no right even to be consulted about the decision to prosecute or choice of sentence: these are all state decisions, to be taken upon public interest principles. The victim's rights at these stages should be those of any other citizen, although there are good reasons for ensuring that the victim is kept informed about the progress of the case and about the general reasons for decisions taken upon it, and decisions not to prosecute should be open to challenge (Ashworth 1986).

We accept that this passage is normative rather than descriptive, but it needs to be set alongside what we take to be the everyday reality of police/victim interaction. Our research demonstrates only too clearly why many assault victims are unable to commit themselves to the processes of arrest and prosecution. Those who have experienced 'domestic' violence may be uncertain, both at the initial stages of making a 'complaint' and through further contact with the police, whether and in what way criminal prosecution of their assailant will meet their needs. This uncertainty compounds the police view of these women as unreliable complainants. For assault victims trapped in other kinds of continuing relationship with the assailant, for example, drug user and supplier, or (less obviously) a common social environment, further contact with the assailant can make it almost impossible to sustain a commitment to prosecution, even where the injuries sustained have been extreme. If pursued, these very serious cases will inevitably be dealt with in the Crown Court; the associated delays add to the pressure on the victim, while police protection is likely to be inadequate in providing anything but the most tenuous sense of security.

The police for their part can hardly be blamed for deflecting unpromising victims so that they do not assume full 'complainant' status, or for not preparing a case file when the victim is ambivalent. Experience has taught the police that they have little chance of establishing the defendant's guilt unless they have a victim who is prepared, if necessary, to tell his or her story to a court. This is confirmed by our observation of the prosecution effort in respect of the very serious assaults perpetrated upon Barker, Freeman, Paxman, and Purnell. In each instance the police and the CPS, perhaps against their better judgment, brought the assailant at least to the point of committal, only for the case to founder in the face of the victim's non-attendance or blatant non-co-operation with the prosecution authorities. The Henderson case displayed similar features in that the police, even more unusually, arrested the alleged assailant before the victim had committed himself to making a formal statement. In this instance the case was discontinued by the CPS in light of the victim's refusal to co-operate. These cases were relatively unusual in that the police attempted, unsuccessfully as it transpired, to overcome the victim's reluctance. But the victim veto proved effective at whatever point it was decisively applied. Indeed, on the basis of our evidence we would say that this veto is *100 per cent effective* in respect of assaults. So whilst we might criticize the police for being too eager to deflect the unsatisfactory complainant, we can hardly say that they are misguided, operationally speaking, to place such a premium upon the victim's commitment to the prosecution process.

What consequences should flow from this reappraisal of the role of assault victims in the justice process? One has to start from what is already conceded. It is Ashworth's view, as it was that of Shapland *et al.* (1985) who wrote from a specifically victim perspective, that the needs of the victim and his interest as a central figure in the offence should not be neglected. The police should inform victims of the progress of the case. Victims should be informed about the state compensation scheme. The police should obtain details of the victim's injury or loss and prosecutors should present this in order to provide the basis for calculating a compensation order. However, we have to recognize that none of this challenges the offence against society model because it does not challenge the priority given to state punishment and the (virtually) exclusive offender focus which follows from this. We are still therefore left with a justice system which, at least in relation to assault, proclaims itself to be operating upon one principle — that of punishing offences against the state — whilst in fact operating upon two different principles at successive stages of the criminalization process. We now offer two alternative ways of reconciling this conflict.

Possible new directions

The first strategy which we identify would involve a significant change in police practice in an attempt to make this consistent with the exclusive focus upon the offender and the offence which is characteristic of court proceedings. One of the assault victims whom we interviewed — Amanda Britton, referred to above — expressed the view that it should be the police, rather than the victim, who bore responsibility for initiating prosecution. This, she suggested, would do much to meet the victim's need for support and security at the point when an assault was reported. Such an approach on the part of the police would declare *the state's* interest in the prosecution of offenders at a very early stage. The burden of decision-making would no longer be borne primarily by victims. The change has already been implemented in some US states in the context of domestic violence. How far this has achieved increased deterrence and the protection (as opposed to further victimization) of women who report domestic violence is still the subject of debate (see, for instance, Morley and Mullender 1992).

Even if it were accepted that crime should be objectively defined and objectively punished, there would remain formidable practical difficulties in seeking to implement such a moral imperative. The case studies referred to in this article give some indication of the vital role played by the victim as witness. The probative burden cannot be satisfied without this evidence. Even were the alleged victim *compelled* to give evidence, such testimony would be of limited value. Also, the practice of 'compelling' witnesses might be considered morally dubious in itself. On the other hand, victims would at least be relieved of the decision whether or not to 'press charges', although the burden of giving evidence would remain and, along with it, the possibility that victims might withdraw their co-operation at that stage. In order to counter this, a greatly improved system of support for victim witnesses might need to be set up. Victim Support has introduced Victim/Witness in Court schemes at many Crown Courts, following the success of seven pilot projects. The report of these experiments (Raine and Smith 1991) suggests a satisfactory 'take-up' of the support offered. Should prosecution for reported assault be made mandatory there would clearly be need for a more effective support network, of which this might be one element. There would also be need for more effective police protection. Taken together, these steps might go some way towards overcoming the tendency for assault victims to withdraw their co-operation with the prosecuting authorities. More important, some of those who find it hardest to seek the law's protection might be empowered to do so. At the same time, the offence against society model would be more consistently applied.

An alternative response, and one which would be consistent with the present absolute reliance upon victim commitment to the prosecution process, would be that both the *form* and the *outcome* of court proceedings be shifted decisively in the direction of addressing the harm done to the individual victim. Once again there are, we should concede, formidable difficulties in the way of such a major shift of emphasis. The arguments for viewing criminal law as a branch of *public* law, in which the state punishes offenders, are frequently rehearsed. The various theoretical justifications for punishment all tend to express the state's interest. The denunciatory theory of punishment is about *societal* condemnation of wrong-doing. Criminal justice is a 'normative moralising symbol' (Bussman 1992). This is what gives it its legitimacy. As Bussman explains, justice is an intangible — it belongs to our 'symbolic world of meanings'. In contrast, making amends — the repair of a private wrong — has little symbolic power.

The utilitarian perspective is also unpromising. It is society, rather than the individual victim, which has an interest in achieving deterrence, incapacitation, or rehabilitation. It is significant that in defending the primacy of the state's interest against that of the victim, Ashworth appears to accept many of the utilitarian arguments for punishment which tend, in their turn, to direct the focus of attention away from the victim interest. He asserts, for example, that the criminal law is concerned with future behaviour as well as past behaviour: it is intended that it should exert influence both upon the individual offender and upon other potential offenders.

It is significant, perhaps, that the Criminal Justice Act 1991 conveys the impression that utilitarian considerations are to weigh less heavily than hitherto. The Act is no more successful than its predecessors in reflecting a single, coherent philosophy, but one must assume that flagging up 'just deserts' signals the re-emergence of retributive theory as the justification for punishment. Of course 'just deserts', as enshrined in the

Act, is concerned with restoring the equilibrium between offender and *society*. None the less, retributive theory, unlike the various utilitarian approaches, is compatible with justice expressed in terms of a requirement that the offender make amends to his or her individual victim (Watson *et al.* 1989; Davis 1992: 11). Both reparation and retribution are 'act-based' (McAnany 1978); that is, they are each concerned with the harm done in the one case rather than with extraneous factors contributing to the offender's character or social circumstances. Both are generally proposed in a form which acknowledges the moral significance of individual autonomy. Furthermore, they are each species of distributive justice: the root metaphor in each case is that of justice as balance; the object is to restore the distribution of rights which existed prior to the offence.

The form which such restoration might take is not a subject which can be addressed in this article. The task of delivering meaningful reparation either through or alongside the criminal courts is a formidably difficult one, as the recent attempts to develop mediation and reparation programmes in this country have demonstrated only too clearly (Davis 1992: *passim*) . The fate of these experiments confirmed the intractability of our criminal justice institutions and demonstrated the remarkable ease with which vested interests in the penal system marginalize ideas which threaten basic assumptions. None the less, the case for some shift in the direction of remedying the harm done to the individual victim (see, for example, Campbell 1984) is sufficiently persuasive to at least demand a reasoned response. Whether or not one accepts this particular argument, it is impossible to defend the logic of an offence against society model which rests as heavily as ours does upon the frailties and foibles of 'the aggrieved'.

Notes

1. In the 1988 British Crime Survey fear of reprisals was given as a reason for non-reporting in 2 per cent of common assaults; in 3 per cent of other assaults; and in 5 per cent of woundings (Dowds *et al.* 1989: 74). We believe that fear of reprisals underpins non-reporting in a significantly higher proportion of more serious assaults and of cases where assailant and victim are known to one another. Hindelang and Gottfredson (1976), reporting the findings of the US National Crime Survey Panel, observed that only 4 per cent of victims gave fear of reprisals as their reason for not reporting an assault, although the percentage doubled in relation to serious cases.

2. Offences Against the Person Act 1861.

3. In this and subsequent examples the names given are pseudonyms.

References

Ashworth, A. (1986) 'Punishment and Compensation', *Oxford Journal of Legal Studies,* 6: 1.

Bussman, Kai-D. (1992) 'Morality, Symbolism, and Criminal Law: Chances and Limits of Mediation Programs', in H. Messmer and H.-U. Otto, eds, *Restorative Justice on Trial.* Deventer: Kluwer.

Campbell, T. (1984) 'Compensation as Punishment', *University of New South Wales Law Journal,* 7: 338-61.

Christie, N. (1977) 'Conflicts as Property', *British Journal of Criminology,* 17: 1.

Davis, G. (1992) *Making Amends*. London: Routledge.

Dowds, L., Elliot, D., and Mayhew, P. (1989) *The 1988 British Crime Survey,* Home Office Research Study 111. London: HMSO.

Hindelang, M., and Gottfredson, M. (1976) The Victim's Decision not to Invoke the Criminal Justice Process', in W. F. McDonald, ed., *Criminal Justice and the Victim*. London: Sage Publications.

McAnany, P. D. (1978) 'Restitution as an Idea and Practice: The Retributive Prospect' in J. Hudson, and B. Galaway, eds, *Offender Restitution in Theory and Action*. Lexington, MA: Lexington Books.

McConville, M., Sanders, A., and Leng, R. (1991) *The Case for the Prosecution*. London: Routledge.

Miers, D. (1992) 'The Responsibilities and the Rights of Victims of Crime', *Modern Law Review*, 55: 2.

Morley, R., and Mullender, A. (1992) 'Hype or Hope? The Importation of Pro-arrest Policies and Batterers' Programmes from North America to Britain as Key Measures for Preventing Violence Against Women in the Home', *International Journal of Law and the Family*, 6: 265-88.

Pannick, D. (1987) *Judges*. Oxford: The Clarendon Press.

Raine, J.W., and Smith, R.E. (1991) *The Victim/Witness in Court Project*. National Association of Victim Support Schemes.

Rock, P. (1991) 'Witnesses and Space in a Crown Court', *British Journal of Criminology*, 31: 3.

Shapland, J., Willmore, J., and Duff, P. (1985) *Victims in the Criminal Justice System*. Aldershot: Gower.

Sparks, R., Genn, H., and Dodd, D. (1977) *Surveying Victims*. Chichester: John Wiley.

Watson, D., Boucherat, J., and Davis, G. (1989) 'Reparation for Retributivists' in M. Wright and B. Galaway, eds, *Mediation in Criminal Justice*. London: Sage Publications.

2. Crime Statistics, Patterns, and Trends: Changing Perceptions and their Implications

Mike Maguire

> At heart the extent of crime is a political as well as a behavioural matter
> ... The figures for crime ... are not 'hard facts' in the sense that this is
> true of the height and weight of physical bodies. They are moral not
> physical statistics.   (Young 1988b: 175)

Introduction

This chapter explores a number of interrelated questions regarding the state of our knowledge about 'crime levels', 'crime patterns', and 'crime trends'. These range from what may sound like (but are not) straightforward empirical and methodological questions, such as 'How much crime is there?', 'How is it changing?' and 'How do we find out?', to broader questions about the relationship between, on the one hand, the kinds of data which are collected and published about crime and, on the other, the perceptions, ideas, and theories which are formed about it.

A changed picture

There is no doubt that the picture of crime painted by such data in Britain in the early 1990s is very different from the image which was presented to our predecessors in, say, the early 1950s by the information available at that time. Most obviously, it differs in terms of the quantity of criminal offences known to have taken place. The annual totals of offences officially recorded by the police and published in Criminal Statistics are now more than eleven times greater (over five and a half million, compared with around half a million).[1] Moreover, repeated 'sweeps' of the British Crime Survey, (conducted in 1982, 1984, 1988, and 1992) have established beyond doubt that the official totals reflect only the tip of an iceberg of crimes known to victims, the majority of which go unreported and unrecorded.

Equally important, the present picture is composed of considerably different types and patterns of crimes. This is quite striking even among officially recorded offences: for example, crimes involving motor vehicles, relatively rare in the 1950s when there were few cars on the roads, now make up a quarter of the total; crimes of violence against the person have overtaken sexual and fraudulent offences, both of which clearly exceeded them in the early 1950s; and offences of criminal damage, then an almost negligible category, now total over 800,000 per year, around 15 per cent of all recorded crime. However, the difference is much more dramatic if one looks beyond police statistics and beyond the British Crime Survey (which focuses on a limited set of

Mike Maguire: 'Crime Statistics, Patterns, and Trends: Changing Perceptions and their Implications' from *THE OXFORD HANDBOOK OF CRIMINOLOGY*, edited by Mike Maguire, Rod Morgan and Robert Reiner (Oxford: Clarendon Press, 1994), pp. 233-291. Reprinted by permission of Oxford University Press.

standard offences), to the studies of criminologists. As noted in the introduction to this volume, the growth of criminology has been remarkable over the last forty years: from a few lone scholars and a small Institute in London to over 300 academics engaged in teaching and research countrywide (many in specialist 'Centres'), regular funding of empirical research, and a flourishing market for publications.[2] As greater resources have been devoted to research, so more and more kinds of criminal activity which formerly remained largely hidden from police and public view have been described and analysed in depth. Important among these are intra-household offences (such as domestic violence and sexual abuse of children), 'white-collar' and corporate offences, and crimes between consenting parties (notably drug offences), none of which attracted any sustained attention in the 1950s.

A third major difference lies in our perceptions of 'criminals'. In the early 1950s, offenders tended to be represented by experts, as well as by politicians and the media, almost as a breed set apart from the rest of society. Conviction for a criminal offence was a relatively rare occurrence in most communities and was likely to bring opprobrium and ostracism from family and neighbours (Morris 1989). Those convicted — in the main, young males from lower-class backgrounds — were seen by most people who described themselves as criminologists, as well as by many working within the criminal justice system, as suffering from something akin to a medical condition — caused, ultimately, by some form of social and/or emotional deprivation — and in need of 'treatment' to reduce their chances of reconviction (see e.g. Bowlby 1953). Forty years later, though media stereotypes of 'criminals' still abound, possession of a criminal conviction is by no means unusual and is much less likely to be stigmatizing: indeed, it is now known from cohort studies[3] that over one-third of all males (though only 8 per cent of females) born in 1953 had acquired at least one criminal conviction for an indictable offence by the age of 31 (Home Office 1989). Furthermore, in-depth and ethnographic research — as well as high publicity for particular cases — has helped to bring about wider recognition that criminal behaviour is not a near-monopoly of poor and deprived young males. For example, the sexual abuse of children (Baker and Duncan 1985), domestic violence (Dobash and Dobash 1992), football hooliganism (Murphy et al. 1990), workplace theft (Ditton 1977; Mars 1982), and drug offences (Pearson 1987) have all been shown to be committed by people from a wide range of age groups and social classes — though, as will be discussed later, much less so by females than males — while a series of major frauds, some with direct financial consequences for large numbers of ordinary people (BCCI, Maxwell, Barlow Clowes, etc.) have demonstrated for all to see that criminals are to be found in suites as well as on the streets (Levi and Pithouse 1992).

None of this is to deny that there exist identifiable groups and individuals, many of them young males from deprived and disturbed backgrounds, who commit substantial numbers of the highly visible 'predatory' kinds of offence like burglary and car theft which make up the bulk of recorded crimes. Indeed, the authors of the Home Office cohort studies have estimated that as many as 65 per cent of all court convictions acquired by the cohort for indictable crimes are accounted for by just 7 per cent of its members, each convicted on six or more occasions (Home Office 1989). Nor is to deny that such persistent offenders, whose activities often seriously damage their own and their victims' lives, are worthy of special attention by researchers. However, it should make us wary of accounts and explanations which proceed as though virtually *all* crime were akin to predatory street crime and *all* offenders were afflicted by social or psychological 'problems'.

In at least three important respects, then — dramatically higher totals of known offences, revelations of major 'new' kinds of criminal activity in previously unprobed areas of the social world, and recognition that many offenders are neither psychologically abnormal nor young males from the lower social classes — the phenomenon of crime appears very different to the informed observer in 1993 than it did to his or her counterpart forty or so years ago. (On a different tack, it is also worth flagging here a fourth difference — much greater awareness of the experience of crime from the *victim's* point of view — the importance of which will be discussed later.)

Of course, the $64,000 question which remains is how much the differences reflect 'real' changes in behaviour over this period and how much they are simply a function of new, improved, or differently tuned channels of communication about what is happening 'out there'. No satisfactory answer to this could be expected without a wide-ranging search for relevant (and mainly obscure) historical evidence; nor, equally importantly, without a thorough consideration of complex epistemological questions which underlie the differences between what Bottomley and Coleman (1981) call the 'realist' and the 'institutionalist' approaches to crime data — tasks which (though the latter questions will be touched upon) are clearly beyond the scope of this one chapter. The more modest aim here is simply to examine the kinds of data on which our perceptions of the phenomenon of crime are built, outlining some of the main developments in criminology, as well as in other sources of information about crime, which have helped to transform and broaden these perceptions. A few general comments will also be made about how convincing or otherwise some of the theories of crime causation which were put forward in earlier years, without the benefit of current sources of data, appear to remain in the light of that new knowledge.

Painting by numbers

The empirical data most often used by modern criminologists, as well as by policy-makers in the Home Office and elsewhere, derive from three main sources: statistical records routinely compiled by the police and criminal justice agencies; large-scale surveys (usually directly commissioned by government); and small-scale surveys and studies conducted by academic and other researchers.

With notable exceptions, the central feature of this raw material, and of the use made of it, is the predominance of *numbers* as a descriptive medium. Indeed, a salient feature of almost all modern forms of discourse about crime is the emphasis placed upon terms associated with its quantification and measurement: 'volume', 'extent', 'growth', 'prevalence', 'incidence', 'trends', and so on. In political and media debates, trends in aggregate crime figures are often put forward as evidence of failures or successes in criminal justice policy, or are treated as a sort of social barometer, supposedly indicative of, for example, declining standards of parenting or schooling. Among policy-makers, arguments for an initiative in response to a particular form of crime are unlikely to cut any ice without a convincing numerical representation of 'the scale of the problem'. Criminologists, too, are well aware of the power of the 'language of figures', and even those orientated primarily towards qualitative research methods routinely produce quantitative data to reinforce and 'legitimate' their findings.

If their limitations are fully recognized, crime-related statistics offer an invaluable aid to understanding and explanation. On the other hand, not only can they can be highly misleading if used incorrectly, but, if presented in mechanical fashion, without any deeper comprehension of their relationship to the reality they purport to represent, they can grossly distort the social meaning of events as understood by those experiencing or witnessing them. Ultimately, indeed, one may ask whether 'crime' (or any particular category of crime) is a phenomenon which can sensibly be described merely by adding up totals of diverse actions and incidents.

It is also important to note that, while changes in regularly compiled statistics have a considerable impact on our perceptions of the crime problem, these are by no means the only — nor necessarily the most influential — sources of information or insights about it. In fact, systematic data collection often *follows,* rather than generates, new insights and perspectives. Spectacular instances of forms of criminal behaviour hitherto considered of only marginal importance may suddenly attract attention from the media and spark off a trawl for similar events, thus 'uncovering' (or, from another perspective, 'creating') a new 'crime problem'. Examples from Britain in the 1980s and early 1990s include the surge in public, academic, and official attention to 'child sex abuse' produced by the Cleveland case (see e.g. Morgan 1988), to 'corporate crime' by the Robert Maxwell pensions fraud, and to 'police malpractice' by the Guildford Four, Birmingham Six, and other major cases revealed as miscarriages of justice (Woffinden 1987; Rozenberg 1992).

Some writers — among the best known being Hall *et al*. (1978) — have argued further that 'crime waves' may be deliberately manufactured (with assistance from the police and the media) by governments suffering unpopularity during economic recessions, when the legitimacy of the class-based economic system is weakened. Hall *et al.'s* main example was the 'mugging' scare in the early 1970s, which was created, they claim, to focus public hostility upon, and justify greater social control over, the unemployed young black populations of inner cities. They pointed out that 'mugging' is a term which does not correspond to a legal offence category, and that the racially differentiated statistics from the Metropolitan Police Department figures which fuelled the scare were highly unreliable [for further discussion, see Chapter 7 in this volume].

Finally, more gradual changes in perception may be brought about either by the dissemination of the work of criminologists with original ideas or by the persistence of groups campaigning to get a particular form of behaviour taken more seriously by the police and criminal justice system, as has happened in the case of racial attacks and domestic violence. But whatever the source of the initial attention, once sufficient public or media interest in a type of crime is generated, researchers are not usually slow to seek grants to investigate the scale of the problem in a more systematic way, while policy-makers may ask agencies to keep new kinds of records. The results, in turn, are likely to feed back into the political domain, thus promoting and continuing a dynamic process of 'amplification'.

Fundamental problems

The above examples serve as a useful introduction to some of the fundamental problems associated with the study of crime, which demand careful attention from anyone wishing to make general statements about its nature and extent. They help, especially, to illustrate the point that the core object of study — 'crime' — is, ultimately, a *social construct*. Looked at as an abstract formal category, it consists of a diverse set of behaviours which have in common (perhaps only) the fact that they are proscribed by the criminal law. The law, of course, changes over time, new offences being created and others being redefined or decriminalized, so that, even if we had god-like vision to spot every possible transgression, it would be difficult to make definitive comparisons between the 'true level of crime' at different points over a period of years (let alone to compare levels in countries with significantly different laws). More importantly, though, such an exercise would lack social meaning, which derives from the application in the real world of the label 'crime' or 'criminal' to specific incidents and people, *out of a much wider set of possible candidates for such a label.* This necessitates recognition by those involved in (or witnessing or hearing about) an incident, both that a crime has been committed and that this fact is of some significance to them or others; in most cases, too, for the event to have any publicly visible consequences requires its notification to the police and subsequent incorporation into official records. As will be illustrated later, despite the apparently precise wording of legislation, such categorization is anything but mechanical and value-free: it is highly selective and value-laden, the product of complex social, political, and organizational processes.

One of the recurrent criticisms made of criminology (particularly by sociologists) has been that, despite the daunting implications of the above points for the status of empirical knowledge in the subject, 'crime' has too often been treated as an unproblematic concept. Partly because of the importance of direct government grants in the funding of research, it has been pointed out, the overall 'agenda' of criminology — including the determination of the range of behaviours to be studied or analysed — has always been heavily influenced, explicitly or implicitly, by relatively short-term, policy-related concerns. Yet criminologists have often forgotten or ignored this, claiming a spurious 'scientific' status for their subject-matter (for an extensive historical critique, see Taylor *et al.* 1973; see also Cohen 1974; Bottomley 1979; Garland's chapter in this volume). While such criticism is less fair nowadays than in the past, it is still easy, for example, for those engaged in government-funded research to be pulled into unquestioning acceptance of policy-driven definitions of particular 'crime problems'. There is also a tendency to present the accumulation of data about unreported crime as the gradual unveiling of more and more of the 'complete picture', the 'true total' of criminal offences committed, when a more appropriate metaphor might be the constant repainting of a canvas of indeterminate size, with new areas highlighted and depicted in greater detail.

Awareness of the shaky foundations of criminological knowledge does not mean that one should abandon the pursuit of statistical data about it: on the contrary, these are vital to the development and testing of ideas, as well as to the very necessary task of description. The important point to stress, however, is that no conclusions should be drawn from any such data without careful qualification and very clear definition of terms.

Changing perspectives: key influences

To gain a broader understanding of how and why perceptions of crime — and approaches to its measurement — have changed, it is necessary to begin by reiterating one or two general points about the nature of criminology in the earlier part of this century and to refer to the crucial upheaval in the subject which occurred in the late 1960s and early 1970s. [These issues are discussed in varying degrees of detail by several other contributors to this volume; see particularly the chapters by Garland and Young.] Two other significant influences will then be briefly discussed: the growing focus, during the 1980s, upon victims of crime; and the increased attention given in Home Office policy to crime prevention and opportunity reduction through alteration of the environment. Both of these, it will be pointed out, played a part in shifting the focus of many criminologists' interests from the mental state of *offenders* to the physical circumstances and distribution of *offences*.

The paradigm shift in the 1970s

For much of the twentieth century, British criminology remained a small and somewhat insular discipline, dominated [though by no means monopolized; see chapter 1 in this volume] by what has since been widely, and often disparagingly, referred to as the 'positivist' tradition.[4] Most early criminologists were people with backgrounds in medicine or psychiatry, for whom the central goal was to understand and explain — and hence point the way to 'treatment' for — the 'criminality' of individual offenders. This was regarded by some as a real and discoverable condition, a propensity towards criminal or other anti-social behaviour, somewhat akin to a disease. Research was typified by the use of supposedly 'scientific' methods, such as systematically comparing the physical or psychological characteristics of groups of 'known offenders' (usually prisoners) with those of 'non-criminal' control groups, in order to identify factors which appeared to distinguish them and might therefore provide clues to the elusive 'causes of crime'. Biological explanations (variants on Lombroso's notion of the 'born criminal') had been largely discounted by the 1920s, being replaced by a variety of psychological and psychiatric theories. Later, as more academics with social science backgrounds entered criminology, interest shifted to 'social' factors such as family structure or unemployment, but the primary focus still tended to be on their possible influence upon individuals' propensity to commit offences — an equally deterministic approach, in which people continued to be seen as passive objects of extraneous forces, rather than as exercising choice, and in which no heed was paid to their own understanding of events. The dominant positivist method of enquiry thus remained essentially unchanged, continuing to thrive well into the 1970s.[5]

Despite their professed commitment to 'science', most British criminologists sought findings with direct relevance to the immediate goals of policy-makers and practitioners. Consequently, positivist criminology was further characterized by the acceptance of narrow, conventional definitions of 'the crime problem'. Many were content to restrict their inquiries entirely to officially defined offenders, focusing upon the predominantly male, lower-class 'recidivists' (repeat offenders) who provided the bread-and-butter work of the police and courts, and the majority of whom were convicted of a limited range of predatory property crimes such as burglary and petty theft. Others preferred to define their focus of inquiry, as advocated by Sellin (1938), according to social, rather than legal, categories of disapproved behaviour, using terms such as 'delinquent' or 'anti-social' or 'socially harmful' behaviour, rather than 'crime' (see e.g. Burt 1944; Bowlby 1953; West and Farrington 1969). However, this clearly involved value-laden choices about what to include: again — particularly during the late 1950s and early 1960s as middle-class fears of the 'youth culture' increased — attention was directed at readily visible kinds of norm-violation, especially in cultural forms commonly displayed by working-class adolescents.[6] In either case, with the emphasis upon finding out what was 'wrong with' those who engaged in such activities, there was relatively little curiosity about other, more 'hidden' forms of crime, particularly those practised by more powerful social groups; and 'crime' itself continued to be treated essentially as an unproblematic concept.

However, since the late 1960s, when, galvanized by a new generation of scholars with a strong interest in sociological theory, the discipline began to expand and burst out of its positivist straitjacket, the task of understanding and explaining crime has been interpreted in a variety of new ways. The immediate impetus came from the work of American sociologists, including the influential 'labelling' theorists (e.g. Becker 1963; Kitsuse 1964), who popularized the argument that 'crime' (or 'deviance') was not an independently existing phenomenon, but simply a label attached for a variety of reasons to diverse forms of behaviour. In the words of Erikson (1964): 'Deviance is not a property inherent in certain forms of behaviour, it is a property conferred upon those forms by the audience which directly or indirectly witness them.'

The influence of these writers, mediated at first in Britain through the work of 'deviancy' theorists such as Rock (1973) and Cohen (1974), helped to initiate a broad shift in the focus of inquiry and level of explanation, away from 'the pathology of the criminal' towards 'the social construction of crime' — the social and political processes by which particular forms of activity and the actions of particular groups within society are (or are not) 'criminalized'. The way was thus opened to the growth of new academic schools such as interactionism, radical criminology, and socio-legal studies, which, though deeply split on many other grounds, shared this basic interest. Some writers engaged in macro-level analyses of the relationships between the interests of the ruling classes, the state, and the shaping of 'crime' through the criminal law (see Taylor *et al.* 1973). Others, influenced by the work of other American sociologists such as Skolnick (1966), Cicourel (1968) and Manning (1977), conducted micro-level studies of the daily interactions through which legal and social rules are interpreted and deviant or criminal identities are created. This included exploration of systematic biases by the police and criminal justice system in the invocation and enforcement of legal rules (see Holdaway 1979; Bottomley and Coleman 1981).

Among their many other influences, such approaches made virtually all criminologists distinctly more wary of accepting, as representations of an 'objective reality', broad pictures of crime and criminals derived from official police and court records. These data, it became widely understood, created not just an *incomplete* picture of crime — the problem, already familiar to all criminologists, of the missing 'dark figure' of crimes which are not reported to the police — but a *systematically biased* picture of crime. Criminal statistics had to be analysed as the product, not of a neutral fact-collecting process, but of a record-keeping process which is geared first and foremost to organizational (primarily police) aims and needs. As such, they may tell us more about the organization producing them than about the 'reality' they are later taken to describe. In the words of Wiles (1971: 188):

> Criminal statistics are based on data collected not by agencies designed to collect information about crime, but agencies designed to enforce the law. The statistics which result are part of the attempt to achieve that goal. The nineteenth century political economists were right in seeing the collection of statistics by such agencies as part of the process of government, but the implication of this for the sociological study of crime is that statistics themselves must be explained, rather than that they provide data for the explanation.

This line of argument led some writers to conclude that there was no point in analysing crime figures for the purpose of finding out anything about the extent of any kind of illegal behaviour — if, indeed, it made any sense to speak of 'real' crime rates at all. For them, crime rates were simply 'indices of organisational processes' (Kitsuse and Cicourel 1963) or 'an aspect of social organisation' (Black 1970), worthy of study only to help one understand the agency producing them.[7] This 'institutionalist', as opposed to 'realist', approach was also broadly the starting position adopted by Bottomley and Coleman (1981) in a major empirical study of crime-recording processes in police stations. However, although the study revealed a great deal about the influence of specific police interests, attitudes and decisions in the creation of official statistics, the authors also reached the important conclusion that the decisions of many other people and agencies (notably personal and commercial victims, who between them initiate the vast majority of recorded crimes) had as much, if not more, to do with the overall 'shaping' of the figures.

The growing belief that official statistics should be studied as an object of sociological enquiry, rather than as a means of describing criminal activity, had the further important effect of raising criminologists' awareness of the rich potential of alternative sources of information about crime, such as ethnographic or participant observation studies and data from agencies other than the police. It also encouraged studies of previously neglected and largely hidden areas of 'deviant' and/or 'criminal' activity, such as drug-taking, workplace 'fiddles', and, later, corporate crime, domestic violence, and sexual violence against women (examples being, respectively, Young 1970; Ditton 1977; Levi 1981; Dobash and Dobash 1979; Hanmer and Saunders 1984).

The new focus on victims

The search for new forms of knowledge generated a fertile period for criminology in terms of theory and ideas, but it should be stressed that, with the emphasis upon understanding social processes rather than upon description or measurement, it did not immediately produce much new information in *statistical* form. On the contrary, there was a period when the climate in many parts of the discipline was distinctly *anti*-statistical, those who employed quantitative methodologies frequently being derided as 'mere empiricists'. In many cases, then, the new information acquired was qualitative (based, for example, on small numbers of detailed case studies) rather than quantitative.

A marked change came about in the early to mid 1980s, fuelled to a large extent by a growth in attention to crime *victims*. This perspective, initially given impetus by feminist campaigns in the USA in the 1970s, has since been embraced in a variety of ways by criminologists from all parts of the political spectrum, informing debates about, *inter alia,* the welfare and rights of victims, policing policy, crime prevention, court processes, mediation, racial harassment, and sexual oppression (for overviews, see the chapter by Zedner in this volume; Walklate 1989; Heidensohn 1989; Lurigio *et al.* 1990; Maguire 1991). More important for our purposes here, it has had the general effect of focusing attention much more upon the *offence* (and its impact) than upon the *offender,* and hence encouraging systematic analyses of where, when, and against whom different types of crime are likely to be committed.

An early British example of this kind of study was Maguire and Bennett's work on residential burglary (Maguire 1982).[8] The researchers described it as a 'crime-specific' study: a detailed look at one particular form of crime, the circumstances under which it is committed, the motives and behaviour of those committing it, and the experiences of its victims. They mapped every burglary recorded by the police over various periods in three separate areas and conducted 'in-depth' interviews with as many of the victims as possible about the precise circumstances of the incident. They also collected information from the police about the known or suspected offenders and interviewed some of those who had been convicted. A number of recurrent patterns were found, such as that burglaries tended to be clustered in poorer housing areas or close to arterial roads on the edges of towns; and that individual houses were more likely to be burgled if situated near road junctions or if they offered good cover (e.g. high hedges or fences) or access (e.g. rear or side alleys) to potential offenders. These patterns were tentatively explained in terms of interactions between, on the one hand, variations in the attractiveness of targets and in the risks and opportunities they offered and, on the other, the aims, thought processes, and behaviour patterns of different types of offender (juvenile and adult, local and travelling, and so on). The findings were generally consistent with offending behaviour as purposive and instrumental in pursuit of gain, rather than as irrational or expressive of psychological disturbance.

Many of these findings were echoed and amplified in further studies (e.g. Winchester and Jackson 1982; Bennett and Wright 1984), which also contributed to interest in the general concept of 'crime as opportunity' (Mayhew *et al.* 1976) or as a by-product of 'routine activity' (Cohen and Felson 1979), as well as in the responses of potential offenders to various kinds of opportunities to steal, the latter finding theoretical expression in, among other approaches, 'rational choice theory' (Cornish and Clarke 1986). They also fuelled new thinking about crime prevention (see next section). All of these approaches, it should be noted, are significantly removed from traditional concerns of criminology, in that they tend to direct attention to questions about the distribution of criminal events and about the physical circumstances in which they take place, rather than to questions about the mental state of those committing them. Interesting and important as the new questions are, the main academic criticism they attract is that they leave on the back burner the theoretical task which many criminologists would still consider to be the ultimate goal of criminology, that of explaining why people commit crime at all [for further comment on these points, see the chapters by Garland and Young in this volume].

Moreover, whatever their usefulness in opening up new lines of thought, the obvious methodological weakness of the above mentioned burglary studies, as of similar research in North America (e.g. Reppetto 1974; Waller and Okihiro 1978; Brantingham and Brantingham 1975) and of other crime-specific studies in the UK (e.g. Banton 1985 on robbery), remains their reliance upon offences recorded by the police. Later in the chapter we shall look at what was probably the most significant development in criminological research in Britain during the 1980s, whereby systematic information has been built up about patterns of *unrecorded* crime: the advent and acceptance of the 'victim survey' (latterly more often called 'crime survey') as a standard method of data collection. Initially conceived primarily as a means of counting crimes not reported to the police, crime surveys have developed into a flexible and rewarding research tool, gathering all kinds of details about the circumstances of offences, the relationships between offenders and victims, and the reactions of victims to what happened. Indeed, so successful have they been, it is already clear that the danger with such surveys, as in the past with official crime figures, lies in the temptation to regard their results as objective reflections of the overall state of crime in the country. This is plainly wrong, not least because surveys measure a limited range of criminal activity and, even within this range, are better suited to eliciting information about some types of offence — and some types of victim — than others. These and other issues will be discussed in a substantial section of this chapter devoted to the British Crime Survey and to the various local surveys which have made their own distinct contribution in recent years, while further comment will be found in chapter 25 [of *THE OXFORD HANDBOOK OF CRIMINOLOGY*, 1994].

New thinking about crime prevention

Another strand of the shift of focus towards the offence, rather than the offender, was the growing disillusionment among influential policy-makers with the idea that crime can be controlled solely — or even principally — through the actions of the police and criminal justice system (cf. Brody 1976; Clarke and Hough 1984). Faced with the apparent failure of the police, courts, and prisons to stem rising crime rates, the Home Office Research Unit, under the headship of Ronald Clarke, began a clear policy shift in the late 1970s towards research and initiatives in the area of crime prevention, in the sense of attempting to alter the physical environment, rather than the offender. This led eventually to the formation of a separate research unit, the Home Office Crime Prevention Unit.

The distinctive contribution of Home Office research during the early and mid-1980s was the development of 'situational crime prevention'. Eschewing any interest in what Clarke (1980) called 'dispositional' theories of crime (which assert that certain people have a predisposition to offend and hence that the key to crime prevention lies in changing them), it set out to use detailed crime pattern analysis to pinpoint areas of the environment which could be altered in such a way as to make it less easy or less attractive for potential offenders to commit particular types of crime. The alteration might take the form of extra physical security, increased surveillance, the marking of property, and so on (for overviews and examples, see Clarke and Mayhew 1980; Bennett and Wright 1984; Heal and Laycock 1986; [and Pease chapter 14 in this volume)].

This 'targeting' approach necessitated detailed knowledge about the prevalence and the geographical and temporal patterning, as well as the physical 'mechanics', of particular offences, thus stimulating more empirical research in these areas. At the same time, the already fast declining proportion of Home Office funding which was granted for research into subjects connected with the psychology or social problems of individual offenders, dwindled virtually to zero.

For these and other reasons, then — including a general expansion of interest in issues such as public sector accountability and managerial efficiency, which led to more research examining the data collection practices of crime-related agencies — criminology began to benefit from a rapidly growing storehouse of empirical data about the frequency, location, and physical circumstances of specific kinds of criminal incidents. Since the beginning of the 1980s there have been, *inter alia,* four national crime surveys, several substantial local crime surveys, various 'victimization' surveys of businesses, 'in-depth' interview studies of victims of specific types of offence, analyses of police message pads (as opposed to the traditional dependence on crime files), and trawls of data held by ethnic minority welfare groups, hospitals, and other agencies to which people reveal 'hidden crimes'. The most influential of these sources will be discussed in some detail below. However, before commenting further on the explosion of new knowledge, it is time to take a closer look at the traditional sources of information and the basic picture of crime they produce.

The official picture

The key official publication in respect of crime figures is *Criminal Statistics,* the annual compilation of data derived from police and court records throughout England and Wales, which is collated and tabulated by the Home Office Research and Statistics Department.[9] Despite the caution with which they are now treated by criminologists and Home Office statisticians alike, and despite the increasingly high profile given in *Criminal Statistics* to comparative data from the British Crime Survey (see below), these statistics remain the primary 'barometer of crime' used by politicians and highlighted in the media. They are also — a use to which they are much better suited — influential in the resource and strategic planning of the Home Office and police forces. We shall now consider, briefly, how the police-generated statistics are constructed and what they indicate about the total volume of crime, the relative frequencies of different offences, their geographical distribution, and broad trends over recent years. Later in the chapter, we shall also examine what the statistics based on court records appear to tell us about the characteristics of offenders.

Total volume of crime

The latest official figures available at the time of writing (Home Office 1993a) indicate that the total number of 'notifiable offences' recorded by the police in England and

Wales in 1992 was just under 5.6 million. Although this is the global figure referred to in most public debates about the extent of crime, it has to be emphasized that, *even as a record of criminal offences officially known to the authorities,* it is anything but complete (unreported offences are another matter, as discussed below). Notifiable offences are largely, though not fully, coterminous with offences which may be tried in the Crown Court.[10] This means that a large number of *summary* offences (i.e. those triable only in magistrates' courts) do not appear in the figures. No records are kept of the totals of such offences, although some statistics are available on the numbers of people officially sanctioned for them. For example, in 1990, about 1.3 million people were convicted or formally cautioned for summary offences: a total, it is worth noting, almost three times that of people convicted or cautioned for notifiable offences.[11]

In addition, the 'official crime figures' do not include offences recorded by police forces for which the Home Office is not responsible, notably the British Transport Police, Ministry of Defence Police, and UK Atomic Energy Authority Police, who between them recorded about 80,000 notifiable offences in 1992.[12] Nor, more significantly in terms of numbers, do they include numerous cases of tax and benefit fraud known to agencies such as the Inland Revenue, Customs and Excise, and Department of Social Security, which have investigative and prosecutional functions but which deal with the vast majority of cases by using their administrative powers to impose financial penalties (Levi 1993). Again, while such agencies keep internal records of the numbers of people dealt with in these ways, or of the total amounts of revenue saved, they do not record the total numbers of 'offences' coming to their notice — a task which, given that a single offender may repeat the same kinds of fraud numerous times over a period, would require complex counting rules.

It might be argued that, for all practical purposes, it is perfectly adequate to judge the size of 'the crime problem' by the total of notifiable offences recorded by the police, on the grounds that these embrace the most serious crimes, for which the vast majority of prison sentences are passed. However, they also include large numbers of incidents which it is difficult to claim are any more serious than many of the summary offences and the offences dealt with administratively, referred to above. For example, among the largest categories of notifiable offences, together making up well over a third of the total recorded, are theft from a vehicle, criminal damage, and theft from shops: most cases in these categories involve relatively small amounts of loss or damage. Again, attempts to commit notifiable offences are included along with completed crimes. Meanwhile, not only do unprosecuted tax and benefit frauds often involve considerable sums of money, but among the uncounted summary offences are common assault, assault on a police officer, cruelty to children, 'drink-driving', and indecent exposure, all of which include acts arguably more serious than many of the abovementioned notifiable offences.

Changing views about the seriousness or otherwise of particular kinds of offence have led on occasion to changes in Home Office decisions about what to include in or exclude from the official crime totals. Most notably, offences of criminal damage of £20 or less — which were not indictable — were not counted prior to 1977, but since that date have been defined as notifiable and included. This decision immediately raised the 'total volume of crime' by about 7 per cent.[13]

In addition to the issue of which categories of offence are included, there are important questions to ask about how individual crimes are counted. Some kinds of offence tend to be repeated many times within a short period, to the extent that, though there may be several separate actions or people involved, they may be considered to form part of one concerted criminal incident. For example, a thief may go through twenty trouser pockets in a changing-room, or try the doors of a whole row of cars, or steal a cheque card and use it many times to obtain goods or cash. Equally, a large affray — for example, at a demonstration or a football match — may involve numerous assaults by many people on many others; or a man may assault his partner virtually every night for a period of months or years.

Prior to 1968, there was little consistency between police forces on how many offences were to be recorded when events of these kinds came to their notice. Following the recommendations of the Perks Committee in 1967, clearer 'counting rules' were established (Home Office 1971),[14] which tidied up some of the discrepancies between forces, but at the same time they appear fairly arbitrary and, undoubtedly, understate the relative frequency of some offences. The general rule is now that, if several offences are committed 'in one incident', only the most serious is counted — unless violence is involved, in which case the rule is 'one offence for each victim'. There is also a broad (and by no means clear) guideline stating that only one offence will be counted in a 'continuous series of offences, where there is some special relationship, knowledge or position that exists between the offender and the person or property offended against which enables the offender to repeat the offence'. Thus, in the above examples, the changing room thief, the cheque fraudster, and the spouse abuser are likely to be credited with only one crime apiece, while the affray may produce quite a large number of offences. If the rule were changed, for example, to allow all cheque frauds to be counted separately, the overall 'official' picture of crime might look significantly different.

The illustrations given here all demonstrate that statements about the 'total volume of crime' have to be hedged about with qualifications, even when they purport only to describe crimes officially known to state agencies: if different notification or counting rules were adopted (let alone new offences being created by legislation), the total could be raised or lowered significantly at a stroke.

However, the problems of police statistics are by no means restricted to formal questions of definition or rules of inclusion and exclusion. Not only do the figures (obviously) not include offences known to the public which fail to come to police notice, but a great deal of discretion remains in police hands about whether and how to record possible offences which do come to their notice. Reports from the public — which are the source of over 80 per cent of all recorded crimes (McCabe and Sutcliffe 1978; Bottomley and Coleman 1981) — may be disbelieved, or considered too trivial, or deemed not to refer to a criminal offence, with the result that they either are not recorded at all, or are officially 'no crimed' later. They may also be excluded ('cuffed') for less defensible reasons, such as to avoid work or to improve the overall clear-up rate (Bottomley and Coleman 1981).[15] Calculations from crime survey data indicate that about 40 per cent of 'crimes' reported to the police do not end up in the official statistics, for good or bad reasons (Mayhew and Maung 1992).

31

Equally, the numbers of offences 'discovered' by the police themselves — either in the course of patrols or observation, or through admissions by arrested offenders — are subject to all kinds of fluctuation. For example, planned operations against a particular type of offence will usually result in a considerable increase in arrests and the uncovering and recording of many new offences. This is particularly true of operations against 'victimless' crimes: for example, a pop festival is almost guaranteed to generate a sudden dramatic boost in an area's recorded drug offences. Conversely, numbers may fall owing to a withdrawal of police interest in a particular type of crime, as in the late 1950s and early 1960s when, pending anticipated legislation to legalize homosexuality, most forces turned a blind eye to instances of 'indecency between males' and the recorded total of such offences declined to half the level previously regarded as 'normal' (Walker 1971).

Types of crime

Criminal Statistics currently lists the notifiable crimes recorded by the police under a total of seventy-one headings, each of them assigned a Home Office classification number (murder is no. 1, attempted murder no. 2, threat or conspiracy to murder no. 3, and so on). These are grouped under eight broader headings, namely 'offences of violence', 'sexual offences', 'robbery', 'burglary', 'theft and handling stolen goods', 'fraud and forgery', 'criminal damage', and 'other notifiable offences'. Most of these groups contain a considerable variety of offences, in terms of both context and seriousness, but most are dominated numerically by just one or two. Thus the category 'violence' includes offences as diverse as murder, causing death by reckless driving, and concealment of birth, but over 90 per cent of its total is accounted for by what is referred to in the tables as 'other wounding etc.' — ie mainly offences of s. 47 assault (which tend to involve fists or feet rather than knives or other weapons). Similarly, 'sexual offences' range from rape to bigamy to indecency between males, but over half consist of indecent assault on a female. In other words, a relatively small number of offence categories play a major part in determining both the overall crime total and the size of each offence group in relation to the others. Moreover, trends in these dominant offence types tend to disguise countertrends in less prolific offences.

Table 1   Notifiable offences recorded by the police, 1992

Offence group	No. (to the nearest 10,000)	%
Theft of/from vehicles	1,540,000	29
Other theft	1,300,000	24
Burglary	1,360,000	25
Criminal damage	690,000	13
Violence (inc. robbery)	250,000	5
Fraud and forgery	170,000	3
Sexual offences	30,000	<1
Other	40,000	<1
Total	5,380,000	100

Source: Adapted from Home Office 1993*a*.

Table 1 shows in simplified form the contributions of the main offence groups to the total number of offences recorded by the police in 1992. It also separates out 'auto crime' (the theft or unauthorized taking of, or theft from, motor vehicles) from other forms of theft.

If one looks at the figures as a whole, the picture of the 'crime problem' which emerges is one dominated by property offences, and above all by theft associated with vehicles. The 'theft and handling' group as a whole, with 2,844,548 recorded offences, constituted well over half of the sum total, with 'auto crime' alone accounting for 29 per cent. Burglary — primarily a property offence, though with the added (and often disturbing) element of trespass — makes up another quarter of the total. The numbers of fraudulent, violent, and sexual offences appear very small in comparison.

The fact that offences against the person make up such a small proportion of all recorded crime has quite often been quoted in a reassuring tone, especially to support the argument that the popular media focus too strongly upon violence and distort its importance within the overall crime picture. However, two points need to be made in this context. First, as pointed out above, the published figures do not include sizeable numbers of offences of common assault or assault on a police officer, which are not indictable crimes. Secondly — a more fundamental problem — the statistics can be misleading without an acknowledgement of the relative importance of violent offences judged by criteria other than sheer numbers: for example, in terms of public concern, the effects upon victims, or the number and length of prison sentences they attract. Sexual assaults, robberies, and woundings have been found to have a profound emotional impact on much higher proportions of victims than is the case with offences of theft (Maguire and Corbett 1987). Fear of violence also severely restricts the social lives of many people (Maxfield 1984; Zedner, chapter 25 in this volume). Strikingly, too, on any one day one cares to select, well over 40 per cent of the total population of convicted prisoners will be found to be serving sentences for violent or sexual offences. By contrast, people sentenced for the much more common offences of theft, handling, fraud, and forgery together make up under 12 per cent of the convicted prison population.[16]

Related comments can be made about fraud. First, as explained earlier, the counting rules cause a great number of repetitive fraudulent acts, especially those involving cheque cards and false entries in accounts, to be recorded as only one or two 'sample' offences. Second, many fraudulent tax or benefit offences are dealt with administratively by the Inland Revenue, Customs and Excise, or Social Security Department. Third, if one measures the importance of property offences in terms of the value of goods stolen, rather than the quantity of incidents, fraud comes out as of enormously greater significance than other categories. For example, Levi (1993) points out that the *mininum* value threshold for a case to be accepted for investigation by the Serious Fraud Office is a fraud of £5 million and that in April 1992, the Frauds Divisions of the Crown Prosecution Service were supervising cases involving nearly £4 billion. By contrast, the combined costs of the common offences of 'auto crime' and burglary for 1990 were estimated by the Association of British Insurers at under £1.3 billion. (Levi also points out that the alleged fraud in any one of several major cases — Barlow Clowes, Guinness, Maxwell, BCCI, Polly Peck — *alone* exceeded the total amount stolen in thefts and burglaries recorded by the police.)

This problem of minor offences 'counting' the same as major offences was recognized many years ago by Sellin and Wolfgang (1964), who devised a weighted index, based on the notional gravity of each recorded offence, which could be used to present an alternative picture of crime in any jurisdiction. This, they argued, would allow more realistic comparisons of the seriousness of the crime problem, either over time or in different cities, states, or countries. In brief, the authors attached a different score to each category of crime, based upon ratings of seriousness derived from interviews with random samples of the population. They found a fair degree of agreement among raters, both about the order in which they placed offences and about the degree of difference in 'seriousness' between them.

Various comparisons were carried out in the USA between changes in officially recorded crime rates and changes in 'crime rates' as measured by the Sellin-Wolfgang index. Some interesting results emerged — for example, Normandeau (1969) found some contrary trends in robbery in Philadelphia, as measured by the index and by the official Uniform Crime Rates — but eventually most criminologists abandoned the index as of both dubious validity and dubious utility. Lesieur and Lehman (1975), for example, doubted whether seriousness is 'one kind of thing' that can be ordered along a scale as on a ruler, let alone whether adding up the scores would produce a total which had any meaning at all (see also Nettler 1978). Such questions, of course, are also pertinent to the current debate about 'just deserts' sentencing systems based on scales of punishment supposedly related to the seriousness of each type of offence (for contrasting views, see Von Hirsch 1986; Hudson 1987).

Finally, a long-standing criticism of the presentation of official statistics (see e.g. McLintock and Avison 1968) has been that they do not give a clear picture of the social or situational context of crimes. For example, 'robbery' includes actions as diverse as an organized bank raid, the theft at knifepoint of the contents of a shopkeeper's till, and a drunken attempt to snatch a handbag or necklace in the street. Knowing that 52,894 robberies were recorded in 1992, or that this represented an increase of 16.7 per cent over 1991, tells us very little about the events, nor whether different styles of robbery are declining or becoming more prevalent. Until recently, the only offences for which any attempt was made in *Criminal Statistics* to illustrate the context were homicide and offences involving firearms. Information is regularly provided in homicide cases about the age and sex of the victim, the relationship between the principal suspect and the victim, and the method of killing used. For example, in 1991 the highest victimization rate, expressed in terms of deaths per million population in each age group, was found among males under the age of one year (53 per million);[17] or, again, 41 per cent of female victims were killed by a current or former spouse, cohabitant, or lover, most commonly by means of strangulation.

A further step in the direction of providing 'context' has been taken in recent years, with the analysis of data (from a small number of police forces) on offences of violence. For example, recorded assaults are subdivided into 'street brawls' (the largest group for male victims), 'pub brawls', 'attacks on a public servant', and 'domestic violence' (the largest group for female victims). There are all kinds of doubts about even the factual accuracy of these data. Nevertheless, particularly when compared to crime survey findings — which show a rather higher proportion of domestic violence — they still raise some interesting questions, both about relationships between gender and violence and about how domestic violence is responded to by the police [for further discussion of this topic, see Levi, chapter 7 in this volume].

Geographical distribution

Criminal Statistics does not include detailed breakdowns of the distribution of recorded crime across the country, but basic figures are supplied separately for each of the forty-three police forces in England and Wales. Some forces, of course, are much larger than others and in order to afford a ready means of comparison, crime rates are expressed for each in terms of numbers of recorded offences per 100,000 population. This is by no means a fully satisfactory way of compensating for the differences between police force areas, as it takes no account of possible difference in the *compositions,* as opposed to the sizes, of the relevant populations. As Bottomley and Pease (1986: 11-12) point out in relation to changes in the same area over time:

> We should beware of easily reaching the conclusion that 'people commit crime, therefore more people can be expected to commit more crime' so that if the ratio between crime and population is unchanged then there can be nothing which requires an explanation. It can be seen at once that underlying such an assumption is an emergent theory about rates of offending, and possibly about rates of victimization, which leaves itself wide open to a series of supplementary questions such as whether all members of a population are equally 'at risk' of offending . . . what significance should be attached to the gender composition of the population . . . [and] given the change in the pattern of criminal opportunities, should one adjust for social changes like the number of cars registered.

It should also be noted that the crime rates produced may not reflect important differences between areas *within* forces. Nevertheless, they do offer some fairly consistent patterns. The most obvious difference between forces lies between those covering metropolitan areas and those covering predominantly rural counties. Table 2, which gives the figures for forces which fall clearly into one or other of these groups, shows that the rate in 'metropolitan' forces is consistently higher than, and sometimes double, that of 'rural' forces.

Apart from those shown in Table 2, there was only one force in the country where the recorded crime rate exceeded 10,000 per 100,000 population: Nottinghamshire showed a rate of 14,810, the second highest in the country. This was not a new phenomenon. Indeed, Nottinghamshire has long been an object of curiosity for its unexpectedly high crime rates and, more recently, has been held up as a prime example of the potentially misleading nature of official statistics. Farrington and Dowds (1985) published a detailed study of police recording practices in the county, from which they concluded that its apparently huge crime rate relative to its neighbouring counties of Leicestershire and Staffordshire (which are socially not dissimilar to Nottinghamshire) was a function of (a) a much greater number and proportion of recorded crimes originating from admissions to the police (25 per cent, compared to 4 per cent and 8 per cent in the neighbouring forces); (b) a greater number and proportion of recorded crimes involving property of little value (48 per cent valued at £10 or under, compared with 29 per cent and 36 per cent); and (c) a somewhat higher 'true' crime rate, indicated by a public survey. The researchers stated:

> 'It is reasonable to conclude that between two-thirds and three-quarters of the difference in crime rates . . . reflected differences in police reactions to crime, while the remaining one-third reflected differences in criminal behaviour . . .

> The research shows once again the difficulties of interpreting official statistics. Almost certainly, Nottinghamshire has never been the most criminal area in the country. (Farrington and Dowds 1985: 70-1)

Table 2   Selected police force areas: notifiable offences recorded per 100,000 population, 1991

	Offences per 100,000 population
'Metropolitan' forces	
Cleveland	14,137
Durham	10,881
Greater Manchester	14,700
Humberside	13,831
Merseyside	10,309
MPD (London)	12,855
Northumbria	15,798
W. Midlands	11,584
W. Yorkshire	14,273
'Rural' forces	
Cheshire	6,913
Devon and Cornwall	7,224
Dyfed-Powys	5,508
Norfolk	8,541
North Wales	6,804
North Yorkshire	7,086
Suffolk	6,201
Wiltshire	6,998

Source: Adapted from Home Office 1992*c*: table 2.6.

Interestingly, Nottinghamshire fell from its top place in the national table in 1981 to fifth place in 1982, a change which, Farrington and Dowds claim, 'is almost certainly attributable to changes in police policies for recording offences, which may have been caused partly by this research project'.

The foregoing discussion provides us with two messages about the capacity of the official statistics to reflect patterns of crime across the country. On the one hand, they show broad consistency in indicating differences in crime rates between the extremes of rural and metropolitan areas — differences one would expect according to most theories of crime causation, as well as in the light of ordinary experience. On the other hand, as the Nottinghamshire example shows, variations in recording practices can have such a great effect on the totals produced as to render 'face value' comparisons between individual areas meaningless. It is only when one probes deeply into the practices generating police statistics that they begin to yield valuable insights.

Trends

Although graphic references to the volume of offences (e.g. 'A Burglary Every Twenty Seconds') are not uncommon, the kinds of statistic most likely to feature in newspaper headlines are those referring to apparent *trends* in recorded crime (e.g. 'Burglary Up 20 Per Cent'). In many cases, such figures refer only to a rise or fall relative to the previous year, or even the previous quarter, paying no attention to the relationship between the latter and the situation in earlier years. Thus — even leaving aside the doubts about whether changes in recorded crime levels reflect real changes in criminal behaviour — they can be highly misleading in terms of longer term trends. Sometimes, too — a practice which, if used deliberately, is simply dishonest — commentators refer to a percentage fall or increase since a particular year (to take a real example, 'burglary has risen over 60 per cent since 1989'), selecting as their baseline year one in which the official total had deviated significantly from the underlying trend.

Serious attempts to identify trends in recorded crime use figures produced at regular intervals over longer periods, and may represent the trend either in the form of a graph or through devices such as 'moving averages'. They also try to take account of changes in recording practice, such as allowing for the exclusion of minor offences of criminal damage prior to 1977, referred to above, as well as adjusting for legislative changes — the most important in the post-war years being the Theft Act 1968, which radically redefined a number of key offences including burglary (Maguire 1982: 8-9).

As can be seen from Fig. 1, the main features of trends in official crime statistics since their inception in 1876 have been a relatively unchanged picture until the 1930s, a clear rise up to and through the Second World War (though tailing off a little in the early 1950s), and an extremely sharp and sustained increase from the mid-1950s onwards. This saw a doubling of the figures within ten years (from roughly half a million crimes in 1955 to a million in 1964), another doubling over the next ten years, and yet another by 1990.

It should be kept in mind that parallel spectacular rises were recorded in most other western democracies over the same period.[18] Indeed, it was from this time on that criminologists worldwide, hitherto used to fairly stable, if gradually increasing, crime rates, began to be faced for the first time with a phenomenon which laid down a serious challenge to most of the 'positivist' explanations of crime which had been put forward and gained broad acceptance during the 'quieter' years. Most of these, as mentioned earlier, postulated some form of pathology in individual offenders, caused by some form of deprivation. How, it began to be asked, in a time of rising prosperity — which would, if anything, predict a *decrease* in crime according to such theories — could there be such an apparently massive increase in individuals with 'problems'?

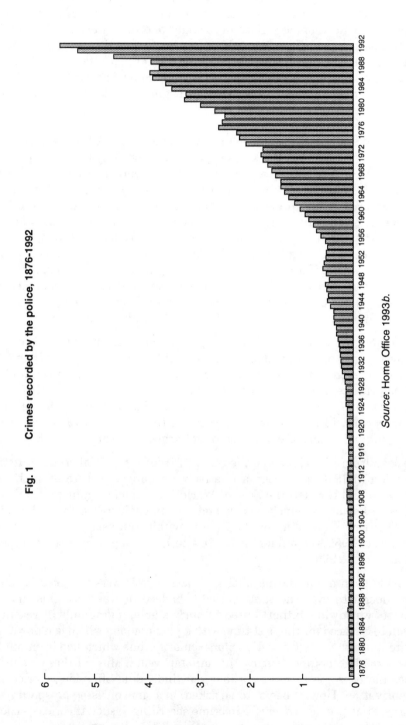

Fig. 1   Crimes recorded by the police, 1876-1992

Source: Home Office 1993*b*.

Other features of the growth in recorded crime since the legal changes in definitions introduced by the 1968 Theft Act include the following:

1. The average annual rate of increase has been in the region of 5 per cent, but there have been many fluctuations, ranging from a rise of 18 per cent in 1974 to a 3 per cent fall in 1979. The late 1980s saw a period of relatively little change, but this was followed by exceptionally sharp rises (of 17 and 16 per cent) in 1990 and 1991.

2. The greatest *percentage* increase has been in offences of criminal damage: from about 13,000 in 1969 to over 900,000 in 1992 (or 690,000 if offences of value £20 and below are excluded, as in 1969), a massive rise of more than 6,000 per cent. In *numerical* terms, as one would expect, the largest increases have been in various categories of theft, especially those involving vehicles. There were around two million more theft offences recorded in 1992 than in 1969.

3. During the 1980s, the offences which appeared to rise most sharply were rape and trafficking in controlled drugs, both exhibiting average annual increases of over 10 per cent. There appear to be special reasons, associated with police practice, in both cases: publicized improvements in the treatment of — and a greater willingness to believe — rape victims (Blair 1985) may have affected both reporting and recording behaviour, while more police and Customs resources have been put into operations against drug trafficking (which, of course, tends to be recorded only when arrests are made).

All other major categories of crime showed more gradual increases over the 1980s, until the figures for theft, burglary, and fraud 'took off' quite dramatically in 1990 and 1991, with 'auto crime' leading the way. In 1992, however, the increases returned to a relatively modest rate.

The advent of crime surveys

Prior to the advent of national crime surveys in the early 1980s, criminologists used to spend a great deal of time debating whether or not the trends apparent in recorded crime reflected 'real' changes in levels of offending, or were primarily a function of changes in the propensity of the public to report crimes and/or of the police to record them. At the extreme, some argued that the 'rises in crime' regularly deplored in newspaper headlines were largely, if not totally, illusory: the result of, *inter alia*, increases in the number of police officers (more people to uncover and record offences), the installation of telephones in more and more houses (thus making reporting easier), the spread of insurance (reporting being necessary to support a claim), reduced levels of public tolerance to violence, and the break-up of traditional communities (the last two factors making people more inclined to call in the police rather than 'sort the problem out themselves'). Hal Pepinsky, in a brief unpublished study in a British city in the late 1970s, produced the interesting finding that local crime rates appeared to have varied in relation to fluctuations in police morale and disputes about resources, offering the interpretation that the figures were manipulated, consciously or unconsciously, for 'political' reasons, such as to support arguments for increased manpower.[19] He claimed, for example, that almost half the year's increase in recorded thefts in one subdivision had been produced by a single prolific offender who stole bottles of milk from doorsteps, efforts having been made (arguably in contravention of the counting rules) to identify and record separately large numbers of his minor criminal acts. At the same time, he found, officers working 'on the ground' had not noticed any difference in levels of criminal activity in the area. Selke and Pepinsky (1984) produced a similar kind of analysis in relation to crime figures in Indiana which, they claimed, had risen and fallen almost entirely in relation to the political needs of the party in power.

While few went as far as Pepinsky in doubting that any 'real' increase at all in conventional forms of criminal activity had been taking place, criminologists in the 1970s generally remained highly sceptical, at least, of the *rates* of increase indicated by police returns. Certainly, little academic writing or debate was devoted to analysis of 'the rise in crime' as a genuine and pressing social problem. By the early 1990s, such sceptical attitudes have become much less common, it having been broadly accepted throughout the discipline that the incidence of certain forms of crime, at least, has substantially increased. This change has been influenced by several factors, not least the high proflle of and acceptance achieved by crime surveys, to which we now turn. Other factors, such as the currency achieved in the 1980s by 'left realist' ideas (e.g. Matthews and Young 1986), will be referred to later.

National surveys

In the mid-1960s, the first serious attempts were made to assess the extent of the 'dark figure' of crimes which were either not reported to the police or, having been reported, were not officially recorded by the police. Two substantial experimental surveys were conducted in the USA (Ennis 1967; Bidermann and Reiss 1967), wherein members of a random sample of households were asked whether anyone in the house had been the victim of a crime within the previous year and, if so, whether the matter had been reported to the police. A similar experiment was carried out in three areas of London in the early 1970s (Sparks *et al.* 1977).

In both countries, despite the many methodological problems identified by the researchers, governments were sufficiently persuaded of the value of such surveys to invest considerable sums of money in running them officially on a large scale. In the USA, the Department of Justice funded regular surveys at both a national and local level from 1972, and while the Home Office was slower off the mark, its crime surveys have moved rapidly into a position where they now rank alongside *Criminal Statistics* as a source of data on crime and crime trends in Britain. Other European countries are quickly following suit. Indeed, the notion of regular *international* crime surveys, building upon those co-ordinated by van Dijk *et al.* (1990) and Van Dijk and Mayhew (1992), is by no means an idle dream.

The British Crime Survey (BCS), undertaken by members of the Home Office Research and Planning Unit, was first conducted in 1982, with further 'sweeps' (the radar metaphor consistently used by its authors) in 1984, 1988, and 1992. The main rationale for the survey — and, in particular, for its expensive repetition at regular intervals — is that, by asking samples of the public to describe crimes committed against them within a given recent period, the vagaries of crime-reporting behaviour and police recording behaviour are neatly avoided, and the responses can be grossed up into an alternative, 'fuller' — and hence, by implication, more 'valid' — picture of crime and its trends in Britain.

Table 3 **Estimated totals of offences in England and Wales, 1991, as derived from the 1992 British Crime Survey and 1991 *Criminal Statistics* where possible comparing crime groups**

	BCS No.[a]	(%)	Police[b] No.	(%)
Comparable offence groups				
Theft of/from vehicles	3,807,000	(25)	1,263,000	(24)
Vandalism	2,730,000	(18)	410,000	(8)
Burglary	1,365,000	(9)	625,000	(12)
Wounding	626,000	(4)	157,000	(3)
Robbery/theft from person	622,000	(4)	82,000	(2)
Bicycle theft	564,000	(4)	225,000	(4)
Subtotals	9,713,000	(65)	2,762,000	(52)
BCS offences not comparable with police data				
Other household theft	1,838,000	(12)	–	
Common assault	1,757,000	(12)	–	
Other personal theft	1,744,000	(12)	–	
Police-recorded offences not covered by/comparable with BCS				
Burglary not dwelling	–	–	595,000	(11)
Vandalism of public property	–	–	410,000	(8)
Theft from a shop	–	–	281,000	(5)
Fraud and forgery	–	–	175,000	(3)
Theft of/from commercial vehicles	–	–	132,000	(3)
Other	–	–	921,000	(17)
Totals	15,052,000	(100)	5,276,000	(100)

[a] All figures are rounded to the nearest 1,000; percentages may not total precisely owing to rounding.
[b] The 'comparable' police figures follow adjustments made by Mayhew and Maung (1992), which include adding some offences recorded by the British Transport Police. These are not included in the overall police total given, so the 'Other' figure in the 'non-comparable' section (921,000), which was arrived at by subtraction from this total, is a slight under-estimate.

Sources: Mayhew and Maung 1992; Home Office 1992c.

Before discussing its shortcomings in this respect, let us look briefly at the way the data from the BCS are compiled and presented. The basic format of the part of the questionnaire which elicits information about crimes known to respondents, and the framework for presenting the figures, were established in the 1982 survey and have changed relatively little since.[20] Respondents, who are residents of households over the age of 16 (though see note 20), are first asked whether 'you or anyone else now in your household' have been the victim of any of a series of crimes, each described to them in ordinary language, since 1st January of the previous year.[21] They are then asked whether 'you personally' have suffered any of a number of other offences. If any positive answers are received, interviewers complete a detailed 'Victim Form' for each incident, though with an upper limit of five. The results of this exercise are analysed to produce estimated national totals of both 'household offences' and 'personal offences', based on calculations using, respectively, the total number of households and the total adult population of England and Wales.[22]

The offence categories produced by the BCS are shown in Table 3. The first important point to note is that by no means all are coterminous with police categories. In fact, when making direct comparisons of 'official' and 'BCS' crime rates, only about two-thirds of the BCS-generated 'offences' can justifiably be used (Mayhew and Maung 1992).[23]

And, vice versa, there are many categories of offence covered in the police-derived statistics which are not measured by the BCS. These include crimes against commercial or corporate victims (notably shoplifting, burglary, and vandalism), fraud, motoring offences, and so-called 'victimless' crimes such as possession of or dealing in drugs. The main BCS schedule also excludes offences against victims under age 16 (though the 1992 'sweep' was designed to generate more information about these: see note 20 above). And sexual offences, though asked about, are reported to BCS interviewers so infrequently that no reliable estimations can be produced.

In other words, as their authors freely admit (see e.g. Hough and Mayhew 1985: ch. 1), national surveys are much less successful in obtaining information about some types of incident than others. They do not produce an overall figure purporting to represent the 'total volume of crime', but concentrate instead upon selected categories of offence, which are usually analysed and discussed individually or in sub-groups. It cannot be too heavily stressed, therefore, that the BCS provides an *alternative,* rather than a directly *comparable,* overall picture of crime to that offered by police statistics: it is 'fuller' than the latter in some respects, but 'narrower' in others.

Let us look first at the areas where the two data sets do overlap, and then at the BCS 'picture of crime' in the round. The main value of being able to compare estimated totals derived from the BCS with police-recorded totals in the equivalent offence categories is that some tentative statements can be made about the famous 'dark figure' of unreported and unrecorded crime — or, more accurately, about the 'dark figure' in each of these categories.

The authors of the initial BCS summarized the results of this exercise as follows:

> Only for one category — thefts of motor vehicles — were the figures similar. For instance, the survey indicated twice as many burglaries as were recorded by the police; nearly five times as much wounding; twelve times as much theft from the person; and thirteen times as much vandalism (or criminal damage) . . The overall ratio *for incidents which had been compared* was one in four. (Hough and Mayhew 1983: 10; emphasis added)

It will be noted from the first section of Table 3 that — though vandalism is an important exception (see below) — most of the above ratios were found to be relatively unchanged in the 1991 survey.

As the authors rightly went on to point out, there is a strong temptation to interpret such figures as showing that there is 'four times as much crime' as the official records suggest: a trap into which many people have duly fallen. The problem lies in the wide variations between offences in terms of their reporting and (to a lesser extent) recording rates. These variations mean that the choice of offence groups to include in any comparison can significantly affect the overall ratio between the survey figures and the police figures. For example, if the comparison included survey data covering some of the offences in the final section of Table 3 — let us say, estimates of instances of shoplifting or pilfering from work or cheque frauds, derived from surveys of employers or shopkeepers or bank employees — where the proportions which end up in police records are known to be tiny (see e.g. Martin 1962; Levi 1993), the overall 'dark figure' would emerge as a very much larger one. (In fact, the overall 'dark figure' estimated by Sparks *et al.* (1977) in their pioneering survey was one of eleven times the police figure, in contrast to the 'four times' estimate of the BCS. The main reason for this seems to be the different spread of offences covered.) These remarks are highly pertinent to the difference between the 'image' of crime presented by the BCS and that presented by some local surveys, which will be discussed in the next section.

How, then, can we summarize the main picture of crime that has emerged from the British Crime Survey? First, the central message sent out by its authors during the initial passage of its results into the public domain was, in essence: the bad news is that there is a lot more crime than we thought, the good news is that most of it is petty. The emphasis upon 'the petty nature of most law-breaking' (Hough and Mayhew 1983: 33) was designed to deflect a possible moral panic in reaction to the huge amount of 'new' crime revealed by the survey,[24] but it also reflected the finding that unreported crimes generally involve much lower levels of financial loss, damage, and injury than those reported to the police.

Secondly, the four 'sweeps' of the BCS, like most surveys in the USA, together suggest that, overall, increases in crime have been less steep than police figures suggest. Between 1981 and 1991, among the sub-set of offences which are comparable, the number of recorded crimes increased by 96 per cent, while those uncovered by the BCS rose by only 49 per cent. This is partly explained by an increase in 'reporting rates' — i.e. the proportion of offences known to victims which get reported to the police — from 36 per cent to 50 per cent (among the comparable sub-set). However, Mayhew and Maung (1992) point out that the increase in reporting was especially marked in the case of vandalism, a factor which significantly distorts the overall picture. In fact, what they call 'acquisitive crime' (burglary, vehicle-related theft, and other personal thefts) appears from BCS results to have increased at a rate close to that indicated by police figures.

Thirdly, the BCS produces a picture of crime not wildly dissimilar in its broad 'shape' to that projected by police records: both sets of figures are dominated by 'auto crime' and both indicate low levels of violent offences in relation to property offences. The main difference in respect of directly comparable offences is that vandalism is more prominent among BCS offences than in the official statistics: it appears that only about one in seven cases known to victims ends up in the police figures.

Finally, and more fundamentally, the BCS, perhaps even more so than the police figures, promotes a picture dominated by the types of crime that are generally *committed by strangers,* as it were 'out of the blue'. Most incidents reported to the survey consist of discrete events in which individuals suddenly and unexpectedly suffer the theft of or damage to a piece of their property, or an illegal entry into their house. Crime in this mode takes on an appearance in many ways akin to an accident, or an 'act of God' — an almost random event which can strike anyone at any time, but which is relatively rare in the life of any individual. This image was strengthened in the first BCS report by the calculation of the 'average risks' of falling victim to various types of offence:

a 'statistically average' person aged 16 or over can expect:

> * a robbery once every five centuries (not attempts)
>
> * an assault resulting in injury (even if slight) once every century
>
> * a family car to be stolen or taken by joyriders once every 60 years
>
> * a burglary in the home once every 40 years.
>
> . . . These risks can be compared with the likelihood of encountering other sorts of mishaps: the chances of burglary are slightly less than the chances . . . of a fire in the home; the chances a household runs of car theft are smaller than the chances . . . of having one of its members injured in a car accident. (Hough and Mayhew 1983: 15)

This manner of describing crime may correspond to many people's experience of it, especially among the middle classes. However, as will be discussed in the next section, it tends to leave out of the picture a number of very different kinds of experience. First of all, there are areas (poor inner city areas, particularly) where even predatory, stranger-to-stranger offences like burglary are suffered by individuals far more often than the above figures suggest. Secondly, there are important kinds of criminal behaviour, inadequately measured by the BCS, which are closely tied up with *continuing relationships between 'offender' and 'victim'.* These include assaults resulting from disputes between neighbours, the battery of women by their partners, and the sexual and physical abuse of children, all of which tend to be suffered many times by the same victims. They also include the repeated threats and harassment from local gangs suffered in some areas by members of racial minorities and by other individuals who become targeted as 'different'.

Local surveys and the radical critique

Concerns about the tendency of the BCS to distort 'real' experiences of crime — especially those of women, ethnic minorities, and the very poor — have been raised by several writers (see e.g. Matthews and Young 1986; Stanko 1988; Genn 1988; Dobash and Dobash 1992). They have also strongly influenced the design of a number of local crime surveys (e.g. Kinsey 1984; Hanmer and Saunders 1984; Jones *et al.* 1986, 1987;

Crawford *et al.* 1990), funded mainly by Labour councils, which have aimed to uncover areas of criminal behaviour not seriously touched by the BCS and, equally important, to examine and emphasize the extent to which victimization is *unequally distributed* among the population.

Some aspects of the distribution of risk were considered in the BCS from the start, but the main angle from which this topic was approached in the first report attracted a good deal of criticism. The main findings highlighted by the authors were that, for crimes of violence, males had higher victimization rates than females, and younger people higher than older; and that the risks were further related to lifestyle — for example, people who frequently went out drinking were more likely to be assaulted. From these findings they concluded, first, that offenders (or, at least, known offenders) and victims of violence shared several of the same social characteristics — the survey, wrote Hough and Mayhew (1983: 25) 'paints a . . . coherent picture of assault victims, in which the people they most resemble are their assailants'; and, second, that, this being the case, the fears of street violence expressed by both women and the elderly (which were much greater than those of young men) were to some extent out of proportion to the actual risks they faced. As will be discussed shortly, this latter point became a key target for some radical critiques of the BCS and the message it appeared to be sending out.

Other points from the first survey which received less attention included the finding that, where burglary was concerned, council properties were more vulnerable than owner-occupied dwellings (Hough and Mayhew 1983, 1985). Preliminary results from the 1992 survey confirm this in more detail, indicating that residents of 'the poorest council estates' face a burglary risk 2.8 times the average and twelve times that of people living in agricultural areas (Mayhew and Maung 1992).[25]

Similar patterns obtain for 'auto crime around the home' and robbery/theft from the person, though the greatest risk for the latter appears to be in 'mixed inner metropolitan areas'. The 1988 survey paid particular attention to differences in risk between racial groups. It was found that both Afro-Caribbeans and Asians were more at risk than whites for many types of crime, the latter being particularly vulnerable to vandalism and robbery or street theft committed by strangers (Mayhew *et al.* 1989).

Although these are all important findings, their impact has to some extent been diluted among the welter of other figures emerging from the surveys. By focusing chiefly upon inner city districts, local crime surveys have brought out much more vividly than the BCS the extent to which crime is concentrated in some small areas — predominantly those blighted by poverty — and, moreover, how particular forms of crime are suffered disproportionately by particular social groups within those areas. For example, the first Islington Crime Survey (Jones *et al.* 1986) indicated that a third of all households had been touched by burglary, robbery, or sexual assault within the previous twelve months (a situation light years away from that of the notional 'statistically average' person referred to in the BCS). It also indicated that young, white females in the area were twenty-nine times more likely to be assaulted than white females over 45. As Young (1988: 171) observes, such massive differences between subgroups illustrate 'the fallacy of talking of the problem of women as a whole, or of men, blacks, whites,

45

youths, etc.' Rather, he insists, criminological analysis should 'start from the actual subgroups in which people live their lives'.

Writing in the same volume, two of the founders of the BCS acknowledged that the increased attention given in later 'sweeps' of the BCS to the distribution of risk was to some extent prompted by criticism of the superficial approach taken earlier on, and in particular of the handling of questions about the relationship between risk of victimization and fear of crime (Mayhew and Hough 1988).[26] Much of this criticism was led by Jock Young and others broadly adhering to the 'left realist' school of criminology (cf Matthews and Young 1986; Young 1988).[27] They attacked in particular the inference, mentioned above, that fear of crime was in some senses 'irrational' because both women and the elderly, who were less likely to be attacked, expressed greater fear than the young men who were 'objectively' at the greatest risk. Young (1988: 173-5) points out that such an approach, like the argument that fears are exaggerated because much crime is 'trivial' in terms of loss or injury, obscures the fact that what are 'objectively' similar events can have enormously different meanings and consequences for different people:

> People differ greatly in their ability to withstand crime . . . The 'same' punch can mean totally different things in different circumstances . . . Violence, like all kinds of crime, is a social relationship. It is rarely random: it inevitably involves particular social meanings and occurs in particular hierarchies of power. Its impact, likewise, is predicated on the relationship within which it occurs . . .

> The relatively powerless situation of women — economically, socially and physically — makes them more unequal victims than men.

The other main strand of criticism concerned the extent to which some forms of crime still remained largely 'hidden' to the BCS, even though questions were asked which appeared to cover them. Efforts to put this right were central to the design of the local crime surveys mentioned above. Perhaps the most significant aspect was the attention given to ways of obtaining more information about sexual and other assaults on women. These included less restrictive wording of questions and greater emphasis on sensitive approaches to these areas in the training and selection of interviewers. The results stand in considerable contrast to the BCS findings: in the first Islington survey, for instance (Jones *et al.* 1986), significantly higher levels of sexual assault were found, while over one-fifth of reported assaults were classified as 'domestic' — more than twice the proportion identified by the BCS. Moreover, questions were asked about incidents which would not necessarily be classified by the police as 'crime', but may be experienced as serious by victims, namely sexual and racial 'harassment'. It was found, for example, that over two-thirds of women under the age of 24 had been 'upset by harassment' in the previous twelve months.

A number of special surveys of women, most conducted by feminist writers, have also found high levels of actual or threatened sexual violence. For example, Hanmer and Saunders (1984) found that 59 per cent of 129 women surveyed in Leeds had suffered some form of threat, violence, or sexual harassment within the previous year; and Hall (1985) and Radford (1987) have produced even more startling figures. Among the most challenging of all has been a survey by Painter (1991), based on a representative sample of over 1,000 married women, which suggests that 14 per cent had been raped by their husbands at some time during their marriage, over 40 per cent of them perceiving the incident as 'rape' at the time.[28]

Of course, there are major questions of definition to be tackled in relation to all the above findings, as well as to those of the BCS discussed earlier. Clearly, different surveys are 'measuring' different things. The large government-run surveys in Britain and elsewhere, while prepared to experiment, have broadly held on to the definitions of crime and the counting rules used by the police in compiling official statistics: this is to allow direct comparison and hence a convincing statement of the 'dark figure' and its fluctuations over time. The surveys carried out by academics have moved further away from official definitions of crime, towards alternative definitions favoured by their designers — which, the latter would claim, are also much closer to 'social reality' and the perceptions and priorities of ordinary people. Thus the 1992 BCS 'filter' question on sexual offences was simply: 'Since 1st January 1991, have you been sexually interfered with, assaulted or attacked, either by someone you knew or by a stranger?', while most local surveys have used much broader definitions in their questions, including threats and 'pestering' behaviour.

Finally, a graphic illustration of the kinds of definitional and counting problems we have been discussing is provided by Genn (1988). Prompted by worries that the survey method leads to serious undercounting of certain types of crime, Genn revisited some of the female respondents to the pilot crime survey in which she was involved, all of whom had said they had been victimized many times. She gives an eye-opening account of the way in which the lives of these women, in severely deprived areas of London, were blighted by frequent sexual and physical assaults, thefts, burglaries, and other forms of mistreatment, many of them from people with whom they had some sort of continuing relationship. Yet this kind of 'multiple victimization', she notes, is lost from view in most surveys, partly because — in order to create comparability with police recording practices — they tend to impose artificial limits (five, in the case of the BCS) upon the number of crimes that can be counted for any one victim, and partly because such victims may be less likely than others to respond to the survey or to admit their victimization to interviewers. (Similar comments could be made about other marginalized groups — the homeless, the mentally ill, those who drift from bed-sitter to bed-sitter, and so on — whose voice is not often heard in the large surveys which draw their samples from the Electoral Register. Such people may also be subject to exceptionally high levels of victimization.) At the same time, Genn raises fundamental questions, touched on earlier in this chapter, about how meaningful it is to 'count' certain crimes at all. She writes:

> In asking respondents about their experiences of crime, victim surveys have tended to use an approach which Skogan has termed 'the events orientation': that which conceptualises crime as *discrete incidents*. This . . . can be traced back to one of the original primary objectives of victim surveys: the estimation of the 'dark figure' of unrecorded crime for direct comparison with police statistics. In order to accomplish this . . . information obtained from victims had to be accommodated within a rigid

'counting' frame of reference. *Although isolated incidents of burglary, car theft or stranger attacks may present few measurement problems, for certain categories of violent crime and for certain types of crime victim, the 'counting' procedure leads to difficulties. It is clear that violent victimization may often be better conceptualized as a process rather than as a series of discrete events.* This is most evident in cases of prolonged and habitual domestic violence, but there are also other situations in which violence, abuse and petty theft are an integral part of victims' day-to-day existence. (Genn 1988: 91, emphasis added)

The 'offender population': young, male, and poor?

Throughout this chapter we have looked at crime mainly from the point of view of those who experience it and of those who chart its incidence, the focus being upon where, against whom, and in what circumstances it is known and perceived to occur. Of course, what is glaringly absent from most of the discussion so far is information about the perpetrators of all these crimes. While it is important to conclude our account with some comments on this topic, these will be kept to a minimum, to avoid trespassing too much on David Farrington's territory [see chapter 12 in this volume] and partly because studies of offenders have become much rarer over the past two decades as criminologists' interests have leaned more towards victims, offence patterns, and the operations of the criminal justice agencies.

Just as the annual statistics compiled by the police produce an 'official' account of the extent of crime, to which victim surveys offer various alternative pictures, so the statistics compiled from court records (together with police cautioning records) produce a picture of all those officially held responsible for recorded offences, while various other studies and surveys — notably 'self-report studies' — have similarly provided alternative pictures of the offender population.

In looking at all those convicted of or cautioned for indictable offences in any given year, the first point to note is that their total is very much lower than the total of offences recorded. Moreover, it has become proportionally lower in recent years: despite the virtual doubling of the recorded crime rate, the numbers of people convicted or cautioned have changed little since the late 1970s.[29] In 1991, for example, about 337,000 were sentenced in court and a further 180,000 were cautioned — small figures compared with the recorded crime total of over five and a half million offences. Taking into account the fact that some offenders are charged with more than one offence, this means that not many more than one in ten offences recorded by the police result in a caution or conviction: in other words, in the vast majority of cases, nothing is officially known about those responsible. Indeed, it has been further calculated (Home Office 1993a: 29) that only about one in fifty of the comparable crimes identified by the BCS result in a conviction — a figure which drops as low as one in 200 where 'vandalism' (criminal damage) is concerned.

This being the case, it can obviously not simply be assumed that the characteristics of 'offenders' as a whole can be inferred from those of adjudicated offenders — a central point which we shall return to in a moment. First, though, let us look at the official figures.

The basic profile of the half million or so offenders convicted or cautioned for indictable offences in 1991 was as follows: 82 per cent were male and 46 per cent were under the age of 21. The 'peak age' for males was 18 and for females it was 15 (Home Office 1992c).[30] It is also known from cohort studies using the Home Office Offenders' Index that a high proportion of those convicted will have had a number of previous convictions: as noted earlier, it has been calculated that two-thirds of all convictions are accounted for by male offenders who have already been before the courts six or more times (Home Office 1989).

Another, more detailed, picture of adjudicated offenders — in this case, the subgroup thought to have offended seriously enough to warrant detention in a custodial institution — is provided by analysis of information held in prison records. The National Prison Survey (Walmsley et al. 1992) gives a breakdown of the social characteristics of 10 per cent of all male, and 20 per cent of all female, prisoners over the age of 17 held in custodial institutions in England and Wales in early 1991.[31] Like the sentenced and cautioned population, the prison population was shown to be predominantly young: excluding juveniles in both cases, 62 per cent of inmates were aged below 30, compared with 25 per cent of the general population. Males were even more strikingly overrepresented, making up 96 per cent of all prisoners.

Disproportionate numbers of prisoners also came from ethnic minorities: 15 per cent of male prisoners and as many as 23 per cent of female prisoners described themselves as black or Asian.[32] Where social class was concerned, 41 per cent of males had had unskilled or partly skilled jobs, compared with 18 per cent of the general population.

Other noteworthy findings included the revelation that over a quarter of prisoners had at some time been in local authority care (compared with an estimated 2 per cent of the general population); 40 per cent of male prisoners had left school before the age of 16 (compared with 11 per cent of all British males); and 13 per cent had been 'of no fixed abode' before coming into prison [for further details, see the chapter by Morgan in this volume].

Taken overall, these data clearly illustrate that the social characteristics of people who are arrested and processed by the criminal justice system — and particularly of offenders who are eventually sent to prison — present a very different pattern from that found in the general population. There are many more males, young people, black people, poor people, poorly educated people and people with disturbed childhoods than one would find in a random sample.

Of course, as pointed out above, if only 2 per cent of known crimes end in a conviction, it is important to ask whether the other 98 per cent are likely to have been committed by a similarly skewed section of the population (or, indeed, by the very same people). This is the province of self-report studies — the technique by which samples of the population are asked in confidence whether they have committed crimes for which they have not been caught. On the one hand, these suggest that crime is committed by a much larger proportion of the population than is officially held responsible for it. On the other hand, convicted offenders tend to admit to both *more serious* and *more frequent* offending behaviour than people who have not been convicted.

Depending upon the age, location, and other social characteristics of the sample questioned, as well as upon the wording of the questions, self-report studies have generally found that between 50 and almost 100 per cent will admit to having committed at least one criminal offence during their lifetime. Most such studies have used samples of young males, often schoolchildren or students. For example, in one of the best early studies, Elmhorn (1965) found that 92 per cent of a random sample of teenage schoolboys in Stockholm admitted to at least one offence, while 53 per cent admitted to at least one 'serious' offence (roughly the equivalent of an indictable crime in Britain), principally theft. Methodologically sound studies of adults are rare, although Farrington (1989) found that 96 per cent of the birth cohort used in the long-term Cambridge delinquency studies — which contains a higher than average proportion of working-class urban males — admitted to having committed at least one criminal offence by the age of 32. Like the authors of most other self-report studies, however (e.g. Short and Nye 1958; Christie *et al.* 1965; Elmhorn 1965; Huizinga and Elliott 1986), Farrington found that a much smaller proportion — predominantly, those who had criminal convictions — admitted to large numbers of offences (see also Farrington 1973). Hence, the general conclusion reached over 20 years ago by Hood and Sparks (1970: 51), after a summary of results of self-report studies from several countries, seems to remain valid today: 'While it may be correct to say that to commit one or two delinquent acts is "normal behaviour" for boys, to be involved in frequent criminal acts is apparently relatively rare.'

An important qualification, however, is that self-report studies have generally covered a limited range of offences, chiefly the less serious forms of street crime. Many, too, have included vaguely defined 'delinquent' or 'anti-social' acts, such as 'defying parents' authority' or 'a fist fight with one other person' (Short and Nye 1958), which would be unlikely to qualify as crimes if reported to the police. These features of their methodology have played a part in what has been the most controversial issue surrounding the results of self-report studies, that of the social class of offenders.

The argument was started in earnest by the abovementioned study by Short and Nye (1958), which indicated that middle-class boys were as likely as lower-class boys to be involved in delinquent acts, despite the fact that adjudicated offenders are predominantly working-class. This finding, supported by some (but contradicted by other) subsequent studies, suggested that there must be some major form of class bias in the processes of arrest and prosecution by which offenders come to official notice. A lively debate ensued over many years, focusing particularly on the reliability of the methodologies employed. Questions were raised about the representativeness of the samples used, the suitability of the method of administering the questions (for example, self-completion questionnaires may elicit a fuller response from middle-class than working-class people), the doubtful status as 'crime' of many of the acts asked about, the possibility of respondents telling lies and, indeed, the definition of 'lower class' — including the possible significance of differences between the urban and the rural working classes (for more detailed accounts of these problems and the related arguments, see Hood and Sparks 1970; Braithwaite 1979; Bottomley 1979; Hindelang *et al.* 1979; Bottomley and Pease 1986; [and the chapter by Farrington in this volume)].

Perhaps the most thorough review of the evidence has been that provided by Braithwaite (1979), who analysed forty-one self-report studies as well as over 250 other studies concerning the relationship between social class and crime. He concluded that, although the evidence was often contradictory and confusing, although police bias probably exaggerates the relative extent of working-class delinquency, and although self-report studies tend to exaggerate the relative extent of middle-class delinquency, the following statements may be made with some confidence:

1. Lower-class adults commit *those types of crime which are handled by the police* at a higher rate than middle-class adults.

2. Adults living in lower-class areas commit *those types of crime which are handled by the police* at a higher rate than adults who live in middle-class areas.

3. Lower-class juveniles commit crime at a higher rate than middle-class juveniles.

4. Juveniles living in lower-class areas commit crime at a higher rate than juveniles living in middle-class areas.

(Braithwaite 1979: 62, emphasis added)

Aside from membership of the lower class, statistical correlations have been claimed between many other social (as well as psychological and physical) factors and self-reported or officially defined offending. No more will be said here about the wide range of factors which are identified and discussed in depth by Farrington in this volume as distinguishing serious and persistent offenders from non-offenders or occasional minor offenders, except to reiterate the point (also emphasized by Braithwaite 1979 in relation to the social class of offenders) that the offences covered in the studies to which he refers are chiefly the common and visible predatory street offences like burglary and 'auto crime' — almost by definition the 'crimes of the poor' — rather than the more hidden kinds of crime which happen within the private space of the commercial world or within the household. Nor will any more be said here about the complex issue of race and crime, which is tackled by Smith in chapter 22 in this volume. However, although a fuller discussion can be found in Heidensohn's contribution (chapter 21), it is important to make a few general points about what is perhaps the most interesting phenomenon of all to emerge from all statistics on offenders: *the overwhelming preponderance of males over females.*

This imbalance seems to be a universal feature of the criminal justice records of all modern countries, enduring over time, and confirmed by self-report studies and other research methods (Heidensohn 1985): it happens, for example, that the male-female ratio of convictions was almost precisely the same in 1892 as in 1992 (Home Office 1993c). Gender differences are also apparent when one looks at the types of offence for which males and females are convicted. For example, 69 per cent of all females cautioned or convicted in England and Wales in 1990 had committed theft, compared with 41 per cent of males; and much smaller proportions of females than males were held responsible for burglaries or violent offences (Home Office 1992b: 7).[33]

There has, it is true, been a very gradual upward trend since the 1960s in the proportion of females among those convicted or cautioned, as well as some small shifts in the pattern of female convictions which suggest greater involvement by women and girls in offences such as robbery and burglary — trends which gave rise to some controversy in the 1970s and early 1980s, around Adler's (1975) argument that the 'emancipation of women' was responsible for a greater number of women engaging in criminal activity, just as it had allowed women to engage in a wider range of legitimate economic and social activities. However, the rise in female cautions and convictions has not been strongly sustained: since the end of the 1970s, the female 'share' of officially defined offenders has fluctuated mainly between 16 and 17 per cent, reaching a high point of 17.6 in 1991, while the total numbers — like those of males — have slightly declined. (Moreover, several writers have commented, with regard to Adler's hypothesis, that the assumed 'female emancipation' is neither a proven phenomenon nor easily measurable — see e.g. Box 1983.)

The argument that the official statistics grossly distort the 'true picture' and that a disproportionate amount of female crime remains 'hidden', likewise finds little evidence to support it. As Heidensohn rightly points out:

> There is little or no evidence of a vast shadowy underworld of female deviance hidden in our midst like the sewers below the city streets. As we have become increasingly aware in modern times, *quite the opposite is true.* There is a great deal of crime which is carefully hidden from the police, from families, friends and neighbours. Much of this takes the form of domestic violence, the abuse of children both physically and sexually, incest and marital rape. *The overwhelming majority of such cases involve men,* usually fathers and husbands injuring or abusing their wives and children. (1989: 87, emphasis added)

Similar points can be made about another major area of crime which remains largely unrevealed by both police statistics and conventional crime surveys: that of corporate crime. As few women are in the high-level positions from which markets can be manipulated or business frauds perpetrated, it is safe to assume that this genre of crime, too, is overwhelmingly a male province.

To sum up, there now appears to be relatively little dispute about the broad validity of the general picture, as reflected in the official statistics, of the relative 'contribution' as offenders of males and females, but there is much more argument about the relative contributions of other major social groups, particularly black people and white people, and people from different social classes. Where the *persistent commission of common predatory street offences* is concerned, it is true, both 'official' and 'self-reported' offenders emerge with a broadly similar profile (partly, one may presume, because few persistent burglars or car thieves succeed in escaping conviction entirely). However, this does not alter the vital point that, just as victim surveys are vastly more effective in revealing 'hidden' instances of some kinds of crime than of others, so the perpetrators of different kinds of offence are not equally well 'revealed' through the medium of self-report studies. Thus, while the (usually young and all-male) respondents tend to be asked in great detail about the relatively visible kinds of anti-social activity which are associated with the court appearances of adolescents, they are not asked whether they have assaulted their partners or sexually abused their children, nor whether they have perpetrated a significant financial fraud. It may be, as many writers on the subject claim, that intra-family violence and abuse are much more evenly distributed throughout the population (see e.g. Morgan 1988; Morgan and Zedner 1992; Dobash and Dobash 1992). And without doubt, the social class distribution of people involved in business fraud is skewed in a different direction from that of burglary and street robbery.

Studies other than surveys

Although the bulk of information relating to the 'crime picture' nationwide comes, by virtue of the vastly greater resources spent on gathering them, from data gathered by the police and criminal justice agencies or by major government-run surveys rather than by individual criminologists, it is important to end this account with some (necessarily brief) mention of empirically based criminological studies which have not used survey methods and have been conducted in only one or two areas, yet have had a considerable influence on how we perceive crime.

At the extreme opposite end from national surveys are ethnographic or 'participant observation' studies of particular small groups or individuals. Most of these have been based upon groups of offenders, although a few have focused upon the lives of victims (especially women subjected to assault by men — see e.g. Genn 1988; Counts *et al.* 1992). Such studies do not use numbers at all, but try to convey the essence of their subjects' lifestyles, behaviour and experiences by means of qualitative analysis, based on field notes acquired through close observation over a substantial period of time. Criminology has a long tradition in this kind of work, rooted in the 'Chicago' studies of the 1930s, which brought to life the dominant lifestyles, motivations, and *modi operandi* of, for example, the 'jack-roller' (Shaw 1930) and the street corner gang (Thrasher 1927; Whyte 1955). However, apart from a period of prominence in the 1960s and early 1970s, this tradition has never really flourished in Britain, remaining largely a 'lone furrow' ploughed by a small number of talented ethnographers.

Even so, studies of this kind have produced important insights which have informed a great deal of other work, both theoretical and empirical. For example, Young's illuminating ethnography of small groups of drug-takers (Young 1970) helped greatly to develop the important concept of 'deviancy amplification' — the process by which deviant behaviour 'escalates' as deviants and control agencies react to each other. Other such studies have done much to reflect the reality of teenage petty theft and 'joy-riding' in an inner-city area (Parker 1974), gang life in Glasgow (Patrick 1973), and violence among female gangs (Campbell 1984). More recently, Hobbs's (1988) ethnographic study conducted in the East End of London produced original ideas about the influence upon both crime and policing of the unusual working-class entrepreneurial tradition in the area.

More common than purely ethnographic studies have been field research studies based on a catholic mixture of quantitative and qualitative methods, usually including face-to-face interviews with samples of offenders and/or victims using a semi-structured questionnaire. The samples may be drawn up primarily from official criminal justice records (like Maguire and Bennett's 1982 and Bennett and Wright's 1984 samples of 'burglars'), recruited from a variety of community schemes for offenders (as in Light's 1993 study of car thieves), or created via a 'snowballing' process of asking interviewees for introductions to potential new informants (as in Cromwell *et al.*'s (1991) study of burglars). While open to question about the 'representativeness' of their samples, such studies have usually carried more weight with policy-makers than have ethnographic studies, owing to the scope they give for producing statements of magnitude (e.g. '50 per cent of burglars interviewed said . . .'). At the same time, they have the advantage over large-scale surveys that they allow the researchers more scope to build up a rapport with those they interview, exploring matters in more depth and teasing out the subject's own understanding of events. Direct quotations from interviews can then be used to counterbalance any tendency of the figures and percentages to lose or distort the reality.

Studies of this kind have played a part in altering both criminologists' and policy-makers' perceptions of various kinds of crime. For example, Dobash and Dobash's (1979) study altered many people's notions of the scale and seriousness of domestic violence; Maguire and Bennett's (1982) study drew attention simultaneously to the relatively minor loss or damage suffered in most burglaries and the severe emotional impact that burglary has on many victims; and Pearson's (1987) study has widely changed the view of heroin use as a swift and automatic path to addiction and dissolution, to one of a culture in which some people can handle regular use of the drug over a long period while still leading an otherwise 'normal' life. In each case, the studies have performed to some extent a 'myth-breaking' function, showing that the picture is not so simple as was previously thought. Other studies have shed new light upon scarcely known fields of crime and victimization, such as Ditton's (1977) and Mars' (1982) examinations of almost routine thefts by employees in all kinds of industries, Levi's (1981) work on long-firm fraud and Morgan and Zedner's (1992) study of child victims. Finally, while one or two scholars (e.g. van Duyne 1993) have made a laudable start, there remains a major gap in our knowledge about the important area of highly organized cross-border crime — activities associated particularly with drug-smuggling and money-laundering, but also many other kinds of illegal financial manipulation at an international level (e.g. frauds involving European Community funds). British criminologists, who have generally focused their attention upon crime within the UK, have only recently begun to identify such cross-border offences as an area of any serious relevance to their field of study (cf. Croall 1992; Levi and Maguire 1992).

Concluding comments

One of the central themes of this chapter has been the extent to which knowledge about 'crime' in all its manifestations has not only greatly expanded, but has shifted in focus over the last twenty or thirty years. A Rumplestiltskin-like criminologist, waking up after, say, a 35-year sleep ready to resume his (he would almost certainly be male) task of 'explaining crime', would find himself confronted with a situation so foreign that he would have difficulty in finding a theoretical perspective in his toolbag with which to make sense of what he saw. Let us end the chapter with a few brief, speculative thoughts about how he might react. These are put forward as no more than quick and crude illustrations of how theoretical work, far from developing in a vacuum, has to take account of developments in criminal statistics and empirical research.

We have identified several major features of the changes with which our criminologist would have to come to terms. First of all, instead of well under a million 'conventional' property and violent crimes, he would have to explain over 15 million (the BCS estimated total). Second, he would be confronted with evidence of widespread intra-familial crime, mainly sexual and physical abuse by men of women and children living with them. Third, he would have to explain numerous massive corporate frauds and many other lesser forms of 'white-collar crime'. Fourth, he would have to explain an apparently major increase in international organized crime, much of it based on the smuggling and distribution of illegal drugs and the laundering of money from that trade. Fifth, he would be confronted with a general switch of interest from 'what makes offenders tick' to how criminal events are distributed in time and space. Sixth, he would find as much written about the institutions which define or respond to crime — the police, courts, and prisons (and, latterly, the media) — as about crime and offenders themselves, all of which draws attention to the extent to which the shape of 'the crime problem' is socially and politically constructed. Seventh, he would find widespread interest in the relevance of gender issues to crime — in why, for example, the sex distribution of victims and offenders is significantly skewed in many different types of crime. Finally, he would be confronted with ample evidence of the stark unpleasantness of crime from the point of view of the victim — and, moreover, the fact that a great deal of it is suffered by the poorest and most vulnerable members of society.

Faced with a picture so much more complex than it had been in the 1950s, he would probably soon abandon any lingering hopes he might still have had then of finding the 'criminologist's stone' — the single 'cause' of crime. The wisdom of embarking upon such a search has been thrown into serious doubt since the 1960s by a combination of the insights of the deviancy and labelling theorists, the revelation of many 'new' kinds of crime in all sections of society, and the continuing upward trend in 'conventional' offences like burglary. To begin with, if, as many of his contemporaries did, our man from the 1950s saw individuals' criminal behaviour as caused primarily by economic and social deprivation, he would have expected crime figures (especially those of minor theft, which make up the bulk of officially recorded crime) to have declined significantly from the mid-1950s onwards, as people generally became wealthier, education and housing improved, and so on. He would therefore immediately encounter serious problems in trying to explain why the trend had gone dramatically in the opposite direction. This unexpected phenomenon was the crux of what Young (1986) has called the 'etiological crisis' — a crisis which seriously undermined positivist criminology. (It should, however, be pointed out that deprivation-based explanations become more convincing when applied to crime trends in more recent years when, although living standards may have increased for the majority, there has been an increase in poverty — both relative and absolute — among those at the lower end of the economic scale: [for discussion of these issues, see Taylor, chapter 11 in this volume.)]

Similarly, our criminologist would also certainly begin to question whether any physiological or psychological theory of why certain people offend and others do not could ever aspire to accounting for both the range and the extent of criminal behaviours now known about. This is particularly true of physiological theories, especially those arguing that crime is genetically determined, which, though they may be defensible where specific forms of behaviour are concerned, would have to assume almost a mutation of the species to explain the overall picture (for reviews of such theories, see Wilson and Herrnstein 1985; Moffitt 1990; [Farrington's chapter in this volume).] Similar comments apply to single-factor psychological explanations. For example, Bowlby's (1953) work linking juvenile delinquency with the separation of children from their mothers in the early years of childhood — originally attractive by virtue of the coincidence of a rise in delinquency with the arrival at adolescence of the generation of children who had been evacuated during the Second World War — not only became increasingly unconvincing as later generations apparently exhibited more delinquency than the evacuees, but is far too simplistic to take proper account of the complexities of modern forms of family life [for further discussion, see the chapter by Pearson in this volume].

Moreover, our criminologist's new knowledge would probably cause him to have reservations about the normative 'strain' theories which were being discussed and developed in the USA in his era — Merton's 'anomie' theory, Albert Cohen's subcultural theory, and subsequently Cloward and Ohlin's subcultural/differential opportunity theory, and so on — which were built on the assumption that crime is committed by people whose legitimate channels to status and success are blocked (for good brief summaries of these theories see, *inter alia,* Chambliss 1988; Heidensohn 1989; [see also Garland's chapter in this volume).] Neither 'crimes of the powerful' nor intra-familial crimes fit these models; nor, indeed, is there any convincing evidence of an unprecedented growth in specific subcultures expressing a search for goals other than those espoused by the dominant middle-class culture. At the same time, the greater awareness now of gender issues — and the more widespread readiness to challenge assumptions in this area — would force the by now confused time-traveller to face such difficult questions as why, if young men turn to crime when their opportunities are blocked, women do not do so to the same degree.

How might he be helped, then, by catching up on later writers? First of all, he would certainly gain a great deal of insight by reading the early 'labelling' and 'deviancy' theorists, who would direct his attention to the role of 'powerful others' in defining certain acts and people as 'crimes' and 'criminals' — a perspective useful in making sense of the shifting patterns of media and public concern about particular forms of behaviour. But while they might help him understand the weaknesses of positivism, the analyses of these writers were much more convincing in relation to the 'marginal' kinds of crime (recreational drug-taking, sexual deviance, and so on) which occupied most of their attention, than they would be in relation to types of behaviour (of more interest to modern criminologists, owing to the apparently enormous increase in their incidence) which would be almost universally described and recognized as criminal, not least by those engaging in them: crimes, that is, such as burglary, robbery and car theft.

He would also find valuable insights in some of the Marxist analyses of crime which were prominent in the late 1970s, although he might be less impressed by their ability to explain some important pieces of empirical data. For example, little evidence has emerged to support the image they often projected of offenders as proto-revolutionaries or latter-day 'Robin Hoods': on the contrary, the evidence of crime surveys, as we have seen, suggests that most criminal victimization is *intra*-class rather than *inter*-class [see also the chapter by Emsley in this volume]. However, he might find more persuasive the general perspective of the 'left realists', who start from criticism of 'the great denial' in which, they claim, criminology (particularly the criminology of the 'idealist' left) became involved in the 1970s — denial, that is, of the seriousness and high incidence of crime. While maintaining a radical approach — in the sense of (a) recognizing that criminal statistics are social constructs, not hard facts, and (b) locating the roots of crime in the fundamental social relationships of class and patriarchy — they have adapted their thinking more than most other theorists to the new evidence about crime that we have been discussing. They have constructed new ideas around questions raised by victim surveys. They have acknowledged unequivocally that crime is a very real social problem which, moreover, most afflicts the poorest and most vulnerable groups. They have taken gender issues seriously. They have also stressed the importance of studying the subjective understandings and choices of those who become involved in crime, rather than seeing offending in purely deterministic terms as the mechanistic product of some biological, psychological, or social force (for overviews of the left realist position, see Young 1986, 1988*a*; Kinsey *et al.* 1986). While their theories of why people commit crime remain undeveloped in several respects — indeed, many would argue that left realism is a 'perspective' rather than a theory — adherents of this school have certainly taken criminology forward by trying to come to terms with the 'facts' of crime as understood in recent years.

Similar points can be made about feminist theories of crime, one of the main growth areas of criminology in the 1980s and early 1990s [for an overview, see the chapter by Heidensohn in this volume]. Feminists, more than the proponents of any other approach, have followed through at a theoretical level the implications of the many research findings which locate a great deal of crime within the home, and of those which show huge imbalances between the sexes in both the commission of crime and the experience of victimization.[34]

Finally, if he wished to eschew radicalism and embrace some very broad theory of individual offending behaviour, our criminologist might be drawn in the general direction of control theory, which starts from the other end, as it were, by asking why some people do *not* commit crime. The assumption that the 'natural' state is one in which, without some form of control being applied, everyone would do so, at least fits with the findings of self-report studies that criminal offences are committed by virtually everyone at some time. However, whether he would agree with the chief progenitor of this theory, Travis Hirschi (Hirschi 1969), that the main mechanism of control is that of 'bonding' with parents, school, or some other body which disapproves of crime, is more doubtful, there being little strong empirical evidence for this [see Garland's chapter in this volume].

More likely, though, coming from an era in which statistical analysis was a central feature of almost all criminologists' work, he would eventually follow the sizeable number of his modern colleagues who, finding a waning of interest in the search for the 'ultimate causes of crime', have switched their attention from data about convicted offenders to the vast amounts of numerical data which have accumulated about the incidence of criminal events, employing their skills to seek explanations for patterns and trends in crime and victimization. The kinds of explanation investigated have included, for example, shifts in economic conditions (Field 1990), patterns of crime in relation to unemployment (Box 1987) and housing (Smith 1986), crime opportunity structures created by routine social activities (Cohen and Felson 1979), and the 'geography' of offence patterns (Evans and Herbert 1989).

Interesting as these avenues have proved to explore, however, he might ultimately find that, despite the vast amount of data generated, there was still something lacking: perhaps a sense of genuine understanding of how those most directly involved — offenders, victims, and criminal justice officials — perceive and experience crime. What seems to be missing, now as in his own time, is good qualitative material about offending, gleaned through the most difficult kind of research of all where crime is concerned — that based upon direct observation and ethnographic methods.

If one broad conclusion can be drawn from the discussion in this chapter, it is that while we may know a lot more about crime, we are less sure about the implications of our knowledge. In 'postmodern' fashion, old certainties have disappeared, and both the phenomenon of crime and explanations of it have become fractured, patterns appearing transient and illusory. Criminological research has become a far more complex and demanding enterprise and there is no clear consensus on the questions that should be tackled or how to tackle them. In sum, the 1980s saw increasing sophistication in data collection techniques and, in particular, important advances in knowledge about previously 'hidden' forms of crime; the challenge of the 1990s seems to be to find new theoretical frameworks to make sense of it.

Notes

1. The total number of notifiable offences recorded in 1992 was 5,594,000. Even when increased population is taken into account, the increase has been more than tenfold, from just over one offence per 100 population in 1950 to 10.6 per 100 in 1992.

2. The Institute referred to was the Institute for the Study and Treatment of Delinquency, whose members were chiefly engaged in medical or psychological studies of convicted offenders (see Saville and Rumney 1992). This was not only the sole criminological centre in Britain. but published the main academic journal, the British Journal of Delinquency, later to become the British Journal of Criminology.

   As stated, the picture is quite different now. In 1993, for example, about 180 papers were given at the now biannual British Criminology Conference; at least ten major publishers commissioned several books each in the criminological field; and, in addition to the substantial Home Office funding of external research, criminologists received grants totalling over £2 million from the Economic and Social Research Council's initiative on crime and social disorder. For useful accounts of the growth of post-war criminology, see Rock's (1988) edited special issue of the British Journal of Criminology.

3. Such studies trace the progress of a given group of people over a long period of time, often from birth to maturity, collecting new data on them at regular intervals. The best known in criminology include cohorts followed by the Gluecks (1950) and by West and Farrington (e.g. 1969), as well as the more recent Home Office studies referred to in the text.

4. Positivism as a distinct, self-proclaimed 'school' is principally associated with the work of Italian scholars such as Ferri (1913) and Garofalo (1914), who had a major influence in the institutionalisation of criminology in the USA in the early years of the twentieth century.

5. Indeed, the tradition still has some distinguished and unapologetic exponents (see Farrington's chapter in this volume).

6. Many 'delinquency' studies included behaviour such as under-age smoking or drinking, 'horseplay' in groups on the street, truanting, and even rudeness to schoolteachers (see e.g. West and Farrington 1969: Belson 1968). Apart from general concern about 'rebelliousness', another reason for the concentration on youth was that this was regarded as one of the areas in which policy interventitm was most likely to have an impact.

7. An alternative view was put forward by Taylor *et al.* (1973), who argued that the statistics could be usefully analysed to reveal truths about the importance attached to various forms of property under a capitalist economy.

8. Several North American studies, illustrating the value of attempting to understand patterns of crime through detailed information from or about victims, had been carried out considerably earlier. These include von Hentig's (1948) classic *The Criminal and his Victim,* Wolfgang's (1959) work on criminal homicide, and Amir's (1971) controversial study of forcible rape. Specifically on burglary, there were similar studies by Reppetto (1974) and Waller and Okihiro (1978).

9. Mention should also be made of the relatively new Digest of Information on the Criminal Justice System (Home Office 1991, 1993a), which provides an excellent 'user friendly' summary of key statistics, using coloured graphs, bar charts, and pie charts.

10. Known as 'indictable' and 'triable either way' offences (see *Criminal Statistics* 1990: 21).

11. See *Criminal Statistics* 1990: 14. More than half of the summary offences were motoring offences, but even excluding these, more people were convicted or cautioned for summary than for indictable offences.

12. A number of these, in fact, overlap with offences recorded by the police, owing to joint operations or joint processing of cases. These agencies have published separate totals of notifiable offences since 1989.

13. This is recognized in *Criminal Statistics;* when comparisons are required between pre- and post-1977 figures, adjustments being made to the relevant tables. However, such comparisons are further complicated by the problem of inflation.

14. These were revised again in 1980.

15. The more 'hopeless' cases, in terms of their potential for detection, that are omitted from the figures, the higher the proportion detected (the clear-up rate) is likely to be. If a division's or force's clear-up rate is exceptionally low, officers (especially those in the CID) can expect criticism from management as well as, in some cases, the media. There is thus some incentive to 'massage' local crime statistics to avoid such criticism (Young 1991).

16. In June 1990, for example, 14,800 out of 34,800 convicted prisoners were serving sentences for violence against the person, sexual offences or robbery, while 4,100 were serving sentences for theft, handling, fraud, or forgery (Home Office 1992). It should be noted that the proportion of violent offenders among receptions into prison is considerably lower: their prominence among the population reflects the disproportionate length of their sentences.

17. The lowest was found among males between 5 and 16 (three per million). Overall, females (11) were calculated to be at slightly less risk than males (15).

18. An interesting exception was Switzerland, which produced such low crime rates that a distinguished American criminologist (Clinard 1978) wrote a book attempting to explain why.

19. Pepinsky, an American professor of criminology, was at the time a visiting fellow at the Oxford University Centre for Criminological Research.

20. However, the follow-up questionnaire, which asks questions of a more general nature, has been altered significantly on each 'sweep', while extra self-completion forms asking about people's own involvement in crime, and a special form for offences against children, were introduced in 1992.

21. The survey is usually conducted in January or February, to allow comparisons to be made with the whole of the previous year's official crime figures.

22. As the total interview sample deliberately includes an over-representation of households from denser urban areas (to maximize the chances of finding 'victims' to interview), the calculated victimization rates are weighted to take account of this.

23. Those not directly comparable are 'common assaults', 'other household thefts' (for example, thefts of milk from doorsteps, the type of minor and very common incident identified by Pepinsky as a potentially misleading element in police statistics) and 'other personal thefts'. Some thefts involving commercial vehicles and vandalism against public and corporate property are also reported to the BCS, but excluded from the analysis.

24. This message has been sent less loudly latterly as (a) the media and the public have become more used to the idea that there is a great deal of unrecorded crime, and (b) the notion of 'trivial' crimes has become less easy to defend as the general level of tolerance for petty theft appears to have fallen. This has been reflected in 1993 in vocal opposition to clauses in the Criminal Justice Act 1991 which appear to allow petty persistent offenders to escape prison, as well as in several cases of 'vigilantism' against suspected local thieves.

25. These are identified in the survey by means of the ACORN classification, which assigns every dwelling to one of 11 categories based on the demographic, housing, and employment characteristics of its immediate surrounding area.

26. A special analysis of BCS data on this topic (Maxfield 1988) was also commissioned by the Home Office.

27. In fairness to the authors of the BCS, it should be pointed out that they had anticipated several of the criticisms in qualifications to their original conclusions (which were anyway tentative), though these qualifications tended to be forgotten in the later controversy.

28. The question used was 'Have you ever had sex with your present husband (or previous husband) against your will, when you had clearly insisted that you did not want to and refused your consent?' This is a legal definition of rape, though despite court decisions which mean that a man can be convicted of raping his wife, it is unlikely that many police officers would arrest on allegations of refused consent by a wife living with her husband, without evidence of violence.

29. In 1980, for example, 556,000 people were convicted or cautioned for indictable offences. In 1990, the total was around 540,000. The fact that these figures have hardly changed while the totals of crimes 'cleared up' by the police have risen (in absolute numbers not percentages) seems to be explained by the growth of practices such as 'prison write offs' and 'informal cautions', whereby minor crimes are 'cleared' in a bureaucratic fashion, with a minimum of fuss and expense.

30. That is, 18-year-old males constitute the age group with the highest proportion of its population cautioned or convicted for indictable offences. In fact, the peak age for males has changed recently, from 15 to 18. Farrington and Burrows (1993) note that this is due mainly to a significant fall in the number of boys under 16 cautioned or convicted for shoplifting — itself explained by a growing tendency of the police to use alternative, informal ways of dealing with them.

31. The survey included remand prisoners as well as those convicted, so was not strictly speaking a subgroup of all adjudicated offenders (a relatively small proportion will subsequently have been found not guilty).

32. For a full discussion of the massive overrepresentation of black people in prisons in the USA and England and Wales, see Tonry (forthcoming). Hood (1992) and Smith's chapter in this volume provide more general discussions of the disproportionate black-white ratios, and the probable extent of racial bias, at each stage of the criminal justice process.

33. The equivalent proportions for burglary were three per cent compared with 13 per cent, and for offences of violence they were 10 per cent compared with 18 per cent.

34. Feminist theory, it should be noted, has also contributed a great deal in the socio-legal field, in particular to the understanding of how social biases and inequalities are built into definitions of crime, the creation of legal rules, and the operation of the criminal justice system.

Selected further reading

A. K., Bottomley and C. A. Coleman (1981) *Understanding Crime Rates,* Farnborough: Saxon House.

A. K. Bottomley and K. Pease (1986) *Crime and Punishment: Interpreting the Data.*

L. E. Cohen and M. Felson (1979) 'Social change and crime rate trends: a routine activity approach' *American Sociological Review* Vol. 44, 588-608.

D. J. Evans and D. T. Herbert (1989) *The Geography of Crime.* London: Routledge.

D. P. Farrington (1989) 'Self-reported and official offending from adolescence to adulthood' in M.W. Klein (ed.) *Cross-national Research in Self-reported Crime and Delinquency,* Dordrecht, Netherlands: Kluwer.

D. P. Farrington and E. A. Dowds (1985) 'Disentangling Criminal Behaviour and Police Reaction' in D. P. Farrington and J. Gunn (eds.), *Reaction to Crime: the Public, the Police, Courts and Prisons.* Chichester: John Wiley.

S. Field (1990) *Trends in Crime and Their Interpretation: A Study of Recorded Crime in Post War England and Wales.* Home Office Research Study No. 119.

H. Genn (1988) 'Multiple Victimization' in M. Maguire and J. Pointing(eds.), *Victims of Crime: A New Deal?.* Milton Keynes: Open University Press.

F. M. Heidensohn (1989) *Crime and Society.* London: Macmillan.

Home Office (1989) *Criminal and Custodial Careers of those born in 1953, 1958 and 1963.* Home Office Statistical Bulletin 32/89. London: Home Office.

Home Office, *Criminal Statistics, England and Wales* 1991. London: HMSO, (annual).

Home Office (1993) *Digest 2: Information on the Criminal Justice System in England and Wales.* London: Home Office Research and Statistics Department.

T. Jones, B. Maclean and J. Young (1986) *The Islington Crime Survey: Crime, Victimization and Policing in Inner City London.* Aldershot: Gower.

P. Mayhew, N. A. Maung and C. Mirrless-Black (1993) *The 1992 British Crime Survey.* Home Office Research and Planning Unit, London: HMSO.

E. Stanko (1988) 'Hidden violence against women' in M. Maguire and J. Pointing (eds.), *Victims of Crime: A New Deal?* Milton Keynes: Open University Press.

J. J. M. van Dijk, P. Mayhrew and M. Killias (1990) *Experiences of Crime Across the World: Key Findings of the 1989 International Crime Survey.*

R. Walmsley, L. Howard and S. White (1992) *The National Prison Survey 1991: Main Findings.* Home Office Research Study No. 128, London: HMSO.

J. Young (1988) 'Risk of crime and fear of crime: a realist critique of survey-based assumptions', in M. Maguire and J. Pointing (eds.), *Victims of Crime: A New Deal?* Milton Keynes: Open University Press.

References

Adler, F.(1975) *Sisters in Crime.* New York: McGraw-Hill.

Amir, M. (1971) *Patterns in Forcible Rape.* Chicago: University of Chicago Press.

Baker, A., and Duncan, S. (1985) 'Child Sexual Abuse: A Study of Prevalence in Great Britain', *Child Abuse and Neglect,* 9: 457-67.

Banton, M.(1985) *Investigating Robbery.* Aldershot: Gower.

Becker, G. (1974) 'Crime and Punishment: An Economic Approach', in *Essays in the Economics of Crime and Punishment.* New York: National Bureau of Economic Research.

Becker, H. S. (1963) *Outsiders: Studies in the Sociology of Deviance.* London: Macmillan

Belson, W. A. (1968) 'The Extent of Stealing by London Boys and Some of its Origins', *The Advancement of Science,* 25: 171-84.

Bennett, T. and Wright, R. (1984) *Burglars on Burglary.* Aldershot: Gower.

Bidermann, A. D., and Reiss, A. J. (1967) 'On Explaining the "Dark Figure" of Crime', *Annals of the American Academy of Politics and Social Science,* November.

Black, D. J. (1970) 'The Production of Crime Rates', *American Sociological Review,* 35: 4, 733-48.

Blair, I. (1985) *Investigating Rape: A New Approach for Police.* London: Croom Helm.

Bottomley, A. K. (1979) *Criminology in Focus.* London: Martin Robertson.

Bottomley, A. K., and Coleman, C. A. (1981) *Understanding Crime Rates.* Farnborough: Saxon House.

Bottomley, A. K., and Pease, K. (1986) *Crime and Punishment: Interpreting the Data.* Milton Keynes: Open University Press.

Bowlby, J. (1953) *Child Care and the Growth of Love.* Harmondsworth: Penguin.

Box, S. (1983), *Power, Crime and Mystification.* London: Tavistock.

—— (1987) *Recession, Crime and Punishment.* London: Macmillan Education.

Braithwaite, J. (1979) *Inequality, Crime and Public Policy.* London: Routledge and Kegan Paul.

Brantingham, P. J., and Brantingham, P. L. (1975) The Spatial Patterning of Burglary', *Howard Journal,* 14: 11-23.

Brody, S. (1976) *The Effectiveness of Sentencing,* Home Office Research Study no. 35. London: HMSO.

Burt, C. (1944) *The Young Delinquent.* London: University of London Press.

Campbell, A. (1984) *The Girls in the Gang.* Oxford: Blackwell.

Carson, W. G. (1982) *The Other Price of Britain's Oil.* Oxford: Martin Robertson.

Chambliss, W. J. (1988) *Exploring Criminology.* New York: Macmillan.

Christie, N. (1977) 'Conflicts as Property', *British Journal of Criminology,* 17: 1, 1-15.

Christie, N., Andenaes, J., and Skirbekk, S. (1965) 'A Study of Self-Reported Crime' in K. O. Christiansen, ed., *Scandinavian Studies in Criminology.* London: Tavistock.

Cicourel, A. V. (1968) *The Social Organization of Juvenile Justice.* New York: Wiley.

Clarke, R. V. G. (1980) 'Situational Crime Prevention: Theory and Practice', British Journal of Criminology, 20: 136-47.

Clarke, R. V. G., and Hough, M. (1984) *Crime and Police Effectiveness,* Home Office Research Study no. 79. London: HMSO.

Clarke, R. V. G., and Mayhew, P., eds. (1980) *Designing Out Crime.* London: HMSO.

Clinard, M. (1978) *Cities with Little Crime.* Cambridge: Cambridge University Press.

Cohen, L. E., and Felson, M. (1979) 'Social Change and Crime Rate Trends: A Routine Activity Approach' *American Sociological Review,* 44: 588-608.

Cohen, S. (1974) 'Criminology and the Sociology of Deviance in Britain', in P. Rock and M. McIntosh, eds., *Deviance and Social Control.* London: Tavistock.

Counts, D. A., Brown, J. K., and Campbell, J. C. (1992) *Sanctions and Sanctuary: Cultural Perspectives in the Beating of Wives.* Oxford: Westview Press.

Corbett, C., and Maquire, M. (1988) 'The Value and Limitations of Victim Support Schemes', in M. Maguire and J Pointing, eds., *Victims of Crime: A New Deal?* Milton Keynes: Open University Press.

Cornish, D. B., and Clarke, R. V. G. (1986) 'Situational Prevention, Displacement of Crime and Rational Choice Theory', in K. Heal and G. Laycock, eds., *Situational Crime Prevention: From Theory into Practice.* London: HMSO.

Croall, H. (1992) *White Collar Crime.* Milton Keynes: Open University Press.

Crawford, A, Jones, T, Woodhouse, T., and Young, J. (1990) *Second Islington Crime Survey.* London: Middlesex Polytechnic.

Cromwell, P. F., Olson, A., and Avary, D. W. (1991) *Breaking and Entering: An Ethnographic Analysis of Burglary.* Newbury Park: Sage.

Ditton, J. (1977) *Part-time Crime.* London: Macmillan.

Dobash, R. E., and Dobash, R. P. (1979) *Violence against Wives.* London: Tavistock.

—— (1992) , *Women, Violence and Social Change.* London: Routledge.

Elmhorn, K. (1965) 'Study in Self-Reported Delinquency among School Children in Stockholm', in K. O. Christiansen, ed., *Scandinavian Studies in Criminology.* London, Tavistock.

Ennis, P. (1967) *Criminal Victimization in the United States, President's Commission on Law Enforcement and Administration of Justice, Field Surveys III.* Washington, DC: US Government Printing Office.

Erikson, K. T. (1964) 'Notes on the Sociology of Deviance', in H. S. Becker, ed., *The Other Side: Perspectives on Deviance*. New York: Free Press.

Evans, D. J., and Herbert, D. T. (1989) *The Geography of Crime*. London: Routledge.

Farrington, D. P. (1973) 'Self-Reports of Deviant Behaviour: Predictive and Stable?', *Journal of Criminal Law and Criminology*, 64: 99-110.

—— (1989) 'Self-Reported and Official Offending from Adolescence to Adulthood', in M. W. Klein, ed., *Cross-National Research in Self-Reported Crime and Delinquency*. Dordrecht: Kluwer.

Farrington, D. P., and Burrows, J. N. (1993) 'Did Shoplifting Really Increase?' *British Journal of Criminology*, 33: 57-69.

Farrington, D. P., and Dowds, E. A. (1985) 'Disentangling Criminal Behaviour and Police Reaction' in D. P. Farrington and J. Gunn, eds., *Reaction to Crime: The Public, the Police, Courts and Prisons,* Chichester: Wiley.

Ferri, E. (1913) *The Positive School of Criminology*. Chicago: C.H. Kerr.

Field, S. (1990) *Trends in Crime and their Interpretation: A Study Of Recorded Crime in Post War England and Wales,* Home Office Research Study no. 119. London: HMSO.

Garofalo, R. (1914) *Criminology*. Boston: Little, Brown.

Genn, H. (1988) 'Multiple Victimization', in M. Maguire and J. Pointing, eds., *Victims of Crime: A New Deal?* Milton Keynes: Open University Press.

Glueck, S. and Glueck, E. (1950) *Unravelling Juvenile Delinquency*. New York: Commonwealth Fund.

Government Statistical Service. (1992) *Criminal Justice: Key Statistics in England and Wales 1991*. London: HMSO.

Hall, R. (1985) *Ask Any Woman: A London Enquiry into Rape and Sexual Assault*. Bristol: Falling Wall Press.

Hall, S., Critcher, Jefferson, T., Clarke, J., and Roberts, B. (1978) *Policing the Crisis*. London: Macmillan.

Hanmer, J., and Saunders, S. (1984) *Well-Founded Fear*. London: Hutchinson.

Heal, K., and Laycock, G., eds. (1986) *Situational Crime Prevention: From Theory into Practice*. London: HMSO.

Heidensohn, F. M. (1985) *Women and Crime*. London: Macmillan.

—— (1989) *Crime and Society*. London: Macmillan.

Hirschi, T. (1969) *Causes of Delinquency*. Berkeley: University of California Press.

Hobbs, R. (1988) *Doing the Business: Entrepreneurship, the Working Class and Detectives in the East End of London*. Oxford: Oxford University Press.

Holdaway, S., ed. (1979) *The British Police*. London: Edward Arnold.

Home Office. (1971) *Instructions for the Preparation of Statistics Relating to Crime*. London: HMSO.

—— (1989) *Criminal and Custodial Careers of those Born in 1953, 1958 and 1963,* Home Office Statistical Bulletin, 32/89. London: Home Office.

—— (1991) *A Digest of Information on the Criminal Justice System*. London: Home Office Research and Statistics Department.

—— (1992a) *Criminal Justice: Key Statistics in England and Wales 1990.* London: Government Statistical Service.

—— (1992b) *Gender in the Criminal Justice System.* London: Home Office.

—— (1992c) *Criminal Statistics, England and Wales 1991*, Cmnd 2134 London: HMSO.

—— (1993a) *Notifiable Offences, England and Wales, 1992, Home Office Statistical Bulletin,* 9/93. London: Government Statistical Service.

—— (1993b) *Digest 2. Information on the Criminal Justice System in England and Wales.* London: Home Office Research and Statistics Department.

—— (1993c) *Criminal Justice Statistics 1882- 1892,* Home Office Statistical Findings, 1/93. London: Home Office Research and Statistics Department.

Hood, R. (1992) *Race and Sentencing: A Study in the Crown Court.* Oxford: Clarendon Press.

Hood, R., and Sparks, R. (1970) *Key Issues in Criminology.* London: Weidenfeld and Nicolson.

Hough, J. M., and Mayhew, P. (1983) *The British Crime Survey,* Home Office Research Study no. 76. London: HMSO.

Hough, J. M., and Mayhew, P. (1985) *Taking Account of Crime: Key Findings from the Second British Crime Survey,* Home Office Research Study no. 85. London: HMSO.

Hudson, B. (1987) *Justice through Punishment.* London: Macmillan Education.

Huizinga, D., and Elliott, D. S. (1986) 'Reassessing the Reliability and Validity of Self-Report Measures', *Journal of Quantitative Criminology,* 2: 293-327.

Jones, T., Lea, J., and Young, J. (1987) *Saving the Inner City: the First Report of the Broadwater Farm Survey.* London: Middlesex Polytechnic.

Jones, T., Maclean, B., and Young, J. (1986) *The Islington Crime Survey: Crime, Victimization and Policing in Inner City London.* Aldershot: Gower.

Kinsey, R. (1984) *Merseyside Crime Survey: First Report.* Liverpool: Merseyside Metropolitan Council.

Kinsey, R, Lea, J., and Young, J. (1986) *Losing the Fight Against Crime.* Oxford, Blackwell.

Kitsuse, J. I. (1964) 'Societal Reactions to Deviant Behaviour: Problems of Theory and Method', in H. S. Becker, ed., *The Other Side: Perspectives on Deviance.* New York: Free Press.

Kitsuse, J. I., and Cicourel, A. V. (1963) 'A Note on the Uses of Official Statistics', *Social Problems,* 11: 131-9.

Lesieur, H. R., and Lehman, P. M. (1975) 'Remeasuring Delinquency: A Replication and Critique', *British Journal of Criminology,* 15: 69-80.

Levi, M. (1981) *The Phantom Capitalists: The Organization and Control of Long-Firm Fraud.* London: Heinemann.

—— (1993) *The Investigation, Prosecution and Trial of Serious Fraud,* Research Study no. 14. London: Royal Commission on Criminal Justice.

Levi, M., and Maguire, M. (1992) 'Crime and Cross-Border Policing in Europe', in J. Bailey, ed., *Social Euorpe.* London: Longman.

Levi, M., and Pithouse, A. (1992) 'The Victims of Fraud', in D. Downes, ed., *Unravelling Criminal Justice.* Basingstoke: Macmillan.

Light, R. (1993) *Car Theft: The Offender's Perspective,* Home Office Research Study no. 130. London: HMSO.

Lurogio, A., Skogan, W. G., and Davis, R. C. (1990) *Victims of Crime: Problems, Policies and Programs.* New York: Sage.

McCabe, S., and Sutcliffe, F. (1978) *Defining Crime: A Study of Police Decisions.* Oxford: Blackwell.

McLintock, F., and Avison, N. H. (1968) *Crime in England and Wales.* London: Heinemann .

Maguire, M. (1991) 'The Needs and Rights of Victims of Crime', in M. Tonry, ed., *Crime and Justice: A Review of Research,* vol. 14. Chicago: University of Chicago Press.

Maguire, M., in collaboration with Bennett, T. (1982) *Burglary in a Dwelling: The Offence, the Offender and the Victim.* London: Heinemann Educational.

Maguire, M., and Corbett, C. (1987) *The Effects of Crime and the Work of Victim Support Schemes.* Aldershot: Gower.

Manning, P. (1977) *Police Work.* Cambridge, Mass.: MIT Press.

Mars, G. (1982) *Cheats at Work.* London: Allen and Unwin

Martin, J. P. (1962) *Offenders as Employees.* London: Macmillan.

Matthews, R., and Young, J., eds. (1986) *Confronting Crime.* London: Sage.

Maxfield, M. G. (1984) *Fear of Crime in England and Wales,* Home Office Research Study no. 78. London: HMSO.

—— (1988) *Explaining Fear of Crime: Evidence from the 1984 British Crime Survey,* Home Office Research and Planning Unit Paper no. 43. London: HMSO.

Mayhew, P., Clarke, R. V. G., Sturman, A., and Hough, J. M. (1976) *Crime as Opportunity,* Home Office Research Study no. 34, London: HMSO.

Mayhew, P., Elliott, D., and Dowds, L. (1989) *The 1988 British Crime Survey.* Home Office Research Study no. 111. London: HMSO.

Mayhew, P., and Hough, J. M. (1988) 'The British Crime Survey: Origins and Impact', in M Maguire and J. Pointing, eds., *Victims of Crime: A New Deal?* Milton Keynes: Open University Press.

Mayhew, P., and Maung, N. A. (1992) *Surveying Crime: Findings from the 1992 British Crime Survey,* Home Office Research and Statistics Department, Research Findings no 2. London: HMSO.

Moffitt, T. E. (1990) 'The Neurophysiology of Juvenile Delinquency: A Review', in M Tonry and N Morris, eds., *Crime and Justice,* vol 12. Chicago: University of Chicago Press.

Morgan, J. (1988) 'Children as Victims', in M. Maguire and J. Pointing, eds., *Victims of Crime: A New Deal?* Milton Keynes: Open University Press.

Morgan J., and Zedner, L. (1992) *Child Victims: Crime, Impact and Criminal Justice.* Oxford: Oxford University Press.

Morris, T. (1989) *Crime and Criminal Justice since 1945.* Oxford: Blackwell.

Murphy, P., Williams, J., and Dunning, E. (1990) *Football on Trial: Spectator Violence and Developments in the Football World.* London: Routledge.

Nettler, G. (1978) *Explaining Crime.* New York: McGraw-Hill.

Normandeau, A. (1969) 'Trends in Robbery as Reflected by Different Indexes', in T. Sellin and M. E. Wolfgang, eds., *Delinquency: Selected Studies.* New York: Wiley.

Painter, K. (1991) *Wife Rape, Marriage and the Law: Survey Report*. Manchester: University of Manchester Faculty of Economic and Social Science.

Parker, H. (1974) *View from the Boys: A Sociology of Downtown Adolescents*. Newton Abbot: David and Charles.

Patrick, J. (1973) *A Glasgow Gang Observed*. London: Eyre Methuen.

Pearson, G. (1987) *The New Heroin Users*. Oxford: Blackwell.

Radford, J. (1987) 'Policing Male Violence', in J. Hanmer and M. Maynard, eds., *Women, Violence and Social Control*. London: Macmillan.

Reppetto, T. (1974) *Residential Crime*. Cambridge Mass.: Ballinger.

Rock, P. (1973) *A Sociology of Deviance*, London: Hutchinson.

—— (1988) 'The History of British Criminology', special issue of the *British Journal of Criminology*, 28/2.

Rozenberg, J. (1992) 'Miscarriages of Justice', in E. Stockdale and S. Casale, eds., *Criminal Justice under Stress*. London: Blackstone Press.

Saville, E., and Rumney, D. (1992) *A History of the ISTD*. London: Institute for the Study and Treatment of Delinquency.

Selke, W., and Pepinsky, H. (1984) 'The Politics of Police Reporting in Indianapolis 1948-78', in W. J. Chambliss, ed., *Criminal Law in Action*. New York: Wiley.

Sellin, T. (1938) *Culture, Conflict and Crime*. New York: Social Science Research Council.

Sellin, T., and Wolfgang, M. E. (1964) *The Measurement of Delinquency*. New York: Wiley.

Shaw, C. (1930) *The Jack Roller: A Delinquent Boy's Own Story* Chicago: University of Chicago Press.

Short, J. F., and Nye, F. I. (1958) 'Extent of Unrecorded Juvenile Delinquency', *Journal of Criminal Law, Criminology and Police Science*, 49: 296-302.

Skolnick, J. H. (1966) *Justice Without Trial: Law Enforcement in Democratic Society*. New York: John Wiley.

Smith, S. (1986) *Crime, Space and Society*. Cambridge: Cambridge University Press.

Sparks, R., Genn, H., and Dodd, D. (1977) *Surveying Victims*. Chichester: Wiley.

Stanko, E. (1988) 'Hidden Violence against Women', in M. Maguire and J. Pointing, eds., *Victims of Crime: A New Deal?* Milton Keynes: Open University Press.

Taylor, I., Walton, P., and Young, J. (1973) *The New Criminology*. London: Routledge and Kegan Paul.

Thrasher, F. M. (1927) *The Gang*. Chicago: Phoenix Press.

Tonry, M. (forthcoming) 'Racial Disproportion in US Prisons', in R. King and M. Maguire, eds., *Prisons in Context*. Oxford: Oxford University Press.

van Dijk, J. J. M., and Mayhew, P. (1992) *Criminal Victimization in the Internationalized World: Key Findings of the 1989 and 1992 International Crime Surveys*. The Hague, Netherlands: Directorate for Crime Prevention, Ministry of Justice.

van Dijk, J. J. M., Mayhew, P., and Killias, M. (1990) *Experiences of Crime Across the World: Key Findings of the 1989 International Crime Survey*. Boston: Kluwer.

van Duyne, P. C. (1993) 'Organized Crime and Business Crime-Enterprises in the Netherlands' *Crime, Law and Social Change,* 19: 103-42.

von Hentig, H. (1948) *The Criminal and his Victim.* New Haven: Yale University Press.

von Hirsch, A. (1986) *Past or Future Crimes.* Manchester: Manchester University Press.

Walker, N. D. (1971) *Crimes, Courts and Figures: An Introduction to Criminal Statistics.* Harmondsworth: Penguin.

Walklate, S. (1989) *Victimology: The Victim and the Criminal Justice System.* London: Unwin Hyman.

Waller, I., and Okihiro, N. (1978) *Burglary: The Victim and the Public.* Toronto: University of Toronto Press.

Walmsley, R., Howard, L., and White, S. (1992) *The National Prison Survey 1991: Main Findings,* Home Office Research Study no. 128. London: HMSO.

West, D. J., and Farrington, D. P. (1969) *Present Conduct and Future Delinquency.* London: Heinemann.

Wheeler, S. (1967) 'Criminal Statistics: A Reformulation of the Problem', *Journal of Criminal Law, Criminology and Police Science,* 58: 317-24.

Whyte, W. F. (1955) *Street Corner Society,* 2nd edn. Chicago: University of Chicago Press.

Wiles, P. N. P. (1971) 'Criminal Statistics and Sociological Explanations of Crime', in W. G. Carson and P. N. P. Wiles, ed., *The Sociology of Crime and Delinquency in Britain.* London: Martin Robertson.

Wilson, J. Q., and Herrnstein, R. J. (1985) *Crime and Human Nature.* New York: Simon and Schuster.

Winchester, S., and Jackson, H. (1982) *Residential Burglary,* Home Office Research Study no. 74. London: HMSO.

Woffinden, R. (1987) *Miscarriages of Justice.* London: Hodder and Stoughton.

Wolfgang, M. (1959) *Patterns in Criminal Homicide.* Philadelphia: University of Pennsylvania Press.

Young, J. (1970) *The Drugtakers.* London: McGibbon and Kee.

—— (1986) 'The Failure of Radical Criminology: The Need for Realism', in R. Matthews and J. Young, eds., *Confronting Crime.* London: Sage.

—— (1988a) 'Risk of Crime and Fear of Crime: A Realist Critique of Survey-Based Assumptions', in M. Maguire and J. Pointing, eds., *Victims of Crime: A New Deal?* Milton Keynes: Open University Press.

—— (1988b) 'Radical Criminology in Britain: The Emergence of a Competing Paradigm', *British Journal of Criminology,* 28/2: 289-313.

Young, M. (1991) *An Inside Job.* Oxford: Clarendon Press.

3. Counting Crimes: Bending and Fiddling the Account

Malcolm Young

Even as commentators on crime statistics acknowledge, they have little objective value as a true reflection of the complexity of social events, so the criminal justice system massively invests in the idea of crime to support its practices. Undue significance continues to be given to crime figures, reinforced for an ill-informed general public by apparently authoritative sources, so that this prime symbol of the procedural drama becomes endlessly and simply regurgitated, and even headlined by an alleged quality press: 'Crime Fall hit by Rise in Sex and Violence' (Guardian, 15 December 1988). As a result, the idea of crime has come to achieve a significance comparable to those ritual metaphors which Turner (1974: 55) attributes with the power of being able to 'instigate social action . . . condensing many references [and] uniting them into a single cognitive and affective field'. Today the statistical record is still as mythological as it was in the 1950s, yet it has assumed what Ditton (1979: 23) describes as an almost 'religious significance'. Hard data has become sacrosanct, so that reflexive enquiry into policing becomes even harder to justify, simply because of this reverence for a quasi-mathematical truth. Furthermore, philosophical research might easily penetrate the inherent deceptions in the metaphor, for in effect the current need to formulate corporate plans, management strategies, and other trappings of this 'business enterprise' still rests largely on the use of this manipulated falsehood.

In such a world, the measurement of a continued expansion in crime becomes a self-evident factor in the institutional mentality, for the institution cannot contemplate its reduction or contraction, nor can it be expected to set out to dismantle itself. The mythology therefore quickly becomes reality, as the idea of crime turns into hard fact and the primacy of the construct is recreated at every turn. In 1980, when a Higher National Certificate in 'Police Studies' was set up at Newcastle Polytechnic, the module on 'Crime and the Criminal' was again introduced by using this idea of a knowable crime return, and attributing an objective nature to the idea of crime statistics:

> it is essential to place 'crime' in quantitative terms . . . [and for the student to explore] the continuing upsurge in recorded crime since the second world war . . . which coincided with a chronic shortage in [police] manpower . . .

This predetermined belief in a world where crime has exploded since the Second World War is set to deny the student the chance to explore an alternative reality, while the stated 'chronic shortage of manpower' pre-empts any real opportunity to analyse

Malcolm Young: Extracts from "'Crime' or 'Offence': A Structuring Principle" in *AN INSIDE JOB* (Oxford: Clarendon Press, 1991), pp. 356-390. Reprinted by permission of Oxford University Press.

reasons for the expansion in policing, except to set them in a predetermined mould, for the introduction to this module seems determined to replicate an overwhelming faith in a numerical truth.[55]

By the 1970s, the newly amalgamated forces began to reverse the claims of the 1950s, when the small forces were indicating an era of social calm and tranquility. New crimes such as TWOC and criminal damage, as well as the wholesale recording of much of what had previously been 'cuffed' seemed to take the executive by surprise and the root metaphor of social stability began to run amok.[56] By the middle of the decade, the forty-three forces were more or less united in presenting a public picture of soaring 'crime' as the prime indicator of their problems. However, by returning a mean 50 per cent detection rate, they also implied that the rising tide of disorder was valiantly, but only just, being held back by these newly consolidated units.[57]

During the 1970s as recording techniques were polished and sharpened, some particularly specific practices were employed by detective departments to ensure their detected crimes remained at 50 per cent of those recorded. At this time the Home Office 'Instructions for the Preparation of Statistics relating to Crime' (1971) allowed 'crimes' to be detected not only when someone appeared at court and was convicted, but also:

(a) when a person is charged and acquitted;

(b) when 'crimes' are 'taken into consideration' after conviction;

(c) when there is some practical hindrance to prosecution, e.g. if the suspect dies or if the victim and/or key witnesses are unwilling to give evidence;

(d) when a person admits a crime and is cautioned or is under the age of criminal responsibility, i.e. 10 years;

(e) when a person who is already serving a custodial sentence admits a crime but it is decided that 'no useful purpose would be served by proceeding with the charge'.

It is apparent that in (c), it becomes possible for a dead man to provide a detection, while in (b), the minor theft from a shop taken into consideration (TIC) can be set against an unsolved robbery to provide a 50 per cent detection rate. In (e) above, the prisoner can 'clear his slate' and perhaps give the divisional 'clear-up' team 'fifty for nowt' (fifty detections for little or no effort). As Skolnick (1966) suggests, such admissions are 'a valued commodity for exchange, a substantial part of the police administrative process and a major indicator of success'.

Let us look briefly at each of these categories in turn.

Crimes detected when a person is charged and subsequently acquitted

At the time a person is charged with any crime from petty theft to murder, the normal practice is for the Officer in Charge of the case to submit a supplementary crime report and be awarded a detection. Any subsequent acquittal might follow months later after remands, adjournments, and trial; but the detection stands. Indeed the traditional party that detectives always hold on any murder inquiry always takes place on the evening of the 'arrest and charge', not on conviction or acquittal; for the case is 'wrapped up' on a charge and only the protracted file preparation follows. By the time the case is heard, many months will have elapsed and detectives on the case will be dispersed to other duties. The crime is detected, however, even if the accused is acquitted.

After conviction, a person can ask for other crimes to be TIC

The accused agrees he has committed a list of crimes, signs to that effect, and these are considered before sentence is passed. In recent years the TIC is a disappearing commodity for exchange. It is often said now that 'only the insane or the first-timers will have TICs', for the simple acquiescence of the 'prig' to an exhortation to 'come clean lad, get it off your chest and you'll feel better with it out in the open' seems to be vanishing, along with the processes of law that went with it. It is now understood that 'only a fool admits TICs . . . with a list of TICs against you, you'll get more bird ...' (Fieldnotes: bridewell 'prig'). However, there are still times when the recovery of a horde of stolen property from parked cars or shops makes one initial arrest into a statistical gold-mine. As one detective said: 'just give me one milk-token thief, or a car-badge-juvenile each month, and everything will be all right'. One juvenile crime file which crossed my desk as I first drafted a seminar paper which was used as a basis for this section, had 134 TICs for the theft of trivia from stores. The injured persons — Woolworths, Boots, and the other High Street multiples, as well as the times and dates of the offences, were carefully arranged to allow each to stand as separate crimes, rather than be counted as one series of crimes which would have reduced the numbers of detections dramatically (and which I will discuss in the next section when I outline aspects of the 'counting rules'). Mawby (1979) found that 40 per cent of crimes in Sheffield were cleared up by TICs and other indirect means, while Lambert (1970: 43) rightly understood the search for TICs had played a main part in the game, and was a major symbol of police success: 'this dependence on getting offenders to confess to maintain a success rate, has . . . important consequences for police administration'. These 'important consequences' are just that! They are crucial to the institution and cause some detectives to have few qualms about bending the rules. The quest for detections is as basic a task for the detectives as it is to 'nail' or 'fix' the 'prig', for it forms a homologous place in the maintenance of position and esteem.

Detected crimes all carry a potential for enhancement of the detection rates. Each detected theft of a social security giro cheque, for example, can hold out the possibility of producing at least two further 'clear-ups'. The initial crime of theft might be followed by a second of forgery when the thief signs the giro with a false name purporting to be the person named on the cheque; while a third could be a 'deception' created when the cheque is presented at the post office — or 'three for one'. The stolen television or video from one crime of burglary, if sold to a second-hand dealer can become a second crime of 'criminal deception' (i.e. the assertion by the thief that he had authority as owner, to sell the goods). Always the ability to have these recorded as separated detections will depend on the skill of the detective and on the diligence of the Force Statistical Officers to search out these attempts to double or treble up one event, an activity which is contrary to the Home Office instructions issued on the 'counting rules'. Of course undetected thefts of giro cheques or television sets are never recorded as two or three crimes committed; not until a 'body' materializes!

Ditton (1979: 39) quotes from the *Newcastle Evening Chronicle* (5 February 1977), when a 17-year-old appeared before the local Crown Court and asked for 31 TICs:

> Judge Roderick Smith rapped Northumbria (Police) for abusing the system where an offender appears in court and has other offences considered. When a 17-yr-old youth appeared before him, the judge was asked to take 31 other offences into consideration, after the youth had been convicted of taking a car without consent. The youth's counsel said the other offences were nearly all for trying to take cars. Judge Smith said: a lad tries to get into 50 different cars, gets into the fifty-first, appears charged with it and 50 other offences to be taken into consideration. All it can be thought to be doing is to improve the detection rate of the Northumbria Constabulary. It is an abuse of the system whereby other offences are taken into consideration. I keep on saying it — no one takes the slightest notice of what I say. Except in this case, these 31 offences will not be taken into consideration.

Even if the accused reneges on his admissions in court (which happens regularly) or the judiciary refuse to allow the TICs, it is still possible for the detective to submit them with the statement of admission taken during the investigation and claim to his senior officer (who may well have been through the same situation), that the crimes were almost certainly committed by the accused, and to ask they be recorded as 'detections — no useful purpose to be served in charging the offender with these and taking him back before the court'. The criminal record of the accused will not show any subsequent account of them, but the crimes can be accepted by the senior officer to be written off as detections in the Home Office returns.

Other more dubious means exist for fiddling TICs and I have listened as detectives discussed ways of 'making one or two for nowt'. One such fiddle was described:

> you get a young juvenile admitting say 5 crimes. You have the five typed up onto 5 separate TIC forms (where there is space for 3 or 4 to be listed). Get the juvenile to sign each and submit the necessary papers to the court. Wait until the case is over and all the papers are in, and then add perhaps one crime to each sheet from the lists of undetected rubbish. No one is hurt, the sheets and the supplementaries go off to HQ and the division gets another half-dozen rubbishy crimes solved, and even the kid's record only shows the original five TICs. The detection rate is better, everyone is happy . . . (From fieldnotes)

The incidence of getting 'two for one' in cases of theft and the subsequent 'deception', or 'theft' and 'going equipped for stealing' (widely used against car thieves) became so prevalent at one time, that a force instruction was issued in an attempt to prevent its occurrence; however, other ways of making 'crime' still occur. I was told of the cautions imposed for 'a theft of a tin of biscuits' passed around a schoolyard which became one theft and several crimes of handling stolen property; while the ten cigarettes stolen from the corner shop became one crime of theft and nine schoolyard 'handlings' of one cigarette. These 'cautioned' crimes (about which I say more below) like TICs, have to be submitted to the HQ stats. department at irregular intervals to avoid the scrutiny which sets out to confound attempts by the detectives to record *series* crimes (claim one detection), as *individual* crimes (claim each detection separately).

It is not always easy for the civilian clerks in stats. departments to spot duplications when handling many thousands of 'crime' reports, and although end totals are often computed, it is curious how slow some forces have been in setting up computerized systems which allow easy cross-reference to culprit, crime-type, and other factors that reveal attempts to get extra detections. By 1983, Northumbria had spent millions on a massive command and control system, but still manually recorded many aspects of 'crime reporting'.

Often it is only luck when the stats. departments spot the duplication, as they chance to see an unusual name of an injured person (or accused) reappearing on new crime reports submitted weeks after the initial record has been catalogued and filed. It was by such a chance that the stats. clerks spotted a theft of a bicycle by three young men acting together had become three separately numbered crimes of theft of a wheel, theft of a wheel, and theft of a frame committed by three individuals. It was a similar chance that revealed one theft of a table from a public house committed by five men had been recorded as five separate detected 'crimes' — two of theft of the table and three of 'handling stolen property': 'sometimes they blatantly duplicate and put the same crime through two or three times with separate numbers, hoping we'll not tie them together' (Crime stats. clerk: from fieldnotes).

Practical hindrance to prosecution: death of witness or suspect or unwillingness of an essential witness

If the suspect to a murder commits suicide after committing the crime, then a detection is almost certainly assured. However, even the burglar who dies while waiting trial can be a source of detections and the counting rules allow any admissions made to be classed as detections, provided a senior officer agrees. The reluctance of a witness to appear in assault cases, which is especially prevalent in the domestic dispute, can also be a steady source of 'No Further Action' detections, and the incidence of detections following an NFA decision in minor assault cases never pursued to prosecution must be considerable.

Admissions by those under the age of criminal responsibility and those cautioned by the police

When a child under the age of 10 years admits crimes or a person agrees to be cautioned rather than prosecuted (often used for juveniles between 10 years and 17 years and for first offenders), the crimes are classed as detected. These can be a great source of detections, and fiddles to extend on these can be considerable.

Most of these manipulations again concern ways in which 'series' crimes can be separated out (and are discussed below in the next section on the counting rules), while others relate to crimes which might not even exist and offenders who are invented because of this demand for detections. One middle-ranking detective of my acquaintance created crimes which had not occurred and which were then admitted by juveniles who were similar inventions of the mind. These mythical juveniles were then cautioned or were allegedly under the age of criminal responsibility, allowing for 'detections' without a court appearance. Two or three such 'crimes' per week (about 1-2 per cent of his subdivisional totals) gave his subdivision a healthy detection rate and may well have helped him in the 'promotion stakes'.[58] Picking fictitious injured persons from the voters' register can be hazardous, however, especially when it is out of date and a crime clerk recognizes the name of a relative who died some two years previous! Of course, on his own 'detection' and fall from grace, his actions were not recorded as a 'crime' of 'criminal deception', although his disciplinary punishment of a 'return to uniform duties' again supports my point about the status of the detective in comparison to 'uniformed patrol'. Another detective was not so lucky; Roger Anderson was gaoled for six months for forgery and perverting the course of justice for much the same sort of activity (*Daily Mail,* 25 March 1980):

> he gave himself less work by reporting the arrest of imaginary people for crimes that never happened... In files for which he was responsible fabrications are two a penny, and almost every document one turns over is false in one way or another . . . The worst thing he did was to invent defendants for real crimes, because the real criminal may have escaped being brought to justice ... the court heard that Anderson invented a man called Mensell to admit a fictitious offence of indecency and then had him pleading guilty to real offences of stealing women's clothing. When Mensell was due to appear in Court, Anderson had him conveniently killed in a motorway accident . .. Nobody suffered as a result of these offences. Nobody could suffer because the people named in the offences were wholly fictitious.

Those in custody who admit crimes and no useful purpose would be served in proceeding with a charge

A person serving 'time' for crimes such as theft or burglary can, as I have suggested earlier, be regarded as socially dead and will not usually be prosecuted for other minor crimes he admits. However, he is still a prime source of detections, and after sentence will almost certainly be visited in prison by a 'clear-up squad' or 'prison visit team'. Their sole task is to follow up convicted 'prigs' and get them to 'cough' as many previously unadmitted crimes as possible. At a time when the TIC has largely disappeared from the scene, the prison visit write-off has taken off as a valuable source of detections, and today 'prigs' often ask for a visit and willingly 'clear the slate' and 'cough' outstanding crimes.

Using his potential for detections as a commodity for exchange as Skolnick (1966) suggested, the convict gains information about his family or contemporaries, and earns some time out of his cell away from his fellow inmates. In addition he solidifies contacts with detectives who will, no doubt, remain his adversaries in the future. He has access to cigarettes and may ask for family favours on the outside, while the detectives can clear perhaps fifty or sixty burglaries or other crimes, which are then written off as detected. The veracity of these 'coughs' can, at times, be somewhat suspect and there are clear indications that not all the crimes submitted as prison visit write-offs might stand up to close scrutiny. Stories of detectives who have left prison with blank statement forms signed by the inmates, which then have admissions of fifty or sixty 'rubbish crimes' written in, are not unknown. On other visits the 'prig' has allegedly run his finger down the lists of outstanding crimes and agreed to take 'some rubbish', as long as each was less than, say, £50 or £60 in value. He then gets on with the real business of making some 'snout' (enhancing a supply of tobacco or cigarettes), talking to the detectives about 'jobs', friends, relatives, and life on the outside.

Occasionally prison visit or 'clear-up' squads have fallen from grace when their bending and fiddling have come unstuck and the admissions by prisoners have been found to be less than accurate. In 1981 the chief constable of Northumbria denied his officers had given prisoners money, tobacco, and cigarettes to admit crimes they had never committed, but it was reported in the *Newcastle Journal* (10 September 1981) that

> he did not deny that five officers had been returned to uniform duties . . . after a detective constable submitted false statements which led to the clearing up of several crimes . . . That officer together with a Sergeant and two other detective officers from the same Sub-Division were transferred to other duties.

Following other disclosures in the national press that crimes were being falsely admitted, some forces dispensed with special units for 'clear-ups' altogether, leaving the responsibility for visits on the officer in charge of each case. In addition, in the same way that questionable dealings with informants resulted in the issue of rules of conduct, so the rules relating to prison visits were tightened up and a list of 'reasons for interviewing persons serving custodial sentences' was issued. At a subsequent Senior CID conference I attended, however, it was agreed it was impossible to discontinue the practice if for no other reason than because of the numbers of detections the 'write-off system produced.

In 1982, a detective inspector about to submit forty-nine burglaries valued at £37,000 as prison visit write-offs complained over a coffee in my office about the institutional desperation for detections which subsequently hit the lowest ranks when this political need forced the constables to 'fiddle'. At the time he was submitting this list to HQ asking they be recorded as 'No Further Action Detections — offender in custody and the court is unlikely to vary the sentence'; he shook his head somewhat woefully, saying:

> What are things coming to Malcolm? . . I can't charge him with any of them; the first one we charge will be the last detection we get this way and the figures would plummet. This 'prison visit' system is a scourge; it's a sickness and yet everyone plays the game until the bloody wheel comes off.

Such admissions have played a major part in the detection figures in the recent past. After the Northumbria system of prison visits was developed, the resulting detections rose from 2,700 in 1974, to 20,500 in 1980 and in one division in 1980 40 per cent of all detections were cleared up in this way. These 'subsequents' or follow-up detections have other idiosyncratic properties and it is always likely that recorded crimes and the detections may appear seriously out of synchronicity. For example, crimes from one year, say 1989, can be detected by a prison visit in 1990 and be set against that year's record of crimes committed, so that detections may well exceed crimes committed, especially in the early part of the year. Another colleague in the CID described how his divisional commander had triumphantly called him in to expose a 'fiddle' that he had spotted: 'I see we've had a dozen indecent assaults this year yet we've got 16 detected in this month's figures [February]: how do you account for that?' My detective friend told me he had to explain 'to that fool of a commander' how 'subsequents' from prison visits had accounted for the majority of the sixteen detections and that out of the dozen reported so far, 'we'd be lucky if we had one or two cleared up'. He went on to describe how the commander had not really understood the whole concept of 'subsequents' until it 'had been spelled out to him in words of one syllable'. 'But then', he concluded, 'he's never been in the department so he obviously knows nowt.'

A similar hiccup or degradation of the system occurred when a good run of early detections from prison visits gave one division a 170 per cent detection rate for house burglary in the first two months of the year. Of course, it was then necessary to hold some back and submit them as the year progressed to ensure the figures matched the expectancies of the hierarchies or some commanders, who often do not seem to understand the nuances of 'doing the business'. It is common for detectives to be asked to hold some detections back until next month if the figures are satisfactory, or alternatively to be asked by the detective inspector to 'pull out any "keepy-backs" you've got tucked away this month, we're running a bit short . . .'. At other times the detective inspector will tell his men, 'Its all right this month, I've get a few in the drawer which will see us out.'

Some years after all this has become regular practice in many county forces, it seems that the Metropolitan Police will belatedly follow the shire forces in taking on the prison visit system. The *Police Review* (14 December 1984: 2406) reported:

> Frank Dobson, the Labour M.P. asked the Home Secretary when he expected the clear-up rate for crime in the Metropolitan Police area to match that of the West Midlands [The West Mids. rate at the end of 1983 was 35.8 per cent; the Met. figure was 17 per cent] Mr. Dobson also asked what steps were taken by the Metropolitan Police to study training methods in Forces with higher clear-up rates...Giles Shaw, for the Home Secretary, said there were regular exchanges to study the...methods of other Forces and that the Met has examined the investigative methods . . .
> He said that an experiment is now taking place in which convicted prisoners are interviewed about unsolved crimes.

It seems hardly surprising that detectives have become cynical about this 'numbers game'. One 'clear-up squad' detective I had worked with as a young CID officer in the 1960s, revealed the inherent irony generated by the system when I visited his station in 1981 and met him for the first time in three or four years. He showed me into the 10' square office he shared with his partner and asked me:

'What do you think of this? 1,500 recorded detections from this room this year, for this division.'

'What percentage of those are genuine?', I asked, with a grin on my face. '50 per cent?'

He assumed a look of mock horror and outrage, placed his hand on his heart, then laughingly said, 'You're being generous, aren't you!'

Both he and I understood these statistical truths were a relative commodity, for the success of the unit was always measured in terms of its 'clear-ups' for the record of detections. The resulting cynicism manifest in our exchange, I would argue, occurred in part because of an unspoken acknowledgement of the obvious complicity which some chief officers and senior detectives play in this scrabble for an acceptable crime figure, for many have engaged in similar practices themselves as they have struggled up the hierarchies, on what Graef (1989) calls their 'obsessive quest for promotion'. And during the amalgamations and the growth in these hegemonic empires, which these statistical 'waves' of crime have helped generate and sustain, these same men have willingly ensured that such practices have taken a deep hold in the collective consciousness of the culture. However, in true hierarchical fashion and in keeping with the current refusal of senior figures in other executive corridors of power to accept responsibility when the 'wheel comes off' or fiddling of the account is revealed, it is left to those at the bottom end to take the discipline and punishment. On more than one occasion when a figure-fiddling exercise was exposed or went wrong it was the firm conviction of those in the department that the buck stopped with the detective sergeant or occasionally the detective inspector, while beyond that rank 'you were safe'.

By the late 1970s the use of 'crime waves' to indicate 'busyness' and a 'backs to the wall' mentality forced the Home Office to introduce controls under the 'Crime Counting Rules'; and in Northumbria we invented the naive simplicities of 'Manpower Provisions', based on the fallacy that crime statistics alone could determine the deployment of manpower. It was proposed to allocate men to divisions solely in relation to their returns of crimes reported. No other measure such as population density, social factors, economic opportunity, road mileages, dispersal of communities, housing types, or any other influence which might have weighted 'crime' was to be included; and no other aspect of police work was to be added to the equation. Only crime was to be used, and each geographical division was to receive its slice of the available manpower dependent on how much crime it recorded.

The result was obvious, for each divisional commander simply ordered his section and subdivisional heads to record all the crime possible. Someone, of course, had to come bottom of the table or list, and when one subdivision reported a 2 per cent drop in crime, and its neighbour had risen by the same amount, it seemed the commander might have to lose 40-50 men from his establishment. Of course this loss would mean his reduced manpower would probably record even less crime in the following year and his subsequent allocation would drop again. The cumulative effect was that by 1980 one subdivision was calculated to need so few men that it was jokingly said the superintendent would be driving the panda, acting as foot patrol, serving as counter clerk, and logging in the prisoner which he would have to go out and arrest!

Elsewhere, a population drift into a new town caused crime to be displaced as residential patterns changed, so that detectives were sent out to find the unreported 'dark' crime in an effort to keep the divisional figures up. Many small shops do not report the petty shoplifting that goes on, for a variety of reasons, not the least because a court appearance as a witness could well close the shop down for half a day. Two sergeants concentrated on this area and were able to come back with several dozens of detections for thefts from shops (usually committed by juveniles and children under the age of criminal responsibility). These deeds had previously been resolved at the store counter by mediation and discretion, but as detected crimes they helped ensure the division could claim its share of the manpower in the following year, and of course helped add to the 'crime wave' that inexplicably was rising year by year at the time. Not unnaturally only detected crimes were really welcomed, for although the commander might want more crimes recorded, the detectives could not afford to jeopardize their system or their career prospects by having a surge in crime and fewer detections. It is only a short step from this type of exercise which has hierarchical weight behind it to the situation I have outlined where someone decides to record 'crimes' which have not happened, and are committed by 'offenders' who do not exist, but who allegedly have been 'cautioned by a senior officer'. For only two or three such detections per week can make a considerable difference to the acceptability of divisional statistics.

When the exercise had been running for three years, I was able to have some influence on its discontinuity, for it was again going to take forty men away from a quieter division and redistribute them. At this time I was in Research and Development and we were able to show that such a measurement of resource allocation was somewhat simplistic,[59] by forecasting that one subdivision would soon have no men at all. As a result, 'Manpower Provisions' was abandoned for three years until I was at a quiet subdivision, when another new superintendent in research[60] reintroduced it on the direction of chief officers, and our division suddenly lost twenty-one officers from its authorized establishment.

The counting rules

Almost inevitably the 'crime wave' which the police found to be so useful an indicator of productivity became untenable to other sections of society, and political measures were introduced to curtail the expansion which the control industry had enjoyed. By 1979 the Home Office became obliged to impose a formula to suggest that less crime was occurring. If properly instituted, this measure would present a less dramatic appearance of disorder and social unrest to the public, for the moral panic and the unleashed tiger were becoming difficult to contain as the forty-three forces trawled up an increasing surge in crime, and then skilfully manipulated the detections to show their efficacy in holding back the tide of mayhem.

Walker (1971: 24-5) has shown how multiple crimes can be generated from one circumstance, making similar points to those I included earlier in my hypothetical case study:

> an advertiser causes a fraudulent advertisement to appear in 16 issues of
> *The Times* and defrauds 80 people; a father has sexual intercourse with

his daughter 10 times before his 'crime' comes to light. A cashier pockets small sums of money each week ... a burglar breaks into a hotel and takes property from 10 guests. How many crimes are involved in each case . . . ?

Again the answer, as Ditton (1979: 21) indicates, has got to be: 'as many as you want (to react to) . . .'.

By 1979, the police were better practised at recording the 'crimes' they wished to react to, and especially those with 'a body' to sustain the detection rate, and in that year the Home Office introduced measures in an attempt to curtail the multiple recording of crimes, such as those described above by Walker (1971). Detailed rules were issued to the police in a document: *Crime Statistics: Counting Rules for Serious Offences — Home Office Requirements,* which set out to ensure that such 'multiples' were recorded as 'only one continuous, or "series crime"...'. These directives were made under Sect. 54 of the Police Act 1964, and their implementation was agreed by ACPO.

The main requirement in the Rules concerns the way numbers of crimes are to be recorded and counted. Only the most serious offence (i.e. crime) in any series of offences will be counted. In other words, in my earlier hypothetical example the 'prig' would statistically have committed only the one crime of rape; i.e. the most serious. Severity is to be determined by the sentence and the Counting Rules set out the penalties for each, in order to determine the most serious:

> At the beginning of each of the three categories (Violence against the person, Sexual offences, Other offences) is a section listing the offences in that part in order of maximum penalty. This is to assist in determining the most serious offence to be counted where several offences are committed in one incident. (Counting Rules, Para. 2(2): 5)

However, in the event of my hypothetical incident ever occurring, it is unlikely the police would only count one crime. It is almost certain they would count one in each of the three sections at least, and the detectives would be sure to try to count many more by the use of administrative lacunae in the local recording processes.

Offences (crimes) which are reported separately by the public, we are informed by the Counting Rules, can be counted separately and allowed to stand as individually numbered crimes when they are cleared up, even if it becomes apparent they form a part of a continuous series. However, the Home Office urge that 'serious consideration must be given, at the time the offences are reported, to the possibility that they are part of a continuous offence' (Counting Rules, Para. 3(2): 6). For over a decade now, these 'continuous' offences have been a source of great dispute, argument, and manipulation by some forces in their efforts to maintain their inculcated presentations of social reality. Some stats. departments seem to be less than scrupulous in allowing separately counted series, while others fight continuous battles with the divisional detectives as they set out to bend the Counting Rules to their favour. On one occasion in 1987 I heard a superintendent (an ex-detective) propose the use of the Force Statistical Officer on a management project, away from the immediate assessment of crime reports. Outlining the value of this move to the management services department, he grinned mischievously as he added 'and it'll do wonders for the crime figures'. For stats. officers are adept at spotting attempts to get 'associated offences' (as the continuous series is also known) recorded separately, and thus getting 'three or four for one'.

Futher changes in the Counting Rules since 1979 seem to reflect the political use of 'crime' as a mirror image or metaphor of social unrest or socio-political dominance, and not surprisingly in these circumstances, they tend to have been accorded only a token acceptance by detectives who understand these changes have a political nuance which lies well outside their daily experiences of dealing with 'prigs'. In the circumstances it should come as no surprise to find they have had few qualms about bending the rules to suit their own needs, for their *habitus* of success, promotion, and status is built on their ability to maintain a suitable 'detection rate'. It is therefore almost a given fact that their interpretation of the Rules will follow and support the existing modes of thought upon which the police system is built.

In my hypothetical example, the youth who took the milk tokens from fifty doorsteps might well have committed fifty crimes, or only one, depending on whether the crimes were reported and recorded separately or in a series. Initially, in 1979, the Rules directed such thefts were associated offences and would be recorded as one continuous crime. If (and this is unlikely) all of these thefts were reported, and no immediate 'body' was anticipated, a detective had different options open to him, depending on his ability to play out the nuances of the system. He could:

(a) record fifty separate *undetected* crimes immediately, if he was foolish enough to try to convince his Detective Inspector that he never considered for one moment that these were a series of thefts committed by one person.

(b) record one continuous *undetected crime,* following the instructions in the Counting Rules to the letter.

(c) hold them back for a few days to see if a 'body' was forthcoming.

Option (a) would earn him few favours, especially if the fifty crimes remained undetected. Option (b) is more attractive, for if the crimes remained undetected he only needs one detection from somewhere else to maintain a 50 per cent detection rate. The third option has attractions, for if the detective finds a culprit, he can then record the fifty as separate crimes, and have 'a nice little roll-up'. Of course he can only allow them to lie unrecorded for a short period, for 'if the wheel comes off' to reveal he has not immediately recorded them, he can be disciplined. However chances are often worth taking, as the following incident illustrates:

> . . . a youth has been brought in for shoplifting in the town centre and is searched. The gaoler turns out his pockets and milk tokens tumble out everywhere . . . We phone the division from which they have been stolen and a detective from the 'clear-up' squad comes down. He arranges to see the youth and his father at his divisional station in two days' time to 'sort out this little business'. By then, he will have recorded these as perhaps 70 separate undetected thefts after he has knocked on a few doors. Then he will 're-arrest' the kid when he comes in, which will allow these 70 to

> stand as separate 'crimes', even though it is 'now apparent' that these
> form part of a continuous offence. (Bridewell fieldnote)

Even if the juvenile is cautioned in this case, it matters not! The counting system is irrelevant to the court proceedings or to cautions. It is merely how crimes are counted for the statistical returns, and the whole transaction is best understood if we note how the detective describes this incident as a 'little business', in which — it could be said — he enhances his capital in the form of statistical returns.

Early in 1983 the Counting Rules were amended once again. Milk tokens or milk stolen from doorsteps of individual houses was now to be construed as 'having remained in the constructive possession of the house'. Such thefts were therefore to stand as separate crimes, having spent the previous four years as continuous offences. In February of that year, I recorded my conversation with a stats. clerk who had just had an argument with a detective friend of mine:

> STATS. Your friend has just had words with us. He's not very pleased. He
> put two crimes through, one for theft of 80 pints of milk and one for 50. I
> told him that he now had to put in 130 separate crimes . . . and he's not
> amused!
>
> ME. Why is that, aren't they still a continuous offence?
>
> STATS. Not any longer.
>
> ME. Weren't they detected?
>
> STATS. Of course not, why do you think he was annoyed?

I then went to the detective inspector on my subdivision, described the same event, and asked him how he would resolve it:

> 'That's easy', he told me, 'you have to argue that as the householders have
> not paid for the milk, it is not in their constructive possession and still
> remains under the constructive possession and ownership of the milkman,
> so only one crime has been committed against him. Mind you, are you sure
> that he's not just making sure he gets 130 recorded and has a body tucked
> up his sleeve to produce in a couple of days?'

'Bouncy' cheques from a stolen cheque book, however, are still to be considered as 'associated' or 'continuous' offences and only one crime of criminal deception should be recorded regardless of the number of cheques issued. Such paradox in the Rules offends the sense of order which detectives operate by and cheque book deceptions are one of the crimes which stats. departments recognize detectives may well attempt to fiddle to get extra 'clear-ups'. The practice is simple, and the detective with a 'body' for ten 'bouncy' cheques might well try to put in ten separate crime reports, each separately numbered to indicate ten crimes committed and ten crimes cleared up. To avoid the stats. clerks spotting each is part of a series which should only count as one crime, he will submit the individually numbered crime reports over a period of days or even weeks, hoping they will be 'lost' in the deluge of reports submitted. If the ten reports are submitted over a month or two, they may well be hidden among 20,000 others that have arrived during that time. As the injured persons will be different on each report (e.g. Woolworth's, Boot's the Chemists, Marks & Spencer, Comet, Dixon's, etc.), the only way the stats. clerks may have of spotting the ten are a series is to check the arrested person or culprit on each report and compare each one against the other. Some stats. department clerks have developed elaborate indices to spot these attempts by the detectives to make ten detections when the Rules only allow one.

Crimes recorded are also defined in the Rules by peculiar temporal measures which specify that an 'occasion' affects the way a crime is to be counted. In burglary, robbery, theft, handling stolen property, fraud, forgery, and criminal damage, the police are instructed to 'record one offence for each victim on each "occasion". An "occasion" is classed as a 24 hour period'. At a CID conference in 1982, those present were reminded that when a series of thefts occurred against the same person with more than 24 hours between each, separate crimes should be recorded, and the copies of the Counting Rules in the stats. departments are sprinkled with bizarre examples of 'continuous offences' and 'separate occasions'. Many of these have been defined by the Home Office or been added to by the clerks as they have consulted the Home Office over some specific ruling, such as page 45 of the Rules, for Rape, Classification 19/1:

A.	Four males rape three girls twice each on the same occasion .	Count 3 offences.
B.	Two males assist a third to rape a woman.	Count 1 offence.
C.	A male rapes a girl, detains her against her will and rapes her again later.	Count 1 offence.
D.	A young person having temporary charge of young children on several occasions admits to having committed 2 rapes on one young child and 1 on another and several indecent assaults and gross indecencies.	If the 2 rapes were on separate occasions count 3 offences. Count the indecent assaults separately if the children were unwilling. Gross indecency (offence 74) is not countable.

For the extremely unusual crime of 'sending unworthy ships to sea', the instruction is to 'record 1 offence for each initial sending, irrespective of the number of intermediate ports the ship calls at'. At p. 26 of the Counting Rules for 'Assault Occasioning Actual Bodily Harm', Classification 8/6, the stats. officers have added:

a husband assaults his wife on a number of different occasions.	Count 1 offence for each occasion.

Under Rule 8, 'Aggravated Burglary in a Dwelling' (Classification 29), there are a number of examples of how to count crimes, which 'also cover classifications 28, 30 and 31'. A number of examples are given, such as:

F.	A wounding (classif. 5/1) occurs in the course of a burglary.	Count 1 offence of wounding and no burglary.

| A wounding (classif. 8/1) occurs in the course of a burglary. | Count 1 offence of burglary and no wounding. |

In these cases, the classification of which crime is to be counted is dependent on the degree of injury in the wounding. When the wounding is categorized as more serious it supersedes the burglary in the rules.

At example L, the stats. clerks have added the following comment:

| L. | Four huts on a building site are burgled; there is a perimeter fence. | Count 1 offence. |
| M. | As example L, but with no perimeter fence. | Count 4 offences. |

Here the perimeter fence affords what is known as 'protection', thus creating only one 'crime'. When I have asked detectives how they would record the incident, they all respond by asking the question which determines their practice: 'is there a body?' If there is not, then there *is* a perimeter fence. If there is a 'body' then any fence is conveniently ignored and they claim four crimes detected. Thefts from cars on car parks will often be statistically determined in a similar manner.

Under 'Other Criminal Damage' (classification 58, p. 92), where the heading instructs: 'One offence for each occasion and offender/group of offenders', the stats. clerks have added several examples, such as:

| A. | A group of offenders damage several different properties on their way home from a party. | Count 1 (continuous) offence because the rule is 1 offence for each occasion and offender/group offenders. |
| B. | An offender damages garden sheds in several roads on several occasions. | Count each date as 1 offence unless the incidents occur within 24 hrs of each other. |

Stats. officers invariably acknowledge that the whole system is played out as a big game, and when the Rules were once again amended in the early 1980s, a stats. officer (who had been on the Working Party considering the amendments) told me that as they came away from the meeting they were asking themselves how long it would take detectives to find loopholes in the new instructions in order to maintain their practices.

At page 80 of the Rules, under classification 53/2 'Obtaining Pecuniary Advantage by Deception', the stats. clerks have added examples which clearly acknowledge these attempts by detectives to obtain statistical advantage:

| C. | A person has obtained money by deceiving a number of people in a variety of ways; this is not discovered until he is interrogated for some other offence. | Count 1 offence of forgery (Rule of deception that is substantially different. |

D.   A self-employed motor cycle dealer forged 140 insurance cover notes with intent to defraud 3 separate insurance companies. He also dishonestly obtained cash from 134 persons by falsely purporting to have arranged insurance cover. These offences were 'discovered' when the offender asked for them to be taken into consideration in court.

Count 1 offence of forgery (Rule 9). Do not count the dishonest obtaining of cash since forgery is the more serious element in the incident.

F.   It is discovered that money was illegally drawn each week from 2 Pension books, one issued by the D.H.S.S. and one by the local County Council, the true recipient having died 15 years earlier. A total of 1560 offences are presented at Court.

Count 2 (continuous) offences as each Pension book provided the means of committing a continuous series of deceptions.

The 1,560 offences 'presented at court' in example F and the 134 offences which were 'discovered' when the offender asked for them to be taken into consideration in court are obvious attempts by detectives to swell their detection rates, and I know of many other occasions when such 'series' crimes became separate 'occasions'.

Throughout the pages of the Counting Rules similar examples emphasize how crime generally relates to minor offences, such as damage to sheds or the theft of trivial items; for rape and aggravated burglaries are thankfully still rare events. And although by the early 1980s Northumbria was claiming well in excess of 100,000 established crimes each year, we might well wonder how many single crimes were recorded as series, or vice versa, and how many actually occurred or were being submitted for misrecording?

In this illusory world which has long dealt in the rituals of 'cuffing', 'creating', 'keepy-backs juggling', 'fiddling', and 'bending', I suggest the way that crime recording is manipulated means that any statistical reality is best considered as a reflection of the semantic values of a xenophobic and defensive institutional system, largely enacted for the benefit of those inside the organization. Meanwhile the theatre surrounding the Counting Rules remains relatively unknown as an aspect of a ritualized drama played out for limited public consumption by skilled actors who operate in a world of 'clear-ups', 'roll-ups', and occasional 'cock-ups' when 'the wheel comes off'.

Other times, other places: same bending, same fiddles

In July 1986 Constable Ron Walker of Kent Police 'went public' in the *Observer* (13 July 1986) detailing various ways in which the Kent detectives had swelled their detection rates:

one division had increased its clear-up rates from 24.4% to 69.5% ... methods used included taking down a random selection of car numbers, obtaining the names of the owners from PNC [Police National Computer] and then persuading an offender to admit stealing the cars... A statement in which an offender admitted 54 burglaries some of which occurred two years earlier was written down in 60 minutes although it included details of addresses and property stolen. *(Police Review,* 6 March 1987)

At this time I was one of thirteen subdivisional commanders in West Mercia Police, with a team of detectives skilled in 'doing the business'. Their immediate reaction was that Walker had 'lost his marbles in going public', especially as he had gone to the Metropolitan Police with his tale of administrative corruption. For it was axiomatic to my CID colleagues that the Met. are perhaps the best of the lot in the field of 'massaging events'. As my detective inspector cynically commented: 'You'll see; that man is really pissing on his fritters.'

Three years later PC Walker was still on 'sick leave' and although West Mercia, along with other forces, had carried out immediate internal inspections of the recording systems, not a lot had changed. Crime and Counting Rule recording practices continued to be manoeuvred to suit the institutional need, while prevailing systems survived more or less intact. And even though a long enquiry was carried out under the guidance of the Police Complaints Authority into the Kent practices and recommended some disciplinary charges, PC Walker moved into a sort of structural limbo at the time of writing *(Police Review,* 16 September 1988).

In November 1986, following a quick internal inspection of the force systems, which reported that all was well, a visit to all our divisions was arranged for the assistant chief constable (operations) who was accompanied by a detective superintendent from HQ. All the senior staff on our division were present and I later wrote up a long fieldnote, from which the following is an extract:

... the meeting is to discuss 'current crime' and Divisional strategies. I am forcibly reminded how all of those present have different perceptions of what 'crime' is all about. The Detective Inspectors have a different reality to these HQ politicians ...

The meeting has an agenda but a crucial item is missing ... afterwards in the canteen it is agreed the visit has had two main thrusts, one of which has been left out of the circulated agenda.

The first concerns the increase in house-burglaries on the divison. Both subdivisions are about 100 up on last year at this time (but compared to the adjacent division in the West Midlands force we have no h/burglaries at all; in the first 10 months they have 3,049 while I have just over 400 but only a slightly smaller establishment). During the meeting I point out that our apparent increase is merely over two ten-month periods, Jan.-Oct. 1985 and 1986, and that comparative analysis on such a data base is relatively unsophisticated. If we look at variations in this small sample or include the 1984 and 1983 figures then some altogether different patterns emerge. The ACC doesn't want to hear this however, and even gets a bit angry. Later on a Detective Inspector says its the first time he has heard him swear.

The non-agenda item relates to the 'Kent' figure fiddling and the recent whirlwind visit by Ch. Supt. *** who has looked at our detections and found us to be whiter than white! Our prison visit 'write-offs' I think are relatively 'clean' (as far as I can tell), but the system is hardly used in some divisions and the Force only makes occasional use of it in comparison to Northumbria. The ACC then mentions that there is value in going to an Injured Person, even months later, and telling them we have someone in prison who admits their 'burglary', and who is now serving a sentence (albeit for a different crime). I look across at the Det. Inspector, who grins. We have just done some research which suggests that we perhaps tell 25% of IPs whose 'crime' is cleared, and then only tell those whom it is 'comfortable' to tell . . . We do not tell them if it is likely to get difficult, e.g.

— those who are cautioned. According to the Crime Admin. Inspector, the IPs often get quite upset and won't accept the 'caution' decision, even though it is not within their power to have any say. 'They enter into lengthy telephone calls or correspondence and fuck the system up. So we don't tell many of them.'

— those where we decide to take no further action. Again it is too difficult to explain to the IP. 'They don't understand Attorney Generals' Guidelines, the Crown Prosecution code, the evidential sufficiency criterion (i.e. 50% plus chance of winning), or the 'public interest' concept; and they just cause trouble if they are informed.

— those whose crimes are admitted on prison visits. Sometimes if it is suitable we do inform the IP, but again it is often too difficult to explain to the public, who just don't understand the business of dealing an NFA agreement in return for 'clear-ups'.

It is obvious that the ACC is oblivious to the fact that we don't tell 75% of the injured persons that their case has been cleared up. The Crime Admin. Inspector tells me that all the Divisions pursue the same policy because of the problems which occur when we do try to tell the public, for they 'want their culprit to be boiled in oil and not to be cautioned or dealt with as an NFA.'

The ACC then staggers the detectives, by asking: 'How about seeing offenders who receive a non-custodial sentence, e.g. probation or a fine, to get them to "clear their slates" with a view to a "No further action — detection"?' Anyone admitting a serious robbery might have to go to court, he warns, but otherwise, 'I think we could offer a guarantee of NFA'. The CID are shocked, but the ACC tells us that our 'write-offs' are low in comparison to other Forces in the 'family' in the CIPFA stats,[61] and the HMI has pointed out that we could increase our percentage 'write-offs'.

If our prison visit write-off situation was being played according to the rules, and no flagrant creation of admissions had been revealed, then the same can hardly be said for 'NFA detections'. In a 1983 Amendment to the Counting Rules, the Home Office defined eleven occasions when an offence (i.e. a crime) will be considered to be cleared up:

Notifiable Offences Recorded by the Police   *Crimsec 1A-2*

Offences Recorded as Cleared Up

An offence is cleared up when:

1. a person has been charged or summoned for the offence (irrespective of any subsequent acquittal);

2. the offence has been taken into consideration by the court;

3. the offender has been proceeded against in another police force area for the offence;

4. the offender dies before proccedings could be initiated or completed;

5. the offender has been cautioned by the police;

6. the offender is ill and is unlikely to recover or is too senile or too mentally disturbed for proceedings to be taken;

7. the complainant or an essential witness is dead and the proceedings cannot be pursued;

8. the guilt of the offender is clear but the victim refuses, or is permanently unable, or if a juvenile is not permitted to give evidence;

9. the offender admits the offence but it is decided that no useful purpose would be served by proceeding with the charge;

10. it is ascertained that an offence has been committed by a child under the age of criminal responsibility;

11. an offence is admitted by a juvenile of the age of criminal responsibility and police take no action other than reporting the particulars to a local authority for action under the Children and Young Persons Act 1963 Section 1.

On the advice of the Home Office, a twelfth category had been added to the Rules. This was a variation on Rule 9 which allowed an NFA 'clear-up' when the offender admitted the offence and 'no useful purpose would be served in pursuing a prosecution'. However, the extra dimension to this NFA detection 'clear-up' rule is that it does not even need the offender to admit the offence, it only requires that 'there is sufficient evidence to charge the offender but the police prosecutions department, the DPP or a senior police officer decides that no useful purpose would be served by proceeding with the charge'. As a subdivisional commander during 1985 and 1986, I found I was authorized to 'mark off' crimes as 'detected NFA'. Once I had appended my signature to this decision, the detection was more or less assured and I found I was processing about 10-15 per month in this category. My concern became aroused when I read one file of evidence where the denial by the accused was so strong and the evidence so weak, that I set out to read an exact interpretation of the Counting Rules. No copy of the Rules existed then on the subdivision and no one in the CID had a copy of this Amendment to the Counting Rules (January 1983) listed above. Eventually I obtained one from HQ and a copy of the 'sufficiency of evidence' criteria set out in an Attorney-General's guide-line of 1983, which required that we had more than a 50 per cent chance of winning before proceeding with prosecution. At this time, some 2-3 years after these changes had been implemented, the chief inspector in charge of prosecution decision-making on the division had never even heard of them and I therefore began to make a note of files submitted to me in this category, e.g.

> Theft: a 17-year-old local villain for perfume valued £20. We would undoubtedly get a Not Guilty Plea and the only evidence is that he was in the shop near the perfume counter, and ran off when asked what he was up too. The theft could have occurred any time over a period and cannot be 51% attributed to him, but as we will have to NFA it anyway, why not ask for it to be an NFA detection — after all, as the officer in charge has said in his covering report, there is no doubt that he is guilty!

> Criminal damage to a car, value £300 by a 29-year-old. We have a motive, but no real evidence. We may have about 40%, but we do not have 51%, however the officers in the case are convinced of guilt and ask for a 'detected NFA'.

It seems such practice was the result of a long history in the force of taking cases that perhaps only had a 40 per cent chance (if that) to court and bluffing a way through. As a subdivisional prosecutions sergeant pointed out, 'the magistrates were on our side and we often got a guilty plea out of the unrepresented idiots we dealt with'. Such practice had ground to a halt in 1983 when a force-wide prosecuting solicitors' department was instituted many years after they had been the norm in other police areas, and the force was now having to grapple with the unwelcome phenomenon of prosecuting solicitors who demanded sufficient evidence to justify the charge as required by the Attorney-General's guide-lines and withdrew a case when it was not forthcoming.

A good proportion of the NFA detections I marked off in my twenty-two months on the subdivision would no doubt have gone to court in the past and made a conviction. Now they were claimed under Rule 12 (above) and one case in my fieldnotes illustrates the significance of these 'clear-ups':

> I have marked up a file 'NFA detection' during my first days in the subdivision for 3 offences of burglary. The accused is a 25-yr-old professional with a long criminal history. A guilty plea is not anticipated! I read the file and discuss it with the Det. Insp. and the detective in the case. There is a little evidence and a lot of suspicion, but not enough to

give it a go at court. Weeks later, I track down the 1983 revised Counting Rules and the Attorney-General's Guide-lines which require a 51% chance before we can decide to take no further action, but claim a detection. Now, on the inspection following Ron Walker's 'bursting the bubble' in Kent, Chief Superintendent *** scours our NFA detection files and rightly declares this one to be invalid. The rest are accepted even though some are very 'iffy', and we are told these three burglaries will have to be reclassified and remain on files as 'undetected'. But too late! I speak to HQ's stats. and find that there is now no way of declassifying them, for they have long since gone into the returns to the Home Office.

At this time, in 1986, the force had claimed 1,261 detections in this category 'NFA — other than by Prison Visit'. Across the thirteen subdivisions the numbers varied from 255 to 29. My own subdivision claimed 105 detections in this category, and the total statistical return at the end of the year showed:

(a) 1,003 crimes cleared by TICs;

(b) 1,876 crimes (previously reported) cleared by cautions;

(c) 1,261 crimes cleared by NFA — other than by 'prison visit write-offs';

(d) 1,372 crimes (not previously reported) cleared by TICs;

(e) 693 crimes (not previously reported) cleared by cautions;

(f) 269 crimes cleared by prison visit write-offs;

(g) 1,138 crimes (not previously reported) cleared by prison visit write-offs.

TOTAL: 7,612

(h) 5,021 crimes cleared, charged at court;

(i) 230 crimes cleared, further charged at court.

TOTAL: 5,251

12,863 crimes cleared in total.

A further 5,627 detected crimes were yet to be broken down into the nine categories. However, by using the percentage norms indicated above, we could expect some 3,319 of these to fall into categories (a)-(g) and many of these to be NFA detections. In effect this means that some 10,931 crimes will be cleared by TICs, prison visit write-offs, cautions, and NFA decisions out of the total 18,490 detections for the year. Much deliberation on the creation of this 59 per cent of the overall detection rate goes unseen, just as it did in 1955 when I started out, but it still continues as an essential prerequisite for the detectives, and is seen as a marker of their ability to 'do the business'.

Some of these 'crimes' raise questions. Why, for instance, had 1,138 detections obtained by prison visit write-offs not been previously reported? At a social occasion, where I voiced this question at a time when I was surrounded by detectives, the various possibilities were outlined:

(i) the public had not bothered — i.e. the 'dark' figure.[62]

(ii) the detectives had 'cuffed' them for a time, knowing they would eventually be admitted when the suspect was sentenced. Had they then not been admitted, they could have vanished forever or have reluctantly been put in as 'undetected' crimes.

(iii) they had never occurred at all, but were figments of the imagination and were 'found' by detectives using electoral rolls and telephone directories to create unwitting injured persons. (From fieldnotes)

This led to a discussion on the unexpected problems caused by the creation of divisional Crime Operational Support Units (Crime OSUs) for the centralized administration of all 'crime papers' and a short-lived attempt to send letters to all injured persons telling them of the progress of their crime and the results of any case. As I have outlined above, many difficulties occurred because IPs were incensed by the decision-making processes; however, another problem came to light in relation to 'previously unreported clear-ups' (listed at *(d)* and *(g)* above). One of the detectives involved in the Crime OSU system told those present: 'injured persons began ringing or writing into the Unit saying they knew nothing of the crime they were allegedly the aggrieved party in. It became very embarrassing; and the OSUs had to stop sending the letters out.' This was an instance when some very experienced negotiators of the statistical drama, with their own deeply entrenched methods of purveying a suitable truth, were suddenly left stranded by the introduction of a new computerized system which was set up as if the whole game was played out according to the Rules. On such occasions rapid adjustments have to be made to avoid revealing the bizarre realities of a historical system which PC Ron Walker seemed, somewhat naively, to believe he could adjust. While similarly deploring the fiddling, others have kept their heads beneath the parapet by anonymously declaiming against the demands of the system:

Tell the truth about crime

Once again it is the time of the year when forces publish their January/ July figures of reported crime and detection rates. You can read it in all the papers: 'Crime Down — Detections Up', or 'Neighbourhood Watch Works'. In my force and in particular my division, I am instructed to 'cuff' minor crimes, including burglary and assaults, where there is no chance of detection. I 'cuff' more crimes than I record at a rate of eight to one. We are always demanding more men and resources, yet we do this. If the true figures were published this country would have a major heart attack. Why do we do this? So that some promotion-mad detective inspector can go to his boss and say 'Look what a good DI I am', and then his boss goes to his boss, and so on. Finally the chief constable can say: 'I've got the best detection and clear-up rate in the country . . .'

Name and Address Supplied

(*Police Review*, 19 August 1988: 1766).

How crime is being cuffed

I write in answer to the letter 'Tell the truth about Crime' (PR Aug 19). I do not know what force the author belongs to, but I agree with everything that was said. I know that cuffing crime does go on in my Force. For example, crimes that should be attempted burglary are often recorded as criminal damage. Burglaries are sometimes crimed as theft, particularly if there is little chance of detection. Other crimes go unreported. Crime figures are adjusted basically to appease 'superior officers' and enhance promotion prospects. But who really benefits? . . . The Police prides itself on honesty and does not easily tolerate corrupt or improper practices, yet we put up with 'crime cuffing'.

Name and Address Supplied

(*Police Review*, 2 September 1988)

After a lifetime's experience of this drama of manipulation I find little has changed in the basic facets of the exercise or in its centrality to the structural process of publicly claiming effective success. In the middle of 1988, at a time when I was writing fieldnotes on the rituals of retirement I was then experiencing, I also noted:

> I listen as 'Val' from Stats. seeks advice from the head of the department about a crime, a burglary, recorded, established and detected. Now, some 3 months later the divisional detectives have submitted another 'detected crime' of 'theft of a key' used to commit the burglary. 'It's two for one under the rules' she is reminded, and the second crime is returned to the division to be deleted and the number to be reallocated to a 'real crime'. . . I have visitors from another Force with me in the Stats dept. at the time. 'Val' has a pile of such 'crimes' to check back with the originating officers — all seem to be attempts to get an extra 'handling' along with a 'theft', a fraud/deception after a credit card theft, and so on — a stream of attempts to get two for one which the rules don't allow . . . I wonder how many of the 5,000 plus 'No crimes' we have had a couple of years back are from such doubling up? The difference between initially *'recorded'* crimes and the eventual return of *'established'* crimes is quite considerable and must be largely a matter of rule interpretation . . . a Detective Sergeant rings while we are there. He has 250 admissions of theft from motor vehicles but has no injured persons, no report of crimes and no property recovered. He is advised he can have those he can prove, i.e. produce an injured person for, but he has none and asks what he should do. Later when I tell a Detective Sergeant about this call, he laughs sadly at this naivety. 'You don't ask, you find IPs. The number of times I've been put down as an IP or M—S—has, . . . i.e. someone who won't create problems if they inadvertently get an IP letter — but then you ensure they are down on the Crime Report as having been informed personally.' The message is that in such a situation you don't look a gift horse in the mouth and you invent IPs to meet the admissions — but not 250 — just enough to meet the numbers necessary to hit the divisional, subdivisional or section norms.

These statistical games are sustaining dramas. They are about 'various regimes and discourses of truth' (Sheridan 1980: 222 on Foucault) which can be lived with; about those the institution can handle openly and those it cannot face. And they occur not just in Northumbria, Kent, or West Mercia, but across the organization. In July 1988 I had the opportunity to assess a new presentation by Cheshire Police in relation to its own statistical truths, when a 60-page analysis of 1987-8 crime was recommended to West Mercia by HM Inspector of Constabulary. I was asked to comment on the document and among the points in my report, I noted that:

> It's thick (60 pages) and if this is an average month then it is 720 pages per year and what analytic skills lie on the Div/Sub-Div to ask of each graph 'okay what does this mean; can we influence it?' Otherwise it will end up like many other publications as so much drawer-liner . . .

> . . . If there are statistically significant aspects where are they addressed and analysed? e.g. very low figures for the categories on pages 3, 5 and 6 for Feb. '87 — result of very bad weather? Beyond police control? Who remembers now? P. 4 shows marked drop in June — but no explanation? P. 6 very high Dec. '87 figure for criminal damage=Xmas mayhem, or result of manipulations of detections and write-offs for the end of year returns? . . .

> . . . Many of the graphs are straight line graphs and are the equivalent of 'statistical background noise' which looks as if it is the norm and will occur regardless of police action; but as the whole document is only a comparison of equivalent months for 1987 and 1988 who can say? With only this comparative data what significant trends can be assessed? This obsession in the service with a 'this year/last year' evaluation makes much of the data somewhat 'skin deep'. . . As a result, on many of the 60 pages the straight line graphs show nothing significant yet add to the bulk. Across a 6-7 year period, however, the data might have shown relevant trends . . .

> . . . Then there are the detection rates! It makes interesting reading to see that Cheshire don't use an end of the year 'adjusted figure' for their detected crimes, but show them monthly. As a result, the 'subsequents' from previous years — usually from prison visit write-offs — give the sort of bizarre results shown on p. 14, where in March 1987 there was a 117% detection rate for 'burglary in a dwelling', but only 4% in April, and then 90% in May. On p. 24 the monthly 'detected' rates for 1987 show 144%, 154%, and 111%, for 3 months out of 12. This sort of statistical assessment renders any credibility as being at least suspect!

And yet this document was being recommended to us by the adviser to chief officers, as a valid way to put out data to the force, even though it was again telling a story which was only one very skewed representation of an institutional truth.

This inability to handle real truth and separate it from an organizational truth causes continual difficulties, which is especially ironic in an organization tasked with implementing law through a system of adversarial trials of truth telling! In February 1987 a young detective constable revealed the gulf which exists between the two categories when he described his promotion board with the chief constable and other senior officers to an understanding canteen audience. This somewhat serious minded young officer regretfully told them:

> you have to toe the party line and I had to tell them the lies they wanted to hear about our unqualified belief in neighbourhood watch, about the usefulness of special constables, and about our keen support for crime prevention and community affairs schemes, such as teaching the unemployed to drive . . .

The laughter this produced repeats the message that such games, like the counting rules, are part of a drama played out for limited public consumption. In this world where an official presentation and the realities of canteen culture both rely on mythology, the 'clear-ups' remove structural dirt and ambiguity, for the idea that crimes can be *cleared up* reasserts a belief in a world where disorder can be brushed away to restore structural purity and where incongruity can be cleaned up to re-create a perfectly ordered universe in which hierarchical principles reign undisturbed. The unending nature of this drama generates the status given to those with the ability to 'do the business', and ensures that the 'bending and fiddling' remains unseen and invisible. Senior detective officers are totally cognizant of the dramatic practices surrounding this use of 'crime' and understand that because its presentation is largely symbolic, such myths require the maintenance and continuity of a closed system, with rewards for those who sustain its many illusions. Revelation of this mythology by an insider, such as PC Walker or the academic researcher, will threaten the integrity of the closed world, for it reveals how the whole fabric is built on precepts which at times seem to border on thc farcical and produce a system which might well be considered to be morally unsupportable or philosophically indefensible.

A continually unspoken need to sustain the magnitude of this myth helps reinforce an obsession with an oft-mentioned idea of the 'dignity of the job', which means that although many grumble in private or send in anonymous letters to *Police Review,* few proclaim openly about the true nature of the game. At a CID conferencc in 1980, I watched with interest as a newish detective inspector shocked the company when he openly complained how 'the political need to appear to be swamped with work at this time, means that all "crimes" were now being recorded and no longer were being cuffed'; so that

> in consequence between 1976 and 1979 there has been a rise of 15,000 minor crimes in our force, and even in the first six months of 1980 we are 6,000 crimes up on last year, even though the Home Office Counting Rules have reduced some by introducing continuous offences and denying the practice of getting two detections for one incident as in the past.

He went on to point out to the conference that Northumbria therefore had 21,000 extra crime reports on which detectives were still required by Force Orders to show times and dates of visits to the scene, and that detectives were making fictitious entries, saying each crime had been visited when it was patently obvious it was impossible for this to have occurred. The system, he complained, was making liars of detectives and he asked that when no visit had been made to a scene of crime, then this should be recorded as such on the crime report.

This frank admission of a functional problem in what is a largely symbolic system was difficult for some to handle. I watched as senior CID officers from ACPO rank down to detective inspectors grappled with this statement that the system was built on a foundation of creative inaccuracies and deceptions. Everyone present knew that it was impossible for all the scenes of crimes to be visited, just as we all knew that many of the 21,000 crimes could be added to those for 'criminal damage' and 'car theft' which had not been crimes only a decade previous. But how could this be admitted or acknowledged, for the mythology had to be maintained? The structure of the police social world and its interlocking ideology and practice requires that the foundation remains inviolate, for an institution which is set up to impose control and define order for society relies heavily on acquiescence from its ranks. They are not required to subject it to any really close examination or philosophical scrutiny, even when they are posted to departments involved in the evaluation of its practices; for in the final analysis when the order comes to 'jump', the response must be 'Yes sir, how high Sir?'; and never 'Why Sir?' This detective inspector had transgressed this basic tenet and improvidently reminded the conference that the 'King's New Suit of Clothes' (to paraphrase Hans Christian Andersen) was a dramatic symbol, which did not really exist until it was produced and directed for an accepting audience.

This mythological disorder of crime has been dramatized and pursued in fashionable, yet archetypal settings. Its use as a metaphor of 'masculine' activity or 'real' policework is directed along well tried and tested lines, which are not confined to one police force nor contained by any specific period of social history. In effect police ideology is sustained by the concept of crime at every turn, for the criminal-justice system is a theatre of make-believe with more than a touch of farce to its systems of production and presentation, and it is difficult for those who are sustained within its structures to admit this to themselves, never mind to the outside world. Many have carved out powerful roles and personae for themselves within the organization, and for these participants to admit to the dramatic or mythological nature of many of their practices would be to interfere seriously with an instilled belief in the dignity of their office and the sanctity of their role in the idea of law.

As a result, open admission that 'bending' or 'fiddling' occurs, or any revelation that arbitrary 'cuffing' and 'trade-puffing' of crime reporting and recording has been standard practice across decades, is, I suggest, a structural impossibility. It is little wonder then, that anthropological research is largely unknown, or that the insider who pursues reflexive analysis will become marginal and remain largely muted, for the system promotes an uncritical reverence for institutional practice, for tradition, and for the doctrines of precedent as part of its belief in 'the dignity of the job'. To admit that 'bending' and 'fiddling' the account is the norm would be to acknowledge the fact that irreverence, disorder, and potential chaos sustains an institution which is allegedly geared to prevent its occurrence. Such a world is not one that police *habitus* is structured to contend with or even acknowledge; for any admission could easily reverse the direction of the application of power.

Notes

55. Braudel (1981) suggests the growth of a belief in the supremacy of statistical numeracy is increasingly being used as a determining basis for everyday structures of action and ideology.

56. Skolnick (1966), Lambert (1970), McCabe and Sutcliffe (1978), Bottomley and Coleman (1981), and Farrington and Dowds (1984) all attempt to show how variable police recording techniques have influenced statistical returns of 'crime'. Farrington and Dowds (ibid.) recognize that 'car theft' and 'criminal damage' statistics have had the marked effect I have set out to demonstrate above, and theirs is one of the few studies to detail the crucial influences of these recent changes in classification.

57. In the 1977 Northumbria annual report, crimes were reported to have increased by 15.1% on the previous year, while the detections at 49.5% were 2% lower than in 1976. The 1978 report indicated another 2.9% rise in crimes recorded and detections at 51.2%. Suffolk reported their 1979 detections at 56.4% and Hertfordshire claimed 54%, while in 1980 South Yorkshire police had 51.16% . By the early 1980s it was noticeable that many forces were now claiming just below 50% and in doing so appeared to reflect the pressures in society, as unemployment and social *Angst* increased. By 1981 Kent were regretting a drop to 47% detections, while Northumbria reported another 9% increase in crime and only 49.6% detections.

58. 'The promotion stakes' is another phrase used constantly within police culture, and is a further indication of the way that policing is considered to be a metaphorical game of chance, lodged in a drama that is enacted by participants skilled in the use of manoeuvres such as the juggling created by the 'bending and fiddling' of crime figures.

59. The desire to deal in such simple statistical 'truths' has a profound influence. As Southgate (1984) pointed out, any hermeneutic exploration of ideas and attitudes is at odds with the accepted methodology of training. Most police courses deal in facts rather than ideas and policemen are less than ready to acknowledge emotions, feelings, and perceptions, for they cannot comprehend such abstractions as having a factual reality.

60. During my bridewell days, this unpopular senior officer acquired the nickname 'nasal spray' = 'a little squirt that gets right up your nose'.

61. In this age of a 'value for money' criteria for many public services, the increasing use of such markers as the CIPFA (Chartered Institute of Public Finance and Accountancy) figures of force comparisons has been noticeable. West Mercia is now included in a 'family' of six other allegedly comparable police units, i.e. Sussex, Essex, Devon and Cornwall, Staffordshire, Northants, and Humberside.

62. At the beginning of 1989 the Counting Rules were amended once again, so that these 'previously unreported' admissions obtained on prison visits could no longer be claimed as detections, but would be recorded as 'No Crimes'. Five months later a detective described how a dozen unreported thefts from shops could still be used to advantage at specific times, such as at the end of the year. Submission of the crimes with the information that the 'offender has been reported', but omitting the fact that he was in prison, had the effect of immediately enhancing detections for the end of year returns. Subsequently these were reclassified as 'No Crimes' after submission of a supplementary report in the new year, when the fact they had been obtained by prison visit write-off was revealed, and these new 'No Crimes' would then be set against the record of actual crimes.

CRIME, GENDER AND GENDER RELATIONS

4.   Understanding Female Criminality
Frances Heidensohn

Social theories

Social theories have a central role to play in making sense of social reality. There is a well-established tendency to react against 'theory' which is seen as 'abstract' and therefore 'unreal' or distorted. Yet knowledge has to be fitted into a framework of some kind in order to be usable; it cannot, indeed be collected in the first place without assumptions being made about its use or the need to solve certain problems. Social theories are important and worth attention because they offer (or attempt to offer) coherent explanations of social happenings. Even if we reject the explanation as ill-founded, theories can be illuminating because their application has produced new and challenging material; few would now accept the ecological theories of the Chicago school, but its ethnographic studies remain fascinating. Finally, ideas do change the world, or at least parts of it. The influence of sociological concepts is frequently underestimated: they affect both the intellectual climate and social policies. Consider for instance, the impact of Bowlby's formulation of 'maternal deprivation' (Bowlby, 1953; Dally, 1982; pp.97ff) or the idea of 'community' presented by nineteenth-century social theorists (Nisbet, 1966, Ch. 3).

Criminological theorising has been particularly abundant. A recent text describes its history as 'tumultuous', 'revolution after revolution', and 'this bewildering and extensive maze of quarrels and claims' (Downes and Rock, 1982, p. vii). Crime and deviance obviously have special characteristics which attract social theorists: they are key social issues, perhaps, after the economy, the major issue. For sociologists, too, social order has been the central issue and the nature of crime is peculiarly problematic, confusing and ambiguous.

In this chapter, I want to look at the attempts which have been made to explain female criminality. As we have already seen, female crime as a subject has not been well-covered in criminological literature, despite the fact that it has certain distinctive and apparently challenging features. Indeed this neglect has generated its own commentary (Heidensohn, 1968; Smart, 1977). In more recent times there have been notable developments and there are articles and at least one text devoted to a critique of criminological theory and its bearing on women and crime (Naffin, 1981; Leonard, 1982). In these studies it is clear that it is difficult to impose a coherent pattern on the works discussed. Analyses of women criminals were very rare before the 1960s. They may therefore have to be studied in arbitrary isolation since they bear little relation to one another. The main schools of criminological thought have little or nothing to say about women offenders and so they have to be presented negatively or not at all. In order therefore to achieve what I hope will be a clear account of theories relating to

Frances Heidensohn: 'Understanding Female Criminality' from *WOMEN AND CRIME* (Macmillan Press Ltd, 1986), pp. 110-124. Reproduced by permission of Macmillan Press Ltd and New York University Press.

women and crime, I have divided them into traditional modern and feminist. In this chapter and the next I shall look at both the occasional 'classical' theories and modern criminology, and in the following one I shall discuss those more recent contributions which, while they differ markedly in approach and conclusions, have in common that women are the central focus of their work.

Traditional criminology

Criminology, mainstream and tributary, has almost nothing to say of interest or importance about women. This is as true of most major modern contributors as it was in the past. Writers on women and crime who have looked to the past, to 'classical' criminology have focussed on those few texts which do deal with women and tended to highlight them (Smart, 1977; Leonard, 1982). Even where Lombroso, Thomas *et al.* are placed in their intellectual and historical context as 'social Darwinist' or 'liberal paternalist' there is a tendency to overemphasise their distinctiveness because they actually wrote about women (and provide us with some detailed case histories and statistics) when their contemporaries were silent. What distinguishes writers on female crime is not only that they represent a particular criminological tradition, but that they seek to rationalise and to make intellectually acceptable a series of propositions about women and their consequences for criminal behaviour. Women, in this view, are determined by their biology and their physiology. Their hormones, their reproductive role, inexorably determine their emotionality, unreliability, childishness, deviousness, etc. These factors lead to female crime. Even a superficial examination shows up the contradictions here.

First, only women are seen as so particularly dominated by their biology. (Lombroso did, it is true, stress genetic factors in male criminals, but in later writings he modified this stress. Nor did he suggest that male sexuality or reproduction affected their criminality, although he believed that male criminals were much uglier than their female counterparts.) Any adequate explanation of female crime in biological terms has to explain why female but not male biology determines deviant behaviour. Moreover, such explanations are over-deterministic in that since most women experience the physiological changes discussed, a much higher crime rate should be predicted for women than for men.

A partial answer to questions about sex differences in criminality is given by all these theorists: not only are women biologically distinct and uniquely behaviourally determined, their deviance is peculiarly sexual. Thus they are seen as engaging in prostitution as an equivalent to normal crime in men (Lombroso, 1895) or as the key symptom of the 'unadjusted' girl (Thomass 1923). Even apparently non-sexual actions such as assault or theft are redefined as evidence of sexual repression (Pollak, 1961, p.142) or of the hysterical abnormality of the 'born female criminal' (Lombroso and Ferrero,1895, p.248).

Curiously, while stressing the innate, physically-based character of female deviance these writers also stress its pathology. 'As a double exception, the criminal woman is consequently a monster — her wickedness must have been enormous' (Lombroso and Ferrero, 1895, p.152). In other words, what occurs in nature, through atavistic inheritance or hormonal influences is at the same time unnatural and evil. A further duality can be noted in these writers' views of women. Women are both wicked and saintly, whores and mothers, the two images are frequently juxtaposed sometimes in very uneasy harmony. These three writers do differ in certain aspects as we shall see, but in these themes they have a great deal in common. What is most important, however, is that they expressed popular views about female crime and gave them mainly spurious scientific support. Far from being swamped by the modern criminological tides which have long washed away biological determinism these ideas have flourished in their intellectual rockpools, amazing examples of survival. Neo-Lombrosian studies of girl-delinquents were still being carried out in the 1970s, prostitution was still seen often as evidence of individual psychopathology rather than a rational economic choice for women in the 1980s (McLeod, 1982). Since their ideas have had great influence and are still with us it is worth looking at these writers in some detail.

Lombroso and Ferrero

Cesare Lombroso was the leading proponent of positivist criminology 'whose theories and writings have influenced the course of thinking more deeply than those of any other criminologists' (Mannheim, 1965, p.213). Although his work with its biological–anthropological base is no longer accepted he played a crucial role in focussing research on individual offenders and their traits and characters. The monograph on women offenders which he published with his son-in-law Ferrero was a relatively late work. Although in other late works (Lombroso, 1913) he acknowledged social and economic factors in crime causation, these are discounted in *La Donna Delinquente*.

Applying the principles and methods of Lombroso's earlier work, he and Ferrero conducted detailed measurements of the skulls, brains and bones of women criminals and prostitutes, and studied their appearance from masses of photographs and their careers from a variety of life histories. Using this material they concluded that there were far fewer 'born female criminals' than males as judged by the characteristic signs of atavistic degeneracy and that prostitutes had more 'anomalies' than female offenders or normal women (Lombroso and Ferrero, 1895, p. 85). 'All the same' they observed it is incontestable that female offenders seem almost normal when compared to the male criminal, with his wealth of anomalous features' (Lombroso and Ferrero, 1895, p. 107). Women, when they do degenerate into atavism, are more likely to become prostitutes 'whose types approximates so much more to that of her primitive ancestress'. According to Lombroso and Ferrero women commit less crime because they have not evolved to the same degree as men and are therefore more primitive and have less scope for degeneration. Really 'women are big children . . . their moral sense is deficient' (Lombroso and Ferrero, 1895, p. 151). Women are much more likely to be occasional than born criminals; even so, the ordinary female criminal is perceived as particularly unnatural, she is masculine and virile and shows 'an inversion of all the qualities which specially distinguish the normal woman; namely, reserve, docility and *sexual apathy*' (Lombroso and Ferrero, 1895, p. 297, emphasis added). The Italian authors frequently asserted that maternity and female sexuality are mutually exclusive — 'her exaggerated sexuality so opposed to maternity'. 'In the ordinary run of mothers the sexual instinct is in abeyance' (Lombroso and Ferrero, 1895, p. 153).

Lombroso became famous as the father of 'scientific' criminology. In fact his work was fanciful rather than scientific. His detailed measurements were not subject to any tests of significance and his 'analysis' of photographs of 'fallen women' is as objective as an adjudication in a beauty contest. What this joint study sets out is an undoubtedly sincere attempt to justify certain beliefs and theories without submitting them to any kind of systematic enquiry. Thus Lombroso and Ferrero confronted the 'eternal anomaly of womankind' — that women could be madonnas but also prostitutes, and although women are 'revengeful, jealous inclined to . . . cruelty' (Lombroso and Ferrero, 1895, p. 151), they nevertheless number few criminals amongst them. Like almost all the writers in this group and in others, Lombroso and Ferrero did not ultimately help our understanding of women and crime. What they did show us was the attempt to rationalise and justify the *status quo,* the existing position of women and the double standard of morals of their day.

Hence, although women are not very criminal, their 'evil tendencies are more numerous and more varied than men's' (Lombroso and Ferrero, 1895, p. 151) and by implication it is appropriate that they should be 'kept in the paths of virtue by ... maternity piety, weakness' (Lombroso and Ferrero, 1895, p. 152). Prostitution is the 'natural' state of regression for women and any women who are criminal are unnatural and more like men, lacking maternal feelings and carrying virile stigmata. In short Lombroso and Ferrero defined distinctive sub-species of women as 'good' and 'bad', 'natural' and 'abnormal' and equated these with conformity and crime. In this they reflected nineteenth-century attitudes to respectable and other women and add another footnote to the debates about 'separate spheres'. But they told us little about female criminality and more, much more about themselves and their ideas about women. Describing a bust of an old Palermo woman poisoner, they

> recall the proverbial wrinkles of witches and the instance of the vile old woman . . . of Palermo who poisoned so many . . . the bust of this criminal so full of virile angularities and above all so deeply wrinkled with its Satanic leer, suffices of itself to prove that the woman in question was born to do evil, and that, if one occasion to commit it had failed, she would have found others (Lombroso and Ferrero, 1895, p. 72).

Thomas

In studying the group of 'classical' criminological writers gathered into this chapter, we shall see how several central themes emerge in their work on women. These themes have remained important and influential in studying female crime, and indeed in its treatment. As scholars who produced full-length studies of women, they were exceptional, but they were not straying outside traditional territory. They used approaches already established and accepted in their fields. What does distinguish them, especially from the American sociologists of deviance at whom we shall look later, is the way in which they make certain ideas explicit.

Their view of women is heavily stereotyped. Women are defined according to domestic and sexual roles; they are dominated by biological imperatives; they are emotional and irrational. At the same time, irreconcilable ambiguities enter the picture. Women are uniquely qualified for motherhood and domestic tasks. It would be foolish and inappropriate to attack these writers for their unsurprising sexism. They were men of their age and subscribed to contemporary ideology and culture. Where they can be criticised is in their failure, despite strong claims of scientific rigour for and by them all (Lombroso and Ferrero, 1895, p. xv; Thomas, 1923, p. xvi; Pollak, 1961, p. xv) to analyse any of their assumptions and to consider whether they might be changed or modified. They remain important then because they crystallise certain views scattered throughout criminology and also because, while they do not in the end help very much towards an understanding of women's crime, they themselves provide us with case study material to develop our own understanding.

W. I. Thomas was himself a pioneer of the use of case study material in social research. His *Unadjusted Girl* is a study of a series of such 'cases' designed to illustrate the dominance of four key 'wishes' in human behaviour: for new experience, for security, for response and for recognition (Thomas, 1923, p. 4). Thomas had earlier produced *Sex and Society* (1907) which was clearly influenced by Lombroso and Ferrero. Like them he assumed a 'natural' male — female dichotomy corresponding to 'active' and 'passive' states. As Smart noted, this was a narrowly selective view for Thomas to take 'as his major concern was the plight of immigrant, often peasant, women in the USA, who not only worked outside the home but often had to rear children single-handed' (Smart, 1977, p.39). Klein (1976) has observed the close parallels between Thomas's early work and Lombroso's — 'they both delineate a biological hierarchy along race and sex lines'. Like Lombroso and Ferrero, Thomas asserted that men are further developed than women in evolutionary terms; 'Man . . . (is) more . . . specialised an animal than women' (Thomas, 1907, p.36) just like the Italian positivists, Thomas linked women and children and 'the lower human races and the lower classes' as being tougher and less sensitive than white males.

Thomas did, however, live through a transitional period in the study of crime and delinquency and in his later work he was much more concerned with social influences and pressures. He still dealt with instincts, especially the maternal 'instinct' in women: 'the child is helpless throughout a period of years and would not live unless the mother were impelled to give it her devotion. This attitude is present in the father of the child also but is weaker, less demonstrative and called out more gradually' (Thomas, 1923, p. 18). What really interested him most, however, were the definitions of their situation which his subjects had. Thus subjective reality was more crucial than any 'facts' of a situation. Women, in Thomas's view, were more likely to be 'unadjusted' because they suffered more and were aware of their deprivations during a period of social change. The 'wishes' could and should be repressed as in the past:

> In the small and spatially isolated communities of the past, where the influences were strong and steady, the members became more or less habituated to and reconciled with a life of repressed wishes (Thomas, 1923, p. 71).

Mature women and young girls suffered in 'the modern revolt and unrest' because they were most excluded and felt most frustrated at their deprivations. 'Costly and luxurious articles of women's wear' Thomas wrote 'disorganise the lives of many who crave these pretty things' (Thomas, 1923, p. 71).

It is clear that Thomas largely equated female delinquency with sexual delinquency. Many of his case histories of unadjusted girls describe lives of promiscuity or adultery rather than of crime. Smart (1977) noted that in adopting anecdotal style he avoided theorising or indeed analysing women's social position. He noted the power of community and family in controlling and repressing women's behaviour in traditional societies, but he did not examine or extend this insight. Nor did he consider how female sexual misbehaviour was stigmatised, but male behaviour was not. Smart (1977) has linked his work with that of Konopka and with a whole school of social pathologists who individualise female delinquency, equating it with sexual delinquency and urging that the girl delinquent should be readjusted to society, to accept her role 'to co-ordinate the girl immediately with the large society in which she lives' (Thomas, 1923, p. 200). That the role assumptions or the prevailing morality might be changed are not ideas that Thomas ever contemplated.

The Unadjusted Girl differs from *La Donna Delinquente* and *The Criminality of Women* in that some 'real' women do appear in it. Thomas did not show the same distaste for his subjects that Lombroso and Ferrero and Pollak did. There is some compassion, albeit of a paternalist kind for the delinquent girls and little of the implicit fear of devious, dangerous femininity present in the other works. But Thomas did share their fears for the sanctity of the family:

> The bad family life constantly evident in these pages and the consequent delinquency of children as well as crime, prostitution and alcoholism are largely due to the over-determination of economic interests (Thomas, 1923, p. 256),

and throughout his work automatically took for granted the doctrine of 'separate spheres' — that the home is women's province, work and public life only for men. Nowhere did he consider that women too may have economic motivations as rational as those of men for their delinquent acts.

Pollak

Pollak's *The Criminality of Women* (1961) was originally published in the USA in 1950. It is the only full-length published study of this period which looks at women and crime. The post-war era did of course, produce a wave of criminological studies; (male juvenile delinquency was its especial focus in works by Cohen, 1955; Kobrin, 1951; Sykes and Matza, 1957, and Cloward and Ohlin, 1961). Pollak's study seems to have been inspired by his mentor, Thorsten Sellin (Pollak, 1961, p. vii) who with Reckless had 'drawn attention to this neglect of the study of the criminality of women'. Although written and published in the USA at a time of high creativity and debate in criminology, Pollak's work seems not to be part of that time at all.

In its careful but statistically unsophisticated handling of figures, its citation of long-dead European authors, its presentation of data from countries with their boundaries as well as their cultures twice dislocated in half a century, Pollak's book is closest to the works of European scholars such as Hermann Mannheim, but in some ways it seems to belong to a much older European tradition than that of the careful Central European scholar. The 1961 paperback edition has a binding with a crudely-coloured illustration of a witch beating a kneeling man.

Pollak's analysis of female crime has two main strands. First he examined data on recorded criminality in several countries and over time and endeavoured to show 'that female crime has been vastly under-estimated' (Pollak 1961, p.153) and that indeed 'female crime is perhaps the outstanding area of undiscovered, or at least unprosecuted, crime in our culture and that its actual amount as well as its relation to male criminality has been greatly underrated' (Pollak, 1961, p. 154). Second, and of greater theoretical interest, Pollak put forward a theory to explain this 'masking'. Here although a sociologist he used none of the existing repertoire of sociological explanations of crime. There are no references at all to Chicago school authors, to Tannenbaum or to Merton. Sutherland rated a passing mention (Pollak, 1961, p. 39), but his theory of differential association is not used. Instead Pollak put forward a view of women as inherently deceitful and vengeful, exploiting a flow of helpless victims and aided by men's besotted chivalry. Although Pollak stressed cultural variables his explanations are rooted in biological 'facts' and are profoundly ahistorical and unsociological.

Let us look first at Pollak's statistical chapters where his 'finding' of heavily masked female crime led him to put forward his theory. His main argument here is that the crimes women commit are more likely to be hidden or under-reported. In particular he cited criminal abortions and shoplifting as examples (Pollak, 1961, p. 44). He even produced figures which reduce the male:female crime ratio from 10:1 to 4.7:1 by including this under-recording. Of course he failed to take account of social and legal changes in abortion law: as successive nations have legalised abortion so illegal abortions have declined in incidence. With shoplifting as with illegal abortionists he made the unsupported assumption that almost all offenders are women. This is not so (see Chapter 1 [of *Women and Crime*]). Pollak was on even shakier ground when he discussed other 'hidden' female crimes: thefts by domestic servants, offences by prostitutes and domestic revenge: poisoning and violence carried out by women on their helpless families. It is hard to take this catalogue seriously, but it should be emphasised that Pollak remained quoted in texts — but uncritically — for nearly twenty years (Heidensohn, 1968) and that his ideas have been influential (Smart, 1977). Pollak's view that women were more criminal than men, more prone to 'revenge desires', somehow more evil seems to have been deeply-rooted. Thus he claimed repeatedly that domestic servants commit crimes frequently against their employers (Pollak, pp. 36,111, 144, etc.) without offering any serious evidence for this. Further in order to refute the notion that men might also commit masked crimes on a large scale, he suggested (Pollak, 1961, p. 54) that male white-collar criminals, whom Sutherland had shown to be largely unprosecuted, employ female servants and therefore their offences cancel each other out! Again he offered no supporting evidence and totally failed to cite the enormous rise in white-collar employment especially amongst *women* in this century and the near-extinction of domestic service (Tilly and Scott, 1978). His discussion of prostitution is very selective. He accepted, as with abortion, the then current US definitions of sex offences of prostitution, adultery and fornication (Pollak, 1961, p. 55) and claimed that male customers are not party to any offence and therefore cannot be used to inflate male crime figures. But he ignored both crimes committed against prostitutes by their customers (the Yorkshire Ripper and his earlier namesake were only the most notorious perpetrators of these) and the whole range of traditionally male activities of pimp, landlord and tout associated with prostitution. In short, Pollak's approach seems rather more ideological than empirical.

It is, however, in his theoretical approach that Pollak's sexist assumptions are most obvious. Women, he argued, are more devious than men: 'for women deceit . . . (is) . . . a socially prescribed form of behaviour' (Pollak, 1961, p. 11). This is because women can fake an orgasm and still have sex whereas 'man must achieve an erection in order to perform the sex act and will not be able to hide his failure'. From what he considered physiological facts, Pollak moved on to social mores. Women were equipped to dissemble and they were also forced to do so by a society in which mention of menstruation, menarche, menopause and pregnancy are taboo. Smart has pointed out the dated sexual politics of Pollak's account and his unquestioning acceptance 'of folklore and stereotypical perceptions of women' (Smart, 1977, p. 48). His negative evaluation of all of the female reproductive cycle is very significant. Even 'pregnancy in a culture which . . . fosters . . . childlessness must become a source of irritation, anxiety and emotional upheaval' (Pollak, 1961, p. 58). He could find little evidence to link gynaecology with criminology (although some later authors have since taken up the challenge (Dalton, 1969): and in particular seems to confuse biological and cultural effects. Thus concealment of menstruation is by no means universal and changed sexual mores have long since made nonsense of his view of passive, receptive females brooding vengeance (Hite, 1977).

Pollak recognised the importance of women's domestic role in society and that women could be 'contained' in their homes in a special way. But he went on to contend that women use the home as 'cover' for a variety of crimes: poisoning their relatives and sexually abusing children. They can do this because they can conceal their crimes better than men, because their victims are vulnerable and unlikely to report them or co-operate with the police, because women use especially devious means such as poison and because men are chivalrous and cannot bear to prosecute or punish women. Once again social and biological factors are intertwined here. Women's domestic role in our society is not inherent in their reproductive role: it is based on economic and historical developments and is not always the same in all social classes. Pollak ignored too the possibility that personal privacy may hide much male crime such as rape and wife-battering and that women may be powerless to prevent these. Nowhere has he accounted for widespread male acceptance of huge hidden waves of domestic slaughter and indecency, nor given indications of its persistence.

Pollak saw women as automata (Smart, 1977, p. 52), impelled by their physiology, their hormonal cycles and their low self-evaluation to commit crimes which, he believed, total as much as those of men. He did not for a moment suggest that *male* criminality has a biological basis and can be explained by greater strength or aggression. Indeed the whole tenor of American criminology at this time stressed the social causation (and indeed function) of crime, its structural (Merton, 1949) or subcultural (Cohen, 1955) origins. Only women were presented in this way as a separate species whose behaviour could be explained in simple 'scientific' terms to which there still cling odours of witchcraft and demonology. Pollak wrote about women and crime, a topic ignored by his contemporaries. It did not fit readily into their sociological theorising and Pollak wrote as though this did not exist. He cannot be said to have helped our understanding of female crime, but his work has been influential because he lacked competitors and the topic interested no one else. As Leonard points out (Leonard, 1982, p. 5), while finding his work 'dismal' and 'ridiculous', issues raised by him recur in much subsequent discussion.

The European tradition

I have called this group of writers the 'European' tradition and have tried to show that in approach and methods they share certain common themes. I would not wish to stretch the parallels too far since each author saw himself producing a new and revealing work which broke with earlier traditions. What they did have in common were their assumptions that women are a different species from men, differently made and motivated. All of them confronted the duality in women's social roles and their moral natures (which they often confused). Women are 'madonnas' and 'magdalenes', 'witches' and 'good wives'. Pollak and Lombroso believed that women are more wicked than men. Rock has argued (Rock, 1977) that to examine the work of such theorists is to act like 'resurrection men' disinterring corpses of long-buried and neglected ideas. But only faint-hearted criminologists flinch at ghosts and ghouls. In fact the ideas of the old tradition have proved powerful and long-lasting.

First, it can be argued that they lend an intellectual respectability to very much older folk ideas about women and their behaviour. Unfortunately, these ideas are never questioned nor criticised in their work. Second, critical analysis of these studies was very limited until recently and the work of Pollak especially, accepted without reservation. Standard criminology textbooks quote him as 'definitive' (Reckless, 1961, p.83) and as giving 'the lie to the current notion that women are less law-abiding than men' (Barnes and Teeters, 1951, p.592). Both these texts also cite Lombroso's analysis of the specifics of female crime. Even far more modern texts are uncritical in their use of these sources (Clinard, 1968, p.247). Mannheim was one of the earlier critics of Pollak, although he was very cautious:

> While many of Pollak's points may be valid, one gets the impression that in his efforts to show that the sex difference in crime rates is actually much smaller than generally assumed, he goes too much to the other extreme (Mannheim, 1965, p.693).

A few pages on and he too was quoting Lombroso as an authority and moving into a magisterial condemnation of the inferior nature of the second sex:

> Political ideals . . . take second place in the female mind . . . [they] . . . lack respect for abstract ideas such as the state and its system of justice (Mannheim, 1965, p.103).

Women, he asserted 'prefer shoplifting to looting' as they can then choose individual items which they want!

That this European tradition has influenced generations of criminologists is only too clear. Smart referred to 'their continuing influence on the development of analysis of criminality by contemporary criminologists' (Smart, 1977, p.54) and Shacklady Smith pointed out that:

> The predominant form of empirical research on the nature of female delinquency published over the last ten years ... owes a great deal to the sexist assumptions inherent in the classical studies of female criminality (cf. Lombroso and Ferrero, Pollak, Thomas). (Shacklady Smith, 1978, p.75).

Cowie and his colleagues, for example, pinpoint characteristics of delinquent girls which sound remarkably like Lombroso's unattractive criminal women. 'They are . . . oversized, lumpish, uncouth and graceless.' (Cowie *et al.* 1968, p.167). As Smart pointed out these factors are seen as constitutionally 'predisposing' girls to delinquency. Further, in this study it is the girls' biological nature and in particular their 'markedly masculine' traits (which they link to chromosome features) which lead them to delinquency. Smart has commented extensively (Smart, 1977, pp.54-60) on their failure to question assumptions about culture, sex and gender, or indeed to consider whether the lumpish, ugly, delinquent girls they observed might have been suffering from the effects of a stodgy diet and lack of beauty aids. It is more pertinent to the present discussion however to note that a neo-Lombrosian study of delinquent girls could be produced in the late 1960s. No anatomist of the dismal history of female crime needs Burke and Hare if the 'corpse' is still alive and kicking!

Richardson, in a fuller and far more perceptive account of young girl delinquents, nevertheless also used Lombroso as a reference point and devoted extensive sections to the physique and appearance of her charges (Richardson, 1969, pp.56-71). Her concern paled beside that of another professional, a member of the Massachusetts Parole Board who described some of her parolees thus:

> The unmarried mother is usually a solitary being who has been wandering about seeking approval or affection. Many times she is extremely plain looking and her normal life has been marred by serious skin disease, partial blindness, or some other disfiguring physical handicap (Sullivan, 1956, p.101).

The Foreword to Konopka's study of delinquent girls made quite explicit links to Thomas's work and even suggested that the Foreword to that work 'might have been (written) of the situation and the need today, 42 years later, and of Dr Konopka's studies and purposes' (Ellington, 1966, p.viii). Konopka shared Thomas's liberal perceptions and her analysis of the emotional needs of women is close to Thomas's 'wishes'. She also used a similar method, avoiding statistical analysis and aiming at case histories and personal accounts. While Konopka claimed to avoid theory and let her girls speak for themselves, she did in fact have similar assumptions to those of Thomas about the role of biology in women's lives and the cultural significance of sexuality and reproduction. As Smart showed:

> Konopka can be seen (like Thomas) to be engaged in a process of weaving taken-for-granted assumptions about the female sex into an explanation of juvenile delinquency (Smart, 1977, p. 66).

Old ideas live on when they are not supplanted by new research enterprises nor by rigorous and thoughtful criticism. Old ideas about female criminality have had a remarkably sustained life. They largely failed to help to demystify female crime because they ignored clear evidence and rested on unexamined stereotypes. Female criminality, although studied in these few works, remained at the fringes of the criminological terrain, an intellectual Falklands remote, unvisited and embarrassing. In the major, dynamic areas of criminology which have flourished in the past half century, women were almost completely ignored within what I shall call the American tradition. Yet — and it is a most curious paradox — a central tenet of many of the theories of male delinquency which this tradition produced is based on assumptions about gender and gender difference.

5. Everyday Life and Symbolic Creativity
Paul Willis

Introduction

The aim of this chapter is to try to give a direct living picture of some of the symbolic work at play in the everyday activities of young people not associated with any specific cultural media or products. Crucially we aim to show something of the terms, strategies and symbolic work used by young people themselves to constitute and understand their own activities in common culture.

This chapter is based mainly on fieldwork conducted in Wolverhampton. Most of our respondents were in their late teens or early twenties, single and, generally speaking, in working-class occupations or from working-class backgrounds. A substantial number were British Asian or British Afro-Caribbean.

We contacted them and spoke to them in a variety of places, including youth clubs, colleges and mother and toddler groups. Sometimes young people were talked to singly, but mostly in groups of up to five. Initial interviews were structured, asking young people what they did from morning until night during the week and on Saturdays and Sundays. Interviews were taped, and the researcher listened to them afterwards, to generate questions for the next interview. Later interviews were less structured, allowing subjects to use their own terms and strategies to discuss their leisure activities.

Perhaps we risk an overly anthropological approach in this chapter in presenting some of the meanings of social practices themselves rather than focusing, as previous chapters do, on the specific uses of particular cultural commodities and cultural media. This is a worthwhile risk, however, in order to emphasize a perspective from which the whole book should be read: that the symbolic creativity of the young is based in their everyday informal life and infuses with meaning the entirety of the world as they see it.

Language is the most fundamental means of symbolic work and throughout this chapter (as in others) we use and quote the words that young people themselves use to express and explore their possibilities.

The biggest single dilemma in writing and editing this chapter has been whether, and if so how, to deal with the 'antisocial' activities of excess drinking and fighting. These things certainly involve large sections of youth, especially those from the white male working class. But they are also the focus for contempt and very widespread, often sensationalized, concern. Violence, particularly, has become the index and displaced image for many troubling questions concerning the quality, direction and meaning of 'life in our times'. We certainly do not wish to fan the flames of sensation. However,

Paul Willis: 'Everyday Life and Symbolic Creativity' from *COMMON CULTURE* (Open University Press, 1990), pp. 98-127.

we have decided to include such activities because we are committed to following through our emphasis on presenting youth meanings both realistically and in their own terms. We cannot avert our gaze selectively and conveniently when trouble looms and miss out whole tracts of social symbolic landscape which actually constitute the terrain underfoot as well as, often, the effective horizon for many young people.

This does not mean that we applaud or support such activities. Apart from their intrinsic destructiveness, they also help to reproduce oppressive race, class and gender structures of feeling, attitude and practice. Nevertheless, common culture teaches us that more than one thing can be true of, or said about, a phenomenon. If we can find a thread of symbolic work and coherent human meaning and feeling even in brutalized conditions and through degrading materials, then our general argument is demonstrated *a fortiori* by this extreme and limited case. This thread of meaning will swell into streams and rivers through sympathetic materials and welcoming symbolic channels.

In part our purpose here is to get behind the tabloid headings, to get at real human contexts and meanings. It is ironic, for instance, that in the case of violence the physical fight on the stage boards or through the celluloid image is accepted as a legitimate climax to other kinds of symbolic fighting. It is taken as an understandable resolution to a tense chain of events connected together through the meanings of plot and situation. Yet our images and understandings of urban violence in real life are ridiculously truncated. We're transfixed by the notion, symbolically, of 'gratuity'. Fights are cut off from prior and surrounding symbolic meanings: from all that went before, from the narratives, contexts and meanings which place and make them, these things which for the participants often remove precisely their 'gratuity'.

To reverse the currently fashionable banalities about screen violence leading to real violence, it is certainly possible to suggest that something of our very capacity to accept and interpret violence in dramatic contexts may well (invisibly) depend on our own informal knowledge concerning the informal dynamics of aggression. This includes understanding the difficulty of seeking appeasement with dignity, appreciating the seemingly irrevocable cast of some events, and accepting that there are moments when no words will do but 'actions speak louder than words'. Violence can have a symbolic as well as a physical part to play in social interaction and in complex human meanings. We aim to draw back a little the veil of public outrage to glimpse more neutrally some of the human meanings and processes behind the apparently 'inexplicable' and 'inhuman' face of violence.

Pub culture and drinking

Drinking in pubs is a central leisure activity, especially for white young men. Three-quarters of the 16-24 age group visit pubs, on average, nearly four times a week.[1] It is much less central for Afro-Caribbeans and for most young Asians.

Young people go to pubs for many reasons. One important reason is simply to escape boredom and often the restrictions of the parental home. As Steve says:

> If you stop in the house with your family, I just moan. I wish I was going out. Even if you go and tidy your room up, they have a go at you . . . So

you've got to go out somewhere. I think if I had to stop in the house, they start getting on my nerves and I start getting on their nerves, after a while, like. You know, they have nothing to do so they start getting on to you...When you're in the house like...it's the same four walls all the time. So it's great to see somebody different, even if you're just sitting in the pub, you're looking at something.

If you are looking for somewhere to go, it's hardly surprising that it should be the pub. It is one of the most, if not the, central leisure institutions of white adult British culture. Young people turn towards it not only for 'something to do' but also as a way of identifying with adults, of becoming more adult and seeking acceptance by adults as an adult. The under-age thrill of successfully ordering alcohol in public, in 'The Public', is one of the markers of passing from childhood.

The pub is also an extremely social environment which announces immediately that here is a place which is about relaxation, leisure and pleasure — polar opposites to the formal qualities of work and school. The direct effect of alcohol relaxes the self and distances the real world, as does the warmth, size, comfort and protection of the pub. But the 'good pub' is one that concentrates many good things. As one of our male (employed) respondents says, 'Women, cheap beer, good beer, loud music'. The media shape young people's leisure activities throughout and the pub is no exception. Pubs are enjoyable partly because they allow young people to see and hear videos of the latest pop hits as well as classic 'evergreens'. They also allow access to expensive media and play-back hardware beyond the reach of domestic finances.

> STEVE: There's one [a satellite dish to receive MTV, the music video television station] in a pub in Bilston, Bull's Head. You used to have to pay for a video in there, 50p for two sides. Now you just sit there and watch MTV . . . The in-thing is CDs, compact discs. You pay 50p for two sides on the CD. The thing is, it's off albums, not just the chart thing.

> NEIL: You get maybe on a juke box a hundred songs. On a compact disc you get 2,000. 'Cause they're only small. They're excellent. On a juke box like, it's singles. You know, the 45s, but on a compact disc, it's the album and you can have what track you want off each album like . . .

From the point of view of space, architecture, design, technology and devotion to pleasure pubs are much grander than the home. That is obviously part of their attraction. But this is not the end of the story. There are more illicit pleasures. For many young men the entry into the pub, especially on a Saturday night, is also the start or the promise of a kind of adventure, reflected symbolically in some of the more outlandish 'theme styling' of refurbished 'leisure pubs'. This adventure or promise is about the suspension of the given, the mundane and the everyday. It starts in the head and in the immediate social group with the physical effects of alcohol, but it produces changes there whose ripple can and does spread to make waves outside.

The social context of drinking operates to maximize consumption for many young men. There's no shame in it. It's done with others. Round-buying reflects and reinforces social and cultural solidarity. It is often a competitive activity. The amount consumed

113

is related to how much of a 'man' you are, and the 'men' encourage each other in their 'manliness'.

> DEAN: When you're drinking, you always want to drink more than the other person. You always think you can take the most. If you go drinking, you're a man.

For young women, by contrast and to underline the case, drinking is not social, nor competitive, nor encouraged by the group. Excess consumption certainly emphasizes public gender identity but in ways which are felt to be negative, especially given the realities of dealing with a predatory and sexist environment:

> SANDRA: It's not feminine [to drink in excess]. My friend, she got drunk and I just left her there and then. 'Cause she was just slaggin' around. And I just, I just said, 'If you're gonna be like that, that's your problem.' And I just walked out. And I went home.

Being drunk produces uncertainty and, with it, potential danger. In particular, however unjustly and unfairly, it runs the risk of being perceived to be 'slagging around', immoderately displaying sexual availability.

For young men, however, there seems to be a positive welcoming of uncertainty and its possible dangers. It defeats boredom and seems to open up symbolic and real possibilities not available in normal life. They view drinking as that which sets up a situation, an atmosphere where anything might happen. The physiological effects of alcohol are interpreted to mean loss of control — an existential freeing of the self to an uncertainty which seems to be 'new' or 'different' every time. It opens the way to adventure whose possibility constitutes a kind of grounded aesthetics of risk and risk-taking. Risk is esteemed. The unexpected adventures which follow might be trivial: a bet, a 'piss-take', cheeking others or elders. They might be nothing at all except a frisson and heightened atmosphere of possibility with your mates in the pub. They might be serious, or escalate into it: setting out to gatecrash a party; being stopped by the police; getting into a fight; passing out in strange places. It's almost as if some young men want to invent, through drink, their own trials by performance in uncertain situations. The kinds of risks they take, the way they structure these risks, the way they deal with them, indicate, of course, components of young masculinity. Such components include improvisation, 'wit', 'guts', indifference to pain resulting from foolhardy actions, 'devil-may-care' irresponsibility.

> DAVID: When you've had a bit of drink, you'd do anything . . . you just feel wild more than anything.

> DEAN: You feel lucky as well.

> DAVID: No matter how big they are, you think, I'll have a go at him.

> ANDREW: Sometimes you go drinking and you go home, pissed out of your brains, and the next day you think, 'Was it reality or a dream ? '

> DAVID: Some time ago me mum found me in the verandah, just lying flat. I must have passed out.

DEAN: I've jumped in the canal pissed and everything, off the bridge. You do all sorts of funny things, don't you?

ANDREW: You find it ever so funny when you do it. I mean, if somebody fell over, you'd laugh your head off.

DEAN: You wouldn't be able to stop laughing. Or someone would say, 'Go and do this.' And you'll go and do it.

ANDREW: You do mad things that you wouldn't dare.

The sense of release, adventure and possibility is partly about the symbolic creativity of overthrowing, ignoring or transcending conventions and normally approved patterns of behaviour and activity. These are seen often as, by definition, restrictive and boring. Many young people feel that they have no possibilities for 'safe adventures'. This may say as much about the conventional possibilities we provide as about the risky and antisocial ones they pursue.

Street survival: the dramatic permutations of 'hardness'

From the point of view of the vast majority of individual young men, it is not their own individual actions or potential actions which make large parts of the urban environment unsafe, threatening or violent. From their point of view it is already unsafe. This is quite independent of their own actions or non-actions. Far from their threatening it, the street threatens them. This is a given for many young men. For them only social theorists and do-gooders have the safety and luxury to worry about how it comes to be like that. The problem isn't to understand why or how urban violence comes about, still less to monitor your own contribution to it. The problem is simply how to survive it. And to survive it with some dignity and humanity. If we look closely here there are some terrible but surprising grounded aesthetics.

The fundamental issue for most young men in urban areas and locations where there hangs a fear of violence is *not* to fight as often as possible, but as little as possible. Most of all, the aim is to maintain honour and reputation whilst escaping intimidation and 'being picked on'. To achieve this you have to grapple with the complexities of 'hardness' in social performance:

JONATHAN: It's a sort of feeling of being known as a hard person. Like sort of going around and knowing that no one's gonna mess with you because you're hard . . . Being hard is all to do with how you put yourself across.

'Hardness' can be both an inner and an outer quality. It is also related directly to masculinity, its codes and public honours. There are several permutations of hardness with performance. All have their relation to masculine reputation.

JONATHAN: How hard you act and how hard you are are two different things. Like there's some people who act really hard but they just aren't at all. Put down in one punch. Whereas other people keep themselves to themselves and you go up to them, you have a fight with them, and they take your punch, no trouble, and when they throw a punch at you, you know about it.

115

> ANDREW: You can be hard and act hard, and you can not act hard and be hard, or you can act hard and not be hard. I think the best of them is to be hard and not act hard . . .

The space between inner and outer meanings is worked through in what can be thought of as a dramatic grounded aesthetic: acting out your own performance and interpreting the public performances of others.

> STEVE: You got to watch people like, and see how they're acting. You can always tell when they're trying to act as if they're hard, you can always tell the quiet ones. They just stand there . . . The quiet ones nearly always turn out to be the hardest.

The worst of the permutations is to be somebody who acts hard but is not really hard 'inside'. Such a person creates an external persona that is unmatched by bodily force and skill. He is not what he appears to be. He is in danger because of this:

> STEVE: If you keep yourself to yourself, nothing will happen, but if you start going around acting hard or something, when you aren't, people are going to come down on you.

Someone who acts and is hard is preferable. At least the exterior is matched by inner qualities. But the most respected permutation is dissimulation, 'to be hard and not act hard'. This is to have substance, the 'right stuff', but not feel the need to display it:

> NEIL: A mate'll respect you if you walk away from drunkenness.

> STEVE: If anyone comes up to you and says 'Do you want a fight?' you say, 'Fuck off.' If they don't, you just beat them up. You give them a chance to walk away. Say 'I don't want to fight, all right? I don't want no trouble, just go away like.' You're still standing your ground, you're standing there saying, 'Go away.'

The one who is provoked speaks before hitting. Respect is gained by negotiating with an antagonist. This is part of 'standing your ground' and is preferable to fighting. None of this works, however, unless you are prepared to fight *in extremis*. The shadow and the substance intertwine. The performance and the inner reality overlap.

There is a tight moral and dramatic economy here. But it can easily break down. External appearances are not a good guide to the reality of danger. It is not easy to judge the line where giving someone 'the chance to walk away' becomes undignified appeasement. It is not easy to maintain both dignity and safety. Symbolic rather than physical management of tension is always preferred by most and provides the norms for behaviour. But real fighting remains the final arbitration. 'Hard-knocks' and 'nut-cases' who seem to like fighting and who can offer unexpected open and demeaning provocation have to be dealt with. For some reason they don't know, or won't play, 'the game'.

More important, drink routinely complicates or destabilizes the balance of the dramatic economy. Its buzz, frisson and grounded aesthetics of risk enable the unexpected; 'one thing leads to another', somebody feels 'lucky' or 'wild' so 'anything can happen'. Drink makes unreasonable attack and foolhardy defence much more likely. Were it not for 'hard-knocks' and drink, the menacing aspects of urban social life might simply resolve into a series of honourable stand-offs. But when the gauntlet is thrown down, masculine honour seems to demand an answer. Aided by drink, the drama becomes compulsive.

Andrew recounted the events surrounding a fight he'd been involved in recently. He and his mate were drunk, his mate had been beaten up, and those around him were then calling him a 'wanker' for not fighting single-handedly against the large group that had beaten up his mate:

> ANDREW: Everyone was calling me a wanker . . . In a way I felt I had to do it [fight] to prove myself I was strong . . . To prove I wasn't scared of them. I mean, I was [scared] . . . I mean, I wouldn't do it if I was sober. I wouldn't go, 'Oh, fuck, let's go and get battered by twenty kids!' I'll just look harder . . . and they won't call me a wanker . . .When you're pissed, you go 'fuck', you can have your head split.

Andrew had to fight, not just to defend his mate, but, more importantly, his own honour and standing. Harsh, it seems unanswerable, judgements and exclusions wait on failure:

> ANDREW: They'd just laugh and leave you out. Say, forget about you. 'He daren't hit back, so we may as well forget him now. '

Sometimes it's necessary to lose physically in order to win psychologically and socially.

Once embarked, however unwillingly, on a violent encounter, there seems to arise another, darker, excitement that eclipses some of the previous moral and social calculus. We can think of it as a nihilistic grounded aesthetic — the incomprehensible buzz of the momentary disappearance of all meaning. Courting this prospect may lead a minority to provoke incidents deliberately, 'nutters' and 'hard-knocks' certainly, but also sometimes 'normal' kids who are drunk, bored 'out of their minds', 'pissed off' about something, or desperate to find energy and excitement from somewhere *that night*. Those who've been involved in fights say that they feel suddenly stronger, experience no pain and find the situation strangely compelling.

> ANDREW: I've found that when I'm drunk, I'm stronger ... When you're drunk as well, you don't feel the pain . . . You feel the force, but not the pain. It's a weird sensation, scary and good. People like to be scared, like on roller coasters . . . scary because it's different, you ain't used to it. That's why it's scary. But it's good 'cause you aren't feeling it. You can go back for longer.

This feeling of reckless strength is essential to any real prospect of winning a fight. It is part of, tests and reproduces 'hardness', being able to detonate all explosion of physicality in extreme situations. Andrew again:

> It's just a waste of time having a fight if you don't feel hard. Then you know you're gonna lose, aren't you? I mean, you got to feel hard to think you've got a chance to win. You have to feel confidence.

117

Crucial to displacing finer feelings and fear with a robotic brutality is the notion of 'losing your temper'. David and Andrew say that they feel no pain in a fight because they 'get in a temper'. 'Losing your temper' seems to be losing yourself as well, losing the humdrum of the everyday, momentarily, for an entirely different state of being:

> KEITH: You don't feeling nothing. When they're hitting you, you don't know.

> ANDREW: You're so busy concentrating . . . You feel the hit, but you don't feel the pain. Pressure, but no pain.

> DAVID: You'd just want to hit him and concentrate on hitting him. If someone just punched you without [you] being in a temper, it would hurt. If it was unexpected. But once you're in a temper, you just don't care. You don't give a toss.

> JC: Is it exciting, then, when you're in a temper? . . . You don't feel anything?

> ANDREW: It's excitement, really, ain't it?

> KEITH: Then it's all over, ain't it! [Laughs] It's over too quick. You don't realize what's happened and then, when you walk away, you say, 'Did I win? Or did I lose? Or what!'

Being in a fight seems to heighten your sense of reality by removing you from its conventions. The usual capacity to see events unfold is lost; there is no past, no future, only a very consuming present. This radical transformation of reality is 'exciting', yet ephemeral, gone as soon as it is experienced. Such intense and consuming absorption in the present makes it difficult to develop a narrative sequence to explain and place events, 'Who won, who lost, or what?'

There's an interesting connection to the media-violence debate here. For these young men it is not that violent media images fascinate because they lead to copycatting. It's more that, whilst their own experience gives a prior basis of interest, the media images add to this and shape it by giving it a grammar and more public language of representation. Media images fascinate because they can be used to name and to make comparisons. They can be used as symbolic material to make sense of that incoherent but exciting experience which in the heat of the conflict seems to be without its own meaningful signs and symbols. Media images can be used to try to make sense of how something can be exciting and incredibly scary at the same time, controlled from outside and numbing but also exhilarating — 'like a roller coaster'. TV images are used to try to convey the terrible fascination and as a way of trying, impossibly, to give a narrative back to the incomprehensible:

> DAVID: It's like you're watching it and it's coming at you, but you can't feel it.

> KEITH: It's like the telly, you can't feel the punches, but you're giving them out like.

> DAVID: It's like someone's punching on the TV screen at you and you can't feel it.

JC: How's that like the telly?

KEITH: 'Cause you watch it and you don't get hurt.

ANDREW: You could give me shit and beat me with anything, sticks, the lot, and it's horrible, it, like, you aren't there, as though you're watching. It's like you see on the telly, it's scary, really. That's the scary part.

KEITH: You could've got killed then and wouldn't have known about it.

ANDREW: It ain't getting beat up that's scary, it's that you can't feel anything and you don't know what's happening.

Later from another discussion:

KEITH: They bust your nose, didn't they?

ANDREW: Yeah, bust me nose up.

KEITH: Right across your face, it was, wasn't it? Like Rocky.

It must now be recognized that violence is irredeemably part of our modern culture. For some young men fighting unleashes a seemingly uncontrolled and uncontrollable power. This power is admired and exciting, yet simultaneously dangerous and frightening. Both emotions are way beyond the range of middle-class and conventional notions of the importance of control at all times, except perhaps in the safe outer reaches of 'art for art's sake'. 'Hardness' has very wide currency and respect. It indicates the readiness, if necessary and under pressure, to risk the self and to try to control the dangerous and contradictory forces of violence.

Ironically the cultural system which limits and places this dangerous power is very much about control and performance: a *drama* of presenting and reading appearance and intention. To be lacking in control is very much looked down on. Control and power, very real physical and social stakes and the inherent risks and meanings of being outside the law make violence and its associated dramas potent symbolic materials to displace or disrupt given official and institutional meanings. These materials help in the construction and reconstruction of alternative ways of being in and seeing the world, of alternative values and ways of valuing people.

Some of these values may be repellent. They undoubtedly help to reproduce a certain kind of masculinity, as well as reproduce a dangerous acceptance of unacceptable violence. This has particular implications for women in the home where symbolic disputes can all too easily find a physical resolution. It can spread over as a threatening quality to the whole of our common cultural experience, making public space unsafe for all, but especially for women.

But these values and identities also concern a desperate kind of honour, a strange respect for the space around dignity and a mad courage which confronts banality with really live drama. Whether we like them or not, these are some of the contradictory living arts of survival — physical, psychic, cultural. Horrifyingly, hypnotizingly, they contain some of their own specific grounded aesthetics. Outside condemnation, without understanding or alternative, shows up the limits of the observer as well as those of the observed. Alternatives to and ideas and plans for the safer resolutions of the compelling dramas of violence should be what exercise our imaginations.

'I'll be better next time around'

Sports and games provide materials, activities and social relationships which have symbolic as well as physical meanings and uses. They provide resources towards the symbolic work of cultural expression and formation of cultural identity. This may not always be planned for by the providers or conducted in the terms which they set out. It may not be so much about the ideal 'ungendered' improvement of health as a symbolic working through and creative testing of more profane everyday senses of what it is to be men and women in this society — but especially men. Whatever else may be said sports and games certainly involve symbolic creativities which must be recognized.

The quantitative importance of sport for young people is easily demonstrated from available statistics for the United Kingdom. While 54 per cent of all men and 35 per cent of all women participated in some sport activity in the prior four weeks, 66 per cent of young men and 43 per cent of young women between 16 and 19 years of age participated during the prior four weeks. The five sports most popular with young participants are walking (18 per cent), snooker/billiards/pool (17 per cent), darts (13 per cent), swimming (12 per cent) and football (10 per cent) (*General Household Survey,* 1983). These figures point to a high degree of interest in minority sports which is increasing at the expense of traditional sports.

Young people's level of participation in sport generally decreases when they leave school. Girls tend to give up sport from around the age of 13, while boys are more likely to continue into their early 20s. While this indicates a significant gender difference in sports participation, this difference has been narrowing during the past decade as women increasingly partake of indoor activities such as keep-fit and yoga. Ethnic differences in young people's sports participation are difficult to determine as there is little documentation on sports activities of ethnic minorities. Finally, there are class differences in sports participation: semi- and unskilled manual labourers are likely to participate least, while professional and white-collar workers are likely to participate most (Greater London and South-east Council for Sport and Recreation, 1982).

Sport, like other leisure activities, involves a growing cultural industry. Over 370,000 people work in sport-related jobs. Sport-related consumer expenditure totals £4.4 billion at 1985 prices. The more popular expenditures include gambling, £1.16 billion; clothing and footwear, £770m; sports goods, £690m; sports participation, £530m (Henley Centre for Forecasting, 1986).

These are the bald figures. What is their symbolic content and meaning for common culture? Perhaps most importantly sports and games facilitate sociability of a wider and more networked kind than the immediate 'neighbourliness' of the street. They multiply many times over the possibility of meeting 'new people' but still on some shared ground of mutual interest and trust; in many urban and inner-city areas this is absolutely necessary when encroaching on other 'territories'. Sport is a neutral flag. It gives an immediate explanation of presence.

ROBERT: We started up a football team, we went in a league which my mum helped us run. So I helped a lot doing that and that's how I really started to know people from off the other estate, 'cause we had asked them to come and play football for us. So they come training to get in the team and I got to know them better. There's a load of them, I'd get to know their friends and so I knew a new group of people....

For young women sociability is also central to their enjoyment of sport with perhaps a greater stress on social relations between team mates rather than with other social groups. As Jane, who plays netball, notes:

We are just all together, we are one big family, like that . . . We go out at least once a month, or once every two months, or something like that, but we're always together, we're great friends, we've got each other to ring up . . . chatting over the phone, and things like that.

Sports and games then supply a set of controllable symbolic resources and connections which radiate outwards socially, but they also radiate inwardly, somatically. They provide ways of thinking about, regulating and developing the body, and through that a sense of self. 'The self' is therefore at an important kind of junction in sport, constructed somatically to one side and socially to the other. This is a complex articulation both of meaning and practice which provides a rich field for symbolic work and creativity and for the development of a bodily grounded aesthetic.

Jane takes a pride in her ability to make her own body move as she wants it to and for as long as she wants. Not everyone's body has these qualities, so it is a comparative pride and distinction too; a social as well as a bodily quality.

JANE: I've been in that club now for five years and I enjoy it. It's a fast game, you've got to be energetic, you've got to be fit to play that game. If you're not fit and you're not energetic, don't bother playing netball. We train for four hours non-stop, train for two hours and play for two hours . . . I love netball because in a way it gets me fit, even though you get tired, you get fit . . .

The nature of bodily grounded aesthetics seems to be different between men and women. The qualities of fitness and control are important for many young women for the prospects of internal wholeness being 'naturally' reflected in external appearances and ambience. For young men it seems to be more that fitness and control are important to increasing *applied skill* over something external, to becoming more effective and better at a game.

GURPRET: If you play a game, any sport, right, you think, okay . . . 'I'll be better next time around.' You try to upgrade yourself really from being at the bottom to as high as you can depending on how serious you want to play that game, so you're always trying to better yourself.

There is also, for young men a sharp distinction between serious competition where the self and perhaps masculinity are really tested, and 'messing about' where skills are still exercised and developed but in a non-threatening context. These are distinct bodily grounded aesthetics for, on the one hand, competitive purposes and, on the other, for expressive purposes. They have different ways of linking the body to the social through sport:

> GURPRET: Serious, right, it means you're out to win. No matter what happens, you go out to win . . . But if you're messing about, right, you go for the shots. Like, say some shots that would be impossible normally, like, you wouldn't do in serious cricket, you take the shots and go for chances and things like that (when you're messing about). You also improve your skills, you can just try new tactics . . . You learn more when you're just practising and that, like messing about.

Spectator sports, in contrast to participative sports, attract many many more males than females. For example, while 32 per cent of all UK males have gone to a football match in the past twelve months, only 8 per cent of all females have gone (MORI, August 1988). This concurs with our fieldwork findings; (white) young men were those who talked most about going to professional football matches.

Though the movement and control of one's own body is not important for the spectator, its sensuous and communicative presence within an immediate mass social spectacle is of the essence. Spectator football combines drama with spectacle in a way which actively involves the watcher. It also allows the individual to transcend local neighbourhood differences and rivalries by absorption into grander and more epic rivalries, into public though still grassroot traditions, into solidarity and traditional loyalties 'under the same flag' — a grounded aesthetic of place and belonging.

> STEVE: I don't like watching it [football] on the telly.
>
> JC: Why?
>
> STEVE: 'Cause there's no atmosphere. Like you get the atmosphere at the match, 'cause there's thousands and thousands of people there, like. You can see their fans, you know, you have a contest with their fans, like . . . I mean like Heathtown, Ashmore Park, they're all Wolverhampton. Like, when we were at the match, there's no, like, difference. It's all the same one, it's all Wolves and that's it . . .
>
> JC: Do you feel that the Wolves are your team?
>
> STEVE: Yeah.
>
> JC: How are they your team, like what do they do?
>
> STEVE: I don't know, like . . . Wolverhampton's where you come from like, it's where you were born, and everything, so you support Wolves, you support Wolverhampton . . . Like I've always supported the Wolves, and that's it, like. My dad's supported the Wolves, and I've supported the Wolves. My son, like, I hope he supports the Wolves.

It is often overlooked that the excitement of spectacle in football relies on strong symbolic communication — tumultuous and powerful, collectively and selectively creative. Each fan carries on a process of communication, mediated by their own grounded aesthetic of the spectacle, with the play, the game and the 'local heroes' on the pitch. This is enhanced beyond measure by being in the crowd which swells his or her voice and presence to epic proportions. Stevie Bull who plays for Wolves was the leading goal scorer of all four leagues in the 88/9 season. This is Charlie, a Wolves fan, on his 'local hero'.

> CHARLIE: It's bloody great, wild, when Bully's charging down the wing, he looks up at the South Bank and there's a huge roar and you're shouting like mad. You know he's gonna do it. You know, he's communicating with the whole of the South Bank. And if he does it, if he puts it in the back of the onion net, he goes mad, we go mad, the whole crowd goes mad. It's wild! Then he goes like an aeroplane with his arms held out, sweeping and diving in front of the South Bank. Then he does a gambol, he's doin' it for the fans and they love it. That's why he's a local hero.

And this strange spectacular communication seems to work in practical as well as emotional ways. Eighty per cent of Stevie Bull's goals this season have been at home matches in front of the home 'South Bank' crowd. The communication is about action as well as symbols. Stevie Bull's goals are willed. The fans are playing too.

Football chants and songs also show a marked degree of collective symbolic creativity. Sung to the tunes of well-known classic pop songs, they arise it seems from nothing, build up and crescendo into mass choruses. No one knows who's made up the words! There are many current songs and chants at Molineux (Wolves' Football Ground). They change continuously. This one is sung to the tune of 'Lily the Pink'. It combines drinking, popular music and football, perhaps the triple alliance of one important form of male working-class culture.

> Have a drink a drink a drink
> To Stevie the King, the King, the King
> Saviour of the Wanderers
> Football T — E — A — M
>
> He's the greatest centre forward
> The World has ever seen.

In contrast to the excitement of mass spectatorship, 'fandom' can also be a very private thing, an intimate communication from the self to the self, but somehow with all the resonances of the spectacle supplied through its connecting grounded aesthetics. Bill is a strong fan. His bedroom is a private temple to the Wolves. It also has a whole social atmosphere. Mostly it's about helping to create his identity as belonging to Wolverhampton as an individual, as a father's son, and as a fan.

> STEVE: I mean, my bedroom, it's [painted] all gold and black . . . I've got a big flag on the one wall, big picture of the team on another. All newspaper clippings on the one, and a scarf hung up on the wardrobe. There's all things about them [the Wolves], there's a couple of T-shirts, like, that was when they were a really big club.

Table and electronic indoor games are not about personal bodily fitness, nor are they about spectacle or local identity. They do, however, especially involve a lot of male young people. They are growing in popularity and provide their own kind of resources towards symbolic work and creativity.

Video games get your adrenalin going and also excite partly because they simulate real challenging situations. They produce the possibilities for a virtual grounded aesthetic.

> GURPRET: There's a new game out where you're actually, you feel like you're driving a car . . . you're sitting in a car, right, the car tilts from side to side, [depending] on the way you're steering. Because it's got a simulation of the road, right, with bumps and that, right, the car moves according to the bumps and that.

Learning new skills and enjoying being skilful is central to the enjoyment of games. Delroy, for example, now enjoys playing table football and pool because he can see he has learnt many skills by investing much time and money on improving his game:

> DELROY: Before, all I used to do was hit the ball anywhere, but now I know what I'm doing with the ball. It makes you feel better. At one stage I used to . . . spend about one pound or two pounds every day on the one football machine . . .

> JC: What makes football more fun than the other ones?

> DELROY: 'Cause I'm good at it, that's why. I'm all right at pool, but I'm better at football. I'd say if you're better than most people at football, it makes you want to play more and well, it makes you feel good, I suppose.

Delroy enjoys developing his technical skills so that he can beat formerly successful opponents. But there's also a complex interplay here between the social and the technical which mirrors that in sports. Partly this is simply enjoying the space for sociability which these games provide. But there are several social possibilities for playing a game depending on how the opponent is perceived.

> DELROY: If the game's good and I play with someone that I know can beat me, I don't talk, but if I'm playing doubles now, right, and I know I'm going to beat the person, we just talk all the time, or we just take the mickey out of him, like try to aggravate him, stuff like that.

One-to-one competition between male equals is a serious affair. In part it's about the construction and reproduction of masculinity as dominance and competence. But this masculinity is creatively tested and constructed in and through dramatic grounded aesthetics: as master, pushing and taunting someone to the point where he gets upset, watching to see if he does so: as victim, responding with good-natured stoicism, controlling yourself and coming up with a witty rebuff or something that might pass as such. If you fail in this latter, you're likely to become the butt of repeated jokes.

Such potentially cruel banter and the competitive spirit surrounding games as well as their aura of masculinity and masculine domination seem to put most young women off participation at least in heterosexual situations.

SANDRA: I don't play any of the games because I don't think it's ladylike to play table football, you know what I mean . . .I can't see myself hitting the ball, you know, and playing pool. I can't see myself doing that. It's not me. I like certain things, but those kinds of things I just see men doing it, and I think it's just because it's for men, you know what I mean.

As this quote and much of our other material show, the physical basis of sports and games symbolism makes them eminently suitable for the — even if creative — reproduction of *conventional* gender identities and definitions. In the case of young men this encourages what verges on, and is sometimes really, anti-social behaviour. Still, the creativity should not be overlooked. Contradictions make and produce cultural life. They energize from the inside many of the grounded aesthetics of common culture. What we wish to show is the balance of contradictions too well-known and understood in their other halves.

Dead old-fashioned

The notion of 'romance' is thought to structure the lives of many young women and to regulate their relationships with young men. Certainly the infamous double standard and fear of being labelled 'a slag'[2] influenced the behaviour of the young women we spoke to. However, for a good proportion the notions of 'romance' and 'courtly love' seemed distinctly outdated. Certainly not infallible guides to action, they were rather simply materials towards the symbolic work of understanding their own position and possibilities. Like so much else, they could be questioned, contextualized, tested. In part this was associated with a particular critical ability with respect to the media; the puncturing of the myth of romance was associated with the operation of grounded aesthetics concerned to read, place and select media stereotypes differentially.

There was certainly a clear sense of what constitutes romance, and one immediately identified through omnipresent media images:

JC: What's romantic love?

YVONNE: Walking in the park, buying flowers.

HILARY: I think it's stupid, romantic love . . . 'Cause I think it's like pretend. Like romantic love is the kind of love that you see on the TV and love in real life is love what's real, you know . . . Romantic love will last a couple of years, but love's there for ever.

JC: But don't you have an element of wanting that, of wanting someone to give you flowers, sweep you off your feet, and tell you he thinks the world of you?

ANNA: Everyone's bound to dream of that, but it just isn't real life, is it?

HILARY: It's what you see on thc TV.

ANNA: It's just adverts. Like the body spray, you know, Impulse. The man gives her flowers (when she's shopping just because she's wearing Impulse). And you don't see that down Bilston Market, if someone's wearing Impulse. I mean, I wear Impulse and I don't even get one pea chucked in my face!

125

In another discussion Katy says that it's 'nice' when a boy is 'jealous' — 'It makes you feel like you've got some hold over him.' Again she goes to the media for illustration and quotes two young men currently fighting over Jane in *Neighbours,* but is immediately interrupted:

> RACHEL: What's the use of fighting? It doesn't prove nothing . . .
>
> GAIL: It's like in the old days, like in the old books, like *Romeo and Juliet,* they're gonna fight over them . . . You read all the old stories in all the old books, so.

Rachel's and Gail's comments suggest that chivalry is not so much dead as dead old-fashioned. Tragic love stories found in 'old' books evoke a way of developing relationships which seems far removed from the lives of these young women. They get more usable ideas from television shows, most notably English soap operas. While American soaps exaggerate ideas about romance and relationships, English soaps, in contrast, seem more realistic:

> ANNA: It [American soaps] seems to be full of passion, they just seem to jump into bed with everyone, don't they?
>
> HILARY: . . . But like *EastEnders* and *Brookside,* you can't forget about the world. Michelle [from *EastEnders*] had everything happen that somebody has in a hundred years! She's had a divorce in a year, she's had a baby at 16 . . .
>
> JC: What kinds of images of love and romance do you get from shows like *EastEnders* and *Brookside?*
>
> HILARY: Don't get married! Don't have a family.

It's not that the puncturing of 'romance' brings a real sense of equality to relations between the sexes. The more negative features of 'romance' seem to linger. Young men are still the prime movers. Bold advances from women are still out of the question. There is much suffering in silence. Suffering is reflected and interpreted immediately in the light of 'feminine' qualities of appearance and personality.

> RACHEL: Boys are bad though, when you fancy boys, oh they love it, don't they?
>
> GAIL: It goes to their heads, they think that they're really . . . if you, you know, let them know you fancy them, they'll let you hang on.
>
> JC: So what do you do if you fancy a bloke?
>
> RACHEL: There's not a whole lot you can do, is there? . . . You can't stop fancyin' them, can you? Have you ever really fancied somebody and know that they wouldn't go out with you?
>
> JC: Yeah.
>
> RACHEL: It's terrible, isn't it? . . .
>
> KATY: It makes you feel ugly, doesn't it? . . .

RACHEL: It makes you feel bad on the inside.

KATY: It makes you feel like you're an alien.

RACHEL: And when you see him, oh God, he's lovely!

GAIL: You can't keep your eyes off 'em!

The critical engagement with 'romance' seems less 'feminist' than 'realist'. The problems of the double standard may not be overthrown but they are negotiated using a tough and creative repertoire of actions and words. This repertoire is far from being drawn wholly from or used in the manner of the 'respectable' end of gender images, behaviour and language:

HILARY: Like what you got to do when you're going out with somebody, right, they always try it on with you . . . A bloke will go off with a slag, right, but when it's time to get married, they'll look for the quiet, well, not quiet, but decent girl . . . So when a bloke tries it on you, you kick him in the donkeys and tell him to get lost . . . When I was going with this bloke, right, he tried it on with me and I thumped him and everything. And after he said to me, 'Well, at least I know you're decent now', you know what I mean. So sometimes it's a test.

Marriage is seen as a goal, but not through rose-tinted glasses:

JC: So do you think you'll ever get married?

HILARY: I will, when I'm 28 . . . I'm gonna get married and have two children . . . I want them all girls.

JC: Why all girls?

HILARY: I don't like boys. They're so aggressive . . . I want it to be an equal relationship [with my husband]. Like he goes to work and I go to work, right. We won't have any kids for about a year, so we'll be able to build up a relationship more, right, and then we come back home and say, the housework, we'll do it together, ... so it's equal ... I want to be a breadwinner because if you're a breadwinner, right, you know, if you bring the money back to the home, you got more say what goes on in the house then. If you're just an ordinary housewife, the bloke seems to get more what he wants and I don't want that happening.

Hilary disapproves of, rather than accepts, male aggression. She also makes some key points that feminists have made; not only is having a job central to a woman's power in the home but, more critically, the housework must be divided between partners so that the woman alone does not end up with a double workload. Yet Hilary's comments are idealistic in their way. By stating that she will put off marriage for ten years Hilary, like many other young women, may be deferring rather than solving problems. Similarly, by claiming that she and her partner will build up their relationship for 'about a year' before they have children, she does not consider that after that time, one of them, she more likely than he, may have to give up a job, if not a career, in order to bear and raise children.

Despite these constraints, Hilary constructs present and future relationships in ways which do not empower her partner at her expense. She mobilizes her symbolic resources in ways which also introduce more of her identity into relationships. She sees where relationships are constraining and tries to anticipate how best to cope so that she can still assert herself. Symbolic work and creativity on received notions of 'romance' — holding, criticizing, qualifying — play a part in this.

Work and creativity

Leisure is the primary space in which young people mobilize and creatively work on and through a wide range of symbolic resources. Even though its loss or non-availability is a calamity, most of our working respondents did not rate their work very highly as a source of satisfaction and human involvement. Some of them, like 17-year-old Ian, who is a dustbin man, find that the best thing about work is the money and the hours. Work is just the huge gap in the middle of the 'good hours'.

> JC: What do you like about work?

> IAN: Money, finishing at half past four. The money is good for me, because I'm only 17 and it's [the work] easy done. Like we have an hour off for dinner and then we finish at about quarter to four and just go back to the depot, play pool until about twenty past four, clock out, and then I come home.

For others the problem is the 'bit in the middle' — boredom. And it can be a physical problem as well as a mental problem, characteristically contrasted with the healths and freedoms of leisure:

> JOHN (an assistant caretaker): I get really bored at work, the time don't seem to pass. I'm full of aches and pains all day as well, I seem to get everything — but as soon as I go home I'm fine, hobbies, watching telly, everythin' . . . Boredom, that's the problem . . . the place is killin' me.

However, symbolic and social activity can be part of work tasks and can produce satisfactions. For a minority we found a sense of creativity in work. Eighteen-year-old Neil, for example, gets great satisfaction from the work that he does with disabled people. He enjoys it for several reasons. First and foremost, he enjoys helping them to expand their leisure activities, participating more in the world which able-bodied people primarily inhabit:

> NEIL: Like George Garnett, he's a cerebral palsy, it took me six months to get him to go to a night club. It's always something he's wanted to do but, because of his shape and disfigurement, he didn't want to go because he thought that people would look at him?

> JC: Did they?

> NEIL: Yes, well, but you know, you have to get the fact over to him that, forget them, they don't mean a thing, you know, what other people think is not important, you should enjoy yourself and make the most out of your life . . .

JC: Have you succeeded?

NEIL: Well, I feel that I've succeeded there because I did change people, not a great deal, but changed them enough for them to enjoy themselves, and ... it just makes you feel good inside, you know, and it boosts your whole outlook on life, just to see people like that enjoy themselves.

To be able to achieve his aims Neil must be able to put himself in the position of and to understand how it might feel to be a disabled person entering a room occupied by the able-bodied. He also must be able to provide the disabled with tools that will help them get beyond this feeling. Both of these tasks require a keen knowledge of emotional life. In talking with them and coming to understand how they live and understand their lives, he comes to understand the human condition more fully through an emotive grounded aesthetic which most work allows no play for. He says that he would like to work with other kinds of disabled people so that he can gather together as diverse and full a picture of the human experience as possible:

NEIL: I'd like to work with disabled kids, young kids, nursery kids. I want a wide scope of life, try and collect as much information as possible, because that's what we're here for, we're all brought down to collect information, like you're collecting information now.

Young mothers

Many of our respondents were young mothers with two or more children. These women note that they have hardly any time during the day to themselves. They are too preoccupied with housework and taking care of the children and perhaps husband or partner.

MARGARET: You don't have time to get bored. Because you've got too much to do. If it ain't housework, it's looking after the kids. If it ain't looking after the kids, it's looking after the husband . . .

LESLEY: ... There's not enough hours in a day. There isn't enough hours to do what you've got to do. You know you don't have time to get bored.

JC: You're busy, are you enjoying it?

MARGARET: It isn't that I don't enjoy it and I do enjoy it, it's got to be done. These [kids] have to be fed, and washed and dressed and everything else, and the house has to be cleaned up, so it's just a normal day, everyday thing. But if I wasn't in a routine, I'd be in a mess.

Clearly, creative expression and symbolic creativity are not uppermost in these women's minds.

Housework and looking after children can be physically exhausting. Of the half-dozen young mothers in our discussion groups two complained of being physically worn down.

ELAINE: I'm on vitamins and iron. The doctor's told me I've got to start and take things easy. Everything's getting on top of me, but he says I'm run down, really under, and he wants to test me water for diabetics [sic] 'cause it's in the family. He says I'm showing some of the symptoms. Probably it's just a lack of sleep, tired.

Neither she nor most of the other married women in our discussion groups had much help with household tasks from their husbands. Even women with unemployed husbands got little help.

Yet all these women make some space for rest and relaxation to be themselves for themselves — and symbolic materials play a part in this. The television gives them the minimum means of escape. Many have the television on all day. Like most viewers, they combine watching the television with other activities. They glance at and listen to it throughout the day. Only when programmes that they like are on, do they try to sit down and watch them. As Elaine notes again: 'It's on all day, it's always on all day. If there's summat on I want to watch, I will sit down and watch it. But if there ain't nothing, I won't bother.'

If these women's daytime viewing is sporadic and involves only partial attention to what is going on, their nighttime viewing is almost the opposite. Lesley, for example, notes that she likes to watch the television by herself at night in a kind of grounded aesthetic of solace.

> Because it's the only time I can watch, usually my husband goes out at about quarter to ten, so that . . . depending on what time he comes in, is my only time on my own that I can unwind. I can't go to bed unless I've watched TV and unwound. . . Last night I went upstairs after tea for an hour and a half, me husband says, 'What were you doing?' I says, 'I was watching telly in the bedroom just so I could be on me own.' I like to be on me own and I just don't seem to get it.

The most liked programmes are soap operas and quizzes. Many watch *Neighbours* and *Sons and Daughters*. Some of them, like Elaine, enjoy game shows because of the 'Excitement, the money, just getting involved in the quizzes and questions they ask, and that, and guessing the answers before they say "um".' Television shows like these invite them to participate, to put themselves in the shoes of the participants.

Young mothers do not constitute a monolithic group. Although most in our discussion groups were somewhat demoralized by the constraints of motherhood and maintaining a house, this was not true for all.

Susan, for instance, took precautions as soon as her son was born, to prevent herself from feeling too enclosed by the new demands of motherhood. She began playing netball:

It's mainly since I had Neil that I wanted to do the sport, to get a bit back, to normal kind of things. I hadn't really bothered since I left school to do anything, really . . . Sometimes I feel like going out. With the netball, I think, 'There's a good break.' When I come home from netball, I feel, if I've gone out in a bad mood, I come back all right, like, so that's my main break at the moment and I enjoy it. I'd sooner go and play netball than sit in the pub drinking.

During her time out she is able to forget about her domestic situation by getting immersed in different and outside social and symbolic materials which then act back on her sense of identity to make her feel 'normal'. Susan also engages in other activities both in and outside the home. She and her unemployed husband Scott bought a video machine which has given them a means of having leisure in the home. They play video games, which enable Susan to intertwine some symbolic creativities into the dry texture of daily domestic chores. She has a way of escaping from routine. Susan also reads books, knits and makes cakes for relatives. She is fairly happy with her life.

The two structural features which distinguish Susan from the others seem to be having an unemployed husband who helps her with chores, and having only one child. These two features free her from some of the constraints that weigh heavily on the other women and open up possibilities for more creative symbolic work and cultural satisfactions.

The young unemployed

The situation is also difficult but in different ways for unemployed young people. Whilst young mothers lack the time and energy for much leisure activity, unemployed young people lack the economic resources necessary for more than a minimal amount of leisure, leisure activities and the possibilities for symbolic lifting through grounded aesthetics which they provide.

A striking feature of unemployed groups in both Wolverhampton and Sunderland is that they live in an increasingly small world as cuts diminish their income and thereby make it more difficult for them to engage in the leisure activities that other people take for granted. They are cut off not only from work, but from access to usable symbolic resources and the creative activities associated with them.

> NEIL: You pay your rent, you pay your food, and you're left with one night out [a week], if that . . . I go out once a week, on a Saturday. Like this week, I'll go out to a pub and I'll go to a club after. Next week, I can just about scrape going to a pub.
>
> JC: So it's like, one week you'll have a really good night?
>
> NEIL: Right, and then next week it's really nothing . . .
>
> REBECCA: I like to go out a lot, so I spend 50 pence a night, and it's getting to the point where you can't spend 50 pence 'cause drinks are 55, something like that. So, I mean, you just don't bother drinking. If you live alone, like if you've got a flat, then you don't see anyone if you don't go out at night. So you gotta keep going out. There are people who are really isolated, 'cause they haven't got the money to go out and meet people.

Going out at night to the pub is, for many of these young people, the only break in their very solitary lives. Some of them, like Neil and Rebecca, go to their local youth club during the day just to break 'the monotony in the days'. Their homes do not seem to be places where they find comfort and solace. This is probably especially true for those who, like Rebecca, have their own flats and therefore spend the whole day alone, unless they go to the local youth club.

Pubs and clubs are not the only places that these young people visit infrequently, or with very slim purses. They find it difficult to engage in other leisure activities as well. For example, Neil used to attend football matches when he was working. Now, however, he hardly goes at all because he 'can't afford to go, four quid to get in now!'

Contrary to what many people might think, it is not the unemployed who are the most violent, at pubs, clubs or football games. They can hardly afford to get into these places, never mind buy enough alcohol to reach the requisite state of intoxication usually necessary to get into a fight.

Unemployed young people find that their severely limited financial resources make their lives very frustrating, and, worse, demoralizing. They seem to feel radically removed from even the possibility of a good life which bites particularly hard if they have children to look after. Some of the measures felt to be necessary to get a bit of the good life — especially those for whom you're responsible — are desperate. As Linda in Sunderland reports:

> When you've been on the dole for as long as us, you just can't afford to go out and it drives you round the bend — day after day. Then the bairn's asking for money or toys or clothes and you can't give any of them to her and you feel terrible — you end up not eating so she'll be the same as other kids at school — not shabby looking. And we've only got one kid — I don't know how people with more kids manage — well, they don't manage, they just live — just survive. And you have to do things that other people wouldn't dream of doing. Last year in the winter — it was a bad winter — me and some other women used to go down the lines pinching coal . . . I couldn't afford to buy coal at £10 a week. So we used to wait till the pubs were out and we used to put hats and things to hide our hair, climb over a great big wall, climb into these dirty trucks getting coal . . . dragging it back across the lines on our hands and knees, getting it across this high wall and then humping it across home. We used to get back at two in the morning. We used to be rotten dirty from head to foot and because you had had no coal the day before, you had no hot water for a bath, so you had to start boiling kettles to get washed. That's the sort of thing you have to do if you're poor and on the dole. People shouldn't have to do things like that.

Nor do most of these young people believe that their lives will change for the better in the next few years. Many of those who went on training schemes found that they learnt very little. They thought that they were pointless, demoralizing and led to no work anyway:

> DICK: I was supposed to be painting and decorating. I only ever seen the bloke twice. So I just give it up. A month and a half I was there . . . He was always away, it was bad. And there wasn't anybody else could teach us . . .
>
> JC: How about you Bob? Have you been on a training scheme?
>
> BOB: Yeah.
>
> JC: What was it?

BOB: It was general maintenance, looking after things.

JC: Did you learn how to look after things?

BOB: More like destruction. Well, they say, like, go and build us a wall. But before we had to build it, we had to knock it down. They don't tell us nothing about that.

REBECCA: They got a training scheme, but they ain't got no work for you.

In an economy which is eliminating many of the old manual labour jobs that working-class young people formerly held, and with no economic resources of their own, many unemployed young people hold out little hope that things will change:

NEIL: I don't look into the future. I live day by day.

And Raf from Sunderland:

I don't think very far ahead. I don't think things are going to get any better. There'll only be full employment again if there's a war. It's technology that's done it, no doubt about that. So things are going to get worse and all you can do is go out and try to create something for yourself — that's all I can think of — and what can you create on this much money?

Despite this poverty and demoralization unemployed people do attempt to express, develop and make themselves through symbolic and social resources. In Sunderland Linda has become the chair of a housing co-op. Holding this post has brought her to perform well a number of tasks which she would have thought impossible for a person as 'thick' as she considered herself to be:

What I've learnt these last three years [as chair of the housing association] is amazing — part treasurer's job, how to do rents, how to organize repairs, chair meetings — and it's just great the things you can do if someone takes the time to help you to learn how to do them. I knew nothing when I first started, but the professional workers helped us and we went on courses. Being as thick as I am, I never thought I could do anything like this . . . But now I'm trusted with thousands and thousands of pounds and people tell me that I'm not thick — and you can learn by being told you're not thick, and that's good.

For others salvation comes from an overriding interest and symbolic creativity in a particular cultural form. Neil is totally involved in heavy-rock music. One kind, gothic rock', is:

NEIL: . . . slowed down punk, really, but it's more morbid. It's got a morbid side to it. Most of it's like about death. Some of it's about love, but mostly death, but they do politics as well.

JC: What kind of politics is it?

> NEIL: It's South Africa and things like that ... Whatever's happening now, they'll write a song about it. Like most of the groups we listen to, it's all politics, ain't it?

Neil also symbolically works on the image that goes with his preferred music. He saves his money to go to gothic-rock concerts. When he goes he creatively and materially fashions his appearance through a bodily grounded aesthetic:

> But the gothics, like they wear make-up just to look more evil and morbid. It's black make-up. Like when I go to see some bands, I'll pale my face out, wear black eye-liner and black lipstick and put grey cheeks in so it looks like you've got a death look.

Only a minority of the unemployed are involved in symbolic work and creativity of a public or spectacular kind. Many young unemployed people have such aspirations but lack the context, possibility or, more importantly, cash. But symbolic work and creativity do not stop because you are depressed, demoralized and often alone indoors. Instead it seems to become part of a twilight domestic world of the imagination enlivened by grounded aesthetics of fantasy. The imagination refuses to give up, but moves in surprising and unlikely ways — often taking on the very forms of normality which most of us are bored with and seek to escape. But working boredoms can be part of a distant or lost world for the unemployed quite as remote and attractive as any imaginative land. The common themes of housebound day-dreaming were, 'Just having a house of your own'; 'Sitting there, typing all day'; 'I fantasize about having a girl-friend'; 'I fantasize about having someone to cook for.'

These prosaic themes of imagination and fantasy can manifest themselves in private action: 'I used to dance in front of the mirror, when I was about 16-17, I still do', or 'When I am in the kitchen cooking, I think I am like her on telly . . . "Now you put the eggs, stir around,"' or 'I move the furniture around in the kitchen and pretend it's a disco.'

The young unemployed work and rework their own imaginative 'cultural scripts' just as would any playwright or writer. They are painfully grounded in 'normality' rather than in radicalism or the transcendental. They certainly show the central *cultural* importance as well as material importance of access to a decent wage. Most importantly for us, however, they show the tenacity of human symbolic capacities fed by the phantoms of cultural media even in the desert. What would more resources and wider possibilities produce?

Notes

1. *General Household Survey*, 1983; P. Willis *et al.*, *The Youth Review*, Avebury, 1988.

2   See for instance, C. Griffin, *Typical Girls*, Routledge and Kegan Paul, 1985: and S. Lees, *Losing Out*, Century Hutchinson, 1980.

6. Violence and Sexuality
Tony Eardley

In our culture male arousal is a real social problem . . .
(Ros Coward)[1]

What is it about male sexuality that makes it a social problem? How have we reached the point where violence is automatically associated with men's sexual behaviour and our relationships with women? Rape and battering are hardly new phenomena and it would be difficult to demonstrate in any conclusive way that men are now more violent than ever before. Yet in the last decade male violence towards women has become a central focus of feminist politics and a contentious social issue in all the countries where women's liberation has emerged in any strength. Previously much 'domestic' violence had been hidden because of the deep and long-standing social consensus which viewed the family as an element of cohesion and harmony, rather than as a site of sharp conflict and sexual antagonism.

The silence this consensus has imposed on women has been broken. Feminist organizations like Women's Aid and Rape Crisis have enabled thousands of women to speak out and to escape the violence they have suffered. But men's response to these developments has been muted, to say the least. Where we have begun to think about our own behaviour and how we are implicated in violence, we are often confused, defensive, self-doubting or self-hating and resentful. A challenge to sexual violence may itself produce a further violent reaction.

It has been variously suggested that men's violence is biologically determined, that it is learnt through cultural socialization, or that it is primarily the result of deprivation and the oppressive divisions imposed by the alienated work process of capitalism. Radical feminism has further argued that men are reluctant to confront the problem of violence simply because men enjoy the power it gives us too much.

I don't find any of these arguments very convincing in themselves as real explanations. I want to look at what lies behind them, to see how they might help — or fail to help — our understanding of the problem. It is a huge subject to deal with in a short chapter, and inevitably I have had to truncate arguments, but I hope I have not distorted them. I cannot claim to have found a comprehensive 'answer' to the many difficult questions raised. I hope only to suggest that the problem of male sexual violence is principally that of the deep psychic construction of masculinity within the social and material meanings our culture ascribes to it. A potential for violence becomes encoded in the way we are defined as men and learn to experience ourselves in relation to women. To change this in any fundamental way will require radical shifts not just in the framework of legal protection and sanctions, or even just in sexual attitudes, but also in the organization of child rearing, in household structures, and in employment patterns which reproduce masculinity as it is currently constructed.

Tony Eardley: 'Violence and Sexuality' from THE SEXUALITY OF MEN, edited by Andy Metcalf and Martin Humphries (Pluto Press, 1985), pp. 86-109.

I always have a problem in writing about men: should I be referring to 'we' or 'they'? It seems more than a self-indulgent quibble to ask this question. The ideology of masculinity is generalized and pervasive, and moulds us all; but men are not simply passive recipients of it, any more than all women have accepted their own ideological designation. Masculinity as a lived experience is different and rather more complex than the sum of male 'roles', and I will suggest that in this discrepancy, this disjuncture, can be found some of the problems men end up trying to resolve with violence.

To talk as 'we' can suggest a false confessional, a communality of feeling with other men that I don't often share, since I have learnt in quite a self-conscious way to distance myself from and question male assumptions. To retreat into 'they' supposes a spurious separation, a making of exceptions, which men are inclined to use when dealing with uncomfortable political ideas. It also denies the shared experience and understanding which should and does link me with other men.

I remember, several years ago, the first of a difficult series of discussions of violence with the *Achilles Heel* collective. One of us distributed copies of an article from the American radical journal *Mother Jones*, which reported the story of the rape and mutilation of Mary Bell Jones, a teenage girl attacked while hitch-hiking in California. We didn't know how to begin talking about it and found ourselves avoiding each other's eyes. When our reactions came they varied from 'I can't bear to read this', and 'we cannot be expected to take responsibility for these atrocities simply because we are men', to 'we have to accept that at bottom this is what men are about'. It soon became clear that any notion of responsibility was meaningless unless we started from our own violence and our experiences both as perpetrators and as victims, as a way to some understanding of how men acquire such a capacity for brutality. We found it was essential to develop a political analysis of male violence which looked towards possibilities for change, and a concept of personal responsibility not based on guilt but on positive challenge to destructive aspects of masculinity.

One can start such a challenge by asking what lies behind men's silence. We seem to have been unable or willing to say very little about how or why violence is apparently so central to our relationships, our sexual practices and desires. Yet we are nurtured, educated and immersed in a culture whose imagery constantly intertwines violence with sexuality, either subtly or blatantly, and describes each in terms of the other. For evidence of this we only have to look at the covers of pulp thrillers which line the shelves of popular bookshops, the constant stream of 'women in jeopardy' films which are shown in mainstream cinemas, and the cult of video 'nasty'. We might also point to the gradual assimilation of sado-masochism chic into high street fashion and advertising. The meaning of these developments may be uncertain and hotly disputed, but their existence is undeniable.

Some feminists have argued that men's reluctance to question this cultural coupling of sex and violence is simply a conscious calculation of the power it brings — that men know which side their bread is buttered on, and are quite happy to exert control and extort sexual and other services by the use or threat of force. There is an undeniable element of truth in this, yet it seems inadequate as an explanation.

136

Men mostly do grow up in selfish expectation of being serviced by women, but they also grow up with expectations of breadwinning, work, family duties and responsibilities. Although ideas about marriage have changed considerably over the last 20 or 30 years the marriage contract is still very widely regarded both by men and women as a reciprocal agreement — a bargain. Research on the distribution of family income, such as that by Jan Pahl,[2] has shown how unequal a bargain financially this often is; men's dependence on the material and emotional support of women is very deep. Nevertheless, it is not clear that the role of 'breadwinner' is automatically such a privileged one, in spite of the oppressive nature of the marriage relationship for many women. Historically, the rigid and oppressive character of most waged labour gave the division between male labour and female servicing a deeply entrenched sense of reciprocity, as both natural and compulsory. The strength of these expectations may have outlived the material circumstances which fostered them, but they are still what underlies the puzzlement and indignation many married men feel when this apparent bargain is challenged.

It is doubtful whether the power to demand or force sexual services from women has led to any widespread sexual satisfaction or happiness amongst men. Surveys in popular magazines and reports from sexologists and sex therapists seem to suggest that anxiety rather than 'cock-sureness' has become a central emotion in male (hetero)sexuality. A snippet on the women's page of the *Guardian* autumn 1983, provides one example. A telephone advice service, mainly for women with sexual problems, had been set up in a large Italian city — the country commonly thought of as the bastion of self-confident male machismo. In the first few months, it was flooded with calls from men in desperate doubt and anxiety about their inability to 'perform' sexually and to live up to their own image of masculinity.

Women's liberation, the growing assertiveness of women with a bit more money and power in the world, is popularly blamed for the wave of male impotence and insecurity that is reported. It seems possible that much contemporary violence against women does result from the challenge women pose to male self-esteem; it could be argued that men are only confused and unhappy because their power is being challenged. But this only raises more questions: what is this masculinity which is so powerful and dominant but also apparently so fragile and vulnerable to challenge? How does a sexuality commonly understood as naturally predatory and aggressive become so set about with doubt and failure?

Violence as male supremacy

In attributing male violence to a conscious and systematic attempt by men to maintain women's social subordination, radical and revolutionary feminists have asserted a universal and trans-historical system of male supremacy in which power is defined by rape, battering and murder. The growing pornography industry is cited as the propaganda arm of the 'patriarchial' system .

It is not surprising that this stark picture of society has achieved prominence, for it corresponds to the deep anger many women feel towards men for the atrocities that they themselves and other women have suffered. It has been a salutory and enlightening experience for men to have felt this anger directed at them. But although the analysis of male violence has inspired a militant and combative activism, the issue is a great deal more problematic if we really expect and hope that anything will change. I cannot discuss here general problems with theories of patriarchy, but I want to make a few points about rape and pornography which I think are relevant.

Susan Brownmiller, in *Against Our Will: Men, Women and Rape*[3] first set out the ground for the idea of rape as a universal system of control. She collected a wide range of persuasive supporting evidence for this theory from different historical periods and from different cultures. The main problem with her argument is that by retaining the viewpoint and the interpretive framework of her own late twentieth-century culture, she fails in the end to distinguish the historical and cultural specifics of others. It then becomes difficult to understand the meaning of any differences which do exist. There is admittedly a danger on questions like rape of falling into a liberal relativism in respect of other cultures — but there are other approaches. Anthropologist Peggy Reeves Sanday, for example, has suggested that there are a number of cultures where rape is quite unknown.[4] Julia and Herman Schwendinger have further argued that the prevalence of rape in societies where it is known seems closely correlated to general social antagonisms and to the extent to which different societies are hierarchically organized.[5] This does not in itself contradict the idea that rape may be one form of the exercise of power and control; clearly it is one almost exclusively practised by men. But it does suggest that in order to understand it we need to concentrate less on its supposed universality and more on the specific features which seem to generate it in particular societies and particular historical periods.

A similar problem exists in radical feminist approachcs to pornography. Anti-pornography campaigners, both in the USA and England, have asserted an unquestionable link between the consumption of pornography and actual violence against women, even though the connection between fantasy, representation and practice is far from being clearly understood. It has become difficult to challenge this orthodoxy, although some feminists both in England and the USA have begun to do so.[6] I doubt whether pornography can be 'read' as a simple description of male sexuality or even of male fantasy (though it is interesting to see how it seems to shape the language and forms within which male fantasy is expressed.)[7] If it says anything coherent at all about male sexuality it seems to be more about passivity or the fear of passivity in the face of the threatening reality of sex. Real erotic feeling dissolves and disintegrates into the solitary pursuit of the illusory substitute offered by the captured and static imagery, and the creams, potions and paraphernalia of techno-phallocracy.

Andrea Dworkin has tried to generalize and universalize a 'history' of pornography in its function as propaganda for patriarchy.[8] Although we can accept that graphic and written material depicting sexual imagery and activity has been in circulation in many different cultures at different times, it is hard to see how we can accept any single meaning or significance in this material. Dworkin and other anti-pornography campaigners base their assertions primarily on the specific form of violent imagery presented in some contemporary hard core porn, but the availability of this type of material and the mass consumption of soft porn are both recent and specific historical phenomena which require a corresponding social explanation beyond ahistorical concepts of male supremacy.

To question these assumptions is not to deny that there is a link between male sexuality, violence and women's subordination. A woman on her own at night in a quiet street has no reason to be confident that the man walking behind her will not harass or attack her. The woman clerk or junior executive cannot always be sure that her boss will not use his position to force sexual advances on her. But to say that all men are rapists must be to define all heterosexual activity, in a society where women are subordinate, as rape, and all heterosexual women as victims. It is possible to argue this, but then rape loses any specific meaning at all. In this argument, all contradiction, all sense of change and development, are denied. It is a static and monolithic picture of society which itself belongs in a curious way to the same timeless and decontextualized zone which is the realm of pornography. Men and women alike are fixed frozen in the same depersonalized tableau of aggressor and victim. All the cultural explanations in the world cannot disguise the biological determinism that lies at the heart of such a theory. In the end it becomes a let-out for men rather than any real challenge. As Vic Seidler says:

> In a strange way the idea [that all men are rapists] can leave many men untouched as they accept this judgement of themselves intellectually. They can credit themselves with supporting the women's movement while not really having to challenge themselves.[9]

Violence as innate aggression

Our biology is still, of course, most commonly regarded as the determinant of sexual violence. Male sexuality is seen as an innate, aggressive 'drive' — a natural legacy of biological evolutionary imperatives of our descent from animality. Culture and environment may be given some credit, but the image of the 'naked ape' still lies at the heart of bourgeois sexual morality. These assumptions about sexual differences between men and women have an ancient lineage, but they were given an important secular and scientific backing in the evolutionary theories of Charles Darwin.

Darwin's study of natural selection in the plant and animal world convinced him that women's evolutionary role was to restrain the animal urges of men (which tended perpetually to threaten human progress towards civilization) and re-channel them into family life. This gave a scientific rationale for the double standard of female chastity and male philandering so characteristic of nineteenth-century bourgeois morality. This model of male urgency and female receptivity still persists despite a wider acceptance of women's own sexual needs and pleasures, and the boundary between rape and mutual sexual activity remains blurred because of it.

The idea of natural male aggression has earlier roots also in the seventeenth century philosophy of Thomas Hobbes. He portrayed man as violent, essentially individualistic and competitive in the selfish pursuit of his objectives. Elizabeth Wilson has pointed out that what Hobbes philosophized as nature was in fact more a description of a particular society in transition from feudalism to mercantile capitalism, and that the violence and aggression Hobbes saw was both a product of and a justification for the morality of the times.[10]

139

Hobbes's pessimistic view of life as 'nasty, brutish and short', and of self-interest as the guiding human motivation, has always been the philosophic base for right-wing economic liberalism. More recently it has also provided the basis for the social and moral onslaught of the new right, especially in the USA. Barbara Ehrenreich has produced a fascinating analysis of what she describes as the 'flight from commitment' in the changing roles and styles of men in American society since the 1950s.[11] She shows how the new 'moral majority' have mobilized as much against these changes in men as against the achievements of feminism. It is in precisely Hobbesian and Darwinian terms that the new right issue warnings about the social consequences of a mass collapse of gender roles. Ehrenreich quotes George Gilder, a leading new right activist and writer: 'The crucial process of civilization is the subordination of male sexual impulses and psychology . . .'[12] Gilder argues that men's nature must be controlled and channelled by women as dependent wives into the socially useful breadwinning role. The single man who fails to marry and take on this role should be regarded not just as selfish or immature but as positively criminal:

> The single man in general is disposed to criminality, drugs and violence.
> He is irresponsible about debts, alcoholic, accident-prone, and venereally
> diseased. Unless he can marry, he is often destined to a Hobbesian life —
> solitary, poor, nasty, brutish and short. [13]

It is not hard to see why the neo-Hobbesian discipline of 'socio-biology' has drawn support from the right in its efforts to reassert the leading role of genetic and biological imperatives in gender behaviour. Much of the scientific evidence used and the conclusions drawn have been shown to be dubious to say the least. The conclusions we can usefully draw for human behaviour from observation of captive sticklebacks seems distinctly limited, as Elizabeth Wilson has pointed out. Yet it is this kind of experimentation which makes up Konrad Lorenz's famous *On Aggression,* often quoted as evidence of man's innate aggressive tendencies.[14]

In the end what matters is not that, scientifically, most of these ideas don't bear much scrutiny, but that they have filtered down into commonsense notions which shape the way men and women interpret their own actions and feelings. Elizabeth Wilson says:

> Biology becomes a giant moral let-out. Such arguments are popular
> because they pander to our inertia. After all, to change one's behaviour
> involves pain and effort. It's much easier to pretend to be a baboon.[15]

And it is, of course, as a kind of human baboon or 'naked ape', unable for a moment to contain his 'urges', that the rapist or batterer is generally portrayed in the popular press and, with monotonous regularity, in the pronouncements of learned judges.

Violence as a response to the environment

Conservative ideas of innate aggression have often been opposed by the left, marxist and social democratic alike, with an argument that violence and aggression are primarily responses to an objectively threatening and brutalizing environment. It has clearly been a progressive and optimistic argument in that it suggests that change is possible and achievable. But Marxism's tendency to reduce social problems to economics has, at its crudest, spawned absurdities like the Socialist Workers Party's initial analysis, in their weekly paper, of the Peter Sutcliffe 'Yorkshire Ripper' murders as a product of unemployment. [16]

Even on a more sophisticated level, the sociological analysis of cultural and environmental causality, on which post-war reform has been based in this country and other western democracies, has been severely limited by its basic commitment to gender as biologically given and unproblematic. Sociologists and radical criminologists have rightly warned against being stampeded by moral panics into assuming that violence, including sexual violence, is running out of control. Difficulties of comparison with other periods, and changing fashions in reporting, make any evidence inconclusive, but it may be the case that violence between individuals is actually less common now than in the late nineteenth century. Mass education, some redistribution of wealth, better housing, health services, divorce reform and political enfranchisement have all clearly contributed to the transition from the society of Zola's *Germinal*, from the murky and dangerous London of Dickens and Mayhew, and from Sinclair's brutal Chicago.

But projects of social reform in England, the USA and Europe have been closely wedded to the notion of the family as a locus of private relations lying, apparently, outside the scope of political intervention. Whatever the origins of this separation of 'public' and 'private' — generally ascribed to the development of capitalist wage labour, or to the penetration among the working class of the bourgeois model of family life — this division is increasingly ideological rather than actual. The state has intervened politically in ways that impinge on every aspect of personal relationships and the family — from the establishment of family planning clinics to old age pensions, taking in divorce reform and social security, the growth or reduction of nursery places, and the power of the social services to remove children from parents. But still these interventions have been presented as necessary but limited incursions on to territory properly belonging to the individual or the private family. This enduring vision of the family as a private 'haven in a heartless world', the place, within a programme of social reform, where children grow 'straight and tall' is precisely the cause of the invisibility of violence against women — and against gay men. The idea that male aggression and violence are products of a brutalizing environment and will disappear with the advent of ameliorative social reform has been entirely undermined by this commitment to the family as unproblematic and naturalistic, even though the family is the place where gender characteristics are first acquired, then fostered and reproduced.

Violence as learnt activity

In the late 1960s the sociological and political consensus on the family began to come under attack from various quarters, including that of R. D. Laing and the anti-psychiatrists, and that of resurgent feminism. Since then the concept of 'socialization' has come to be used extensively to analyse the process of gender acquisition. The great value of this work has been in its ability to break from notions of gender as given, and to examine how gender characteristics which reflect social norms are learnt. Studies have shown how children are influenced by the idealist representation of family values in children's books, school textbooks, and other cultural imagery. These ideas are reinforced by gender-differentiated practice in child care and education, by the dominant representation in public imagery of a naturalistic gender division of labour, and by peer group pressure. There has been relatively little specific study of the formation of masculinity within this perspective, although Andrew Tolson's work shows clearly how decisive the influence of work and work expectations is on men and boys.[17]

But violence is not just learnt as male activity. It is part of what actually shapes the contours of masculinity. Vic Seidler describes how violence becomes encoded with boys' bodily stances:

> As boys, we have to be constantly on the alert to either confront or avoid physical violence. We have to be ready to defend ourselves. We are constantly on our guard. This builds tension and anxiety into the very organization of our bodies. You get so used to living with it it comes to feel normal. Masculinity is never something we can feel at ease with. It is always something we have to be ready to prove and defend.[18]

The coercive nature of this process must be emphasised. It is not optional — all boys in our society have to go through it to some degree. Julian Wood's research on boys suggests that the traditional assumptions of characteristics of masculinity are widely and deeply ingrained at an early age.[19] Yet not all boys fall so clearly into these patterns. Some find themselves, as young gay men increasingly do, resisting this socialization and the assumptions on which it is based. The fact that some do resist this process, for reasons that are not always clear, throws up one of the difficulties with socialization theory — its implicit functionalism.

The mechanics of socialization presuppose the influence of a body of predetermined ideas and roles which equip the subject to take a particular functional position in society. But how are these roles and functions determined? Traditional sociology has suggested that they have evolved as a contribution to the harmonious workings of society, but this view has merely served to obscure and conceal the existence of conflict, as I have already argued.

Proponents of the 'male supremacy' thesis might argue that male socialization serves men's own interests. Men have certainly come to hold and defend power as men in society, even when their class or racial positions renders them relatively powerless, but men seem increasingly to be reaching the conclusion that power is often wielded at considerable expense to their own humanity. This does not necessarily always include a recognition of how women are oppressed in this power relationship. It is a contradiction which Barbara Ehrenreich has emphasized when she argues that much of the shift in male sex roles in the USA has been caused less by feminism than by men seeking to shrug off self-oppressing aspects of traditional male roles.

Marxists have traditionally held the view that gender socialization is demanded by the needs of capital, and there is considerable evidence to support this view. Gender divisions, particularly the gender division of labour, have become deeply embedded within capitalist ideology and the economic and social policies of capitalist nations. The family, and familial ideology, has in certain senses been extremely efficient at reproducing class and gender relations, servicing and reproducing a workforce, and at organizing and maximizing consumption. Andrew Tolson's work, as mentioned, supports the view that the demands of capitalist production are deeply influential on the formation of masculinity.

Nevertheless, there are many aspects of sexual divisions which are hardly inherent in the logic of capitalism. Even though it has been recognized that sexual divisions in the working class have weakened its ability to mount a resistance to capitalism, masculinity has also been crucial to the traditions of this resistance. Men's propensity for violence is not just against women but also in areas such as street violence, football hooliganism, and the 'problem of youth' (really the problem of *male* youth); these forms of violence can specifically be seen as positively dysfunctional for the capitalist state.

Michele Barrett has pointed out that socialization theory also has problems in explaining and incorporating the variations of sexual practice because its main mechanism is seen as social pressure to conform.[20] Studies of sexual behaviour from the famous Kinsey Institute reports of 1948 and 1953 up to more recent work, such as that of Shere Hite, have suggested that surprisingly little conformity in sexual practice actually exists beneath apparent conformity to gender expectations.[21]

In the Hite report on male sexuality large numbers of men described practices and feelings which it would be extremely difficult to encompass within a unitary notion of male sexuality based on potency, unemotionality, predatory desire, dominance and control. If we are to see men as functionally socialized into roles as workers, breadwinners, soldiers, power wielders, how are we to explain the widespread occurrence of homosexual practice (distinct here from homosexual identity), male masochism, and a whole range of practices which fall outside of the pattern generally associated with proper male socialization?

At the same time, it is also true that the majority of men interviewed listed most of these attributes as essential to their ideas of being a proper man. They regarded intercourse as still the central and most important part of sex (even though, for many it was not the most pleasurable) and felt that they did not have sex often enough. These comments are fairly typical:

> I have to take to bed as many women I can, as often as I can, the more often the better, to be a real man.

> I am ashamed to tell you how often I have intercourse, it is so infrequent.

> Of late the frequency is rare, my wife does not have the drive I have.[22]

It appears that men still absorb the accepted ideas of what sex is supposed to be, even if it does not necessarily correspond to their own experiences and their own practices; so it would be wrong to suggest a clear break between gender socialization and sexual practice. There are nevertheless discontinuities which I believe are important and which have perhaps widened as personal relationships and sexuality have become more and more a matter of public interest and enquiry. What we are seeing may be partly a variation among men reflecting uneven shifts and changes in sexual attitudes in the face of feminism and the 'sexual revolution'. More than that there seems to be a tension within masculinity itself — a tension between the compulsive and regimenting demands of masculine socialization and the desire to express a variety of needs and emotions which may run counter to this socialization, and often have little intrinsically to do with sex at all. As Andy Metcalf has put it:

> Wanting to have sex a lot, feeling a great need for it, is often quite tied up with misery. There's no direct link between feeling sexy, feeling erotic, having desire for someone else, and wanting sex . . . I think sex is a vehicle for many needs and feelings; making things better when you're feeling tense, anxious; feeling out of contact with somebody and out of contact with yourself. It's the easiest way to connect to somebody and to yourself.[23]

This is not in itself gender specific. Women too learn to channel a variety of non-erotic needs and feelings into sex. But for men it becomes heavily charged because of the emotional illiteracy which is part and parcel of male socialization. So often sex then becomes a bottleneck of pent-up and misdirected yearnings, frustrations and anger. The pressure of this mass of undigested and unexpressed emotion which clusters around sexuality is perhaps what gives the myth of male urgency its subjective power for men. Relationships with women are really the only socially permitted area for uncircumscribed expression of male emotion and vulnerability, in so far as this is permitted at all. But although there is now more general public acceptance of the idea that men should be able to express emotion more openly, the communication of this emotion in relationships with women can become a minefield where there is little shared language of emotionality and little subjective experience in common.

Despite legislative regulation of sexuality, bourgeois ideology defines the act of sex as essentially a private one, where two people meet in 'free exchange', casting off the world with their clothes and becoming anonymous, lost in oneness with their partners. In fact, nothing could be further from the truth. Angela Carter remarks:

> No bed, however unexpected, no matter how apparently gratuitous, is free from the de-universalizing effect of real life. We do not go to bed in simple pairs; even if we choose not to refer to them, we still drag there with us the cultural impedimenta of our social class, our parents' lives, our bank balance, our sexual and emotional expectations, our whole biographies — all the bits and pieces of our unique existences. [24]

Still it is not only the social, economic, or even physical power inequality between women and men which is the problem. Social and physical power gives men license to resolve conflict and contradiction by force, but it is not in itself the root of this violence. More fundamentally, it is the process of gender construction which creates in men a deeply ambivalent feeling towards women. Nancy Friday subtitled her collection of men's sexual fantasies 'The Triumph of Love Over Rage'. This might be considered as an unreasonably optimistic conclusion to have reached, but it does express the ambivalence of men's feelings. To see what this ambivalence is and how it arises I feel we can usefully look to more recent explorations in psychoanalysis and the physical construction of gender.

Illusions of independence

Feminists and socialists have approached psychoanalysis in recent years in two ways. First, in a personal way, as an attempt to grapple with conflicts in our own lives, as apparently intractable patterns of feeling which have been rejected intellectually seem to resurface again and again. Secondly, in an attempt to understand the place these feelings have in the construction of gender. As a project it has not been without its problems. Michele Barrett has usefully discussed the difficulties of reconciling psychoanalysis and materialism.[25] She points out the applicability and the historical specificity demanded by a materialist approach, and how it occupies a cloudy zone between the biological and the social, where any kind of synthesis with feminism or Marxism is highly problematic.

While accepting these serious limitations, I want to suggest that the psychoanalytic framework can still shed some useful light on how the psychosocial construction of masculinity in a capitalist society predisposes men towards sexual violence.

In Freud's account of a boy's sexual development, emotional rejection of the mother is an essential stage in the proper resolution of the Oedipal conflict through which heterosexuality is developed. The consequences of this rejection are not examined as a potential problem except in so far as a failure to reject may result in fixation at a stage of homosexual inclination. Nancy Chodorow has argued that Freud undervalued the importance of the mother/daughter relationship and the crucial role it has in transmitting the qualities of nurturing, which reproduce the social aspects of mothering and other activities which society associates with mothering.[26] I want to suggest that the rejection of the mother by the son under the social pressures which draw him towards the external world of the father (or of men, whether the father is actually present or not) has also been given too little consideration. We do not have to see this process as universal or transhistorical. Anthropologists have found enough evidence from other cultures to suggest that this particular pattern of psychic development is not inevitable. It is the consequence of socially defined gender expectations, and it is in turn the structure through which expectations are reproduced. The tensions within masculinity itself, to which I have referred above, arise because economic and political changes have allowed the possibility of these definitions and expectations to be questioned. Yet the basic problem continues, even if in our society it is not formally marked by the rituals and ceremonials of initiation.

This rejection of the mother, and the relationship of nurturance which binds mother and son together, is in itself a violent and dehumanizing process because it involves an internal rejection and suppression of the son's own potential qualities of nurturing, in favour of the coercive but compensatory attributes held out to him as his reward for achieving malehood. Part of this process is the devaluation in the son's eyes of the gender to whom those rejected qualities are assigned. 'Big boys don't cry' will be drummed into him through his early ears as a constant reminder of his internal struggles: suppression of the language of emotional expression is an inevitable consequence, as Peter Bradbury describes:

> How do we learn in the first place to speak a language of domination?
> There are many reasons, some of which can be seen if we look at what

145

happens as we go from birth to adulthood. The language we speak to our mothers moves in that time from the most intimate and sensual — the shared utterances of skin and first speech — to the tyrannical, the instrumental and the dismissive. At some time between birth and say 20, we learn to recognize our mothers as servant, nurse, giver of birth — that is, as socially inferior beings from whom, by a process we learn to ignore or disparage, we have somehow sprung. In this conflict between recognition and denial we lose the language of intimacy and the knowledge of our mothers we must have once have had. The reality of the woman who gave us birth and brought us up is reduced in our perceptions to its physicality.[27]

When in adolescence boys begin to re-attach to girls as their 'object-choice', a pattern has been established which makes it difficult to perceive women in any other than an instrumental way. Yet this way of seeing women becomes deeply contradictory. While men expect the service they receive from their mothers, and casually despise women for the inferior status this expectation consigns them to, they find that women now possess unexpected powers of sexual 'attraction'. Women are now also seen to possess arcane skills of emotional intensity and expression — all the feelings men have learnt to deny but which they now look at with some envy. Men start to discover in women an unsettling power which contradicts and undermines their own more obvious social and physical power.

Wendy Holloway has observed how the re-attachment of unconscious feelings about mothers on to women lovers creates a dependence/independence dilemma for heterosexual men.[28] Because men are brought up to associate being a man with qualities of independence this dilemma is often resolved by displacing feelings of dependency on to women. Men's vulnerability is thus shielded and the illusion of masculine independence preserved. Holloway goes on to argue that men's fear of dependence and their fear of women's sexuality is associated with anxieties about potential engulfment in unconscious desires for the totality of the mother/child relationship. In this light it is also possible to see that the power women often feel men have in relationship stems in part from men's defensive reaction to these anxieties rather than existing as something innate.

Men nevertheless continue to seek out these dependency relationships, often quite unaware of who is really dependent on whom. Social definitions of women as dependent mean that women too will very often find themselves colluding in this mutual self-deception. But if men's dependence and their emotional weakness within a relationship is exposed and challenged they may well perceive it as a deep threat to their identity and their security. All men's worst fears about themselves and all the ambivalent feelings they have towards women can emerge at these moments, and they may react with defensive hostility or outright violence. It is as though men attempt to exercise, in the only way they know how — by force — the fear of accepting what they are and what they may have lost in the process of becoming what they are.

Within the traditional power structures of the patriarchal family, the areas of power and control men exercise could veil the reality of men's unconscious ambivalence towards women; direct physical control was legitimate and socially acceptable. Social changes such as women's mass entry into the labour market, male unemployment and de-skilling, and the increasing state management of family life, have all tended to undermine the material basis for men's power without fundamentally altering the familial ideological structures within which masculinity is constructed. Faced with this, men may be increasingly inclined to view women as 'too powerful' or dominating. Sexual autonomy or independence shown by women strikes at the heart of this male insecurity and fuels the rage which battles with love.

Amanda Spake, an American journalist, writes about the man who raped and mutilated Mary Bell Vincent:

> What Lawrence Singleton did was to act out a profound, almost mythic rage, an angry fear, a peculiarly male emotion. On that September day, Singleton decided to strike — in his view strike back — at what he perceived to be female domination of his life, his sexuality, his psyche. His acts were sadistic, but his rage is generic.[29]

If we look at the more extreme instances of male violence against women we often expect to find psychopaths and sadists. In reality, research into domestic violence and rape suggests that batterers and rapists are not necessarily specially disturbed, come from all walks of life, and in most respects are ordinary men. What does come out clearly in the Dobash pioneering work, for example, is that the wider the gulf between a man's notion of proper masculine character and behaviour and his own perception of himself, the more likely he is to be violent.[30] The more ill-equipped to deal with these contradictions emotionally, the more likely he will react to any challenge by lashing out. It is a common feature that men become almost amnesiac about violent incidents, as if to admit or recognize them is to see their tenuous security undermined even further. To admit that all they have is physical power is in real terms a confession of absolute weakness.

Similarly, an American study of the psychology of 500 convicted rapists found that few were in any way psychopathic, but that the majority did exhibit certain common characteristics:

> [the rapist] is not much in touch with his own needs and feelings, and except for anger his emotional life seems impoverished . . . anxiety and restless dissatisfaction with the existing circumstances of his life and/or with unfulfilled emotional need resulting from a feeling of powerlessness. He feels menaced by his situation and helpless to remedy the situation . . . At the root of all this are deep-seated doubts about his adequacy and competence as a person.[31]

This strikes me as not too unfair a description of the end product of 'normal' masculinity rather than anything unusual or extraordinary. While not all men are overtly violent or coercive towards women, the potential violence within male sexuality is unlikely to disappear in any general and fundamental way as long as men continue to be constructed as emotional illiterates with self-deluding ideas of independence and deep ambivalence between love and fear, attraction and antagonism, towards women.

Where do we go from here?

I have tried to argue that sexual violence is not innate in men in any biological sense, and that it cannot be seen simply as a means of defending men's own power and privilege. It is not a product of capitalism but the consequence of a form of gender construction which is very deeply embedded within capitalist social relations. Where does this leave us — particularly as men? It is not enough to conclude on a note of millenial pessimism that nothing will change till we change the whole world. That's another let-out. We are not cyphers, and we make choices for which we are responsible and should be held responsible.

This is not the place to argue the pros and cons of greater legal sanctions against violent men or to discuss the shortcomings of the penal system. Women need legal protection, safe transport, housing and income opportunities which guarantee their independence. Legal, political, or educational programmes which strengthen women's power to oppose violence should be supported.

How men will change is rather a different question. Men changing their own behaviour is an important starting point, but individual change has only a marginal effect whilst all the material and ideological structures of society are geared towards the reproduction of a masculinity which so often relies on violence to resolve emotional crises or protect fragile egos. One development in collective action by men in the USA which has excited considerable interest in England is counselling for violent men. The American pioneer group in this field is EMERGE. Based in Boston, EMERGE was set up in 1977 with the co-operation of the women's shelter (refuge) network, and the collective of men, including ex-batterers, who run it provide counselling, community education, and training for other agencies. An (as yet) unpublished document puts the position of the collective:

> we are all committed to the principle that serious attack on women abuse must include an equalizing of power relationships between men and women, on a personal as well as a social level. It must also include a challenge to some widely-held stereotypes about what is and what is not appropriate 'male' behaviour.[32]

EMERGE recognize that the initial motivation of many men who come to them for counselling is to re-establish a relationship which has broken down, or to encourage the return of a woman who has left them. Critics of services like EMERGE argue that this rehabilitative emphasis, and its work with men as individuals, fails to tackle the institutional structures which give men social power and which shape the contours of masculinity itself.

It remains to be seen whether projects of this kind will develop in the English context. Clearly there are a great many difficulties and contradictions. But the real potential which does exist in the development of programmes like EMERGE seems to lie not just in the individual counselling of violent men or in the public education, but in the very contradictions such work raises.

To push at and beyond the limitations of individual change in men is to bring us right up against the fundamental construction of masculinity, the sexual division of child rearing which reproduces gender, the employment structures which maintain this division, and the political system which defines our aspirations towards equality. It is also a means to ending oppressive and violent sexuality.

Notes

1. Rosalind Coward, 'Pornography: Two Opposing Feminist Viewpoints', *Spare Rib*, Issue 119, June 1982.

2. Jan Pahl, 'Patterns of money management within marriage', *Journal of Social Policy*, Vol. 9, Part 3, 1980.

3. Susan Brownmiller, *Against our Will: Men, Women and Rape*, London: Penguin, 1977.

4. Peggy Reeves Sanday, 'The Sociocultural Context of Rape — A Cross-Cultural Study', *Journal of Social Issues*, Vol. 37, no. 4, 1980.

5. Julia & Herman Schwendinger, 'Rape, Sexual Inequality and Levels of Violence', *Crime and Social Justice*, No. 16, 1981.

6. See for example Deirdre English, 'The Politics of Porn: Can Feminists Walk the Line?', *Mother Jones*, Vol. 5, No. 3, April 1980, and Paula Webster, 'Pornography and Pleasure', *Heresies*, Vol. 3, No. 4, Issue 12, 1981.

7. See for example Nancy Friday, *Men in Love: Men's Sexual Fantasies*, London: Arrow Books, 1980.

8. Andrea Dworkin, *Pornography: Men Possessing Women*, London: The Women's Press, 1981.

9. Vic Seidler, 'Raging Bull', *Achilles Heel*, No. 5, p. 8, 1980.

10. Elizabeth Wilson, *What is to be Done about Violence Against Women?*, London: Penguin, 1983, pp. 19-23.

11. Barbara Ehrenreich, *The Hearts of Men: American Dreams and the Flight from Commitment'*, London: Pluto Press, 1983.

12. George Gilder, *Sexual Suicide*, New York: Quadrangle, 1973, p. 23.

13. George Gilder, *Naked Nomads,* New York: Times Books, 1974, p. 10.

14. Konrad Lorenz, *On Aggression*, New York: Bantam, 1969.

15. Elizabeth Wilson, *Violence against Women*, p. 27.

16. *Socialist Worker*.

17. Andrew Tolson, *The Limits of Masculinity*, London: Tavistock, 1977.

18. Vic Seidler, 'Raging Bull' in *Achilles Heel*, p. 9.

19. Julian Wood, 'Boys will be Boys', *New Socialist*, No. 5, May/June 1982.

20. Michele Barrett, *Women's Oppression Today: Problems in Marxist Feminist Analysis*, London: Verso 1980. pp. 63-4.

21. A.C. Kinsey et al., *Sexual Behaviour in the Human Male*, W.B. Saunders, 1948 and *Sexual Behaviour in the Human Female*, Philadelphia: W.B. Saunders, 1953. Shere Hite, *The Hite Report*, and *The Hite Report on Male Sexuality* London: MacDonald, 1981.

22. Shere Hite, *The Hite Report*, pp. 378-81.

23. Andy Metcalf and Paul Morrison, 'Motorway Conversations: Sex in Long-Term Relationships', *Achilles Heel*, No. 6, p. 20, 1982.

24. Angela Carter, *The Sadeian Woman*, London: Virago, 1979, p. 9.

25. Michele Barrett, *Women's Oppression Today*, pp. 58-61.

26. Nancy Chodorow, *The Reproduction of Mothering*, Berkeley: University of California Press, 1979.

27. Peter Bradbury, 'Sexuality and Male Violence', *Achilles Heel*, No. 5, p. 23, 1981.

28. Wendy Holloway, 'Heterosexual Sex: Power and the Desire for the Other' in Sue Cartledge and Joanna Ryan (Eds) *Sex and Love*, London: The Women's Press, 1983, pp. 124-40.

29. Amanda Spake, 'The End of the Road: Analysing a Sex Crime', *Mother Jones*, Vol. 5, No. 3, April 1980.

30. R. Emerson Dobash and Russell Dobash, *Violence Against Wives*, London: Open Books, 1980.

31. A. Nicholas Groth, and H. Jean Birnbaum, *Men Who Rape: The Psychology of the Offender*, New York: Plenum Press, 1979.

32. Emerge Inc., *Organising and Implementing Services for Men who Batter*, unpublished.

7. Women, Property and Rape
Lorenne Clark and Debra Lewis

We began this book by probing the contradictions in public attitudes towards rape, contradictions which are also present in the theory and practice of the law. During the course of our study, we found ourselves confronted with further questions about the treatment and definition of rape in our society. The one clear and absolutely striking pattern revealed by our research, was the extent to which reported rapes are acknowledged to be "real" only if they involve certain types of victims. As the data clearly shows, the ultimate disposition of a rape report — whether or not it will lead to a charge and proceed to further phases of the criminal justice system — is determined almost entirely by the character and behaviour of the reporting rape victim. Nevertheless, it was clear to us, and is often, we believe, clear to the police as well, that rapes reported by women who do not conform to stereotypes of "respectability" are nonetheless genuine rapes. Obviously, some explanation of this contradiction is required. We need a theoretical framework which explains both the social causes of rape, and the social function of rape laws. Why does rape happen, and what purpose is served by rape laws which offer protection only to a restricted segment of the female population? It is our belief that the explanation for both of these questions lies in the history of women's status as a form of private property.

Women as forms of private property

From its beginnings in Ancient Greece, western political and legal theory has rested on two main assumptions. The first is the assumption that individuals have a right to own private property and that inequality in the distribution of such property can be traced to natural differences between men. Thus, a fundamental cornerstone of western liberal democracy is the belief that private property and inequality in its distribution are justified. The second is the assumption that men are naturally superior to women and that this inequality can be traced to natural differences between the sexes.[1] Thus, an equally fundamental cornerstone of western liberal democracy is the belief that legal, social and economic inequality between men and women is also justified. The first assumption laid the basis for a class society characterized by inequality between individuals and, ultimately, between classes of individuals. Those who held the greatest share of private wealth were held to be more "noble", "magnanimous", "just", or "wise", and later, more "rational" and "industrious" than those who did not own property. The second assumption laid the basis for a sexist society characterized by inequality between the sexes. The specific form that this inequality took made women the objects rather than the subjects of property rights: women were among the forms of private property owned and controlled by individual men. This inequality in the distribution of property rights was considered to be justified by differences between males and females. Those attributed with such rights were held to be stronger, more

Lorenne Clark and Debra Lewis: 'Women, Property and Rape' from *RAPE: THE PRICE OF COERCIVE SEXUALITY* (Women's Educational Press, Toronto, 1977), pp. 111-124.

able, rational, and capable of realizing the loftier aspirations of the human spirit. Those denied such rights were held to be weaker, less able, emotional rather than rational, and incapable of rising above the demands of necessity imposed on them because of their unique capacity to bear children.

The law reflected these two assumptions, and institutionalized them within the social, legal and economic structure. The legal system confirmed, supported and perpetuated unequal relationships between individual men, and between sexes. Women simply were not considered to be "persons" under the law. They could not own property; they were denied access to the productive labour market; and, within marriage, they and their children were the property of their husbands. Their economic status was determined by that of their father or husband, and their unique status as women within this system was determined by their sexual and reproductive capacities.

An explanation of the origins of private property and of the nature and functioning of class society is a task well beyond the scope of this book. However, it is impossible to understand the problem of rape without understanding the historical evolution and development of the legal offence of rape, and it is impossible to do this without understanding the historical position of women. How is it, then, that women became forms of private property, and how did their transformation affect the development of laws against rape?

The origin of sexual and reproductive property

The emergence of a system of private property under individual ownership brought with it the need for a mechanism which could transfer accumulated private property from one generation to another. In order to keep assets intact across generations, determinate future individuals had to be identifiable as the future owners of those assets. Property was held by individual families, in which sole authority for the present and future disposition of property rested with the father. Families required offspring in order to preserve the family line, and preservation of lineage was itself necessary to keep family property intact over time. Since the father of the family was the legally entitled owner of its property, it was the father who needed an heir on whom to devolve the family assets, and the only available mechanism for determining future property rights was biological inheritance.

As is well known, a system of private property under individual ownership necessitated ownership of the means and products of production by the propertied classes. But as is much less well known or appreciated, it also required control of the means and products of reproduction, in order to ensure that there would be determinate heirs to function as the designatable future owners of individually-held accumulations of private property. Under this system of property distribution, in which property moved through family and blood lines, the primary function of the legal and social system was to provide adequate institutions and practices designed to preserve both blood lines and private property.

A system of biological inheritance could, however, work properly only if the family's biological heirs were clearly and certainly identifiable. And since the personality of the family was vested in the husband alone,[2] this meant that certainty of paternity was necessary if biological inheritance was to be an adequate institution for the preservation of family property across generations. Certainty of paternity was, therefore, a necessary feature of this system of property disposition, and certainty of paternity was possible only if the male property owner had exclusive access to one (or more) women. The husband had to be protected in his right of exclusive sexual access and in his right to control over the products of reproduction, and so he became the owner of his wife and children.

Ownership is simply the most efficient form of control. "Ownership" is nothing more than a set of legal rights and duties which ensures the most effective control over some form of property, whether it be a TV set, land holdings, stocks and bonds, or wives and children. Typically, this set of rights includes the right to exclusive use and disposition of the property in question, and it imposes a duty on others to return any property to the lawful owner which is his. The set of legal rights and duties articulating the structure of relations between the sexes, designed to ensure to male "heads of households" exclusive sexual access to the women they married and exclusive rights to the children they produced (but only, of course, where certainty of paternity was secure), amounted to a set of legal relations which gave the husbands property rights in the wife and children. Husbands had rights to their wives' sexual and reproductive capacities, were under no obligation to maintain any minimum standard of care for their families, and had an absolute right to dispose of any family property as they saw fit, regardless of the needs of their wives and children.[3] But wives, on their part, had a duty to obey and submit to their husbands, were legally prohibited from leaving them, and were liable to serious penalties for adultery. Children were also under an obligation to obey their father — at least until they reached the age of majority — and had no legal claim on family property independent of his will. Thus, the conversion of women and children into forms of private property resulted from the evolution of social and legal institutions designed to ensure effective control to men over the certainty of their future offspring, and thereby to fulfill the need for a settled principle of inheritance which could preserve property through time.

Marriage itself was one of the institutions designed to facilitate the transference of property.[4] Chief among the rights it gave to the husband was an absolute right to exclusive sexual access to his wife, and an absolute right to exclusive disposition of family property. It denied the wife any right to sexual or reproductive autonomy vis-à-vis her husband; it also denied her any right to share in the ownership (and hence, control and future disposition) of family property, regardless of the fact that she may well have made, and almost certainly did make, as much of a contribution to any increase in these holdings as he did.[5] The husband's rights with regard to his wife and the family property, together with her lack of rights with respect to family property and her duties to her husband, articulated a legal state between them in which the wife was a form of private property exclusively under the ownership and control of her husband. And husbands were expected to exercise both authority and control, frequently being penalized when or if they failed to do so.[6]

Thus it was that women became forms of private property. And thus it was too that the sexual and reproductive capacities of women became the sole qualities which gave women value. The function of a wife was to have babies and to provide another pair of hands for work that had to be done.[7] A barren wife was worthless, but a woman who could produce an heir was guaranteed a certain amount of security and respect. Even today, many women feel that they have an obligation to provide their husbands with a son; this accomplishment both validates their existence and solidifies their status as "good wives".

Rape as an offence against property

Parallel to marriage law, rape law developed as another form of social control designed to regulate the orderly transfer of property. Under Anglo-Saxon law, rape, along with most other offences, was punished by orders to pay compensation and reparation. If a woman was raped, a sum was paid to either her husband or father, depending on who still exercised rights of ownership over her, and the exact amount of compensation depended on the woman's economic position and her desirability as an object of an exclusive sexual relationship. The sum was not paid to the woman herself; it was paid to her father or husband because he was the person who was regarded as having been wronged by the act.

Rape is simply theft of sexual property under the ownership of someone other than the rapist. When women are forms of private property, owned by fathers or husbands, with a value determined by their sexual and reproductive capacities, rape is an act of theft and trespass against the legal owner of the sexual property (that is, the woman) in question. In having intercourse with a woman who does not belong to him, a man is guilty of trespassing on the property of whoever does own her, and of stealing access to female sexuality to which he has no legal right. From the beginning, rape was perceived as an offence against property, not as an offence against the person on whom the act was perpetrated, and it has not lost the shrouds of these historical origins.

The fact that rape was originally perceived as an offence against one form of property owned by men, and that it has developed historically and legally within this conceptual framework, had several important consequences. First, just as with any other property offence, the punishment had to fit the crime. The punishment corresponded to the value of the goods stolen, and to the amount of damage done in the trespass: the more "valuable" the rape victim, and the more damage done to her property value, the harsher the penalty. And "value", where a woman was concerned, depended strictly upon her economic status as determined by her father or husband, and her desirability as an object of an exclusive sexual relationship.

Thus, the economic position of the rape victim, and her status as a desirable, marriageable property, were the two features assessed in determining the extent of punishment to be meted out to the rape offender. Under Anglo-Saxon law, the higher the economic or social position of the woman's husband or father, the higher the fee exacted from the rapist. And that rule of thumb continued well past the point at which Anglo-Saxon law was superseded by a more sophisticated legal system which moved beyond simple reparation and compensation for offences. The punishment of rape has never lost its connections with the economic status of the rape victim. The higher the socio-economic status of the victim, the greater the likelihood that she will be considered "credible", and granted her day in court. As we have already seen from the data presented, this is as true today as it was six hundred years ago. All that has changed is that the economic position of the victim's husband or father is no longer seen to be the sole measure of her economic worth. With women's greater participation in the productive labour force, some women have begun to earn an economic rating for themselves, and this rating is, as we have seen, reflected in the data presented.

But the relationship between a rape victim and her husband or father is, as we have also seen, by no means irrelevant to the question of whether or not she will be seen as a credible rape victim: those women who are most clearly dependent upon a male owner/protector will most readily be viewed as meriting protection from rape. And the reason for this lies in the popular belief that one of the major attributes of "real" rape is the subsequent diminution of the victim's value as a desirable marriage "partner". From the earliest times to the present, virgins have been considered "credible" rape victims, because the loss of virginity most drastically and obviously affects the social value women have as desirable objects of exclusive sexual access. When a woman's value consists in her sexual and reproductive capacities, and when the object of marriage is to gain access to the exclusive use of a woman's sexuality, virginity is, of course, a woman's greatest treasure. Loss of virginity (or, if married, loss of one's status as an object of guaranteed, exclusive sexual access) markedly affects a woman's property value. This is why the law has always favoured rape victims who are virgins under the ownership and protection of their fathers, or chaste wives under the ownership and protection of their husbands. The right of men to preserve valuable sexual property — either for their own use, or for the use of a husband, in which case the daughter's virginity was a great asset at the bargaining table — was one of the rights which rape laws were meant to protect. It is hardly surprising, therefore, that virgins and chaste wives are the most highly protected forms of sexual property within the system, and that these are the women which the law perceives as credible rape victims. In their endorsement of the idea that virginity and marital chastity are the primary features which give woman value — features which belong to women's husbands or fathers — contemporary rape laws reflect their historical origins. Rape laws were simply one of the devices designed to secure to men the ownership and control of those forms of property, and to provide a conceptual framework which would justify punishing men who violated the property rights of other men in this respect.

The development of our modern criminal offence of rape began in the Middle Ages as a specific response to the problem of bride capture. Under this system, marriages were frequently accomplished by means of abduction and rape.[8] Sexual intercourse with a woman had long been regarded as establishing a primary right to possession and, ultimately, to ownership through marriage with the woman in question. The legal articulation of an offence of rape was not meant to undermine the validity of this method of establishing a basis for marriage. Abduction and rape remained valid ways of establishing a legal and sanctified marital relationship; indeed, this practice is still followed in many communities, where marriage is often regarded as the only "honourable" course to be followed once a rape has occurred. But rape laws were designed to prevent legitimate transfers of property through marriages established this way.

155

Under the marriage laws of the time, any property which a woman owned, or to which she might become entitled upon marriage (such as a dowry), automatically became the property of her husband. Her rights to such property were, as they say in the legal trade, "extinguished" upon marriage, and for the most part they remained extinguished forever after, although in some few instances they "revived" on the death of her husband.[9] Understandably, fathers had a vested interest in preventing marriages between their daughters and men who had nothing to offer. Men of property with eligible daughters wanted to marry them off in the ways best calculated to secure and, if possible, increase their property holdings. They wanted their daughters to "marry well", and marriages were, at least among the propertied classes, business mergers rather than the wedding of kindred spirits.[10]

In order to prevent unscrupulous and upwardly-mobile men from acquiring rights to family property through abduction and rape, men of property developed rape laws. Rape did not nullify a marriage, but it did nullify the rights of the husband to his wife's property if the marriage was established by this means. Marriage and rape laws were twin mechanisms, designed to ensure that transfers of property would and could be accomplished only in accordance with the express wishes of a woman's father, or of whatever other male had authority over her. The primary function of rape laws, therefore, was to deny rights of ownership in property to men who were not acceptable to the families of the women in question, and who attempted to get around such familial disapproval by abduction and raping the daughter of the family. The secondary function of rape laws was to protect men in their ownership of daughters who were, because of their virginity, valuable properties in their own right. Thus, the social function of rape laws was the protection and preservation of patrimonial property, both in the form of real property (land), and in the form of desirable female sexual property (virgin daughters) .

Once rape laws had become effective in preventing unscrupulous men from gaining access to power and position by abducting and raping wealthy heiresses, their chief purpose became the protection of men in their ownership of desirable female sexual property. The only women rape laws were designed to protect were women of high socio-economic status and those who were highly desirable as objects of an exclusive sexual relationship. But since the offence was conceived as a wrong to the man entitled to rights of ownership over a woman, the law did not view her as the party injured by rape. She was, again as they say in the trade, merely a third-party "beneficiary" of the law. She was protected because the law sought to protect men in the ownership of such valuable women, and not because she herself had any right to autonomy — sexual or otherwise — which the law sought to protect. Rape was not perceived as a violation of the rights of women at all, and the present treatment of rape continues to reflect its historical roots. This is precisely why it is that dependent women, women living at home under the control of parents, or with a husband, are the rape victims the system most strongly supports. Independent women, on the other hand, are seen as quite literally having no right to complain of rape: since they cannot own themselves, and since rape is an offence against the owner of sexual property, such women are not viewed as having a legitimate complaint if they are raped. Instead, they are viewed as "vindictive" or "unreasonable", unless, of course, they sustained serious and preferably permanent physical damage.

156

If physical injury does occur, then the law is prepared to take these women seriously because the act can be seen as causing a net loss in their sexual attractiveness, and therefore in their value. In the absence of such disfigurement, however, rape victims who are independent of parental or matrimonial control are not thought to have anything to complain about. They have not suffered a significant loss in their potential to be desirable objects of exclusive sexual access, and no rights of ownership have been infringed. No ownership, no wrong.

In the application of rape laws as infringements of rights of ownership, the legal structure has simply extended the same rules of lawful appropriation to sexual as to other forms of private property. The only property which deserves the full protection of the law is that which is already owned, and the most severe punishments are reserved for offenders who infringe rights of ownership already established by someone else. If presently unowned property is at least potentially valuable, it deserves to be protected from wanton mutilation or destruction. But if an object has no perceivable value, either actual or potential, then no property rights can be violated, and no harm can be done. Only an object with an actual or potential value qualifies for the protection of the law. It makes little difference whether the object in question is a tree in the forest or a woman in the street.

Rape is treated as an offence against the person, as a direct harm to the woman attacked, only if it results in severe injury to the victim, and even then, an evaluation of the victim's "value" affects judgments made about the gravity of the offence. One is regarded as having suffered a harm only if one has lost possession of something valuable, and since a woman's value lies in her desirability as an object of an exclusive sexual relationship, she is not viewed as having suffered a harm if she has already lost that which gave her such a status. This is why a non-virgin is immediately suspect as a credible rape victim, even when she is injured by the attack; and physical injuries are themselves perceived as legitimating her complaint only if they lead to a demonstrable loss in her property value. The degree of physical harm suffered by the victim, and her prior and present value as sexual property, are among the major factors which determine her standing as a credible rape victim. But if she had little sexual value to begin with, and was not seriously injured by the attack, where is the harm in the rape?

The commoditization of female sexuality

However, there is more to the issue of sexual value than has so far been discussed. While it is obvious that loss of virginity is a major setback to women, given that it forever prevents them from being desirable as objects of an exclusive sexual relationship, this does not in itself explain why the law apparently refuses to protect women who are somewhat more "liberal" in the distribution of their sexuality. Why is it that certain types of rape victims are popularly viewed as women who "got what they deserved", "were asking for it", or, simply, as women who are not credible because of their "promisicuity" or "lewd and unchaste" behaviour? The simple explanation is that women who voluntarily give up that which makes them desirable as objects of an exclusive sexual relationship are seen as "common property", to be appropriated without penalty for the use, however temporary, of any man who desires their services. What this public attitude seems to entail is that the voluntary granting of sexual access outside the parameters of sanctified matrimony leads to the loss of sexual and physical autonomy. Once a woman parts with her one and only treasure, she never has the right to say no again.

But that would seem to imply that women have the right to sexual autonomy at least at some point in their lives. Up to the point at which virginity is irretrievably lost, a woman may say "yes" or "no" with some hope that her wishes will be honoured. It is, we believe, false to construe this as in any way constituting a woman's right to sexual autonomy. With the conversion of women into forms of private property, with a value determined by their sexuality, female sexuality ceased to be a quality over which women exercised rights of ownership. It became a quality held in trust by their fathers for their potential husbands, and thus, a quality of themselves which women also held in trust for their potential owner/husbands. From that time up to the present, women did not have rights of ownership over their own sexuality and reproductivity. The sexuality of women became a commodity to be traded on the marriage market, bargained and paid for in the marriage contract between father and prospective husband. This is the explanation for the legal qualification that a husband cannot rape his own wife. What a husband gets when he gets a wife is rights of ownership to her sexuality, and what this means is the right to use her sexuality whenever and however he pleases. Her wishes in the matter are simply irrelevant. Husbands have a legally protected right to the sexual services of their wives, and wives have a legal duty to honour the "conjugal rights" of their husbands. Women certainly do not have sexual autonomy within marriage, and any question of their "consent" to sexual relations is utterly without meaning in this context.

Prior to marriage, a woman's sexuality is a commodity to be held in trust for its lawful owner. Making a "free" use of one's sexuality is like making a "free" use of someone else's money. One can act autonomously only with things that belong to oneself. Things held in trust for others are surrounded with special duties which place the trustee under strict obligations for the care and maintenance of the assets in question, and also place the trustee under a strict duty to avoid unreasonable risks. If I hold money in trust for someone else, any act of mine which diminishes the assets held, other than those expenses necessarily incurred for its preservation and increase, is an act of theft. I am legally prohibited from using the assets to further my own interest, and must justify all actions involving the assets as being in the interest of the person for whom the trust is established. And so it is with female sexuality. Women are not regarded as being entitled to use their sexuality according to their own desires because their sexuality is not theirs to use for such purposes. Their duty is to preserve it in the best possible condition for the ultimate use and disposition of its rightful owner. Thus, women who behave in a sexually autonomous manner are stealing from those to whom their sexuality properly belongs, and are no more deserving of protection or redress than persons who are free spenders with other people's money. They are to be punished rather than protected.

Moreover, just as trustees are legally prohibited from taking unreasonable risks with the assets they hold, so women are expected to avoid taking any risks with their sexuality. Women who place themselves in "compromising" situations, who frequent "low" areas of the city or associate with "undesirables", are seen as taking risks with themselves which they ought not to take, and as being either reckless or negligent in the protection of that which they have a duty to preserve. Since the taking of unreasonable risks means that the victim contributes to the commission of the offence by assumption of the risk, she is regarded as being undeserving of redress in the event that the risk materializes. This is what lies behind the popular phrase: "she got what she deserved". Women who place their sexuality in jeopardy do not deserve protection because they are doing something which they ought not do in the first place; and if they are raped they deserve no redress, because they voluntarily incurred the risk. So the theory goes. Women who use their sexuality as they themselves desire, who appropriate to themselves an alleged right to sexual autonomy, are "outlaws" and "renegades". They are making free with a commodity which they have no right to dispense, and therefore they fall well beyond the definition of the "respectable" women who were meant to be the beneficiaries of rape laws. For in the end, "respectable" women are just women who agree to live by the rules of the society in which they find themselves, who regard themselves as wives and mothers, who accept their status as forms of private property and relinquish any claim to ownership rights in their own sexuality and reproductive ability. Women who refuse to accept these rules and limitations are viewed as relinquishing any right to be protected, and are thereby punished for making that choice.

The open territory victim

Refusing to abide by the rules is tantamount to accepting for oneself a status as "valueless", and entails that one can fairly be regarded as "common property", up for grabs by any man who wants sexual contact. As the data clearly shows, the law gives little protection to women who are judged to be "valueless", and what leads to that judgment is having broken free of parental or matrimonial control, and of having tried to be autonomous, sexually and otherwise. The law does not penalize men for appropriating what is regarded as abandoned or "common" sexual property any more than it penalizes them for appropriating other forms of abandoned or unowned property. So it is that "promiscuous" women, women who are "idle", "unemployed" or "on welfare", living "common law", "separated" or "divorced", "known frequenters of Yorkville", "drug users", "alcoholics", or "incorrigible", are all perceived as women who are not credible rape victims, for they have all, by their behaviour, placed themselves at risk and hence forfeited any right to either protection or redress. And these "valueless" women are real persons; they are the women we described in [chapter 5] as the "women who can't be raped", women whose cases are classified as unfounded because the police know that they will not make "convincing" witnesses in court.

It is virtually impossible for those women to complain of rape and have their complaint taken seriously. Because they are perceived to be valueless, a rapist may attack them with impunity, without fear of either retribution or rebuke. They are perceived as women who take unreasonable risks, who ought to know what they are getting into, who may drink in bars and even go home with the men they meet there, who solicit or accept rides from strangers. And if the worst happens, then the risk which was taken must have been unreasonable. And so, the victim is construed as being responsible for her own disaster. Open territory victims, then, are women with an already diminished sexual and reproductive value, or women who have forfeited this value by defying traditional expectations of respectable, acceptable, female behaviour. This flaunting of tradition is no mere social impropriety, but a direct threat to the stability of the sexual status quo. As the champion of all forms of the status quo, the law cannot protect these women against rape. It will either ignore their complaints, on the rationale that nothing of value has been lost, or penalize them even further for placing themselves at risk and wilfully damaging that which gave them a property value.

But as is clear from this discussion, the present treatment and handling of rape and rape victims within the Canadian criminal justice system does not arise from any malfunction in the administration of the law or any gross bias on the part of those who administer the system. Given the conceptual framework out of which rape laws developed, and within which rape evolved as a criminal offence, the results are exactly what we would expect. Rape laws were never meant to protect all women from rape, or to provide women with any guaranteed right to sexual autonomy. Rape laws were designed to preserve valuable female sexual property for the exclusive ownership of those men who could afford to acquire and maintain it. Thus, it is not at all surprising that the present practices are what they are given the historical context of the legal offence of rape.

The system of inequalities which has determined the formulation and application of rape laws is also, we believe, the root cause of rape itself. Women and men do not face each other as equals in our society, and their sexual relations are scarcely ever a simple expression of mutual sexual interest in one another. Sexual relationships are inextricably bound up with economic relationships of dependency and ownership, and very often they involve some kind of trade-off, calculation or coercion. As we shall discuss in the next chapter, rape is only an extreme manifestation of the coercive sexuality that pervades our entire culture. It is an inescapable by-product of a system in which sexual relationships are also power relationships, in which female sexuality is a commodity, and in which some men have no source of power except physical force. The logical conclusion of this analysis is that in order to eliminate rape, we must alter the underlying social structure which produces it.

Notes

1. For an elaboration of these themes, see Lorenne M.G. Clark, "The Rights of Women: The Theory and Practice of the Ideology of Male Supremacy"; Lynda Lange, "Reproduction in Democratic Theory"; and Mary O'Brien, "The Politics of Impotence", in *Contemporary Issues in Political Philosophy*, Canadian Contemporary Philosophy Series, ed. J. King-Farlow and W.R. Shea (New York: Science History Publications, 1976).

2. R.E. Megarry, *A Manual of the Law of Real Property*, 2nd ed. (London: Stevens & Sons, Ltd., 1955) p. 538.

3. Ibid., p. 291: "From the Fourteenth Century to 1939 there was in general no restriction upon a testator's power to dispose of property as he thought fit: for good reasons or bad, he might give all his property to a mistress or to charities and leave his family penniless."

4. Edward Shorter, *The Making of the Modern Family* (New York: Basic Books, 1975). For a thorough discussion of the extent to which marriage before 1750 was "held together by considerations of property and lineage" rather than by ties of affection, see especially

chapter 2, from which the above quotation is taken (p. 55). This point is further elaborated in chapter 4, in which is argued that interest rather than affection was the main factor determining who married whom. The following is from p. 142: "Make no mistake: the parents of the couple *had* to approve, because to spite parental will was to risk disinheritance, and in a society where capital was inherited, not accumulated, exclusion from your patrimony automatically consigned you to a marginal existence — not to mention having to endure the anguish of community opprobrium if you started keeping house without the proper sanctification."

5. Recent Supreme Court decisions in the *Rathwell* and *Murdoch* cases make it quite clear that no matter how much a wife may contribute to family assets, she is not entitled to an equal share of such property in the event that the marriage is dissolved.

6. Shorter, *The Making of the Modern Family*. Chapter 6 outlines the methods of community control exercised in "traditional society" in order to enforce socially acceptable practices and to discourage those out of keeping with community norms. He points out, on p. 222, that "the community, sensitive to any usurpation of husbandly authority, was especially quick to strike down public manifestations of feminine strength."

7. Ibid., p. 75: " . . . women's work was found in sex and reproduction: sleeping with their husbands on demand and producing babies up to the limits set by community norms." According to Shorter, women were regarded as little more than baby machines, and were regarded as easily replaced (pp. 57-58 and p. 77). He remarks further, on p. 145, that "the need to marry big, strong women able to shoulder their full share of work may have blinded peasants to the delicacy of line and fineness of feature that constitute our modern ideal of feminine beauty."

8. Adelyn Bowland, "The Source and Development of Rape Law in England to 1820", unpublished. We are greatly indebted to this work for its thorough analysis of original sources and for its absolute verification of the hypothesis that rape laws were primarily intended to limit the acquisition of property rights.

9. Megarry, *A Manual of the Law of Real Property*, p. 538.

10. Shorter, *The Making of the Modern Family*. This book points out that during the Middle Ages, when our modern offence of rape first begins to emerge, the vast majority of people never formally "married" at all. "In the eyes of medieval society, a couple who plighted their troth without undergoing the formality of a legal ceremony would still be considered as married by the surrounding society, even though the offspring might be recorded as illegitimate" (p. 85). Marriage was not fully sacramentalized until the Reformation and was, prior to that time, more a secular than a religious rite. The further back one goes the clearer it is that the roots of marriage lay in the necessity of providing a settled method of property transfer. Thus, during the medieval period, the persons most likely to go through the formalities were precisely those who had property to worry about.

8.   The Structure of Sexual Relations
Sue Lees

Girls walk a narrow line: they must not be seen as too tight, nor as too loose. Girls are preoccupied in their talk with sexuality, and in particular with the injustice of the way in which they are treated by boys. Defining girls in terms of their sexuality rather than their attributes and potentialities is a crucial mechanism of ensuring their subordination to boys. 'Nice girls don't' is a phrase all girls understand, even if standards of sexual morality are more liberal. The terms of abuse are so taken for granted that girls do not question them and are themselves drawn into judging other girls in terms of their reputation. One reason for this is that to mix with girls whose reputation is suspect can be 'contaminating' to one's own reputation. The only security girls have against bad reputations is to confine themselves to the 'protection' of one partner. Yet such a resolution involves dependency and loss of autonomy precisely because women's position in the family is subordinate and unequal.

Girls and boys talk about sexuality in quite different ways. For boys respectability is not crucial. On the contrary, their sexual reputation is enhanced by varied experience: bragging to other boys about how many girls they have 'made'. As Jacky, a working-class sixteen-year-old, and Leiser, a middle-class eighteen-year-old girl, described:

> A boy can be called a stud and people like and respect him — they have no responsibilities, they can just be doing what they want and if they are called a stud then they think it's good, they think it's a compliment . . . It's a sort of status symbol. (Jacky)

> I think it's made a sin for women to enjoy sex. From the time we begin enjoying sex we're called slags, or we can't have too many friends that are men. The ones who have good rapport with boys are called slags and the ones who don't are simply called tight bitches. 'Never get close to her', y'know, 'prude', and I don't think it ever stops. (Leiser)

A boy boasts about sex, but a girl is desperate to keep it quiet: her reputation is under threat, not merely if she is known to have sex (except with a steady) but for a whole range of behaviour often quite unconnected with sex. This is because she is always seen in terms of her sexuality, subjected to verbal and sometimes physical sexual abuse. For a boy, reputation depends on many other things, like being tough, witty, smart or good at sports. His standing in the world is not only determined by his sexual status or conquests. Equally important is his sporting or fighting prowess, his ability to 'take the mickey' or be one of the boys. As Paul Willis comments in *Learning to Labour*:

> It is the capacity to fight which settles the final pecking order. It is not often tested ability to fight which valorizes status based usually and

Sue Lees: Extracts taken from 'The Structure of Sexual Relations' in *SUGAR AND SPICE: SEXUALITY AND ADOLESCENT GIRLS* (Penguin Books, 1993), pp. 29-33; 48-51; 52-53; 57-63.

interestingly on other grounds: masculine presence, being from a famous family, being funny, being good at 'blagging', extensiveness of informal contacts (Willis 1977).

For a girl it is the defence of her sexual reputation that determines her standing with girls and boys, certainly around the age of fifteen or so. The emphasis on assumed sexual experience to a girl's reputation is shown by a whole battery of insults that are in everyday use among young people. The effect of this verbal abuse is to silence girls, to make it difficult for them to discuss their sexual desires and to throw each girl back on her own resources to protect her reputation. For boys, talking about sex, whether bragging or putting down girls, enhances camaraderie among them. Their experience is voiced, yet it is a distorted form of experience. Pressure is on them to boast about their conquests, about domination and performance, not about how close they felt to a girl and how well they got on with each other.

Sexism appears to be an important feature of male bonding, where denigration of girls and women is a crucial ingredient of camaraderie in male circles. The masculine tradition of drinking and making coarse jokes usually focuses on the 'dumb sex object', 'the nagging wife' or, more derogatively, 'horny dogs' and 'filthy whores'. Learning to be masculine invariably entails learning to be sexist: being a bit of a lad and being contemptuous of women just go 'naturally' together. Paul Willis in his study of working-class boys talks of boys' relations to girls as 'Exploitative and hypocritical. Girls are pursued, sometimes roughly, for their sexual favours, often dropped and labelled "loose" when they give in' (Willis 1977:67).

The asymmetry between girls and boys is illustrated by the term 'slag', which can be used in a whole range of circumstances. It implies that a girl sleeps around, but this may in fact have nothing to do with the case in point. A girl can be referred to as a slag if her clothes are too tight, too short, too smart or in any way sexually provocative, if she hangs about with boys, if she talks to another girl's boyfriend, if she talks too loudly or too much. It is an ever-present threat; a mechanism whereby boys can control girls' behaviour, whether sexual or otherwise, although no equivalent term exists for boys. Any girl is in danger from the 'slag' label at any time, and the girls agreed that the one way to redeem yourself is to get a steady boyfriend. For a girl to admit to feelings of sexual desire is a transgression of this code and can lead to a sullied reputation.

In the media, paradoxically, a girl's body is salaciously discussed, displayed naked on billboards, desired and denigrated. A man's body is concealed and it is even against the law to portray an erect penis publicly. Learning to be a girl, therefore, involves learning to conform to, resist and somehow survive the blatant sexism all around and to be reticent about your own desires. Camaraderie among girls is rarely enhanced by sexist talk as there is no vocabulary of abuse to level at boys. Criticizing the sexism of boys labels a girl a man-hater or a lesbian. It in no way enhances femininity. Quite the contrary. Girls who contest the unfair subordination of girls are likely to be regarded as show-offs or lesbians. There is no commonly used equivalent to the word misogynist, a man who hates women.

Amrit Wilson (1978) who undertook the first British study of Asian girls in the late 1970s described how in conversations she had with girls from many language groups and religions, in every part of Britain, 'reputation came up all the time'. It was not just important but was the 'bane of their lives from adolescence to the early years of marriage. It controls everything they do and adds a very tangible danger to any unconventional action' (Wilson 1978:102). Girls as young as twelve are frightened to go out with boys as they are afraid of the reputation they would get. Sofia, a Muslim girl of nineteen, described how if you go out with a man in Southall

> He will go around and boast to his friends that he's been out with this girl
> and he's done this to her and that to her. Even if he hasn't, he'll boast
> about it. Then they get the girl's name bad. That's why girls try and keep
> it quiet when they're going out with a bloke, because they don't want
> anyone to know. It's quite different for boys. They can get away with it.
> Their names can't ever get spoilt.

Reputation is a conservative force controlling everything in Asian societies, as male pride, or *izzat*, depends on it. Disgracing your family means harming the family *izzat*. A girl's family can be disgraced by the clothes she wears, the way she talks, where she is seen and all the various indicators of a girl's reputation, indeed any indication that she is independent. Some girls do take risks and go out with boys. Asian families do vary. Some Asian girls and women have argued that they do not experience lack of freedom in not leaving their families and communities. They affirm their need to be free within the family and criticize specific aspects of their cultures, including particular kinds of arranged marriages, but they also recognize that the black family, like the working-class family, can be a bastion of defence against class or racial oppression (Amos and Parmar 1987, Brah and Minhas 1985). There is no clear basis for inferring that Asian girls are more oppressed than white girls.

What is the meaning of sexist language for boys and men and why does it depend to such an extent on denigrating women? It is the means of maintaining power over girls and women. Achieving manhood involves a permanent process of struggle and confirmation. Madeleine Arnot (1982) sees this as a dual process of men distancing women and femininity from themselves and maintaining the hierarchy and social superiority of masculinity by devaluing the female world. Calling girls slags accomplishes exactly these two processes. It both distances boys from girls and keeps girls in control. To be a real man, to grow to manhood, involves differentiating oneself from all that is female. Boys therefore abuse each other by using words such as 'woman' or 'motherfucker', and even 'poof', words denoting femininity, to gain solidarity with each other.

* * * * * *

In reviewing her study of fourteen-year-old girls, Angela McRobbie found that there was a disparity between her 'wheeling in' of class in her report and its complete absence from the girls' talk and discourse. She concluded that being working-class meant little or nothing to these girls, but being a girl over-determined their every moment (McRobbie 1982). Girls are aware of class differences in income, accent, access to a wider social life and better opportunities, but the objectification of girls occurs regardless of class, though middle-class girls may have access to greater linguistic practices to deal with abuse. However, any girl or woman can be brought down to size by being rendered a bitch, a cow or a cunt, which girls regard as deeply offensive, but is also one of the few words to describe the female sex organs. One distinction that did emerge in the discussions with middle-class girls was a greater awareness that the defining characteristic of 'slag' was not in fact actual promiscuity. As Silvia, a middle-class white girl from a single-sex school, explains:

> There are some people I know who have slept with lots of different people, but they don't conduct themselves in a way that I would call a slag, they don't do it on purpose, they don't sort of treat boys in a completely different way — grease up to them and change their whole personality because someone they like is in the room kind of thing, and some people who have slept with different people I wouldn't define as a slag.

Q Why would you have defined the two girls as slags?

> Because they were using people and became very flirtatious. You wouldn't recognize them as the same people. You could be having a conversation with them one minute. Someone they like comes into the room, suddenly they change their whole personalities. They don't talk to you sincerely. It's tits out. And then all they want of the boys is to get off with them. They'd go off with two, three boys.

Q Do you mean they'd be sleeping with three people?

> Oh no, I didn't mean they'd be sleeping, but, I mean, that would be a bit hard.

The girl here is describing behaviour that would be regarded as natural in a boy. It is natural for a boy to chat up girls. Here if a girl is seen to be appearing to chat up boys or perhaps talking to three different boys in succession she is in danger of being regarded as a slag. What Silvia fails to appreciate is the constraints on a girl, the limits on her freedom to move around, to talk to whoever she wants and behave independently. Such behaviour would be categorized as inappropriately forward, attention-seeking and 'sluttish'. There are ways in which stereotypes of class, such as low intelligence and rough language, overlap with sexist abuse. In the same way that 'slut' denotes both promiscuity and low social class, Anna Marie describes Tania, whom she regards as stupid, in this way:

> This girl I know — she couldn't even pass her entrance into Woolworths. And usually they come from very poor families. I never ask them to go out with us.

Peter Wilmott, in his study of boys, found a connection between swearing and assumed looseness. He quotes one of the boys he interviewed as saying: 'You can always get a bit with the girls with big mouths, but that kind of thing turns you off after a while — you realize that if you can get it so can anyone else' (Wilmott 1969).

The effect of sexist abuse

The crucial point about the label 'slag' is that it is used by both girls and boys as a deterrent to nonconformity. No girl wants to be labelled 'bad', and 'slag' is something to frighten any girl with. As Laura said, 'Everyone thinks lower of them than what they did before.' The effect of the term is to force girls to submit voluntarily to a very unfair set of gender relations. A few girls did reject the implications of the label and the double standard implicit within it, but even they said they used the term to abuse other girls.

To call a girl a slag is to use a term that, as we have seen, appears at first sight to be a label describing an actual form of behaviour but into which no girl incontrovertibly fits. It is even difficult to identify what actual behaviour is specified. Take Helen's description of how appearance can define girls, not in terms of their attributes as human beings, but in terms of sexual reputation:

> I mean, they might not mean any harm. I mean, they might not be as bad as they look. But their appearance makes them stand out and that's what makes them look weird and you think: 'God, I can imagine her, y'know?' . . . She straight away gets a bad reputation even though the girl might be decent inside. She might be good. She might still be living at home. She might just want to look different but might still act normal.

You cannot imagine a boy's appearance being described in this way. How she dresses determines how a girl is viewed and she is viewed in terms of her assumed sexual behaviour. Whether she is 'good' or not is determined by how she is assumed to conduct her sexual life; that sexuality is relative to male sexual needs. Girls are aware that appearances may be deceptive, but this does not lead them to really contest the categorization:

> You can't tell a slag walking down the street. I mean, you might see someone who looks a real — debauched, sort of mess, make-up run everywhere, but you don't know the reason. You might call her a slag, but, I mean, she could just have been beaten up by her husband or something. So really a slag is usually someone you know and you just have evidence of what they've done.

Rather than attempt to specify what particular behaviour differentiates a slag, it is more useful to see 'slag' as what Sumner (1983) terms a category of 'moral censure': as part of a discourse about male conceptions of female sexuality that run deep in the culture. They run so deep that the majority of women and men cannot formulate them except by reference to these terms of censure that signal a threatened violation.

> Their general function is to denounce and control, not to explain . . . They mark off the deviant, the pathological, the dangerous and the criminal from the normal and the good . . . [they] are not just labels . . . [But] . . . They are loaded with implied interpretations of real phenomena, models of human nature and the weight of political self interest (Sumner 1983).

What Sumner fails to explore is how these forms of moral censure are gendered. In effect exactly the behaviour which would be extolled in a boy is censured in a girl. 'Slag' is literally the coal dust that is 'cast off' on to the slag heap, or, in sexual terms, the woman who is fucked and discarded. However, it is also one of the few words to imply active female sexuality, personified in the prostitute. The term is of course highly derogatory, yet it refers to a woman who behaves in the way men are expected to behave. A slag is a woman who is 'after one thing', someone 'who does not really care', or 'uses sex for other motives' rather than love (the whore who has sex for money). For a man to have sex without a relationship is fine, to be expected, part of 'natural male sex drive'. In one discussion with adolescent boys, Nico, hearing I had had discussions with girls, was curious as to what they had said about sex. 'Do girls like sex?' he asked as though the question had never crossed his mind before.

* * * * * *

For girls to have sex for its own sake makes them into 'prostitutes'. It could be argued that both prostitutes and men separate their bodies from their emotions: the prostitute has sex for money, the man for conquest. So for a girl sex is only legitimate when she interacts with the boy, when she 'recognizes' the boy, when she likes him, not when she treats the boy as an object of her desire. To demand sex for itself makes her dirty, destroys her 'womanliness'. This is relevant to the construction of female sexuality. The loss of virginity represents a cheapening of the woman, a drop in her value. Amazingly, in the interviews I undertook with boys, many of whom were actively having sex with girls, they still voiced a commitment to finding a virgin to marry. In some cultures a loss of virginity precludes the possibility of marriage. Paul Willis suggests that there is a fear that unleashing the woman's desire will lead to uncontrolled promiscuity. In analysing the term 'slag' as a representation he comments: 'Woman . . . as a sexual object is a commodity that becomes worthless with consumption and yet as a sexual being, once sexually experienced, becomes promiscuous.' He quotes one of his lads as saying: 'After you've been with one, like, after you've done it, like, well, they're scrubbers afterwards, they'll go with anyone. I think that once they've had it, they want it all the time, no matter who it's with' (Willis 1977).

The term slag therefore applies less to any clearly defined notion of sleeping around than to any form of social behaviour by girls that would define them as autonomous from the attachment to and domination by boys. It acts as a censure against being unattached. In other words, any independent behaviour — such as going places on your own, or talking back to a boy, or standing your ground in a dispute — opens a girl up to sexist abuse. A second important facet of 'slag' is its uncontested status as a category. Although it connotes promiscuity, its actual usage is such that any unattached girl is vulnerable to being categorized as a slag. In this way the term functions as a form of control by boys over girls, a form of control that steers girls into 'acceptable' and dependent forms of sexual and social behaviour. The term is uncontestable. All the girls agreed that there was only one defence, one way for a girl to redeem herself from the reputation of slag:

> To get a steady boyfriend. Then that way you seem to be more respectable,
> like you're married or something.

'Going steady' establishes the location of a sexuality appropriate for 'nice girls', and that sexuality is distinguished from the essentially dirty/promiscuous sexuality of the slag. Sex with a steady boyfriend is easy to get away with:

> If you had it away with your boyfriend, right, and you didn't tell no one,
> no one else needs to know, do they?

It is the young unattached woman who is likely to be regarded as a slag, rather than the sexually active girl who sleeps with her boyfriend. The term slag functions as a pressure on girls to submit to a relationship of dependence on a boy, leading eventually to marriage. It is this complex nexus of constraints that lies behind the importance all girls lay on finding a boyfriend and leads to girls often colluding in their own oppression. Being unattached carries risks:

> If you went round with someone, right, or you don't know her but you
> always see her and every time you see her she's got a different fella with
> her, you get to think she's a slag, don't you? She got a different fella every
> minute of the day.

*   *   *   *   *   *

Racist and sexist stereotyping

In the same way that girls are aware of class differences, they are also aware of ethnic differences. Black girls are not a homogeneous group, and very different types of gender relations exist among different groups.

The relation between cultural backgrounds has already been mentioned in relation to the importance of *izzat* or family honour in some Asian households. Religious customs and beliefs operate in such a way as to control female sexuality in so far as most religions lay down moral codes relating to virginity and sexual behaviour. One of the main ethnic differences that emerged was the amount of freedom girls are allowed, to go out late, or at all, and to mix with boys of religions different to those of their own families. Some girls' lives are much more constricted than others, which is as much related to their families' religious beliefs as to race. Work is also liberating many women from total dependence. In the case of Asian women during the last ten years, going out to work, if only part-time, is breaking the knot of total dependence some experienced (see Westwood and Bhachu 1988).

There is a sense in which racist and sexist stereotyping are intertwined and related. The sexist category of 'slag' is part of the raw material out of which racist views are elaborated. Sexist and racist stereotypes operate in ways which, although not identical, are in some respects similar. Both sets of stereotypes are difficult to pin down to any hard or specific content that could be shown to be untrue and thus lead to the withdrawal of the label. For 'slag' this is because of the ambiguous way in which it is used; in the case of racist stereotypes this results from a refusal to allow any exceptions. Gordon Allport (1954), an American social psychologist who, after the Second World War, carried out a classic study of prejudice to try and throw light on the horrors of the Holocaust, called this re-fencing.

169

There is a common mental device that permits people to hold to prejudgements even in the face of much contradictory evidence. It is the device of admitting exceptions. 'There are nice Negroes but . . .' Or, 'Some of my best friends are Jews but . . .' This is a disarming device. By excluding a few favoured cases, the negative rubric is kept intact for all other cases. In short, contrary evidence is not admitted and allowed to modify the generalization; rather it is perfunctorily acknowledged but excluded (Allport 1954:23).

This process of acknowledging and then excluding exceptions is illustrated by a snippet of conversation where Karen elaborates on the sexual and racial prejudices of herself and her friends:

Like me . . . Pam and me and Susan . . . and we were sat in those flats talking, and I just said . . . A Paki come along, and Pam says, 'Oh, I hate Pakis,' and I go, 'Oh, I hate Jews,' and Susan goes, 'I hate black people.' And I go, 'How can you hate black people? Sybil's black,' and, like, Susan and Pamela and me were all white, and she goes, 'I don't really' . . . She goes, 'I hate golliwogs.' 'My best friend's black,' and she goes, 'Yeah, so's mine,' so I go 'Yeah? So how can you hate them?' and Pamela goes, 'I hate Pakis.' . . . No reason, she just hates them. I hate Jews for a reason.

Karen's reason for hating Jews is that:

A Jew knocked my dog down and he died, so ever since then I've hated Jews and I hate all Jews.

Q You think all Jews are like that?

Yeah now. Only them that wear the black thing and . . . I had a Jewish friend and I didn't know she was Jewish and I was watching Jesus of Nazareth up her house one day and I said to her when the Jews come on, I said, 'Oh, look, the Jews,' and she said, 'I'm Jewish,' and her dad was there and all and she goes her dad's Jewish — he's not one of them Jews that wear the black thing . . . Ever since then I don't play with her.

Q Do you like her?

No not a lot. That weren't the only reason I didn't like her. There were other reasons but that made it worse.

Karen's incoherence illustrates both sides of the process that Allport was describing. On the one hand, a counterfactual example to a racist generalization will happily be incorporated without disturbing the generalization, and on the other hand, a single instance will be held up as sufficient reason for subscribing to a generalization about an ethnic or religious group.

Thus both the 'slag' and racist categorizations are forms of labelling that are difficult to pin down to any specific content that could be shown to be untrue and lead to a withdrawal of the label. For 'slag', this is because of the ambiguous way in which it is used. In the case of race it is by refusing to allow any exception to modify the basic racist stereotype. It is easy to see how 'slag' can come to fulfil the requirements of racism. Racist stereotypes of blacks and whites occur among the girls through the familiar devices of 'slag' and bitching, which are at the same time being used by both girls and boys in ways that end up constraining the freedom of girls, irrespective of ethnic group. The processes by which girls are labelled 'slags', irrespective of race, can become one component out of which racist views are elaborated. It is not just that 'slag' is a label that has a fluidity similar to racist stereotypes. Racism is able to absorb and work through sexist categories. In *Black Women in White America* Gerda Lerner explains the centrality of sexual mythology concerning black women:

> By assuming a different level of sexuality for all blacks than that of whites and mystifying their greater sexual potency, the black woman could be made to personify sexual freedom and abandon. A myth was created that all black women were eager for sexual exploits, voluntarily 'loose' in their morals, and therefore deserved none of the consideration and respect granted white women. Every black woman was, by definition, a slut according to racist mythology; therefore to assault her and exploit her sexually was not reprehensible and carried with it none of the normal sanctions against such behaviour (Lerner 1981, quoted in hooks 1981:59).

This 'animal' sexual appetite and behaviour of the black woman finds a reflection in a comment by a white girl in this study:

> They look black and somehow stronger. If you got a white girl and a black girl you say, 'Oh she looks stronger 'cos she's black.'

Appearance is important in the process of racial as well as sexual stereotyping. The awareness of dress differences is a key theme in the feelings of racial antagonism between black and white girls in the public spaces outside the classroom. Jane, a white girl, describes how it is the black girls she is most frightened of when she goes out, and that if you dress like some black girls — wearing brightly coloured cotton — then you are 'asking for it':

> Then we went to the Lyceum, all of us looked really smart, and there was this group of black girls and they were all going 'Tchch' and looking us up and down, and you feel uneasy with them.

Black girls feel themselves on the receiving end of innuendo concerning dress from white girls. Wilma complains about the way

> They tease you about the way you dress, sometimes the way you walk . . . [The white girls] think they're perfect, that's why. They say something to you and when you say it back they say, 'What did you say it about me for?' They don't like it. They can say it to you but you can't say it to them.

This is echoed by Sharon:

> Some of [the white girls] are all trendy, the sort of dresses and that, and then there're some of them that are really bitchy. The thing that gets me is they take the piss out of our clothes and then half of their clothes come from jumble sales. I couldn't get my clothes from a jumble sale.

This bitching about clothes is of course no different from relations between girls in terms of subcultural styles. A white girl talks about trendies in much the same way:

> They might not mean any harm, they might not be that bad, as bad as they look, but their appearance makes them stand out and that's what makes them look weird and you think, 'God, I can imagine her'. . . Straight away she gets a bad reputation even though she might be decent inside.

What this illustrates is not that racism is 'just another' form of bitching between girls over dress and style of behaviour, but rather that racism constructs its stereotypes out of the content of everyday interpersonal interaction which is then institutionalized (otherwise racism appears as only interactive). The processes by which girls are labelled slags, irrespective of race, are one component of the way in which racial stereotypes are constructed and perpetuated. Black women are therefore seen by these girls to be particularly sexy. As Lynne Segal (1987:102) indicates, western images of sex are also quintessentially racist.

We have seen that the vocabulary used to describe girls divides them into good and bad, the promiscuous and the pure, the tasty and the 'dogs'. It is not only the boys that categorize girls in this way but girls use the same terms to categorize and 'police' each other. Embodied in this vocabulary is a contempt for women which emerges if they are seen to be actively sexual and unattached. What is particularly pernicious about this language is that it is accepted as part of nature, or of common sense, by the girls themselves.

Sometimes other members of the family are brought into arguments about a girl's reputation. Both fathers and brothers were reported to call girls slags, which gives the nasty impression that they might be involved in other forms of abuse, perhaps sexual abuse. Sadie said that when her dad called her a slag, her mum retorted:

> Look at your sister. She was pregnant at sixteen. So you can't talk about your daughter like that.

Sybil, when asked what she thought about her brothers, replied:

> I ain't got no brothers really. All they do is call me names, especially the eldest one. Then the other two join in.

Sexual abuse in childhood and adolescence can be a devastating experience for women in terms of their body image and overall self-esteem. American studies estimate that as many as one in three girls are sexually abused (Russell 1984). Alice Miller outlines the drastic effects if children are beaten, humiliated, lied to and deceived, and how anger, if unexpressed, does not disappear but is transformed with time into a more or less conscious hatred against either the self or a substitute person (Miller 1987).

Conclusions

An absence of any form of expression of sexual desire among girls except in terms of an exclusive 'love' relationship is one significant finding. Yet there is talk about who did what, with whom and how far they went. But all this talk is circumscribed and checked by the invocation of the category 'slag'. Far from being personal and private, sexuality reflects unfair power relations between the sexes. Girls are categorized as passive objects who can only wait and hope to be chatted up without being insulted, to make love and not be talked about afterwards. The terms on which their dilemmas are handled are always socially organized and largely socially determined. Girls may have more freedom, but they have to develop strategies for dealing with day-to-day sexism. Some are voicing their rejection of the double standard. There may be little collective protest but some girls are questioning sexism. Girls tease each other for playing up to boys. Girls are having fun, and can be humorous, self-assured and full of spark. Girls do not passively accept their subordination. Yet feminism is more popular among women who have had children than among adolescents, who are too preoccupied with developing ways of surviving the contradictions of female identity.[1]

In this chapter I have shown how femininity and masculinity are socially constituted and reconstituted through social practices and are not biologically determined. For the adolescent girls I spoke to feminine identity rests to a great extent on their sexual reputation. The only terms for active female sexuality are derogatory. Otherwise, girls are categorized as passive objects. The terms on which their dilemmas are handled are always socially organized and largely socially determined. Defining girls in terms of their sexual reputation rather than their attributes and potentialities is a crucial mechanism of ensuring their subordination to boys. The lack of specific content of the term 'slag' means that girls are in a permanent state of vulnerability, for the way they dress and speak, for being too friendly to boys or not friendly enough. The terms of abuse are so taken for granted that girls do not often question them; they use the terms of abuse themselves against other girls. The only security against abuse and a bad reputation is to confine themselves to the 'protection' of one partner. Yet such a resolution involves dependency and loss of autonomy, as I shall elaborate in [Chapter 3].

Notes

1. Gloria Steinem (1979) found that older women become more radical as a result of their experiences with men. Younger women are more conservative.

9. Preventing Domestic Violence to Women

Rebecca Morley and Audrey Mullender

Prevention of domestic violence to women can be conceptualised in two ways: preventing violence occurring in the first place, or, more commonly, preventing repeat attacks. The vast bulk of work worldwide has focused on attempting to reduce the incidence of repeat victimisation by provision of legal, welfare and social supports for women; and to a more limited extent attempting to control and change male offenders. The emphasis should continue to lie with prevention of repeat violence since support systems and resources remain inadequate for protecting women and stopping men. This report thus focuses on preventing repeat victimisation.

However, reducing repeat violence will not bring an end to the problem. There is little evidence that the prevalence of domestic violence has declined since becoming a recognised social problem in the mid 1970s, and this is not surprising. As the Metropolitan Police's *Working Party on Domestic Violence Report* states:

> At present, women are not regarded as, or treated as, equal to men in terms of their social and economic rights. There is discrimination against women in employment and education and women are grossly under-represented in key areas of political life, in Parliament, Local Government, Trade Unions. Part of the total climate of sexual discrimination is the whole issue of women's *[sic]* rights to sexual freedom. It is clear from evidence on rape, prostitution, sexual harassment, etc., that women are vulnerable to abuse and mockery. It is in this climate of contempt for women that domestic violence thrives.
>
> (Metropolitan Police Working Party 1986: 63)

Thus, to eliminate domestic violence to women, 'values and social structures which promote and condone violence, as well as values and social structures which emphasise the power of men over women and children must be identified and changed' (MacLeod 1989: 15).

This section of the report briefly summarises the results of an inquiry carried out between October 1990 and June 1991 into preventive responses — primarily to repeat offending — overseas, in Britain, and on the project estates. The discussion focuses mainly on policing, with short summaries of the civil law and of community supports for women, although it must be acknowledged that other major areas of service provision have a vital role to play, notably housing, social services, and the health care professions. Developments since 1991 are included where possible. Before examining specific provision, however, some general remarks are needed regarding prevention of repeat attacks.

Rebecca Morley and Audrey Mullender: *PREVENTING DOMESTIC VIOLENCE TO WOMEN*. Police Research Group Crime Prevention Unit Series: Paper No. 48. (London: Home Office Police Department), pp. 11-46. © Crown Copyright 1994. Crown copyright is reproduced with the permission of the Controller of HMSO.

Effective early intervention is vitally important if men are to stop their violence and women are to be protected: very few men stop of their own volition, and violence usually increases in frequency and severity over time. Violence is much more difficult if not impossible to stop, except by separation, when it progresses into a patterned feature of the relationship (e.g. Dobash *et al.* 1985, Bowker 1986, NiCarthy 1987, Kelly 1988). Therefore the best hope for effective prevention is *very early* effective intervention.

However, women typically do not seek help from outside agencies until the violence has become established. For example, a Canadian study found that women had been assaulted an average of 35 times before contacting the police (in Jaffe *et al.* 1986a: 38). The decision to involve outsiders is, in fact, an extremely difficult, as well as a potentially *dangerous,* one. There is evidence that women are most likely to be murdered by their partners when attempting to get outside help or to leave the relationship. In 1987/1988, more than 90% of women killed by their partners in Minnesota, USA were actively seeking help from an outside agency or attempting to separate (Pence 1989: 345; see also Browne and Williams 1989). The quality of intervention at this initial stage and its perceived effect on the violent partner's behaviour are crucial in determining whether a woman will continue to seek help (see Dobash *et al.* 1985) as well as in ensuring her immediate safety.

Dobash *et al.* 1985, amongst many others, point out that any one particular attempt to seek help may not directly correspond to the severity of the specific violent attack to which it is linked:

> It is important for professionals to recognise that it may not be the severity of a particular attack that leads a woman to seek help. Rather, it may be the cumulative effect of persistent violence and intimidation, decreasing acceptance of the man's justifications for violence and repeated failures to solve the problem alone. Even then, the decision to approach a formal agency is so fraught with misgivings and trepidation that the nature of response can easily lead to discontinuation of contact. (Dobash *et al.* 1985: 154-5)

Thus professionals who respond only to the perceived severity of the presenting violent incident risk missing the context of the *continuing* violent *relationship* in which it is most probably embedded, and may well judge the victim to be undeserving of help, leaving her in an even more precarious situation. It is vital therefore that all service providers who come into contact with women suffering domestic violence should have a perceptive understanding of the context of this crime and its effects on victims.

Finally however, as the Home Affairs Committee (1993a: paras 35, 37) points out, a small minority of women exists in the UK for whom access to help from formal agencies and the potential for escaping violence are particularly problematic. The *Statement of Changes in Immigration Rules* (House of Commons 251, 1990) states that spouses of persons entitled to settle in the UK who do not themselves have such entitlement are allowed to stay in the UK initially for a period not exceeding 12 months, and only if they have the intention of living permanently with their spouse and can be accommodated and maintained without recourse to public funds.

Non-entitled spouses who leave the marital home or who attempt to make use of public services during the 12 month probationary period are liable for deportation. Cases have been documented of women who, as a direct consequence of these Rules, have been deported after fleeing violent husbands or have remained trapped within abusive relationships, fearing deportation and unable to apply for benefits or rehousing (e.g. Inquiry interviews; *The Guardian* January 9, 1991, October 28, 1992; *The Observer* June 2, 1991; *National Union of Public Employees Journal* 1992, no.5, p.3; Roshni 1992; Home Affairs Committee 1993b: Appendix 9). In its response to the Home Affairs Committee (Cm. 2269 1993, paras 35, 36), the Government indicated that Home Office officials are to consider the possibility of developing practical ways of ensuring that women who feel vulnerable are informed of their status and the help and advice available to them.

The police

The police are the only 24 hour emergency protection service available in every locality to respond to violent attacks. Therefore they are uniquely situated to provide immediate aid to victims of domestic violence. UK studies of women's help-seeking undertaken during the 1970s and 1980s (Dobash and Dobash 1980, Binney *et al.* 1981, Evason 1982, Homer *et al.*1984, Pahl 1985, Mama 1989: ch. 6, McGibbon *et al.* 1989) showed that the police were one of the *most* frequently contacted agencies, but rated as one of the *least* helpful.

These studies (see also Montgomery and Bell n.d., Edwards 1989, Bourlet 1990)found that police often told victims that they were not empowered to intervene in 'domestics', since these constituted civil matters. Thus, women were sometimes advised to take out a private prosecution or a civil injunction, to contact a welfare agency, or given no advice at all. Frequently police 'mediated' or 'conciliated' the 'dispute', often by suggesting that the victim modify her behaviour in exchange for the assailant's promise not to commit further violence, leaving her without protection and at risk of escalating violence (see also Hague *et al.* 1989). Only infrequently did police arrest the assailant, even when the victim requested it and the violence was severe (see also Smith 1989: 43). In a minority of cases, the police failed even to arrive at the scene. Black victims often reported, in addition, racist treatment (e.g. Mama 1989). Women's lack of confidence in thc police was consistently cited as a major reason for not reporting attacks.

Police disregard for domestics was reflected in their recording practices (e.g. Metropolitan Police Working Party 1986, Edwards 1986, 1989; Smith 1989). Some calls were not recorded in station message books. Some were written up as 'no call for police action', even when considerable time had been spent at the scene. Some were recorded in categories which precluded their identification as domestic violence. Some were recorded as incident reports rather than crimes even with clear evidence of a criminal offence, one aspect of a more general tendency to 'crime down' domestic offences. A high proportion of incidents initially crimed were subsequently 'no-crimed', disappearing from the statistics altogether. Finally, injunctions with powers of arrest were often improperly stored at the station, making retrieval difficult or impossible.

Overall, police responses appeared to be grounded in a well-documented *reluctance* to intervene in 'domestics', viewed as private (civil) matters rather than 'real crime work', a view firmly entrenched in police training manuals (e.g. Bourlet 1990:14-18, 72-6) Indeed, legal criteria (whether an offence had been committed) were frequently superseded by 'moral' criteria (often a suspicion that the woman was to blame for the violence) or by a belief that domestic violence victims withdraw charges (e.g. Stanko 1985, 1989; Edwards 1989; Hanmer 1989), even though the extent of victim withdrawal was debatable (e.g. Faragher 1985, Sanders 1988). The crux of the argument from victims and their advocates was that by making intervention contingent on an assessment of the woman's worthiness as a victim or on the likelihood that she would carry through with a prosecution, *'the police abrogate their protective role'* (Faragher 1985: 117, emphasis added).

The police began to respond to criticisms of their approach to domestic violence in the latter half of the 1980s. In this they followed trends elsewhere in the world, notably in North America and Australia.

Recent international developments

Similar criticisms of the police in North America and Australia led many jurisdictions in those countries to institute legal and policy reforms encouraging, and in some cases mandating, tougher criminal justice system (CJS) responses grounded in *arrest*. These moves were accompanied by directives to provide support for victims through transport to a place of safety, information about and referral to other agencies, and the like.

Arrest has been advocated on several grounds (e.g. Buel 1988, Buzawa and Buzawa 1990: 84-8): it provides immediate protection by removing the assailant; it sends messages to the assailant, victim and community that domestic violence is a serious *crime*; and it gives the police a tangible product for work which is conventionally viewed as a waste of time. Most fundamentally, however, arrest is believed to *deter* offenders from repeating their violence, that is, to have a *direct* preventive effect.

Two 'classic' studies are cited in the literature to support the deterrent argument. The most influential is the 'Minneapolis Experiment' (Sherman and Berk 1984) which compared the effectiveness of three police responses — arrest, advice/mediation and separation — on misdemeanour domestic assaults. Arrest produced the least repeat offending in the six month follow up period, independently of any other action by the CJS. The US National Institute of Justice subsequently commissioned six replications of the Experiment in different cities throughout the USA. Of the five replications for which findings were available in 1992, only two found evidence for a deterrent effect of arrest during the first six months (Sherman 1992 30; see papers in *The Journal of Criminal Law and Criminology* 1992, vol. 83, no. 1 for a fuller discussion). However, though the authors of the three replications which failed to reproduce the Minneapolis findings all reject *mandatory* arrest policies on grounds of deterrence, two (Dunford *et al.* 1989, Hirschel *et al.* 1991) stress the importance of arrest and the need to clearly define domestic violence as a crime.

Indeed, Dunford *et al.* (1989: 64) appear to favour a *pro-arrest policy* which 'encourages, but does not mandate arrest', for two reasons. First, it would enable police to heed the wishes of victims who do not want arrest This consideration is important, given the increasingly expressed concern that mandatory policies generally may disempower victims by removing their control over the criminal justice process (e.g. MacLeod and Picard 1989; personal communication, Office of the Solicitor General Canada, May 1991; Morley and Mullender 1992). Second, arrest could provide 'an entry point into a *coordinated criminal justice system* rather than an end point, [which might] shift the burden of deterrence from a single official police intervention (arrest) to a sequence of other interventions, each of which may have some salutary effect' (p. 64, emphasis added).

The term 'coordinated criminal justice system response' refers first to coordination *within* the CJS — *between* police, prosecution and sentencing; second to coordination between the CJS and community services. Several studies suggest that both are needed to make arrest an effective preventive response. The most notable is the second 'classic' research — the London, Ontario pro-charging studies (Jaffe *et al.* 1986a, Jaffe *et al.* 1991) — which found that, while police intervention *per se* was effective in reducing repeat violence, charging was more effective than not charging. In London, Ontario most offenders whose cases are recorded as crimes are also charged *and* prosecuted (coordinated CJS); and the police fund a 24 hour crisis intervention service and training. Moreover police responses are embedded within interlinking community services including a victim advocacy clinic providing legal advice and counselling, a programme supporting victims throughout the court process, shelters (refuges) and longer term housing, treatment for batterers, and a comprehensive public education programme. As the researchers state: 'These services provide an important community context in evaluating police services and policies ....Other communities that do not provide the same level of support for victims may vary in the effectiveness of a police policy to lay charges against perpetrators of wife assault' (Jaffe *et al.* 1986a: 48).

Indeed other evidence suggests that arrest/charging without these supports may in some cases increase risk to the victim of reprisals from an angry partner (e.g. Davis 1988: 365, Steinman 1990; see also Ministry of the Solicitor General of Canada 1986: 3). Certainly, fear of reprisal appears to be a major reason why many women withdraw charges, or do not call the police (e.g. Dobash and Dobash 1980, Mama 1989). Clearly this is not to reject arrest as a potentially useful response — it may offer immediate, short term, life-saving protection. However, it would be surprising if one discrete police *act,* isolated from any other means of controlling the man or protecting the woman, would deter violent behaviour which has often developed over many years.

Coordinated CJS responses may, in fact, have two effects. First, they may bring offenders under further control and offer victims protection and support. Second, they may change the nature of the initial police intervention itself, since in jurisdictions with good CJS/community coordination the police often demonstrate a commitment to tackling domestic violence (e.g. Jaffe *et al.* 1991).

This second point is pertinent to police *policy* on domestic violence, where the international evidence shows that even mandatory arrest policies do not remove discretion in police decision-making, and that without strong leadership, monitoring, and a structure of accountability to the community, policy does not translate into practice (e.g. Ferraro 1989; Balos and Trotsky 1988; personal communication, Office of the Solicitor General Canada, May 1991). Jurisdictions where policies appear to have produced positive effects on practice are ones where the CJS is an integral part of a comprehensive, coordinated community response, and *accountable* to women through continued internal and independent monitoring (e.g. Gamache *et al.* 1988, Pence 1989, Jaffe *et al.* 1991, Hirschel and Hutchinson 1991). These jurisdictions also demonstrate high levels of victim satisfaction with the police.

A number of models exist throughout the USA for providing this coordinated community response (Goolkasian 1986, Cahn and Lerman 1991, Edleson 1991). They are based in organisations staffed predominately by victim advocates linked to local shelters who help women deal with the CJS, civil courts and welfare agencies, and who work closely with these agencies for change in policies and practices. All are grounded in the philosophy that domestic violence is criminal behaviour, that the abuser must take responsibility for his behaviour which requires primary focus on CJS sanctions, and that the victim should be supported and most importantly empowered through the interventive process. The most successful organisations appear to be ones that are organised *independently* of the CJS (Cahn and Lerman 1991, Edleson 1991), notably Community Intervention Projects (Edleson 1991), pioneered in Duluth, Minnesota (Pence and Shepard 1988) and spreading throughout jurisdictions in Minnesota and elsewhere in the USA. (See also McGregor and Hopkins 1991, for discussion of a successful crisis intervention service in Australia which operates as an independent victim advocate service in close collaboration with the police.)

Recent UK developments

In the United Kingdom, the police were the first statutory agency to tackle the need to improve their response to domestic violence. Pioneering policy changes in the Metropolitan and West Yorkshire forces were followed in July 1990 by a Home Office Circular 60/1990 (and parallel circulars in Scotland and Northern Ireland).

The Circular recommends that police forces develop policy statements and strategies grounded in an understanding that domestic violence is a crime as serious as assaults by strangers, and that the primary duty of police is to protect the victim and her children and to take positive action against the assailant. Police are reminded of their extensive powers to deal with domestic violence under the criminal law and warned of the dangers of attempting conciliation between victim and assailant. They are advised to take positive action in every incident, rarely to attempt conciliation, to interview the victim separately from the assailant, to prepare information leaflets for victims, to arrange for medical assistance, to escort victims to a place of safety if requested, to consider arresting and charging the assailant and *not* to be affected by the fact that some women withdraw charges, to provide continued support for victims during the pre-trial period, to liaise with other agencies, to set up (where practicable) dedicated domestic violence units, to ensure that all offences are properly recorded and not 'no-crimed', and to make records easily retrievable.

There is widespread agreement that the Circular provides a sound foundation for developing sensitive and effective police responses to domestic violence (e.g. Home

Affairs Committee 1993a: para 14). The critical issues concern the degree to which forces have changed their policies in line with the Circular and, most crucially, the degree to which policy changes have been translated into practice. By July 1991, all forces in England and Wales had formulated policy statements on domestic violence (in Home Office Memorandum to Home Affairs Committee 1993b: 2). Comprehensive and detailed information concerning the Circular's impact on force policy and practice is as yet unavailable, though the Home Office is currently undertaking an impact study, to be completed in 1994. Nonetheless, existing though patchy evidence from police statistics, small scale research including this Inquiry, accounts of service providers and victims, and the recent Home Affairs Committee investigation into Domestic Violence (Home Affairs Committee 1993a, 1993b) suggest that recent policy changes have had a positive impact on practice in many areas, although some very important concerns remain.

Police dispositions

Improvements in police dispositions have been documented. Edwards (1989) analysed police statistics in two London divisions, comparing the situation before and one year following the inception of the Metropolitan Police force order in 1987. During that period, incidents logged at the station increased by 77%, the percentage of incidents recorded as crimes increased from 12% to 21%, the percentage of incidents resulting in arrests increased from 2% to 17%, and the percentage of crimes subsequently 'no crimed' decreased from 83% to 64% (figures calculated from Edwards 1989: 202-3, Tables 6.2, 6.3). Metropolitan Police statistics for London as a whole show that recorded domestic violence increased from 770 in 1985 to 9800 in 1992, the latter figure representing 26% of all recorded assaults in London. Further, in 1992, arrests were made in 45% of recorded domestic violence.

Domestic violence units

A particularly notable advance has been the creation of domestic violence units (DVUs). The first was established in Tottenham, London in 1987. By the end of 1992, DVUs existed in 62 out of the 69 Divisions in the Metropolitan Police, and in 20 of the 42 other police forces in England and Wales (Home Affairs Committee 1993a: para 23).

There is some evidence that divisions with DVUs do better than those without. Edwards (1989) compared two London divisions in 1988, one with and one without a DVU. The division with the DVU did better on a number of measures. For example, more arrests were made for crimes and for breach of the peace, more incident reports were written, and more cases were referred to the Crown Prosecution Service (pp. 205-6). Edwards also pointed to figures for Tottenham in March 1988 showing that 29 of the 36 crimed cases were reported to and pursued by the Crown Prosecution Service (pp. 206-7). While these findings are indicative, they are not controlled studies, and thus it cannot be concluded that the results were due to the existence of DVUs rather than to a positive generalist practice regarding domestic violence.

Another study compared two divisions with DVUs with one which had no DVU but where every case was followed up by a uniformed officer (personal communication, Jayne Mooney 1991). Results suggested that victims favoured the DVUs. They preferred relating to Unit officers over uniformed ones, indeed they did not respond well to uniformed officers. Moreover, the DVUs appeared to play a valuable role in linking the police with other agencies, the major problem being the shortage of adequate back-up support services from other agencies, particularly refuges and counselling services. Finally, the researcher expressed concern that the organisation and running of DVUs is left to the initiatives of individual officers, and that little coordination exists between them.

Hanmer's study of the West Yorkshire Police one year following its policy changes (1990: 44, 53-4) suggested that victims and agency workers were broadly in favour of their Domestic Violence and Child Abuse Units. Arrests were more likely to occur with Unit involvement than with local stations. However, some negative responses were noted, in one case involving a victim being told she would have to wait two weeks before the Unit could take her statement. Agency workers generally liked the Units but expressed concern about the shortage of staff and resources for the Units and the consequent use of an answerphone, about the attitudes towards domestic violence of some officers, and about the fact that not all Unit officers are women.

More recently, a Women's Aid Federation England (WAFE) survey of 102 refuges in England and Wales (in Barron *et al.* 1992: Appendix 3) found that nearly one half of the refuges had a DVU in their area and a similar number had been involved in liaison/consultation with a DVU. Nearly 75% of refuges with local DVUs said they knew what their Unit's role was and 70% said they had found the Unit helpful in improving the overall response to domestic violence.

Overall, research for this Inquiry suggested that DVUs had in most cases improved relations between the police and other agencies, and were viewed as sympathetic to victims. However, a number of concerns about DVUs were raised, some of which have been noted above, and most of which were echoed nearly two years later in the Home Affairs Committee Report (1993a: paras 23-32).

The lack of a systematic approach to DVUs within most forces or between forces is a major concern (Inquiry interviews, Home Affairs Committee 1993a: paras 25, 26). There is no overall coordination or monitoring of units, agreed standards of operation are lacking, and officers have no formal job description or training. The way DVUs are set up is often left entirely to officers from local stations. This means that DVU roles differ from unit to unit, as do their relations with 'mainstream' policing activity, their lines of support, and their accountability.

There appears to be general agreement that a key role of DVUs is to support the victim (e.g. Inquiry interviews, Metropolitan Police Community Involvement Policy Unit, n.d., Victim Support 1992: 2.20). But disagreement exists concerning exactly what this can and should entail. Providing information and support regarding the criminal justice process, making referrals to other agencies, and assisting in gathering evidence for legal proceedings through interviewing the victim are important activities which fit comfortably within a policing remit. However, some DVU officers offer strictest confidentiality to their victim clients (see, for example, Metropolitan Police Community Involvement Policy Unit, n.d.: Appendix 3). The police are clearly not in a position to promise this, since they are obliged to follow up information which a victim might inadvertently give implicating herself or her assailant in illegal activities.

Indeed, some black women have expressed the view that police are often more interested in investigating the 'criminality' of their partners or in conducting immigration investigations than in offering protection from violent men (e.g. Mama 1989, who also found that victims have themselves been arrested pending immigration investigations; Inquiry interviews with victims and service providers). This view was given weight by comments of DVU officers in a division serving a large black population in interviews for this Inquiry. These officers expressed a heightened enthusiasm for working in the DVU based on the opportunities it provided for collecting intelligence concerning the illegal activities of the partners of women seen by the Unit.

A further danger is that the boundaries of the role of the DVU officer have not been sufficiently clearly drawn. Some DVU officers go beyond their policing roles, attempting to engage in 'social work' activities inconsistent with these roles (e.g. Inquiry interviews, Home Affairs Committee 1993a: para 28, 29): for example, trying to coordinate all support services for women or offering support already provided by independent women's advocates, notably Women's Aid (see 'Inter-agency liaison' below). Some of these issues are illustrated by the debate surrounding the role of the Islington Domestic Violence Crisis Intervention team highlighted in Home Affairs Committee inquiry (Home Affairs Committee 1993b: QQ22-7). This pilot project, launched in early 1993, is to provide 24 hour civilian back-up within a police station.

Although the project provides civilian counsellors, their location within a police station has been questioned. Recent research from the USA and Australia (see 'Recent International Developments' above) suggests that a more successful model is one where independent advocates work in close conjunction with the police, but are accountable first and foremost to women victims (an accountability which the police cannot provide) and who are clearly seen by victims to be independent.

An extreme example of the dangers inherent in the police going beyond their law enforcement role was the tragic case of the fatal stabbing of a woman by her husband inside a London DVU in April 1991. The DVU officers had left the couple alone in a room, apparently at their own request, to discuss their troubles. Defending this practice, the Chief Superintendent told reporters:

> Officers dealing with domestic violence cases perform a difficult dual role of police officer and social worker.... They're allowed a great deal of discretion and allowing parties to talk through their difficulties is a legitimate option. If both parties agree, this can be done in private. Many cases have successfully resolved using this very method. (Independent Newspaper April 30, 1991).

This practice however is directly contrary to the Circular (see above), to the Metropolitan Police's Domestic Violence Best Practice Guidelines which warns that 'Police Officers are not trained counsellors' (Metropolitan Police Community Involvement Policy Unit, n.d.: 35, original emphasis), and to assertions made in all recent police documents that the victim's safety should be the primary consideration in policing domestic violence. In fact, the Metropolitan Police are currently reviewing their DVU guidelines in the light of this tragic case (Home Affairs Committee 1993b: Memorandum 4, p. 28).

It may be significant that the couple concerned were Asian. Interviews undertaken for this Inquiry with a range of Asian professionals in various parts of the country indicate that police officers may be especially reluctant to intervene in Asian communities, because they believe that these communities prefer to deal with marital conflicts through conciliation and that 'cultural' differences should be respected (see also Home Affairs Committee 1993a: para 33). However, as Siddiqui and Patel argue in the context of the DVU killing: 'the adoption of such differential strategies denies Asian women the choices and alternatives that are often available to other women...such dangerous thinking...silences women and strips them of their rights' (Siddiqui and Patel 1991). In their quest to promote good race relations and 'multi-culturalism', the police may inadvertently define as 'the community' those who have the power to speak; that is, primarily male leaders.

Concerns have also been expressed that DVU officers do not always adequately carry out their advice-giving and referral roles. The Home Affairs Committee Report (1993a: para 28) noted evidence that DVU officers sometimes give incorrect advice, for example that all civil injunctions have powers of arrest attached, or concentrate on other agencies' roles and on civil remedies rather than on their own law enforcement powers. Moreover, although now against national Victim Support policy (Barron *et al.* 1992: para 6.4; see also Victim Support 1992: para 6.27), officers in some areas still automatically refer women to local Victim Support groups (as well as other agencies) without seeking women's prior consent, a practice which may put their safety at risk

Perhaps the most widespread criticism of DVUs is that they tend to be marginalised from mainstream policing (e.g. Inquiry interviews, Home Affairs Committee 1993a: para 27, 1993b: Q27, Memorandum 20: 71, Memorandum 22: 102). Indeed, the most striking finding from interviews with service providers for this Inquiry was that, although relations with DVUs were generally positive and helpful, more work needs to be done in changing the attitudes and behaviour of front-line officers (see also McGibbon *et al.* 1989: 100-1; Home Affairs Committee 1993a: para 16, citing evidence from a range of sources). While accounts were given of sensitive and appropriate emergency responses, officers were accused often of not responding promptly when called, not taking protective action, not arresting or charging even when clear evidence existed that a crime had been committed, misinforming women about their legal options, not informing of other supports, including the DVU, and disclosing confidential refuge addresses. Some service providers felt that even in areas where the emergency response to victims was improving, this was the case mainly for 'respectable' victims — notably, white, middle class women with conventional lifestyles. Moreover, some DVU officers complained of difficulties in getting their colleagues to notify the DVU of cases, to record cases fully, to consult DVU files, to pass to DVU officers injunctions delivered to the station, and to properly tag incoming calls.

Agency workers, including some DVU officers, were concerned that most DVUs are open only during the daytime and are often under-resourced and under-staffed, limiting the service available to women and sometimes endangering their lives. The use of answerphones in DVUs was particularly disliked. Indeed, use of answerphones together with a lack of emergency response at some stations has fuelled a fear among some workers that the police may regard DVUs as being *the* solution to dealing with domestic violence, without a commitment to integrating them within mainstream policing or to resourcing them adequately (e.g. Inquiry interviews, Barron *et al.* 1992: para 6.7). Rights of Women (Mavolwane and Radford 1992) have documented cases where women phoning the police, desperate for help, have had their call transferred by the duty officer to the DVU answerphone. Similar problems were identified in memoranda of evidence presented to the Home Affairs Committee (1993b). For example:

> When women ring to report an incident of violence, the desk officer insists on transferring them to the domestic violence unit. Frequently the officers are not in, so the client fails to get any service at all. (Appendix 9: 233) Most domestic violence units are staffed by one or two officers only. This means that any woman calling the unit will invariably receive an answerphone message requesting her to leave her name and number so that an officer can get back to her. This is useless to women who have no home phone or who are staying in Bed and Breakfast or other temporary accommodation, who feel unable to give out a refuge number or who are fearful that their abuser may intercept a call intended for them.
>
> (Memorandum 22: 102)

Clearly, the overall level of resources available to the police is not under their control, and it is important to acknowledge that the Service is extremely stretched. In his testimony to the Home Affairs Committee, the Chief Constable of Gloucestershire and Chairman of the Association of Chief Police Officers' Crime Committee made this point strongly (1993b: QQ181-188) . In particular, he defended not having DVUs in his own force by referring to lack of resources. However, in so doing he also demonstrated that, despite Circular 60/1990, the belief that domestic violence is a lesser problem has not died: 'As a Chief Constable, one cannot look at domestic violence in isolation. In my county alone, crime has doubled in five years and that needs to be addressed: a lot of that is *serious crime like burglaries* which have gone up by leaps and bounds' (Q186, emphasis added). The significance of this comment was not lost on the Home Affairs Committee (1993a: para 16). If the police genuinely believe domestic violence to be a crime as serious as assaults on strangers, then justifiable concerns about resource shortages cannot absolve them of their duty to prioritise domestic violence. In their Report, the Home Affairs Committee stated: **'We do not believe that resource limitation should be used as an excuse for an inadequate response to domestic violence.** ... a response to violent crime, whether it occurs in the home, the pub or the football match, is a core function of the police' (1993a: para 20, original emphasis).

Some commentators, including some police officers, argue that special units inevitably marginalise, and suggest that while DVUs exist, domestic violence will not be taken seriously by other officers. Some divisions have attempted to deal with marginalisation by creating alternatives to DVUs; for example, designating a sergeant in charge of domestic violence for every relief. However none of the alternatives discussed in interviews for this Inquiry were viewed as successes, and some divisions had returned to DVUs. Indeed, marginalisation may not be a necessary consequence of special units. A problem in many divisions appears to be that although DVUs may have the support of senior management, that support does not take the form of active daily supervision and monitoring. Most DVUs are staffed by one or two (usually women) uniformed officers. Rarely do these officers have sufficient rank to challenge their colleagues or to institute and effectively monitor procedures. Junior officers cannot be expected to enforce policies.

West Yorkshire, on the other hand, appears to have had some success with specialist units headed by sergeants who are responsible for daily monitoring of practice on their divisions. This task is considerably aided by a force-wide Domestic Violence Index which holds information on every domestic violence call. The controller checks the Index when calls come in, informing responding officers of any history *before* arrival on the scene. The police also run a 24 hour helpline, directly connected to the control room, which is especially important outside Unit opening hours. Finally, in addition to daily monitoring, the Force undertakes periodic monitoring research, and independent monitoring occurs through outside research and local authority sponsored inter-agency domestic violence forums (see Hanmer and Saunders 1991).

Nonetheless, Hanmer's (1990) survey of victims showed that there were still problems in West Yorkshire. Although advice given by uniformed officers was in line with the new policy in 55% of cases, in the remainder the response was not, and included advising victims that nothing could be done because 'you are man and wife' or 'it is up to her to bring charges' (p. 34). Where assailants were present on police arrival, 40% were arrested, but in 25% of cases the police did not even speak to the man. Nor were police arresting for breach of injunctions. Not being present when the police arrived appeared to be the most effective means of avoiding police intervention. When asked whether the police were helpful, half of those women who had phoned the police once in the past year said 'no', as did nearly two-thirds who had phoned more than once. The most helpful responses consisted of advice and information to the woman regarding ways of protecting herself and children, and firm action to control the man. Unhelpful advice included doing nothing, taking the man's side, blaming the woman, and racist harassment. Some police simply did not turn up when called. Finally, over half of women said the police did not help in the way they wanted, which in most cases was a stronger response.

Inter-agency liaison

This Inquiry found strong support from service providers for a closer, more effective and hospitable working relationship with the police, and indeed the international evidence demonstrates the central importance of inter-agency coordination in achieving an effective preventive police response (see 'Recent International Developments' above). It is clear that in many areas liaison between DVU officers and other agencies has begun and has markedly improved perceptions of police by these other agencies. DVU officers also expressed feelings that positive working relationships were being established.

Of crucial importance are signs in many areas of improved relationships between the police and Women's Aid, widely acknowledged as *the* key agency supporting women who experience domestic violence (e.g. Women's National Commission 1985: paras 21-24, Victim Support 1992: paras 6.14-6.21; see also 'Community supports for women' below). Mutual training by police and Women's Aid has occurred in some locations and has helped to remove prejudices on both sides which are often unfounded (personal communication, WAFE 1992). This may be a necessary first step towards evolving formal consultation mechanisms with respect both to local police policy and practice development and monitoring, and to dealing with individual cases. However, in some areas police and local Women's Aid groups have not discussed policy and practice (personal communication, WAFE November 1992), clearly indicating that further work is needed.

In many areas, the police are also involved in inter-agency work through local domestic violence forums which bring together a wide range of statutory and voluntary sector agencies (see Victim Support 1992: Ch. 7) Indeed, some inter-agency groups have been organised by the police, in line with policy statements suggesting that police *initiate* local inter-agency groups or *coordinate* the work of other agencies (e.g. Metropolitan Police Working Party 1986: para 13.2.1, Home Office Circular 60/1990: para 10). This Inquiry found evidence that attempts by DVU officers to coordinate inter-agency groups had created suspicion and ill feeling in some areas, with agency workers refusing to attend meetings because they felt that the police had insisted on setting the agenda for the group and were using other agencies for their own ends (see also Southall Black Sisters 1989, Home Affairs Committee 1993a: para 28). Forums 'brokered' by local councils or the voluntary sector and including strong representation from local refuge and other support groups for women — as for example in Hammersmith and Fulham, Nottinghamshire, Leeds, and Wolverhampton — have been more successful in bringing together a range of agencies, including a positive role for the police, and setting and implementing concrete agendas (Inquiry interviews, Victim Support 1992: Ch. 7).

Streatham's deferred cautioning policy

A well publicised claim that policy has improved police practice in dealing with domestic violence concerns Streatham's deferred cautioning policy (extended throughout Metropolitan Police District 4 Area [Victim Support 1992: para 2.18]). This policy encourages arrest followed by cautioning after a two month deferral period for domestic violence offenders who have caused *minor* injury only, who admit their offence, who are first-time offenders, and whose victims do not want to prosecute. Data on police dispositions appear to support the policy's success when compared with the pre-policy situation at Streatham and a comparison division with no domestic violence policy: both comparisons showed the policy to produce more recorded crime, arrests, and charges and less 'no criming'. Further support is claimed from official re-offending rates and interviews with victims (see Buchan and Edwards 1991).

However, it is unclear whether the improvement in dispositions resulted from the *cautioning* policy *per se* or from a strong interventionist policy on domestic violence generally plus a DVU, both of which were absent in pre-policy Streatham and the comparison division. Further, only 35% of victims (a total of 23 women) whose partners were cautioned were interviewed, and those victims not interviewed may have been more likely still to be living in dangerous situations since 'the interview sample was drawn without having to make contact with victims who were living with difficult offenders'(Buchan and Edwards 1991: 56). Indeed, in the course of discussing interview contact (p.57), the researchers make a number of statements which suggest that the circumstances of some victims were extremely precarious; for example, two women who were interviewed had left their homes, fleeing violent partners; one woman, who was finally tracked down by methods which included leaving a letter with the offender, said she was depressed and did not want to be interviewed; at one house, the offender answered the door, and 'was very rude and abusive stating that the woman was not at home and in any case would not wish to be interviewed'.

In addition, concern has been expressed over the legality of the cautioning policy, its potential for symbolically trivialising domestic violence, and the possibility that it may divert cases from prosecution (e.g. Horley 1990, Inquiry interviews). This last concern, contrary to the researchers' claims, has not been refuted since the dispositional comparisons mentioned above were not well controlled. To the extent that practice has improved at Streatham, it is most likely to be the result of commitment by the Chief Superintendent to take domestic violence seriously, and careful monitoring of cases. A cautioning policy could well backfire where this is lacking.

Towards an effective police response to domestic violence

Overall, the limited evidence discussed above suggests that the UK has made some very important strides in improving police responses to domestic violence. Using survey data collected from 100 refuges in September 1992, WAFE summarised the situation as follows:

> In a number of areas, police officers are giving a higher priority to domestic violence, are giving out more information to women, are following up cases and are generally becoming more sympathetic and understanding of women's situation. The response is, however, very uneven, and in some areas, police attitudes seem largely unchanged.
>
> (Barron *et al.* 1992: 6.2)

The Home Affairs Committee Report (1993a) came to similar conclusions: 'It was clear that the picture varied both between different police forces and within individual forces, and a recurrent description of the police response was that it was "patchy" (para 17). The Report noted evidence both of positive attitude change and responses (para 15) and of the continuing failure of many officers to take domestic violence seriously (para 16).

The Report (Home Affairs Committee 1993a: paras 33-7) also highlighted the following evidence suggesting that much work is still needed to ensure that black and minority ethnic women are given equal access to and treatment by the police: black and minority ethnic women lack confidence in police, they are particularly likely to find the police unhelpful if not openly racist and are thus less likely to contact them. Asian women may suffer from police reluctance to intervene in their communities and a minority of women may be inhibited from using the police due to immigration legislation. In addition, some women may be silenced by lack of police sensitivity to language problems and lack of interpreters (e.g. Mama 1989, Inquiry interviews Home Affairs Committee 1993b: Appendix 9). Police sometimes speak only to and through the violent man, or use friends or relatives who may, instead of interpreting put pressure on women not to seek help or to request police action to the detriment of their own wishes and safety.

The international evidence shows that effective policing requires more than policy change. It requires, above all, *coordination* between the police and other criminal justice and community agencies, *police accountability to women victims* through continued internal and independent monitoring, and well funded *independent victim advocacy and support* services which work closely with the police (see 'Recent International Developments' above).

The UK has only just begun to tackle the need for truly comprehensive and coordinated CJS responses (see generally, Home Affairs Committee 1993a, 1993b). Although cooperation between the police and other agencies is beginning in some areas, often through inter-agency forums, the development of something approaching community coordination will take time, effort and a great deal of commitment on all sides. A small number of innovative pilot projects which aim to produce a more coordinated response are already under way or about to begin. For example, two court-mandated re-education programmes for violent men exist in Scotland, a civilian crisis intervention team based within Islington Police Station has recently begun operation, and victim advocacy services for women dealing with the CJS are being developed in Leeds and Nottinghamshire.

Much work also still needs to be done to establish police accountability to victims. No formal mechanisms yet exist for police liaison and consultation with Women's Aid or other victim advocates. Internal and independent monitoring is extremely limited and patchy.

Finally, community services for women, notably Women's Aid, have inadequate resources to provide the level of support and advocacy required to enable women safely and effectively to use the police (see Barron *et al.* 1992: Appendix 2, Home Affairs Committee 1993a: para 130). This is clearly outside the control of the police, as the Home Affairs Committee Report acknowledges (1993a: para 22). Nevertheless, the Committee states: 'in our view there is not much point in making the work of the police more efficient and effective if at the end of the line there is inadequate refuge provision available for victims' (para 22; see 'Community supports for women' below for a discussion of refuges and other victim supports).

Recommendations for an effective local police response

Despite the shortcomings noted above, it is clear that the police in many locations have moved further than other statutory agencies in developing positive policies and practices towards domestic violence to women. Listed below are a number of recommendations, some of which build on practice already occurring in various locations, but all of which are intended to sharpen up the police response.

i.   Acceptance of women's experiences and understandings of domestic violence.

ii. Prompt and sensitive response to calls: a. ensure victim's (and children's) safety; b. never attempt conciliation; c. interview victim away from perpetrator; d.

provide accurate and precise advice, supplemented by multi-lingual advice leaflets for women, and e. transport victim and children to a place of safety if requested.

iii. Policy encouraging arrest when evidence allows. Victim's wishes should always be considered.

iv. Readily available independent interpreters, with officer training regarding their use.

v. Equal service to women of all communities and circumstances.

vi. Integrated, coordinated and adequately resourced DVUs headed by senior staff to provide: a. prompt follow-up of cases in conjunction with CID; b. visible contact point for women to obtain information and advice concerning criminal justice matters, information regarding community supports, and referral to other agencies *with prior consent of the victim;* c. liaison with relevant health and social welfare agencies, including in particular local Women's Aid refuges, and support groups, concerning all aspects of police policy and practice; d. advice to and training of officers; e. daily monitoring of division practices; f. accurate and comprehensive records, and g. links with local inter-agency forums.

vii. Extension of DVU opening hours.

viii. Where no DVUs exist or their establishment is not practicable, implementation of functions listed in vi. above through a specialist officer or the generalist system of policing.

ix. Computerised domestic violence index.

x. Mutual training of police and relevant support agencies including, in particular, Women's Aid.

xi. Coordination of police with other agencies, ideally through local inter-agency forums.

xii. Public accountability through independent monitoring.

Civil law remedies

Since the mid 1970s, many jurisdictions worldwide have passed civil laws designed to protect women suffering domestic violence through the provision of two types of injunction (order): i. protection, restraining or non-molestation orders which require the abuser to stop harassing or assaulting the victim (and/or her children), and ii. exclusion or ouster orders which require that the abuser leave the home or, if he has already left, remain away from it.

A major advantage of injunctions is that they are designed explicitly to *protect* victims from *future* violence. As the Law Commission states 'most acts of violence are also crimes, but the object of the criminal law is primarily to punish and deter the offender, whereas the object of family law is primarily to protect the victim' (Law Commission 1989: 1). In fact, the international evidence suggests that injunctions, properly enforced, have a vital role to play *in conjunction with* criminal justice sanctions, as part of a coordinated community response (e.g. Pence 1989) In addition, the exclusion order in particular 'gives a victim of abuse an enforceable right to be safe in her home, and establishes that the abuser rather than the victim should bear the burden of finding another residence' (Lerman 1980: 272).

In England, however, the failure of injunctions to provide effective protection has been widely documented. The following major problems are acknowledged:

i.   exclusion orders granted *ex parte* (in emergency without notifiying the respondent) are very difficult to obtain;

ii.   judges dislike granting *exclusion orders* under any circumstances due to concerns about the property rights of respondents; where granted they are temporary, usually limited to three months, and are therefore not a long term housing solution;

iii.   powers of arrest are hardly ever attached to *ex parte* injunctions;

iv.   injunctions with *powers of arrest* attached are difficult to obtain even at full hearings (*ex parte* provision and powers of arrest are essential for effective protection, since women are often in imminent danger);

v.   women are frequently offered *undertakings* at county courts instead of injunctions, which amount to informal 'promises' by assailants without the need to admit guilt or give evidence, and without provision for powers of arrest;

vi.   injunctions are inadequately enforced (recent evidence suggests that half of all injunctions are breached on one or more occasions [Barron 1990: 65]): police rarely arrest for breach of injunctions even when powers of arrest are attached, solicitors are often reluctant to take breaches back to court, and judges rarely commit men to prison for breaching injunctions;

vii.   injunctions are restricted to married or cohabiting couples, providing no cover to ex-partners (except under limited conditions) or to partners who have never cohabited;

viii.   the civil law is cumbersome and complicated to use due to the existence of different statutes with varying eligibility criteria and powers, and

ix.   injunctions are rarely used jointly with criminal justice sanctions, rather they tend to be viewed as alternative measures; indeed, the existence of bail conditions prohibiting the abuser from returning home may deny the victim the possibility of obtaining an exclusion order.

(For a fuller discussion, see Homer *et al.* 1984: 61-6, McCann 1985, Parker 1985, Freeman 1987, Law Commission 1989, Mama 1989, Barron 1990.)

Many of the above points are addressed in the recommendations and draft bill published by the Law Commission in May, 1992. The Commission's recommendations include:

i.   extending the categories of people who can apply for orders (paras 3.26, 4.9);

ii.   confirming that the courts should consider all the circumstances of a case and that it is their *duty* to grant occupation orders (formerly exclusion orders) to applicants without property rights 'if it appears likely that the applicant or any relevant child will suffer significant harm if an order is not made and that such harm will be greater than the harm which the respondent or any relevant child will suffer if the order is made' (para 4.33), where 'significant harm' is defined as 'ill-treatment or impairment of physical and mental health' (para 4.34);

iii. *requiring* courts to consider factors such as 'risk of significant harm to an applicant or a child if the order is not made immediately' (para 5.10) when deciding whether to grant *ex parte* orders;

iv. *requiring* courts to attach powers of arrest to injunctions where violence has occurred or is threatened, *unless* the applicant or child is adequately protected without such power (para 5.13);

v. *enabling,* but not requiring, courts to attach powers of arrest to *ex parte* orders when violence has occurred or is threatened and the court is satisfied that significant risk of harm exists if the power is not immediately attached (para 5.14);

vi. extending the duration of *ex parte* occupation orders granted to applicants without property rights up to six months in the first instance (4.37) and those with property rights for any specified time or until further notice (para 4.36), and

vii. *empowering* the police to apply for injunctions on behalf of victims (para 5.20).

The Commission's recommendations have received widespread, though not universal, support (see Home Affairs Committee 1993a: Section C, 1993b). However, even if enacted in full, the legislation does not and cannot effectively cover all areas of concern for victims wanting to use the civil law. For example, solicitors representing victims are not always fully cognisant with domestic violence law and thus give inadequate advice; some solicitors fail to consult closely with victims throughout all stages of the legal process or pressurise them into making decisions without adequately discussing alternatives; the courts are often very distressing and potentially dangerous places, with no facilities to enable women to avoid contact with their partners; and hearings can be extremely intimidating (e.g. Barron 1990) (although steps are being taken to make courts less intimidating this, following the Home Affairs Committee report). Moreover, legislation cannot ensure enforcement of orders and effective remedies against breaches.

Women's access to civil remedies generally is threatened by legal aid restrictions recently agreed by Parliament (*Guardian,* 1/4/93). These come at a time when solicitors are increasingly withdrawing from legal aid work and when women are increasingly being denied legal aid for injunctions (Home Affairs Committee 1993a: para 125). In some cases, refusal of emergency legal aid is apparently being rationalised by reference to recent policy changes in policing (Barron *et al.* 1992: Appendix 3). This ignores the fact that policy changes towards arrest and prosecution have not as yet been fully implemented and that criminal justice and civil remedies fulfil different functions and may need to be used together. Because of legal aid restrictions, the Home Affairs Committee expressed its concern that civil remedies will effectively be denied to 'a very large number of victims' (para 126) who seek 'simply the right to live [their] life without being molested' (para 127).

This right is also threatened by recent moves in family proceedings towards conciliation and joint agreements regarding children's welfare, supported by the Law Commission's (1990) divorce reform proposals and the Children Act 1989; and by the growing emphasis on paternal responsibility for continuing care and support of children following family breakdown, enshrined in the Children Act 1989 and Child Support Act 1991. Although the Children Act in particular is specifically concerned with the welfare of children and not the protection of women from domestic violence, the two are obviously related and a broad view needs to be taken in assessing the best interest of the child. The Children Act makes no mention of domestic violence, for example, and the Child Support Act allows for the duty of lone parents to supply information regarding the whereabouts of the absent parent to be waived if there are reasonable grounds for believing this would lead to risk of harm or distress, but does not indicate how this is to be proved. These two Acts may thus make permanent escape from violent men problematic for many women (see Home Affairs Committee 1993a: paras 123, 124). Cases have been documented where women have suffered further abuse, sometimes severe injury, as a direct result of their whereabouts being given to a partner in a contact order granted under the Children Act 1989 (Singh 1992). Moreover, residence orders have been awarded to violent men for children as young as ten months, sometimes on the grounds that a refuge is not a suitable place for a child. Some solicitors and Women's Aid groups, attuned to the dangers surrounding the Acts, are advising women not to attempt *any* civil action against their partners (personal communication, WAFE 1993).

Community supports for women

The international evidence demonstrates a clear need for an integrated range of services for women (see below). Women needing these services range from those experiencing abuse for the first time, through those who have suffered it for years but feel they have no option but to stay; those on the point of leaving and needing somewhere to go, to those who have left and need further support of various kinds. Organisations which are provided by women for women (only) are best suited to take the lead in offering these forms of help (e.g. Victim Support 1992 paras: 6.14-6.21, 6.24). They have received the most positive evaluation from earlier research (Smith 1989) and have years of relevant experience and training (see publications of Women's Aid Federations in England, Wales, Scotland and Northern Ireland).

Refuges

Refuges are a particular success story (Smith 1989). Run by women for women, they admit on an emergency basis and offer secure and confidential shelter for an indefinite period, thus providing safety for many thousands of women and their children who otherwise would be further abused or killed by violent men. In a USA-wide study covering 1981, 1982, and 1983, (Stout 1989: 25, 27) found a strong negative correlation between the rate of shelters (refuges) in a state and femicide: states with a higher coverage of shelters had fewer killings of women by their partners than did those with a lower coverage.

In the UK, there are about 290 local refuge groups of which about 200 are affiliated to one of the four national coordinating bodies — Women's Aid Federation England

(WAFE), Welsh Women's Aid, Scottish Women's Aid and Northern Ireland Women's Aid (Barron *et al.* 1992: Appendix 1). Each year about 25,000 women and children use refuges and more than 100,000 contact Women's Aid for support (Barron *et al.* 1992: Appendix 2). London Women's Aid alone deals with over 5,000 callers a year looking for a place to go and 4,000 more wanting advice or information (undated factsheet: About London Women's Aid).

Women typically do not find their way to refuges without enduring many years of violence. The women in Binney *et al.*'s (1981, 1985) survey — still the only nationally funded refuge survey in Britain — had suffered violence for periods ranging from a few months to 30 or 40 years, the average being 7 years. Their ages ranged from 17 to 70 (average, 31 years), the violence usually having started when the woman was in her early twenties. Most had wanted to leave from the first year of their marriage but had nowhere to go, having not heard of refuges at that time. Some told of spending the night in a telephone box, public lavatory or on a park bench. Two thirds tried staying with families or friends usually resulting in overcrowding, but were easily found and gave in to pressure (often involving physical force or threats to themselves or their hosts) to return home.

In that it succeeds in helping women escape from constantly repeated violent attacks, the provision of refuges is vital. In playing such an important role in their provision, Women's Aid plays arguably the biggest crime prevention role of any agency involved in domestic violence. Local groups running refuges are, however, seriously under-funded and often there are not enough places. The figure still generally quoted as an absolute minimum is that of one family place per 10,000 of the population, which was originally recommended as an initial target by the Parliamentary Select Committee on Violence in Marriage in 1975. This figure has never come anywhere near being met. Binney *et al.*'s (1981: 27) 1978 figures showed that 150 groups were providing about one sixth of this number in 200 houses in England and Wales, and were unable to meet current demand. Many areas remained without refuge provision at all, and women from such areas rarely found their way to refuges elsewhere (p.27-8). The 200 plus groups existing by 1988 (1988 reprinting of same text, new foreword, p. i.) cannot have exceeded a quarter of the recommended target figure. Indeed, WAFE considered that they represented no net improvement in provision since rehousing had become far harder to achieve and women were having to stay longer in refuge places. London Women's Aid was able to find refuge for only 40% of women requesting accommodation in 1990 (Barron *et al.* 1992: Appendix 2). The Government's view on this is that refuges (being essentially local organisations) are best provided in response to local need, and can and do receive help from local authorities. Nevertheless, by the end of 1992, there were still fewer than one third of the Select Committee's recommended number of refuge places (Barron *et al.* 1992: Appendix 2). It is a tribute to their commitment that they have been able to do so.

Women who have used them state that refuges are the only agencies which meet their needs (Smith 1989). Further, they are the only agencies which tend to be consistently positively evaluated in research; the only criticisms relating to factors resulting from inadequate funding, for example poor and overcrowded premises. Bowker and Maurer's US sample (1987: 39) rated women's groups and shelters as the most effective of all the sources approached for help in dealing with violence. Smith (1989: 99) lists tributes paid to the refuge movement by official reports from the Women's National Commission (Advisory Committee to the Cabinet Office), the Council of Europe, and the United Nations. The major problems are that only a minority of women hear about refuges or find out how to contact them, and more women could not easily be accommodated in existing provision.

Russell (1989: 39-43) points to the need to identify and target groups marginalised due to ethnic origin, disability and age. Specialist black refuges have not yet been established in sufficient numbers to make escape a real option for many minority ethnic women, and mixed refuges may operate in racist ways (Mama 1989), although they are working to counteract this (Inquiry interview). Women from particular ethnic groups (South Asian, Chinese and others) use refuges less than their numbers would indicate might be the case (Russell 1989: 41-2) because of limited provision, inadequately targeted publicity, language issues, and the additional difficulties for such women in even attempting to escape from violence. Disabled women are also less likely to see publicity on how to reach safety, especially if they are housebound or heavily dependent on their abusers. Furthermore, the age and state of most refuge buildings makes access and other provision for most disabled women a virtual impossibility. Specific funding for outreach staff and for purpose-built accommodation would need to be the starting points of effective provision for this doubly jeopardised group of women (personal communication, WAFE, November 1992). Ironically, severe and repeated violence can be the cause of the very disability which then cuts women off from hearing about or receiving help.

Support groups and follow-up

Groups, or house meetings in refuges, appear more effective than therapy in assisting women to rebuild their emotional strength (Rodriguez 1988:242). They also play a crime prevention role in teaching women they have the right to remain safe and how to go about doing so. Groups for Asian women, communicating in mother tongues where appropriate, can help women understand their own particular experience of abuse and the way this is compounded by welfare agencies' inappropriate responses — for example, rehousing to areas where racial attacks are common or demanding to see passports (Guru 1986: 162-3). Such groups can help women who are unlikely to be accepted back into traditional communities, build a new identity and new support networks (Guru 1986: 163).

Through participation in groups, women's guilt and stigma are reduced. They learn that they are not the only ones to have suffered abuse and that it can only really be understood as a wider social problem (e.g. Clifton 1985: 51-2, Condonis *et al.* 1989: 8-9). Support groups in refuges and afterwards also combat isolation and empower women to take further preventive steps most suited to their own circumstances. For women to make the shift from being victims to being survivors, support groups are absolutely crucial. Removing the abuser from the scene and giving the women a personal alarm, for example, may assist the woman to summon help. But if it is the sole response, this action may leave the woman isolated and perhaps in permanent fear. Membership of a group, on the other hand, may well help her to find the courage to construct an entire plan for a future life lived in safety, perhaps even in a different area (Inquiry interviews).

The international evidence confirms this stance (e.g. Pence 1987, Dutton-Douglas and Dionne 1991) and also suggests the need for coherent follow-up programmes and funded workers to run them. Based on research on readmissions to shelters in the USA, Wilson *et al.* (1989: 282) regard continual contact with former residents as a crucial supportive network in preventing women returning to further violence and in helping with reintegration into the community. This contact may be particularly difficult in rural areas where refuges are likely to need to take on a range of extra roles to cover the shortfall in support around issues like rape and incest (e.g. Noesjirwan 1985: 84- 5).

Interviews for this Inquiry confirmed the need, reiterated consistently by WAFE in its publications over the years (most recently as evidence to the Home Affairs Committee, see Barron *et al.* 1992), for funded workers to offer longer-term support. These workers would be available to help women locate local resources, groups and forms of support needed to 'make a go' of a new life, and to assist women in negotiating with public agencies. A refuge worker interviewed for this Inquiry thought this kind of help could significantly cut the number of women who return to their husbands after being rehoused, only to leave again later; thus representing a real saving to the public purse by rehousing such women only once. One woman, described in an interview, had been in and out of a refuge eight times in three months because, after 25 years as a housewife, she found the hurdles of police, courts, housing, poll tax, schools, and the humiliation of going to the Department of Social Security too much to cope with. With adequate support, however, she is now rehoused and is doing voluntary work in her local community. Local refuge workers currently have the expertise but not the funded time routinely to offer this effective form of help (Inquiry interviews). Evidence from other countries demonstrates that advocacy schemes, operating independently of public agencies and linked to refuges and other women's organisations, constitute an effective way of offering such support in negotiating with legal and welfare agencies (e.g. London Battered Women's Advocacy Clinic 1985, Pence and Shepard 1988: 290-1, Cahn and Lerman 1991, Edleson 1991).

A range of crisis services

Mugford (1990: 4, citing research conducted for the Office of the Status of Women, 1990, Department of the Prime Minister and the Cabinet in Australia) refers to the crucial need for 24-hour crisis intervention services. Existing health and social services are often not geared up to deal with domestic violence as appropriately as they should and are not available at the most necessary times. Helplines, with responses available in a range of languages, backed up with posters and other public education, also in a range of languages, and in appropriate media including the minority ethnic press, are a crucial crisis service. Russell (1989: 8) points to the need for disability organisations to have appropriate information and for outreach workers to contact abused disabled women.

Hanmer and Saunders (1987: 293) highlight the need for provision of drop-in centres or 24- hour safe houses where women can go for advice and help. Wharton (1987: 158) lists services for battered women as including crisis lines, counselling, and providing information about community resources; but always with a shelter as the central form of service that women need to know they can fall back on. Each refuge in New Zealand, being government funded, is able to run programmes for women and children in their own areas, provide training and education for local community groups, and give talks in schools and elsewhere (National Collective of Independent Women's Refuges Inc. n.d.).

Women's Aid groups in the UK undertake some of this work but are always hard pressed owing to insecure and inadequate funding. Notably, the coordinating body of the WAFE provides a National Helpline (and has recently been awarded £140,000 over three years by the Department of Health to support this). London Women's Aid operates an emergency telephone line during office hours and coordinates an emergency rota run by the refuges themselves at night.

There is growing recognition that other agencies who come into contact with women suffering the effects of domestic violence should develop their services in ways which complement, but do not attempt to duplicate, the work of Women's Aid and other women's organisations that have developed considerable expertise over the years (e.g. Victim Support 1992: chapters 6 and 7). In particular, there is a danger in involving untrained or inadequately trained personnel — particularly volunteers — in life-threatening or complex situations. Consequently, organisations such as Victim Support are not well placed to play the primary role in this field of work. Nevertheless, they do have a role to play. Inter-agency forums and joint training initiatives may provide effective mechanisms for coordinating and expanding the work of a range of agencies.

Cocooning the victim/survivor

One interesting preventive initiative rated highly by women and which, it appears, has no full-scale equivalent in Britain is the Safe Space Project in Duluth, Minnesota, organised under the widely-known Domestic Abuse Intervention Project (DAIP) there (Pence 1987: 101-2). It was designed for women whose male partners are on court-mandated batterers' programmes, but staff also contacted every woman with a protection order and every woman whose partner had been charged with a domestic assault related crime. The project aimed to extend into the wider community the attitude change achieved with the police and criminal justice system; that is, to encourage people to place the blame on the offender rather than the woman he abused. For example, three support group members who had the same employer as another member persuaded management to agree to call the police if her husband came near, and to screen her calls so that he could no longer threaten her. Another group explained to a social worker that she was being used as an instrument of the husband's harassment (in constantly checking on standards of child care because of his allegations, for example).

The Safe Space Project brought family and friends together to design for every woman a safe space plan in a structured way. This might involve the group in enlisting the support of a minister, doctor, employer, or whoever could help 'to strategize together on enlisting the cooperation of community members in protecting women'. It included follow-up meetings to review the plan. Each woman defined her own support system: e.g. friends, family, shelter and DAIP staff and volunteers, police, courts, church members. Any or all of these might 'help her establish safety and hold her abuser accountable to her' (Pence 1987: 102). This was in addition to ensuring that women knew how to use the courts if they choose to.

Conclusion

There is a very great deal which police at the local level can do — in conjunction with other agencies targeting domestic violence and civil law remedies — to assist women in becoming and remaining safe from men's violence. Such work is long-term, must permeate all levels of the Service, and must always take the safety of women and children as its linchpin.

A coordinated approach, established by an inter-agency group, has been found elsewhere to be a key starting point. Inter-agency forums in the UK, however, are only beginning to be independently evaluated — a matter of great urgency since they are currently proliferating at a rapid rate. Existing women's organisations, including in particular local Women's Aid and other voluntary sector women's groups, play a key role in such forums. They can offer the greatest expertise in advising, through training and other inter-agency contact, what forms of intervention are likely to prove safe. Special efforts should always be made to involve groups representing minority ethnic women.

It is also crucially important to listen to victims. The very fact that they know their abusers over many years makes this one area of violent offending where the criminal mind holds little mystery. The imposition of any blanket policy, when individual women do not consider it to be safe, is unlikely to prove helpful in the longer term.

This report has shown that the long neglect of domestic violence as a crime in the UK — true of police and government alike until quite recently — was badly misplaced and counterproductive. There is a pressing need for effective measures of prevention. They need to be accompanied by adequate resourcing and efficient coordination in order to build effectively on new evidence of a willingness to take men's crimes against women seriously. The involvement of central government is essential for this to occur. Without such concerted and pro-active developments, the term 'prevention' will retain a hollow ring.

It is thus appropriate to end this report by noting that much needed action is now beginning to be taken at national level to combat domestic violence. A ministerial group on domestic violence has been established, headed by the Home Office — the newly appointed 'lead' department for coordinating work nationally. The Home Affairs Committee (1993a) has reported on an inquiry into domestic violence. Among its many recommendations are: 'that the need to tackle domestic violence effectively is given appropriate priority by all Departments' (para 132); 'that the Treasury should be invited to participate in the Ministerial and Official Working Groups on Domestic Violence' (para 135); and that 'the first priority for Government action on domestic violence should be the establishment of a central, co-ordinated policy for refuge provision throughout the country' (para 124).

These moves are warmly welcomed. They may herald, at long last, an era in which genuine attempts to improve policies and practice, by the police and others, will not be hampered through lack of an infrastructure of other forms of escape and support for women. They may also mean that those who exhibit a reluctance to change will be spotlighted as unacceptably out of step and out of date. These will be the ultimate tests of national pronouncements and local action.

References

Andrews, B. and Brown, G.W. (1988) 'Marital violence in the community: a biographical approach'. *British Journal of Psychiatry,* 153: 305-312.

Balos, B. and Trotsky, K. (1988) 'Enforcement of the Domestic Abuse Act in Minnesota: a preliminary study'. *Law and Inequality,* 6: 83-125.

Barron, J. (1990) *Not Worth the Paper. . ? The Effectiveness of Legal Protection for Women and Children Experiencing Domestic Violence.* Bristol: Women's Aid Federation England Ltd.

Barron, J., Harwin, N. and Singh, T. (1992) *Report to Home Affairs Committee Inquiry into Domestic Violence.* Bristol: Women's Aid Federation England. (Also published as Memorandum 22 in Home Affairs Committee (1993b) *Domestic Violence.* Vol.II. Memoranda of Evidence, Minutes of Evidence and Appendices. London: HMSO.)

Binney, V., Harkell, G., and Nixon, J. (1981) *Leaving Violent Men: A Study of Refuges and Housing for Battered Women.* Leeds: Women's Aid Federation England.

Binney, V., Harkell, G., and Nixon, J. (1985) 'Refuges and housing for battered women'. In J. Pahl (ed.) *Private Violence and Public Policy: The Needs of Battered Women and the Response of the Public Services.* London: Routledge and Kegan Paul.

Borkowski, M., Murch, M., and Walker, V. (1983) *Marital Violence: the Community Response.* London: Tavistock.

Bourlet, A. (1990) *Police Intervention in Marital Violence.* Milton Keynes: Open University Press.

Bowker, L. H. and Maurer, L. (1987) 'The medical treatment of battered wives'. *Women and Health,* 12(1): 25-45.

Bowker, L.H. (1986) *Ending the Violence.* Holmes Beach, Florida: Learning Publications.

Browne, A. (1987) *When Battered Women Kill.* New York: The Free Press.

Browne, A. and Williams, K.R. (1989) 'Exploring the effect of resource availability and the likelihood of female-precipitated homicides'. *Law and Society Review,* 23(1): 75-94.

Buchan, I. and Edwards, S. (1991) *Adult Cautioning for Domestic Violence.* London: Home Office. June.

Buel, S.M. (1988) 'Mandatory arrest for domestic violence'. *Harvard Women's Law Journal,* 11: 213-226.

Buzawa, E.S. and Buzawa, C.G. (1990) *Domestic Violence: The Criminal Justice Response.* Newbury Park, California: Sage.

Cahn, N.R. and Lerman, L.G. (1991) 'Prosecuting woman abuse'. In M. Steinman (ed.) *Woman Battering: Policy Responses.* Cincinnati, Ohio: Anderson Publishing.

Clifton, J. (1985) 'Refuges and self-help'. In N. Johnson (ed.) *Marital Violence.* London: Routledge and Kegan Paul.

Condonis, M., Paroissien, K., and Aldrich, B. (1989) *The Mutual-Help Group: A Therapeutic Program for Women who have been Abused.* 67 Smith Street, Wollongong, NSW 2500, Australia: Cider Press Pty Ltd. Funded by the Office of the Status of Women.

Davidoff, L. and Dowds, L. (1989) 'Recent trends in crimes of violence against the person in England and Wales'. In Home Office Research and Planning Unit *Research Bulletin,* No. 27. London: HMSO.

Davis, N. (1988) 'Battered women: implications for social control'. *Contemporary Crisis,* 12: 345-372.

Dobash, R.E. and Dobash, R. (1980) *Violence against Wives: a Case against the Patriarchy.* Shepton Mallett, Somerset: Open Books.

Dobash, R.E., Dobash, R.P, and Cavanagh, K. (1985) 'The contact between battered women and social and medical agencies'. In J. Pahl (ed.) *Private Violence and Public Policy: The Needs of Battered Women and the Responses of the Public Services.* London: Routledge and Kegan Paul.

Dunford, F.W., Huizinga, D., and Elliott, D.S. (1989) *The Omaha Domestic Violence Police Experiment.* Final Report. National Institute of Justice and the City of Omaha, June.

Dutton, D.G. (1988) *The Domestic Assault of Women: Psychological and Criminal Justice Perspectives.* Boston: Allyn and Bacon, Inc.

Dutton-Douglas, M.A. and Dionne, D. (1991) 'Counselling and shelter services for battered women'. In M. Steinman (ed.) *Woman Battering: Policy Responses.* Cincinnati, Ohio: Anderson Publishing.

Edleson, J.L. (1991) 'Coordinated community responses'. In M. Steinman (ed.) *Woman Battering: Policy Responses.* Cincinnati, Ohio: Anderson Publishing.

Edwards, S.S.M. (1986) *The Police Response to Domestic Violence in London* . London: Central London Polytechnic.

Edwards, S.S.M. (1989) *Policing 'Domestic' Violence: Women, the Law and the State.* London: Sage.

Engelken, C. (1987) 'Employee Assistance: Fighting the Costs of Spouse Abuse'. *Personnel Journal,* 66(3): 31-4.

Evason, E. (1982) *Hidden Violence: Battered Women in Northern Ireland.* Belfast: Farset Co-operative Press.

Ewing, C.P. (1987) *Battered Women Who Kill: Psychological Self-Defense as Legal Justification.* Lexington, Massachusetts: D.C. Heath and Co.

Faragher, T. (1985) 'The police response to violence against women in the home'. In J. Pahl (ed.) *Private Violence and Public Policy: The Needs of Battered Women and the Response of the Public Services.* London: Routledge and Kegan Paul.

Freeman, M.D.A. (1987) *Dealing with Domestic Violence.* 'Family law for practitioners'. Bicester: CCH Editions Limited.

Gamache, D.J., Edleson, J.L. and Schock, M.D. (1988) 'Coordinated police, judicial and social service response to woman battering: a multiple-baseline evaluation across three communities'. In G.T. Hotaling, D. Finkelhor, J.T. Kirkpatrick and M.A. Straus (eds) *Coping with Family Violence: Research and Policy Perspectives.* Newbury Park, California: Sage.

Gayford, J.J. (1975) 'Wife battering: a preliminary survey of 100 cases'. *British Medical Journal,* January: 194-7.

Gelles, R.J. (1974) *The Violent Home.* Beverly Hills, California: Sage.

Goolkasian, G.A. (1986) *Confronting Domestic Violence: a Guide for Criminal Justice Agencies.* Washington, D.C.: National Institute of Justice.

Guru, S. (1986) 'An Asian women's refuge'. In S. Ahmed, J. Cheetham and J. Small (eds) *Social Work with Black Children and their Families.* London: Batsford.

Hague, G., Harwin, N., McMinn, K., Rubens, J., and Taylor, M. (1989) 'Women's Aid: policing male violence in the home'. In C. Dunhill (ed.) *The Boys in Blue: Women's Challenge to the Police.* London: Virago.

Hanmer, J. (1989) 'Women and policing in Britain'. In J. Hanmer, J. Radford, and E.A. Stanko (eds) *Women, Policing, and Male Violence: International Perspectives.* London: Routledge.

Hanmer, J. (1990) 'Women, violence and crime prevention: a study of changes in police policy and practices in West Yorkshire'. Violence, Abuse and Gender Relations Unit Research Paper No. 1. Department of Social Studies, University of Bradford. December.

Hanmer, J. and Saunders, S. (1987) *Women, Violence and Crime Prevention.* Report of a research study commissioned by West Yorkshire Metropolitan County Council. University of Bradford. November.

Hanmer, J. and Saunders, S. (1991) 'Policing violence against women: implementing policy changes'. Paper presented to the British Criminology Conference, July.

Hanmer, J. and Stanko, E.A. (1985) 'Stripping away the rhetoric of protection: violence to women, law and the state in Britain and the U.S.A'. *International Journal of the Sociology of Law,* 13: 357-74.

Hart, B., Stuehling, J., Reese, M. and Stubbing, E. (1990) *Confronting Domestic Violence: Effective Police Responses.* Reading, Pennsylvania: Pennsylvania Coalition Against Domestic Violence.

Hirschel, J.D. and Hutchinson, I. (1991) 'Police-preferred arrest policies'. In M. Steinman (ed.) *Woman Battering: Policy Responses.* Cincinnati, Ohio: Anderson Publishing.

Hirschel, J.D., Hutchinson, I.W., Dean, C.W., Kelley, J.J., and Pesackis, C.E. (1991) *Charlotte Spouse Assault Replication Project: Final Report.* January.

Home Affairs Committee (1993a) *Domestic Violence.* Vol. I. Report together with the Proceedings of the Committee. London: HMSO.

Home Affairs Committee (1993b) *Domestic Violence.* Vol. II. Memoranda of Evidence, Minutes of Evidence and Appendices. London: HMSO.

Home Office (1990) *Domestic Violence.* Home Office Circular 60/1990. London: Home Office.

Home Office (1992a) *Criminal Statistics: England and Wales 1990.* London: HMSO.

Homer, M., Leonard, A.E., and Taylor, M.P. (1984) *Private Violence — Public Shame: A Report on the Circumstances of Women Leaving Domestic Violence in Cleveland.* Middlesbrough: Cleveland Refuge and Aid for Women and Children.

Horley, S. (1990) 'A caution against cautioning'. *Police Review,* March: 484-5.

Jaffe, P., Reitzel., D., Hastings, E., and Austin, G. (1991) *Wife Assault as a Crime: The Perspectives of Victims and Police Officers on a Charging Policy in London, Ontario from 1980-1990.* Final Report. April. London, Ontario: London Family Court Clinic Inc.

Jaffe, P., Wolfe, D.A., Telford, A., and Austin, G. (1986a) 'The impact of police charges in incidents of wife abuse'. *Journal of Family Violence,* 1(1): 37-49.

Jaffe, P., Wolfe, D.A., Wilson, S., and Zak, L. (1986b) 'Emotional and physical health problems of battered women'. *Canadian Journal of Psychiatry,* 31: 625-629.

Jaffe, P.G., Wolfe, D.A., and Wilson, S. K. (1990) *Children of Battered Women.* Newbury Park, California: Sage.

Jones, T., MacLean, B. and Young, J. (1986) *The Islington Crime Survey: Crime, Victimization and Policing in Inner-city London.* Aldershot, Hants: Gower.

Kalmus, D. (1984) 'The inter-generational transmission of marital aggression'. *Journal of Marriage and the Family,* February: 11-19.

Kaufman Kantor, G. and Straus, M.A. (1987) 'The "drunken bum" theory of wife beating'. *Social Problems,* 34(3): 213-230.

Kelly, L. (1988) *Surviving Sexual Violence.* Cambridge: Polity Press.

Langan, P.A. and Innes, C.A. (1986) *Preventing Domestic Violence Against Women.* Bureau of Justice Statistics Special Report. Washington D.C.: U.S. Department of Justice.

Law Commission (1989) *Domestic Violence and Occupation of the Family Home.* Working Paper No. 113. London: HMSO.

Law Commission (1990) *The Ground for Divorce,* Law Com. No.192, London, HMSO.

Law Commission (1992) *Family Law, Domestic Violence and the Occupation of the Family Home.* Law Com. No. 207. London: HMSO.

Lerman, L.G. (1980) 'Protection of battered women: a survey of state legislation'. *Women's Rights Law Reporter,* 6(4): 271-84.

London Battered Women's Advocacy Clinic (1985) *Final Report.* London, Ontario: London Battered Women's Advocacy Clinic.

MacLeod, L. (1987) *Battered but not Beaten....: Preventing Wife Battering in Canada.* Ottowa, Ontario: Canadian Advisory Council on the Status of Women.

MacLeod, L. (1989) 'Wife battering and the web of hope: progress, dilemmas and visions of prevention'. Discussion paper for *Working Together: 1989 National Forum on Family Violence.* Ottowa, Ontario: The National Clearinghouse on Family Violence.

MacLeod, L. and Picard, C. (1989) *Toward a More Effective Criminal Justice Response to Wife Assault: Exploring the Limits and Potential of Effective Intervention.* Working Paper. Research and Development Directorate: Policy, Programs and Research Sector. Department of Justice Canada. June.

Mama, A. (1989) *The Hidden Struggle: Statutory and Voluntary Sector Responses to Violence Against Black Women in the Home.* London: London Race and Housing Research Unit.

Mavolwane, S. and Radford, J. (1992) 'Domestic violence unit'. *Rights of Women Bulletin,* Summer: 15-6.

McCann, K. (1985) 'Battered women and the Law: the limits of the legislation'. In J. Brophy and C. Smart (eds) *Women in Law: Explorations in Law, Family and Sexuality.* London: Routledge and Kegan Paul.

McFarlane, J. (1991) 'Violence during teen pregnancy: health consequences for mother and child'. In B. Levy (ed.) *Dating Violence: Young Women in Danger.* Seattle, WA: Seal Press.

McGibbon, A., Cooper, L. and Kelly, L. (1989) *"What Support?" Hammersmith and Fulham Police Committee Domestic Violence Project. An Exploratory Study of Council Policy and*

Practice, and Local Support Services in the Area of Domestic Violence within Hammersmith and Fulham. London: The Community Research Advisory Centre and the Child Abuse Studies Unit, Polytechnic of North London.

McGregor, H. and Hopkins, A. (1991) *Working for Change: The Movement against Domestic Violence.* North Sydney: Allen and Unwin.

Metropolitan Police Community Involvement Policy Unit (n.d.) *Domestic Violence Best Practice Guidelines.* London: Metropolitan Police.

Metropolitan Police Working Party (1986) *Report of the Working Party on Domestic Violence.* London: Metropolitan Police.

Millar, J. (1992) 'Lone mothers and poverty'. In C. Glendinning and J. Millar (eds) *Women and Poverty in Britain: The 1990s.* London: Harvester Wheatsheaf.

Ministers Responsible for the Status of Women (1991) 'Building blocks: framework for a national strategy on violence against women'. Tenth Annual Federal-Provincial-Territorial Conference of Ministers, Responsible for the Status of Women. St. John's, Newfoundland, Canada. June 18-20.

Ministry of the Solicitor General of Canada (1986) 'Statement from the Ministry of the Solicitor General of Canada for the UN Expert Meeting on Violence in the Family'. Ottowa: Solicitor General of Canada.

Montgomery, P. and Bell, V. (n.d.) *Police Response to Wife Assault: a Northern Ireland Study.* Northern Ireland Women's Aid Federation.

Mooney, J. (1993) *The Hidden Figure: Domestic Violence in North London.* The findings of a survey conducted on domestic violence in the North London Borough of Islington. Islington Council.

Morley, R. (Forthcoming) *Men's Violence to Women in Intimate Relationships.* London: Harvester-Wheatsheaf.

Morley, R. and Mullender, A. (1992) 'Hype or hope: the importation of pro-arrest policies and batterers' programmes from North America to Britain as key measures for preventing violence against women in the home'. *International Journal of Law and the Family,* 6: 265-88.

Mugford, J. (1990) 'Domestic violence in Australia: policies, practices, and politics'. Australian Institute of Criminology, Canberra. November.

National Collective of Independent Women's Refuges Inc. (n.d.) *Home Is Where The Hurt Is.* Wellington, New Zealand: National Collective of Independent Women's Refuges Inc. (leaflet).

New South Wales Women's Co-ordination Unit (1991) *New South Wales Domestic Violence Strategic Plan: 3. Costs of Domestic Violence.* Haymarket, NSW: NSW Women's Co- ordination Unit.

NiCarthy, G. (1987) *The Ones Who Got Away: Women Who Left Abusive Partners.*, Seattle, Washington: The Seal Press.

Noesjirwan, J. (1985) 'Ten years On. 1975-1985'. *Evaluation of Women's Refuges in NSW.* New South Wales, Australia: publisher unstated.

Office of the Status of Women (1990) 'Country report on violence against women: Australia'. Presented by Helen L'Orange to the Commonwealth Ministers Responsible for Women's Affairs, Ottowa, 8-12 October. Office of the Status of Women, Department of the Prime Minister and the Cabinet.

Okun, L. (1986) *Woman Abuse: Facts Replacing Myths.* Albany, N.Y.: State University of New York Press.

Pagelow, M.D. (1981) *Woman-Battering: Victims and their Experiences.* Beverly Hills, California: Sage.

Pagelow, M.D. (1984) *Family Violence.* New York: Praeger.

Pahl, J. (1985) 'Violent husbands and abused wives: a longitudinal study'. In J. Pahl (ed.) *Private Violence and Public Policy: The Needs of Battered Women and the Responses of the Public Services.* London: Routledge and Kegan Paul.

Painter, K. (1991) *Wife Rape, Marriage and the Law.* Survey Report: Key Findings and Recommendations. Faculty of Economic and Social Studies, University of Manchester, Department of Social Policy and Social Work.

Parker, S. (1985) 'The legal background'. In J. Pahl (ed.) *Private Violence and Public Policy: The Needs of Battered Women and the Response of the Public Services.* London: Routledge and Kegan Paul.

Parliamentary Select Committee on Violence in Marriage (1975) *Report from the Select Committee on Violence in Marriage Together with the Proceedings of the Committee. Session 1974-75.* Vol. 2. Report, Minutes of the Evidence and Appendices. London: HMSO.

Pease, K., Sampson, A., Croft, L., Phillips, C., and Farrell, G. (1991) 'Strategy for the Manchester University Violent Crime Prevention Project'. August.

Pence, E. (1987) *In Our Best Interest: A Process for Personal and Social Change.* Duluth, Minnesota: Minnesota Program Development Inc.

Pence, E. (1989) *The Justice System's Response to Domestic Assault Cases: a Guide for Policy Development.* Duluth, Minnesota: Minnesota Program Development Inc.

Pence, E. and Shepard, M. (1988) 'Integrating feminist theory and practice: the challenge of the battered women's movement'. In K. Yllo and M. Bograd (eds) *Feminist Perspectives on Wife Abuse.* Newbury Park, California: Sage.

Pizzey, E. and Shapiro, J. (1982) *Prone to Violence.* London: Hamlyn.

Roberts, G. (1988) 'Domestic violence: costing of service provision for female victims — 20 case histories'. In Queensland Domestic Violence Task Force *Beyond these Walls: Report of the Queensland Domestic Violence Task Force.* Brisbane.

Rodriguez, N.M. (1988) 'A successful feminist shelter: a case study of the Family Crisis Shelter in Hawaii'. *The Journal of Applied Behavioral Science,* 24(3): 235-250.

Rosenbaum, A. and O'Leary, K.D. (1981) 'Marital violence: characteristics of abusive couples'. *Journal of Consulting and Clinical Psychology,* 49(1): 63-71.

Rosenbaum, A. and O'Leary, K.D. (1986) 'The treatment of marital violence'. In N. Jacobson and A. Gurman (eds) *Clinical Handbook of Marital Therapy.* New York: Guilford Press.

Roshni (1992) 'Forwarding the struggle' conference report. Organised by Roshni (Nottingham Asian Women's Aid). 11 April.

Roy, M. (1982) 'Four thousand partners in violence: a trend analysis'. In M. Roy (ed.) *The Abusive Partner: An Analysis of Domestic Battering.* New York: Van Nostrand Reinhold.

Russell, M. (1989) *Taking Stock: Refuge Provision in London in the late 1980s.* London: London Strategic Policy Unit with financial assistance from the London Borough of Southwark.

Sampson, A. and Phillips, C. (1992) 'Multiple Victimisation: Racial Attacks on an East London Estate'. *Police Research Group Crime Prevention Unit Series Paper 36.* London: Home Office.

Sanders, A. (1988) 'Personal violence and public order: the prosecution of "domestic" violence in England and Wales'. *International Journal of the Sociology of Law,* 16: 359-82.

Shepard, M. and Pence, E. (1988) 'The effect of battering on the employment status of women'. *Affilia,* 3(2): 55-61.

Sherman, L.W. (1992) 'The influence of criminology on criminal law: evaluating arrests for misdemeanour domestic violence'. *The Journal of Law and Criminology,* 83(1): 1-45.

Sherman, L.W. and Berk, R.A. (1984) *The specific deterrent effects of arrest for domestic assault. American Sociological Review,* 49: 261-272.

Siddiqui, H. and Patel, P. (1991) 'Policing domestic violence'. Letter to the editor. *The Guardian,* 4 May.

Singh, T. (1992) *Implications of the Children Act for Women's Aid.* Information Update November 1992. Bristol: Women's Aid Federation England.

Smith, L. (1989) *Domestic Violence: an Overview of the Literature.* Home Office research study no. 107. London: HMSO.

Southall Black Sisters (1989) 'Two struggles: challenging male violence and the police'. In C. Dunhill (ed.) *The Boys in Blue: Women's Challenge to the Police.* London: Virago.

Stanko, E.A. (1985) *Intimate Intrusions: Women's Experience of Male Violence.* London: Routledge and Kegan Paul.

Stanko, E.A. (1989) 'Missing the mark? policing battering'. In J. Hanmer, J. Radford, and E.A. Stanko (eds) *Women, Policing, and Male Violence: International Perspectives.* London: Routledge.

Stark, E. and Flitcraft, A. (1985) 'Woman-battering, child abuse and social heredity: what is the relationship?' in N. Johnson (ed.) *Marital Violence.* London: Routledge and Kegan Paul.

Stark, E., Flitcraft, A. and Frazier, W. (1979) 'Medicine and patriarchal violence: the social construction of a "private" event'. *International Journal of Health Services,* 9(3): 461-494.

Steinman, M. (1990) 'Lowering recidivism among men who batter women'. *Journal of Police Science and Administration,* 17(2): 124-132.

Stout, K.D. (1989) '"Intimate femicide": effect of legislation and social services'. *Affilia,* 4(2) Summer: 21-30.

Straus, M.A. Gelles, R.J.and Steinmetz, S.K. (1980) *Behind Closed Doors: Violence in the American Family.* Newbury Park: Sage.

Torgbor, S. (1989) 'Police intervention in domestic violence: a comparative view'. *Family Law,* 195-8.

Victim Support (1992) *Domestic Violence: Report of a National Inter-Agency Working Party on Domestic Violence.* London: Victim Support.

Walker, L.E. (1983) 'The battered woman syndrome'. In D. Finkelhor. R.J. Gelles, G.T. Hotaling, and M.A. Straus (eds) *The Dark Side of Families: Current Family Research.* Newbury Park, California: Sage.

Walker, L.E. (1984) *The Battered Woman Syndrome.* New York: Springer.

Wharton, C.S. (1987) 'Establishing shelters for battered women: local manifestations of a social movement'. *Qualitative Sociology,* 10(2): 146-163.

Women's National Commission (1985) *Violence Against Women: Report of an Ad Hoc Working Group.* London: Cabinet Office.

THE MEDIA AND THE
CONSTRUCTION OF
CRIME AND DEVIANCE

10.   Deviance and Moral Panics
Stanley Cohen

Societies appear to be subject, every now and then, to periods of moral panic. A condition, episode, person or group of persons emerges to become defined as a threat to societal values and interests; its nature is presented in a stylized and stereotypical fashion by the mass media; the moral barricades are manned by editors, bishops, politicians and other right-thinking people; socially accredited experts pronounce their diagnoses and solutions; ways of coping are evolved or (more often) resorted to; the condition then disappears, submerges or deteriorates and becomes more visible. Sometimes the object of the panic is quite novel and at other times it is something which has been in existence long enough, but suddenly appears in the limelight. Sometimes the panic passes over and is forgotten, except in folklore and collective memory; at other times it has more serious and long-lasting repercussions and might produce such changes as those in legal and social policy or even in the way the society conceives itself.

One of the most recurrent types of moral panic in Britain since the war has been associated with the emergence of various forms of youth culture (originally almost exclusively working class, but often recently middle class or student based) whose behaviour is deviant or delinquent. To a greater or lesser degree, these cultures have been associated with violence. The Teddy Boys, the Mods and Rockers, the Hells Angels, the Skinheads and the Hippies have all been phenomena of this kind. There have been parallel reactions to the drug problem, student militancy, political demonstrations, football hooliganism, vandalism of various kinds and crime and violence in general. But groups such as the Teddy Boys and the Mods and Rockers have been distinctive in being identified not just in terms of particular events (such as demonstrations) or particular disapproved forms of behaviour (such as drug-taking or violence) but as distinguishable social types. In the gallery of types that society erects to show its members which roles should be avoided and which should be emulated, these groups have occupied a constant position as folk devils: visible reminders of what we should not be. The identities of such social types are public property and these particular adolescent groups have symbolized — both in what they were and how they were reacted to — much of the social change which has taken place in Britain over the last twenty years.

In this book, I want to use a detailed case study of the Mods and Rockers phenomenon — which covered most of the 1960s — to illustrate some of the more intrinsic features in the emergence of such collective episodes of juvenile deviance and the moral panics they both generate and rely upon for their growth. The Mods and Rockers are one of the many sets of figures through which the sixties in Britain will be remembered. A decade is not just a chronological span but a period measured by its association with

Stanley Cohen: 'Deviance and Moral Panics' from *FOLK DEVILS AND MORAL PANICS* (Basil Blackwell Ltd, 1980), pp. 9-26.

particular fads, fashions, crazes, styles or — in a less ephemeral way — a certain spirit or *kulturgeist*. A term such as 'the twenties' is enough to evoke the cultural shape of that period, and although we are too close to the sixties for such explicit understandings to emerge already, this is not for want of trying from our instant cultural historians. In the cultural snap albums of the decade which have already been collected[1] the Mods and Rockers stand alongside the Profumo affair, the Great Train Robbery, the Krays, the Richardsons, the Beatles, the Rolling Stones, the Bishop of Woolwich, *Private Eye*, David Frost, Carnaby Street, The Moors murders, the emergence of Powellism, the Rhodesian affair, as the types and scenes of the sixties.

At the beginning of the decade, the term 'Modernist' referred simply to a style of dress, the term 'Rocker' was hardly known outside the small groups which identified themselves this way. Five years later, a newspaper editor was to refer to the Mods and Rockers incidents as 'without parallel in English history' and troop reinforcements were rumoured to have been sent to quell possible widespread disturbances. Now, another five years later, these groups have all but disappeared from the public consciousness, remaining only in collective memory as folk devils of the past, to whom current horrors can be compared. The rise and fall of the Mods and Rockers contained all the elements from which one might generalize about folk devils and moral panics. And unlike the previous decade which had only produced the Teddy Boys, these years witnessed rapid oscillation from one such devil to another: the Mod, the Rocker, the Greaser, the student militant, the drug fiend, the vandal, the soccer hooligan, the hippy, the skinhead.

Neither moral panics nor social types have received much systematic attention in sociology. In the case of moral panics, the two most relevant frameworks come from the sociology of law and social problems and the sociology of collective behaviour. Sociologists such as Becker[2] and Gusfield[3] have taken the cases of the Marijuana Tax Act and the Prohibition laws respectively to show how public concern about a particular condition is generated, a 'symbolic crusade' mounted, which with publicity and the actions of certain interest groups, results in what Becker calls *moral enterprise: '. . .* the creation of a new fragment of the moral constitution of society.'[4] Elsewhere[5] Becker uses the same analysis to deal with the evolution of social problems as a whole. The field of collective behaviour provides another relevant orientation to the study of moral panics. There are detailed accounts of cases of mass hysteria, delusion and panics, and also a body of studies on how societies cope with the sudden threat or disorder caused by physical disasters.

The study of social types can also be located in the field of collective behaviour, not so much though in such 'extreme' forms as riots or crowds, but in the general orientation to this field by the symbolic interactionists such as Blumer and Turner.[6] In this line of theory, explicit attention has been paid to social types by Klapp,[7] but although he considers how such types as the hero, the villain and the fool serve as role models for a society, his main concern seems to be in classifying the various sub-types within these groups (for example, the renegade, the parasite, the corrupter, as villain roles) and listing names of those persons Americans see as exemplifying these roles. He does not consider how such typing occurs in the first place and he is preoccupied with showing his approval for the processes by which social consensus is facilitated by identifying with the hero types and hating the villain types.

The major contribution to the study of the social typing process itself comes from the interactionist or transactional approach to deviance. The focus here is on how society labels rule-breakers as belonging to certain deviant groups and how, once the person is thus type cast, his acts are interpreted in terms of the status to which he has been assigned. It is to this body of theory that we must turn for our major orientation to the study of both moral panics and social types.

The transactional approach to deviance

The sociological study of crime, delinquency, drug-taking, mental illness and other forms of socially deviant or problematic behaviour has, in the last decade, undergone a radical reorientation. This reorientation is part of what might be called the *sceptical* revolution in criminology and the sociology of deviance.[8] The older tradition was *canonical* in the sense that it saw the concepts it worked with as authoritative, standard, accepted, given and unquestionable. The new tradition is sceptical in the sense that when it sees terms like 'deviant', it asks 'deviant to whom?' or 'deviant from what?'; when told that something is a social problem, it asks 'problematic to whom?'; when certain conditions or behaviour are described as dysfunctional, embarrassing, threatening or dangerous, it asks 'says who?' and 'why?'. In other words, these concepts and descriptions are not assumed to have a taken-for-granted status.

The empirical existence of forms of behaviour labelled as deviant and the fact that persons might consciously and intentionally decide to be deviant, should not lead us to assume that deviance is the intrinsic property of an act nor a quality possessed by an actor. Becker's formulation on the transactional nature of deviance has now been quoted verbatim so often that it has virtually acquired its own canonical status:

> . . . deviance is created by society. I do not mean this in the way that it is ordinarily understood, in which the causes of deviance are located in the social situation of the deviant or in 'social factors' which prompt his action. I mean, rather, that *social groups create deviance by making the rules whose infraction constitutes deviance* and by applying those rules to particular persons and labelling them as outsiders. From this point of view, deviance is *not* a quality of the act the person commits, but rather a consequence of the application by others of rules and sanctions to an 'offender'. The deviant is one to whom the label has successfully been applied; deviant behaviour is behaviour that people so label.[9]

What this means is that the student of deviance must question and not take for granted the labelling by society or certain powerful groups in society of certain behaviour as deviant or problematic. The transactionalists' importance has been not simply to restate the sociological truism that the judgement of deviance is ultimately one that is relative to a particular group, but in trying to spell out the implication of this for research and theory. They have suggested that in addition to the stock set of *behavioural* questions which the public asks about deviance and which the researcher obligingly tries to answer (why did they do it? what sort of people are they? how do we stop them doing it again?) there are at least three *definitional* questions: why does a particular rule, the infraction of which constitutes deviance, exist at all? What are the processes and procedures involved in identifying someone as a deviant and applying the rule to him? What are the effects and consequences of this application, both for society and the individual?

Sceptical theorists have been misinterpreted as going only so far as putting these definitional questions and moreover as implying that the behavioural questions are unimportant. While it is true that they have pointed to the dead ends which the behavioural questions have reached (do we really know what distinguishes a deviant from a non-deviant?) what they say has positive implications for studying these questions as well. Thus, they see deviance in terms of a process of becoming — movements of doubt, commitment, sidetracking, guilt — rather than the possession of fixed traits and characteristics. This is true even for those forms of deviance usually seen to be most 'locked in' the person: 'No one,' as Laing says, 'has schizophrenia like having a cold.'[10] The meaning and interpretation which the deviant gives to his own acts are seen as crucial and so is the fact that these actions are often similar to socially approved forms of behaviour.[11]

The transactional perspective does not imply that innocent persons are arbitrarily selected to play deviant roles or that harmless conditions are wilfully inflated into social problems. Nor does it imply that a person labelled as deviant has to accept this identity: being caught and publicly labelled is just one crucial contingency which *may* stabilize a deviant career and sustain it over time. Much of the work of these writers has been concerned with the problematic nature of societal response to deviance and the way such responses affect the behaviour. This may be studied at a face-to-face level (for example, what effect does it have on a pupil to be told by his teacher that he is a 'yob who should never be at a decent school like this'?) or at a broader societal level (for example, how is the 'drug problem' actually created and shaped by particular social and legal policies ?).

The most unequivocal attempt to understand the nature and effect of the societal reaction to deviance is to be found in the writings of Lemert.[12] He makes an important distinction, for example, between primary and secondary deviation. Primary deviation — which may arise from a variety of causes — refers to behaviour which, although it may be troublesome to the individual, does not produce symbolic reorganization at the level of self-conception. Secondary deviation occurs when the individual employs his deviance, or a role based upon it, as a means of defence, attack or adjustment to the problems created by the societal reaction to it. The societal reaction is thus conceived as the 'effective' rather than 'original' cause of deviance: deviance becomes significant when it is subjectively shaped into an active role which becomes the basis for assigning social status. Primary deviation has only marginal implications for social status and self-conception as long as it remains symptomatic, situational, rationalized or in some way 'normalized' as an acceptable and normal variation.

Lemert was very much aware that the transition from primary to secondary deviation was a complicated process. Why the societal reaction occurs and what form it takes are dependent on factors such as the amount and visibility of the deviance, while the effect of the reaction is dependent on numerous contingencies and is itself only one contingency in the development of a deviant career. Thus the link between the reaction and the individual's incorporation of this into his self-identity is by no means inevitable; the deviant label, in other words, does not always 'take'. The individual might be able to ignore or rationalize the label or only pretend to comply. This type of face-to-face sequence, though, is just one part of the picture: more important are the symbolic and unintended consequences of social control as a whole. Deviance in a sense emerges and is stabilized as an artefact of social control; because of this, Lemert can state that '. . . older sociology tended to rest heavily upon the idea that deviance leads to social control. I have come to believe that the reverse idea, i.e. social control leads to deviance, is equally tenable and the potentially richer premise for studying deviance in modern society'.[13]

It is partly towards showing the tenability and richness of this premise that this book is directed. My emphasis though, is more on the logically prior task of analysing the nature of a particular set of reactions rather than demonstrating conclusively what their effects might have been. How were the Mods and Rockers identified, labelled and controlled? What stages or processes did this reaction go through? Why did the reaction take its particular forms? What — to use Lemert's words again — were the 'mythologies, stigma, stereotypes, patterns of exploitation, accommodation, segregation and methods of control (which) spring up and crystallize in the interaction between the deviants and the rest of society'?[14]

There are many strategies — not mutually incompatible — for studying such reactions. One might take a sample of public opinion and survey its attitudes to the particular form of deviance in question. One might record reactions in a face-to-face context, for example, how persons respond to what they see as homosexual advances.[15] One might study the operations and beliefs of particular control agencies such as the police or the courts. Or, drawing on all these sources, one might construct an ethnography and history of reactions to a particular condition or form of behaviour. This is particularly suitable for forms of deviance or problems seen as new, sensational or in some other way particularly threatening. Thus 'crime waves' in seventeenth century Massachusetts,[16] marijuana smoking in America during the 1930s,[17] the Teddy Boy phenomenon in Britain during the 1950s[18] and drug-taking in the Notting Hill area of London during the 1960s[19] have all been studied in this way. These reactions were all associated with some form of moral panic and it is in the tradition of studies such as these that the Mods and Rockers will be considered. Before introducing this particular case, however, I want to justify, concentrating on one especially important carrier and producer of moral panics, namely, the mass media.

Deviance and the mass media

A crucial dimension for understanding the reaction to deviance both by the public as a whole and by agents of social control, is the nature of the information that is received about the behaviour in question. Each society possesses a set of ideas about what causes deviation — is it due, say, to sickness or to wilful perversity? — and a set of images of who constitutes the typical deviant — is he an innocent lad being led astray, or is he a psychopathic thug? — and these conceptions shape what is done about the behaviour. In industrial societies, the body of information from which such ideas are built, is invariably received at second hand. That is, it arrives already processed by the mass media and this means that the information has been subject to alternative definitions of what constitutes 'news' and how it should be gathered and presented. The information is further structured by the various commercial and political constraints in which newspapers, radio and television operate.

The student of moral enterprise cannot but pay particular attention to the role of the mass media in defining and shaping social problems. The media have long operated as agents of moral indignation in their own right: even if they are not self-consciously engaged in crusading or muck-raking, their very reporting of certain 'facts' can be sufficient to generate concern, anxiety, indignation or panic. When such feelings coincide with a perception that particular values need to be protected, the pre-conditions for new rule creation or social problem definition are present. Of course, the outcome might not be as definite as the actual creation of new rules or the more rigid enforcement of existing ones. What might result is the sort of symbolic process which Gusfield describes in his conception of 'moral passage': there is a change in the public designation of deviance.[20] In his example, the problem drinker changes from 'repentant' to 'enemy' to 'sick'. Something like the opposite might be happening in the public designation of producers and consumers of pornography: they have changed from isolated, pathetic — if not sick — creatures in grubby macks to groups of ruthless exploiters out to undermine the nation's morals.

Less concretely, the media might leave behind a diffuse feeling of anxiety about the situation: 'something should be done about it', 'where will it end?' or 'this sort of thing can't go on for ever'. Such vague feelings are crucial in laying the ground for further enterprise, and Young has shown how, in the case of drug-taking, the media play on the normative concerns of the public and by thrusting certain moral directives into the universe of discourse, can create social problems suddenly and dramatically.[21] This potential is consciously exploited by those whom Becker calls 'moral entrepreneurs' to aid them in their attempt to win public support.

The mass media, in fact, devote a great deal of space to deviance: sensational crimes, scandals, bizarre happenings and strange goings on. The more dramatic confrontations between deviance and control in manhunts, trials and punishments are recurring objects of attention. As Erikson notes, 'a considerable portion of what we call "news" is devoted to reports about deviant behaviour and its consequences'.[22] This is not just for entertainment or to fulfill some psychological need for either identification or vicarious punishment. Such 'news' as Erikson and others have argued, is a main source of information about the normative contours of a society. It informs us about right and wrong, about the boundaries beyond which one should not venture and about the shapes that the devil can assume. The gallery of folk types — heroes and saints, as well as fools, villains and devils — is publicized not just in oral-tradition and face-to-face contact but to much larger audiences and with much greater dramatic resources.

Much of this study will be devoted to understanding the role of the mass media in creating moral panics and folk devils. A potentially useful link between these two notions — and one that places central stress on the mass media — is the process of deviation amplification as described by Wilkins.[23] The key variable in this attempt to understand how the societal reaction may in fact *increase* rather than decrease or keep in check the amount of deviance, is the nature of the information about deviance. As I pointed out earlier, this information characteristically is not received at first hand, it tends to be processed in such a form that the action or actors concerned are pictured in a highly stereotypical way. We react to an episode of, say, sexual deviance, drug-taking or violence in terms of our information about that particular class of phenomenon (how typical is it), our tolerance level for that type of behaviour and our direct experience — which in a segregated urban society is often nil. Wilkins describes — in highly mechanistic language derived from cybernetic theory — a typical reaction sequence which might take place at this point, one which has a spiralling or snowballing effect.

An initial act of deviance, or normative diversity (for example, in dress) is defined as being worthy of attention and is responded to punitively. The deviant or group of deviants is segregated or isolated and this operates to alienate them from conventional society. They perceive themselves as more deviant, group themselves with others in a similar position, and this leads to more deviance. This, in turn, exposes the group to further punitive sanctions and other forceful action by the conformists — and the system starts going round again. There is no assumption in this model that amplification *has* to occur: in the same way — as I pointed out earlier — that there is no automatic transition from primary to secondary deviation or to the incorporation of deviant labels. The system or the actor can and does react in quite opposite directions. What one is merely drawing attention to is a set of sequential typifications: under X conditions, A will be followed by A1, A2, etc. All these links have to be explained — as Wilkins does not do — in terms of other generalizations. For example, it is more likely that if the deviant group is vulnerable and its actions highly visible, it will be forced to take on its identities from structurally and ideologically more powerful groups. Such generalizations and an attempt to specify various specialized modes of amplification or alternatives to the process have been spelt out by Young[24] in the case of drug-taking. I intend using this model here simply as one viable way in which the 'social control leads to deviation' chain can be conceptualized and also because of its particular emphasis upon the 'information about deviance' variable and its dependence on the mass media.

The case of the mods and rockers

I have already given some indication of the general framework which I think suitable for the study of moral panics and folk devils. Further perspectives suggest themselves because of the special characteristics of the Mods and Rockers phenomenon, as compared with, say, the rise of student militancy or the appearance of underground newspaper editors on obscenity charges. The first and most obvious one derives from the literature on subcultural delinquency. This would provide the structural setting for explaining the Mods and Rockers phenomenon as a form of adolescent deviance among working-class youth in Britain. Downes's variant of subcultural theory is most relevant and I would substantially agree with his remarks (in the preface of his book) about the Mods and Rockers events intervening between writing and the book going to press: 'No mention is made of these occurrences in what follows, largely because — in the absence of evidence to the contrary — I take them to corroborate, rather than negate, the main sociological argument of the book.'[25] At various points in these

215

chapters, the relevance of subcultural theory will be commented on, although my stress on the definitional rather than behavioural questions precludes an extended analysis along these lines.

Another less obvious orientation derives from the field of collective behaviour. I have already suggested that social types can be seen as the products of the same processes that go into the creation of symbolic collective styles in fashion, dress and public identities. The Mods and Rockers, though, were initially registered in the public consciousness not just as the appearance of new social types, but as actors in a particular episode of collective behaviour. The phenomenon took its subsequent shape in terms of these episodes: the regular series of disturbances which took place at English seaside resorts between 1964 and 1966. The public image of these folk devils was invariably tied up to a number of highly visual scenarios associated with their appearance: youths chasing across the beach, brandishing deckchairs over their heads, running along the pavements, riding on scooters or bikes down the streets, sleeping on the beaches and so on.

Each of these episodes — as I will describe — contained all the elements of the classic crowd situation which has long been the prototype for the study of collective behaviour. Crowds, riots, mobs and disturbances on occasions ranging from pop concerts to political demonstrations have all been seen in a similar way to *The Crowd* described by Le Bon in 1896. Later formulations by Tarde, Freud, McDougall and F. H. Allport made little lasting contribution and often just elaborated on Le Bon's contagion hypothesis. A more useful recent theory — for all its deficiencies from a sociological viewpoint — is Smelser's 'value added schema'.[26] In the sequence he suggests, each of the following determinants of collective behaviour must appear: (i) structural conduciveness; (ii) structural strain; (iii) growth and spread of a generalized belief; (iv) precipitating factors; (v) mobilization of the participants for action; (vi) operation of social control.

Structural conduciveness creates conditions of permissiveness under which collective behaviour is seen as legitimate. Together with structural strain (e.g. economic deprivation, population invasion) this factor creates the opening for race riots, sects, panics and other examples of collective behaviour. In the case of the Mods and Rockers, conduciveness and strain correspond to the structural sources of strain posited in subcultural theory: anomie, status frustration, blocked leisure opportunities and so on. The growth and spread of a generalized belief is important because the situation of strain must be made meaningful to the potential participants. For the most part these generalized beliefs are spread through the mass media. I have already indicated the importance of media imagery for studying deviance as a whole; in dealing with crowd behaviour, this importance is heightened because of the ways in which such phenomena develop and spread. As will be shown, sociological and social psychological work on mass hysteria, delusions and rumours are of direct relevance here.

Precipitating factors are specific events which might confirm a generalized belief, initiate strain or redefine conduciveness. Like the other factors in Smelser's schema, it is not a determinant of anything in itself — for example, a fight will not start a race riot unless it occurs in or is interpreted as an 'explosive situation'. While not spelling out in detail the precipitating factors in the Mods and Rockers events, I will show how the social reaction contributed to the definition and creation of these factors. Mobilization of participants for action again refers to a sequence present in the Mods and Rockers events which will only be dealt with in terms of the other determinants.

It is Smelser's sixth determinant — the operation of social control — which, together with the generalized belief factors, will concern us most. This factor, which 'in certain respects . . . arches over all others'[27] refers to the counter forces set up by society to prevent and inhibit the previous determinants: 'Once an episode of collective behaviour has appeared, its duration and severity are determined by the response of the agencies of social control.'[28] So from a somewhat different theoretical perspective — Parsonian functionalism — Smelser attaches the same crucial importance to the social control factors stressed in the transactional model.

A special — and at first sight somewhat esoteric — area of collective behaviour which is of peculiar relevance, is the field known as 'disaster research'.[29] This consists of a body of findings about the social and psychological impact of disasters, particularly physical disasters such as hurricanes, tornadoes and floods but also man-made disasters such as bombing attacks. Theoretical models have also been produced, and Merton argues that the study of disasters can extend sociological theory beyond the confines of the immediate subject-matter. Disaster situations can be looked at as strategic research sites for theory-building: 'Conditions of collective stress bring out in bold relief aspects of social systems that are not as readily visible in the stressful conditions of everyday life.'[30] The value of disaster studies is that by compressing social processes into a brief time span, a disaster makes usually private behaviour, public and immediate and therefore more amenable to study.[31]

I came across the writings in this field towards the end of carrying out the Mods and Rockers research and was immediately struck by the parallels between what I was then beginning to think of as 'moral panics' and the reactions to physical disasters. Disaster researchers have constructed one of the few models in sociology for considering the reaction of the social system to something stressful, disturbing or threatening. The happenings at Brighton, Clacton or Margate clearly were not disasters in the same category of events as earthquakes or floods; the differences are too obvious to have to spell out. Nevertheless, there *were* resemblances, and definitions of 'disaster' are so inconsistent and broad, that the Mods and Rockers events could almost fit them. Elements in such definitions include: whole or part of a community must be affected, a large segment of the community must be confronted with actual or potential danger, there must be loss of cherished values and material objects resulting in death or injury or destruction to property.

In addition, many workers in the field claim that research should not be restricted to actual disasters — a potential disaster may be just as disruptive as the actual event. Studies of reactions to hoaxes and false alarms show disaster behaviour in the absence of objective danger. More important, as will be shown in detail, a large segment of the community reacted to the Mods and Rockers events as if a disaster had occurred: 'It is the perception of threat and not its actual existence that is important.'[32]

217

The work of disaster researchers that struck me as most useful when I got to the stage of writing up my own material on the Mods and Rockers was the sequential model that they have developed to describe the phases of a typical disaster. The following is the sort of sequence that has been distinguished:[33]

1. *Warning:* during which arises, mistakenly or not, some apprehensions based on conditions out of which danger may arise. The warning must be coded to be understood and impressive enough to overcome resistance to the belief that current tranquillity can be upset.

2. *Threat:* during which people are exposed to communication from others, or to signs from the approaching disaster itself indicating specific imminent danger. This phase begins with the perception of some change, but as with the first phase, may be absent or truncated in the case of sudden disaster.

3. *Impact:* during which the disaster strikes and the immediate unorganized response to the death, injury or destruction takes place.

4. *Inventory:* during which those exposed to the disaster begin to form a preliminary picture of what has happened and of their own condition.

5. *Rescue:* during which the activities are geared to immediate help for the survivors. As well as people in the impact area helping each other, the suprasystem begins to send aid.

6. *Remedy:* during which more deliberate and formal activities are undertaken towards relieving the affected. The suprasystem takes over the functions the emergency system cannot perform.

7. *Recovery:* during which, for an extended period, the community either recovers its former equilibrium or achieves a stable adaptation to the changes which the disaster may have brought about.

Some of these stages have no exact parallels in the Mods and Rockers case, but a condensed version of this sequence (*Warning* to cover phases 1 and 2; then *Impact*; then *Inventory*; and *Reaction* to cover phases 5, 6 and 7) provides a useful analogue. If one compares this to deviancy models such as amplification, there are obvious and crucial differences. For disasters, the sequence has been empirically established; in the various attempts to conceptualize the reactions to deviance this is by no means the case. In addition, the transitions within the amplification model or from primary to secondary deviation are supposed to be consequential (i.e. causal) and not merely sequential. In disaster research, moreover, it has been shown how the form each phase takes is affected by the characteristics of the previous stage: thus, the scale of the remedy operation is affected by the degree of identification with the victim. This sort of uniformity has not been shown in deviance.

The nature of the reaction to the event is important in different ways. In the case of disaster, the social system responds in order to help the victims and to evolve methods to mitigate the effects of further disasters (e.g. by early warning systems). The disaster itself occurs independent of this reaction. In regard to deviance, however, the reaction is seen as partly causative. The on-the-spot reaction to an act determines whether it is classified as deviant at all, and the way in which the act is reported and labelled also determines the form of the subsequent deviation; this is not the case with a disaster. To express the difference in another way, while the disaster sequence is linear and constant — in each disaster the warning is followed by the impact which is followed by the reaction — deviance models are circular and amplifying: the impact (deviance) is followed by a reaction which has the effect of increasing the subsequent warning and impact, setting up a feedback system. It is precisely because the Mods and Rockers phenomenon was both a generalized type of deviance and also manifested itself as a series of discrete events, that both models are relevant. While a single event can be meaningfully described in terms of the disaster analogue (warning–impact–reaction), each event can be seen as creating the potential for a reaction which, among other possible consequences, might cause further acts of deviance.

Let me now return to the original aims of the study and conclude this introductory chapter by outlining the plan of the book. My focus is on the genesis and development of the moral panic and social typing associated with the Mods and Rockers phenomenon. In transactional terminology: what was the nature and effect of the societal reaction to this particular form of deviance? This entails looking at the ways in which the behaviour was perceived and conceptualized, whether there was a unitary or a divergent set of images, the modes through which these images were transmitted and the ways in which agents of social control reacted. The behavioural questions (how did the Mods and Rockers styles emerge? Why did some young people more or less identified with these groups behave in the way they did?) will be considered, but they are the background questions. The variable of societal reaction is the focus of attention.

Very few studies have been made with this focus and the term 'reaction' has become reified, covering a wide range of interpretations. Does 'reaction' mean what is *done* about the deviance in question, or merely what is *thought* about it? And how does one study something as nebulous as this, when the 'thing' being reacted to covers juvenile delinquency, a manifestation of youth culture, a social type and a series of specific events? Using criteria determined by my theoretical interests rather than by how concepts can best be 'operationalized', I decided to study reaction at three levels, in each case using a range of possible sources. The first was the initial on-the-spot reaction, which I studied mainly through observation, participant observation and the type of informal interviewing used in community studies. The second was the organized reaction of the system of social control, information about which I obtained from observation, interviews and the analysis of published material. The third level was the transmission and diffusion of the reaction in the mass media. A detailed description of the research methods and sources of material is given in the Appendix.

To remain faithful to the theoretical orientation of the study, my argument will be presented in terms of a typical reaction sequence. That is to say, instead of describing the deviation in some detail and then considering the reaction, I will start off with the minimum possible account of the deviation, then deal with the reaction and then, finally, return to consider the interplay between deviation and reaction. In terms of the disaster analogue this means starting off with the inventory, moving on to other phases of the reaction and then returning to the warning and impact. The book divides into three parts: the first (and major) part traces the development and reverberation of the societal reaction, particularly as reflected in the mass media and the actions of the organized system of social control. This consists of three chapters: the *Inventory;* the *Opinion and Attitude Themes* and the *Rescue and Remedy Phases.* The second part of the book looks at the effects of the reaction and the third locates the growth of the folk devils and the moral panic in historical and structural terms.

Organizing the book in this way means that in the first part, the Mods and Rockers are hardly going to appear as 'real, live people' at all. They will be seen through the eyes of the societal reaction and in this reaction they tend to appear as disembodied objects, Rorschach blots on to which reactions are projected. In using this type of presentation, I do not want to imply that these reactions — although they do involve elements of fantasy and selective misperception — are irrational nor that the Mods and Rockers were not real people, with particular structural origins, values, aims and interests. Neither were they creatures pushed and pulled by the forces of the societal reaction without being able to react back. I am presenting the argument in this way for effect, only allowing the Mods and Rockers to come to life when their supposed identities had been presented for public consumption.

Notes

1. For example, Christopher Booker, *The Neophiliacs: A Study of the Revolution in the English Life in the Fifties and Sixties* (London: Collins, 1969); David Bailey and Francis Wyndham, *A Box of Pin-Ups* (London: Weidenfeld and Nicholson, 1965); Bernard Levin, *The Pendulum Years* (London: Jonathan Cape, 1970); and (in a different way) Jeff Nuttall, *Bomb Culture* (London: Paladin, 1970).

2. Howard S. Becker, *Outsiders: Studies in the Sociology of Deviance* (New York: Free Press, 1963), Chaps 7 and 8.

3. Joseph Gusfield, *Symbolic Crusade: Status Politics and the American Temperance Movement* (Urbana: University of Illinois, 1963).

4. Becker, op. cit. p. 145.

5. Howard S. Becker (Ed.), *Social Problems: A Modern Approach* (New York: John Wiley, 1966).

6. See Herbert Blumer, 'Collective Behaviour' in J. B. Gittler (Ed.), *Review of Sociology* (New York: Wiley, 1957); Ralph H. Turner, 'Collective Behaviour', in R. E. L. Farris (Ed.), *Handbook of Modern Sociology* (Chicago: Rand McNally, 1964), and Ralph H. Turner and Lewis M. Killian, *Collective Behaviour* (Englewood Cliffs, N.J.: Prentice-Hall, 1957).

7. Orrin E. Klapp, *Heroes, Villains and Fools: The Changing American Character* (Englewood Cliffs, N.J.: Prentice-Hall, 1962).

8. The sceptical revolution can only be understood as part of a broader reaction in the social sciences as a whole against the dominant models, images and methodology of positivism. It is obviously beyond my scope to deal here with this connection. For an account of the peculiar shape positivism took in the study of crime and deviance and of the possibilities of transcending its paradoxes, the work of David Matza is invaluable: *Delinquency and Drift* (New York: Wiley, 1964) and *Becoming Deviant* (Englewood Cliffs, N.J.: Prentice-Hall, 1969).

9. Becker, *Outsiders: Studies in the Sociology of Deviance*, op. cit. p. 9.

10. R. D. Laing, *The Divided Self* (Harmondsworth: Penguin, 1965), p. 34.

11. A fuller account of these and other implications of the sceptical position is given in my Introduction and Postscript to Stanley Cohen (Ed.) *Images of Deviance* (Harmondsworth: Penguin Books, 1971). Some examples of work influenced by this tradition can be found in that volume but more directly in Rubington and Weinberg's excellent collection of interactionist writings: Earl Rubington and Martin S. Weinberg (Eds), *Deviance: The Interactionist Perspective* (New York: Collier-Macmillan, 1968).

12. Edwin M. Lemert, *Social Pathology: A Systematic Approach to the Study of Sociopathic Behaviour* (New York: McGraw-Hill, 1951) and *Human Deviance, Social Problems and Social Control* (Englewood Cliffs, N.J.: Prentice-Hall, 1967).

13. Lemert, *Social Pathology*, op. cit.

14. ibid. p. 55.

15. See John I. Kitsuse, 'Societal Reaction to Deviant Behaviour: Problems of Theory and Method', *Social Problems* 9 (Winter 1962), pp. 247-56.

16. Kai T. Erikson, *Wayward Puritans: A Study in the Sociology of Deviance* (New York: John Wiley, 1966).

17. Becker, *Outsiders: Studies in the Sociology of Deviance*, op. cit. Chaps 7 and 8.

18. Paul Rock and Stanley Cohen, 'The Teddy Boy', in V. Bogdanor and R. Skidelsky, *The Age of Affluence: 1951-1964* (London: Macmillan, 1970).

19. Jock Young, 'The Role of the Police as Amplifiers of Deviancy, Negotiators of Reality and Translators of Fantasy: Some Aspects of our Present System of Drug Control as seen in Notting Hill', in Cohen, op. cit.

20. Joseph Gusfield, 'Moral Passage: The Symbolic Process in Public Designations of Deviance', *Social Problems* 15 (Fall, 1967), pp. 175-88.

21. Young, op. cit. and *The Drug Takers: The Social Meaning of Drug-Taking* (London: Paladin, 1971).

22. Erikson, op. cit. p. 12.

23. Leslie T. Wilkins, *Social Deviance: Social Policy, Action and Research* (London: Tavistock, 1964), Chap. 4. I have made a preliminary attempt to apply this model to the Mods and Rockers in 'Mods, Rockers and the Rest: Community Reaction to Juvenile Delinquency', *Howard Journal of Penology and Crime Prevention* XII (1967), pp. 121-30.

24. Young (1971) *The Drug Takers*, op. cit.

25. David H. Downes, *The Delinquent Solution: A Study in Subcultural Theory* (London: Routledge and Kegan Paul, 1966), p. ix.

26. Neil J. Smelser, *Theory of Collective Behaviour* (London: Routledge & Kegan Paul, 1962).

27. ibid. p. 17.

28. ibid. p. 284.

29. Early journalistic accounts of disasters have given way to more sophisticated methods of data collection and theorization. The body in the U.S.A. most responsible for this development is the Disaster Research Group of the National Academy of Science, National

Research Council. The most comprehensive accounts of their findings and other research are to be found in: G. W. Baker and D. W. Chapman, *Man and Society in Disaster* (New York: Basic Books, 1962) and A. H. Barton, *Social Organisation Under Stress: A Sociological Review of Disaster Studies* (Washington, D.C.: National Academy of Sciences, 1963). See also A. H. Barton: *Communities in Disaster* (London: Ward Lock, 1970).

30. Robert K. Merton, Introduction to Barton, *Social Organisation Under Stress*, op. cit. pp. xix-xx.

31. C F. Fritz, 'Disaster', in R. K. Merton and R. A. Nisbet (Eds), *Contemporary Social Problems* (London: Rupert Hart-Davis, 1963), p. 654.

32. I. H. Cissin and W. B. Clark, 'The Methodological Challenge of Disaster Research' in Baker and Chapman, op. cit. p. 30.

33. From: Barton, *Social Organization Under Stress,* op. cit. pp. 14-15; D. W. Chapman, 'A Brief Introduction to Contemporary Disaster Research', in Baker and Chapman, op. cit. pp. 7-22; J. G. Miller, 'A Theoretical Review of Individual and Group Psychological Reaction to Stress', in G. H. Grosser *et al.* (Eds), *The Threat of Impending Disaster: Contributions to the Psychology of Stress* (Cambridge, Massachusetts: M.I.T. Press, 1964), pp. 24-32.

11. The Interpretation of Violence
Philip Schlesinger

How do frameworks of interpretation affect how we think about the question of
violence in contemporary liberal democracies? It is obvious that we have to address
questions of definition and categorization. I shall therefore begin by commenting
briefly upon some theoretical perspectives in the social and human sciences. This leads
me to consider the importance of control over the operation of social memory for
contemporary perceptions of violence and sets the stage for a discussion of current
official concern about the mass media and political violence in the chapters that follow.

The problem

There is no well-demarcated, widely accepted concept of violence. On the contrary, as
many contemporary commentators have pointed out, 'violence' is a term that suffers
from conceptual devaluation or semantic entropy. It is used as part of a discourse of
social pathology in which we are perpetually threatened with disorder and decline, a
discourse which is 'more than alarmist; it is catastrophist' (Chesnais, 1981: 8). As the
historian Eric Hobsbawm has observed, for most citizens of liberal democracies such
dark imaginings are not connected with the realities of everyday life, for physical
violence narrowly understood is still a remote experience:

> Directly, it is omnipresent in the form of the traffic accident — casual,
> unintended, unpredictable and uncontrollable by most of its victims . . .
> Indirectly, it is omnipresent in the mass media and entertainment . . .
> Even more remotely, we are aware both of the existence in our time of
> vast, concretely unimaginable mass destruction . . . and also of the sectors
> and situations of society in which physical violence is common and
> probably, increasing. Tranquillity and violence coexist. (Hobsbawm, 1977:
> 209-10)

But is our *sense* of the present tranquil? Probably, since Hobsbawm wrote the passage
quoted, some two decades ago, consciousness of the balance of terror has become more
acute in many sectors of the populations of Europe, and in the post-Chernobyl years to
be aware of what the aftermath of nuclear war would mean is surely vividly present to
all who think. The past two decades have also seen the growth of various forms of
political violence, often nationalist in origin, sometimes anti-systemic, used both
within national confines and across them. This has gone under the label of 'terrorism'
and has contributed to a sense of instability out of all proportion to its material, as
opposed to its symbolic, importance. In the case of 'transnational terrorism', deriving
from theatres of conflict such as the Middle East, physical violence is often transported
from one context to another. The same could be said when sectoral conflicts such as

Philip Schlesinger: 'The Interpretation of Violence' from *MEDIA, STATE AND NATION: POLITICAL
VIOLENCE AND COLLECTIVE IDENTITIES* (London: Sage Publications Ltd, 1991), pp. 5-16. Reprinted
with permission of Sage Publications Ltd.

that in Northern Ireland are fought out on the British mainland. But these are only the best-publicized faces of terrorist violence, the internal repression practised by states against their own citizens on the whole receiving much less attention.

To talk of contemporary violence, then, carries with it the risk of being all-embracing, of aggregating many diverse manifestations of the use of force and their effects: these might include all or any of criminal violence, public disorder and military actions. How can we make the issue intelligible? A starting-point, I suggest, is to look at practices of interpretation and to point to some of the problems involved in these. This does not make violent phenomena disappear by any means. But it can, at the very least, make us think more clearly about what we are doing and the underlying choices that are being made by opting for one or other evaluative framework.

One necessary step in considering the place of violence in contemporary society is to consider its relationship to the modern state. This, in turn, requires us to distinguish between types of state. But before dealing with either of these points let us briefly consider what might be meant by 'violence'.

The limits of defining

It needs but the slightest acquaintance with the literature on violence and terrorism to recognize the hazards of definition. Of course the process of defining and classifying acts and processes is far from neutral in this connection, for it is closely tied up with the question of legitimation and delegitimation. The well-known slogan that one man's terrorist is another man's freedom-fighter is perhaps the most simplistic way of making this point, directing us as it does to underlying frameworks for evaluating a given use of force and the status of the agent who uses it.

If there is a stand to be taken for the purposes of rational analysis, then it is surely with those who argue for restricting the scope of the term 'violence'. This may give us a sense of proportion about just how violent our times actually are and counter the inflationary effect of treating violence indiscriminately. There is little to be gained by lumping together such diverse manifestations as symbolic protest, the damaging effects on the poor of inegalitarian economic decision-making, the injustices of the routine and impersonal workings of bureaucracy, and the killing and maiming of persons. Although to take such a conceptually conservative stand is easy in principle it is difficult in practice. I have selected several restrictive definitions of violence, almost arbitrarily, in order to illustrate the analytical problems involved.

To take one recent example, Alain Chesnais, author of a study of violence during the past two centuries, proposes that: 'Violence in the strict sense, the only violence which is measurable and indisputable is *physical* violence. It is direct injury to persons; it has three characteristics: it is brutal, external and painful. It is defined by the material use of force' (Chesnais, 1981: 12). Much along the same lines is this formulation by the sociologist Robin Williams (1981: 26): 'the clearest cases of violence are those which cause physical damage, are intentional, are active rather than passive, and are direct in their effects.' Yet a further attempt to circumscribe what is meant by violence comes from the philosopher Ted Honderich (1980: 153), who suggests that 'An *act of violence* . . . is a use of considerable or destroying force against people or things, a use of force that offends against a norm.'

There would be little difficulty in compiling an entire volume of such definitions, and indeed this has been done (cf. Schmid, 1984, ch. 1). We could, moreover, attempt to classify them in various ways. For instance, in our three illustrative cases the 'basic' meaning of violence is stipulatively proposed (a) as physical violence to persons alone; *or* (b) as causing physical damage to unspecified categories of object, whether animate or inanimate, plus restrictive conditions about intentionality, directness and so forth; *or* (c) as involving both persons and things, together with a clause that locates the discussion of violence within a normative framework.

It could be said, fairly enough, that there is no great distance between these various definitions, and that some compromise reformulation could incorporate the essential elements of all three to the satisfaction of all concerned. However, the problem goes deeper. For to define 'violence' is not by any means to offer a protocol for its study and analysis. We might agree on a definition but still disagree about the details of subsequent categorization and what is to count as an adequate method for assembling evidence.

Thus, Chesnais categorizes violence as either 'private' or 'collective'. Under 'private' comes crime, suicide and accident. Under 'collective' come Soviet state terrorism and Western anti-state terrorism. Williams (1981: 28, 31) distinguishes collective from individual violence. In the first category come 'internal wars, revolutions, guerrilla wars, insurrections, rebellions, political purges, genocide, strikes with violence, vigilante actions, pogroms, riots, sabotage, political executions and assassinations'. In the second category come homicide, manslaughter, rape, assault, vandalism and attacks on persons and property. For his part, Honderich is concerned pre-eminently with examining the principle of violence from below directed towards changing a democratic political system.

Faced with such divergent strategies, it is tempting to abandon the rationalist road of definition and to say, as does the political scientist W.J.M. Mackenzie (1975: 160, 117), that the problem may be 'better stated by myth than definition', given his view that violence is 'itself symbol and metaphor'. Undoubtedly, when discussing whether our times are more or less violent than others we cannot fail to address how communication in its broadest sense constructs our perceptions of present dangers for us, and the role which violence as everyday drama plays in our lives.

This, however, is merely one intellectual line to be pursued. The broader question of how violent contemporary societies are can only be made intelligible in empirical terms by a process of rigorous comparison across space and time, a strategy that raises enormous problems of data collection, as Alex Schmid (1984: ch. 3) has pointed out in the case of political violence and terrorism. Ideally, this would require us to meet the following conditions: that (i) an agreed categorization of types of violence is employed during (ii) a clear-cut period in which (iii) comparable social formations are investigated (iv) using evidence or data adequate to support theoretically informed generalizations.

I do not wish to labour the point. But it is clear that even where we are being explicit and go to the lengths of enumerating given types of action within a society to be categorized as violent, this is an area in which normative assumptions are going to affect what we select in a major way. For example, when Britain mobilized for the recent war in the Falklands in the dominant view this was a legitimate use of force where diplomacy had failed. If we then refer to official concern about violence in the United Kingdom during the past decade, this 'small war' and its dead and wounded would scarcely register as something to be counted in (somehow) together with football hooliganism, terrorist bombings and fighting on the picket line during the miners' strike.

A second obvious point concerns the most conventional 'objective' measure of violence in society, namely crime statistics, which are frequently used as the basis for international comparison (cf., for example, Chesnais, 1981). As is well known, however, not only do categories of violent crime and understandings of motivation differ as between cultures, but the reporting of crimes, stringency of enforcement, success in apprehending criminals, sentencing policy, and so forth, all vary across time even within a single society. Such difficulties do not, of course, make comparative discussion of violence impossible. But it is always going to be problematic.

Power, violence and the state

As W.J.M. Mackenzie rightly observes, one route into the problem 'is to relate the problem of violence to that of political power, treating political power as a necessary basis for collective decision-making' (1975: 117). Our concern with the extent of violence in a society has to consider the ways in which it is inherently bound up with a system of rule.

According to Max Weber, control of the means of violence is an essential feature of the modern state — though not by any means the only one — and holds the key to the exercise of power within the political order: 'the state is a human community that (successfully) claims the *monopoly of the legitimate use of physical force within a given territory* . . . The state is considered the sole source of the "right" to use violence' (Weber, 1948: 78). A later eminent historical sociologist, Norbert Elias, also contends that the formation of the centralized, national state has brought with it the creation of territorially based monopolies of force, observing that 'When a monopoly of force is formed, pacified social spaces are created which are normally free from acts of violence' (Elias, 1982: 235). By violence in this context Elias means the exercise of physical force by non-authorized individuals or groups. In the modern era, 'physical torture, imprisonment and the radical humiliation of individuals has become the monopoly of a central authority, hardly to be found in normal life. With this monopolization, the physical threat to the individual is slowly depersonalized' (Elias, 1982: 237).

The 'right' to monopolize violence results in the depersonalization of its exercise through the decision-making processes of judicial authorities and law-enforcement bodies. This has been described by René Girard (1977: ch. 1 *passim*) as, in effect, the rationalization of revenge — an 'interminable, infinitely repetitive process' — from which the 'resounding authority' of the state is there to protect us (Girard, 1977: 15,22). But those who claim to be in the business of social protection must in turn protect themselves from attacks upon their monopoly of force by invoking the mystique of legality and legitimacy: this then permits them to use violence in ways accepted as different in kind from the ways of those who act against the state. For, as Eugene Walter has pointed out in his study of political terror:

226

When a violent process is socially prescribed and defined as a legitimate means of control or punishment, according to practices familiar to us, the destructive harm is measured and the limits made clear. Social definition as an authorized method often extracts it from the category of violence — at least from the standpoint of the society — and places in it the same domain with other socially approved coercive techniques. (Walter. 1969: 23)

If one accepts this broad line of argument, therefore, one of the immanent possibilities of the state's monopoly of violence is the transgression of those very legal frameworks which in theory act to limit its arbitrariness. It is at this point that we talk of states becoming terroristic, or of employing unacceptable techniques (such as torture) whose use they themselves would wish to deny, dissimulate or euphemize.

Forms of state

Throughout the period of the Cold War — now officially dead — we tended to differentiate between types of state and the place of violence within them. At its most simple, at least until the revolutions of 1989-90 in the former Communist bloc, the dominant world-picture was of a capitalist (democratic) West confronted by a socialist (totalitarian) East. Although by the time the Berlin Wall had collapsed it was widely conceded that state socialism was not in most places a regime of Stalinist terror, it was nonetheless still rightly seen as inherently repressive and authoritarian, with violent origins that still continued to exert influence upon the policing of dissent (Curtis, 1979; Friedrich *et al.*, 1969). By contrast, however, the violent origins of most liberal democracies tended (and still continue) to be conveniently forgotten. But we will return to this point.

Liberal democracy, therefore has stood, and still stands, as the contrast case to totalitarianism. As Ted Honderich (1980: 157) has pointed out, it is widely assumed 'that democracy and violence somehow conflict'. However, such a view does need to be tempered by a good dose of realism. If the Weberian view of the state is correct, it applies as much to liberal democracy as it does to totalitarianism: the differences are a matter of degree rather than of kind. This line of argument has recently been pursued to its logical conclusion by the social theorist Anthony Giddens (1985: 301), who has argued that ' "totalitarian" is not an adjective that can be fruitfully applied to a type of state, let alone to soviet-style states generally. It refers rather to a *type of rule*.' For Giddens all nation-states are potentially subject to the implementation of totalitarian rule, whose primary element, he suggests, involves 'an extreme focusing of surveillance, devoted to the securing of political ends deemed by the state authorities to demand urgent political mobilization' (1985: 303). To this he adds the more usual characteristics of moral totalism, terror and prominence of a· leader figure.

We are not obliged to accept the view that all contemporary regimes are immanently totalitarian in this sense. A less far-reaching position is this: that *in extremis*, the liberal-democratic state may suspend all civil rights in defence of the social order itself. Pertinent here are the hard-nosed insights of Carl Schmitt (1985: 8, 12), who, anticipating the transition from the Weimar Republic to the Third Reich, said:

> Sovereign is he who decides on the exception. . . What characterizes an
> exception is principally unlimited authority, which means the suspension
> of the entire existing order. In such a situation it is clear that the state
> remains, whereas law recedes. Because the exception is different from
> anarchy and chaos, order in the juristic sense prevails even if it is not of
> the ordinary kind.

That is as blunt a recognition as one could wish that 'Law and order', usually spoken of as an indissoluble couple, can pull in opposed directions.

The *état d'exception* in such a far-reaching sense is not unknown to us: Greece and Turkey, for instance, have both offered examples of the suspension of democracy in recent years. And exceptional measures have been taken in combating insurgency, as for instance in Northern Ireland, which offers an intermediate, sectoral, case: it is a not entirely successful attempt to insulate the wider polity from the effects of suspending business as usual in one province (cf. Faligot, 1980; Pistoi, 1981).

Nor is the democratic state a guarantee against a use of force that no one — anywhere — willingly admits to: namely, torture. As the historian Edward Peters remarks in his study of this form of political violence, with the emergence of the nation-state, conceptions of treason have expanded. From *lèse-majesté*, focused on royal persons and households, we have moved to *lèse-nation*, in which the threat to 'a people or a state' has become 'both a larger and less specific offence'. Peters goes on to say: 'Paradoxically, in an age of vast state strength, ability to mobilize resources, and possession of virtually infinite means of coercion, much of state policy has been based on the concept of extreme vulnerability to enemies, external or internal'(Peters,1985: 105,7). Moreover, although in the twentieth century torture first appeared in the Soviet Union and the Third Reich and under Spanish and Italian fascism, it has also been found 'in some circumstances, under ordinary legal authority' (Peters, 1985: 105).

The classic example which crystallized post-war debate was the use of torture by the French administration during the Algerian independence struggle, a fact concealed for as long as possible (cf. Vidal-Naquet, 1972). In the case of Northern Ireland, 'counter-terrorist' operations involving the use of sensory deprivation and violent interrogation have been well-documented; instead of being labelled 'torture' it has been euphemized as 'ill-treatment' (McGuffin, 1974: Taylor, 1980). We are not obliged to say, as does Anthony Giddens, that all states tend towards totalitarianism to recognize the force of Peters' argument that the increasing salience of the nation-state as the basis of moral-political judgement, together with the growth of state security apparatuses, 'is perhaps the ultimate cause of the reappearance of torture in the twentieth century' (1985: 114)

Hence, the euphemization of a particular form of violence in the context, say, of a counter-insurgency campaign opens up a struggle over forms of classification, and consequently over the perception and measurement of 'violence'. The same arguments have been central to the debate about the origins of current terrorism in the West. In this connection, one can hardly forget the major efforts made by the first Reagan administration, at the beginning of the 1980s, to forge the ideological connections between international terrorism and Soviet communism. One decade on, and the post-Cold War climate has rendered this irrelevant. It is the Middle Eastern bogyman of 'Islam' that occupies centre stage at this time of writing.

The ideological argument against communism has been linked with US support for repressive regimes, in particular in Latin America and South-East Asia. The disappearance of the Soviet Union as chief ideological adversary will not render this redundant elsewhere. It was at the outset of the 1980s that so much was made of the distinction between 'authoritarianism' and 'totalitarianism', the former label being attributed to politically acceptable regimes of the right. It has also been the key to the running of what Edward Herman and Frank Brodhead (1984) have called 'demonstration elections' in places such as the Dominican Republic, South Vietnam and El Salvador. Given the association of democracy with consent, to make regimes look democratic is also to make them look legitimate and therefore to bring about the recodification of state terror as acceptable force.

Political frameworks and social memory

But it is not the current scene alone that poses problems of analysis. One theme too little explored in much contemporary discussion, given its fixation with the immediate, is the role of what we might call received social memory in structuring perceptions of the kind of society in which we live. Every eruption of violent political conflict, each 'crime wave', is heralded as though it were unprecedented, and an index of novel social pathology. This directs our attention to the ways in which frameworks of interpretation are created, sustained and contested by the activities of those acting for diverse political interests, intellectuals cast in the role of moralists or commentators and the journalistic imperatives of mass media.

Various commentators have noted how manifestations of political violence and 'crime waves' are greeted with surprise, as though they were novel events alien to the democratic political culture of the nation in question, and a telling index of unprecedented decline in civil conduct. The foreshortened temporal perspective at work has major consequences for the way in which the role of violence in the democratic order may be popularly conceived.

One pertinent example comes from the United States of the late 1960s in the wake of the urban riots in the black ghettos, student protest about the Vietnam War and the political assassinations of the Kennedys and Martin Luther King. As is well known, the Kerner Commission was appointed by the Johnson administration to investigate the 'civil disorders' in 1967, and the Eisenhower Commission to consider the 'causes and prevention of violence' was set up the following year.

One product of the latter commission's work was some historical research on violence in America in comparative perspective. One of the themes which emerged clearly from many of the studies conducted was the extent to which collective violence was a central part of American political culture, whether in the form of vigilantism, urban rioting, racial violence or violence on the industrial front. (Interestingly, and very tellingly, genocide is not one of the categories used.) Noting the parallels with Europe, the book's editors comment that 'group violence has been chronic and pervasive in the

European and American past' and that 'both Europeans and Americans have a noteworthy capacity to forget or deny its commonality' (Graham and Gurr, 1969: xxxi).

In his survey of major Western European countries, the historical sociologist Charles Tilly has likewise observed that 'The collective memory machine has a tremendous capacity for destruction of the facts' and that the amnesia in question centres on the well-established finding that 'Historically, collective violence has flowed regularly out of the central political processes of western countries' (Tilly, 1969: 8, 4). Tilly, who considers the transformation of countries such as Britain, France, Germany, Italy and Spain into urban and industrial national states and economies, argues for a political interpretation of collective violence. Central to the various types which he identifies — whether primitive, reactionary or modern — is a 'struggle for established places in the structure of power' (Tilly, 1969: 10). In the contemporary context, argues Tilly, violent collective action tends to be organizationally based in forms of association such as political parties, unions and special interest groups and ought to be seen as interacting with the continual effort of authorities to 'monopolize, control, or at least contain' it (Tilly, 1969: 41). What Tilly calls the 'repertoire of collective action' has changed over long periods of time as social relations have changed with the advance of capitalism and the centralizing tendencies of the national state. Nevertheless, typical nineteenth-century forms such as demonstrations, strikes and armed actions — albeit with different protagonists — are still used today (Tilly, 1983: 73-8). The essential point is the *normality* of collective violence in political life, in the democratic era as before it.

These points about the social memory of historical development also apply to a different type of concern with violence. Whereas Tilly concerns himself with collective forms that might be considered 'political', the sociologist Geoffrey Pearson has examined what he calls the history of respectable fears about criminal violence. Taking the British example, which could undoubtedly be extended to other cases, Pearson (1983: 207) points to a history which is 'a seamless tapestry of fears and complaints about the deteriorated present' in which the leitmotiv is the moral decline of the British people.

One of the dominant themes of British political life, particularly accentuated under Mrs Thatcher's successive administrations, has been 'law and order', in which fighting the country's crime wave and its supposed decline into lawlessness has figured large. The pronouncements of conservative politicians, top policemen and the bulk of the press all share assumptions about the essentially pacific nature of the British nation and project a pre-war idyll of tranquillity and good behaviour. It is worth underlining the importance of images (indeed myths) of the nation in forming such debates. As Pearson (1983: 227) observes: 'Viewed in this light, culture is to be seen not so much as a control upon violence, but as an incitement to violence: a form of regulation to be sure, but a regulation that defines, promotes, organizes and channels violence.' This directs our attention to the role of the mass media which will be discussed in [Chapters 2 and 3].

Antisocial forms of violence, such as gang warfare on the streets, vandalism, football hooliganism, street crime, Pearson convincingly argues, are perceived by each generation as a malaise of the present, when in fact they have an unbroken history. This, he contends, is rooted in 'the social reproduction of an under-class of the most poor and dispossessed' which 'is the material foundation to these hooligan continuities' (1983: 236). A further element, again paralleled elsewhere (as for instance in France, Italy and Germany today) is the way in which successive waves of immigrants or aliens are held responsible for violent crime: in Britain, this is particularly noticeable in the case of the black community which is seen as the principal source of 'mugging' . However, this label was imported from the United States, with the effect of disowning as ' "unBritish" the old-fashioned crime of street robbery', the history of which long predates World War II (Pearson, 1983: 20; cf. Hall *et al.*, 1978: ch. 1).

To say all this is not in any way to belittle justifiable public concern about contemporary forms of violence. It is, however, to place such anxieties in a broader context in which historical continuities put the crises of the present into perspective.

Symbolic violence?

To appeal to historical analyses of the place of violence in collectivities is but to invoke one more cultural practice of interpretation. It is obvious that rational reconstructions cannot easily avoid consideration of the symbolic dimension of violence. In conclusion, it is now time to address this issue more explicitly.

One relevant line of argument conjoins the symbolic and the violent in the concept of 'symbolic violence' which the German communication theorist Harry Pross (1981: 69; his emphases) has defined as 'the power to make so effective the *validity* of meaning through *signs* that others *identify* themselves with it . . . Symbolic violence is bound up with the materiality of signs.' For the French sociologist Pierre Bourdieu (1977: 196), who coined the term, 'symbolic violence is the gentle, hidden form which violence takes when overt violence is impossible'.

I would question whether we should conceive the effects of symbols as more than *metaphorically* violent, although it is easy to see the attraction of the analogy between the regulation of mental life within hierarchical social relations and control over human bodies through the exercise of physical power. However, to go further and insist seriously that symbolic violence and physical violence are variants of a single phenomenon opens up the whole question of scope and definition once more. How, if at all, we might apply a calculus to symbolic effects is one of the unresolved issues of contemporary media theory, and has been the object of repeated reconceptualizations and operationalizations throughout the era of mass communication (cf. McQuail, 1987: chs 8, 9; Wolf, 1985: chs 1, 2).

'Symbolic violence' may be deconstructed into two analytically useful ideas: (i) that the symbolic domain *is* coercive with respect to those who live within a collectivity (although differently according to social location and endowment with cultural capital); and (ii) that symbolic violence offers an alternative to physical coercion where political circumstances permit, and that under some conditions it may also be complementary to it. This question is central to the influential work of Antonio Gramsci, whose analysis of the relations between coercion and consent by a ruling class in the pursuit of hegemony has shaped much contemporary debate.

At the heart of these concerns is the notion that the symbolic domain is a locus in which struggles for ideological domination — for hearts and minds takes place. This is widely accepted across the political spectrum (although not always honestly stated) as witness the quest in regimes of all colours, using a variety of means, for control over propaganda, the imposition of censorship and state secrecy, and the management of information.

The symbolic and the violent come together in another way, namely the obsessive interest in whether the mass media — today, television in particular — cause political and criminal violence and forms of antisocial behaviour that threaten the stability of liberal-democratic states. Although substantial research has been conducted with approaches ranging from behaviourist psychology to ethnography, the results remain inconclusive (cf. Gerbner, 1987). As the next chapter shows, the arguments are bound to continue, fuelled by the strong conviction amongst politicians, counter-insurgents and moral entrepreneurs that mass-mediated violence must somehow have deleterious effects, even if they cannot be pinned down decisively. Hence the common assumption that it is crucial to control the symbolic domain of communication in fighting enemies of the state.

References

Bourdieu, P. (1977) *Outline of a Theory of Practice*. Cambridge: Cambridge University Press.

Chesnais, J.C. (1981) *Histoire de la Violence en Occident de 1800 à Nos Jours*. Paris: Laffont.

Curtis, M. (1979) *Totalitarianism*. New Brunswick. NJ: Transaction Books.

Elias, N. (1982) *The Civilizing Process (Vol. 2): State Formation and Civilization*. Oxford: Blackwell.

Faligot, R. (1980) *Guerre Spéciale en Europe: Le Laboratoire Irlandais*. Paris: Flammarion.

Friedrich, C.J., Curtis. M. and Barber, B.R. (1969) *Totalitarianism in Perspective: Three Views*. London: Pall Mall Press.

Gerbner, G., with the assistance of Signorielli, N. (1987) 'Violence and Terror in the Mass Media: A Consolidated Report of Existing Research'. University of Philadelphia. Unpublished paper.

Giddens, A. (1985) *The Nation-State and Violence: Volume Two of a Contemporary Critique of Historical Materialism*. Cambridge: Polity Press.

Girard, R. (1977) *Violence and the Sacred*. Baltimore, Md. and London: Johns Hopkins University Press.

Graham, H.D. and Gurr, T.R. (eds) (1969) *The History of Violence in America: Historical and Comparative Perspectives. A Report Submitted to the National Commission on the Causes and Prevention of Violence*. New York, Washington and London: Praeger.

Hall, S., Critcher. C., Jefferson. T., Clarke, J. and Roberts, B. (1978) *Policing the Crisis: Mugging, the State, and Law and Order*. London: Macmillan.

Herman, E.S. and Brodhead, F. (1984) *Demonstration Elections: US-Staged Elections in the Dominican Republic, Vietnam and El Salvador*. Boston, Mass.: South End Press.

Hobsbawm, E.J. (1977) 'The Rules of Violence', in *Revolutionaries: Contemporary Essays*. London: Quartet.

Honderich, T. (1980) *Violence for Equality: Inquiries in Political Philosophy*. Harmondsworth: Penguin.

McGuffin, J. (1974) *The Guineapigs*. Harmondsworth: Penguin.

Mackenzie, W.J.M. (1975) *Power, Violence, Decision*. Harmondsworth: Penguin.

McQuail, D. (1987) *Mass Communication Theory: An Introduction*, 2nd edn. London: Sage.

Pearson, G. (1983) *Hooligan: A History of Respectable Fears*. Basingstoke and London: Macmillan.

Peters, E. (1985) *Torture*. Oxford: Blackwell.

Pistoi, P. (1981) *Una Comunità sotto Controllo: Operazioni Contro-Insurrezionali delle Forze di Sicurezza Britanniche nel Quartiere Cattolico di Ballymurphy, Belfast*. Milan: Franco Angeli.

Pross, H. (1981) *Zwänge: Essay über Symbolische Gewalt*. Berlin: Kramer.

Schmid, A. P. (1984) *Political Terrorism: A Research Guide to Concepts, Theories, Data Bases and Literature*. Amsterdam: North-Holland: New Brunswick, NJ: Transaction Books.

Schmitt, C. (1985) *Political Theology: Four Chapters on the Concept of Sovereignty*. Cambridge, Mass: MIT Press.

Taylor, P. (1980) *Beating the Terrorists? Interrogation in Omagh, Gough and Castlereagh*. Harmondsworth: Penguin.

Tilly, C. (1969) 'Collective Violence in European Perspective', in Graham and Gurr (1969). pp. 4-45.

Tilly, C. (1983) 'Violenza e azione collettiva in Europa: riflessioni storico-comparate', in D. Della Porta and G. Pasquino (eds), *Terrorismo e Violenza Politica*. Bologna: Il Mulino. pp. 51-87.

Vidal-Naquet, P. (1972) *La Torture dans la République: Essai d'Histoire et de la Politique Contemporaines (1954-1962)*. Paris: Editions de Minuit.

Walter, E.V. (1969) *Terror and Resistance: A Study of Political Violence with Case Studies of Some Primitive African Communities*. London. Oxford and New York: Oxford University Press.

Weber, M. (1948) 'Politics as a Vocation', in H.H. Gerth and C. Wright Mills (eds), *From Max Weber: Essays in Sociology*. London: Routledge & Kegan Paul. pp. 77-128.

Williams Jr, R.M. (1981) 'Legitimate and Illegitimate Uses of Violence: A Review of Ideas and Literature', in W. Gaylin. R. Macklin and T.M. Powledge (eds), *Violence and the Politics of Research*. New York and London: Plenum Press. pp. 23-45.

Wolf M. (1985) *Teorie delle Comunicazioni di Massa*. Milan: Bompiani.

12.   Mugging as a Moral Panic: a Question of Proportion
Peter Waddington

Summary

Hall *et al.*'s, claim that official and public concern about 'mugging' during the early 1970s was a 'moral panic' (Hall *et al.*, 1978) is seriously flawed. First, their analysis of official statistics designed to show that the crime problem was not 'dramatically worse' confuses *rates* of change with *increments* of change, thus producing a misleading picture. In fact, the evidence cited by Hall *et al.*, supports the opposite conclusion to that drawn by the authors themselves. Second, the lack of any criteria of proportionality allows no distinction to be drawn in general between a 'sober, realistic appraisal' of a problem and a 'moral panic'. The difficulties posed by the absence of such criteria are explored in relation to the problem of 'racial attacks'.

1 Introduction

The notion of 'moral panics' has become firmly established in the conceptual apparatus of criminologists. It is used to explain public anxiety about, and official reaction to, increases in the reported rate of specific offences (Cohen 1973, Young 1971, Hall *et al.* 1978) or crime in general (Taylor 1981, Bottomley and Coleman 1984, *New Society* 1982).

To describe an expression of public and official anxiety as a 'moral panic' suggests that the scale of this response is disproportionately greater than the scale of the problem. There may, indeed, *be* a problem, but it is one which, in a moral panic, becomes overblown by media exaggeration and hyperbole. Consistent with media hysteria, the official reaction tends to be more severe than it need be. Thus, Cohen (1973), in his pioneering study of the moral panic surrounding 'mods and rockers' during the 1960s, does not deny that there was a disturbance during the miserable Easter weekend in Clacton, 1964. What he *does* maintain, however, is that the disturbance was not markedly different from other incidents that had occurred on similar occasions in the past, but which failed to spark media interest and, consequently, official reaction.

Of course, the principal difficulty with this notion of 'moral panics' is that of establishing the comparison between the scale of the problem and the scale of response to it. Studies which have employed this concept have tended to concentrate upon the scale of the response and paid much less attention to the scale of the problem itself (For example, Cohen 1973, Young 1971).

One exception is the highly influential study by Hall *et al.* (1978), of the 'mugging' panic during the early 1970s. Whilst they do not attempt to deny that offences which could be described as 'mugging' did occur, nor that distinct issues emerged regarding

P.A.J. Waddington: 'Mugging as a Moral Panic: a Question of Proportion' from *THE BRITISH JOURNAL OF SOCIOLOGY* (June 1986), Vol. XXXVII, No. 2, pp. 245-259. Reproduced by permission of Routledge.

disaffected young blacks, they argue that the scale of the reaction was unjustified by the actual crime situation. Using official statistics to support their argument, they state quite explicitly their reasons for their view.

This article will attempt to show that the central thesis of Hall *et al.* (1978) — that public and official concern about 'mugging' was unjustified by the actual scale of the problem — is both empirically and conceptually unsound. Empirically, the evidence which appears to suggest that the authorities, especially the police, over-reacted is unconvincing. In fact, the evidence cited by the authors supports the opposite conclusion. Conceptually, the notion of a 'moral panic' lacks any criteria of proportionality without which it is impossible to determine whether concern about *any* crime problem is justified or not.

2 'Mugging' — the scale of the problem

Hall *et al.* (1978), argue that the furore surrounding the apparently sudden appearance of 'mugging' as a crime problem during the early 1970s was an orchestrated reaction to the worsening crisis of legitimacy. By scapegoating young blacks, it allowed the police to go onto the offensive against a section of the population with whom they already had poor relations and prepared public opinion for the introduction of increasingly authoritarian measures designed to keep the 'reserve army' of the unemployed quiescent (ibid.: 362-97). The importation of the term 'mugging' from the USA capitalized upon a persistent theme of racialism in British culture, giving the appearance that deteriorating social conditions were the responsibility of the black community (ibid.: 18-28).

The keystone for this elaborate argument is the claim that in fact there was little, if any, justification for the concern about the growth of 'mugging' expressed by the police, the courts, government ministers and aired by the news media (ibid.: ch 1-3). Hall *et al.'s* (1978) examination of the official crime statistics purports to show that there was no objective basis for these expressions of concern. They argue:

1. There is no legal category of 'mugging' as such: 'muggings' actually span a number of legal categories, most notably robbery and theft from the person. This makes any attempt to infer trends from the official statistics inherently difficult, since not all 'robberies' or 'thefts from the person' will be 'muggings'. Moreover, by including the much more numerous 'thefts from the person' as 'muggings', relatively petty offences are treated as though they were much more serious incidents, thus artificially creating alarm. (pp. 5, 9-10, 15-16)

2. A misleading impression also resulted from media concentration on the most serious incidents, in which death or serious injury was caused. By applying the much wider label of 'mugging' to such incidents the media gave the spurious impression that the problem was more serious than was, in fact, the case. (pp. 1-9)

3. There was nothing novel about 'mugging', it was simply a new label for an old crime. The type of incident labelled as a 'mugging' in the 1970s had been known a hundred years previously as 'garrotting' and 'muggers' had been described in the past as, for example, 'footpads'. (pp. 4-6)

4. During the late 1960s and early 1970s — the period immediately antedating the panic — the general crime situation and the trends in robbery and related offences showed not a deterioration, but an improvement. (pp. 9-11)

5. The association of 'mugging' with young blacks, especially those living in South London, resulted from selective police harassment. This increased the likelihood that young blacks in South London would be detected for whatever offences they might have committed. It also provoked hostility which led to resistance to such police action, resulting in arrest for offences such as 'obstruction', 'assaulting the police', and so forth. (pp. 42-52)

Others have subsequently added the observation that robbery and theft from the person (the two legal categories most closely associated with 'mugging') constitute only a small proportion of total recorded crime (Smith 1982, Ramsey 1982).

3 Assessing the evidence

Does the evidence presented by Hall *et al.*, (1978) actually support the view that concern about 'mugging' was a moral panic? Was there nothing to justify the concern expressed by the police, the courts and the mass media?

3.1 *Quantitative evidence*

Hall *et al.*, state

> Thus, whatever statistics are used, whether the over-all 'crimes of violence' figures, or, more specifically those referring to 'robberies' or 'muggings', it is *not* [original emphasis] possible to demonstrate that the situation was dramatically worse in 1972 than it was in the period 1955-65. In other words, it is impossible to 'explain' the severity of the reaction to mugging by using arguments based solely on the objective, quantifiable, statistical facts (1978: 11).

In fact, *the evidence, as they present it, does not support their view that the situation was not 'dramatically worse'*. The reason is that they refer almost exclusively to *rates of increase* in crime when seeking to establish that the crime situation had not worsened. This ignores other measures of change such as the *amount of deterioration* in the crime situation. The result is to obscure the fact that, contrary to their assertion, the crime situation *had* seriously deteriorated during the period immediately preceding the 'mugging panic'.

Let us begin by considering the contention that total crime, in the period immediately antedating the onset of the concern about 'mugging', was not showing a marked increase. Hall *et al.*, (1978) claim

> The seven years from 1966 to 1972 saw a decreased rate of increase [in the crime rate] . . . the period of the greatest crime increase had passed by 1972. We were then in a rather mixed and indeterminate period — not at the crest of a 'crime wave' . . . The rise, in short, was neither particularly new in 1972, nor sudden. . . . In statistical terms, it was, temporarily anyway, past its peak (p. 10).

Let us be clear that 'a decreased rate of increase' is still an increase. The situation is getting worse, albeit at a slower rate. Even if the rate of reported crime began to decline subsequently, the period of which the authors write would still have been the 'crest of a crime wave' (Figure I). The 'crest' of any wave is its pinnacle, not the point of fastest increase. The sheer fact that the *rate* of increase had declined, does not mean that there had been a decline in the absolute level of crime nor, therefore, that there was no justification for concern at the *level* which crime had reached.

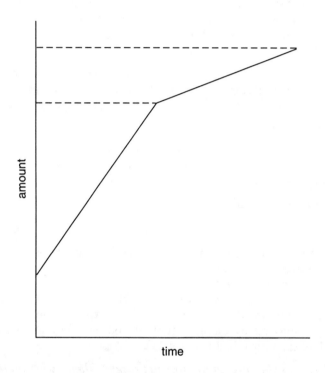

Figure I   A Hypothetical Example of a Decreased Rate of Increase

Does a 'decreased rate of increase' in crime mean that the situation is *not* deteriorating as rapidly as the police, the courts and the media were suggesting at the time? According to the statistical information provided by Hall *et al.,* (1978) between 1955 and 1965 the 'average annual increase was about 10 per cent', compared to 5 per cent in the period 1966-72. From this observation the authors seem to infer that the situation was deteriorating *less* rapidly. However, this obscures an important and fundamental distinction between *a rate of increase* and *increments of growth*. Comparisons between *rates of increase* involve sophisticated notions regarding compound effects of annual increases or decreases. Thus, even when a rate of increase in crime is constant, at say 5 per cent per annum, the crime situation will be deteriorating by *successively increasing amounts*. That is, the *gradient* of annual increases in the number of offences is becoming steeper. Hence, whilst the rate of increase in crime may have been reduced by half during the period 1966-72 compared to 1955-65, crime continued to rise by more or less constant increments (Figure II). By any normal standards, the situation *was* 'dramatically worse'. To say otherwise is to say that if there was a hypothetical increase during one year from five to ten crimes, followed by an increase the following year from ten to twenty crimes, the situation would be no worse because the rate of increase had remained constant at 100 per cent.

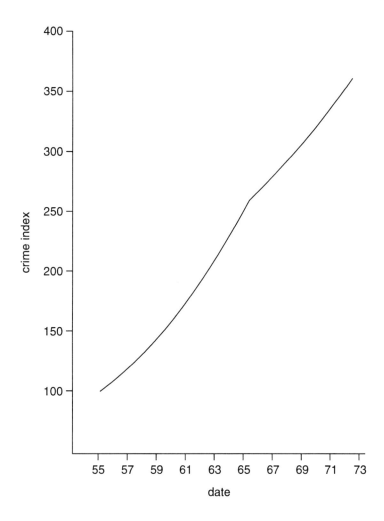

Figure II   Total Recorded Crime. An example of a 10% annual increase followed by a 5% annual increase. (Crime index, base = 100)

Moreover, it is possible that a situation may continue to get rapidly worse whilst still exhibiting a 'decreased rate of increase'. The failure of Hall *et al.,* (1978) to consider this possibility is made evident in their attempt to discredit the then Home Secretary's expressed concern at an increase in crimes of violence of 61.9 per cent between 1967 and 1971. The authors point out that during the period 1957-61 these crimes had increased by 68 per cent. However, as Figure III illustrates, even if there had been *no* increase in crimes of violence between the two periods at issue (a highly improbable assumption), the increment of growth during the later period would *still* have been *steeper* than that during the earlier period because it started from a higher base. Had there been no change in the rate of increase between the earlier and later periods (the 'adjusted' curve), the increase in the later period would have been even steeper.

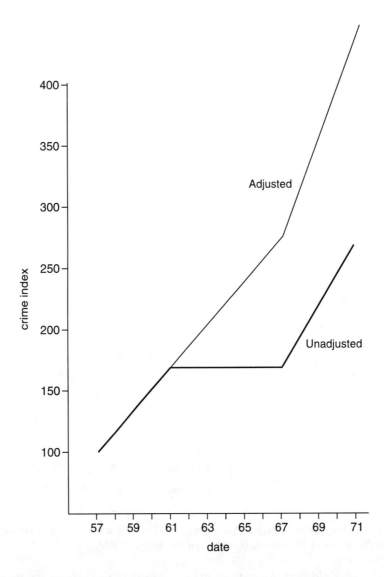

Figure III Recorded 'Crimes of Violence'. An example of a 68% increase (1957-61) followed by a 61.9% increase (1967-71). (Crime index, base = 100)

In short, Hall *et al.,* (1978) confuse ordinary language terms, such as 'dramatically worse' by evaluating the crime situation by the much narrower and more precise concept of 'rates of increase'. In so doing, they fail to take account of compound effects. It ill-behoves those who interpret the data so loosely to describe the Home Secretary as 'cavalier' in his use of statistics.

This same failure to consider compound effects is to be found in their analysis of figures on robberies

> During the ten years between 1955 and 1965 'robberies' increased by 354 per cent. Between 1965 and 1972, however, they increased by only [sic] 98.5 per cent. Expressed as a percentage, the average annual increase between 1955 and 1965 was 35.4 per cent, but during the seven years between 1965 and 1972 it was only 14 per cent (p. 11).

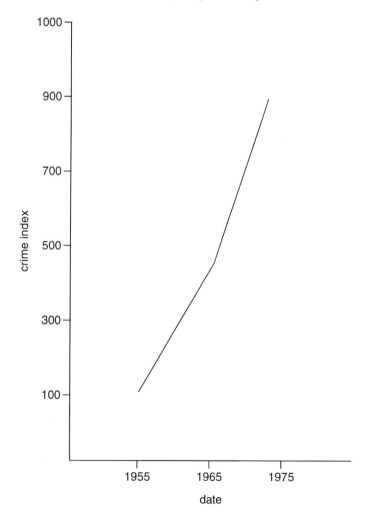

Figure IV **Recorded 'Robbery and Assault with Intent to Rob'. An example of a 354% increase between 1955-65 followed by a 98.5% increase between 1966-72. (Crime index, base = 100)**

Two points can be made about this statement. First, another way of stating the first half of the claim, is to say that during the *ten years,* 1955-65, robberies increased three and a half times and *then virtually doubled during the succeeding seven years.* Again, that represents a *steeper* increase in the number of reported offences (Figure IV). Second, the latter part of the claim actually confirms that the authors themselves do not understand the effect of compound increases. If there *had* indeed been an annual increase of 35.4 per cent for ten years followed by an increase of 14 per cent per year for seven years, the total increase over the seventeen year period would have been *sixty-fold.*

To conclude from these figures, as do Hall *et al.*

> The situation with relation to crimes roughly categorisable as 'muggings' was certainly no worse in 1972 than it was between 1955-65 and, it could be argued statistically that it was, if anything, slightly better (1978: 11).

is simply bizarre. The only valid conclusion to be drawn from the figures presented by Hall *et al.*, (1978) is the opposite one to that drawn by the authors themselves. It is that crime during the period immediately preceding the onset of concern about 'mugging' was indeed increasing and doing so by increasing increments. The only criticism of the police, courts and media is that they were too sloppy in their use of precise terms such as 'rates of increase'. That they had every reason to be concerned about the crime situation cannot, on the evidence presented by Hall *et al.*, (1978) be doubted.

Fortunately, we are not wholly reliant upon Hall, *et al.*'s, (1978) somewhat eccentric interpretation of the statistics. Michael Pratt's detailed examination of 'mugging' (Pratt 1980), based largely upon crime complaints received by the police, shows a very different picture to that described by Hall *et al.* He shows how reported robberies in London have increased recently at a rate unprecedented during this century (p.72) and that since 1957 the increase in robberies has been steeper in London than in the rest of England and Wales (p. 76). He also shows that robberies were increasing more rapidly than were other categories of crime in London (p. 77). Finally, 'mugging' was increasing more rapidly than other forms of robbery (pp. 78-9). All this would seem to have justified police concern about the rise in crime generally and explain the way this concern focused on 'mugging' in particular.

Pratt's research also clarifies a point which Hall *et al.*, (1978) confess bemused them.

> The much publicised 1973 headlines that London 'muggings' were 129 per cent up over the four years 1968-72 seem to have their base in *'Robbery and Kindred Offences in the Metropolitan Police District, 1968-72'*. Their precise origin remains a deep mystery to us. Our efforts to 'crack' them have been in vain. Since there is no legal offence called 'mugging', the figures cannot be derived direct from the Annual Reports. . . . The graph in the 1973 *Report* must, therefore, be a back-projection: but based on what? Since none of the existing 'robbery' figures for 1968, or the other years, square with the reconstructed 'mugging' figures, these must be a selective conflation of proportions of a number of different sub-categories within the overall 'robbery' figures (Hall *et al.* 1978: 13-14).

In fact, Pratt (1980) reveals that since the early 1960s, following McClintock's pioneering research on robbery in London (McClintock and Gibson 1961), the Metropolitan Police have used a system of classification for robberies which does not rely on legal categories (Pratt 1980: 35-8). One such category is 'robbery in the open following sudden attack', which, as he remarks, is as good an operational definition of 'mugging' as one could reasonably hope for (pp. 37-8). His own research is based upon incidents falling into this category. Just as he is able to analyse the scale of 'mugging' in London, so too, at a lower level of expertise, were the Metropolitan Police. Of course, Hall *et al.*, (1978) were not to know this; but it is surprising that their analysis is still so widely accepted without this qualification.

Pratt's quantitative analysis is also important regarding the issue of whether the concentration of police anti-mugging operations in South London were a response to the problem or initiated by them in order to go on to the offensive against the black community with whom they had poor relations. This contention has been criticized on other grounds (James 1979); however Pratt's evidence (Pratt 1980) clearly shows that complaints of mugging made by members of the public concentrated in two areas of London — the West End and the Lambeth police division, particularly the latter (pp. 93-4, 110-17). Also there was evidence that complainants often identified their assailants as black (that is, the Metropolitan Police's identity code 3) (p. 95). As he remarks, and other studies of how the police come to learn of crime confirm, these patterns are largely beyond the power of the police to influence. The police *response* to these complaints may well have involved the aggressive use of 'stop and search' or 'sus'; but this would have had little effect on reported 'muggings'. It seems clear from Pratt's more detailed analysis that the police did not create the 'mugging' problem, whether out of malign motives or otherwise.

3.2 *Qualitative evidence*

Pratt's analysis is also relevant to the question of whether 'mugging' was merely an old crime with a new Americanized label. What his data show (Pratt 1980) is that there had been a distinct shift in the location for such attacks away from 'avoidable' places, such as commons, towpaths and the like, to the less 'avoidable' space of the street (p. 103). Thus, whilst it is correct for Hall, *et al.*, (1978) to say that incidents comparable to 'muggings' had occurred previously, there was still a novel aspect to the offence which surely justified greater attention being paid to it. This is a very significant qualification of Hall *et al.*'s, analysis which does not seem to receive consideration when it is cited by others.

In two other respects, however, Pratt's analysis can be taken as supporting the general case for claiming that concern about 'mugging' was a 'moral panic'. First, 'muggings' comprise only a small proportion of total crime (Pratt 1980: 80, see also Smith 1982). Second, reported 'muggings' do not correspond to the stereotyped media image. The typical victim of a reported 'mugging' is not the little, white-haired old lady, left bloody and distressed in the gutter as a gang of youths make off with her pension book. The typical victim is usually male, aged between 17-50, attacked between 10.00 p.m. and midnight, by no more than two assailants, who carry no weapons, cause no injury and steal items of modest value (pp. 87-93). This analysis has been strengthened further by the British Crime Survey which found that, taking reported and unreported 'crimes of violence' together, victims were often intoxicated young men who admitted to having committed acts of violence themselves (Hough and Mayhew 1983: 20-1).

The objection to the conclusion that mugging is a more serious offence than is often supposed, is that it confuses legal definitions of what is 'serious' or 'petty' with wider social and ethical considerations. It also confuses questions of value with those of statistical frequency. Both of these confusions have been recently attacked at a broader level by Lea and Young (1984), who point to the fallacies of 'the equal offence' and the 'equal victim' (pp. 33-7). As they argue, simply because robberies constitute only a small proportion of total crime does not mean that they are unimportant. One crime cannot be so simply regarded as interchangeable with another, for they differ in their gravity. Likewise, the statistical under-representation of vulnerable groups in the population amongst victims of crimes such as 'mugging' is no justification for complacency. Injuries that would be considered minor for a young man, may be calamitous to an elderly woman. The case that has been made out for regarding public concern about 'mugging' as a moral panic, seems to be a particularly apt example of the kind of minimization of working-class criminality of which Lea and Young (1984) are rightly critical.

4 'Mugging' — the scale of the reaction

The problems of defining and estimating the 'seriousness' of 'mugging' leads to wider conceptual issues surrounding the whole notion of 'moral panics', particularly the claim that public and official concern about a contemporary crime problem is *disproportionate* to the actual scale of the problem.

> When the official reaction to a person, groups of persons or series of events is *out of all proportion* [original emphasis] to the actual threat offered, when 'experts', in the form of police chiefs, the judiciary, politicians and editors *perceive* [original emphasis] the threat in all but identical terms, and appear to talk 'with one voice' of rates, diagnoses, prognoses and solutions, when the media representations universally stress 'sudden and dramatic' increases (in numbers involved or events) and 'novelty', above and beyond that which a sober, realistic appraisal could sustain, then we believe it is appropriate to speak of the beginnings of a *moral panic* [original emphasis] (Hall *et al.* 1978: 16).

Presumably, a response that *was* proportionate would not be a panic. It would be a 'sober, realistic appraisal'. However, we are provided with no criteria for determining what a proportionate, as opposed to disproportionate, response would be.

A way of approaching the problems raised by this lack of criteria for determining proportionality is to consider crime problems which are widely believed to receive *less* attention from the authorities than they should. A particularly appropriate example for these purposes is that of 'racial attacks', for many of those who describe concern about 'mugging' as a 'moral panic' also draw attention to the lack of concern expressed about 'racial attacks' as evidence for double standards amongst the authorities (Smith 1982). Particular attention is drawn to the Home Office report which, in 1981, revealed that black people were 36 times and Asians 50 times more vulnerable to 'racial attacks' than were whites (Home Office 1981). Following a series of incidents during the summer of 1985, including an arson attack in which an Asian family died, this concern about 'racial attacks' became a focus of mass media attention.

Suppose we now apply to this modest expression of governmental and media concern about the problem of 'racial attacks' the logic of 'moral panics', what would we be obliged to conclude? First, we would have to note that, like 'mugging', 'racial attacks' is a term that corresponds to no legal category. The term 'attack' connotes violence, but as the text of the Home Office report makes clear it is concerned with 'inter-racial incidents'. These incidents are defined

> as an incident, or alleged offence by a person or persons of one racial group against a person or persons or property of another racial group, where there are indications of racial motive (Home Office 1981: 7).

It acknowledges that most of these involve offences such as criminal damage (the daubing of racially offensive slogans) or using threatening, abusive or insulting words and behaviour (shouting racialist epithets). Thus, *any* offence could be considered as a 'racial attack' if it was motivated by racialism. The correspondence between 'mugging' and offences such as robbery, theft from the person and so on, is much closer than that between 'racial attacks' and any of the offences to which it might relate.

Second, and by the same token, if the stereotyped image of 'mugging' is misleading, reflecting only the most serious incidents to which it refers, then so too is the stereotyped 'racial attack'. The term 'racial attacks' suggests acts of gross personal violence, whereas many of the incidents referred to in the Home Office report are of a much less serious nature. For example, 26 per cent were 'incidents not normally recorded by police as an offence, e.g. harassment, abuse, slogan writing' (Home Office 1981: 11).

Third, we would have to acknowledge that 'racial attacks' comprise less than one quarter per cent of total crime and 'only' three per cent of all crimes of violence against the person. This compares to 3-4 per cent of total crime comprising 'muggings'. On the logic of 'moral panics', 'racial attacks' would merit, at most, only one-twelfth the concern reserved for 'mugging'. We might add that since the statistical under-representation of vulnerable groups, such as elderly women, amongst victims of crime is taken as grounds for complacency about 'mugging' amongst proponents of the 'moral panic' approach, so too must the lower rates of victimization amongst Asians revealed by the PSI report (Smith 1983: 60, 305, 337).

Fourth, the Home Office report on 'racial attacks' provides no evidence regarding the rate of increase in this problem. However, it is difficult to imagine that had it shown a rate of increase comparable to that of 'mugging', those who protest about the lack of official attention paid to this problem would not have been outraged — and rightly so.

In comparing 'muggings' and racial attacks' I do not wish to suggest that expressions of concern about the latter problem are misplaced. On the contrary, it is a public scandal that so little attention is paid to it. The point is simply that if one applies the logic of the concept of a 'moral panic' to this crime problem one is obliged to conclude that if official and public concern about 'mugging' was unjustified then the lack of official concern about 'racial attacks' is appropriate, given the scale of the problem. Were greater concern to be forthcoming, it, like the concern about 'mugging', would constitute a moral panic.

Without some clear criteria of proportionality, the description of publicly expressed concern, anxiety or alarm as a 'moral panic' is no more than a value judgment. It simply says that the person using the term does not believe that the particular problem is sufficiently serious to warrant these expressions of concern or actions designed to remedy the problem.

5 Summary and conclusion

Hall *et al.*'s, argument that official and public concern about 'mugging' was merely a 'moral panic' suffers two fundamental flaws. First, the evidence cited in support of the view that the situation with regard to crime in general and 'muggings' in particular was not getting dramatically worse, and in some respects showed an improvement, does not, in fact, support this contention. Indeed, in the form that Hall *et al.*, (1978) present it, it supports exactly the opposite conclusion. Second, without criteria of proportionality, it is impossible to say whether official concern is or is not appropriate. Whether or not concern is justified is essentially a value judgment which cannot be reduced to quantitative indices about the frequency and distribution of offences. It is regrettable that the flaws in Hall *et al.*, (1978) have gone without comment for so long.

Of course, there remains the genuine issue of why 'mugging' was identified as a problem during the early 1970s and not at some other moment during the period 1955-1970. Objectively, this was a period of continuing deterioration, but concern about the problem of 'mugging' did not seem to grow proportionately. It is possible that the importation of the Americanized term 'mugging' or a particular incident did alert police to the scale of the problem.

Equally, the issue of why certain types of crime generate official consternation whereas others do not, also remains. Recent analyses of the 'crimes of the powerful' have pointed to the objective harm done by a range of criminal activities from corporate violations of safety and pollution regulations to motoring offences (Box 1983). Yet, these offences have not grabbed the headlines to the extent to which 'mods and rockers', 'pot-smokers' and 'muggers' did, and in the latter case continue to do.

Analysis of either of these issues is likely to be inadequate unless the wider social and cultural context is taken into consideration. It is to the analysis of this wider context that much of Hall *et al.*'s, book (1978) is devoted. However, the validity or otherwise of this wider analysis does not depend upon the view that 'mugging' is not serious or does not merit official concern. It is, of course, perfectly possible to panic about even the most genuine problem. People may panic in a fire, but this does not imply that the building is not burning nor that there is no threat.

However, the way in which the term 'moral panic' is used to describe official and media concern about specific crime problems suggests that it is a polemical rather than an analytical concept. It seems virtually inconceivable that concern expressed about racial attacks, rape, or police misconduct would be described as a 'moral panic'. This is because the term has derogatory connotations: it implies that official and media concern is *merely* a 'moral panic' without substance or justification. If official reaction to crime and deviance is to be analysed adequately perhaps it is time to abandon such value-ladened terminology.

Acknowledgement

The author wishes to thank Christie Davies, Robert Reiner, Barrie Irving, Peter Schofield, Keith Bottomley, Clive Coleman, Paul Rock, David Downes, Tony Jefferson and Eugene Trivias for their helpful and often critical comments on an earlier draft of this article.

References

Bottomley, K. and Coleman, C. (1984) 'Law and order: crime problem, moral panic, or penal crisis?', in Norton, P. (ed.), *Law and Order and British Politics*. Aldershot: Gower.

Box, S. (1983) *Power, Crime and Mystification*. London: Tavistock.

Cohen, S. (1972) *Folk Devils and Moral Panics*. Oxford: Martin Robertson.

Hall, S. *et al.*, (1978) *Policing the Crisis*. London: Macmillan.

Home Office (1981) *Racial Attacks: Report of a Home Office Study*. London: Home Office.

Hough, M. and Mayhew, P. (1983) *The British Crime Survey: First Report,* Home Office Research Study Number 76. London: H.M.S.O.

James, D. (1979) 'Police-Black Relations: The Professional Approach', in Holdaway, S. (ed.), *The British Police*. London: Edward Arnold.

Lea, J. and Young, J. (1984) *What Is To Be Done About Law and Order?* Harmondsworth: Penguin.

McClintock, F.H. and Gibson, E. (1961) *Robbery in London*. London: Macmillan.

Editor (1982) 'Editorial'. *New Society* 59: 24 March.

Pratt, M. (1980) *Mugging as a Social Problem*. London: Routledge & Kegan Paul.

Smith, D.J. (1983) *Police and People in London, vol 2, A survey of Londoners*. London: Policy Studies Institute.

Smith, S. (1982) *Race and Crime Statistics,* Race Relations Fieldwork Background Paper No. 4. London: Board for Social Responsibility, Church of England.

Taylor, I. (1981) 'Crime Waves in Post-War Britain'. *Contemporary Crisis* 5: 43-62.

Young, J. (1971) 'The Role of the Police as Amplifiers of Deviancy, Negotiators of Reality and Translators of Fantasy', in Cohen, S. (ed.), *Images of Deviance*. Harmondsworth: Penguin.

13. Folk Devils Fight Back

Angela McRobbie

The current set of moral panics being orchestrated by the Conservative government surfaced early in February 1993 with the death of two-year-old James Bulger. The flurry of debate which followed revolved around the breakdown of the family, the growth of crimes committed by children, and the powerlessness of the police and judiciary in many cases to do anything more than caution young offenders. By the time the two boys were tried for murder several months later, the language of causality had been further reduced by ministers and media to a denunciation of 'evil'.

The rhetoric of blame and the targeting of socially vulnerable groups to bear its burden is familiar enough to those who, like Stuart Hall, have paid close attention to the modes of managing consent which the Conservatives have developed from the mid 1970s on — relying on sectors of the mass media to pursue these panics with relish, and indeed to make them their own. Yet there are nonetheless quite significant changes between the mobilization of consent up to and during the Thatcher years, and the frantic attempts of the Tories in the last year to repeat the successes of the past. The Bulger case occupies a pivotal place in this extraordinary bid to panic the populace into expressing their wholehearted support for tougher measures for young offenders. Part of the panic is in fact that of the Tories themselves who see that for some reason the bonfire of blame has failed to ignite. Horror, consternation and even disbelief were more reflective of public opinion than any gung-ho call for punishment.

In the months that followed this incident, the twin themes of law and order and welfare dependence came to dominate news and current affairs. The absence of hard parliamentary news during the summer break offered a prime opportunity for scattering the seeds of moral panic in the expectation that by the autumn the groundwork would be done and the media, together with its platoons of moral guardians and experts, would be independently conducting its own fullblown crusades. These would pick up on and amplify the themes addressed by various MPs, thus winning consent to the kind of legislation which might seem appropriate in the light of these dangerous or undesirable social phenomena. First there were the attacks on single mothers, and on girls getting pregnant and 'married to the state' rather than to a male breadwinner. In fact the question of single mothers has been simmering under the surface for some time now. Rhodes Boyson's 1985 comment that 'the state should not encourage bastardy' was echoed at the last Tory party conference and in Peter Lilley's insulting remarks about 'young ladies'. The increasing instability of the family in contemporary Britain is unarguably a deep-seated source of Tory concern. Another minister could devote the greater part of a well-timed speech to the subject of girls preferring to remain single and becoming mothers for the benefits (including housing) that this status entitled them to. Alongside this there was the corresponding focus on young offenders. Throughout the summer the unctuous voice of Michael Howard was

Angela McRobbie: 'Folk Devils Fight Back' in NEW LEFT REVIEW (January/February 1994), No. 203, pp. 107-116.

heard almost daily on the key radio and TV programmes promising tougher measures for young offenders and demonstrating the resolve on the part of the government to 'do something about' crime. This debate to-ed and fro-ed its way across the airwaves throughout July and August, surfacing in every conceivable media spot that would accommodate its agenda.

Stuart Hall has recently documented the political significance of this campaign, which continued through the Tory party conference in October to the Queen's speech in November, culminating in John Major's 'Back To Basics' speech which attempted to maintain these items high on the political agenda and visibly on the front pages and TV screens.[1] Hall connects this ideological obsession with the family and law and order with the broader Conservative commitment (elevated to the level of doctrine by Mrs Thatcher) to radical social restructuring through a break-up of the postwar settlement of the welfare state. This process of dismantling allows for further privatization and deregulation which in turn paves the way for substantial reinvestment in areas which allow the 'free market' to flourish (private pension plans, right-to-buy schemes and so on).

These practices of government have been so focused, so sustained, so able to withstand deep-rooted disagreements and wranglings within the Conservative party itself, that the 'exceptional state' which ensues is, as Hall previously described it, also an 'authoritarian populist' one.[2] Or at least it was during the Thatcher years. There have been several shifts, especially in the style of government practised by the Conservatives, which suggest that we need to adjust this model of a strongly hegemonic form. While Major's deliberate distancing from Mrs Thatcher's strongly personalized style has been acknowledged right from the start of his leadership, the broader questions of why the present government is neither convincingly authoritarian nor obviously populist have received scant attention. It cannot be thanks to Labour — that much seems certain. In his recent lecture Hall points to the failings of the Left and of Labour to provide an opposition 'with conviction'. Elsewhere there has been a good deal of talk of the capitulation of that sector of the Left which has espoused a 'new realist' position;[3] so the waning of the authoritarian populism of the Right cannot be attributed to the success of those 'realists' who have directed their energies towards transforming what they perceive as outdated Left policies and creating a new kind of modern or even postmodern politics. (The Demos group might be seen in these terms.) But what is absent from this round of discussions on 'Majorism' are those forces of opposition which come not from Labour or, for that matter, the Liberal Democrats, but from the margins, from the realms of pressure groups, associations, voluntary organizations and other forms of local, grassroots or campaigning politics. There has not been, it seems, a serious assessment of these admittedly scattered and fragmented and in some ways disassociated groups. How best can we understand their place in the dynamics of change, and perhaps also of crisis, in British society today? It will be part of my argument that these forms of political activity now play a key role in providing convincing opposition to the Conservatives. It is here that conviction politics is alive and well. Choosing to ignore their existence, pushing them to the margins of political culture, or questioning their validity within the democratic political process, can only hinder a fuller analysis of the range of forces engaged in contestation and popular radical democratic struggle today.

New moral minorities

The term 'moral panic' which started its life in textbooks of radical sociology in the early 1970s has since entered the realm of political common sense. Indeed it is not unusual to hear a radio or TV journalist ask rhetorically whether it is not the media itself which is to be blamed for creating this or that particular panic. In academic terms however the most important theory of moral panic was supplied by Stuart Hall's *Policing the Crisis*.[4] This remains a remarkably important book because of its rich interweaving of a political and cultural history of Britain in the postwar years with the more specific task of documenting and explaining the moral panic of the mid 1970s which grew up around the phenomenon of mugging. With great insight, and drawing on Gramsci's concept of hegemony, the authors of this book presented an account of the years running up to the Conservative victory of 1979. They argued that the groundwork which was built in those years through the orchestration of a moral panic reverberating across the mass media, from the local evening papers in Wolverhampton to the full force and presence of Robin Day on TV, successfully won the Tories the consent of the electorate to what Hall called a 'law and order society'.

Many of the strands of thinking which went on to become familiar rallying cries throughout the Thatcher years and beyond, particularly the damaging consequences of sixties permissiveness and the threat to law and order posed by 'inner city youth', were first rehearsed in the early to mid 1970s. By the end of the decade they had coalesced to become a fullblown ideology, a whole vocabulary which knitted together these strands and succeeded in creating an apparent 'unity' of consent. What was particularly distinctive about this moral panic was its emphasis on race, first on black youth, then on the black community as a whole, and then also on the question of migration and the drain on resources, welfare resources in particular, posed by Asian immigrants and their extended families. It was against this background that more intensive policing and fiercer legislation on law and order were introduced by the incoming government. The Thatcher administration continued to wield this 'moral' majority that had brought them to power against the 'ethnic minorities' who had been the folk devils during the run-up to the 1979 election.

Looking back, it is now clear that the demonization of black youth during those years under the guise of widespread social fears about mugging marked a decisive shift. It was not just that the moral-panic vocabulary, by constructing and intensifying such fears, virtually criminalized an entire section of the young black population. It went much further and became a more sustained battle to define who 'we' are and what kind of society this is. It was a transformative ideology designed to eradicate what remained of radical thought and practice in Britain following the liberalism of the sixties, and it attempted to do this by means of a more aggressive attack on outsiders, 'others', and those who would not or could not comply. In this way a new hegemony was sought through a rearticulation of both 'nation' and 'society'.

I want to suggest that things are not the same now as they were then, despite apparent similarities in the deployment of moral panic as a strategy for drawing new lines of consent and marking new boundaries between 'us' and 'them'. But before exploring these points, it might briefly be signalled that the main vehicle for transporting the moral panic round its various ports of call has undergone profound changes in the intervening years. There have been enormous developments in media technology. While some have argued that global communications have merely reinforced media power in the hands of a few, others have suggested that such an expansive system also has its own porosity, its spaces for opposition and contestation. I will come back to this below, but what is relevant here is that while the tabloids — above all the *Sun* and the *Daily Mail* — still use moral panic as a means of communicating with their readerships, terrifying them and setting alarm bells ringing across British society, the absolute force and vitriol of these crusades are somewhat deflated by the simple fact that the moral panic has now become a standard rather than an exceptional means of reporting, a typical rather than an atypical way of transforming news and current affairs into a narrative and a source of excitement as well as fear.

The emergency status of the moral panic has given way to something less unusual. Even the *Guardian,* perhaps with a touch of postmodern irony, runs headlines like THEY'RE PACKING PISTOLS IN MANCHESTER as the caption for a lead story on guns in its tabloid section. The feature which followed this attention-grabbing headline continued the sensational language of moral panic with the more measured kind of commentary generally associated with that newspaper. This suggests a kind of blur in the intensity and focus of the 'classic' moral panic, at least in relation to the press.

In television the question is slightly different. Political debate and 'good television' both require strongly argued positions. For there to be balance there has to be opposition and what has been a remarkable feature of the current round of moral panics has been the lack of opposition from Labour and the silence from those close to Labour when it comes to speaking out against the scapegoating of the new folk devils. No doubt this reflects current Labour policy. There is little desire on their part to be associated with the so-called anti-family values reflected in the rise in one-parent families and the growth of single motherhood. While figures like Tony Blair acknowledge the damage to the family done by poverty and unemployment, his own publicized image is very much that of the 'family man'. Memories of being too closely linked with gay and lesbian groups in the 1980s have frightened the Labour Party, as Stuart Hall in his recent lecture again reminds us. This produces an unimaginatively narrow response. Likewise on the question of crime. There is good reason why Labour should attempt to demonstrate to the electorate that it takes the fear of crime seriously and that it understands the anger and fear of those living in violent, crime-ridden housing estates. But the absence of a clear or convincing strategy on Labour's part for dealing with crime allows Michael Howard to make almost nightly appearances on programmes like *Newsnight* virtually unchallenged by the official Opposition.

Where then do the TV and radio producers look for well-argued opposing views? It is this search which leads to the substance of my argument. To ensure that balance is maintained producers turn to experts. Experts used to be either academics or else 'moral guardians' like Mary Whitehouse or Victoria Gillick. But in the past few years the old moral guardians have dispersed and fragmented, or else become either less vocal or more transparently eccentric. In televisual terms this makes them less attractive an option. (Lady Olga Maitland, for example, whose views on the danger to public morality posed by teenage magazines seem completely hysterical, falls into this

252

camp.) In place of these people whose views now seem unrepresentative as well as unconvincing, a new band of experts has appeared. These are not the academics who used to fill this role in the past, but are instead extremely articulate and televisually skilled representatives from pressure groups and voluntary organizations. It is they who now do the job of defending the folk devils who are the figures of fear and fantasy wielded by the orchestrators of moral panic. It is they who provide balance, analysis and information to counter the often uninformed discourses of the politicians. They steadily counter the seemingly endless stream of moral panics currently being dreamt up by cabinet ministers on a 'thought for the day' basis. They defend from government attack a whole array of folk devils. They can be seen or heard on every available media, whenever they are called upon to do so. The vocality of this 'opposition' (spokespersons from the National Council for One Parent Families, from Mind, from NACRO . . . the list is endless), speaking confidently and persuasively on the *Today* programme at six in the morning, with all the relevant facts at the tips of their fingers, offsets and draws attention to the strange silence of Labour.

Withholding consent

This lack of response from Labour leaves the Tories all the more surprised and confused, as if fearing that their multiple moral crusade is somehow failing to stick. Despite their still recent electoral mandate, the Tories are in power but seemingly devoid of support. Without an evident location or rationale, there seems to be a popular groundswell of discontent expressed in a witholding of consent to the daily scapegoating and culture of blame which is becoming the permanent sign of a government desperately searching around for a 'big idea'. After the Bulger trial, for example, various government spokespersons expressed disappointment at the Church for not condemning more loudly or actively supporting their calls for a return to traditional family values and tougher punishment. Indeed why 'the Church' (no longer the unity it once was) was reluctant to participate in this hysterical outbreak about evil and punishment is an interesting question. Like many of the major 'ideological state apparatuses' of our time it may well be that the Church is also undergoing a process of inner fragmentation and intensified internal dissent. (There is certainly now a vocal feminist presence at almost every level in the various religious denominations.) It need hardly be said that beside the brutally individualistic values of Thatcher and contemporary Conservatism, the Church has indeed represented something more humane. It has connected with the desire among at least some sectors of the public to protect the weak, to 'forgive', and to foster a sense of community, when economic forces work directly to undermine such a concept. In this sense the Church might even be seen as existing alongside the pressure groups, the charities and the voluntary organizations which when taken as a whole represent a strong body of public opinion.

This withholding of consent pushes the Tories to dream up new folk devils in a way which soon becomes embarrassing even to themselves. Having blamed parents for not passing on the right kind of values to their children, and then teachers for failing in their duty, the blaming of the 1960s en bloc and then of the parents of that decade whose own fathers were away in the Second World War showed the Tories stretched to the limit. But fear not: the following days saw them suggest a Truancy Brigade which would involve good citizens stopping children in the street and asking them why they were not at school. Then there were the plans to put all children into school uniform to make them more identifiable as truants or potential offenders, to punish single mothers who had more children by witholding their benefits, and to force young single mothers to live at home with the 'grandparents'. Then to everyone's complete confusion there was Major's call for a 'welfare society', a concept so ill-considered that his 'Back to Basics' campaign announced days later shone out like a beacon of ideological clarity. Underpinning these uninformed attempts at pop sociology there has been nonetheless a sustained attempt to turn the tide of public opinion away from welfare as we know it, and to do this through playing up the dangers of family breakdown and the rise in juvenile crime.

Given the horror of the Bulger case, the brutal killing of Suzanne Capper, and the visible reality of a spiralling culture of criminality — not just in the large urban centres but still more acutely on the housing estates of the North-East and even in towns and villages which in the past saw crime as not their problem — there is a real question about the muted public response to the Tories' recent law-and-order campaign. Likewise with the attack on one-parent families. There are few who would argue that bringing up children alone is easy or ideal, or that the poverty of being a single mother is somehow tolerable. And yet again, given the ferocious campaign to vilify this group, what is significant is how this vilification has not really succeeded. It has not entered the vocabulary of 'common sense'. To understand why these moral panics are not working the way they were intended, three social forces have to be taken into account. First the people, second the media, and third the pressure groups and the 'folk devils' they represent.

As far as the people are concerned, it might be argued that the experience of many people during and after Thatcher has been one of disenchantment, particularly those who were 'first time Tory voters'. The outcome of this disenchantment is not to steer them back towards Labour but rather to encourage them to participate in this refusal to blame. If these groups of people were taken in by the promise of 'popular capitalism', if they bought into the property-owning democracy only to see their homes at risk of being repossessed, if they set up business under the flagship of enterprise culture, often investing hard-earned redundancy payments, only to see how self-employment more often than not meant self-exploitation, it is not surprising that they now demonstrate firm resolve not to agree again with the scare-mongering Tories.

Most people in their everyday lives now understand the reality of single parenthood, either directly or by close observation. Women of all ages, all social and ethnic backgrounds, know what unhappy marriage can mean, and they are not going to endorse a return to traditional family values, with the misery and violence these have so often entailed. It is extraordinary that the Tories do not realize the depths of opposition to this idea from the ranks of women, and that even now they have not taken into account the centrality of women and their opinions in political culture today. They only need to look round their own ranks. It is difficult to find a single Tory woman willing to blame single parents and to argue for this return to conventional family life. On a recent Sunday lunchtime talk show on single mothers, a programme targeted to a popular and 'downmarket' audience, the producers could only come up with two Tory men, one young MP representing Conservatives For Family Values and with him Norman Blugeon, to face the formidable figure of Sara Keays who was supported by a whole array of individuals and pressure groups. But more important perhaps was the anger on the part of this overwhelmingly female audience at the undermining of the strengths and capacities of single mothers in the face of economic hardship.

The same kind of argument could be made about the attempt to run down welfare by pointing the finger at those who depend on it. There are few working-class or middle-class people who do not 'depend' on some aspect of welfare for some part of their lives. And if they are fortunate enough not to have experienced the cold wind of unemployment themselves, they might well be fearful for their teenage children's future in this respect. The idea of pruning down welfare so that only those who 'really need it' will get it is frightening even to those who might appear to be relatively affluent but who can see their future on a meagre and emaciated pension. Once again, women are more likely to experience poverty in old age than their male counterparts. And if the change in family structure through divorce and remarriage is also taken into account the likelihood is multiplied. This kind of fear puts the equally unpleasant fear of crime at least in context.

The old boundaries which the Conservatives throughout the 1970s sought to maintain, between black and white, between 'us' and 'them', have also to a certain extent broken down. Through a generation of young people who have grown up and been educated in a multicultural society, those divides are slowly being blurred. This is not to say that racism is a marginal problem, but there is evidence to suggest that mixed-race friendships and relationships as well as new communities in mixed-race neighbourhoods have constructed something other than the kind of 'absolutist' difference which most politicians still subscribe to and assume still exists. The experience of black people themselves must also be taken into account. If they were 'them' during the 1970s, in the 1980s they turned the tables on those who sought to police and regulate their communities. The black community as folk devil fought back and became politically empowered in the process. It is interesting how the new folk devils of the past months display white rather than black ethnicity.

The politics of pressure

The second force to be taken into account in explaining this refusal to blame is of course the media. It is not just the expanded scale of the media today or its 'porosity' alone that produces these new spaces for the opposition voices, nor is it simply in the interests of balance that we find representatives from NACRO or the Child Poverty Action Group express their opinions. Folk devils can also fight back by producing their own media, given the relative cheapness and availability of new technology. Even the homeless have their own voice, as *The Big Issue* demonstrates. This communicative flow challenges the voices of those at the top. It also reminds us that political debate of this type takes place not only in the current-affairs flagships of the four main channels. Daytime TV and in particular programmes like *Kilroy Silk* and *This Morning* also provide important spaces for 'ordinary people' to participate in precisely these kinds of debate. These are now as good a gauge of public opinion as any opinion poll. They are also 'open spaces' where pressure groups can effectively broadcast.

In short it appears that the new centre of conviction politics resides in those groups described variously as social movements, pressure groups, voluntary organizations and charities, and in fact encompasses them all. Of key significance however have been the women's movement, the gay and lesbian movement and of course the whole range of anti-racist organizations. It is this dynamic set of 'agencies' which now provide oppositional views and alternative information and analysis. Armed with up-to-date research and trained in-house on how to deal with the media and with aggressive questioning, their representatives can stand firm against cabinet ministers trained in the Oxford Union.

These organizations emerged not only from the activist and campaigning politics of the sixties and seventies, but also more recently from the vacuum opened up by Mrs Thatcher's generous offer to 'free people from the burden of responsibility of politics', leaving them, as Martin Jacques recently put it, 'free to jog'. But this is also a vacuum which Labour, with its archaic vision of political activism, the slowness of its procedures and the hierarchies of its branch committees must also take responsibility for. Into this space has developed a thriving sector of local and issue-based political activism. These groups provide support and 'self-help' as well as feeding into the broader political culture in terms of public debate. They are also 'people friendly', they welcome newcomers and provide people with little or no experience of campaigning politics with a distinctive learning environment. They also bring together people from an incredibly wide set of social backgrounds. A more thorough documentation of the scale and number of these groups, as well as of their strategies and internal organization, is long overdue.

One of their most important functions lies not just in challenging the discrimination against folk devils but also in actively redefining the agenda. Organizations like the Howard League For Penal Reform played a leading role all summer in doing precisely this kind of work. Working in this case with an independent TV production company, the Howard League sought through a drama-documentary about juvenile crime to point to the experiences of neglect and abuse which so many young offenders suffer long before they commit their first offence. This public role also appears to be a space of engagement which is particularly open to women. As radical professionals in this kind of field, Sue Slipman (National Council For One Parent Families), Vivien Stern (NACRO) and Frances Crook (Howard League) are possibly most familiar. But across the country groups like Victim Support, the Citizen's Advice Bureaux, National Children's Home and nearly all the self-help groups are largely run by women. The black and Asian communities have also established a large number of campaigning and support groups and services and these too are moving to become fully professional agencies. Often it is personal experience which triggers involvement — the Suzy Lamplugh Trust was set up by the mother of Suzy Lamplugh who was abducted while working as an estate agent in London. Recently the widow of the young man stabbed to death by a schizophrenic stranger on a London underground platform announced her involvement in MIND, the mental health charity, partly as a means of coming to terms with her tragic experience. It seems as though this kind of involvement in groups which adhere to democratic decision-making practices is a more attractive alternative to old-fashioned politics. Running a help line and faxing off information to the major news media outlets must also feel more effective than anything that the local Labour Party might have to offer.

There is no point in being nostalgic for a kind of Left unity that never was. The old days of mass party politics were culturally exclusive to many people despite being ostensibly 'open to the masses'. What is more, the Left was always fragmented and was characterized as much then by diversity and difference as the new politics which I have described above is today. However my intention has not been to offer a neat solution to what has been seen by some as the decline, if not disappearance of radical class-based politics. Perhaps part of the problem lies in the concept of the Left itself as though it were some central organizing body, some point of unity. Maybe it is time that this 'imagined community' was temporarily de-centred, even if only to allow for some fresh thinking. For example gay politics around HIV could hardly be seen as the political centre of gravity, and yet together with anti-racism and feminism it has achieved an absolute global centrality.

Perhaps too the 'new realism' that really counts is the one that requires us to learn, once again as Stuart Hall has put it, to 'live with difference'. This poses fundamental questions, particularly about the role of political parties. Laclau has warned against the dangers of construing the proliferation of politics of the margins merely as pluralism. The task as he sees it is not only to think continually about alliances but to pay close attention to the boundaries and barriers which define the political worlds of these groupings yet are by no means fixed. Fluidity, change, alliances and interactions must, it seems, also be a requirement if the politics of pressure and association is to be extended. But what is important in the first instance is to recognize the energy of commitment and the pleasure of involvement which can be seen in these groups which now span the whole expanse of civil society. Those who participate in the politics of hospitals, health and self-help, in parent-teacher associations, in prisoners' rights groups and organizations like that run by ex-prisoner Jimmy Boyle in Edinburgh designed to help violent men out of their 'dangerous masculinities', those who also fight against sexual harassment in the workplace or for high standards of health and safety for all employees, those women who establish tenants' associations on the worst and most run-down estates in the country to make them a better place for their children, display a sustained level of enthusiasm often in the face of social disaster and 'economic emergency'. As permanent points of struggle and contestation on the political landscape, it is foolish not to say downright suicidal of Labour to devalue the role they have to play. A new Labour politics of alliance and association would need to set itself the task of allowing the party to become, in the first instance, more of a listening body, rather than one — as it is right now — virtually stunned into silence.

(The author would like to thank Mike Fitzgerald for his useful comments.)

Notes

1. Stuart Hall, 'Thatcherism Today', *New Statesman*, 26 November 1993.

2. Stuart Hall, 'The Toad in the Garden', in *Marxism and the Interpretation of Culture*, London 1989.

3. See for example Hilary Wainwright, *Arguments for a New Left*, Oxford 1993.

4. Stuart Hall et al., *Policing the Crisis*, London 1978.

THE INSTITUTIONS
OF THE
CRIMINAL JUSTICE SYSTEM

14.   The Drift to Military Policing
John Lea and Jock Young

The harassment of the public, or sections of it, by the police has become a major political issue. Lord Scarman characterized the Brixton riot of summer 1981 as 'a spontaneous act of defiant aggression by young men who felt themselves hunted by a hostile police force' (3.25). He went on to note that 'the weight of criticism and complaint against the police is so considerable that it alone must give grave cause for concern' (p. 65). How has such a state of affairs come to develop? In this chapter we attempt to give an explanation of what has been happening to policing in the inner-city areas and (the two largely overlap) to policing in areas with a high concentration of the ethnic minorities. In order to do this, it is necessary to begin by contrasting at a very general level two types or styles of policing. The first might be called 'consensus policing' or 'policing by consent' and the second, rather more bluntly, 'military policing'.

Consensus policing

As the name implies, consensus policing is policing with the support of the community. The community supports the police because it sees them as doing a socially useful job. They are protecting the community against crime and crime is something that the community recognizes as harmful to its well-being. Of course, there may be other ingredients behind the support of the community for the police. In Britain during the last century there was considerable resistance to policing on the continental model, and the establishment of police forces acceptable to the British public was very much associated with the fact that constables had no more legal powers than those of the ordinary citizen. As Patricia Hewitt remarks, the accountability of the police to the law in the same way as the ordinary citizen is often regarded as sufficient accountability. Michael Brogden has noted in his recent book on policing that the gaining of acceptance by the police in working-class areas was a slow process. Brogden, surveying historical studies of the police-public relations, concludes:

> By the Edwardian period, varying relations had been constructed between the police institution and the different social classes . . . the merchant capitalists, the business proprietors, the professionals, the shop-keepers, and the new ancillary strata of clerical workers gave increasing consent, a support that was most visible at times of crisis. For the urban industrial workers and their kin — the 'respectable' strata of Victorian England — by the 1900s the relation with the police institution had assumed the features of a truce, a grudging acceptance, with occasional direct confrontations in thc course of an industrial dispute. For the lower classes, the participants of thc street economy . . . attitudes to the police institution throughout the first century of policing remained essentially

John Lea and Jock Young: 'The Drift to Military Policing' from *WHAT IS TO BE DONE ABOUT LAW AND ORDER? CRISIS IN THE NINETIES* (Penguin Books, 1984), pp. 169-198.

> unchanged. They were subject to continuing, occasional, and apparently arbitrary 'culls'. (p. 181)
>
> Working-class response to the police institution during the first century varied over time, by region, and by strata. In general, by the end of that period the relations that had developed were not so much ones of consent but rather a grudging acceptance, a tentative approval, that could be withdrawn instantly in the context of industrial conflict.

But whatever the ingredients of community support for the police, to the extent that this exists, a second important characteristic of consensus policing follows. We have already mentioned the crucial role played by information flowing from the public to the police in the detection of criminals. Where the community is supportive of the police, then it can be expected to maintain a reasonably high flow of information concerning crime, or at least those types about which information exists. Police requests for members of the public who saw the incident concerned, or 'saw anything suspicious', to come forward can be expected to yield results. From this high flow of information follows a third characteristic of consensus policing: what we might call the 'certainty of detection'. Most policing is preventative, concerned with public order and deterring crime, rather than the investigative pursuit of crimes that have already been committed. Under consensus policing the close relationship between police and the community as regards the sharing of information and thus the likelihood of successful detection act as a deterrent upon the potential criminal. After the event, it is that same close sharing of information that will lead investigative policing to a likely successful conclusion.

There is another characteristic of consensus policing that is worth mentioning since it will become important in our later discussion: the role of stereotypes. All policing involves the use of stereotypes. No police force can operate on the basis of suspecting all sections of the community equally when a particular crime has been committed. Some notion of what *type* of person (from what social group, however defined; what area of the city; etc.) has to be employed to enable investigation to get off the ground. What can be said, however, is that the closer the relationship between the police and the community as regards the sharing of information (that is, real information, not pseudo-information generated by the prejudices and stereotypes held by the community at large), the more the police can begin their investigations following actual leads and the less recourse to stereotypes becomes the basis for starting investigations.

Some or all of the features of this description of 'consensus policing' are often held to describe the British police system either in the past, or both in the past and at the present time. We are not making such a claim here. More particularly, we are not claiming that the ethnic minority communities in Britain have at any stage in the past enjoyed a relationship with the police which could be said to correspond to a situation such as we have described. The description we have given of consensus policing is intended to serve two purposes. First, it describes a situation which policing practices in the inner city are moving away from. Second, it describes a system of policing which we believe is the only possible one for a civilized society compatible with freedom and the rule of law.

Military policing

If policing in the inner city and as regards the ethnic minorities is moving away from consensus policing, what is it moving towards? The opposite pole to consensus policing we have termed military policing. By this term we are not referring to the activities of the Royal Military Police or the army generally (in Northern Ireland, for instance), though such a situation could certainly be taken as an example of military policing. What the term describes is a policing style which is linked to a certain type of relationship between the police and the community being policed. The characteristics of military policing can be largely specified simply by reversing the conditions of consensus policing.

Military policing is, therefore, first and foremost policing without the consent, and with the hostility, active or otherwise, of the community. The community do not support the police because they see them as a socially or politically oppressive force in no way fulfilling any protective functions. This general alienation between the community and the police may, though not necessarily, be reflected in a general support by the community for the criminal. If the police are enforcing a legal system which the community does not take to reflect its own concepts of morality, as would be the case with an occupying army holding down a subject population, then the 'criminal' may be seen by the community as a symbolic rebel, to be secretly admired, and if circumstances permit, to be offered shelter and assistance in escaping from the police.

Under such circumstances the flow of information from the community to the police concerning 'crime' can be expected to approach zero. If the community has this information to give and can identify those who commit what it, as opposed to the occupying forces, identifies as crime, then the emergence of some type of surrogate policing from within the community may well occur. Vigilante squads may clandestinely operate, or if there is a guerrilla force attempting to overthrow the occupying military force, then it may well take on certain policing functions on behalf of the community. On the other hand, the community may be so disorganized and demoralized by the effects of war, or simply by poverty and deprivation, that the channels whereby information could accumulate are weakened and ineffective.

Either way the police force under such circumstances will not be in a position to receive the type of information from the community which would enable its activities to be characterized by the principle of 'certainty of detection'. The crucial consequence of this situation is that an important part of police activity will come to constitute the random harassment of the community at large quite irrespective of involvement in crime. This randomness of activity is the central characteristic of military policing, and has two closely interrelated functions.

Firstly, it constitutes a method of obtaining information. Where the community will not voluntarily offer information to the police, then to the extent that the police are still determined to track down criminals, the necessary information will have to be prised out of the community, if necessary by force. A network of paid informers is, of course, indispensable, but also what might be termed 'high-profile' activities assume a crucial role: stopping people randomly in the streets, raiding premises, taking people in for questioning not on the basis of information already received, but as part of an attempt to secure information. These types of activities, aimed at forcing the community to yield up its supply of information, become central in military policing. But secondly, activities such as stopping people randomly in the streets and searching them, besides being attempts to obtain information, become in themselves forms of generalized deterrence. The certainty of detection, with its dependence upon a smooth flow of information to the police, becomes replaced by the arbitrariness or randomness of penalty as the main form of deterrence. 'Do not do anything in case you are stopped by the police at a road block or in some sudden and random street search' becomes the form of deterrence replacing the 'do not do anything because you are sure to be caught eventually' of consensus policing. Indeed, it could be said that a certain type of 'goal displacement' characterizes these random activities. That is to say, even if the strategy of 'sweeps' of the public through mass arrests, searches, etc., starts off as a device for gathering information, its effectiveness in this respect is so dubious and random that its role as a generalized deterrent inevitably comes to the fore.

Finally, under systems of military policing the investigative activities of the police are maximally dependent upon the use of stereotypes. To the extent that the police are determined to track down particular offenders for a crime under conditions of zero information, they will have to begin their investigations with a stereotype of the social group or milieu from which the offender is most likely to have come and to begin their investigations there.

As with consensus policing, what we are concerned with at this stage is capturing the essential characteristics of a style of policing rather than accurately describing any particular situation. It is, of course, easy to think of situations which our description would fit without modification: the American army in South Vietnam, the British in Northern Ireland, the policing of rebellious colonies, etc. But for our discussion of what is happening to policing in mainland Britain the description of military policing fulfils two functions. First, it describes a situation which we see, for reasons we are going to discuss, policing in the inner cities approaching. Second, it describes a type of policing which we see to be incompatible with freedom and the rule of law and as a general form of policing to be closely linked with the authoritarian state. We will return to this point later.

Towards military policing

In his evidence to the Scarman Inquiry, Chief Superintendent Plowman of the Metropolitan Police claimed: 'In Brixton . . . there is no information that comes from the black community to the police . . . We are very short of the co-operation of the community' (Scarman Inquiry, Day 4, p. 17). There is no reason to doubt Plowman's statement. What it reflects is the seriousness of the state of affairs as regards policing Brixton and similar areas up and down the country. Consensus policing is dead, if it ever existed, in Brixton. What exists in its place? It is our argument that, firstly, over the last decade and a half the signs have been of a drift towards military policing in areas like Brixton; and, secondly, that this drift is self-reinforcing. It results in a vicious circle in which moves in the direction of military policing undermine whatever elements of consensus policing may remain, and lay the conditions for further moves in the direction of military policing. The crux of the matter is that the police come to view the population in such areas as generally criminal. Where, as in Brixton, that population is black, the assumption of criminality becomes linked to race and the racial stereotype quickly crystallizes: all blacks are potential criminals.

There have always been areas of large cities which the police have defined as crime-prone; so what is new about the situation that has been developing over the last decade and a half? It is the way in which the definition of a population as crime-prone has been the occasion for acting towards it in terms of styles of policing which have drawn progressively closer to the military model: random stopping and searching, raids on youth clubs and houses, operations often involving the more explicitly 'military' sections of the police such as the Special Patrol Group (SPG) and up until recently the massive use of the Vagrancy Act (or 'sus', as it was known) by some police forces, largely against black youngsters.

During the 1970s one set of statistics in particular illustrates the changing nature of policing. The Institute of Race Relations in its submission to the Royal Commission on Criminal Procedure compiled the table (1) showing the numbers of people stopped and questioned by the Special Patrol Group of the Metropolitan Police in operations involving random stopping of people in the street and at road blocks.

Table 1

Year	Number stopped
1972	41,980
1973	34,534
1974	41,304
1975	65,628
1976	60,898

The figures are compatible with the development of some of the characteristics of military policing. The growth in the number of people stopped and searched indicates a situation in which the police are not so much stopping people on the basis of some particular suspicion, based on information that the individual concerned is likely to have committed a crime, but as part of a generalized screening of the population of that area for information, and as a generalized deterrent. The police officers concerned in such activities acted on the basis of a stereotype, that the population of the area — young blacks — were 'very likely' to have committed crimes.

A second indication of the changing style of policing in areas like Brixton during the 1970s was the widespread and growing use of 'sus' as an offence. In 1976, for example, in the Metropolitan Police District, of 2,112 people arrested under the 1964 Vagrancy Act 42 per cent were black compared to a general arrest rate for all offences of black people of 12 per cent. The use of 'sus' against young black people can come to function as a generalized disciplinary mechanism against a whole category of the population since it needs very little evidence to secure a conviction in a particular case. The 'convenience' of sus as a component of generalized deterrence strategies against the black community was well summarized by the National Council for Civil Liberties in its evidence to the Home Office Working Party on Vagrancy and Street Offences in 1975:

> The evidence is invariably given by Police Officers only. Because by definition no substantive theft, or even sufficient proximate act to charge an attempted theft, takes place, the question for the court becomes one of interpretation of a few actions which may or may not indicate an intent ... We would suggest that convictions for this offence are largely based on probability rather than certainty.

The widespread use of 'sus' and the effective campaign against it resulted in its repeal on the recommendation of the Royal Commission on Criminal Procedure. It remains to be seen to what extent the Criminal Attempts Act will be used in a similar way, or whether other offences will fill the gap left by the repeal of 'sus'.

To return to the question of stop and search, the example now best known to the public is undoubtedly the famous 'Swamp '81' operation in which over one thousand people were stopped and searched in the central part of Brixton but fewer than one hundred were charged with criminal offences. Two features of Swamp '81 and similar types of operations stand out. Firstly, their inefficiency at catching criminals, and secondly, the effect of antagonizing a large number of people. Swamp '81 serves as a tailor-made example of how to antagonize the greatest possible number of people while at the same time achieving the minimum control of a particular type of crime, in this case footpad robbery. As it was unlikely that a snatch theft was going to take place directly in front of the eyes of police officers, the operation involved the random stopping of 'suspicious' youth. As the NCCL remarked: 'Even if police officers behaved with impeccable courtesy towards every person stopped and searched and apologized to those found not to be carrying suspect items, many people would resent being treated as suspects when innocently walking to the tube or home' (Evidence to Scarman, p. 14).

With operations like Swamp '81 as a normal aspect of policing strategy the move to military policing has taken a decisive step. Deterrence is no longer based on the certainty of detection but on the randomness of stop and search, and information provided by the community to the police is replaced by stop-and-search procedures as the basis of the detection of offences. The 'goal displacement' from catching actual offenders or gaining useful information to generalized deterrence of the population at large is illustrated by the very low number of actual arrests resulting from Swamp '81.

But why have these changes in policing been taking place? An obvious explanation would be to point to the generalized recession of the capitalist economy, the emergence of long-term structural unemployment among youth in general and black youth in particular, and the increased unwillingness of such groups peacefully to acquiesce in poverty, discrimination and lives of despair. This is especially so when they have been conditioned through the mass media and the education system to expect something different. From this point of view the move towards military policing in the inner cities is part of a general move in state policy towards the 'pole of coercion' in the control of a new generation of unemployed, and to keep down new forms of struggle against the capitalist crisis (cf. Friend and Metcalf). There is a substantial body of evidence for this analysis, but we have two disagreements. Firstly, such a view can easily lead to an exaggerated focus upon the initiatives of the centralized state apparatus, as if they were consciously formulated, even if behind closed doors. In contrast, we shall develop an argument which stresses the dynamic movement at ground level within the inner city, and the relationship between the police and the community itself which drives policing towards the military model. Often the initiatives of the central state are attempts to come to terms with and respond to what is already happening 'spontaneously' at ground level.

Secondly, this view can easily slip into the rather simplistic view that what military policing is keeping the lid on is a progressive struggle for emancipation by those suffering the consequences of economic crisis. Such a view necessitates imposing a general label of political struggle on the variety of activities in the inner city that are, in the last analysis, a response to deprivation. Precisely because, as we have already argued, the culture of deprivation includes a variety of activities including forms of crime that are genuinely antisocial, harmful and destructive to the communities within which they occur, retaining the simple dichotomy of repressive state bottling up struggles against oppression involves an inability to come to terms with the existence of crime. Once it is recognized that among the responses to deprivation are to be included anti-social activities, then both the dynamics of the drift towards military policing at ground level and the legitimacy that such a move has for the population at large can be more clearly understood.

Our disagreements, therefore, are based on the issue of analysing solely from the point of view of the total system. While we cannot simply focus on the level of day-to-day interaction between the police and the community, if we ignore the dynamic at that level, we are in danger of projecting on to the community beliefs which fit the grand theory well, but only approximate to reality.

The shift towards military policing is to be attributed to three closely related factors. Firstly, a combination of rising rates of street crime and the assimilation of the lifestyle of the petty criminal with the general lifestyle. Both of these result from unemployment and deprivation. Unemployment on a massive scale means that large numbers of young people are hanging out on the street. In other words, the younger members of the community as a whole come to take on a lifestyle which in the eyes of the police is associated with petty crime. This assists the police in stereotyping a whole community as 'crime-prone'. It is the opposite of the situation of organized crime in which criminals may constantly hide behind a respectable business lifestyle which is defined by the police, following the conventions of society at large, as non-criminal.

The second factor is racial prejudice within the police force. Whenever this issue is raised it is usually in terms of the 'bad-apple theory'. A rather condescending version comes from the 1977 report of the House of Commons Select Committee on Race Relations and Immigration on the West Indian community: 'Occasionally they [the police] will act wrongly, but this should be seen as a reminder that despite their inordinate burden they are after all human' (Evidence, p. 187). This scurrilous identification of racism or police law violation with 'being human' is, of course, insupportable. We do not expect our police officers to be criminals or to be racially prejudiced. Lord Scarman, in a more serious discussion of the problem, admits its existence: 'Racial prejudice does manifest itself occasionally in the behaviour of a few officers on the streets' (p. 64). Scarman continues: 'It may be only too easy for some officers faced with what they must see as the inexorably rising tide of street crime to lapse into an unthinking assumption that all young black people are potential criminals. I am satisfied, however, that such a bias is not to be found among senior police officers' (ibid.). Scarman has identified the important factor: it is not simply that individual officers may be racists but that in a situation in which a whole community is becoming defined as crime-prone, and large sections of that community are black, then a fertile breeding ground for racism is created. The sentiments of the individual officer become less important than the general form that policing takes. If black youngsters are being routinely harassed by the police, then individual officers, whatever they may feel about black people in moments of cool reflection, will in their operational duties become conditioned into a view of the black community in which racism makes a lot of sense. Thus it is difficult to square Lord Scarman's remarks about 'a few officers' and 'occasionally' with the very next page where he notes the massive weight of criticism and complaint against the police from the black community. Yet, of course, it is a fact that only a minority of the black community, as with any other section of society, are criminals. The generalized racialist sentiments which are currently so pervasive in British society undoubtedly facilitate the smooth transition in the mind of the police officer from the proposition that certain areas with a high black population also have a high crime rate to the proposition that all blacks are potential criminals. Such thinking in turn smooths the path for the transition to military policing.

A third factor has also undoubtedly assisted the transition towards military policing. The changes in policing methods following the introduction of modern technology and communications have been concisely summed up by John Alderson (p. 41):

> The impact of science and technology on the police over the thirteen years from 1966 to 1979 was very considerable . . . it has had a profound effect on police methods, public image and reputation, to say nothing of police psychology. The police have been helped considerably, even crucially, by technology . . . Stemming from the universal introduction of personal pocket radio . . . together with the availability of cheap motor vehicles and later on expensive computerized command and control systems, what was basically a preventive foot-patrolling force has become a basically reactive patrolling force.

Alderson goes on to note how the reactive or 'fire-brigade' style of policing involving fast response to incidents minimizes a normal, day-to-day, peaceful contact with the public. This type of contact, of course, is a vital aspect of consensus policing; it is both a source of information, and a familiarization of the public with the police officer as an individual human being, and the conditions are created whereby the public willingly passes on information to the police. Alderson's 'technological cop' faces a dilemma: on the one hand, modern data recording and storage-retrieval systems are at his service; on the other hand, the weakening of the link with the public that 'fire-brigade' policing has involved means that there is less reliable information to store in the system. This paradox — rather than any deliberate policy formulated at State level — probably accounts for growing public concern at the extent to which police computers reflect what Alderson identifies as an 'innate tendency to want to record almost anything'. Where there is little useful information coming from the public to the police then inevitably a tendency arises to record almost anything on the grounds that it might conceivably be of use in the future (see Baldwin and Kinsey).

The vicious circle

Once the move in the direction of military policing is established, as a result of factors we have just been discussing, a vicious circle is set in motion whereby the initial moves to military policing themselves create the conditions in which further moves in the same direction are encouraged and made more plausible. There are three broad areas in which this vicious circle can be identified.

The first and most obvious effect of military policing is that it antagonizes a large number of people; it helps to turn the community against the police. The more the stop-and-search procedures, the road blocks, the house-to-house searches, and the raids on youth clubs become a normal part of police activity in the inner city and ethnic minority areas then the more the flow of information from that section of the community dries up and the situation described by Plowman (above, p. 175) comes into existence. An example culled from the Report of the Working Party into Community Police Relations in Lambeth (p. 36) brings this out well:

> The area is patrolled regularly by plain clothes and uniformed police within a radius of 100 yards and there are frequent raids involving 50 or more police with dozens of vehicles and police dogs.

> As some of the schoolchildren were arriving from school and waiting at the gate of the playground for the leader to arrive, about six to eight of the members in school uniforms were frisked and searched by two plain clothes policemen. The young people were annoyed and so were their parents when they knew.

> The observations of young people and their parents at the time indicated that the SPG were being totally successful in keeping everyone off the streets — even to the point of preventing them coming to and from their club. The Working Party were told that the areas just outside the clubs are where 'groups of young blacks leaving [the clubs] are picked up by the police waiting at the end of the road. It's the roughness, the whole brutality, it's sickening'.

The reinforcement process lies in the fact that the easiest police response to a situation in which information from the community has dried up is *more military policing*. More road blocks, more Swamp '81s, desperately to try and catch street criminals and, of course, the easier the transition becomes from attempts to catch criminals to general harassment of the community at large. The end result is a further distancing of the community from the police, a further reduction of information (if it has not entirely dried up anyway), and if nothing is changed, a further drift towards military policing. Military policing produces the alienation of the community from the police and the alienation of the community from the police produces military policing.

The second component of the vicious circle is what might be called the 'spread effect' of alienation. The effect of military policing, though it may initially be directed against a particular section of the community (young people, and young black people in particular) is to spread out to other sections of the community in such a way that the conditions leading to military policing are reinforced. This spread effect takes the form of the undermining of other social institutions in the community which under a system of consensus policing might be expected to promote social control and integration, leading young people into non-criminal forms of behaviour and out of a form of contact with the police characterized by conflict. Three examples of this process readily come to mind.

1 *The effect on the family*

Lord Scarman noted that 'one of the most serious developments in recent years has been the way in which the older generation of black people in Brixton has come to share the belief of the younger generation that the police routinely harass and ill-treat black youngsters' (p. 65). On the simplest level, this is simply a question of parents observing what is going on. But the point about military policing is that, by its very nature, harassment of the young tends to spread into the harassment of the parents as well.

Consider the following example. In an environment in which information coming from the community concerning crime is low, and the police are already relying heavily on stop-and-search procedures in an attempt to contain street crime, and the community within which they are operating already has to a considerable extent become stereotyped as crime-prone, a black youngster is stopped by police officers while carrying a piece of hi-fi equipment. Given the background factors, the police suspect the youngster of having stolen the equipment with no more evidence than the simple fact that he has it in his possession. This is the first stage of the process. The next stage is familiar from countless complaints and reports of police behaviour over the last decade: the police 'know' he is guilty but, because of the general lack of information from the community about crime, they have no information to back up that assumption. So they 'prise' that evidence out of the community. Here is a harrowing account from the Lambeth Report (p. 37):

> At approximately 6.45 a.m. I had just got up but had not dressed when I heard a banging on the front door.
>
> I went downstairs not thinking that there was anything serious and with the intention of just opening the door and sticking my head round to see who was there. When I did open the door there were four police officers in plain clothes and they did not give me time to invite them in or ask them if they had a warrant. They just said 'Is X (my son) here?' brushing me aside as they were saying this. I said 'Just a minute' and got in front of them and went up the stairs.
>
> They followed me and passed me at the top of the stairs and held me back. In fact they barred my way. Two of them went to my daughter's room and opened it. I should say that both children have their names written on the

doors so it was quite obvious whose room belonged to who. I objected to two of the officers going into her room, but I was completely ignored. They banged loudly on my son's door and after a little while he opened the door. I wanted to be there but they barged in and I did not have a chance to get in. I was kept back. They shut the door in my face. Two of them were in the room and two of them were outside on the landing. They came out of his room with my son and I asked what it was all about. I said either 'What are you charging him with?' or 'What are you arresting him for?' They said 'Attempted murder of a policeman.' I did say that he would not do that but I was completely ignored and they bundled him downstairs and out of the house.

Our concern here is not simply to point out the injustices involved nor to get into an argument about the extent of such activities. Undoubtedly, some police raids on homes are justified if properly conducted, but it is equally clear that many are not: extensive complaints are testimony to that. Our point is that this type of activity on the part of the police is an inevitable component of military policing. The relationship between arrest and evidence is becoming *reversed*. Under policing by consent, information from the community enables the police to restrict their incursions into the private lives of citizens to those whom investigations and information have made suspect. In investigative policing as traditionally understood a raid on premises is a response to information already received and is carried out in the expectation that it will result in further important evidence leading to an arrest with a chance of conviction by the courts. Under military policing, however, until the raid is conducted there is no evidence, since there are no other sources of information. Where virtually everyone is under suspicion in a community stereotyped as crime-prone, it becomes an option to apprehend almost any young person found in possession of a consumer durable — given that the area suffers a high crime rate — by a raid on his/her home in the hope that further evidence, proving the item was stolen, might be obtained. In this sequence of events police racism acts not as the cause but as a facilitating factor: no doubt racist officers will more willingly crash through the homes of black families than others, but the practice is an inevitable ingredient of military policing rather than a consequence of the sentiments of police officers.

The effect on the family is severe. Parents, experiencing the same treatment at the hands of the police quite irrespective of their involvement in crime, develop the same antagonism towards the police as these children do. This, of course, is part of the process whereby military policing dries up the supply of information from the community. But more fundamentally, this parental antagonism changes the relationship between the police and the family. Under a system of consensus policing the police could be expected to see the family as an institution with which they work in concert, and the police constable undertakes a paternalistic role towards a juvenile involved in minor offences. For more serious offences the trend of juvenile justice since the 1960s has been towards a combination of detention with various forms of intermediate treatment. The latter, like all forms of community treatment, presupposes a cooperative relationship between the police, social-work agencies and the family. Pitts has argued that the simultaneous growth during the seventies of both detention and more control-oriented forms of intermediate treatment, combined with the activities of the police Juvenile Bureau, represented a spreading of the net of the juvenile justice system into areas which would previously have been left to the family and social-work agencies. Within this system the growing antagonism between black parents and the police would lead to the expectation that a higher proportion of black juvenile offenders would find themselves in detention centres with less reliance by the courts on supervision orders involving social-work agencies and the family. This is borne out by Landau. An accentuation of this trend can follow from the decision of area police commanders as to which offences by young people should be referred to the Juvenile Bureau with the automatic notification of social workers prior to court appearances, in which case a recommendation for a supervision order is less likely to be made in court and a custodial sentence becomes more likely.

This state of affairs can also create antagonism between parents and children. On the one hand, parents, scared that their kids, out in the streets, will get into trouble with the police, will put pressure on them to stay indoors, which will result in conflict:

> In October 1979 I sent my son, 15, out to get fish and chips. He was stopped in the street by two men, plain-clothes, who searched him and asked him where he got his money. They showed nothing to say they were police officers and my son was very shaken by the experience. Since then I take him to and from the youth club every week; he is very embarrassed, but I have to do it. I lock their shoes up at the weekend so they can't go out when I am sleeping in the day. (Lambeth Working Party)

2 The effect upon social-work agencies

We have already mentioned a tendency for social-work agencies to get excluded from sentencing processes. But far more widely than this, military policing tends to create a situation which undermines the activity of youth workers and other volunteers who would normally keep young people off the streets. The effect of police raids on clubs looking for suspects or evidence can be disastrous:

> Recently one of the club members aged 15 was picked up for creating a disturbance and it was said that he was found to have drugs in his possession. This resulted in police visits to the club, which caused much unrest and so the leader told the police that these visits were causing havoc. They appeared to understand but the visits continued until at last the youth said to the leader: 'For the sake of the club members, I will not come again, so you will be left in peace.' So he left the club.

> During November 1978, when the SPG were in Brixton, the activities of the Youth Project were severely affected. Our chief club night, on Thursdays, was reduced to a handful of attending members. Through January and February, it recovered to the usual 100 mark. (Lambeth Working Party)

3 The effect upon community relations

Part of the attempt by governments in the sixties and seventies to link the ethnic minority communities to the existing political structure was the system of Community

Relations Councils (CRCs) under the aegis of the Community Relations Commission (now the Commission for Racial Equality). We shall discuss the effect of these councils in the next chapter. Here our concern is with the effect of military policing upon a more specific component of community relations, that conducted by the police itself. Local CRCs were encouraged to set up police liaison committees, and during the 1970s the Metropolitan Police expanded its community relations initiative. In 1972 Humphrey and John claimed: 'The jobs in Community Relations go only to "dogsbodies" and "liberals". There is no mileage in such positions for promotion, the turnover is frightening in posts where years of experience are necessary.' Since then community relations training and what is now called 'human awareness' training has been stepped up and the number of Community Liaison Officers expanded. In 1976-7 a variable rank structure was applied to CL posts permitting promotion within such posts and enabling career-minded officers to regard community relations as more than a passing interest.

What is very clear from Scarman's report is that the development of military policing as a general strategy undermined and continues to undermine the effectiveness of police-community dialogue. Indeed, the expansion of community-relations work by the police can be seen as an attempt to recreate some of the characteristics of consensus policing in the context of a generalized drift to high-technology military policing. Scarman showed how in Brixton saturation operations like Swamp '81 'provoked the hostility of young black people who felt they were being hunted irrespective of their innocence or guilt . . . However well intentioned, these operations precipitated a crisis of confidence between the police and certain community leaders. In particular they led to the breakdown of the formal arrangements for liaison between the ethnic minority communities, the local authority, and the police.'

But Scarman failed to see the contradiction between police-community liaison schemes as at present constituted and military policing. He went on to recommend *both* that 'hard' policing (by which he meant much the same as our term 'military' policing) should necessarily continue, that this 'requires the use on the streets of stop-and-search powers and the occasional "saturation" operation' *and* a statutory requirement for police-community liaison at borough level. Scarman tries to straddle the contradiction between military policing and community liaison (p. 92):

> I appreciate, of course, that secrecy is essential to the success of certain operations and that consultation will not be possible or appropriate in those cases. Neither will consultation always produce an agreed result: in the end it will be necessary for the responsible police commander to take a decision. But the object must be to enable the community to understand fully why the police regard such an operation as necessary, and there must be a willingness on the part of the police to listen to community views and to be prepared to modify their plans in the light of them.

One can understand why this sort of proposal has cut little ice with police commanders at ground level who believe both that military policing is the only solution to rising crime rates and that this, by definition, does not permit a consultation approach to the community which is going to bear the brunt of it. One can sympathize with Deputy

Assistant Commander Leslie Walker of the Metropolitan Police who on the ITV London Programme in January 1981 complained: 'He [Scarman] says that a police operation of that sort will at times be essential [but] when the commander of an area having embarked on a large scale exercise is told by community leaders "I think you may be getting a disturbance this weekend" he is going to be committing professional suicide if he doesn't call off the operation.'

This inability of the police to discuss their tactics with community-liaison committees in situations where operations depend upon secrecy (the prior publication of something like Swamp '81 would simply have the result that all criminals vacate the area for the duration rendering the exercise useless) can be exacerbated by a local commander who is not oriented towards a community-relations approach. Thus, in another case of breakdown in September 1980, Hackney Council for Racial Equality ended its relationship with the local police. According to the local paper:

> In Hackney it has been made clear time and again that while the HCRE can raise issues, the police reserve the right to be complete masters of their policing policy and that a liaison commitee has only the function of airing issues . . . Hackney CRE received a continuous stream of complaints and with a police commander who has applauded the SPG, made some very outspoken remarks in favour of 'sus', and whose attitude towards minority communities has left a strong suspicion, HCRE has felt that its role must be that of a monitoring agency which makes representations to MPs and the Home Office. (*Hackney Gazette*, 2 September 1980)

The third component of the vicious circle can be called 'the mobilization of bystanders'. The phrase originated in discussions of the consequences of massive intervention by law-enforcement agencies in the American riots of the late 1960s where it was noticed that massive and indiscriminate police response often had the effect of provoking people who otherwise would not have participated in the rioting to join in. The same sort of process can be identified as a general characteristic of military policing. As we have seen, military policing involves the blurring of the distinction between offender and non-offender. The essence of the mobilization of bystanders is that this tendency on the part of the police is reproduced within the community itself. Firstly, the attitude of the community towards the actual offender starts to change. The experience of the community as a whole becomes assimilated to the experience of the criminal: treatment at the hands of the police becomes more and more indistinguishable for both categories. Also, since both, due to unemployment and deprivation, and the declining effectiveness of other institutions of social control, lead a life fundamentally centring on the streets, then they intermix freely. As Scarman remarks: 'There he meets criminals, who appear to have no difficulty in obtaining the benefits of a materialist society.'

The result of this process is that the offender temporarily comes to be regarded as a sort of symbolic rebel by the community. At least he is hitting back, and so crime can come to be seen as a sort of quasi-political response by youngsters. Since one is equally likely to be harassed by the police whether or not one is a criminal, then actual criminality can come to be seen as defensive activity on behalf of the community against the sources of collective oppression. This is the thinking behind the remark of Stuart Hall and his colleagues in an earlier study (pp. 34-5):

> Mugging for some . . . supplied the necessary bread to kill long periods of time where little can be done for nothing, and where little time is likely to be spent at home. It allows an identity of toughness and physical superiority, a channel to a dented identity . . . It is perhaps a 'non-ideological politics'.

But there is a second aspect to this. The other side of the coin is that there is a loss of confidence by the community: when they witness someone being apprehended by the police, they doubt that this is anything other than a case of symbolic attack upon the community as a whole. Under conditions of consensus policing, where the police act upon solid information, if the community witnesses anyone being apprehended, there is the presumption that the police must have good reason for their action, and in any case the consequent process of clearly formulated charges, access to a solicitor, and, if necessary, trial by jury guarantee that only those guilty of crimes will be punished. Under the conditions we are describing here, the process is very different. The assumption becomes that the person being apprehended is probably innocent and, secondly, that his apprehension by the police is going to be the first step in a long process of harassment involving him and his family while the police attempt to 'construct' the information leading to a successful conviction. This, of course, puts the police in a difficult position, since once this type of atmosphere becomes generally established in the community, then, even if reasonably responsible local commanders take care to ensure that arrests only occur where there really is evidence — a difficult enough state of affairs to achieve under general conditions of military policing, as we have already seen — it will, in the short term at least, be regarded in exactly the same light by other members of the community who happen to be bystanders at the event.

The end result of this process, and something that had been noticed long before the riots, was the tendency for collective resistance to arrest to develop among black youths. In its evidence to the House of Commons Report on the West Indian Community, the Metropolitan Police noted that:

> Recently there has been a growth in the tendency for members of London's West Indian communities to combine against police officers who are effecting the arrest of a black person or who are in some other way enforcing the law in situations which involve black people. (Evidence, p. 178)

The most large-scale example of such situations, prior to the 1981 riots, were, of course, the events at the Notting Hill Carnivals of 1976 and 1977. In the context of generally deteriorating relations between the black community and the police, what was regarded as an overbearing police presence at the Carnival itself made it very likely that *any* police action, including genuine attempts to apprehend pickpockets, would provoke a collective response. The result of such a situation is illustrated by the 1977 Carnival in which there were 170 police injuries, 217 arrests and reported crimes totalling 580!

The general dynamics of the self-reinforcing drift towards military policing are summarized in Figure 1. The general features of this vicious circle are clear. Initial moves in the direction of military policing result in antagonizing the older generation of blacks, and in a further reduction of the flow of information; the weakening effectiveness of other institutions of social integration result in more youngsters spending more time on the streets and in contact with the police, which reinforces the processes of stereotyping the community as a whole as crime-prone; and the propensity to collective resistance to arrest, when unchecked, threatens to make any attempt at policing a major military operation in the literal sense of the term.

Figure 1.   The self-reinforcement of military policing

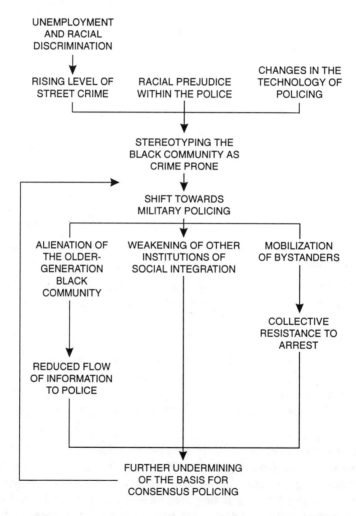

Before we conclude this discussion it is worth asking a simple question: why has it taken so long — why, in fact has it taken the summer of 1981 and the threat of its repetition — to open up a space for some serious political discussion of the nature of policing in the inner city? There have been enough warnings of what was to come. A decade ago the House of Commons Select Committee on Race Relations and Immigration in its 1971-2 session report concluded that:

> To state that a sizable proportion of the West Indian community no longer trust the police is to confer a euphemism upon a situation which for many has reached a level equal to fear, and we are convinced that if urgent action is not taken to give effect to the grave issues at hand, violence on a large scale cannot be ruled out.

Why were the gathering storm clouds of the 1970s ignored? One response, not uncommon on the left, is to see the move to military policing, with its attendant risk of large-scale violence on the streets, as more or less a conscious act of state policy in order to bottle up the new generation of unemployed youth in the inner city and counter, at the same time, the rising militancy of the organized working class by the creation of a 'moral panic' concerning rocketing crime rates. There is an important element of truth in this view. A generation of young people surplus to requirements in the strict economic sense do really pose new problems of social control. Some of the aspects of this we shall look at in the next chapter. But to argue from this that simply bottling up this population through military policing and an escalating technology of repression culminating in water cannon and plastic bullets is a conscious act of state policy is to oversimplify matters considerably.

The broad aim of government policies in the late sixties and seventies was to create, by state intervention, mechanisms of integration into mainstream social and economic life for those groups which the changing structure of capital accumulation had excluded from it. This ranged from the Race Relations legislation, through initiatives to persuade the trade unions to take black workers seriously, to the various components of the urban programme and the Manpower Services Commission youth opportunity schemes. Such policies have been weak and have failed by and large to influence the situation over the last decade. They have failed, above all, through government financial constraints, as well as opposition by employers to strong anti-discrimination legislation.

It is the *failure* of central government policy to avert the crisis of the inner city and unemployment among youth and ethnic minorities which has created the structure within which the development of military policing has taken root. The failure of central government to stem deprivation has resulted in higher crime rates. Other general social forces associated with economic decay have fuelled the fires of racial prejudice in British society and so some of the crucial factors setting off the vicious circle of military policing have been generated. These processes have taken the form of pressures to deal with an already developing situation: pressure from police officers for more power and resources — witness the Police and Criminal Evidence Bill — and from the judiciary to increase the scope of summary jurisdiction to deal with crime rates.

From this standpoint it is easy to see how the warning could be ignored and how the drift to coercive policing policies at ground level could occur without great opposition from public opinion. Three factors stand out. Firstly, the move to military policing in the inner city among the ethnic communities has been absent from the middle-class suburbs and their enclaves within the inner city. Rather than the moral panic concerning crime in the inner city being a deflection of rising struggles at the 'core' of society, it has been precisely the fact that the consensus at the core has been secure *despite* increasing economic crisis that has laid the basis for a move to a more repressive policing policy at the periphery. As Brogden notes (p. 205):

> Consent to policing does not of itself necessarily imply support for what police institutions actually do. Inner City residents believe that police work is crime work and support policing in general . . . Public order police work is conceived of as a kind of accidental by-product of the primary duties of police officers, engaged in the 'war against crime' . . .

> But suburban residents recognize the objective function of police work — maintaining social and public order. The concentration of police officers in the Inner City, on public order duties, and on the prevention of incursions into suburbia, are functions which fit that conception.

Secondly, the drift to military policing has taken the form, as far as the majority of the British public have been concerned, of a fight against crime, and street crime in particular. The niceties of the theorization of crime as a form of 'non-ideological politics' escape the ordinary citizen concerned about his property and personal security. But finally — and this factor will constitute the starting-point of our discussion in the next chapter — the population that has borne the brunt of military policing has been largely a population *about* which we talk, but rarely a population *with* whom we talk. A section of society has arisen that lacks, in effect, one of the basic features of liberal democracy: a means of expressing its grievances and interests at the level of national politics. It is a population in our midst without a political voice.

15. Black Youth, Crime and the Ghetto: Common Sense Images and Law and Order

John Solomos

Introduction

As I have argued above no discussion of the ideologies, policies and forms of state intervention in relation to young blacks can be complete without reference to wider political issues and the general political climate on 'race' questions. The value of this procedure is particularly clear when one looks at the evolution of policies and ideologies during the 1970s, a period during which many of the inputs which went into the racialisation of British political life were mediated via popular and policy concern about the 'problem' of young blacks growing up in 'ghetto environments'. As shown in [chapter 2], images of young blacks as 'children of the ghetto' had already become common during the 1960s, but it was during the 1970s that these images reached full maturity.

In this chapter I shall discuss the genesis and evolution of ideologies and policies in relation to young blacks around three issues: (a) the supposed link between 'race', youth and criminality; (b) mugging and street crime; and (c) policing and law and order. The three issues will be used to illustrate the articulation of debates about the black youth question as a highly politicised dimension of contemporary political debates about 'race relations' and the transformation of policy images about black youths. Additionally, however, I shall aim to explore the complex reasons for this change and the contradictions which resulted from it. This will then make it possible to link the history of the black youth question, as a general phenomenon, to the more recent politicisation of the black youth unemployment question and the outbreak of urban unrest during the 1980s.

Before turning to these aspects, however, it is necessary to make a few remarks about the historical context which has shaped the emergence of 'black crime' and 'street violence' as primary concerns in public policy in relation to young blacks.

Crime and 'race'

Ideologies linking immigrants as a general category, and black immigrants in particular, with crime have a long history in British society.[1] This is not to say that these ideologies have been constant throughout this history, or that they were monolithic. They have undergone numerous transformations over the years, and ideologies which link immigrants to crime have not been universally accepted even by those who opposed migration. But it is certainly true that whether one looks at the Irish migrants of the nineteenth century, Jewish immigrants in the period 1880-1914,

---

John Solomos: 'Black Youth, Crime and the Ghetto: Common Sense Images and Law and Order' from *BLACK YOUTH, CRIME AND THE GHETTO* (Cambridge University Press, 1991), pp. 88-118.

or other significant groups of migrants the issue of crime has been a common theme in the construction of ideologies and policies towards them (Garrard, 1971; Gainer, 1972; Holmes, 1978; Lunn, 1980).

Black seamen who settled in port towns such as Cardiff, Liverpool and London were similarly stereotyped. The areas in which they lived were seen as localities in which the presence of migrants combined with social deprivation and poverty to produce not only patterns of criminal behaviour but social values outside the mainstream of the majority society. A number of studies of black communities during the period from 1900 to 1940 have noted how important such images were in determining both the form and content of dominant ideologies of the 'Negro problem' within both official circles and local voluntary associations (Little, 1947; Banton, 1955; Fryer, 1984; Ramdin, 1987).

An important early study of St Clair Drake provides a detailed account of the processes through which the Tiger Bay area of Cardiff was constructed in this manner. He shows how the inhabitants of the area were defined as a 'problem' by outside institutions, and how the black inhabitants were seen as a specific 'problem' group. Even though many of the Tiger Bay inhabitants expressed the view that 'the colour-bar is the problem; not the coloured people', the black inhabitants of the area were attributed with characteristics which helped to define them as the 'problem'. Within the general category of the black population of Tiger Bay the younger generation of 'half-caste' children was seen as a particular problem group (Drake, 1954: 69-129).

Other studies have shown how the areas into which post-1945 black settlers moved rapidly became identified as localities with crime-related behaviour and other 'social problems', including decaying housing, lack of social amenities, and low levels of community involvement (Carter, Harris and Joshi, 1987; Harris and Solomos, forthcoming). In areas such as Notting Hill and Brixton in London, Handsworth and Balsall Heath in Birmingham, and in similar localities in other cities the question of rising crime and law and order became intimately identified with the broader question of the impact of black immigration on these areas. Questions about the involvement of specific groups of migrants with criminal activities were asked both in and out of Parliament and became a topic for popular concern in the press (*The Times,* 28 March 1958). Such questions became even more pronounced during and after the 1958 riots in Notting Hill and Nottingham, which helped to politicise the issue of black migration and to influence the direction of both local and central government policies.[2] Indeed during the late 1950s and early 1960s the issue of immigration control was intimately tied to the question of the involvement of black migrants in criminal activities. Even before the 1958 riots a number of pro-immigration-control MPs had attempted to politicise the issue of 'black crime' (*Hansard*, vol. 578, 1957: cols. 743-76; vol. 585, 1958: cols. 1415-26). The political climate in the aftermath of the riots proved to be conducive to those ideologies which blamed the rising levels of 'racial tension' on the arrival of 'undesirables' from the colonies. At the 1958 Conservative party Conference Norman Pannell moved a resolution calling for the deportation of such 'undesirables'; whom he defined as those migrants who were not of good character, not in good health, or lacked sufficient means to avoid becoming a liability on public funds (*The Times,* 13 October 1958).

Along with the broader processes of racialisation which I have already analysed in [chapters 1 and 2], the 1960s saw a growing politicisation of this question, and continuous attempts by the police and by government to deal with the danger of conflict between the police and black communities. The concerns at this stage were about the growing number of complaints of racial discrimination by the police against blacks, the future of younger blacks if their social and economic position deteriorated, and the fear that an American-type situation of racial violence and disorder could be reproduced in major cities.[3] In July 1967 the Home Office issued a circular to all Chief Constables on *The Police and Coloured Communities,* which advised them to appoint, particularly in areas of black settlement, liaison officers whose task would be to develop better relations with black communities and educate the police themselves on the dilemmas of policing such areas.[4] This was followed by a number of consultative meetings to discuss the policing of particular localities and to analyse the long-term prospects of future conflict between the police and black communities. In the period from 1967 to 1970 a number of articles appeared in specialised journals which discussed the policing of multi-racial localities, the specific problems faced by young blacks and accusations of discriminatory behaviour by the police in relation to the black communities in areas of London, Birmingham and other localities.[5]

The police themselves began to recognise, somewhat hesitantly, the need to develop an understanding of the context of policing in multi-racial areas. In 1970 a conference of US and British specialists and practitioners was held under the auspices of the Ditchley Foundation to discuss 'police-community relations' on both sides of the Atlantic (Clarke, 1970). Other meetings and seminars were also held to discuss this issue, and from 1970 onwards the annual Reports of the Commissioner of Police of the Metropolis contain some discussion of the specific issues related to the policing of multi-racial localities (Reports of the Commissioner of Police for the Metropolis, 1970-86) .

In this context an article written by Robert Mark, who was then Deputy Commissioner of the Metropolitan Police provides an enlightening insight into the emergent ideology of the police on the question of 'race'. While being quite clear that 'there is no evidence to show that migrants commit a disproportionate amount of crime', Mark argued that a minority become involved in frequent contact with the police. He linked this to two issues:

(1) the involvement of a small number of migrants in prostitution, gaming and the fringes of criminal activity; and

(2) the involvement of other migrants in public order offences, family disputes or noisy parties (Mark, 1970: 4-5).

For Mark such situations of conflict were partly the result of the newness of the migrants and their socio-economic position in British society, but also the result of a failure by the police and other institutions to deal with the 'special problems posed by migrants' (*ibid.* 5). But he saw the situation as one which would not damage relations between the police and the migrant communities on a permanent basis:

Traditionally the protector of all groups and classes, irrespective of race, colour or creed, we believe that we, the police, have done no less than any other public service to promote the welfare and security of the migrant in his transition from his homeland to an alien highly industrial, urban society; and we are not unduly discouraged that we should be attacked and criticised by representatives, self-appointed or otherwise, of the very people that we are trying to help.

(*Ibid.*)

The implicit optimism about the effectiveness of 'positive action' by the police was not shared, as Mark points out, by a growing number of critics of the overall strategy and tactics of the police in policing multi-racial areas. In fact it was partly in response to increasingly trenchant criticisms of the police role from both within and outside the black communities that the police began to develop and articulate an ideological legitimation for their policies in relation to 'black areas' (Lambert, 1970; Humphry, 1972).

This debate was carried forward in the national media, as well as in specialised 'race' journals like *Race Today,* which was at the time published by the Institute of Race Relations.[6] The public nature of the debate helped to politicise the question of 'race and policing' to a new level during the early 1970s, particularly as pressure mounted from within the black communities for investigations into cases of harassment by the police, and for 'greater equality before the law' (Nandy, 1970; John, 1970; Hall *et al.*, 1978). It should also be remembered, of course, that it was during this period that the question of 'immigration and race' came to occupy a central role in debates about domestic social policies at both a national and a local political level [see chapter 1]. This broader process of racialisation helped to increase the impact of the policy debate about the inter-relationship of crime and 'race', since this issue served to give further credence to the Powellite warnings that immigration was undermining the whole of the social fabric of inner city localities. The imagery of black involvement in criminal activities and in public order offences helped to fuel and give a new direction to the increasingly volatile public debate about 'race relations'.

For the purposes of this chapter I will not explore in detail this wider context of the interplay between images of 'race' and images of crime, since my main concern is with the issue of how a particular category of the black community, namely 'black youth', came to be seen as caught up in a vicious circle of poverty, homelessness and criminal activities. The roots of this phenomenon lie in the wider process I have touched on above, but this need not prevent the analysis of the politicisation of the question of the involvement of young blacks in crime from the early 1970s onwards in its own particularity. This is particularly important since, while a number of general accounts of the interplay between 'race and policing' have been written, the specific nature of the black youth question within this process has not yet been analysed in much detail.[7] It is to this question that I now turn.

Black youth, crime and ghetto life

The convergence of images of criminality and delinquency with the wider set of concerns about the future of young blacks in British society has already been touched on in [chapter 2]. Throughout the late 1960s fears about the increasing alienation of young blacks from the mainstream of British society were regularly expressed in the media and policy documents, and became a constant refrain in both academic and policy writings on the subject.[8] But by the early 1970s it became clear that this was not merely a passing phenomenon which would disappear with the 'integration' of young blacks into the mainstream institutions of British society.

This was so for at least two major reasons. First, it became clear that the calls for action to help 'coloured school leavers' gain equality of opportunity in employment and other arenas did not necessarily result in the development of effective policy measures to put such calls into practice. Evidence of high levels of unemployment, low levels of attainment in schools and homelessness among young blacks continued to accumulate during the early 1970s. The evidence tended to show that, even in the space of a few years, the picture painted in *The Problems of Coloured School Leavers* in 1969 had been overtaken by events. Far from the positive measures which had been called for in this Report, the net result of the intense debates during the 1970s seems to have been inaction and a deterioration of the socio-economic condition of young blacks.

Second, by the early 1970s it also became clear that the condition of young blacks was rapidly becoming one of the central concerns within the black communities. In various forums, both locally and nationally, black political activists were discussing issues such as education, employment and policing in relation to young blacks. They were also questioning the failure to take positive measures to tackle the root causes of racism and racial inequality.[9] Such political debates from within the black communities helped to emphasise the centrality of this issue within the context of racialised political debates, and to force state institutions to review the nature of their interventions.

At a symbolic level the commitment to the principle of equal opportunity was still part of the climate of political opinion. The Conservative Home Secretary, Robert Carr, restated this commitment in context of the debate on race relations issues at the 1973 Conservative party Conference:

> Our principle is that there should be no second-class citizens in Britain. Everyone who was born here or has come here legally should be equal before the law and not only that but they should be treated equally in the practices of everyday life. I know we do not live up to that perfectly but that is our commitment and that is what my colleagues and I will do our best to achieve.
>
> (*The Times*, 11 October 1973)

But such symbolic promises did not answer the fundamental question which was raised by the reproduction of young blacks, along with their parents, as second-class citizens: namely, why and how were the inequalities and problems faced by the first generation of black migrants being reproduced within the second generation? What were likely to be the medium- and long-term consequences of this process both for young blacks and for society as a whole? Symbolic promises of future action did not touch upon the substantive issues, but deflected attention onto the prospect of a 'better future'.

The reality of the situation in the early 1970s, however, was made clear in a number of reports which highlighted the dismal prospects for young blacks and the potential of conflict with the police.[10] In 1970 Gus John published his influential study of Handsworth called *Race and the Inner City*, and in the same year John Lambert published a study of *Crime, Police and Race Relations*. Both studies attracted attention because they came out at a time when the issues of relations between the black communities and the police and the involvement of young blacks in crime. During the period from 1969 to 1973 a number of feature articles and reports in the press discussed various aspects of the growing tension between the police and the black communities, both at a national level and in relation to specific communities.[11] The complaints against the police by the black communities themselves, which had been articulated as early as 1966 in Hunte's *Nigger Hunting in England*, reached new levels during the early 1970s and were rapidly becoming a political issue.[12]

John's study of Handsworth was a particularly important document in this growing debate. Written by a black researcher who had spent some time living within the black community in Handsworth it highlights the question of policing and the position of young blacks as the core concerns of local residents. It was written at a time when the police themselves were discussing their role in the policing of multi-racial inner city areas and formulating their ideologies and practices on this issue (Humphry, 1972). Additionally, media coverage at the time talked of the growing tensions between the police and black communities, and 1969-70 saw a number of minor street confrontations with the police in areas such as Notting Hill.[13] John began his account of Handsworth with an analysis of the area and the contrasting perceptions offered by local residents of the changes in its social structure and population make-up during the post-war period. But the core of his report, and the issue which gave rise to a full debate in the press, is the description which it offers of relations between the local black community, particularly younger blacks, and the police.[14] John reports that one police official had pointed out to him that the 'growth of black crime' in the area was the work of a 'hard core' of forty or fifty youngsters (John, 1970: 20). But his own perceptions of the situation were more complex, and he summarised them as amounting to three main issues:

(1) the prevalence of rumours, fears and explanations of black involvement in criminal activities;

(2) a tendency by police to blame the 'hard core' of young blacks for 'giving the area a bad name'; and

(3) deep resentment by older and younger blacks with their social position and the discrimination they had to endure.

Additionally he warned that there were signs of 'a massive breakdown in relations between the police and the black community', and that if nothing was done the situation was likely to lead to confrontations between black residents and the police and outbursts of urban unrest:

> In my view trends in Handsworth are a portent for the future. A decaying area, full of stress and tension, which also happens to be racially mixed, is

going to find it increasingly difficult to cope with the root problems because racial animosities and resentments have taken on an independent life of their own. The problem is not, and can never be, simply one of law and order.

(*Ibid.* 25)

It was this context, argued John, which explained why both young blacks and the police saw the situation in the area as one of open 'warfare' (*ibid.* 28-9).

Some aspects of John's account of relations between the police and the black community were criticised as overstated and impressionistic. Yet there is a certain symmetry between his account of the situation and that described later on in the 1970s by John Rex and Sally Tomlinson in their detailed empirical analysis of the political economy of race and class in Handsworth (Rex and Tomlinson, 1979). Additionally other studies of the interplay between 'race' and policing during the early 1970s indicated that the relaltionship between young blacks and the police was becoming an issue of public concern in other areas similar to Handsworth.[15]

Evidence from black communities across the country highlighted three particularly contentious issues. First, complaints by young blacks that they were being categorised as a 'problem group' by the police, and that they were therefore more likely to be questioned or arrested. Second, allegations that the police used excessive physical violence in their dealings with black suspects. Finally, it was argued that such attitudes and forms of behaviour by the police were helping to fuel popular rumours about the involvement of young blacks in crime, and to drive a wedge between the police and the black communities.

Perhaps most significantly in the context of my general argument is that the shifting emphasis on young blacks as a problem category for the police and for society as a whole was being framed increasingly around the question of 'police–community relations'. This shift became particularly clear when (a) the question of policing was investigated by the Select Committee on Race Relations and Immigration during 1971-2, and (b) popular and media debate focused on the involvement of young blacks in forms of street crime which were popularly defined as 'mugging'.

As argued above, the politicisation of the question of crime in relation to young blacks is best seen within the broader context of official and public concern with the interplay between ghetto life, the social position of young blacks and criminal activities. The Select Committee on Race Relations and Immigration investigation of *Police/Immigrant Relations*, which was carried out during 1971-2, represents a useful starting point for understanding the concerns of the state, the police and the black communities in relation to policing and law and order.[16]

The Committee's Report, two substantive volumes of evidence, and the government response to its recommendations (which was published in 1973) were, in effect, the first coherent official statement on the inter-relationship between race, crime and policing.[17] Young blacks were a central issue in the deliberations and the conclusions of the Committee, since it was the younger generation who were both popularly and officially seen as the 'source of the problem'. The Committee took evidence from community groups, police officials, local authorities and government departments on the causes of 'growing tension' between the police and sections of the black communities. Although the popular press and John's report on Handsworth had shown that police on the ground perceived a section of blacks disproportionately involved in criminal activities, the Committee concluded that this claim was not supported by the evidence:

> The conclusions remain beyond doubt: coloured immigrants are no more involved in crime than others; nor are they generally more concerned in violence, prostitution and drugs. The West Indian crime rate is much the same as that of the indigenous population. The Asian crime rate is very much lower.
>
> (Select Committee, 1972, Report: 71)

It did point out, however, that there was one major source of conflict between the police and black communities: namely, the 'explosive' relations between the 'younger generation of West Indians' and the police. The source of this conflict was seen as lying in a combination of factors, most notably in the situation of young blacks themselves and the attitude of the police *(ibid.* 68-9).

The Committee's Report saw young West Indians as becoming increasingly 'resentful of society' and expressing their anger and frustration against the police because they were an obvious authority symbol. It explained this situation as arising from three factors:

(1) pressures faced by young blacks in competing for jobs and housing;

(2) the nature of West Indian family discipline, which although 'Victorian' for younger children did not extend to the West Indian youngsters aged between 16 and 25; and

(3) conflict between the younger and older generations of West Indians *(ibid.* 69).

The Report did accept that there were problems of discrimination faced by young blacks, but significantly it did not prioritise these processes in its explanation for growing tension between them and the police. It pointed out that much of the evidence presented by black community groups argued that there was a process of 'nigger hunting' and a tendency for 'the police to pick on black youths merely because they are black'. But it balanced this out by adding that the evidence of the Metropolitan Police showed that 'in London black youths are stopped and/or arrested proportionately no more than white youths'.

On the question of allegations that policemen were engaged in practices ranging from harassment, assault, wrongful arrest and detention, provocation, fabrication, planting of evidence and racial insults, the Committee was much more reticent to come to any conclusions. It accepted that much of the evidence by various black groups or individuals, and the evidence submitted to it by the Community Relations Commission, contained claims that such practices were common in many localities (Select Committee, 1972, Evidence: vol. II: 65-8; vol. III: 716-35; vol. III: 765-71). While accepting that these claims were believed by many black people, it found it impossible to 'prove or disprove' them, with the truth lying somewhere in between the claims of the police and their critics (Select Committee, 1972, Report: 20-1). Rather, it saw these claims and counter-claims as the natural outcome of a lack of communication between the police and sections of black youth. This lack of communication helped to build stereotypes and to reproduce situations of conflict. The Committee explained this process thus:

> There are examples throughout our evidence of the way in which a simple situation builds up to a confrontation. A policeman's mode of address is resented by a black youth sensitive to insult; the youth replies with what the policeman sees as insolence, often accompanied by gesticulation; the policeman counters with what the youth sees as hostile formality. Neither understands the other's point of view; each sees the other as a threat. The youth says he is being picked on because he is black and the policeman is immediately in a dilemma. If he takes firm action he can be accused of racial bias by black people, if he doesn't he is open to the same accusation by white people.
>
> *(Ibid.* 69)

The Committee recommended that a programme of action should be implemented to improve communication, including more training and schemes to improve relations with the black communities in 'problem areas' *(ibid.* 92-5). It concluded that such a positive programme of action could ensure that better relations were re-established between young blacks and the police:

> If the best examples of leadership in police and immigrant relations prevailed throughout forces in the United Kingdom, many of the difficulties we have dwelt upon would, within a reasonable space of time, diminish. In some places they could wither away.
>
> *(Ibid.* 92)

From this perspective the situation in some localities, although 'explosive' and dangerous, could be defused if the pressures which produced tension between young blacks and the police were dealt with.

This was a hope that was to remain unfulfilled throughout the 1970s, since the production of the Select Committee's Report on *Police/Immigrant Relations* coincided with a marked politicisation of debates about black youth, and police and crime during the period 1972-6. This politicization, occurring as it did at a time of upheaval about 'race and immigration' more generally, was reflected in frequent media reports, official documents, and speeches by politicians, police officers and other opinion leaders.[18] From the summer of 1972 it focused particularly on the supposed involvement of young blacks in forms of street crime popularly defined as 'mugging'.[19]

'Mugging', social control and young blacks

The social construction of the question of 'mugging' and black youth during the early 1970s represents perhaps the clearest example of how the politicisation of this issue came about. The genesis and development of official, police and media ideologies about 'mugging' has been analysed and commented on from a number of angles during the last fifteen years, and I do not want to retrace the steps of existing accounts. In this section I shall focus on one aspect of this phenomenon; namely, the inter-play during the early 1970s of images of 'black youth' and 'mugging' and the consequences of this process for policy and practice in relation to young blacks.

As I have shown in [chapter 2], during the 1960s the political debate about the 'second generation' of young blacks became synonymous with images of alienation, despair, a lack of equal opportunity and urban disorder. The concern by the early 1970s, as we have already seen in the previous section, was beginning to shift towards the involvement of young blacks in 'muggings' and other forms of street crime.[20] This shift reached its peak during the period from 1972-6, when the 'moral panic' about the mugging issue was at its height in both the press and in official discourses, reaching the point where Enoch Powell could publicly declare mugging to be essentially a 'black crime' (*The Guardian*, 12 April 1976).

The history of the media and popular response to the 'mugging' issue has been analysed in some detail by Hall *et al.* in *Policing the Crisis* (1978). The premise of this study is that the construction of black communities as 'social problems' was the ideological bedrock on which the black youth/urban deprivation/street crime model of mugging was constructed during the early seventies. Mugging as a political phenomenon, according to Hall *et al.*, became associated with black youth because they were seen as:

(a) a social group which suffered the most direct impact of the cycle of poverty, unemployment and social alienation which afflicted inner city areas; and

(b) suffering from the added disadvantage of belonging to a racial group with a 'weak' culture and high levels of social problems, such as broken families and lack of achievement in schools (Hall *et al.*, 1978: chapter 10)

The power of these images according to this study derived partly from popular common sense images about 'race' and the 'inner cities', but also from the feelings of uncertainty which were developing within British society as a whole about the position of black communities and their role within the dominant institutions (*ibid.* 346-9).

This contradictory response to the growth of permanent black communities in many inner city areas coincided with growing concern about 'inner city problems' and the impact of multiple deprivation on the residents of localities with a combination of problems arising out of:

(a) the rising levels of crime and violence which afflicted particular areas of cities;

(b) the emergence of racial disadvantage and inequality as a particular aspect of the social conditions of inner city areas; and

(c) the development of 'ghetto areas' with distinct cultural values and attitudes towards law and order and the police.[21]

Such concerns about the changing character of the inner city areas were intrinsically imbued with racial overtones as well, since the localities which were defined as particularly problematic — in terms of poverty, poor housing, lack of jobs, broken families and crime — were those of high levels of black settlement. Problems of the 'inner city' were therefore often synonymous with questions about 'race'.

Hall *et al.* note, for example, that even in areas where young blacks were a small minority of the total youth population, the issue of crime on the streets became intimately tied with the category of 'black youth'. This ideological construction became possible because during the period from the early 1970s onwards a dominant concern about the 'ghetto areas' focused on the supposed drift of young blacks into a life of crime and poverty. According to Hall *et al.*,

> For all practical purposes, the terms 'mugging' and 'black crime' are now virtually synonymous. In the first 'mugging' panic, as we have shown, though 'mugging' was continually shadowed by the theme of race and crime, this link was rarely made explicit. This is no longer the case. The two are indissolubly linked: each term references the other in both the official and public consciousness.
>
> (Hall *et al.*, 1978: 217)

This convergence of concerns about race, crime and the 'ghetto areas' onto the category of black youth thus involved a combination of images which linked particular areas to specific types of crime, and these crimes to a specific category of the local population. The definition of 'criminal areas' in everyday police practices thus gained a clear racial dimension, which was in turn further accentuated by the wider social and economic processes which confined black communities to inner city localities and excluded them from equal participation in the labour market and in society more generally.

The politicisation of the 'mugging' question occurred with reference to a number of issues which preoccupied both government agencies and the police. Chief among these were (a) a breakdown of consent to policing in certain areas; (b) confrontations between the police and young blacks; and (c) a concern that Britain was becoming a 'violent society'. I shall comment on each of these themes in turn before moving to the broader question of the racialisation of crime and the threat of urban disorder.

(a) Breakdown of consent and 'problem areas'

A glimpse of the everyday confrontations and conflictual situations between the police and sections of the black community can be found in the evidence collected by the Select Committee during 1971-2 on *Police/Immigrant Relations,* the press coverage of this issue during the early 1970s and the activities of various groups within black communities which prioritised the issue of policing as a central complaint. But it was during the period of 1972-6 that the issue of declining consent to policing and the development of volatile problem areas became a major theme in public debate about policing (Humphry, 1972; Alderson and Stead, 1973; Cain, 1973; Pulle, 1973). This was a theme also in the government's response to the Select Committee Report, which was published in October 1973. After noting that the question of policing black communities was not just a problem for the police, it went on to argue that

The police are of course only one element of the society which is confronted by this challenge. While part of the test is the extent to which coloured people are treated by the police on the same terms as white people, any failure of the rest of society, in employment, in housing and elsewhere, to accept coloured citizens on equal terms would undermine the efforts made by the police and leave them facing forms of discontent which spring from causes outside their control.

(Home Office, 1973: 5)

This image of wider forces at work which delegitimised the role of the police pervades the government's response, although it also makes the point that only a 'small minority' of young blacks were opposed to the police, while the majority were 'law-abiding'.[22]

At a more popular level this issue of a lack of consent to the police role was regularly mentioned in press coverage in both the popular and the serious press.[23] The imagery of American writings on the black ghettoes was transposed onto the British situation — with areas such as Brixton, Notting Hill and Handsworth being compared to the streets of Harlem, Watts and other black ghettoes.[24] The questions being asked amounted to asking: Why are young blacks being driven to crime? How can they be re-socialised into the dominant values of society?

Within the terms of this debate the central preoccupation was how to reverse past patterns and ensure that the growing tensions between young blacks and the police did not result in them becoming permanently 'alienated' from British society and its values. Indeed one writer argued that the alienation of many black youngsters from the police was already complete, and that it would require a fundamental programme of positive action at a national level to reverse the situation.[25] Writing in the *New Statesman* in October 1972 Colin McGlashan, a perceptive journalistic observer of the race relations scene, commented that

> It is hard not to feel that race relations in England are at five minutes to midnight. The 'second generation' of black teenagers, born in this country or formed by it, are starting to have children of their own. Far too often they are growing up without fathers, in areas that are not racially exclusive but which in most other ways increasingly resemble in their institutions and attitudes the US ghettoes. Having been left outside most of society's benefits, their morality does not involve staying inside its rules.

(McGlashan, 1972: 497)

In the numerous official, political and media references to 'community relations' and 'police/immigrant' relations this concern about the consequences of growing black 'alienation' and exclusion for society and for public order remained an underlying theme. Whilst not necessarily stated in these terms the main fear was that the growth of black disadvantage, and the involvement of sections of the black community in criminal and semi-criminal activities, would produce a political response from both the black communities and the white majority that would threaten social stability and order. This was seen to be a particularly important phenomenon in certain localities where the factors I have discussed above had produced tension between young blacks and the police.

The issue of 'mugging' was therefore intimately linked to wider conceptions about the social problems faced by young blacks in areas of the country that were popularly and officially identified as 'problem areas'.

(b) Confrontations between young blacks and the police

During the early 1970s it also became clear that everyday confrontations about minor issues could easily escalate into open conflict and acts of collective protest on the streets. This phenomenon had already been noted in media coverage and in the Select Committee's 1971-2 Report, but the level of tension mounted during 1973-6 in a sequence of incidents which can now, with the benefit of hindsight, be seen as presaging the larger-scale disturbances during the 1980s.[26] This included the widely reported confrontation in June 1973 between black youth, the police and the wider black community in Brockwell Park, south London. The events were widely reported in the popular and serious press, and in black journals such as *Race Today*.[27] One of the features of the reporting of this event centred on the image of the events as a 'race riot' and as a sign of larger riots and disorders on the horizon. This theme became more pronounced once it was clear that the Brockwell Park incident was not merely an isolated incident, and that outbreaks of a similar kind were becoming part of the everyday experience of many inner city localities.

The immediate causes for such outbreaks were often small incidents which escalated through rumour and counter-rumour, leading to the arrival of more police and more young blacks to join in the fray.[28] But the underlying conditions which helped to create the basis for such confrontations were a much more complex issue . As early as 1970 John's study of Handsworth had noted that 'the massive breakdown of relations between the police and the black community' held the potential for violent unrest. Attempting to describe black feelings about the local police he says:

> The police station in Thornhill Road is one of the buildings most dreaded and most hated by black Handsworth. It is commonplace to hear references made to 'the pigs at Thornhill Road', or 'Babylon House', or 'the place where the thugs hang out'.
>
> (John, 1970: 22)

Attitudes such as this helped to create a climate of opinion in areas such as Handsworth where the actions of the police were being questioned and at times actively resisted both by young blacks and older members of the community. At the same time the police themselves were adopting in practice a belligerent attitude to all forms of black cultural and social activity which could be described as either 'alien' or 'deviant'. Thus, during the period from 1969 onwards there were numerous reports in the media of confrontations between the police and young blacks and the police in places such as youth clubs, restaurants and other locations which had become identified as 'trouble spots' or as places where criminal activities thrived. Notable examples include the confrontations at the Mangrove restaurant in Notting Hill and the Metro youth club in the same locality.[29] Confrontations between young blacks and the police were also reported in places such as Brixton, Chapeltown in Leeds, Handsworth in Birmingham, Liverpool, and Moss Side in Manchester.[30]

While the extent and scale of the confrontations cannot be compared to the post-1980 riots (which I shall discuss in chapters 6 and 7) their impact was sufficient to produce a sharp debate on the issue of police–black relations and the policing of inner city localities in both the national media and in black journals and police journals.[31] The underlying themes in much of this debate, which to some extent continue to influence perceptions of this issue today, revolved around three fundamental questions:

(1) What factors explained the increasingly volatile and confrontationary relationship between young blacks and the police?

(2) What were likely to be the medium- and long-term consequences of this confrontationary situation?

(3) How could the causes of this situation be tackled so that the likelihood of future violent confrontations be reduced?

The highly politicised nature of these questions, however, meant that the answers provided to these questions by different interests reflected differing interpretations of the reasons why the confrontations between young blacks and the police were becoming more evident on the streets of inner city localities. Thus, while the police journals tended to emphasise such issues as lack of communication and the influence of politicised black groups, the tenor of comments in the black journals and newspapers focused on such issues as police harassment or maltreatment and the racism of British society more generally.

Such contrasts and conflicting interpretations of the relations between young blacks and the police were themselves a reflection of wider preoccupations about the future of 'race relations' in urban localities that were experiencing major transformations in their economic, social, political and cultural institutions (CCCS Race and Politics Group, 1982; Gilroy, 1987). During this time the racialisation of political debates about urban policy and social policy more generally was reaching new heights through the interventions of Enoch Powell and the articulation of public concern about the immigration of Ugandan Asians. It was also during this period that the imagery of 'violence' and 'decay' became synonymous with those inner city localities in which black migrants had settled and established themselves.

(c) Towards a 'violent society'

The final factor which helped shape the politicisation of the 'mugging' issue was the wider picture of societal concern about the 'growing problem' of violence, disorder and a breakdown of law and order in British society. Although this phenomenon was not always linked to popular and official perceptions of 'race, crime and policing', the volatile racialisation of political debate during the early 1970s helped to bring the two issues together in popular discourse.[32]

In an important debate on the Queen's Speech to Parliament at the height of the public debate about 'mugging' the linking of arguments about 'black crime' to this wider concern became apparent. The debate was ostensibly on the general theme of 'social problems' and was called by the Labour opposition. But as Shirley Williams pointed out in her opening remarks, this was one of the few sessions when the House of Commons had discussed in detail 'the future directions in which our society is moving', particularly the 'crisis in the cities' *(Hansard,* vol. 863, 1973: col. 315). For Williams the situation in many inner city localities was the most critical in over a century, particularly in relation to policing, social deprivation, housing, education and juvenile delinquency. The centrality of youth to this scenario was made clear by the remark that

> Young people, white and black, in increasing numbers (are) moving into cities such as Birmingham and London, often in desperate and futile pursuit of better pay, amenities and conditions. They have themselves become a large floating element among the homeless and ... an element that is particularly disturbing to the police, because it is this reservoir of homeless youngsters who, unless emergency action is taken, will become the young criminals of the next decade.
>
> *(Ibid.* col. 320)

This was a theme taken up throughout the debate by MPs from all political parties, and also by sections of the media covering this and other debates in parliament during this period.[33] Indeed the Home Secretary, Robert Carr, emphasised the importance of ensuring that law and order was maintained in the inner city localities, and that disadvantaged groups were not allowed to drift into a vicious circle of disadvantage, alienation, violence and crime *(ibid.* cols. 327-9).

In most of the speeches during this, and related debates of the time, the connection between the 'growing problem' of violence and disorder with 'race' was established in coded terms: largely through references to 'urban problems' and 'pressures on services'. But some MPs, most notably John Stokes and Ivor Stanbrook. linked the growth of violence to the issue of immigration and their impact on urban localities. Stokes used a number of examples from his West Midlands constituency to show how 'mugging' and growing violence were linked to the admission of 'very large numbers of coloured immigrants', a phenomenon which he saw as fundamentally changing the cultural values and relationships that had shaped such areas over the centuries. He warned that if successive governments uprooted indigenous people to make way for 'new, quite alien peoples', that the country would lose the basis of its national identity and cultural fabric *(ibid.* cols. 371-2).

Views such as these, along with those of Powell, were still not acceptable to the main ideologues of the Conservative party, and were certainly a minority viewpoint.[34] But within the wider public debate the questions of immigration and crime became closely interwoven. 'Jobless young blacks' became a powerful symbol that helped link the issue of 'race' to crime and violence, and a politically sensitive symbol as well. In sharp contrast to the reporting of riots during the 1980s, for example, the BBC report on the Brockwell Park incident of June 1973 omitted to mention that the youths involved were black. In response the Monday Club accused the BBC of trying to cover up a 'race riot' in order to avoid open debate about the 'consequences' of immigration. Describing the situation in Brixton during the aftermath of the Brockwell Park incident Paul

Harrison described local black leaders as seeing the events as 'an outbreak of spontaneous anger at what appeared an obvious injustice' (Harrison, 1973: 672). After cataloguing the examples of injustice which were reported to him by local residents, including the tactics of the local police of the Special Patrol Group, and the 'harassment' of young blacks, Harrison prophetically concluded that 'there will certainly be more confrontations, more unnecessary arrests, and more tension. It is a self-fuelling process' (*ibid.* 673).

By the mid-1970s therefore, confrontations on the streets between the police and young blacks had become a central feature of the political agenda about race.[35] Yet, the consequences of this politicisation remained to be worked out in practice.

Policing, racialisation and 'black crime'

The question of the involvement of young blacks in 'mugging' and other forms of street crime remains very much a current issue in political and policy debates. This can be seen partly in the regularity with which stories in the media about mugging refer either directly or in coded terms to the involvement of young blacks.[36] But since the 1970s the issue of 'mugging' *per se* has been overdetermined by other preoccupations about 'black crime', which involve broader issues about 'race relations' as well.

At least two processes seem to be at work. First, the growing politicisation of debates about the social and economic conditions within the black communities has broadened concern out from a preoccupation with young blacks as such towards the wider communities within which the younger generation lived. In this sense debates about 'black crime' signify concern about the crisis of the 'urban black colonies' (Hall *et al.*, 1978: 338-9). Second, the period since the mid-1970s is one in which the question of 'black youth' has become intimately tied to the broader issues of disorder and violent protest, particularly in localities of high levels of black settlement.

The period from 1974-8 saw a number of examples of the material importance of these shifts in political language. The most important were the attempts by Enoch Powell and other politicians to politicise the debate about 'black crime', and the occurrence of small-scale riots in areas such as Notting Hill in 1976 and 1977, and in other localities from 1977 onwards.

(a) 'Black crime' and the political agenda

As we saw earlier the 1971-2 Select Committee Report on *Police/Immigrant Relations* had concluded that on balance 'coloured immigrants are not more involved in crime than others'. But it seems clear from John's research in Handsworth and from much of the evidence in the Report's appendices that a stereotype of areas of black settlement as 'criminal areas' was already deeply entrenched in police mythology. The Report itself notes that despite the lack of evidence to support a link between blacks and crime

> There seems to be a fairly widespread feeling, shared, as we found in informal discussion, by some police officers, that immigrants commit more crime than the indigenous population.
>
> (Select Committee, 1972, Report: 22)

The public debate about 'mugging' helped to amplify and popularise the perception, and the issue of 'black crime' was firmly placed on the political agenda. A number of stages in this process were particularly important.

First, the release in January 1975 by the Metropolitan Police of figures from a study of victims' descriptions of assailants in the Brixton area of London. This claimed to show that 79 per cent of robberies and 83 per cent of offences of theft from the person were carried out by black people.[37] This study was widely reported in the media and helped to attract attention to the 'growing problem' of black involvement in crime and the destabilising role of young disillusioned blacks.

Second, in May 1975 Judge Gwyn Morris jailed five young West Indians for 'mugging' offences in south London. In sentencing them he commented:

> These attacks have become a monotonous feature in the suburbs of Brixton and Clapham, areas which within memory were peaceful, safe, and agreeable places to live in. But immigration resettlement, which has occurred over the past 25 years has radically transformed that environment.
>
> *(The Guardian, 16 May 1975)*

He went on to argue that youngsters such as them were collectively a 'frightening menace to society', and that they represented 'immense difficulties' for those interested in the maintenance of law and order.

Third, and perhaps more important in terms of its public impact, Enoch Powell's speech of April 1976 about 'mugging' being a 'racial phenomenon' helped to articulate a wider undercurrent of concern about the inter-relationship between 'race and crime'.[38] Powell's speech was in turn linked to the evidence submitted by the Metropolitan Police in March 1976 to the Select Committee on Race Relations and Immigration. The committee was investigating *The West Indian Community*. In its evidence to the 1972 Select Committee Report on *Police/Immigrant Relations* the Metropolitan Police had not raised black crime as a major problem, but the intervening period had obviously transformed their image of this issue. In the very first paragraph of its evidence the Metropolitan Police mentioned the 'uneasy nature of the relationship between police officers and young blacks' in some localities. Although the memorandum did not argue for a direct link between crime and 'race', and it mentioned the social disadvantages which were common in such areas, it went on to argue that:

> It is not part of our position that there is a causal link between ethnic origin and crime. What our records do suggest is that London's black citizens, among whom those of West Indian origin predominate, are disproportionately involved in many forms of crime. But in view of their heavy concentration in areas of urban stress, which are themselves high crime areas, and in view of the disproportionate numbers of young people in the West Indian population, this pattern is not surprising.
>
> (Select Committee, 1977, Evidence vol. 2: 182).

Whether surprising or not this analysis was to prove extremely controversial, and was directly criticised in the evidence submitted by the Community Relations Commission, to which the Metropolitan Police responded with additional evidence to support their claims.[39] The public debate over these statistics helped to push 'black crime' onto the political agenda in a way which gave legitimacy both to popular concern about crime on the streets and to the arguments of politicians such as Powell who called for 'repatriation' as the only solution to crime and disorder.

(b) Riots and violent disorder

As argued above the symbolic threat of violent disorder was a theme in official political language about young blacks from the late 1960s onwards. But in August 1976 it became a material reality, on the streets of Notting Hill. During the annual Carnival in the area a major confrontation took place between young blacks (and to some extent young whites) and the police.[40] Although not on the same level as the events in St Paul's, Brixton, Toxteth, Handsworth and Tottenham during the 1980s the symbolic significance of this event was clear at the time and has been reiterated with some regularity ever since. In a recent speech, for example, Kenneth Newman has argued that the events at the 1976 Notting Hill Carnival were at the time a unique phenomenon, and represented an important watershed in the severity of public disorder that the police had to deal with (Newman, 1986: 9). He argues:

> In relation to public disorder, the major changes over the last decade can be easily followed. In 1976, following the riot at the Notting Hill Carnival, defensive shields were introduced; five years later, after petrol bombs were used, we added flameproof clothing and metal helmets; and last year, after the police were shot at, plastic baton rounds were deployed, but not used.
>
> (*Ibid.* 9)

The unstated issue which links all these events together was that the confrontations mentioned all involved young blacks in one way or another. Other less major confrontations also took place in November 1975 in Chapeltown (Leeds), and in other localities. During this period police activities under the 'sus' legislation and through the Special Patrol Group often led to frequent instances of lower level confrontations between the police and young blacks (Demuth, 1978; Hall *et al.*, 1978; AFFOR, 1978). More broadly the concern with the 'growing problem' of black crime helped to make the police on the ground suspect of all black youngsters, and particularly those who congregated in groups. The imagery of violent street crime combined with that of violent street disorders and confrontations to make every young black, or particularly groups of them (such as Rastafarians), a potential suspect in police eyes. They were suspect not only because of social perceptions about their involvement in street crime, but because they were black, because of the areas in which they lived, their style of dress and social contact, and their leisure activities. This is certainly how an increasing number of younger blacks, along with their parents and independent researchers, saw the situation in many inner city localities — particularly those that were seen as 'immigrant areas'.

It was because of this 'growing problem' that Robert Mark, the Metropolitan Police Commissioner, chose to highlight in his annual Report for 1975, even before the Notting Hill disturbances, the fact that there was a tendency within black communities 'for groups of black people to react in violent opposition to police officers carrying out their lawful duties' *(Report of the Commissioner of Police of the Metropolis for the year 1975,* 1976: 12). This was a theme taken up in articles in police journals and by official police documents during this period. The widely publicised Metropolitan Police evidence to the Select Committee investigation on *The West Indian Community* stated the official police wisdom and common sense on the subject when it noted that

> Recently there has been a growth in the tendency for members of London's West Indian communities to combine against police by interfering with police officers who are affecting the arrest of a black person or who are in some other way enforcing the law in situations which involve black people. In the last 12 months forty such incidents have been recorded. Each carries a potential for large scale disorder; despite the fact that very few situations actually escalate to the point where local police are unable to cope. Experience indicates that they are more likely to occur during the summer months and that the conflict is invariably with young West Indians. They can occur anywhere in the Metropolitan Police District, but are of course more likely in those areas which have a high proportion of West Indian settlers.
>
> (Select Committee, 1977, Evidence, vol. 2: 178)

This perception was repeated across the country in the areas where confrontations between young blacks and the police, and growing tension between them, had become a major local issue. Within this context references to urban disorder and street violence became a synonym for confrontations between young blacks and the police.

During 1976 and 1977 other widely reported incidents helped to fuel public and policy debate about the policing of multi-racial areas, particularly in a context of growing tension between young blacks and the police. First, the killing of an Asian youth, Gurdip Singh Chaggar, in Southall during June 1976 sparked off concern about a lack of concern by the police about racial attacks on young blacks as opposed to their preoccupation with 'black crime'.[41] Second, the 1976 Carnival violence was repeated again in 1977 and led to public concern about whether such outbreaks of violent disorder were becoming a regular feature of 'police–black youth' confrontations in inner city localities.

Third, in August 1977 confrontations took place in the Ladywood area of Birmingham and the Lewisham area of London. Both these disturbances involved clashes between the National Front and anti-fascist groups, but it was the involvement of young blacks and the police that became the central issue.

These three incidents helped to ensure that public debate about 'black crime' and 'street violence' in predominantly black localities reached a new crescendo during 1977 and 1978. In Lewisham, for example, the National Front claimed that they were demonstrating against 'mugging', claiming that the local police had long known that the area was a centre of 'black crime'.[42] Indeed they referred to the fact that in October

1976 the police in Peckham had issued a statement which drew attention to the rise in 'muggings' carried out by young blacks. In the case of the 'Ladywood riots' press coverage drew attention to the underlying issue of 'the gradual souring and separation of black youth and authority' *(The Observer,* 21 August 1977).

Apart from the national trends discussed above, it is also clear that the response of the police in areas such as Notting Hill, Brixton, Handsworth and Moss Side further accentuated the stereotype of young blacks (or at least a section of them) as members of a 'criminal subculture'. At a common sense level the everyday contact between young blacks and the police was interpreted through police ideologies as involving a clash between the cultural values of the majority community and those of the minority communities caught up in a web of poverty, unemployment, racial disadvantage and alienation. But such notions about the nature of the 'racial problem' which the police faced in many urban localities were in turn supported by common sense notions about the localities in which the black communities tended to be concentrated in, and the socio-economic conditions which confronted young blacks in inner city localities. This helped to create symbols which the police could easily identify as the source of the problem, whether at the individual level (in terms of 'criminal' young blacks) or at the level of geographical localities ('criminal areas'). This process in turn helped to give further support to the notion that the source of the problem lay in the culture and attitudes of young blacks, with racism and discrimination seen as playing only a subsidiary role.

Gus John, to whose 1970 study of Handsworth I referred earlier, has characterised this position as one in which there is an ascription of certain fixed attributes onto the category of 'black youth'.

> The state, the police, the media and race relations experts ascribe to young blacks certain collective qualities, e.g. alienated, vicious little criminals, muggers, disenchanted, unemployed, unmarried mothers, truants, classroom wreckers, etc. The youth workers, community workers, counsellors and the rest, start with these objective qualities as given, and intervene on the basis that through their operations they could render young blacks subjectively different, and make them people to whom these objective qualities could no longer be applied. When this is done in collaboration with control agents themselves, as in police–community liaison schemes, or instances in which professional blacks collaborate with schools in blaming black kids for their 'failure', it is interpreted as progress towards 'good community relations'.
>
> (John, 1981: 155)

Such categorisations of young blacks helped to deflect attention from the legitimacy of any grievances that they actually had about the police, about racism, or other aspects of their daily lives and focus policy concern on their characteristics or the 'problems' caused by their communal or family backgrounds. During the period of the mid- to late 1970s this process became clear in relation to young blacks who adopted the style and cultural values of Rastafarianism, and who in areas such as Handsworth and Brixton became an easy target for police stereotyping and attracted the attention of other central and local government agencies.[43] Some observers had argued forcefully that the central question about young blacks was not what is wrong with them, but what is wrong with the society which denies them justice and equal rights (McGlashan, 1972; Humphry 1972; Moore 1975). But such arguments about the origins of the problem in social inequality and unequal power relations were easily lost in the maelstrom of common sense images and explanations about the 'problem of criminal and unemployed young blacks'.

The situation in Handsworth during 1976-7 is an example of the impact of such debates on particular localities. The police in the Handsworth area had for long been at the forefront of initiatives which aimed to improve relations between young blacks and the police. In the evidence submitted by the Birmingham Police to the Select Committee investigation on *Police/Immigration Relations*, the police had noted that they did not believe an 'isolated police effort' could deal with the young unemployed West Indians of Handsworth, and they recommended an 'integrated social resources' approach (Select Committee, 1972, Evidence, vol. 2: 446-7). Yet the area became known as Birmingham's 'angry suburb', and as an area with a massive potential for disorder and conflict. In a series of articles during May 1976 on Handsworth the *Birmingham Evening Mail* analysed the tensions below the surface of the area, the plight of unemployed young blacks, and the everyday tensions between young blacks and the police.[44] A year later, in the aftermath of the 'Ladywood riots' *The Observer* provided the following vivid description of one confrontation between young blacks and the police:

> Birmingham's Soho Road at half-past nine last Monday night: fluid groups of edgy young blacks on the pavements. A blue-and-white police Allegro cruises over the traffic lights. With a sudden jagged movement, a group hurls bricks, sticks and bottles at the car, crunching into the windows and bonking on the metalwork
>
> . . .
>
> Missiles clatter on shop doors and one shatters plate glass. The car slews to a stop and half a dozen youths bombard it from 15 feet. 'Babylon' yells a voice, and the blacks dart outwards, sprinting around corners as a police squad with riot shields and the occasional dustbin lid moves to the stranded panda car.
>
> (*The Observer*, 21 August 1977)

At the same time the local press in Birmingham during this period is full of stories about young West Indians confronting the police in the Bull Ring Shopping Centre and other localities.[45] Such events helped to create a climate in which the local police became centrally preoccupied with the issue of 'young unemployed blacks'.

This concern was in turn fuelled by the study carried out in 1977 by John Brown into the question of relations between young blacks and the police in Handsworth. Published in November 1977 under the title *Shades of Grey*, the essence of the study was an analysis of the issues of crime and violence in the area, particularly as they related to a group defined by Brown as consisting of 200 or so 'Dreadlocks' who 'form a criminalised sub-culture' and whose actions helped to create and reproduce tensions between the black community and the police (Brown, 1977: 7-8). For Brown the activities of this group of 'criminalised' youngsters needed to be counteracted by a combination of improved police contacts with the local communities and wider social policy measures. One result of the study was the strategy of 'community policing' developed by Superintendent David Webb during 1977–81, which aimed to create through direct police intervention more peaceful contacts between the local black communities and the police.[46] But perhaps its broader impact was to help popularise the notion that the 'Dreadlock' minority of black youth was the source of the problem. In their detailed sociological study of the Handsworth area John Rex and Sally Tomlinson commented that *Shades of Grey* fitted in with the popular image in the media that British society was being threatened by a 'menacing group of strangers', and that they found no evidence in their study for the existence of a group of 200 'Dreadlocks' who terrorized the area and committed crimes (Rex and Tomlinson, 1979: 231-2). Such reasoned critiques of Brown did not prevent his sensational account of Handsworth from gaining wide coverage in the press and thus helping to popularise dominant police stereotypes of the situation.[47]

Brown's sensational account of the Handsworth situation notwithstanding, the late 1970s saw a further escalation of concern about police–black youth relations — particularly in the context of growing black youth unemployment. Tensions were reaching new levels and the evidence of conflict and violent confrontations was becoming more clear as time went by.

Describing the situation in areas such as Brixton and Handsworth during October 1972, Colin McGlashan painted a gloomy picture:

> Relations between police and black youngsters in some areas where the SPG and similar local squads have been repeatedly employed are now poisonous to a degree that is truly frightening; two moderate and unexcitable community workers separately described them to me as 'warfare'.

> (McGlashan, 1972: 497)

If anything the scenario during the late 1970s was one of even more open hostility and conflict. The depth of opposition to police intervention in 'problem areas' was reaching the stage where violent urban unrest was widely accepted as both inevitable and perhaps necessary by sections of the black communities.

A local resident of Handsworth described the groups of young blacks and other residents marching on Thornhill Road police station as 'more pleased than if they'd won the pools' *(The Observer,* 21 August 1977). Such a depth and intensity of opposition to the police was only partly overcome by the 'community policing' approach adopted by the local police in Handsworth from the mid-1970s onwards. Indeed, as we shall see in [chapters 6 and 7] the background to the violent unrest of the 1980s lies precisely in this history of tension and confrontation between young blacks and the police in many localities. The 1970s may not have experienced violent protests of the same level as we have recently seen but the foundations for the breakdown of relations between young blacks and the police were laid during this period.

'Race', crime and statistics

The 1970s then witnessed a complex process by which young blacks came to be seen as intimately involved in (a) particular forms of street crime and (b) confrontations with the police which represented a challenge to the maintenance of law and order. I shall explore the further development of debates about the second issue in [chapters 6 and 7]. For the moment, however, a few remarks are necessary about how the early 1980s marked a further politicisation of the 'black crime' question.

The early 1980s were an important period in the racialisation of debates about law and order, crime and policing in at least two ways. First, the politicisation of the black youth unemployment issue helped to focus attention on the inter-relationship between unemployment and crime. Second, the riots during 1980-1 forced the issues of 'black crime' and violence on the streets onto the mainstream political agenda. The widespread coverage given to the issue of 'race' in connection with the riots helped to open up a wider debate about issues such as 'mugging' and 'black crime' under the wider concern of 'the future of British society'.

In the aftermath of the 1980-1 riots in Bristol, Brixton, Toxteth and elsewhere, one of the most important public debates about 'race and crime' took place during 1982-3. It followed the decision of the Metropolitan Police in March 1982 to release a racial breakdown of those responsible for street robberies, a statistical breakdown which it had not published previously, although it had been collating such statistics for some time (Scotland Yard, *Press Release,* 10 March 1982: *The Guardian,* 11 March 1982). The police statistics showed a marked rise in street robberies, but the crucial statistic which the press and the media picked on was concerned with the 'disproportionate involvement' of young blacks in street crimes such as 'mugging', purse snatching and robbery from stores. The press reaction to the press release varied from sober commentaries on the nature and limitations of the statistics, sensational headlines about 'black crime', to *The Sun's* 'The Yard blames black muggers'. But a common theme was the argument that the statistics, along with the riots during 1980-1, were further evidence of the consequences of letting in alien communities to settle in the very heart of Britain. *The Daily Telegraph* articulated this argument succinctly:

> Over the 200 years up to 1945, Britain became so settled in internal peace that many came to believe that respect for the person and property of fellow citizens was something which existed naturally in all but a few. A glance at less fortunate countries might have reminded us that such respect scarcely exists unless law is above the power of tribe, or money, or the gun. But we did not look; we let in people from the countries we did not look at, and only now do we begin to see the result. Many young West Indians in Britain, and, by a connected process, growing numbers of young whites, have no sense that the nation in which they live is part of them. So its citizens become to them mere objects of violent exploitation.
>
> (11 March 1982)

Such an argument amounted to a direct link between 'race' and 'crime'. A similar tone was adopted by papers such as the *Daily Mail* and *The Sun,* which went even further in their use of images of 'mugging' — harking back to Powell's 1976 definition of mugging as essentially a 'black crime'. A year later the intervention of Harvey Proctor, the right-wing Tory MP, helped to secure the release of similar figures by the Home Office and led to a similar wave of articles in the press about the 'rising wave' of crime in areas of black settlement.[48] Since then the Metropolitan Police have been much more reticent about publishing such statistics (although they continue to be kept), because of their potentially volatile political impact.

Not surprisingly, however, the issue of the involvement of young blacks in criminal or quasi-criminal activities remains a key area of concern for the police and other institutions, both locally and nationally. Because of this climate of official concern the issues of 'crime' and 'violence', which I have analysed in some detail in this chapter, remain central to the full understanding of how contemporary ideologies about young blacks as a social category were formed and how they are being transformed .

What is clear is that the successive shifts in political language about the black youth question throughout the period since the early 1970s have involved the issues of policing and 'black crime' as a central theme. Whether in terms of specific concerns about 'mugging', 'street crime', or with more general concerns about the development of specific subcultures, such as Rastafarianism, among young blacks, the interplay between images of 'race' and 'crime' has remained an important symbol in political language. Since the late 1970s, and particularly after the 1980–1 riots, political debates about the 'black crime' issue have also been overdetermined by the phenomenon of urban unrest and civil disorder. But even within this context the issues of 'race, crime and the ghetto' which I have analysed in this chapter remain the bedrock for the shifts in official ideologies and public debate about 'black youth'.

This also helps to explain the increasingly politicised nature of the response to the two issues which I shall analyse in the rest of this book: namely, black youth unemployment and violent urban unrest. The ideological construction of the involvement of young blacks in mugging and other forms of street crime provided the basis for the development of strategies of control aimed at keeping young blacks off the streets and keeping the police in control of particular localities which had become identified both in popular and official discourses as 'crime-prone' or potential 'trouble-spots'. It also helped to bring to the forefront a preoccupation with the social and economic roots of alienation and criminal activity among young blacks. This was reflected in the debate about the impact of unemployment on young blacks, which I shall analyse in detail in [chapters 4 and 5]. But it was also reflected in the increasing preoccupation of the police and other social control agencies with particular localities where relations between the police and sections of the black community were becoming tense and politicised. This issue will be analysed in [chapters 6 and 7], particularly in relation to the experience of urban unrest since 1980.

Conclusion

What, then, was the nature of the concern with the 'problem' of the increasing involvement of young blacks in 'crime'? To recap briefly, it has been argued in this chapter that throughout the 1970s there was a tendency to pin down the dangers posed by specific groups of the black population: particularly the young, the criminalised, the militants, the Rastafarians, and finally the unemployed. While recognising in some form the relevance of deep social inequalities and urban decay as factors determining the position of young blacks, a continuing preoccupation throughout the 1970s was the connection between deprivation and supposedly pathological or weak black cultures which produced 'special' problems for young blacks. This ideology had the effect of externalising the source of the 'problem', and locating it firmly within the black communities themselves. The net result of this process of externalisation was that official thinking and policy initiatives were constructed on the basis that young blacks were a 'social problem', which was taking shape within the very heart of the major inner city areas. The phenomenon of street crime, particularly mugging, was a symbol of a broader process through which young blacks were constructed both in policy and popular discourses as caught up in a vicious circle of unemployment, poverty, homelessness, crime and conflict with the police. This was encapsulated in Enoch Powell's statement in 1976 that mugging was a 'racial crime', with black youth as the main actors.

By the late 1970s the image of the areas of black settlement as urban ghettos which bred a culture of poverty, unemployment and crime came to dominate both official reports and media coverage of black youth questions. In the short space of time between the late 1940s and 1970s the question of young blacks had shifted from a marginal item on the policy agenda of state and other institutions to become a major preoccupation of the main race relations institutions, government departments, the police, local authorities and a number of voluntary agencies. But this transformation was to be superseded by the substantive changes in (a) the employment prospects of young blacks from the late 1970s onwards, and (b) by the massive transformations in the politics of racism and urban unrest during the decade from 1976 to 1986. It is to these issues that the rest of this book will be devoted, since they tell us much about the articulation between class, 'race' and youth issues in contemporary Britain, as we move towards the 1990s.

Notes

1. The early twentieth-century anti-immigrant political mobilisation was resonant with references to the link between crime and immigration. See for example the account of this theme in Gainer, 1972: 51-3, 203-6. This is not to argue that the images applied to the largely Jewish immigrants of that time were the same as those applied to the black migrants of the post-1945 period. But the continuities are ones which do warrant some closer examination; see Miles and Solomos, 1987.

2. See Harris and Solomos, forthcoming; for a more general review of this question, but one which does not analyse the historical issues in any detail, see Gilroy, 1987.

3. The 1969 report on *Colour and Citizenship* by Rose *et al.*, contained numerous examples of how the questions of law and order and policing were beginning to surface as important areas of concern for the black communities and for the official institutions themselves.

4. The circular was linked to an overall rethinking of government policy on race and policing, which evolved along the lines that there was a need for 'special measures' to foster good relations between the police and black communities. See Lambert, 1970: 177-87.

5. Examples of this trend are the following: *IRR Newsletter*, 'Immigrants and the police', September 1967; H. Rose, 'The police and the coloured communities', *IRR Newsletter*, October 1968; D. Nandy, 'Immigrants and the police', *Race and Immigration*, October 1970.

6. For a general overview of the history of the debate about 'race and policing' see Gordon, 1985. On the specific period of the late 1960s and early 1970s see: *Race Today*, June 1969; September 1970; June 1972; November 1972; and December 1973.

7. The assumption seems to be that one can treat the issue of policing as almost synonymous with the 'youth' question. But this has meant that the particular reasons for the confrontations between the police and young blacks, as opposed to the black communities as a whole, have remained unexplored.

8. This theme has been explored in some detail in Solomos, 1985, where I show how the construction of the 'alienation' issue depended on the policy concerns of both central and local government institutions. See also Gaskell and Smith, 1981.

9. An exploratory analysis of the dynamics of black political mobilisation and state responses can be found in Mullard, 1982. Few attempts have been made to analyse the complex processes which led to the formation of a 'black political consciousness'. But for a descriptive account see Ramdin, 1987.

10. A review of other reports and studies of this period can be found in Gordon, 1985.

11. See Suganya Ranganathan, 'Race relations, law and order and policing', PhD Thesis, Aston University, in preparation.

12. One measure of this concern is the increasing coverage given to this issue in journals such as *Race Today* and in papers such as *The Times* and *The Guardian*. See also the regular coverage of this question in the Runnymede Trust's Race and Immigration during 1969-73.

13. *Race Today*, October 1970 and November 1971.

14. *The Observer*, 15 November 1970, 'It's hell to be young (and black) in Handsworth'; *The Sunday Times*, 4 January 1970, 'Must Harlem come to Birmingham?'

15. For a general review of this history see Benyon, 1986b; but in particular see: Humphry, 1972; Banton, 1973; Pulle, 1973; Demuth, 1978. See also the theoretical and analytical arguments in Jefferson and Clarke, 1973, and Hall *et al.*, 1978.

16. See the discussion of the language and interpretation of this report in Clarke *et al.*, 1974, for an explication of its role in articulating political ideologies about the police-community relations dynamic.

17. This is not to deny the pertinence of analysing the origins of official ideologies about this issue before this report, and this is something that clearly needs to be done. But the purposes of this study are best served by analysing the genesis and impact of this report in some detail. For the analytical problems posed by the analysis of official texts and discursive frameworks see Burton and Carlen, 1979.

18. This public debate is itself closely reflected in the evidence submitted to the Select Committee, but also in the coverage of 'race and policing' issues in the national and local press. The language used to describe this process was resonant with categorisations of young blacks as a danger to social order and stability.

19. For the social history of the political debate about mugging see Jefferson and Clarke, 1973; Hall *et al.*, 1978.

20. Demuth, 1978, provides a detailed analysis of the legal and policing practices that characterised this shift, particularly in relation to the use of the 'sus' legislation as a mechanism for the social control of young blacks.

21. On the intermingling of political concerns about the 'inner city' with popular concerns about 'race' see Edwards and Batley, 1978; Higgins *et al.*, 1983; Edwards, 1987.

22. This imagery of a 'small minority' working to undermine society from within is something to which I shall return in [chapters 6 and 7].

23. *The Times*, 13 October 1971, 'Police responsibility in race harmony'; *The Sunday Times*, 28 November 1971, 'The life and needless death of the man society spurned'; *The Guardian*, 1 November 1973, 'Police deny catalogue of brutality to immigrants'; *The Sunday Times*, 3 July 1973, 'The disturbing truth behind a mythical "race" riot'.

24. *The Guardian*, 6 February 1970, 'Alabama Staffs'; *The Sunday Times*, 23 July 1973, 'The growing danger of the jobless young blacks'; *The Sunday Times*, 5 January 1975, 'Danger signals from the streets of Lambeth'.

25. P. Harrison, 'Black and white', *New Society*, 21 June 1973.

26. These 'everyday confrontations' have received surprisingly little attention, though they are clearly of great importance to any rounded understanding of the subsequent history of urban unrest and disorder. It is beyond the scope of this study to discuss them in any detail, though it would clearly be of value to see more detailed case studies of the social history of black communities during this time.

27. See various issues of *Race Today* during 1970-6. Also see *Black Liberator*, vol. 2, nos. 1, 2 and 4.

28. See, for example, the reporting of such an incident in *The Sunday Times*, 3 July 1973. Such events were also described in the Select Committee's reports on *Police/Immigrant Relations* (1972) and *The West Indian Community* (1977).

29. *Race Today*, November 1971, 385; A. X. Cambridge, 'On the Metro Saga', *Black Liberator*, 1 (4), 1973, 155-68; P. Medlicot, 'The Brixton scene', *New Society*, 12 April 1973, 64-6.

30. An overall chronology of some of these events can be found in Sivanandan, 1982 and Gilroy, 1987.

31. See the detailed content analysis of these sources in Suganya Ranganathan's 'Race relations, law and order and policing', PhD Thesis, Aston University, in preparation.

32. The linkages between growing official concern about violence and disorder and racialised political discourses are explored in Solomos *et al.*, 1982; Benyon, 1986b; and Gilroy, 1987.

33. *The Times*, 2 November 1973, 'Problems of full employment: immigrants no longer arriving to fill urban jobs'.

34. Such views were criticised widely from within the Conservative party, even though they were supported by a group of MPs belonging to the fringes of the party. But they were widely reported in the press and widely circulated in popular debates about 'race' and immigration issues.

35. This may perhaps be seen as a somewhat exaggerated statement for the period I am discussing here. Yet what the recent riots have made clear is that the expectation of violent confrontations with young blacks is by no means a 1980s phenomenon. See e.g. Newman, 1986.

36. See e.g. J. Shirley, 'Mugging: statistics of an "unacceptable crime"', *The Times*, 14 March 1982; R. Butt, 'Mugging: facing the hard facts', *The Times*, 18 March 1982; R. Butt, 'Who pays for the blues in the night?', *The Times*, 1 April 1982; P. Worsthorne, 'Cant about colour and crime', *The Sunday Telegraph*, 27 March 1983.

37. *The Sunday Times*, 5 January 1975, 'Danger signals from the streets of Lambeth'. But see also Select Committee, 1977, *The West Indian Community*, vol. 2, 'Memorandum by the Community Relations Commission'.

38. *Birmingham Post*, 12 April 1976 and 13 April 1976.

39. Select Committee, 1977, *The West Indian Community*, vol. 2; 'Memorandum by the Metropolitan Police'; 'Memorandum by the Community Relations Commission'; 'Additional Memorandum by the Metropolitan Police'.

40. *The Guardian*, 1 September 1976; *Birmingham Post*, 1 September 1976; *The Guardian*, 31 August 1977; *Birmingham Post*, 31 August 1977; *The Economist*, 4 September 1976, 'London's black carnival'; The Economist, 20 August 1977, 'England's hot summer'.

41. *The Sunday Times*, 8 June 1976, 'Killing stokes new fears of race violence'; Birmingham Post, 9 June 1976, 'Jenkins in surprise visit to Southall'.

42. *The Observer*, 21 August 1977; *The Sunday Times*, 21 August 1977.

43. *Birmingham Post*, 23 March 1976, 'The wild bunch'; *Birmingham Post*, 25 March 1976; *The Economist*, 17 April 1976, 'Not black and white'.

44. *Birmingham Evening Mail*, 11-13 May 1976, 'The angry suburb'; see also readers' responses in the 20 May edition.

45. See references in n. 43.

46. On the social and political context of community policing in Handsworth see Rex and Tomlinson, 1979; Gilroy, 1982; Brown, 1982.

47. *Birmingham Post*, 30 November 1977; *Birmingham Evening Mail*, 8 December 1977; see also the correspondence in the *Birmingham Post* on 6 December 1977.

48. *The Guardian*, 24 March 1983; *The Times*, 24 March 1983; see also New Society, 31 March 1983.

16. Public Perception and Contact with Police

Trevor Jones, Brian Maclean and Jock Young

"It is essential for an organization which lays claim to the description of 'professional' to make every effort to attune itself to the wishes of the public. The Metropolitan Police has an especial obligation in this respect for a number of reasons. Firstly, because its work rests upon the exercise of authority — and occasionally force where necessary — and the legitimacy of that authority rests not only on the fact of the law but also on the will of the community; remove either and the police become oppressive. Secondly, being a huge organization numerically, structurally and geographically, we have been inclined to be impersonal and to have arrogated to ourselves the judgement of what was 'good for' the public. Thirdly, having a centralised headquarters structure in a huge metropolis can work against a local shaping of Force policy."
(K. Newman, *Report of the Commission of Police of the Metropolis,* 1984, p. 7).

In this chapter we analyze the experience of the citizens of Islington in terms of their contacts with the police, their expectations of a reliable police force and their views as to the priorities of tasks in which an effective force should be engaged. We shall start with their priorities.

Public prioritization of policing

As the police have limited time and resources we asked the public to say out of seventeen types of offences — ranging from burglary to racialist attacks — which *five* the police should spend most of their time and energy on.

The highest priorities were as follows:

Table 1   Public priorities of various offences

1.	Robbery with violence in street	70.7%
2.	Sexual assaults on women	69.3%
3.	Use of heroin or hard drugs	59.1%
4.	Burglary of people's houses	58.1%
5.	Drunken driving	43.5%
6.	Racist attacks	39.2%
7.	Vandalism	26.8%
8.	Bag snatching	25.2%
9.	Glue sniffing	22.8%

Trevor Jones, Brian Maclean and Jock Young: 'Public Perception and Contact with Police' from *THE ISLINGTON CRIME SURVEY: CRIME, VICTIMIZATION AND POLICY IN INNER-CITY LONDON* (Gower Publishing Company, 1986), pp. 106-156.

Table 1 (cont/d)   Public priorities of various offences

10.	Unruly behaviour at football matches	21.8%
11.	Use of cannabis	12.8%
12.	Rowdyism in the streets	9.8%
13.	Theft of motor cars	9.1%
14.	Burglary of shops/offices	8.3%
15.	Prostitution	7.5%
16.	Company fraud and embezzlement	6.0%
17.	Shoplifting	3.1%

We have included the full list of the public's five choices of offences on which the police should spend most of their time and energy in order to illustrate the high public consensus over the top five offences and the very low priorities given to many other offences. This is confirmed for the lowest priority offences, when we asked what are *four* offences that the police should spend *least* time on. These were prostitution (53.3%), shoplifting (43.0%), company fraud (37.3%) and rowdyism in the streets (27.7%). Perhaps, more to the point, when we asked which offences the police "spend more time on than is necessary" we found once again prostitution, shoplifting and company fraud but also that 24.3% of the public believed that undue attention was given to cannabis.

Table 2   Offences on which the public believe the police spend more time than necessary

1.	Prostitution	32.7%
2.	Cannabis	24.3%
3.	Shoplifting	19.0%
4.	Company fraud	15.4%
5.	Unruly behaviour at football matches	12.8%
6.	Rowdyism in the streets	10.8%

That a third of the population of Islington think too much time is spent on prostitution and a quarter that undue attention is given to cannabis is a direct indication of public desire to direct resources to more important areas. It also shows in the case of cannabis that the public distinguish quite clearly between soft drugs and hard drugs such as heroin — the latter of which is the third highest policing priority. In the aftermath of the 1985 Handsworth riot *The Guardian* editorial noted "It is (genuinely it is) hard to draw the line between a resolute refusal to allow 'merchants of powdered death' — black or white — to ply their trade unhindered and the systematic harassment of youths who hang around the local pub smoking the odd joint. After all, if drug dealing is the menace it has been portrayed as being this year, then it would be intolerable to ignore it in ghetto areas. On the other hand, to legitimise heavy policing of the ghetto areas on the ground that drugs are involved, is to invite violent unrest. There is a fine and desperately difficult line here" (September 11, 1985). Our survey shows that for the people of Islington such a line is not at all desperate or difficult.

Such a listing of priorities provides us overall with very clear guidelines as to the public will, obedience to which Commissioner Newman rightly acknowledges to be in line with police legitimacy and professionalism. And the five priorities are also precisely the same as those found in the PSI Report covering London in general (D. Smith, 1983a) and the Merseyside Crime Survey (R. Kinsey, 1984).

Table 3   Comparison between priorities in Islington, London as a whole and Merseyside (percentages) (rank order in brackets)

	ICS	PSI	MCS
Robbery with violence in street	(1)71	(2)73	(1)75
Sexual assault on women	(2)69	(1)79	(2)73
Use of heroin	(3)59	(5)40	(4)55
Burglary	(4)58	(3)44	(3)68
Drunken driving	(5)44	(6)28	(5)57
Racialist attacks	(6)39	(4)40	—

Thus a remarkable consensus occurs with regard to seriousness of crimes. Violence whether against women or in street robbery is clearly the utmost public priority and burglary is viewed with a uniform concern. The public evidently displays a sophisticated discrimination between the dangers of different sorts of drugs, both legal and illegal. Thus the effects of one of the most dangerous legal drugs — alcohol — are clearly recognized, as are the dangers of illicit heroin use.

Important to note here is the extent to which racialist attacks are taken seriously by the Islington public — as they are in London as a whole. Thus at sixth place, they are seen as more serious an offence than, for example, either vandalism or bag-snatching.

The solid basis of this consensus over serious crimes in public opinion is clearly substantiated by looking at the breakdown in terms of age, race, gender and income.

It is often argued that we live in a culturally pluralist society where different sections of the population have widely varying forms of behaviour. However true this may be of differences of dress, accent, language and cuisine it is plainly not true in terms of the prioritization of serious criminal offences. All sections of the community, young, old; black, white; male, female; high income, low income; Council house tenant and home owner view, for example, street robbery as a very serious offence which should be high on police priorities. And this is also true of all the major offence categories. There is no difference, for example, in the very high priority which women and men give to the policing of sexual attacks against women. There are variations, of course, between the categories in Table 2 but they occur almost totally with an overall agreement as to the top five categories of offences. Young people, for example, are more likely to prioritize sexual assaults on women, heroin abuse, and racialist attacks than are the older age range. But all age ranges take these crimes very seriously. Burglary, as one might expect from the victim statistics discussed in [Chapter 2], is not an exclusive concern of the home owner or the rich but is a major concern of all income groups, of home owners and squatters, as well as Council tenants.

Similarly, there is a consensus as to those offences which the police should spend least time on. Prostitution, cannabis, rowdyism in the street, shoplifting, and company fraud consistently came at the bottom of all lists of priorities whether it is by age, race, men or women. There are a few deviations to this generalization: for example, older white people are distinctively less tolerant of cannabis use. But, in general, the scale of priorities from those which the police should put at a high premium to those which should be of least concern is widely shared within all sections of the community.

It might be argued, however, that such a simple pluralism is not the problem. Rather that what has occurred is that certain sections of the population because, perhaps, of economic and social deprivation, are marginalized from the vast majority of the community, and it is in this region that one might find subcultures which have radically different views on the nature of crime. Of all the groups to which such an ascription is usually made, none is more frequently cited than young blacks. Let us, therefore, compare their priorities to those of the general population.

The profile that young blacks have in terms of the crimes to which the police should give most attention are as follows: (1) racialist attacks (77.9%), (2) sexual attacks on women (74.9%), (3) robberies in the street where violence is used (65.3%), (4) use of heroin (64.3%), (5) burglary (50.3%), (6) drunken driving (33.8%). These are exactly the top six crimes prioritized by the population as a whole and the ordering is identical, with the understandable exception that racialist attacks move into first place and that, in common with all young people, sexual attacks on women are seen as the highest category of assault. Does this look like a subculture which is alienated from the wider community? Does this look like an alien minority who despise the notion of policing in principle? It might be argued that we are pitching the sub-cultural differences at too high a level. Instead we should be asking about more minor matters, say drugs or attitudes to boisterousness in the streets.

Table 4   A comparison of young blacks and the total population on opinions as to offences on which the police spend more time than necessary

%	Young Blacks	All
Rowdyism	10.8	10.8
Sexual assaults on women	0	1.2
Bag snatching	7.4	4.1
Burglary	0	1.8
Street robbery with violence	2.1	1.8
Cannabis	37.3	24.3
Heroin	4.2	3.4

With regard to "hard" drugs it should be noted that black youths — like the general population — see heroin as one of the major police priorities. Indeed slightly more see it as a top five priority than the general population (64.3% c.f. 59.1%). But let us look at how young blacks compare with the total population on a range of offences of which it is deemed that the police spend "more time" than necessary.

On all the more serious offences young blacks agree with the general population. They are slightly more lenient about cannabis but then so is the general population as a whole: indeed it is only the over 45 year old whites who have a particularly anti-cannabis disposition. 51.6% of those under 25 feel that the police should spend least time on cannabis, 49.0% of those from 25-44 but only 14.2% of those over 45.

Thus there is little indication that the profile of police priorities held by young blacks is different on most offences from the public as a whole, both in terms of high priorities and areas where deprioritization is advocated.

To conclude this section it is useful to look at a breakdown in an area where the figures reveal extremely high levels of public concern. Sexual attacks on women are of course a top public priority: 69.3% of the population place this offence in the top five offences. If, however, we do a breakdown by gender, age and race, we see wide variations albeit usually still within the level of high prioritization.

As can be seen, young white women have an extremely high level of prioritization which probably reflects their high victimization rates. So, of course, do young white men — although to a lesser extent — which demonstrates the principle that it is not so much actual victimization *per se* which shapes attitudes as knowledge of victimization to people that one knows closely.

Table 5   **Prioritization of sexual attacks on women (by age, race and gender) (% placing in top 5 offences)**

	White			Black			Asian		
	16-24	*25-44*	*45+*	*16-24*	*25-44*	*45+*	*16-24*	*25-44*	*45+*
Women	90.6	80.2	52.8	81.7	69.0	76.2	82.4	57.6	46.7
Men	83.2	79.8	60.0	65.2	75.0	62.5	52.3	35.6	48.0

Public assessment of the police: ability to deal with crime

"Public surveys conducted by independent research groups at our request are an instrument of growing sensitivity and therefore offer more accurate and credible findings. Whilst it would be wrong to deny that we look at the ratings of satisfaction with our services, consistently in the region of 75 per cent, with some degree of pleasure, it is also emphasised that we scrutinise with great care and interest the 25 per cent level of dissatisfaction (which includes those who are merely undecided) and the difference between areas, ages and opinions."
(K. Newman, *Report of the Commissioner of Police to the Metropolis*, 1984, p. 8)

As an independent research group, let us look at the Islington public's rating of police services.

In order to audit the public's assessment of the police efficacy in dealing with crime we asked them to evaluate police performance in seven areas ranging from sexual assault to street fights. The results were as follows:

Table 6   Public evaluation of the police as being unsuccessful at dealing with various crimes

1.	Mugging/Street robbery	61.5%
2.	Burglary	65.7%
3.	Teenage rowdiness	45.3%
4.	Street fights	29.8%
5.	Vandalism	65.9%
6.	Sexual assaults on women	56.9%
7.	Women being molested or pestered	61.7%

In terms of the Commissioner's own criterion of dissatisfaction (25%), the public would be clearly extremely dissatisfied with police performance in each of these categories of offence. But let us take a less stringent 50% — that is whether a bare majority of the public were satisfied.

As can be seen we have included three of the crimes in the high public priority category (street robbery, burglary, and sexual assaults on women), one in the intermediate priority category (vandalism), two which relate to rowdiness, the least in terms of public priorities (teenage rowdiness and street fights) and a further question on sexual harassment in general (women being molested or pestered).

In five out of seven of the offences a majority of people interviewed see the police as unsuccessful in dealing with crime. These five include the three public priority crimes, vandalism and sexual harassment. The two crimes which the police are seen to be successful by over 50% of the population are dealing with teenage rowdiness and street fights, and only barely in the case of rowdiness. Furthermore, these types of crimes come very low in public prioritization of police activity. As far as we have seen, only 10% of the population prioritize street rowdiness in terms of police activities.

This would seem on the face of it a very severe public criticism of police effectiveness. It is as if an end of term report written by the people of Islington on police performance in seven major subjects, failed them in five, narrowly passed them in one and gave a clear pass in the least deserving area. And all of this involving a pass mark half as stringent as the Commissioner himself recommended.

Once again, a better understanding of the situation and the extent of the problem can be illuminated by breaking down the population by age, race and gender. Thus Table 7 allows us to map the differences and agreements of public assessment of police performance.

Given Newman's criteria (25%) there is simply no group which sees the police as successful in any of these offence categories. In terms of our less stringent 50%, a public assessment of the police's inability to deal with crime is revealed in every category of age, race and sex for mugging, burglary and vandalism. It is perhaps more interesting if we look at those categories which have a higher appraisal of police efficacy. One group clearly stand out and that is the over 45s. They are the only group in which a majority see the police as being successful at dealing with sexual assaults on women and sexual harassment. True, over 50% are dissatisfied with police performance in terms of mugging and burglary but they are much less critical than the younger age groups.

Table 7   Public evaluation of police performance for seven offences (age, race and gender) (% who see police as unsuccessful)

Offence	All	Age			Race			Gender	
		16-24	25-44	45+	White	Black	Asian	Male	Female
Mugging or street robbery	61.5	68.6	71.9	50.4	61.4	63.1	57.6	68.4	55.0
Burglary	65.7	67.7	77.9	55.6	65.1	69.5	71.7	70.8	60.9
Teenage rowdiness	45.3	51.1	51.4	38.2	43.5	58.4	55.3	48.6	42.0
Street fights	29.8	37.8	30.5	25.7	28.4	37.5	44.7	32.2	27.4
Vandalism	65.9	77.2	74.9	54.5	65.4	68.8	69.6	70.7	61.5
Sexual assaults on women	56.9	68.7	67.0	43.3	55.5	66.0	71.3	57.2	56.6
Women being molested or pestered	61.7	73.0	71.3	48.7	60.0	71.7	75.6	63.0	60.6

In contrast, if we examine these groups which have an exceedingly sceptical level of police ability to tackle crime (say over 66% seeing the police as unsuccessful) we find that we have in the case of:

— mugging: everyone under 45, all whites and blacks, all men.

— burglary: everyone under 45, all blacks and Asians, all men.

— sexual assault: everyone under 45, all blacks and Asians.

In general those under 45 are more sceptical than those who are older, blacks and Asians more than whites, men rather than women.

It is the older age groups which have, of course, the lowest victimization rates which help depress these figures even at the very highest level of assessment of police ineffectiveness. Thus if one turns to the area of sexual assaults on women (Table 8) we can plainly see how the already high levels of dissatisfaction are, in fact, depressed by the category of older white women. Both black and Asian women have extremely high levels of dissatisfaction irrespective of age, and white women and under 45s are in marked contrast to these in the older age group.

Table 8   Women's assessment of the police's inability to deal with sexual assaults on women (by age and race)

	All Women	White Women			Black Women			Asian Women		
		16-24	25-44	45+	16-24	25-44	45+	16-24	25-44	45+
Sexual assaults on women	56.6	71.5	64.9	39.0	75.0	67.4	73.7	72.7	73.9	80.0
Sexual molestation of women	63.0	73.6	70.6	40.3	79.7	71.5	78.9	71.5	88.5	83.4

In terms of actual victimization rates, as we have seen in [Chapter 2 (Table 2.29)], white women over 45 are much less likely to be sexually assaulted than those under 45 and thus there would seem to be some relationship with beliefs in police efficacy. And the same would be true of older Asians who have high rates of sexual assault. However, the patterning of assessment of police effectiveness and sexual assault rates is not at all 1:1 as is demonstrated by the high rate of scepticism in young black women and black women over 45 despite their low victimization rates.

The high rate of scepticism of young women about the police ability to deal with sexual assault is illustrated if we up the criteria of success even further and ask whether the police have any success *at all* at dealing with sexual assault. A full quarter of young white women believe the police are not at all successful at dealing with this offence and this rises to one third of young black women.

As can be seen from Table 9 people's beliefs in the effectiveness of the police on each of these individual offences declines with the degree to which they have been criminally victimized *in general*. Thus, whatever crimes committed against them, people become more sceptical about the police ability to deal with each specific offence whilst the rank order of ineffectiveness from vandalism/burglary down to rowdiness and street fights remains relatively independent of the degree of victimization.

Table 9 **Beliefs in police effectiveness (by extent of victimization) (% believing police unsuccessful)**

	Extent of Criminal Victimization		
Offence	*0*	*1 or 2*	*3+*
Mugging or street robbery	53.7	63.0	69.8
Burglary	58.0	66.0	74.2
Teenage rowdiness	37.5	42.4	55.2
Street fights	26.3	29.8	33.8
Vandalism	57.1	66.5	76.0
Sexual assaults on women	49.4	56.3	66.0
Women being molested or pestered	53.4	61.5	71.3

The paradox of public priorities and police successes

If we rank (comparatively) public estimation of police effectiveness against crime, public perceptions of the changes in frequency of various crimes and public priorities regarding policing, we can see the extraordinary disparity between public demand on policing and public perceptions of policing.

As we can see, there is a tendency for the public to see the police as unsuccessful at dealing with those crimes which they prioritize and see as becoming more common, and vice versa (see Table 10).

Table 10 Public views on policing successes, changes in frequency of offences and policing priorities

	'The police are not successful'	'Offence has become more common'	'The police should prioritize'
Mugging	70.2	60.7	70.7
Vandalism	65.8	53.0	26.8
Burglary	65.5	67.6	58.1
Women being molested and pestered	61.7	47.8	—
Sexual assaults on women	57.0	48.1	69.3
Rowdiness	45.2	44.3	9.8
Street fighting	29.8	31.0	—

Public use of 999 calls

999 calls are the most vital emergency link between the police and public. They are not the major route of contact — other telephone calls and personal visits to police stations are more predominant — but even on a quantitative level they are not far behind (20% c.f. 16%). Furthermore, as we see, the public place police response to 999 calls as the very top of their priorities (9% perceive this as a very important task) (Table 11).

Table 11 Public perceptions of policing priorities

	Tasks Perceived as Very Important
Immediate response to 999 calls	98.6%
Crime investigation	93.2%
Deterrent presence on the streets	87.0%
Control sports grounds & public meetings	80.1%
Contact with children at schools	73.5%
Crime prevention advice	69.9%
Keep a check on shops & offices	64.8%
Traffic control	54.2%
Youth community projects	49.5%

The proportion of people making 999 calls in the last year in Islington was 16%. This is higher than the proportion for London as a whole, of which the PSI report remarked "a remarkably high proportion of people — 11 per cent — said they had made a 999 call to the police in the past 12 months" (D. Smith, 1983a, p. 85). Of these a third were dissatisfied with the result — twice as many as in London as a whole (35% c.f. 17%). *Thus the demand on the police in terms of emergency calls is considerably higher in Islington than in London and the dissatisfaction with the results even more so. The population in terms of ethnic groups, whether white, black or Asian, make calls in* almost identical proportions. Furthermore, there is no great difference in general between the levels of satisfaction by different sub-groups although older people are, to a degree, more satisfied. What is crucial is the level of victimization. In general those who have never been criminally victimized have a high level of satisfaction with 999 calls (presumably they made service related calls) whilst those who have been multiply victimized show very high levels of dissatisfaction (see Table 13).

Lastly, it should be noted that the highest level of dissatisfaction with the police lies in the area of 999 calls. In general the less urgent the matter the more satisfied are the public (see Table 13).

Table 12   Proportion of population dissatisfied with police responses to 999 calls (by age, race, gender and level of criminal victimization)

		Age				Race	
	All	*Under 25*	*25-44*	*45+*	*White*	*Black*	*Asian*
% dissatisfied	34.5	34.7	41.0	25.9	33.6	37.1	42.2
	Gender			*Victimization*			
	Male	*Female*	*0*	*1-2*	*3+*		
	39.0	38.7	18.0	33.1	40.4		

Table 13   Levels of public satisfaction with the police (by different methods of contact)

Public-initiated Contact	*Dissatisfied*
999 calls	34.5%
Other telephone calls	25.6%
Personal visit to police station	23.7%
Approaching police officer	10.9%

The secret social service?

> "The average citizen thinks of the police as an organisation primarily concerned with preventing crime and catching criminals. When the crime rate goes down or criminals go uncaught, the conventional public response is to demand more or better policemen... for some time, persons who run or study police departments have recognised that this public conception is misleading. The majority of calls received by most police are for services that have little to do with crime but a great deal to do with medical emergencies, family quarrels, auto accidents, barking dogs, minor traffic violations and so on."
>
> (J.Q. Wilson, 1985, p. 61).

Thus writes James Q. Wilson, President Reagan's adviser on crime and, internationally, perhaps the most influential scholar writing about the police and policing. Such an approach to policing has had considerable impact in Britain on the thinking of certain key Chief Constables, on the Home Office and on the majority of sociologists working in the field. Broken down this portion suggests:

(i) That the public view of the police is primarily as a crime control organization.

(ii) That public demand on the police is in the majority of instances concerned with tasks of a "non-criminal" kind. Thus Wilson's classic study of citizen's complaints radioed to patrol vehicles in the American city of Syracuse had the following breakdown of calls (excluding information requests).

Citizens' Complaints Radioed to Police Vehicles, Syracuse Police Department

Service Calls (e.g. "accidents, lost animals, lost property")	48.1
Order Maintenance (e.g. "gang disturbance, family trouble, assaults, neighbour trouble")	38.6
Law Enforcement (e.g. burglary, check on car, making arrest)	13.2

(Source: Wilson, 1968)

(iii) That success at this service role has to be recognized as an important indicator of police performance. Thus Morris and Heal write in the Home Office Research Study *Crime Control and the Police*: "it is important to recognise that police *effectiveness and crime-control effectiveness* should not be confused. The importance of this distinction can be recognised by considering that one consequence of measurement in any organisation is for members to concentrate on those activities that are capable of being measured — in the present case recorded crime, arrests, clearance rates etc — at the expense of those less tangible areas of activity which are difficult if not impossible, to measure, such as crime prevention, social assistance and the maintenance of public order" (1981, p. 15).

Let us look at these propositions in terms of the logic of their argument and in the light of the data from the Islington Crime Survey.

(a) The prioritization of crime control

We have seen in the last section how the public prioritize crime control. The problem is that they are dissatisfied with the police's ability to achieve these crime control goals.

(b) Crime control as a minority demand on the police

It is argued that the public — despite prioritizing crime control, in fact, make only a minority of their demands on the police in this area and have a misconception as to the complex role that the police play. This notion of the role of the police has become a conventional wisdom of extraordinary tenacity particularly in Home Office circles. Thus Ekblom and Heal write in their study *The Police Response to Calls from the Public*:

"The data confirmed the by-now well established finding (Punch and Naylor, 1973; Comrie and Kings, 1974; McCabe and Sutcliffe, 1978; Hough, 1980) that only a small proportion of calls for police assistance are related to crime matters. Of all calls received from the public over six days at the sub-divisional control room studied only 18% required the preparation of a fresh crime report. Calls relating to 'plight' (locked out of car or home, lost property, person missing from home), administrative matters (sudden death, various licence renewals or the revision of alarm keyholder records), disputes (commercial and domestic), disturbances and nuisance (e.g. rowdy children or noisy neighbours) made up by far the greater proportion of demand."

(1982, p. 3)

More recently, Southgate and Ekblom in their review of the BCS findings on contacts between police and public write

"Like other studies, the BCS clearly shows that most public contacts with the police are apparently unrelated to crime. Public demands for the provision of general advice and assistance, the resolution of conflict and the control of nuisance and disorder greatly outnumber requests for dealing with crime and enforcing the law."

(1984, p. 25)

Indeed, earlier they summarize the basis for this seemingly rock-hard generalization

"A number of studies have analysed the nature of public calls made on the police, consistently showing crime-related calls to be in the minority. The greater proportion of demand consists of service calls dealing, for example, with lost property, missing persons, sudden deaths, licensing, and order problems (including disturbances, nuisances and disputes). Within this overall pattern, however, there is some variation in the size of the crime to non-crime ratio observed, a variation that probably reflects differences in the definitions used to classify requests to the police, many of which are complex in nature. Thus, Ekblom and Heal (1982) found that of all calls received at one sub-division, only three out of ten were crime-related; Punch and Naylor (1973) found only 41% of requests for police help relating to law enforcement; Comrie and Kings (1975) found 34% of calls to be concerned with crime; Hough (1980) found that 36% of incidents attended by patrols involved crime; Jones (1983) found that 43% of contacts made by the public were crime-related."

(1984, p. 11)

Let us first examine this portion in terms of its logic. In order to assist this process we have summarized the existing data in Table 15.

The crucial data are the ratio of non-criminal-related to crime-related public requests of the police in the final column. The ratio is generally acknowledged to show a majority of non-crime-related requests. Two exceptions to this are the new town in Punch and Naylor's study of three Essex towns and the recent controversial finding by the MCS of a ratio directly in contradiction to the conventional wisdom on the subject.

As the *Howard Journal of Criminal Justice* put it with regard to the MCS, "one unexpected finding from Merseyside is the high proportion of police-public contacts which are crime-related, far more than in the British Crime Survey" (Vol 24/2) May 1985, p. 136). Indeed, for a while there were a flurry of exchanges between scholars and other interested authorities casting doubts on the findings of the MCS and in particular the accuracy of the calculations involved. As we shall see the importance of this debate is not merely scholarly — it has quite crucial implications in the policy field.

Table 14   Summary of research on public initiated contacts with the police

Author(s), Date	Area of Study	Part of Policing Process	% Crime Related	% Order Related	% Service Related	Ratio Non Crime to Crime (Ratio)
J.Q. Wilson, 1968	Syracuse, USA	Citizens complaints radioed to police vehicles	13.2	38.6	48.1	6.6 :1
Punch and Naylor, 1973	New Town, Essex; Old Town, Essex; Country Town, Essex	Personal and telephone contacts from public	50.7 38.9		49.3 61.1	0.97 :1 1.6 :1
Comrie and Kings, 1975	England and Wales	Incidents attended by patrols	34.0	17.0	49.0	1.9 :1
Hough, 1980	Strathclyde	Incidents attended by patrols	36.0	19.0	45.0	1.8 :1
Ekblom and Heal, 1982	Humberside	Telephone calls from the public	30.0		70.0	2.3 :1
Jones, 1983	Devon and Cornwall	Public contacts	43.0		57.0	1.3 :1
Southgate and Ekblom, 1984 (BCS)	England and Wales	All public initiated contacts	22.4		77.6	1.3 :1
R. Kinsey, 1984 (MCS)	Merseyside	All public–police contacts (minus social)	57.0	7	36.0	0.8 :1

Before we look at how the results of the ICS help clarify this matter, it is necessary first of all to clear up some of the confusion in the area. For even at first glance the table displays the rather shaky basis of the conventional wisdom. Firstly, the stage in the process of policing and the routes of public-police demand are extremely mixed. Wilson, for example, bases his classic work on citizen's complaints which have already been filtered at the police station then radioed on to police vehicles; Hough's work concerns incidents being attended to by police vehicles; Ekblom and Heal concentrate on telephone calls from the public; whilst Punch and Naylor focus on all public contacts. Secondly, the distinction between crime and order-related incidents is extremely confusing. Wilson's list of order offences includes, for example, "assaults", "gang disturbances" and "family trouble". It is difficult to see how these are not in the majority of cases crime-related. Surely what has happened is that the criminologists are merely reflecting the distinctions often made by police officers between "real" crime and "rubbish" crime? (See D. Smith, 1983b). And if the police deprioritize certain crime such as domestic disputes, there is no reason why the criminologist — or the concerned member of the public for that matter — should follow suit. Thus the arbitrary distinction between crime and order offences systematically reduces the correlated figure. Thirdly, the distinction between order and service demands is also suspicious. What, for example, are we to make of Punch and Taylor's remark that "Obviously, some calls did not fall easily into this (law enforcement) category. For instance, family quarrels or noisy parties are potential breaches of the peace but, as they rarely result in prosecution and often require the exercise of social skills, we put them in the service category" (1973, p. 358). It is, of course, the police unwillingness to prosecute in instances of domestic violence that has led to considerable criticism (see Hanmer and Saunders, 1984). But a considerable proportion (28.5%) of Punch and Naylor's "service" calls are domestic disputes. Indeed it is the most frequent of all their service categories. Thus once again the "non-crime"-related calls are artificially inflated. Lastly, these breakdowns derive from very different settings: different countries, different parts of the country, large towns and small towns and rural and urban areas. This may explain the wide variation in non-criminal to criminal incident ratios and, of course, the "exceptional" findings of a comparatively low ratio in the new forum in Punch and Naylor's study and a much lower ratio in Merseyside.

The central question which the Islington Crime Survey is able to cast light upon is: what is the public demand pattern in an inner-city area? Or more directly, what is the pattern of public demand in those areas of high criminal victimization where the public have high demands on the police and where the majority of police resources and manpower are centred? In the ICS we have been scrupulous to restrict service demand to non-criminal areas and, whilst retaining for comparative purposes the category of order demands have strictly avoided including those events — such as domestic violence — which are clearly criminal.

In Table 16 we have divided up public-initiated contacts with the police by the rate of contact. Following the usual practice, we have calculated the ratio of non-crime-related to crime-related contacts (Ratio 1). This ratio has almost invariably indicated a majority of non-crime-related contacts ranging up to the region of 3:1.

As can be seen immediately from Table 15 the primary pattern of public contact with the police in Islington is crime-related and the majority of public initiated contacts are about crime, and this narrow majority is transformed when one looks at the different

320

types of contact. Telephone contact — about half of the total — is predominantly crime related. 66% of all telephone calls are about crime and this rises to 76% if we include public order complaints. This flies totally in the face of studies such as Ekblom and Heal who find only 30% of telephone contacts to be crime related. What it does corroborate, however, is the MCS which found that 57% of all public calls (*excluding* social calls) on police time were about crime and an almost identical pattern of contact to the ICS in terms of the various routes. It would seem, therefore, that the conventional wisdom with regard to police-public contact in terms of the inner city, which is the major focus of police activity and resources, is incorrect.

The ratio we find in the ICS is basically 1:1, that is in contradiction to the majority of the previous work with the exception of the MCS. The generalization about the high rate of crime-related public requests in urban settings would seem to hold both in Islington and Merseyside. The controversial Merseyside finding would still seem remarkably atypical, however, and at 0.8 to 1 it is considerably lower than the ICS finding. But, there are two simple reasons for this — one, the MCS did not include social calls (a minor reason) and, more importantly, the MCS includes a miscellaneous category of "difficult to code" reasons which was subsequently distributed equally between the crime, order and service categories. If these were placed — as is more likely — in the service category we find results of 1.1: 1; that is virtually identical with the ICS findings. Furthermore, we have continued to follow the conventional practice of having order as a separate non-criminal category. If we were to include order in crime, given that a majority of public order occasions are potentially criminal, then we would have ratios which show that the public relation with the police is predominantly crime-related (see Ratio 2, Table 15).

Table 15   Public initiated contacts with the police (by various types of contact)

	All	*999*	*Non-999 Telephone*	*Calling in Police Station*	*Approaching Police Officer*
% of all contacts	100.0	22.4	28.5	27.7	21.6
A. Crime related	50.8	65.9	65.0	44.0	25.0
B. Public order related	5.6	16.0	7.0	—	—
C. Service related	40.8	18.0	28.0	56.0	62.0
D. Social	3.0	0	0	0	14.0
Ratio 1 $\frac{(B+C+D)}{A}$	1.0	0.5	0.5	1.3	3.0
Ratio 2 $\frac{(C+D)}{(A+B)}$	0.8	0.2	0.4	1.3	3.0

(c) The policy implications of a finding of high public crime-related demand on policing

Let us first spell out the policy implications of the conventional wisdom that the police have a majority service role. It is argued that there is a peculiar cognitive lapse on the part of the public — on the one hand that they expect the police to be predominantly crime fighters but, on the other, they demand a wide range of services from the police.

The police are — as Maurice Punch nicely put it — "the secret social service" (1979). This results, as members of the BCS urge, in a situation where there is divergence of priorities between the police who emphasize (among the lower ranks, at least) dealing with serious crime, and the public, who expect a far wider range of services. Thus they conclude "much avoidable misunderstanding can be removed by ensuring that myths and selective views of policing are kept in check by a wider and more realistic knowledge of the entire spectrum of police-public contact" (Southgate and Ekblom, 1984, p. 33).

The next stage in this process is the notion that there is a link between such a predominant social service role and the low performance levels of the police at clearing up crime. A Canadian author, John Hagan, spells this line of thought out very clearly:

> "The problem, it seems, is that when in doubt or desperation, we call the police. As a result, the police become our front line gatekeepers of deviance, responding to all kinds of day-to-day variations from the norm, and deciding at this point of entry which of these many acts require further agency attention. Two factors encourage the police to persist in this role. First, it allows the police to avoid an exclusive image as oppressive keepers of the law (instead, they are able to perform a social service role as well). Second, the police frequently are the only 24-hour service agency available to respond to those in need. The result is that the police handle everything from unexpected child-births, skid row alcoholics, drug addicts, emergency psychiatric cases, family fights, landlord-tenant disputes, and traffic violations, to occasional incidents of crime. The latter wording is deliberate, for Canadian and American studies agree that relatively little police time is spent on actual criminal cases. A Montreal study reported by Evans (1973): indicates that the police of that city spend as little as 13 per cent of their total working hours on 'anti-criminal' activity. Similarly, across Canada, Evans estimates that the average police officer brings criminal charges against only 1.25 individuals every month. Even in a major city like Toronto the volume is not much higher — with district detectives and patrol officers averaging 15.5 criminal charges per year. The explanation of this pattern seems to lie in the character of the requests the police receive. Thus, in an American study, Wilson (1968) reports the following distribution of calls: 21.1 per cent asking for information; 37.1 per cent requesting service; 30.1 per cent seeking maintenance of order; and only 10.3 per cent dealing with the enforcement of laws. The importance of these varied demands on police time will become apparent, that the public gets, to a surprising extent, much of what it asks for."

(1977, p. 144)

Such a position has been taken up readily in influential government and policing circles in this country. Because the police are seen to have a very large public demand on them, much of which is non-crime-related, then this explains their low clear-up rate. For there can be no doubt there *is* an extraordinarily high level of inefficiency that has to be explained. *After all, there were only 4.2 crimes cleared up per police officer per year in the Metropolitan Area in 1984* (see Kinsey, Lea and Young, 1986). Indeed, the recent Home Office study on police effectiveness is quite clear on this subject. It reiterates the conventional wisdom

> "Dealing with crime is only one of the many tasks performed by the police. They also maintain order on the streets, marshal crowds, control traffic, cope with emergencies such as fires and floods, and provide a miscellaneous round-the-clock service of help and advice to the public. And even if the police and others have laid great stress on their 'crime fighting' role, only a small proportion of the incidents they have to deal with are directly related to crime. The report does not consider the effectiveness with which the police handle their non-crime functions, though any assessment of optimum manning levels must take these into account. The research reviewed here therefore offers no direct guide to the appropriate size of the police service."
>
> (Clarke and Hough 1984, pp. 2-3)

And then, after an exhaustive review of the literature, they conclude

> "It could be said that limitations on police effectiveness in controlling crime should not be discussed in public because, for example, this might undermine public confidence or encourage offending by those who are deterred at present. But apart from any general arguments of openness it is important that there should be a wider understanding of what can be expected from the police and what the public should expect to do for themselves. It may not be helpful to think in terms of a 'war on crime' fought between criminals and the police, as this may increase unnecessarily public anxieties and fear of crime. The clearest implication of the research reviewed above is that there are few proven grounds for indiscriminately allocating further resources to traditional deterrent strategies. The evidence about police effectiveness, coupled with financial constraints, led some American police departments to reduce manpower in the late 1970s; the New York Police Department reduced its work-force by a fifth. One result was that recorded crime continued to rise — but no faster than before — and arrests for serious offences actually rose. Some police authorities in this country have also entertained the idea of reducing manpower. However, levels of police resources should not be assessed simply in terms of their effect on crime. Manpower is needed to perform the many functions of policing besides law enforcement, and it is doubtful whether the police could provide the same level of service with fewer officers.
>
> Clearly a completely objective formula for deciding police resources will never be devised, but it might be possible to make decisions better informed. This will require several things to be achieved. The public must receive better information about police work and about the effectiveness of crime control efforts. There must be more informed discussion about the tasks which the police should and should not perform. (Here the police

authorities and the recently established consultative committees have an important part to play). The police must confront questions about the efficiency and effectiveness of their non-crime work. And survey techniques and other research methods must be deployed to support them in this task; developing adequate 'output measures' for the totality of police work — difficult though this may be — must therefore rank high on the research agenda."

(1984, pp. 20-1)

Here we have it starkly put. Although there is little real argument for extension of police resources in terms of crime control, the "predominant" service function makes it difficult to generate a very clear indicator of police performance and is a major argument against force reduction. And its conclusion that survey results are of great importance in ascertaining police performance of both a crime-related and service kind, has, of course, great relevance to the significance and uses of this first ICS.

The argument that crime control is a minority task of policing and that a substantial proportion of crimes prioritized by the public cannot be dealt with by the police (burglary, for example) has been taken up enthusiastically in London police circles. As Commissioner Newman put it "over a half of recorded crime is of a capricious and opportunistic nature, upon which police, acting without public help, would never be likely to make any serious impact" (1984, p. 4). Thus much of the type of policing which the public demand ("reactive" policing in response to 999 calls etc.) is liable to be fruitless and there needs to be a move towards greater service provision.

"An alternative to the reactive model, emphasising crime control, is for the police to take the initiative by acting upon the environment rather than merely responding to it and by working with the public and other social agencies to prevent crime. Within this model, the prevention of crime within the community is raised to at least the same level of importance as that of detection; the emphasis moves away from a focus upon the individual offence and offender to more active consideration of the preconditions for offences and thought for the potential victim of crime."

(*Ibid.*, p. 8)

And Kenneth Newman repeats his conclusion in this year's report

"The police service has to a large extent become trapped in a reactive role based upon an understandable and conventional preoccupation with crime committed. Last year I urged the Force to move towards a greater feeling for the preventative role, which accords readily with well-documented research locating the vast majority of police work in the 'service' functions peripheral to crime investigation."

(1985, p. 19)

Thus the Commissioner very neatly acknowledges the existence of a large service provision of the police, together with the low performance in crime control, by arguing for an *expansion* of the service provision, a movement away from a role-reactive to public demands *vis à vis* crime as the only way forward in crime control.

This movement towards a focus on the service rather than the crime control aspect of policing is reinforced by a parallel shift from a focus on crime control to order maintenance. Here, once again, the influence of the work of James Q. Wilson is influential in British policing policy. Once again the Home Office Research Study *Crime and Police Effectiveness* sums up this viewpoint well in the context of the current argument about community policing:

> "Community policing provides a rationale for 'putting bobbies back on the beat' in terms of better relations between the police and public. Recently a second — and to some extent conflicting — rationale has been offered in terms of the foot patrol officer's task of maintaining order on the beat. This suggests that certain levels of disorderly behaviour (on the part of drunks, tramps, rowdy youths, prostitutes and other undesirables) can trigger a spiral of neighbourhood decline, with increased fear of crime, migration of the law-abiding from the area, weakening of informal social control and, ultimately, increases in serious crime. According to this view, beat policemen should be assigned long terms to areas at risk to break the spiral, clamping down on the 'incivilities' which lead to decline.
>
> Such ideas amount to an extension — or at least consolidation — of the police function of 'order maintenance' at a time when many have argued that this aspect of police work should be performed with a very light touch (especially in the multi-racial inner cities). At the risk of distortion it might be said that the beat policeman would arrest offenders or move them on, whilst the community constable would shepherd them back to the fold. Thorny issues about civil liberties and due process arise with informal policing of the local 'roughs' on behalf of the local 'respectables' — especially in areas where there is little consensus about acceptable public behaviour. There is nevertheless some support for the hypothesis. (A Study) in Newark found that the introduction of foot patrols led to reductions in fear of crime, because, the authors argue, they secured a marked reduction on levels of public disorder — patrols moved on drunks, vagrants and beggars, for example, and youths were not allowed to gather in rowdy groups on the street. A more recent study also found that the presence of street disorder stimulates crime levels and fear of crime, and erodes informal control processes."
>
> (Clarke and Hough, 1984, p. 17)

This is the basis of the Wilson-Kelling hypothesis (see Wilson, 1985, Ch.5) which argues that, although the police's effectiveness in directly dealing with crime is limited, the regulation of order in a community can stimulate the weak informal systems of social control back into action and thus in the long run begin to help the community regulate itself for more serious offences (see Kinsey, Lea and Young, 1986). It is easy to see how this argument corresponds with Newman's conception of prevention through community intervention and the service role rather than the direct control of crime.

Fairness to different groups

We now turn from questions of police efficiency and public priorities to questions of police legitimacy — the public's evaluation of their ability to work within the rule of law.

"A community consenting to be policed by its own members gives constables an implied mandate to preserve the peace, to prevent crime and to bring offenders to justice. Such consent rests upon the legitimacy — both actual and perceived — of the methods used by the police to discharge their mandate and of the styles of policing employed in doing so, both of which must be consonant with the demands of a vigilant and energetic democracy.

The level of police professionalism will be gauged by the extent to which the service is able to establish that legitimacy in the eyes of the people."

(K. Newman, 1985, p. 1)

We asked our sample whether the police in the area treated all sorts of people fairly and equally. This is a crucial question in that it points directly to the degree of equality demanded by the law and, in terms of these groups which see themselves as unfairly treated (whether because of age, or race, or class), it provides a potential basis for alienation from the police. A full one third of respondents thought that such unfairness occurred, which is roughly equal to that found in the PSI Survey of all Londoners. This sizeable proportion varies widely when we examine the main background variables.

Table 16   Police do not treat all people fairly and equally

AGE	16-24	54.1%
	25-44	46.6%
	45+	13.5%
RACE	White	29.4%
	Asian	30.2%
	Black	61.1%
GENDER	Male	32.2%
	Female	32.6%
EMPLOYMENT STATUS	Employed	38.6%
	Unemployed	45.2%
ALL		32.5%

One of the most striking differences is with age, in that very few people over 45 see the police as being unfair whereas over half of 16-24 year olds do as well as 46.6% of those in the 25-44 age group. *The other remarkable difference is with race. For whereas white and Asian respondents are almost identical in their appraisal of police fairness, over twice as many blacks — two thirds in all — view the police as acting unfairly*. If such a question is an indication of police fairness by minority groups then it might be noted that the wide differences between Asians and blacks would suggest very difficult relationships with the police. For although a sizeable proportion of Asians maintain that there is police unfairness, a substantial majority — 70% — do not .

In terms of gender there is little difference between the assessment of the police by men and women, whereas the unemployed are somewhat more likely to see the police as unfair when compared to the employed.

326

How do these relationships appear when we control by age, race and gender? If we look at Table 17 we see that the groups which see the police as most unfair are young blacks and that there is little difference between men and women. It is startling that three quarters of this section of the black population believe the police to be unfair.

At the other extreme, it is whites over 45, irrespective of gender, who have the highest confidence in police fairness. This rate of 90% confidence in police fairness is not approached by any other category.

Over 45 non-whites do not exhibit this high level of confidence. The high black lack of confidence in the police in respect to fairness occurs at all ages and in both genders. The most startling difference in the black population is between over 45 men and women, the latter having a considerably lower confidence. We have discussed the exceptional case of older black women earlier in [Chapter 1].

The confidence of white people in the police, in general, is not high, just under half of all men and women under 45 perceiving them as acting unfairly — it is only the very high rates of confidence of the over 45s that brings the overall figure down to 29% . Asians have a higher estimation of police fairness than whites in all categories, except the over 45s, and a much higher estimation than blacks in every category.

Table 17   Belief that the police treat some groups unfairly (by age, race and gender)

	White	Black	Asian
Male 16-24	46.5	77.5	32.0
Male 25-44	48.8	57.7	25.0
Male 45+	10.1	43.5	28.6
Female 16-24	53.5	75.0	45.8
Female 25-44	44.5	54.8	23.1
Female 45+	9.9	64.7	36.4

Unemployment and perceptions of unfairness

As we have noted, unemployment has overall an effect on perceptions of police unfairness. The relationship becomes clearer when we break down by age and race.

The considerable proportion (about a half) of whites aged 16-44 and blacks over 25 who see the police as unfair, is not particularly affected by unemployment. There is, however, a difference between unemployed and employed young blacks — 80% compared to 71% perceive police unfairness. But both these figures are very high and the fact of being young and black is obviously of much greater relevance than work status. Where unemployment does have impact, however, is with young Asians where more than double those unemployed compared to those employed perceive police unfairness.

Table 18   Belief that the police treat some groups unfairly (by age, race and work status)

			Race	
	Age	White	Black	Asian
	16-24	48.8	70.9	20.7
Employed	25-44	45.8	56.1	27.0
	45+	8.3	52.9	30.7
	16-24	51.3	80.3	49.7
Unemployed	25-44	47.5	55.8	23.5
	45+	12.9	51.6	33.2

Relationship between income and perceptions of police unfairness

To note that there is greater tendency for unemployed people to say that the police are unfair does not mean that within the ranks of the employed that those better off are more inclined to believe in police fairness. In fact, a higher income *tends* to *increase* the public's perception of police unfairness irrespective of the race of the person concerned (see Table 19). Young blacks, for example, with incomes greater than £8,000 a year tend to have an extremely high (80%) tendency to suspect police unfairness, and the highest proportion of whites who perceive the police as unfair are those aged 25-44 who earn over £12,000. Those groups with the lowest proportion of people believing that the police are unfair are both 45+, but they present a sharp contrast — 65% of the poorest whites and 40% of the highest income blacks.

Table 19   Belief that the police treat some groups unfairly (by income, race and age)

Income/Age		White	Black
	(16-24	47.1	70.4
£3,000 –	(25-44	41.2	53.4
7,999	(45+	6.5	46.4
	(16-24	51.4	83.4
£8,000 –	(25-44	43.6	66.7
11,999	(45+	14.5	55.7
	(16-24	51.4	82.2
£12,000 +	(25-44	57.8	67.0
	(45+	16.5	40.0

Table 20 below indicates belief in the fairness of the police by our three scales.

Thus people who are highly satisfied with their neighbourhood are very unlikely to see the police as acting unfairly whereas those who are dissatisfied are more likely to be critical of the police on this score. Importantly those who believe themselves likely to be victims of crime are much more likely to doubt the fairness of the police than those who see victimization as unlikely. The level of fear of crime itself is unrelated to views on police fairness.

Table 20   Belief that the police treat some groups unfairly (by scales A, B & C)

	High	Medium	Low
A. Satisfaction with neighbourhood	5.6	25.9	53.4
B. Fear of crime	31.3	32.7	37.1
C. Likelihood of crime	40.9	32.6	21.7

The disquiet felt about police fairness by those who see themselves as likely to be victims of crime is underscored by the data concerning those who have actually been victimized (see Table 21).

Table 21   Belief that the police treat some groups unfairly (by incidence of criminal victimization)

	Personal Victimization	Household Victimization
0	21.8	27.4
1 or 2	35.7	34.4
3+	43.2	51.2

Here we see dramatically that beliefs in the unfairness of the police increase with the chances of being criminally victimized. Such a close relationship between multiple criminal victimization and doubts as to the fairness of the police is true when one controls age and race. For example, if we look at young people by levels of victimization, we can see the following in [Table 22] :

Table 22   Belief in unfairness of the police (by degrees of criminal victimization and race amongst 16-24 year olds)

Victimization	White	Black	Asian
Nil	43.3	65.2	27.6
Multiple	56.5	82.7	40.9

Here we have the same pattern of a rising degree of dissatisfaction with the police from Asians to whites to blacks. And, in each case, there is an increase in belief in unfairness rising to an extremely high 82.7% amongst multiply-victimized young blacks.

Lastly, we find that the number of contacts with police relate closely to public evaluation of the police reacting unfairly to certain groups. Thus:

Table 23   Police reacting unfairly to certain groups (by contacts with police)

Contacts	0	19.5%
	1	39.3%
	2+	45.7%

Police understanding of problems in the area

Overall one third of the sample did not think the police had a good understanding of the problems of the area. This was considerably larger (36% c.f. 25%) than the proportion of people at Merseyside asked the same question. Once again it varied with the main social characteristics.

Table 24   Belief that police do not have a good understanding of the area (by age, race, gender and employment status)

AGE	16-24	58.7%
	25-44	44.7%
	45+	20.6%
RACE	White	33.6%
	Asian	41.6%
	Black	54.6%
GENDER	Male	34.6%
	Female	34.7%
EMPLOYMENT STATUS	Employed	40.5%
	Unemployed	50.6%

As with the public judgement of the fairness of the police to different groups, the pattern is repeated. By age, it is the 45+ age group who are exceptional in their belief in the understanding of the police. Almost half the 25-44 age group do not and this rises to 59% with the under 24s. In terms of race a substantial one third of whites doubt police knowledge of Islington and this rises to over half (55%) in the case of blacks. Asians are in an intermediate position. The unemployed are more doubtful about understanding than are the employed and, once again, there is little to choose from between men and women.

In terms of our three scales an almost identical pattern to the previous section occurs (see Table 25).

Table 25   Lack of good police understanding of the area (by scales A, B & C)

	High	Medium	Low
A. Satisfaction with neighbourhood	4.7	31.3	53.6
B. Fear of crime	39.3	35.3	31.7
C. Likelihood of crime	51.0	33.7	28.2

Once again people with a high satisfaction of their neighbourhood have an extremely high confidence in the police and those with low satisfaction are much more doubtful. Fear of crime does not vary as much — although high fear of crime is more likely to be combined between one's estimation of the likelihood of being a victim of crime and doubts as to police understanding of the area.

Table 26   **Lack of good police understanding of the area (by criminal victimization and contact with the police)**

	0	*1 or 2*	*3+*
Personal victimization	26.6	39.9	44.5
Household victimization	30.5	39.0	53.1
Contacts with police	26.9	36.6	47.0

Once again, doubts in the abilities of the police increase with the degree in which members of the public experience criminal victimization. And the more the public have contact with the police the less they feel the police have an understanding of the area.

Serious police misconduct

Following the PSI report for London as a whole, we asked a series of questions in Islington as to public beliefs with regards to police malpractices. The four areas of serious misconduct we will examine are: the use of undue force in the arrest situation, violence on people held at police stations without undue reason, police officers planting evidence and officers taking bribes.

Table 27 reveals that about one half of the survey believe that such malpractices occur and a substantial minority of those interviewed believe that they occur on a regular basis: 1 in 5 believe this is true of use of undue force and planting evidence, 1 in 6 that the police use undue violence at police stations and 1 in 8 that the police take bribes. *Furthermore, there is a consistent difference between the ICS and PSI results — people in Islington are more likely than those in London in general to believe that police malpractices occur.*

Table 27   Police malpractices: a comparison of ICS and PSI

%	*Undue Force on Arrest*		*Violence at Police Stations*		*Plants*		*Bribes*	
	ICS	*PSI*	*ICS*	*PSI*	*ICS*	*PSI*	*ICS*	*PSI*
Never/hardly ever	45	68	50	64	53	57	45	44
Sometimes	34	18	34	23	35	33	42	47
Often/very often	21	14	16	14	21	10	13	9
Happens more than it used to	58	23	48	20	33	20	30	28

About one half of those interviewed believed that undue force on arrest and at the police station was on the increase, and one third that plants and bribes were more frequent today. All of those figures are substantially greater than those obtained by the PSI and suggest that, as far as Islington is concerned, there is a particularly acute perception of deteriorating police standards within the Borough. We have chosen throughout this chapter on policing to use the PSI report as a backcloth. Substantively, this is because it allows a comparison with all of London but it must also be noted that the PSI itself recorded a substantial level of criticism of the police and a considerable belief in the drop in standards. It is for this reason that politicians, criminologists, police officers and journalists have taken its results so seriously. For the ICS, then, to indicate considerably greater problems of public confidence in the police within an inner-city area underlines the dramatic nature of the present survey's conclusions.

It might be argued that these beliefs in police malpractices are merely a function of a sensationalist mass media which emphasize a high level of police violence and deviation from official standards, but it is difficult to understand why beliefs about the high frequency of police misconduct are more prevalent in Islington than in London as a whole. It surely cannot be a result of a greater addiction to the mass media in the inner city.

A telling piece of information as to formation of such beliefs as to police malpractice is the replies to the question "how have you come to know about it?". The answers are as follows:

Table 28 Sources of information with regard to police using undue violence on arrest

Actually happened to you or someone you know	39%
You or someone you know seeing it happen to someone else	45%
Seeing news pictures on TV of it happening	87%
Hearing it discussed on radio or television	84%
Reading about it in the newspapers	83%

Thus one moves along a continuum from direct experience to reports in the mass media. What is important to underline is the large number of people who claim that it actually happened to them or someone they knew. *Thus a full 39% of those who believe that the police use unfair force on arrest base this on actual experience.* A much greater proportion (over 80%) have also received information from the mass media with regard to the police using undue force. On one level this dismisses the common conspirational (or functionalist) notion that the mass media are a force largely supportive of the *status quo* on all issues. For if this were so why should over 87% of those who believe that the police have acted beyond the bounds of the rule of law have received information to the contrary via the "establishment" mass media? But it might be argued that the quantity and quality of such information is extraordinarily distorted within the media. After all, police drama is a major genre on television and it involves quite extraordinary ideas of the high level of clear up rate of the police and the prevalence of investigative police work (J. Young, 1986) combined with a literary structure which justifies undue violence in the course of the common good (J. Palmer, 1978). And, if there were only a small proportion of direct experential information about police work in the context of the undoubtedly large and distorted mass media input, then we could easily talk of public fantasies with regard to police work which have little relationship to reality. But, in fact, we find that there is a substantial *rational core* to the public's belief in police violence which is based on actual experience. Thus the mass media are effective because they play on existing anxieties, however distortedly, but they seldom create public concern where there is no concern to play upon (J. Young, 1981).

The figures in [Table 29] refer, of course, to the proportion of the population who do believe the police use undue force. The proportion of *total informants* who claim that they have direct or semi-direct experience of undue police violence is as follows:

— actually happening to you or someone you know 24%

— you or someone you know seeing it happen to someone else 28%

Table 29   Belief that police use more force than necessary (by age, race, gender, contact and level of victimization)

	All	Age Under 25	Age 25-44	Age 45+	Race White	Race Black	Race Asian	Gender Male	Gender Female	Contact 0	Contact 1	Contact 2+	Victimization 0	Victimization 1 or 2	Victimization 3+
Never/ hardly ever	45.2	24.3	28.9	65.4	47.2	23.3	49.8	44.1	46.0	54.6	40.1	34.4	54.1	44.7	34.8
Sometimes	34.3	38.8	42.9	26.1	34.1	36.0	39.1	34.2	34.4	32.6	36.0	35.9	33.4	33.3	35.7
Often	20.5	36.9	28.1	8.4	18.8	40.7	11.2	21.6	19.6	12.9	24.0	29.7	12.6	22.0	29.4

These are exactly double the figures found in the PSI report of which David Smith drily commented "12 or 14% are not large proportions, but they represent a large number of Londoners — perhaps 700,000 — who will be hard to convince that this kind of misconduct does not occur" (1983a, p. 260). Well 24 or 28% *are* sizeable proportions — a quarter of Islington's population, some 30,000 people, and there can be no doubt that such experiences leave an indelible mark on police-public relations in the Borough. But, of course, these beliefs as to police malpractices are not equally spread across the population. They reach much higher levels in terms of particular sub-groups.

In terms of age, Table 29 illustrates that there are extremely wide variations: 37% of those under 25 believe the police use undue violence on arrest as against only 8% of over-45s. This reproduces the differences that we have already seen in terms of attitudes to the police with regard to fairness between different groups (see Table 19). Once again the over-45s present a very different picture when compared with the rest of the population. As far as race is concerned there is a very substantive difference between blacks and other groups with, as usual, Asians being less critical than whites. Important here is the fact that beliefs in the police using excessive force rise with contacts and with the extent of criminal victimization. Thus, the general rule is substantiated that the public are more critical of the police in those instances where

(a) they have a high degree of contact with them
or
(b) they are subject to a high level of criminal victimization.

If we further break down our analysis into age, race and gender we find that the belief in the police using excessive violence is extraordinarily high in young blacks, over half of men and women believing such violence occurs. The proportions of young whites is also considerable although not as great: one third of men and women having such knowledge of violence occurring. Of course, such beliefs may be fantasies but, as we have seen, they would seem to be based to an important extent on a rational kernel of direct or semi-direct experience. The most simple question must be asked: how can it be that there is such a wide variation between sub-groups of the population? Is it that white males and females over 45 with their miniscule beliefs in police violence (7% and 6% respectively, see Table 31) are correct whilst the beliefs of both black and white young people are fantasies, or is it that they reflect qualitatively different police-public encounters in the Borough? Is not the likely cause that these widespread differences within the population represent quite radically different experiences of encounters with the police?

If we look at Table 30 we find a very interesting split between direct or semi-direct experiential contact with the police compared to information obtained via the mass media. Nearly 80% of all sub-groups claim that they have obtained information with regard to undue force being used by the police from the mass media. But claims to experiential knowledge vary widely between sub-groups. Thus the mass media becomes a constant unvarying background of information. But direct experience of violence varies widely and it increases precisely in terms of those people who have either directly or indirectly (in terms of relatives and friends) a great deal of police attention focussed upon them.

Table 30 Sources of information with regard to undue police violence (by age and race)

Information Route %	All ICS	Age			Race		
		Under 25	25-44	45+	White	Black	Asian
Actually happened to you or someone you know	38.9	58.6	39.8	21.8	37.8	51.5	18.6
You or someone else you know seeing it happen to someone else	45.4	64.7	48.8	24.9	44.6	55.1	28.8
Seeing news-pictures on TV of it happening	86.9	83.9	85.9	90.7	87.5	85.7	78.0
Hearing it discussed on radio or TV	83.7	81.4	83.6	85.9	83.7	85.5	80.8
Reading about it in newspapers	83.3	79.4	81.6	88.9	84.2	81.3	67.4

Deterioration in police–public relations over time

Lastly, if we look at the sample views on whether police–public relationships have deteriorated over time with respect to undue violence (Table 32) we find that the number of people who believe that there has been an improvement is minute, regardless of age, gender or race. But those who believe it has worsened are in the majority of cases over half of the population. What is important here, perhaps, is that older people experience the situation as having worsened. Particularly noteworthy is that contact with the police or experience of criminal victimization increased views of deterioration.

Table 31 Belief that police often use excessive force (by age, race and gender)

	White Male			White Female			Black Male			Black Female			Asian Male			Asian Female		
All	16-24	25-44	45+	16-24	25-44	45+	16-24	25-44	45+	16-24	25-44	45+	16-24	25-44	45+	16-24	25-44	45+
20.5	36.4	29.0	7.4	34.5	26.0	5.6	61.1	40.5	37.5	51.5	38.4	25.0	11.3	15.2	3.8	18.7	8.8	14.3

Table 32 Belief that police use undue violence more today than in the past

	All	Age			Race			Gender		Contact with Police			Level of Criminal Victimization		
		Under 25	25-44	45+	White	Black	Asian	Male	Female	0	1	2+	0	1 or 2	3+
Less	2.8	3.7	3.0	1.9	2.5	4.0	5.3	3.0	2.7	3.0	2.3	2.9	2.7	4.3	2.4
About the same	13.0	36.8	37.9	42.9	38.4	39.4	53.9	41.3	37.0	42.9	42.7	33.7	44.8	36.6	35.2
More	58.2	59.5	59.1	55.4	59.1	56.6	40.8	55.7	60.4	54.1	55.0	63.4	52.5	59.1	62.4

Willingness to cooperate with the police

In order to gauge the degree to which the public are willing to cooperate with the police we have followed the format of the survey PSI in presenting our sample with three hypothetical situations:

A. If you had seen a traffic accident in which someone had been badly hurt and the police were looking for witnesses. . .

B. If you had seen a couple of youths knock a man down and take his wallet and the police were looking for witnesses. . .

C. If you had seen a couple of youths smash up a bus shelter and the police were looking for witnesses. . .

In each situation the interviewee is asked would they (a) tell the police what they had seen? (b) be prepared to identify the people who had done it? (c) be prepared to give evidence in court about it? Thus we have three graduated types of offence from a traffic accident, to a less serious criminal act such as vandalism, to a fairly serious street robbery, coupled with a graduated degree of involvement with the judicial process — from helping the police, through identifying the offender(s), to witnessing in court.

It is vital to stress here the crucial nature of such public involvement in the judicial process. As we have seen in [Chapter 2], the vast majority of offences are made known to the police by the public — something in the region of 95%+ — and the process of judicial enquiry depends very largely on public witnessing. Successful policing demands high public cooperation; where this is missing the whole process becomes unstuck.

If we examine Table 33 we can immediately discern distinct trends. Our very first category — the case of letting the police know about a serious accident — is a useful base line of cooperation. Here we can see that with the exception of the Asian sample — of which more later — there is no great variation (at least on this level of analysis) between the various groups. Regardless of age, race, gender or income, all groups would be willing to tell the police of the incident at a level of 95% or above (i.e. 5% or less unwillingness to cooperate).

As would be expected, willingness to cooperate with the police declines quite dramatically with the level of involvement in the judicial process. This is true for all social groups and all categories of offences. Thus, even in the instance of the traffic accident — where the police have the highest degree of cooperation — there is much less willingness to cooperate as witnesses in court and a much greater variation between the different groups. As would be expected of the three offences, the serious accident evokes the highest degree of public cooperation, followed by the fairly serious criminal offence and lastly the instance of youthful vandalism.

Let us look next at the overall figures. They reflect, in every instance, a greater degree of lack of public cooperation with the police in Islington than the PSI figures which cover London as a whole. This corroborates the PSI findings that there is a lower rate of cooperation in inner-city Boroughs of high deprivation (PSI, p. 200) but the differences are much more striking than found in that Report. Thus, if one looks at unwillingness to appear in court, it is 44% greater in Islington than in London as a whole for serious accidents, 38% greater for street robbery and 52% greater for vandalism. In its more marked form it is striking that 1 in 5 of the inhabitants of Islington would be unwilling to give evidence in court with regards to a violent street robbery and 1 in 4 would be unwilling to even tell the police about the vandalism of bus shelters.

In this context of the markedly greater lack of police-public cooperation, it is useful to look at the differences between social groups. In terms of age, young people (under 25) are the least willing to cooperate with the police, followed by the over 45s, with the 25-44 age group the most willing to cooperate. As David Smith noted in the PSI report this is probably due to a greater hostility on the part of youth and a higher fear of reprisal on the part of the elderly (*ibid.*, p. 198). As far as race is concerned, we find that blacks are less likely to be willing to cooperate than whites. Thus 40% of blacks would be unwilling to testify in court with regards to street robbery as against 19% of whites. This is an early indicator of what we shall see is a marked level of alienation which corroborates the PSI findings. The most dramatic figures, however, are for the Asian population. Here just under 1 in 5 would not tell the police about a serious accident, a half would be unwilling to testify in court about street robbery and nearly 1 in 3 would not inform the police about vandalism. This is in sharp contrast to the PSI report which found only a slight difference between Asians and whites as to willingness to help the police.

Table 33   Unwillingness to help the police: three situations (by age, race, gender and income)

Incident	% Lack of Cooperation	PSI Comparison	ICS All	Age Under 25	25-44	45+	Race White	Black	Asian	Gender Male	Female	ICS Income £ Under 3000	3000-7999	8000-11999	12000+
A. Serious accident	Unwilling to tell police	3	4	3	2	5	3	4	17	2	5	5	4	2	1
	Unwilling to identify offender	–	7	8	4	8	9	12	23	5	8	10	7	4	2
	Unwilling to give evidence in court	9	13	18	7	15	11	20	33	8	17	17	14	8	5
B. Youths robbing a man of his wallet	Unwilling to tell police	4	7	9	5	8	6	13	25	6	9	9	9	5	4
	Unwilling to identify offender	9	15	21	10	15	12	29	35	11	19	18	17	11	7
	Unwilling to give evidence in court	16	22	31	15	23	19	40	49	16	29	27	25	15	13
C. Youths smashing up a bus shelter	Unwilling to tell police	17	27	40	21	26	26	34	34	24	30	31	30	22	16
	Unwilling to identify offender	23	36	51	30	35	35	46	48	30	42	43	39	29	23
	Unwilling to give evidence in court	29	44	61	38	41	42	56	58	35	51	52	47	34	30

In terms of gender we see clear differences. Women in general are less likely than men to cooperate with the police, particularly at the level of court room involvement. Presumably, in the case of traffic offences this is merely about the embarrassment of public appearances but in terms of criminal offences most probably this is about fear of reprisals. Lastly, there is a distinct rise in cooperation by income. The top income group (over £12,000) is the most likely to cooperate across the board with the police when compared to any other group on our chart.

What can we make of these differences? There seems to be a pattern such that those groups which have a comparatively high view of police fairness (women, the elderly, Asian) and yet a lower level of willingness to cooperate are probably worried over fear of reprisals. Whereas those groups which have a very critical view of police fairness (young people, blacks) and a low level of cooperation are less willing to help police because of a greater degree of alienation. Further research is necessary to substantiate this hypothesis but there are indications that this is correct if we further refine our analysis in terms of age, race and gender.

If one examines Table 34, we can examine the degree of cooperation with the police with much greater precision. If we set up arbitrarily a criterion that a reasonable degree of cooperation would be if 90% of the public were willing to help the police (i.e. a 10% refusal rate) then we find that public cooperation of the subsamples is reasonably high. Nine (one half) of the subsamples fall into this category and we can increase this to eleven if we include the two groups which are only just marginally outside.

This gives us the category groups inside our criterion:

— All white groups

— All black groups apart from young men and women

— Only middle-aged male Asians

and outside

— All Asians apart from middle-aged males

— Young black males and females.

What we have, therefore, is a distinct unwillingness on the part of the Asian community and of young blacks to cooperate with the police. There are clear indications that this may be a product of fear of reprisals and alienation from the police respectively. It is significant that in the Asian community it is women who are less cooperative than men and older people than younger people.

In contrast, in the black community it is young males who are exceptionally alienated and the majority of the black community is willing to cooperate with the police. There is, for example, no difference between elderly black and white women and precious little difference between elderly men. Furthermore, if one looks back to Table 18 where we documented the age, race and gender breakdown by beliefs that the police act unfairly towards certain groups, we find the ranking of perceptions of unfairness closely corresponds in blacks with their degree of unwillingness to cooperate with the police. There is no such correspondence of rankings amongst white or Asian sub-groups.

It should be noted that we have found no difference between black youths and the rest of the community in terms of their views as to the seriousness of street robbery. *What we have is not an alienation of young blacks from the community so much as their alienation from the police.*

It could, of course, be argued that the alienation of young blacks is simply a function of their higher offence rate, particularly in the area of street robberies. There are many problems with such an argument. Firstly, it is obvious that much unwillingness to cooperate with the police occurs in groups with very low offence rates. It is difficult to imagine a group with a lower rate of street robbery than Asian women over the age of 45, but they have the very highest rate of lack of cooperation. Secondly, although casual delinquency is common amongst all adolescent males, only a very small proportion of any sub-group would commit serious crimes such as mugging. Thirdly, this is borne out by the fact that such a high proportion of young blacks rate robbery as a very serious crime. Fourthly, although there is undoubtedly some difference between the offence rates of white and black youths, it is nothing like as different as the popular mass media sometimes make out with their gross stereotype of the "black mugger" (Lea and Young, 1984). It certainly would not be reflected in the extraordinary difference between the willingness of white and black youths to cooperate with the police on this simple level of "telling the police what you had seen" — 33% of black youths would not cooperate with the police in this respect compared to only 6% of white youths (see Table 34). All of this points tentatively to very different relationships between police and public in the cases of black and white youths.

Table 34   **Unwillingness to help the police in the case of street robbery (by age, race and gender)**

% Lack of Cooperation	All	White Male			White Female			Black Male			Black Female			Asian Male			Asian Female		
		16-24	25-44	45+	16-24	25-44	45+	16-24	25-44	45+	16-24	25-44	45+	16-24	25-44	45+	16-24	25-44	45+
Unwilling to tell police	7	6	3	5	5	6	10	33	8	6	16	11	10	21	11	28	31	29	40
Unwilling to identify offender(s)	15	17	5	9	15	10	20	55	16	24	34	29	28	33	23	28	43	42	60
Unwilling to give evidence in court	22	25	8	10	25	16	33	70	32	29	51	35	43	39	46	40	63	50	67

If we look at the highest level of public involvement in the judicial process — giving evidence in the courts — there are signs of a much greater unwillingness to cooperate. We must remember that street robbery is an offence which is given a very high policing priority by all sections of the community (see Table 1). Yet the only sections of the community willing to cooperate to the level of 90% are white men aged over 25 (i.e. Groups 25-44 plus 45+). Every other one of the eighteen sub-groups is unwilling to cooperate on this level and indeed fifteen of the groups have over a quarter of their members unwilling to give evidence in court. It should be stressed that such a lack of cooperation does not split on white/ethnic group lines. If white males aged 25-44 with their remarkable 97%, 95% and 92% *willingness* to cooperate on each of the three judicial levels are perhaps the ideal typical witnesses, other white sub-groups are much less so. Thus a quarter of young whites both male and female are unwilling to cooperate, as are a third of all white women over 45.

Table 35   **Ranking by blacks of perceptions of police unfairness and unwillingness to cooperate with the police**

Unwillingness to Cooperate with Police	Belief in Police Unfairness to Specific Groups
1. Young Male	1
2. Young Female	2
3. Middle aged Male	4
4. Middle Aged Female	5
5. Older Female	3
6. Older Male	6

The problem at its most severe is encountered when we turn to the highest level of non-cooperation, where we have over half of Asian women unwilling to cooperate, half of young black families and a staggering 70% of black youths. Much has been written on the dire consequences on policing of public unwillingness to communicate evidence to the police (Kinsey, Lea and Young, 1986) but the hiatus in cooperation at the court level is of much greater severity. Its consequences are virtually to cripple the criminal justice system; and as can be seen from Table 34, the level of unwillingness to give evidence in court is even greater for minor offences such as vandalism. Even in the case of the most wealthy group of individuals who are exceptionally liable to cooperate with the police, one third would not, whilst nearly two thirds of those under 25, over half of the blacks and the Asians and of the poorest income groups would not cooperate. All of this makes it exceedingly difficult for policing to produce results. For the essence of good policing is public cooperation at each level of the judicial process. Without it, clear-up rates must inevitably fall and protection against crime severely diminish.

Stop and search

Policing is conventionally divided into *reactive* and *proactive* policing. Reactive policing is in response to public demand, proactive policing is initiated by the police themselves. As we have argued, a large amount of the demand on police time stems from public demand particularly given that 95% of crimes are reported to the police by the public. As for the other 5% this is crime within the scope of proactive policing. Part of this process involves the police stopping and searching members of the public. There is considerable debate as to the efficacy of stop and search as a method of crime control. The PSI report presents the dilemma very clearly:

> "The findings certainly show that the present stopping policy produces a significant 'yield' and make it clear that there would be a substantial price to be paid if the policy were to be suddenly abandoned and nothing put in its place. At the same time, the cost of the present policy, in terms of the relationship between the police and certain sections of the public, is shown to be substantial, and most stops are wasted effort, if they are seen as purely an attempt to detect crime. The findings therefore suggest that the police should look for other more efficient and less damaging methods of crime detection to replace those stops that are currently carried out for no very specific reason."
>
> (D. Smith, 1983a, p. 117)

Therefore, on the one hand, stops in London as a whole "yield" an estimated 45,000 non-traffic and 75,000 traffic offences a year whilst, on the other, the great majority of people stopped are innocent people who are liable to be annoyed and alienated by this process. *As far as public dissatisfaction with stop and search is concerned, we found that 41% of those stopped in Islington were dissatisfied with the conduct of the officer concerned. This is a far higher figure than the 19% found dissatisfied by the PSI in London as a whole.* Further, at searches a half of all people stopped on foot thought there was insufficient reason, as did 47% of those whose car was searched.

All of this might be neither here nor there, if the yield from such stops were sufficient. It is often suggested that the percentage of those arrested as a result of stop and search is so low that this automatically invalidates the procedure (L. Christian, 1983; P. Hillyard 1981). In fact the 11% of stops resulting in an arrest in the London area is surprisingly high. If it were any higher it would suggest that the police were guilty of telepathy or of even worse offences. What has to be looked into is the *quality* of yields. For if the yield of stop and search were high in terms of crimes such as sexual assault, burglary and violent crime, we might justifiably argue that it was worth alienating some sections of innocent people. But there is no evidence that this is the case. For example, in the notorious Swamp 81 operation in Brixton 943 stops were made of which only 22 people (2.3%) were arrested for the offences of robbery, theft and burglary at which the operation was supposedly aimed. Similarly a study in the *Guardian* of stops in Brixton found the most common categories for arrest were drugs, drunkenness and offensive weapons. The largest category by far were cannabis violations. The article commented "It sounds like a doubtful crusade against petty crime, with cannabis smokers elevated to public enemy number one. What about the most worrying local crimes — robbery and burglary?"

(*Guardian*, 19.4.83, See the commentary by L. Christian, 1983, Section C).

Further, as Louis Christian points out

"Another factor is the extent to which stop and search creates crime. This could be measured in part by counting the number of offences, such as obstruction or assault on police, which can be said to arise out of the stop and search itself."

(1983, p. 37)

The yield then is derisory not because of the numbers nor the percentage of those arrested but from the quality of the results. Note that one of the major offences which stop and search reveals is possession of cannabis — one of the crimes which a substantial proportion of the people of Islington believe the police should spend less time in tackling. There is an obvious reason why stop and search is an ineffective exercise and this lies in the nature of serious crime itself rather than in any reflection on the abilities of the police officers concerned. Namely, that although the number of crimes in the inner city is high, the number of people at any one time who have just committed a crime is extremely low. Further, even if they are in the most unlikely event stopped within an hour of committing their crime it is extremely unlikely that they will be carrying substantial evidence around with them. Burglars simply do not walk the streets with stolen television sets in their arms and stolen money is very difficult to identify. Similarly, violent offenders only use weapons in a minority of offences, and therefore there is simply nothing to be found on searching them. There are exceptions to this rule — young people may frequently carry around cannabis for their own consumpton — but this is a crime which the public sees as extremely minor. Heroin dealers, in contrast, would scarcely parade their wares in the street, and would be unlikely to be picked up by these procedures. More positively, drunken driving — which *is* rated as a major crime by the public — can be detected by police stops and the use of the breathalyser. The important lesson is to distinguish between those activities which result in a low quality of yield because of the nature of the crimes which are ostensibly being pursued and those which justify stop and search.

Stop and search in Islington

Let us now examine the pattern of stop and search in Islington. The results show that 1 in 9 of the population of Islington have been stopped by the police in the last twelve months (see Table 36). Particularly affected is the under-25 age group, a quarter of whom have been stopped. In terms of race, blacks are twice as likely to be stopped as whites, and in terms of gender, men are over twice as likely as women. Asians overall have a very low stop rate. More seriously, the proportion of people stopped and searched varies remarkably by age; you are seventeen times more likely to be searched if you are under 25 than over 45, whilst you are four times more likely to be searched if a man rather than a woman. By race, blacks are twice as likely to be searched than whites and Asians have a search rate of one third of blacks and 70% less than whites. It is noteworthy that the difference between black and white search rates is largely due to the fact that the former have a high rate of car searches — the two groups do not differ in terms of searches whilst on foot. If we continue to subdivide by race and age we can gauge the degree of focus of police stops. As we can see from Table 37 the focus is on youth. A quarter of white youths are stopped but this rises to one third in the case of black youths (Asian figures are not sizeable enough, in this instance, to make a comparison).

Table 36   Stop and search rates over the last 12 months (by age, race, gender)

	ICS All	Age			Race			Gender	
		Under 25	25-44	45+	White	Black	Asian	Male	Female
A. % Population stopped	12.1	24.2	13.1	5.4	10.9	19.1	8.5	16.9	6.9
B. % Population stopped and searched on foot	4.0	12.7	3.4	0.4	4.0	4.6	1.4	6.6	1.6
C. Population cars searched	3.1	7.5	3.7	0.8	2.6	7.9	2.5	4.9	1.5
D. Total population searched* (B + C)	7.1	20.2	7.1	1.2	6.6	12.5	3.9	11.5	3.1

Excluding home searches

Even more revealing, however, is if we control by gender — because the focus of police attention on the streets is the young male.

Table 37   Rate of stops: comparison of white and black (by age)

Age	% White	% Black
Under 25	23.4	35.1
25-44	13.3	12.2
45+	5.0	10.9

Thus fully one half of young black males and one third of whites have been stopped in the last year. In common with all young people a high proportion who are stopped are searched (84% of all young people male and female are searched compared to 22% of those over 45). This focussing of the police on young people, and black youths in particular, is a stark fact of policing. Thus we might contrast the white male over 45 where under 7% are stopped in a year and under 2% searched, with the black male under 25 where over 50% are stopped and 44% searched. If we find sharp differences in attitudes to the police amongst our population we must remember that different sub-groups live in totally different universes of policing.

Table 38   Under 25, male stop and search

	% Stops	Search whilst on Foot	Search in Car	Total Searches	% Searched
Black	52.7	24.4	19.1	43.5	82.5
White	31.6	19.9	8.9	28.8	91.1

Public opinions of stop and search

Such marked differences in the populations targeted for stop and search is reflected in widespread differences in opinions about the practice (Table 39). Thus only 8% of those over 45 believe stop and search occurs often in their area compared to a quarter of those under 25. Similarly, criticism of stop and search increases with youth, with black rather than white and with the degree of contact with the police and the number of times a person has been a victim of crime.

Table 39   Public beliefs with regard to stop and search (by age, race, gender, contacts with police and levels of criminal victimization)

	All	Age Under 25	25-44	45+	Race White	Black	Asian	Gender Male	Female	Contact 0	1	2+	Victimization 0	1 or 2	3+
Stop and search occurs often in the area	16.8	25.3	22.9	7.6	15.4	29.5	17.6	16.6	16.9	–	–	–	–	–	–
Stop and search should occur less	20.6	32.1	28.0	9.0	17.8	46.2	16.8	–	–	12.6	25.8	28.3	14.5	21.4	26.9
Stop and search occurs without sufficient reason	38.4	59.4	51.9	19.5	37.0	55.0	26.8	38.7	38.1	–	–	–	–	–	–

Complaints against the police

"I am encouraged by the continuing research into public attitudes towards the police: the findings of the National Opinion Poll survey carried out in the spring of 1984 identify a positive public endorsement of our performance. The other major overall indicator I believe to be of worth is the level and seriousness of complaints. There have been substantial falls in the volume of both serious and less serious complaints, assisted in the latter case by the early experiments with conciliation. When considered alongside the rise in recorded crime and other workloads and the results of opinion surveys, the fall in complaints suggests that the performance of

Metropolitan Police Officers in a difficult working environment is received with some understanding and favour by the general public."

(K. Newman, 1984, p. 16)

We have seen how our survey shows no such level of endorsement of police performance in general. Let us, therefore, turn to the second indicator — complaints against the police.

What is of interest is that despite the level of dissatisfaction and annoyance with police performance there exists a substantial minority of people who would not make a complaint against a police officer if they were "seriously dissatisfied".

If we examine Table 40 we can see the level of the problem. Although, in general, only a small minority of people would not complain to the police when seriously dissatisfied, if we break down by sub-group a much greater level of unwillingness to complain is revealed. Thus, just under a quarter of all those under 25 would not complain, a quarter of all blacks, a third of young blacks, and from a quarter to half of all Asians. The paradox here is, of course, that the people who would most willingly complain to the police are those most satisfied with the police and vice versa. Thus it may well be true that over 90% of whites aged 45 and over would complain to the police if seriously dissatisfied but, of course, this group has very little to be dissatisfied about. *The main social groups from whom the bulk of complaints should emanate are the most reluctant to complain.* Lastly, we should note that contact with the police tends to diminish willingness to complain as does the level on which the respondent has been a victim of crime.

All in all, this evidence makes it difficult to recognize the level of complaints against the police as an effective indicator of police-public relations. Some explanation for its inability fully to gear into the problems of the most relevant publics is no doubt the fashion in which such complaints are dealt with internally by the police force and which have extraordinarily low levels of conviction (Kinsey, Lea and Young, 1986, Chapter 3).

Who should control the police?

We asked the interviewers who should be in control of the police, giving them the alternatives of the police themselves, the Council, the Home Secretary, local people and a combination of all of these. As we can see from Table 41, the existing political situation, namely that control of the London police is vested in the Home Secretary, received a derisory level of approval. Only 3% of the total population thought the Home Secretary was appropriate and in no subsection of the population did this rise above 5%. As for control by the police themselves — a situation which many claim that in terms of the majority of policy is in fact the case — only 17% overall thought that this was desirable. But there was a variation here, in that this was a policy which was upheld by a quarter of the over 45s but was unpopular particularly amongst the young (12% in favour) and blacks (9%). What is significant is that there was a marked decline in opinions favourable to police control of the police depending upon the more contacts the public has with them and, also, the more they had been criminally victimized.

344

Sole control by the Council was not at all popular, but control by the local people had the same support as control of the police by the police. Almost a quarter of young people wanted control by local people and the popularity of the option increased both with victimization and the amount of contact the individual has with the police. By far the most popular option was a combination of control: over half of the people plumped for this mode of control.

Table 40   Percentage of the public who would not make a complaint against a police officer if seriously dissatisfied (by age, race, contact with the police and level of victimization)

All		15.3
Age	Under 25	23.3
	25-44	16.3
	45+	11.4
Race	White	13.6
	Black	25.1
	Asian	35.7
White/Age	Under 25	21.6
	25-44	14.8
	45+	9.7
Black/Age	Under 25	30.2
	25-44	27.7
	45+	18.5
Asian/Age	Under 25	28.8
	25-44	24.2
	45+	51.5
Contact with police	None	12.4
	One	15.4
	Two+	19.2
Level of victimization	None	12.9
	One or two	13.6
	Three+	18.9

How can we translate these findings into viable policy alternatives? If we divide the various choices into three packages:

(a) *Present Situation* (police plus Home Secretary): approximately the present state of affairs.

(b) *Radical Democratic*: Council plus local people — a decentralized direct democracy.

(c) *Police Authority*: combination of options, which to the extent that it involves a degree of actual control by the Council and local people would be more democratic than the existing Police Authorities outside of London.

Table 41 **Who should decide how the local area is policed (by age, race, gender, contact with police, level of criminal victimization and income)**

	All	Age Under 25	25-44	45+	Race White	Black	Asian	Gender Male	Female	Contact with Police None	One	Two+	Level of Victimization None	1 or 2	3+	Income Under 3,000	3000-7,999	8000-11,999	12,000 +
The police	17.0	8.2	11.7	24.8	17.9	7.8	19.4	18.4	15.8	20.6	17.1	12.1	21.8	17.2	11.5	21.5	16.3	15.0	13.3
The Council	7.6	6.4	7.1	8.5	7.6	7.6	8.9	9.0	6.4	8.0	6.7	7.6	8.0	5.4	8.1	9.3	8.5	6.1	5.7
The Home Secretary	3.2	1.2	2.2	5.0	3.4	3.3	1.4	4.7	2.0	3.1	3.3	3.6	3.4	2.1	3.6	2.4	3.0	2.9	4.8
The local people	17.8	22.5	19.6	13.5	16.6	22.2	23.2	17.1	17.6	15.6	17.0	20.0	14.5	14.2	21.9	19.1	19.0	15.9	13.0
Combination of above	54.8	61.6	59.4	48.2	54.5	59.1	47.1	50.9	58.2	52.7	56.0	56.7	52.3	61.0	54.9	47.7	53.1	60.1	63.3

Table 42 **Three policy alternatives in terms of control of the police (by age, race, gender and income)**

Policy Options	All	Age Under 25	25-44	45+	Race White	Black	Asian	Gender Male	Female	Income Under 3,000	3,000-7,999	8,000-11,999	12,000 +
A. Present situation	20	9	14	30	21	12	21	23	18	24	19	18	18
B. Radical Democratic	35	29	27	22	25	29	32	26	24	28	28	22	19
C. Police Authority	55	62	59	48	55	59	47	51	58	48	53	60	63

As is obvious from Table 42, the idea of a Police Authority is by far the most popular option. The least popular preference is for the situation we have at the moment. Indeed the radical democratic model is 75% more popular than the present system and is more popular for every subsection of the population we investigated, apart from the over 45s.

A clear mandate arises, therefore, for a change in the system and it points in the direction of a Police Authority with a considerable amount of direct democratic input.

Our findings should be put in the context of a major shift in public opinion among Londoners on the question of who should control the Metropolitan Police Force. A recent Marplan Poll found that 59% of Londoners were in favour of a "Democratically Elected Police Authority" for London and that 80% of a separate poll of blacks and Asians were in favour (*Guardian* 14.10.85). A *Times* newspaper poll (30.9.85 and 2.10.85) found that 60% of Londoners favoured "Local Control of the Police" compared to 33% in a similar poll taken in 1981. Clearly, a majority of Londoners favours

346

achange from the *status quo* and some kind of locally orientated, democratically elected Police Authority, but all research polls to date, including this survey, have failed to pinpoint public views on the range and scope of powers that should be exercised by a democratically elected London Police Authority. However, it is clear that public opinion envisaged a democratically elected police authority having greater power than police authorities outside London set up by the 1964 Police Act, and would not support the inclusion of an undemocratic element, such as Magistrates.

Public perception of the term "control" needs to be more sharply defined as do, in the case of the ICS, terms like "combination of above". Although over half of the respondents favouring a "combination of above" specified the "council and local people" it would be erroneous and premature to draw any firm conclusions from that. In fact, this raises a number of further questions. Is the term "local people" in the minds of some people synonymous with "the Council" or vice versa? Does the coupling of the two imply a distance between "the Council" and "local people" in some people's minds? Does this further imply a desire for some kind of decentralization of some powers from the Town Hall? Only future research will reconcile these contradictions.

In conclusion, our question on control of the police was not finely tuned enough to go beyond ascertaining definite public support for a change in the *status quo* in a democratic direction. The precise policy parameters favoured by the public are yet to be ascertained. Future surveys will have to be designed to establish public opinion, not only on the general question of a democratically elected police authority (for London) but also on public perception of what should be its terms of reference, functions and powers.

17.   Justice and Symbolic Interaction
Stephen Hester and Peter Eglin

In this chapter we shall be considering symbolic interactionist work on the administration or 'construction' of justice. We begin by introducing the interactionist tradition of inquiry into the role of 'accounts' in social action, with particular reference to excuses and justifications offered by defendants in court. We then consider lawyers' application of conceptions of delinquents in courtroom interaction before turning to studies of the organizational context of the work of lawyers and judges in plea negotiation and sentencing. Fourthly, we examine the professional dominance thesis in relation to lawyer–client and court–defendant interaction.

'Accounts' and courtroom interaction

It is perhaps not surprising that symbolic interactionists have paid particular attention to the use of 'accounts' in their studies of courtroom processes since the court is a prime site where persons can be expected to explain themselves, justifying their actions, offering excuses for their behaviour, etc. Indeed, it is partly on such accounts of their conduct, in response to allegations, that the court's verdict and the judge's sentence (if any) will be based. Accordingly, in this section we shall consider symbolic interactionist work on accounts with particular reference to their role in courtroom interaction.

Probably the earliest symbolic interactionist work on the connection between accounts and conduct is that of C. Wright Mills and Sutherland, though what they had to say was rather brief. In his article, 'Situated Actions and Vocabularies of Motive', Mills (1940) referred to socially defined and available 'vocabularies of motive' as permitting the 'release' of the energy required to perform an action. These 'vocabularies' were 'good reasons', 'justifications', 'excuses', etc., in terms of which action could be said to make sense both prior to and after its occurrence. Sutherland (1939) made use of a similar notion in his theory of differential association and, in particular, his theory of white-collar crime (Sutherland 1949). In the former he proposed that a person 'becomes delinquent because of an excess of definitions favourable to violation of law over definitions unfavourable to violation of law'. These 'definitions' referred not only to techniques of committing crime, but also to 'a collection of motives, rationalizations, excuses and justifications for committing crimes'. In his study of white-collar crime Sutherland indicated that an 'ideology' for illegal business practice is learned which 'helps the novice to accept the illegal practices and provide rationalizations for them'.

The first major symbolic interactionist study in this genre was Cressey's (1953) work, *Other People's Money*. After interviewing numerous persons convicted of embezzling from their places of employment, Cressey theorized that in addition to being in positions of financial trust and experiencing 'nonshareable financial problems'

Stephen Hester and Peter Eglin: 'Justice and Symbolic Interaction' from *A SOCIOLOGY OF CRIME* (Routledge, 1992), pp. 189-207.

embezzlers employed 'vocabularies of adjustment' which permitted them to engage in embezzling behaviour. Such permission not only preceded these illegal acts but it was also necessary, argued Cressey. This was because the offenders conceived of themselves as essentially non-criminal. Vocabularies of adjustment or rationalizations such as the characterization of the act as only 'borrowing' enabled the embezzler to take the money and at the same time preserve a sense of him or herself as non-criminal, at least for the initial acts of embezzlement.

The explanatory role into which motives and rationalizations were cast in the work of Mills (1940), Sutherland (1949) and Cressey (1953), and the conception of the criminal and delinquent as basically conformist and in need of linguistic constructs through which they could accommodate crime with a conventional identity, were continued in the work of Matza on *Delinquency and Drift* (1990 (1964)). Matza's aim is to counteract the misleading tendency amongst criminologists to envisage the delinquent as essentially different from conformist youth and as committed to their delinquency. Such a view is that of the 'positive delinquent', says Matza — one who is committed to their misdeeds and constrained by the values and norms of a 'delinquent sub-culture'. Not so, says Matza. Rather than being committed to delinquency, the delinquent 'drifts' into situated acts of delinquency by virtue of a collection of ideas which permit its occasional occurrence. These ideas include five 'techniques of neutralization' which excuse or justify delinquent acts. These are (1) the denial of the victim, (2) the condemnation of the condemners, (3) the denial of responsibility, (4) the denial of injury and (5) the appeal to higher loyalties. They enable a kind of 'moral holiday' for the youth, an episodic release from the constraints of conformity. Thus, the 'denial of responsibility' permits the youth to say he or she did not mean it to happen, that it was an accident. The denial of the victim permits the delinquent to say he or she 'did it in self-defence'. The condemnation of the condemners involves pointing to the 'far worse' crimes committed by more conventional and typically more powerful persons and groups (for example, 'alcohol is far more harmful, so why bust us for marijuana?') The 'denial of injury' permits the claim that 'no one was hurt'. Finally, the 'appeal to higher loyalties' provides for the explanation that the delinquent act was 'required' or 'demanded' in some way by a 'higher authority'.

These symbolic interactionist studies were later subjected to conceptual clarification in an article by Scott and Lyman (1968) entitled 'Accounts'. They indicate that, for the most part, this corpus of work was referring to one of two varieties of 'accounts': excuses or justifications. Thus excuses admit wrongfulness but deny responsibility whilst justifications admit responsibility but deny wrongfulness.

In later studies the role of accounts has been examined not in relation to how they facilitate criminal behaviour in the first place but with respect to their role after the offender has been charged and put on trial for such behaviour. Two studies are of particular note here. The first, by Taylor (1972), is concerned with sexual offenders' accounts of their crimes. The second, by Emerson (1969), examines the use by delinquents of excuses and justifications in the juvenile court.

Taylor: sex offenders' accounts of their motives

Taylor's study is interesting because it not only provides a description of the range of accounts used by sexual offenders, it also examines the relative acceptability of those accounts for the courts. As far as the former is concerned, accounts range from the involuntary to the voluntary. Involuntary accounts cited factors which were beyond the individual's control at the time of the offence and they deprecated the role of a conscious motive for the assaults. Out of a total of ninety-four accounts offered in the study, forty-one thus cited some form of 'breakdown in mental functioning' such as temporary insanity, a blackout or fit or some kind of cortical disturbance. Twelve explained the behaviour in terms of an 'inner impulse' such as instinct or an overwhelming desire which 'compelled' the offender to act against his will. In this regard offenders spoke of being 'sex-mad' and 'over-sexed', mere spectators while their irreversible and uncontrollable urges took over. Another twelve 'involuntary' offenders spoke in terms of 'defective social skills'. For them their assaults were a 'mistake'. They thus claimed things like 'I didn't know what I was doing', 'I just stumbled into the situation', and 'I didn't mean to frighten her. I was trying to ask her to go out with me'. Voluntary accounts, on the other hand, admitted the active role played by the offender in the commission of the offence. Six accounts 'implicated the victim', saying they were tempted and willingly went along with the temptation, seven reported a desire for special experiences, three confessed a wish to frighten or hurt the victim and another five reported a refusal to accept the normative constraints surrounding sexual relations; they insisted on the importance of allowing 'free play'. One of these last stated 'I'll do it to anybody. It's all a laugh to me.'

Turning to the relative acceptability of these accounts, Taylor found that with respect to twenty-six magistrates questioned there were marked differences in acceptability. The magistrates were offered the various categories of accounts and were asked how likely they thought it was that the statement was true and how likely it was that the remark would be made by a sexual deviant. This was done in relation to three offences: rape, indecent assault and indecent exposure. The relative acceptability was consistent across these three offence categories. Thus the most acceptable accounts were those mentioning 'involuntary factors' whilst the least acceptable were those of the voluntary variety. Thus:

Account	*Number of judgments of acceptability as true*
Defective social skills	49
Breakdown in mental functioning	40
Inner impulse	38
Wish to frighten or hurt	36
Implicating the victim	34
Desire for special experiences	26
Refusal to accept normative constraints	22

These results show that magistrates are more likely to accept as true those accounts which cite 'involuntary' factors.

Emerson: typical delinquencies in the juvenile court

Symbolic interactionism has had a long-standing interest in the use of social types, classifications and labels in social interaction. This is in keeping with its concern for illuminating the 'actor's point of view'. As we shall show in the [next chapter], this interest in 'typification' is one which it shares with phenomenology and ethnomethodology, but with certain key differences in approach. We review these differences in the [next chapter]. It remains true, however, as we noted in [Chapter 5], that ethnographic studies in symbolic interactionism and ethnomethodology are often quite similar since their authors frequently draw on both of these traditions (see Hawkins and Tiedeman 1975). A major example of this is the work of Emerson on *Judging Delinquents*. He examines the interactional practices and the typifications used by court staff in dealing with alleged juvenile offenders.

With respect to the typifying work of the court he found that an initial distinction could be drawn between those cases typified as involving 'trouble' and those not. Of course, all youths brought before the court are regarded by someone as trouble; every complaint is a plea for the court to do something about the defendant. However, Emerson found that the court has its own ways of judging or typifying trouble. For the court 'trouble' is a 'predictive construct'. It is the 'inferred potential for committing serious delinquent acts'. Trouble relates to the type of person the offender is, not simply to the type of offence he or she has committed. The nature of the offence may assist in typifying the trouble but it will not be the only criterion. Serious offences create a 'presumption of trouble', but trouble is also predicted on the basis of the presence of adverse patterns of behaviour and social circumstances which typically precede delinquency.

The court's focus on the offender rather than the offence flows from its commitment to treatment rather than simple sanctioning of the juveniles who come before it. As Emerson puts it, the court's concern is not so much 'what happened' but 'what is the problem here'. Once it has decided that it has trouble on its hands, it looks in greater depth at the juvenile's overall behaviour, personality and family and social circumstances. There then occurs what Emerson calls a 'second sorting' which involves establishing or typifying the juvenile's 'moral character' (recall Sacks on the assessment of moral character, in [Chapter 6]).

Assessments of moral character provide for the kind of special handling that cases require. That is, assessments of moral character differentiate kinds of trouble and provide accounts for the delinquent behaviour. Three general types of moral character were distinguished by the court: the 'normal', the 'hard-core' and the 'disturbed'. The juvenile with a 'normal' moral character was seen as being like most kids, acting for basically normal and conventional reasons, despite some delinquent behaviour. Those seen as 'hard-core' were typified as criminal-like delinquents, motivated by malice and hostility, consciously pursuing illegal ends. The 'disturbed' moral character belongs to those who were driven to acting in senseless and irrational ways by obscure motives and inner compulsions. These distinctions echo those described in Cicourel's earlier (1968) study of juvenile justice.

The significance of the categories of juvenile moral character is that they provide institutionally relevant means for explaining the juvenile behaviour and they provide justifications for the court's actions. Thus, to decide that a youth is 'disturbed' is to account for his or her behaviour and to provide the relevance of psychiatric care, whilst to typify the youth as 'hard-core' explains the behaviour as a product of that kind of criminally motivated actor who needs punishment and restraint. The decision that the juvenile is 'normal' explains the behaviour as the result of conventional motives and provides justification for routine handling, for example, probation.

If these are the types of moral character used by the court in examining and dealing with individual cases the question is then raised as to how moral character is decided. Emerson suggests that in general it is a product of social interaction and communicative work involving the delinquent, his or her family, enforcers, complainants generally and the court. In particular, it involves two types of social process. The first is the presentation by the prosecuting and defence lawyers of different versions of moral character. The second is the use of protective strategies by the juvenile.

There are two types of character presentation used by the lawyers: pitches and denunciations. Pitches are directed to obtaining a more lenient disposition than would initially seem appropriate. They tend to emphasize the sterling moral qualities of the defendant. Denunciations, on the other hand, seek a more severe disposition than could be expected. They aim to soil and discredit the juvenile's character. Both focus on the delinquent act and both emphasize the delinquent's general behaviour, including personal and social background, arguing that these provide evidence of moral character. Successful pitches manage to depict the act as a typical product of a normal actor and thus establish the normality of the youth's biography. Successful denunciations establish the present act as that typically committed by delinquents of a criminal-like character and they manage to construct a delinquent biography that unequivocally indicates someone of such character.

In presenting both pitches and denunciations the lawyers focus on (1) the offence and (2) the defendant's biography. With respect to the offence, they make use of the notion of 'typical delinquencies' (see Sudnow in [Chapter 10]). These consist of the typical features of regularly encountered delinquent acts and delinquents, embodying the court's experience with and common-sense knowledge of the situations and settings of delinquent acts. Each typical delinquency or delinquent is composed of typical elements or features. For example, the typical shoplifter is a mild type, not a serious delinquent, with no previous record, from a well-to-do family, who takes goods for kicks, is seldom in trouble, not a thief at heart, succumbing to the temptation of the moment. On the other hand, the typical handbag snatcher is a pretty serious delinquent, known to other courts, maybe on parole or probation and is aggressive. Furthermore, typical delinquencies as a whole were divided into three classes by the court. Thus, for example, the 'normal' assault is a fight comprising a street scene, young boys, fists (weapons only in the 'heat' of battle) and equal contributions by both parties. By contrast, the 'criminal assault' is an attack on a stranger, typically motivated by robbery, and is vicious, causing serious harm, sometimes murder. The 'disturbed assault' has no apparent motive, involves strangers, and is typically an irrational outburst. The job for the denouncer, if he or she is to be successful, is to demonstrate that the features of a typical criminal assault were present. For a successful pitch, the task is to show that those of the normal assault were present.

With respect to the defendant's biography, denunciations seek to place the delinquent act at or near the ultimate stage in the youth's delinquent career, that is, a hopeless case. Pitches demonstrate that the youth has rehabilitation prospects, that the person's delinquent involvement is inconsequential, and that they are growing out of it. Both denunciations and pitches attempt to do this first by 'establishing a pattern'. The denouncer therefore presents a history of both official and unofficial prior delinquency, uses reports to accentuate the significance of the present incident and emphasizes the youth's bad attitude, trouble at school, truancy and bad companions. The pitch's pattern-making, on the other hand, involves minimizing the significance of prior trouble, the youth's cooperation and good attitude. Secondly, the denouncer and the pitcher refer to 'family background and sponsorship'. Here both try to show the presence or absence of the typical background and circumstances associated with the type of delinquency which they are recommending to the court.

Emerson's work shows the importance of typification in judging delinquents. However, before leaving it we must emphasize that this is not to say that dealing with delinquents is solely a one-sided cognitive process. The juvenile does at least have the opportunity to provide a version of the events leading to the court appearance. Emerson thus refers to three types of 'defensive strategy' employed by the juveniles in courtroom discourse: (1) the plea of innocence, (2) justifications and (3) excuses. These are the sort of accounts we discussed earlier in the chapter on the role of accounts in symbolic interactionist work. Coleman (1976) provides a useful symbolic interactionist analysis of 'grievance accounts' in traffic court, an analysis that may be compared to the ethnomethodological studies of traffic court interaction by Pollner, whose work we examine in [Chapter 10].

The organizational imperatives of courtroom work

As Peter Berger (1963) says in his famous, if now somewhat dated, short *Invitation to Sociology*, the discipline has a reputation for debunking official and 'respectable' images of society. A large part of this reputation is owed to the ethnographic (that is, descriptive) studies by symbolic interactionists of a huge variety of everyday settings, both those that are nominally 'exotic' (nude beaches, massage parlours) and those that are, superficially, closer to home (buses, shopping malls, factories). Indeed, in some quarters, such work has been accused of amounting to advocating partisanship on behalf of the 'underdog'. As Cuff and Payne (1984: 129-131) argue, however, this effect arises, not from some 'political' intention on the part of the inquirer, but from symbolic interactionist studies adhering to their own methodological principles, namely, to tell the story from the 'inside', as the participants to the setting see it, that is in terms of their 'definitions of the situation'. Inevitably, this will mean giving equal weight to viewpoints that standardly are not heard — the prostitute's, the janitor's, the bus-driver's, the drug-pusher's, the 'deviant's'. This attitude is expressed, for example, in the title of an article by Stoddart (1982) which we cited in [Chapter 5], 'The enforcement of narcotics violations in a Canadian city: heroin users' perspectives on the production of official statistics.' Indeed, for most members of a modern society with its highly variegated division of labour the work settings of others are, in many cases, 'foreign' territory. Just to learn how such settings routinely operate can be a source of news. We pass through or by the doctor's office, the bus, the mall, the office building, the factory, the bar, the hospital. How is it for those who spend their working lives there? How does it really work?

The criminal justice system has been no exception to this debunking phenomenon. We saw in [Chapter 5] how, in order to do what they regard as good police work, police were seen to have recourse to extra-legal features of an encounter to select that which was criminal. Similarly, we shall see that in order, as they see it, to make the court system work legal personnel engage in a variety of practices that lie outside the strict legal description of their jobs. This is not something they see themselves as having an option about. That is, they feel compelled in order to fulfil the mandate contained in their job descriptions, indeed their professional vocation, to be responsive to what we will call the 'organizational demand characteristics' or 'organizational imperatives' of the work setting itself. The expression 'demand characteristic' comes from experimental psychology where it refers to those features of an experiment which are influencing the results but which are not intended parts of the research design. Thus in the court system the desired outcome, namely justice within the law, must be achieved not only according to the rules of due process and according to the facts of each case, but with due respect for the following inescapable organizational matters: the resources available, the time at hand, the working relationships that must be sustained between setting co-inhabitants, the division of labour, the flow of cases, the availability of witnesses, the sentencing practices of particular judges, the presence of interpreters and so on. According to Blumberg (1976 (1967)) the court's 'problem' can be reduced to the dilemma of managing huge caseloads while preserving due process. He describes the court's 'solution' as comprising 'a large variety of bureaucratically ordained and controlled "work crimes", short cuts, deviations, and outright rule violations adopted as court practice to meet production norms' (*ibid.*:150).

Blumberg mentions the following 'stratagems' to dispose of too-large caseloads:

> threatening a 'potentially harsh sentence . . . as the visible alternative to pleading guilty, in the case of recalcitrants'
> 'tailoring' of probation and psychiatric reports to meet organizational needs, or to be 'at least responsive to the court organization's requirements for the refurbishment of a defendant's social biography, consonant with his new status'
> judges' pressing into service '[s]tenographers and clerks, in their function as record keepers . . . in support of a judicial need to "rewrite" the record of a courtroom event'
> using bail as a 'weapon . . . to collapse the resistance of an accused person'.
> (Blumberg 1976 (1967):150-151)

As these practices suggest it is appropriate to think of court personnel as a 'closed community'. Such a community embraces all who are 'regulars' in that setting, including the judges, crown attorneys, the Office of the Clerk of the Court, the

Probation Division and the press. It also includes the defendant's lawyer, especially if s/he is a court-appointed duty counsel (Canada) or public defender (USA): 'The accused's lawyer has far greater professional, economic, intellectual and other ties to the various elements of the court system than he does to his own client' (Blumberg 1976: 149). Consequently, the defendant is regarded as an 'outsider', one who in Blumberg's phrase is the 'mark' in a legal 'con game'. 'Goffman's (1962) "cooling out" analysis is especially relevant in the lawyer-accused client relationship' (Blumberg 1976: 154).

If the court's problem is too many cases, the court community comes together to solve it by focusing on getting the defendant to plead guilty, thus avoiding a trial and all the work, expense and time that involves. A 'plea bargain' is '[a]ny agreement by the accused to plead guilty in return for the promise of some benefit' (Griffiths *et al.* 1980: 159). The standard benefits on offer are as follows:

> reduction of a charge to a lesser or included offence
> withdrawal of other pending charges or a promise to do so
> a promise about a sentence recommendation (type, severity)
> a promise not to oppose the defence's sentence recommendation
> a promise not to charge friends or family
> a promise to proceed summarily in dual offences
> the shortening of 'dead time'
> concealment of actual criminality (e.g. from parole board)
> freedom from further investigation of prior offences
> (from Griffiths *et al.* 1980: 159-160; Skolnick 1975 (1966): 175)

According to Klein (1976) defendants mostly do 'deals' directly with the police. Police benefits are cited as recovery of illegal or stolen property (such as explosives, firearms or drugs), the improvement of clearance rates and the maintenance of the flow of information. Indeed, on occasions such as the Olsen case and the Kirby case, both in 1981–82 in Canada, the police will buy information from defendants or witnesses. Brannigan cites data from 'A Longitudinal Study of the Cumulative Effects of Discretionary Decisions in the Criminal Process' carried out by the Centre of Criminology of the University of Toronto in the middle and late 1970s showing police pressing their views in particular cases on the prosecuting crown attorney. Indeed, according to one of the major reports on this study — the only large-scale (and interactionist) study of such matters in Canada — 'detectives frequently participated in plea discussions and were often acknowledged by the defence lawyer and crown attorney to be the key participant because they had the most intimate official knowledge of the case and thus were deemed to be in the best position to decide the limits of negotiation' (Ericson and Baranek 1982: 115). According to Tepperman 'the process of turning arrests into conviction statistics usually takes place in a prosecutor's office' (1977: 82) and takes place between an accused person's lawyer and the prosecutor (1977: 80). But in the end it appears to be the defence lawyer, whether retained privately or through legal aid who must sell the deal to the client and so get the guilty plea from him or her (Blumberg 1976: 162-163; Snider 1988: 296). 'In sum, police, crown attorneys, and lawyers collaborate in collectively achieving an outcome that serves their respective interests' (Ericson and Baranek 1982: 123).

The actual discussions that may or may not result in an agreement as to plea are not standardly conducted in open court (although, especially in the United States, they must be reported there) but 'in various "low visibility" contexts out of court. Charge alterations, possibilities for evidence submission, and ranges of sentencing are discussed in a variety of locales, e.g. in the courthouse corridors and offices, in the judge's chambers, at a lunch counter, and over the telephone' (Ericson and Baranek 1982: 111). There are structural limits to the scope of 'bargaining' set by, for example, mandatory minimum penalties for certain repeated convictions and, conversely, by the considerable sentencing discretion in the hands of the judge in Canada: a reduced charge may not mean much if the judge can give the same sentence for it as for the original charge.

> In addition to the limits framed by the penalty structure, and by sentencing practices of judges, there are substantial influences coming from other sources. Chief among these is the charging practices of the police, which frame what the other parties have to discuss once the case reaches the court stage . . . Alschuler (1968) states, 'The charge is the asking price in plea bargaining, and the drafting of accusations is therefore an integral part of the negotiating process.' . . . [O]ur observation of the police in constructing cases against our accused respondents (Ericson, 1981, 1982) led us to conclude that an established practice was to charge every accused in a case with everything possible as a means of creating a maximal starting position for plea discussions. This was undertaken even on some occasions when the police explicitly stated that some of the charges against some of the accused would clearly not be upheld in court.
>
> (Ericson and Baranek 1982: 115)

Furthermore, much that is relevant to plea discussions is tacit. That is, as in many an organization, 'silent bargains' are struck between various players as to what will be the preferred course of action in some given state of play. When such circumstances arise, nothing need be said; matters are simply understood. Again it is arguable to what extent participation in these 'games' is optional:

> Prosecutors establish reciprocal relationships with those who are able to reciprocate, resulting in the neglect of those who are unable to do so. Reciprocity is largely confined to those defence lawyers who have been admitted to the social circle, dependent as it is on the quality of their relationship with the prosecutor. Reciprocity results in discrimination, for benefits are limited to those lawyers who happen to be suppliers of benefits. Lawyers who do not supply their 'quota' of guilty pleas and contest every case are subjected to 'the bare bones of the legal system'.
>
> (Grosman 1969: 80; cited in Griffiths et al. 1980: 161)

This admittedly 'impressionistic' result from Grosman's interview study of crown prosecutors in the county of York, Ontario is nevertheless supported by a parallel observation in Sudnow's (1976 (1965)) study of 'sociological features of the penal code in a public defender office' in a metropolitan California community, a study we examine in greater detail in [Chapter 10]. The first of the practices Blumberg cites (see p. 198) whereby defendants are induced to plead guilty refers specifically to 'the case of recalcitrants'. In Sudnow's court 'recalcitrants' are called 'stubborn defendants'. 'These are cases for which reductions are available, reductions that are constructed on the basis of the typicality of the offense and allowable by the D.A.. These are normal crimes committed by "stubborn" defendants' (Sudnow 1976: 136). Stubborn defendants are those who insist on pleading not guilty. For the team of the public defender and the district attorney the question here is not one of guilt or innocence, but of 'reasonableness'; they take the guilt of the defendant not to be in question. Consequently, when the case of such a defendant who will not play the game gets to court, the defence provided by the public defender amounts to what Sudnow calls minimum 'adequate legal representation'. That is, while the lawyer will

> conduct his part of the proceedings in accord with complete respect for proper legal procedure . . . [H]e will not cause any serious trouble for the routine motion of the court conviction process . . . In 'return' for all this, the district attorney treats the defendant's guilt in a matter-of-fact fashion . . . [and] 'puts on a trial' (in their way of referring to their daily tasks) in order to, with a minimum of strain, properly place the defendant behind bars. Both prosecutor and public defender thus protect the moral character of the other's charges from exposure.
>
> (Sudnow 1976: 139-140)

> The routine trial, generated as it is by the defendant's refusal to make a lesser plea, is the 'defendant's fault': 'What the hell are we supposed to do with them? If they can't listen to good reason and take a bargain, then its their tough luck. If they go to prison, well, they're the ones who are losing the trials, not us'.
>
> (Sudnow 1976: 138)

In short, the 'punishment' for the stubborn defendant of minimum, adequate legal representation seems quite akin to that of 'the bare bones of the legal system' visited on the lawyers who will not play the game.

The professional dominance thesis and the law

The 'professional dominance thesis' was originally developed to explain the social organization of medical care (Freidson 1970). It is a 'structural' thesis. Cross features of the phenomenon in question, namely the provision of medical care, are seen to be consequences of a certain arrangement of the social structure, namely that medicine is organized in the form of a profession and that profession has come to dominate the provision of that care. But from the beginning the thesis has received an interactional interpretation. Not only is professional power institutionalized in that the relationship between service provider and service seeker is carried on as one between a 'professional' and a 'client', but, it is argued, that power is exerted and expressed in the forms of 'control' by which the doctor dominates the patient in the consultation itself (Scheff 1968; Strong 1979: 128ff.).

So interpreted the thesis is attractive to those looking for the sociological missing link — the bridge between micro- and macro-levels of analysis. Indeed the result has been what Robert Dunstan (1980: 74) calls 'interactionism for Marxians', an area of inquiry in which the two perspectives have somewhat converged. (There have also been important contributions from that area of linguistics known as 'discourse analysis' or 'pragmatics', and in the work of West (1984) and others an important gender component has been added.)

The thesis has been extended from medicine to more or less the whole range of professional/client 'service encounters'. In its general form the thesis holds that such encounters are

> arenas of conflict, struggle or, at least, negotiation
> over the definition of the situation, the interactional agenda
> and the time and resources available
> between contending parties with competing interests in the
> matter at hand.

The professional service provider is portrayed as one concerned to define the presenting 'complaint' in terms that suit his or her professional, bureaucratic or, indeed, ruling-class interests: the professional is interested in the disease rather than the patient's health, a manageable classroom rather than the student's education, a smoothly operating courtroom rather than justice for the defendant. To enforce those interests, and this is where the specifically interactional claims arise, the professional is said to employ various strategies for controlling the service encounter. Among these are specifically sociolinguistic ones. Particular significance has been accorded to interruptions, questions and silences (Eglin and Wideman 1986).

The following is a characteristic statement of the thesis as it applies to lawyer-client interaction.

> In contrast to the traditional depiction of lawyers as providing loyal disinterested service to clients, analysis of one lawyer-client interaction in a legal aid office revealed that the lawyer used language to control the client's presentation of the case, and to define it in terms of convenience to the organization rather than the expressed wishes of the client. Three types of linguistic strategies relating to the control of talk were examined: (1) management of structural features; (2) choice of instrumentality; and (3) management of interactional features. Structural strategies of interruptions and topic control served to display the lawyer's expertise, while preventing the client from enhancing his status. The form of the directives controlled the client's responses, forcing him to react to the lawyer's assertions rather than serving as the primary source of information, while the use of performatives and other elements of the formal register served to highlight the lawyer's control. Frequent challenges to the client's adherence to the maxim of quality by the use of repetitions, requests for outside confirmation, reformulations, repeat questions without waiting for a reply, and unfounded presuppositions combined with the other features to establish a dialogue that is very much like cross-examination.
>
> (Bogoch and Danet 1984: 249)

While the above is stated for the case of lawyer–client interaction in a legal office virtually identical claims have been made for the character of spoken interaction in the courtroom between judge or lawyer and defendant (Danet and Bogoch 1980; O'Barr 1982).

Particularly prominent in professional dominance studies have been analyses that have attempted to show that it is through the professional's use of interruptions and particular kinds of questions that power and control are exercised. By interrupting the client or defendant or witness, by being the one who asks the questions, and by asking particularly yes/no questions, the professional (lawyer or judge) is said to control topic choice, topic development and answerer's options. Thereby the defendant is coerced.

Of course, before it can be assessed whether or not questions and interruptions do produce these interactional effects they have to be identified as such in the record of the talk to be analysed. This is where problems begin to arise for this Marxian–interactionist enterprise. The mere identification in the transcript of some syntactic form such as an interrogative or declarative does not guarantee that the one is doing the work of 'asking a question' and the other 'answering'. For questions can be asked without using interrogative syntax, and utterances with such a form may be doing an accusation rather than asking for information. As Dunstan says:

> The proposal that almost every one of a lawyer's turns will have 'the illocutionary force of a request for information' [Danet and Bogoch, 1980] appears to be patently insensitive to the work done in and through 'questioning'. As has been pointed out elsewhere, such turns are only 'minimally describable' as questions for they are also variously produced and treated primarily as accusations, counter-denials, displays of disbelief, repair initiations, pre-sequencers, and so on [see Atkinson and Drew in (Chapter 10), this volume]. Furthermore, in only a small fraction of instances are the questions asked in cross-examination genuine requests for information. It is, as consultation of trial manuals will reveal, a primary 'rule' for cross-examination, that one should never ask a question to which one does not know the answer.
>
> (Dunstan 1980: 64)

Similarly, there is no syntactic or other coding rule which will uniquely capture interruptions, since interruptions are a form of deviance and symbolic interactionism itself teaches that the identification of deviance rests on the interpretive judgments of participants, not observers. Overlapping talk, for example, may result from simultaneous starts by both parties to the talk or may constitute what conversation analysts call 'third-turn overlapping repair'. In neither case is interruption involved. Nevertheless, without regard for this fundamental point Bogoch and Danet (1984) proceed to code their case for interruptions.

Their initial finding is that 12 per cent of utterances are interrupted by the other speaker, and that 'the difference in the rate of interrupted utterances between the speakers is not great (14 per cent for the client and 9 per cent for the lawyer)' (*ibid*: 254). This surprises them since the literature would lead one to expect that the lawyer 'who is the superior in the interaction' would interrupt more often. However, they realize that not all interruptions are alike, and distinguish two types, 'cooperative' and 'competitive', the former occurring at the end of utterances and signalling co-participation, the latter in mid-utterance and signalling attempts to control.

> The distribution of these two sorts of interruptions between the lawyer and the client is highly revealing. While over three-quarters of the interruptions of the client's speech occurs in mid-utterance, reflecting the lawyer's bid for control, 70% of the interruptions of the lawyer's speech occur at the end of her utterance, most likely indicating active cooperation by the client.
>
> (Bogoch and Danet 1984: 255)

The authors display the following example of each type, where overlaps are indicated by square brackets.

COOPERATION

Lawyer: What happened [to you]
Client: [He asked me] to leave

COMPETITION

Lawyer: Private? A private complaint?
Client: Yes yes [it]
Lawyer: [The man] who is the attacker, what's his name?

Notice (1) that without the lawyer's next utterance in the first case it is impossible for the reader to know how the lawyer took the claimed interruption. (2) Again, without the client's preceding utterance it is impossible to know whether, as seems likely from the client's answer, the completion of 'What happened' could be projected by the hearer; were that so then it is quite common for next speaker not to wait for the end of the turn but to come right in at the first point that understanding has been achieved and so produce overlap with the end of the current speaker's turn. It is doubtful in such interactional circumstances whether anyone would find this to be an interruption.

In the second case notice: (1) that the client answers the lawyer's question perfectly adequately, whereupon the floor quite legitimately returns to the questioner for the next turn; (2) that the answerer chooses to try to extend the turn produces the overlap with the questioner's next turn; (3) after one word in overlap answerer drops out. If this is an interruption by questioner it is immediately acceded to by answerer. Competition would seem to be noticeable by its absence.

This is not how it appears to Bogoch and Danet who go on to assert that the lawyer's 'interruption' denies opportunity to the client to 'display his knowledge of legal matters', 'indicates that what he had to say was not worth hearing' and asserts the lawyer's 'right to control the topic' (*ibid*: 255). These claims are advanced without any evidence presented from the client's talk of struggle, challenge or competition that might indicate that he shares the analysts' perception and evaluation of the situation. Bogoch and Danet conclude by noting how like courtroom cross-examination this encounter is and clearly find it thereby objectionable. That this is a collaborative accomplishment of the two parties, that they produce the interactional features of an interview or consultation (not unlike the medical sort), that socialization of the client to the standard format for such an encounter may be a feature of it (see Hughes (1982) for the medical case), and that it is specifically a feature of (first) legal interviews that the lawyer *does* 'cross-examine' the prospective client are considerations not to be found in their account.

The foregoing critique of elements of the interactional version of the professional dominance thesis as applied to one form of legal encounter has drawn on ideas from a species of ethno-methodological conversation analysis that deals with the organization of turn-taking in conversation and related speech exchange systems. We examine this approach in detail in the next chapter [(Chapter 10)] as it applies to courtroom interaction, and so will not say anything further on that topic here.

18.　Creation of the Modern Prison in England and Europe (1550-1850)

Dario Melossi and Massimo Pavarini

Bridewells and workhouses in Elizabethan England

> The process, therefore, that *clears the way* for the capitalist system, can be none other than *the process which takes away from the labourer the possession of his means of production;* a process that *transforms*, on the one hand, the social means of subsistence and of production *into capital;* on the other hand, the immediate producers into *wage-labourers.* The so-called *'primitive accumulation'* therefore, is nothing else than the *historical process of divorcing the producer from the means of production.* It appears as primitive because it forms the *pre-historic stage of capital* and of the mode of production corresponding with it. The economic structure of capitalistic society has grown out of the economic structure of feudal society. The dissolution of the latter set free the elements of the former.[1]

This well-known passage in which Marx outlines the essential meaning of the 'so-called primitive accumulation' is the key to a reading of those historical events which are the subject of our enquiry. The same process, *of divorcing the producer from his means of production,* is at the root of a dual phenomenon: the transformation of means of production into capital; and the transformation of the immediate producer tied to the soil into *a free* labourer. The process manifests itself concretely in the economic, political, social, ideological and moral dissolution of the feudal world. The first aspect of the question, the creation of capital, does not concern us here. Rather it is the second aspect, *the formation of the proletariat,*[2] that constitutes the more fruitful area of research.

'The disbanding of feudal retainers, the dissolution of the monasteries, the enclosures of land for sheep-farming and changes in the methods of tillage each played their part'[3] in the great expulsion of peasants from the land in fifteenth- and sixteenth-century England. But according to Dobb's classic thesis, the feudal mode of production was being drained by its own inefficiency even before these events;[4] as the system demanded heavier workloads of the peasants, the only escape routes left open to them were vagabondage in the countryside or flight to the towns. The decline of feudalism and the corresponding brutality in social relations was marked by the intensification of the class struggle in the countryside, the prime expression of which was the desertion by the peasantry from increasingly intolerable conditions. [5]

Dario Melossi and Massimo Pavarini: 'Creation of the Modern Prison in England and Europe (1550-1850)' from *THE PRISON AND THE FACTORY: ORIGINS OF THE PENITENTIARY SYSTEM* (Macmillan Press Ltd, 1981), pp. 11-62.

Thousands of dispossessed workers in the countryside flocked to the towns which, with the development of economic activity, especially commerce, already represented a notable pole of attraction; the dispossessed now became the mass of the unemployed — beggars, vagrants and in some cases, bandits.

In its quest for expansion, capital displayed its most ruthless class savagery in the movement for the enclosure of common land. When referring to the relevant eighteenth-century legislation, Marx was to define the rape of the countryside which drove the first ranks of the future proletariat into the towns, as 'decrees of expropriation of the people'.[6] Thomas More gave this lucid description of the phenomenon in his *Utopia* as early as 1516:

> Your sheep that were wont to be so meek and tame, and so small eaters, now as I hear say, be become so great devourers and so wild, that they eat up, and swallow down the very men themselves. . . For look in what parts of the realm doth grow the finest and therefore dearest wool, there noblemen and gentlemen . . . leave no ground for tillage, they inclose all into pastures; . . . by one means therefore or by other, either by hook or crook they must needs depart away, poor, silly, wretched souls, men, women, husbands, wives, fatherless children, widows, woeful mothers, with their young babes, and their whole household small in substance and much in number, as husbandry requireth many hands . . . And when they have wandered abroad till that be spent, what can they then else do but steal, and then justly pardy be hanged, or else go about begging. [7]

The state's initial response to what was at the time a social phenomenon of unprecedented proportions is quite clearly described by Marx:

> The proletariat created by the breaking up of the bands of feudal retainers and by the forcible expropriation of the people from the soil, this 'free' proletariat could not possibly be absorbed by the nascent manufacturers as fast as it was thrown upon the world. On the other hand, these men, suddenly dragged from their wonted mode of life, could not as suddenly adapt themselves to the discipline of their new condition. They were turned en masse into beggars, robbers, vagabonds, partly from inclination, in most cases from stress of circumstances. Hence at the end of the 15th century and during the whole of the 16th century throughout Western Europe a bloody legislation against vagabondage. The fathers of the present working class were chastised for their enforced transformation into vagabonds and paupers. Legislation treated them as 'voluntary' criminals, and assumed that it depended on their own good will to go on working under the old conditions that no longer existed.[8]

Marx goes on to cite examples of the growth during the fourteenth, fifteenth and sixteenth centuries of draconian legislation against vagabondage, begging and — to a lesser extent — crime, in the face of which traditional medieval structures, based as they were on private and religious charity, proved impotent. Moreover, the secularisation of ecclesiastical wealth following the reformation in England and Europe had the twofold effect of contributing to the expulsion of peasants from church property and of leaving those hitherto dependent on the charity of the monasteries and religious orders without means of subsistence. The greater the scale of proletarianisation, therefore, the less the effectiveness of the campaign of terror,[9] while, at the same time, the development of the economy, and of manufacture in particular, demanded an ever greater quantity of labour from the countryside. More pointed out the only logical solution as early as 1516 when he strongly advocated the necessity of placing this 'idle sort' [10] in useful employment. An Act of 1530 made the registration of vagrants compulsory. For the first time a distinction was made between those unable to work ('the impotent poor'), who were authorised to beg, and the rest, who were forbidden any kind of charity on pain of being flogged until the blood ran. [11]

The principal instruments of English social policy remained whipping, banishment and capital punishment until the middle of the century, by which time conditions were evidently ripe for what was to prove a model experiment. At the request of certain representative clerics alarmed at the amount of begging in London, the King consented to the use of Bridewell Palace as a place where vagrants, idlers, thieves and petty criminals would be housed. [12] The aim of the institution, which was to be run with an iron hand, was threefold: to reform the inmates by means of compulsory labour and discipline; to discourage vagrancy and idleness outside its walls; and, last but not least, to ensure its own self-sufficiency by means of labour. [13] Work mainly centred around textiles in accordance with the need of the time, and the experiment must on the whole have been crowned with success since houses of correction, indiscriminately referred to as Bridewells, soon appeared in various parts of England.

Even so a comprehensive policy was reached only under the various acts of the Elizabethan Poor Law, which were destined to remain in force without any real alteration until 1834. An act dated 1572 set up the general system of relief based on parishes. Parishioners paid a poor rate for the maintenance of their local 'impotent poor' whilst sturdy 'rogues and vagabonds' were to be furnished with work.[14] Since this last provision was to be satisfied only when the impotent poor had been catered for,[15] in fact no effective assistance was given to the unemployed, who simply continued to be the object of repression.[16]

Four years later, the entire problem was tackled by the introduction of houses of correction throughout the country so that refractory or unemployed workers could be set to work.[17] As in Bridewell, the prototype, their population was extremely mixed: paupers' children 'so that youth might be accustomed and brought up to labour', those looking for work, and all the categories noted in the first Bridewells: petty offenders, vagabonds, petty thieves, prostitutes and poor people refusing to work. [18] If the inmates received differential treatment at all, it was based on the grading of heavy jobs. The only act to which a real criminal intention seems to have been attributed was the refusal to work. As we can see, under the Act of 1601 (wrongly judged to be the principal statute of the old Poor Law whereas it merely completed preceding legislation) judges were vested with powers to despatch 'idle blockheads' to the common gaol.[19] However, it is necessary to clarify exactly what 'refusal to work' actually meant in the sixteenth century. A series of statutes promulgated between the fourteenth and sixteenth centuries fixed maximum wages. It was unlawful for anyone to exceed the stated limits. It was impossible for workers to negotiate wages or to conduct collective bargaining. Labourers were obliged to accept the first available job on whatever conditions the employers cared to establish.[20] In this way, forced labour in workhouses or houses of correction was geared towards breaking working-class resistance; it compelled labourers to accept the most exploitative conditions.

On this point, it is interesting to consider the hypothesis advanced by G. Rusche and O. Kirchheimer. Their view is that the introduction of forced labour in Europe during the late sixteenth century and in particular, as we shall see, the early seventeenth century, is related to the seventeenth-century population decline throughout Europe which must have contributed to the strength of the working class on the market.[21] They argue that the period between the fifteenth century and the early sixteenth century witnessed a bloody and ruthless repression of the mass of the unemployed at a time when there was a plentiful supply of labour. But with the approach of the seventeenth century, the labour supply dwindled and nascent capital needed state intervention to guarantee the high profits brought about by the so-called 'price revolution' of the sixteenth century.[22] Even if all this holds good it is also necessary to consider, as Marx noted[23] in the above passage, that the demand for labour by no means proceeded *pari passu* with labour supply, particularly in the 'primitive' phase of capitalism, where organising sufficient capital to make full use of the available labour is much the slower process. In fact, the growing supply of labour in the second half of the sixteenth century could not meet the demands of the prosperous and turbulent times of Elizabethan England. Forced labour had to be resorted to if the new proletariat was to be prevented from taking advantage of this situation. It thus kept down labour costs on the free market right from the start. Nor must one forget, as Marx noted, that this newly formed proletariat was reluctant to enter the totally alien world of manufacture. As F. F. Piven and R.A. Cloward observed:

> Bred to labour under the discipline of the sun and season, however severe that discipline may be, they may resist the discipline of the factory and machine, which, though it may be no more severe, may seem so because it is alien. The process of human adjustment to these economic changes has ordinarily entailed generations of mass unemployment, distress and disorganisation.[24]

I will return to this problem later, since it is fundamental in understanding the historical role of forced labour in segregated institutions such as the Elizabethan houses of correction. Suffice it to say, for the moment, that this type of institution was the first and most important example of secular detention involving more than mere custody in the history of prison; its characteristic features, its social function and its internal organisation are, as far as the final form of the institution is concerned, already to a large extent those of the classic nineteenth-century model of prison.

Manufacture and the Amsterdam Rasp-huis

It was, however, in Holland during the first half of the seventeenth century [25] that the new institution of the workhouse reached its highest form in the period of early capitalism. A juridical history (that is, the history of ideas, the history of 'the spirit') would characteristically have us believe that this new and original form of punitive segregation sprang from the individual genius of some reformer. However, given that the earlier English initiatives (Bridewells) had no *direct* influence on those of the seventeenth-century Dutch ones, it is apparent that the origins of the workhouse were rooted in the whole of capitalist development.[26] We can point to two factors around the late sixteenth and early seventeenth centuries impelling Holland to adopt a system of forced labour which was to become a model for the whole of Reformation Europe: first, as a result of the struggle for independence led by the urban mercantile class and sanctioned by the Union of Utrecht in 1579, the northern provinces of the Netherlands took over the secular state of Flanders which suffered impoverishment and strangulation at the hands of Philip II.[27] The golden age of Amsterdam followed. Secondly, the precipitant growth of trade inflated the demand for labour without a plentiful supply being available on the market (as there had been in England) at a time when Europe was undergoing a serious decline in population.[28] There was a risk that rising Dutch capital would find itself faced with a high cost of labour and a proletariat which would in some way be in a position to bargain over the sale of its labour-power despite repressive constraints. According to Rusche and Kirchheimer's interpretive hypothesis,[29] this was the economic and social situation which caused the young Dutch Republic to change its punitive methods in an effort to avoid wasting as little of the workforce as possible whilst controlling and regulating its use as capital required.

It needs to be stressed, of course, that a hypothesis restricted largely to the relationship between the labour market and forced labour (in the sense of unfree labour) cannot exhaust the entire thematic of workhouses. As we have already seen in the English case, these institutions were by no means the only instrument used in the attempt to depress wages and control the labour force. Nor, for that matter, was this the only use to which workhouses were put. As regards the first point, such instruments were accompanied, (as we have seen in England, although the point is generally valid for this period) by legally fixed maximum wages, the lengthening of the working day and the prohibiting of association and meetings, etc.[30] In reality, the fact that they were always confined to a relatively small scale means that it is better to see them as an *index* of the general level of class struggle rather than as an influencing factor. The function of workhouses was undoubtedly much more complex than that of being a simple regulator of free labour. To put it a different way, one could say that this last objective taken in its fullest sense means *control of the labour force,* its education and training. As Marx states in a passage already cited,[31] adaptation 'to the discipline of their new condition', that is, the transformation of the ex-agricultural worker expelled from the land into wage labourer, with all that that implies, is one of the principal tasks the first capitalists had to undertake. Workhouses and many other similar organisations respond especially to this need. Evidently this question is inseparable from that of labour supply. This is not simply because the institutionalisation of (however limited) a section of the labour force in workhouses has a dual effect first on free labour as already outlined, and secondly on forced labour, generally the most rebellious, in the sense of learning a discipline — but also because the extent to which a nascent working class displays docility or opposition depends on its relative strength in the market. Clearly, its capacity for stubbornness, opposition and resistance grows with the scarcity of labour. It may be expressed spontaneously through crime, increased aggressiveness and revolt rather than in a conscious or organised form but it still tends to endanger the social order and becomes objectively political. [32]

367

In the wake of studies by von Hippel and Hallema, Thorstein Sellin's book *Pioneering in Penology*[33] provides us with the richest and most meaningful reconstruction of the structure and function of a workhouse during the seventeenth century. The intimately bourgeois character of the movement which began to emerge on the penal question around the time of the Renaissance and which found its first expression in English and particularly in Dutch Humanism, appears very clearly in the principal thesis of a pamphlet on vagabondage by D. V. Coornhert. Rather like More in *Utopia,* Coornhert reasons that since slaves in Spain are worth 100 to 200 guilders, free Dutchmen, the majority of whom were skilled in some way, ought to be worth more alive than dead. It would be more fitting, he argues, to put anybody committing crimes to work.[34] It was not long before the work of Coornhert (and of succeeding reformers) was put into practice. In July 1589, the Amsterdam Magistrates decided to set up a house:

> where all vagabonds, evildoers, rascals and the like could be imprisoned
> for their punishment and could be given labour for periods of time which
> the magistrates found suitable considering their offences or misdeeds.[35]

After further discussion, the new establishment was inaugurated in 1596 in what had formerly been a convent. The institution was expected to support itself by means of the inmates' labour. There was no individual profit either for the governors, who received an honorarium, or for the warders, who were given a regular wage. This distinguished it from the old English custodial prisons where warders could constantly extort money from prisoners, a factor contributing in no small measure to the terrible conditions to be found, for example, in the county gaols of late medieval England. The Dutch institution's population was similar in composition to that of its English forerunners: young petty offenders, [36] beggars, vagrants and thieves. They were admitted either by administrative or by juridical order. Sentences tended to be short and for a stated period which could be altered depending on the prisoner's behaviour. Of course, the Dutch *Rasp-huis* did not provide a complete substitute for the whole range of punitive measures already in existence any more than did the English workhouses or houses of correction or others which subsequently developed in Europe. It stood somewhere between the fine, pure and simple or light corporal punishment on the one hand and deportation, exile and the death penalty on the other hand. The important point here is that those destined for the workhouse were labelled as the 'criminological types' of the time; the origins and development of these criminal categories lay in the birth and development of capitalism itself.

The institution was based on cells, each containing more than one inmate. Work was carried out in the cells or, weather permitting, in the large central courtyards. It was a question of applying the dominant productive model: *manufacture.* Dutch workhouses became widely known as *Rasp-huis* because the type of work mainly performed was the pulverisation with a multiple-blade saw of a certain wood for use in dyeing textiles. This process could be carried out in one of two ways: either with a millstone, a method commonly adopted by employers of free labour, or, as in the workhouse, by placing the hard South American wood across a bench with two inmates standing at either side and using a heavy saw to make the sawdust. This particular method was considered most suitable for the lazy and idle, who often broke their backs — quite literally — whilst doing it. Such was the justification for choosing this most fatiguing method. Incidentally, it is interesting to note that buyers of *Rasp-huis* sawdust complained of its inferior quality compared to what they obtained from the mill, but the fact is that the Amsterdam workhouse had an effective monopoly of this sort of work and indeed, the municipality became involved in legal disputes with other local authorities seeking to establish more advanced production methods. This system, based on the distribution of privilege and monopoly, is typical of the mercantilist outlook of an age in which capital was still in its infancy and required the active support of the state to make up for its weakness.[37] The initiation of a public policy, as in the management of pauperism through poor relief and workhouses, is an integral part of this particular approach to economic relationships. What is interesting here, however, is the specific relationship that came to be established between the chosen technique of production and the aim and function of houses of correction. This can be seen from the outset in terms of the problematic nature of the economic relationship between free and forced labour which looms ever larger as the development of capital accelerates the growth of its fixed component.

During what could be described as the 'preparatory studies' carried out prior to the opening of the workhouse, Dr Egbertszoon, whose proposals were to to be adopted by the Amsterdam administration, criticised a number of points advanced in the programme of the utopian Spiegel. In particular, he attacked the latter's views on prison labour. Egbertszoon held that since most prisoners were of low intelligence, they would be most efficiently employed in a single trade because teaching them a skill involved time and money. Moreover, the work ought to be based on minimum investment and maximum profit and pay should not be fixed once and for all but left to the discretion of the warders who could regulate it according to 'behaviour'.[38] It is significant that the form of manufacture involved little use of machinery, capital being mainly invested in raw materials. Forced labour was accompanied by a minimal use of capital; production was low in quality and volume, and profits were ensured by exceptionally depressed wages. It was the very *protectionist* nature of this type of industry as against the free market that permitted its survival. In this sense, there were obvious conflicts with those seeking to introduce grinding machines. They wanted to deal with a reduction in the labour force to which workhouses largely owed their existence, by introducing machines — in this instance, one of the oldest machines of all, the mill. In other words, they sought to intensify the extraction of surplus value.[39] The curbing of the class struggle by means of segregated institutions also put an immediate restraint on the development of capital itself. It was not only free workers who opposed the idea (for obvious reasons), but also capitalist interests excluded from privilege. The choice of the roughest and most tiring production methods depended on the possibility of extracting high profits without heavy capital investment, given a situation in which the classical monopoly of mercantilism enjoyed protection against external competition. But this choice had another side to it which is hidden amongst the half-truths mouthed by the ideologues of the age about the punitive character of fatiguing work or the 'low intelligence' of the labour force which filled the *Rasp-huis*. Manufacture recruited its labour essentially from two kinds of small producer ruined by the development of capitalism: the ex-artisan and the ex-peasant. Basically it was the latter who filled the houses of correction and clearly artisans were more suited to the new mode of production than the peasantry. Furthermore, manufacture had developed, as Marx stated:

> in every . . . handicraft that it seizes upon, a class of so-called *unskilled labourers*, a class which handicraft industry strictly excluded. If it develops a one-sided speciality into a perfection, at the expense of the whole of a man's working capacity, it also begins to make a speciality of the absence of all development.[40]

These 'unskilled workers' are precisely those working in the kind of production examined here which generally forms part of the first operations of production. However, such workers remained a minority in manufacturing while those who retained some residual skill as artisans displayed a capacity for insubordination and resistance towards capitalist manufacture which had not yet been shattered by the arrival of machines.[41] Hence, given the problem of managing a section of workers that needed to be disciplined and coerced into its place in the world of manufacture, clearly the most suitable method of production would tend to be that which could render workers most docile and which would demand the least knowledge and skill of them lest they be furnished with the means of resistance.

In any event, no matter where the workers came from and whether they were skilled or not, at this stage the monotonous and heavy practice of *rasping* best suited what was at the time the basic function of corrective institutions: disciplinary training for capitalist production. As Sellin notes,[42] proposals elaborated by Spiegel in his primitive programme for giving vocational training to inmates were completely rejected. Instead, it was emphasised that the aim of the institution was to prepare its guests to follow a 'life of laborious honesty',[43] an objective to be fulfilled by regulating their behaviour and by obtaining their submission to authority. This attitude must have been most evident when it came to work. It is no coincidence that the most serious infraction of discipline, necessitating re-appearance in court rather than internal sanction or extension of sentence, was the refusal to work for the third time. This accords with the ascetic view of life typical of Calvinism in the young Dutch republic.[44] A view of life according to which the work ethic and ideological subordination were to be reinforced in the houses of correction, as parts of the more general bourgeois-Calvinist *Weltanschauung*. Only then did it concern itself with exploitation and the extraction of surplus value. To sum up, it seems very clear to me, even from these early examples of workhouses, that the inefficient and backward form in which exploitation took place in this institution (a backwardness which could only exist in so far as state violence permitted exceptionally low wages compared to external levels) does *not* indicate a dysfunction in relation to the system as a whole. The workhouse was not a true and proper place of production, it was a place for teaching the *discipline of production*. As a matter of fact, low wages in this sense were extremely useful in that they make work methods particularly oppressive and pave the way for obedience outside. The particularly severe conditions inside houses of correction had a further effect on the outside world: jurists call it 'general prevention', that is, the intimidation of free labourers into accepting the general conditions of life and work imposed on them as being at least preferable to those inside prisons or workhouses. Hence, quite apart from the absolute pre-eminence assigned to work, the internal regime in workhouses tended to accentuate the role of that total bourgeois *Weltanschauung* to which the free proletarian never entirely commits himself. The prominence given to order, cleanliness, uniforms, hygiene (except of course when it came to working conditions), the rules against swearing, using slang or obscene language, reading, writing or singing ballads unless allowed by the governors (in a place and time characterised by the struggle for freedom of thought!), the prohibitions on gambling and the use of nicknames, etc. — all of this constituted an attempt both to impose the newly discovered way of life and to smash a radically counterposed underground popular culture which combined forms of the old peasant way of life with new methods of resistance called forth by capitalism's incessant attacks on the proletariat. If one cannot understand the close connection between the worker in manufacture and later in the factory with social relations as a whole; if one cannot understand the thoroughness with which, even in the early stages of its development, capital tried in every possible way to pull together a proletariat for itself and to secure the most favourable conditions for the exploitation of labour, one will not succeed in seeing how a series of factors and social events, far from being insignificant, reveal meaning and direction which link them up with manufacture during this period. The general significance of this relationship is well described by Marx in his depiction of the worker in manufacture:

> ... manufacture thoroughly revolutionises it, and seizes labour-power by its very roots. It converts the labourer into a crippled monstrosity, by forcing his detailed dexterity at the expense of a world of productive capabilities and instincts; just as in the States of La Plata they butcher a whole beast for the sake of his hide or his tallow.[45]

The role assigned by the worthy Calvinists to the seventeenth-century workhouse will later be assumed by the modern prison: to ensure the supression of a *world of productive capabilities and instincts* in order to concentrate upon that minute part of the individual useful to the capitalist work process. The total impoverishment of the individual takes place in manufacture and in the factory; but preparation and training is ensured by a string of ancillary institutions from which basic features of modern life have already begun to develop by this time: the nuclear family, school, prison, the hospital and later the barracks and the mental asylum ensure the production, education and reproduction of the workforce for capital.[46] Resistance is the only alternative. At first, spontaneous, unconscious, *criminal*; later organised, conscious and *political* as the proletariat begins to learn opposition both in the factories and in the various institutions mentioned above. The relationship between capital and labour determines the general course of development once the new society is born and the new terms of struggle are posed. A number of observations made by Sellin in his discussion of the *Rasp-huis* may provide us with evidence on this. He reports on collective punishments meted out for refusing to work.[47] It is interesting to note that by the first half of the eighteenth century the number of blades used on saws had been reduced from twelve to eight, then to six and finally to five. At the same time, the amount of sawdust produced per week by each inmate fell from 300 to 200 lbs. Naturally this must have been due to the use of an obsolete method of production, out of date since its inception, as well as to the more general evolution of workhouses over the centuries. However, the opposition in this institution to which Sellin refers (despite his lack of interest in reconstructing this aspect of the workhouse) must have been a contributory factor of no little significance.

Genesis and development of prisons in other European countries

We will now consider the situation more generally. Before the development of capitalism in England, forms of capitalist production arose in certain areas of Italy, Germany, Holland and, somewhat later, in France.[48] It is not relevant here to examine how and through what complex of historic events the precocious development of capitalism in these areas later became much inferior to the development of capitalism in England (or indeed, how Italian capitalism actually regressed). The important thing is that capitalist develpment in these areas coincided with the creation of a 'roaming, landless, depressed class, competing for employment' [49] and of a vast stratum of workers excluded from corporations, for example the Florentine Ciompi (wage-earners in the wool industry).[50] The so-called 'price revolution' caused real wages to fall in sixteenth-century France, Flanders and Germany at a time when there was a plentiful supply of labour.[51] In this situation, the 'bloody repression of vagabondage' was complemented by the equally ruthless repression of the unemployed masses: free association, strike action and abandonment of work were severely dealt with, wide use being made of the *galley*. Houses of *correction* multiplied. In Paris, where the *Royaume des Truands* was built, the number of vagabonds amounted to one third of the total population.

One of the first reactions to this situation was to replace the old system of private and religious charity with public assistance co-ordinated by the state. This was in social terms one of the most significant consequences of the confiscation of ecclesiastical property during the Reformation.

Luther himself undertook the interpretation and diffusion of new ideas about charity in his *Letter to the Christian Nobility* which clearly stated that begging ought to be abolished, each parish providing for its own poor.[52] He later elaborated a detailed scheme of assistance which Charles V was to apply throughout the empire.[53] However, measures to remove assistance to the poor from purely private initiative were not simply confined to Protestant countries. The development of a commercial bourgeoisie and a national state in Catholic France, for example, gave rise to a similar problem and a similar solution. Take the case of Lyons, a trading and commercial centre where the population doubled during the first half of the sixteenth century.[54] After the continual agitation among artisans, day-labourers and the poor in 1529, 1530, and 1531, a decision was made to set up a centralised, comprehensive scheme of welfare. Two years later the system was extended to every parish in France by decree of Francis I. At the same time, the French created their version of the workhouse: *l' Hôpital*, which was based much more on confinement as such rather than on work as was typical of institutions in the countries of the Reformation. On the other hand, confinement only became general in France (within limits, as we shall see) during the second half of the next century — a notable delay in comparision with England and the Protestant states. Undoubtedly, however, this was not simply due to religious influences; the fact that workhouses and houses of correction flourished in Flanders, the Netherlands and Northern Germany considerably earlier had much to do with the more advanced stage of capitalism reached in these parts. Nevertheless these dynamic societies undergoing a process of total transformation did, it is true, provide the most favourable conditions for the existence and growth of both the Reformation and the new attitude to poverty alike. There is no denying that Catholicism could not compare with the various strands of Protestantism, especially Calvinism, in furnishing a complete vision of the world and of life based on the *work ethic*, that *religion of capital* which gave life to the first segregated institutions. [55]

In the transition from medieval peasant society to bourgeois-industrial society, the worker is no longer subject to the direct, immediate ties of the Seigneur — ties which were juridically and militarily guaranteed, and justified on an ideological level by a completely theocratic vision of life. Now he is governed by a much more indirect force, that of economic coercion. Moreover, it is only in its fully-developed form that capitalism comes to exercise so complete a material and ideological hegemony over society that it can use need on its own as a means of compulsion in the running of society. In the long period of transition we are now considering, during which an interpenetration of peasant and urban economies persisted, the 'outlawed' worker went through the novel experience of being, as Marx observed, 'free' and 'dissolved of ties'. It was only an illusory freedom, of course — the freedom to die of hunger, a freedom to which authority frequently responded with drastic terroristic measures. None the less, the social relations which emerged in this period did present the worker with a series of alternatives which, though often quite dramatic and desperate, had not existed in previous social structures.

It is no coincidence that this was the day of the vagabond, the brigand, the rural thief, peasant revolt and the beginnings of class struggle in the towns. The bourgeois monarchies still depended on the use of violence for the control of the lower classes, although it was necessary to build a world where violence as a generally valid instrument of control could be largely avoided. The workers' 'liberty' will be expressed in the Enlightenment law through the concept of the *contract*. This marks a great change even if, as the Marxist critique was to show, this apparent liberty is nothing but the sanctioning of a different kind of force no longer juridical-military or political, but economic. Clearly, social organisation is considerably different where labour is allocated through the impersonal workings of the market (however terribly concrete), as against that in which it is exploited under the personal and perpetual supervision and control of the exploiter. This is the structure upon which the whole dialectic between the principle of liberty and the principle of authority is based. It began with bourgeois society and the Reformation was its first basic expression. Authority in the medieval system weaves together the social relations of an undifferentiated peasant community which derives internal cohesion and all-embracing structure from its very penetration by the religious, political and economic hierarchy. In the *dialectic* of the peasant *liberation* and the transformation of the peasantry into proletarians, this hierarchical order ends in destruction: while the principle of authority becomes the very basis of capitalist production *inside the factory*, it contracts and withdraws from *certain areas of external social life*. The more the principle of authority progresses inside the factory, the more it controls the organisation of exploitation, the more the struggle for liberalism and democracy advances outside (that is, at least for as long as the canons of 'classic' eighteenth-century capitalism remained valid). In any event this opened up a profound contradiction between the world of the factory and the external world. It is no coincidence that this contradiction was to become one of the major areas of struggle for the organised proletariat. Moreover, authority in the factory is an impersonal, *mute* authority; it has lost the rich ideological character of religious medieval society. Thus, authority in the factory must always be accompanied by external control over the labour force — indeed such control began to unfold on more than one level during this period. It was a question of inducing in the worker a natural and spontaneous tendency to submit to factory discipline, whilst reserving the use of open force merely for a minority of rebels. Such control — and here the importance of religious reform and its connection with the early forms of confinement is evident — developed in two ways: within the individual (and within the family) and within the *segregated institutions*. [56] In his early works, Marx very succinctly expresses all this in a few lines:

> Luther, to be sure, overcame servitude based on devotion, but by replacing it with servitude based on conviction. He shattered faith in authority by restoring the authority of faith. He transferred the priests into laymen by changing the laymen into priests. He liberated man from external religiosity by making religiosity that which is innermost to man. He freed the body of chains by putting the heart in chains . . . it was no longer a question of the layman's struggle with the priest outside of him, but of his struggle with his own inner priest, his priestly nature.[57]

The disintegration of the peasant community, the isolation of the worker as an individual in the face of the individual capitalist, the struggle against the Catholic church and its 'external' forms of communion devoid of inner faith, their replacement by the isolation of man from man and man before God — all these went hand in hand. When Luther spoke of divine activity, he was really talking about capital: 'For God has fully ordained that the under-person shall be alone into himself and has taken the sword from him *and put him in prison*'. [58] The struggle for freedom of conscience and of religion, the 'private' reading of the holy scripts, the direct rapport between man and God, the devaluation of good works and of the world in the face of faith are profound transformations in the religious, social and above all in the psychological *habitus* of the individual which tended to internalise authority and violence. The psychological chains of the pious man largely replaced the visible chains between serf and glebe. At the same time, extraordinary prominence is given to 'educative' instruments, *imprimis* to the family. It has been noted that it was precisely in this period and under the impact of Protestant doctrine that the classical form of the patriarchal bourgeois family assumed a new and particular vigour; it was at this point that the father became a social figure endowed with great power to whom public authorities could delegate control over his children's education and over his wife.[59] It is no accident that in this period one of the primary aims of workhouses and other institutions examined here was the socialisation of the young. It was to a case concerning a youth and to a general preoccupation with juvenile delinquency that the famous *Rasp-huis* in Amsterdam owed its existence. Houses of correction for the young appeared at the same time as those for the poor. Parts of the workhouses were often set aside for the young — some, from good families, having been sent by their fathers.[60] Clearly, it was fully recognised that the new order of ideas, without precedent from previous centuries (at least not on any large scale), the new 'spirituality' of order and repression, had to be taught and inculcated from infancy — indeed particularly in infancy. For Luther and Calvin, 'God, the Father and the Master' was the perfect trinity.[61] Other institutions gradually emerged outside the family, particularly workhouses and houses of correction. The function of these institutions was marked by a certain ambivalence: were they genuine places of production or were they educative instruments of the 'paternalistic' type? Though this ambivalence persisted, we will see that the latter gradually triumphed.

With the Reformation, poverty was seen in a different light. It no longer possessed the 'positive mystique' it had had for medieval Christianity. Now poverty was a sign of divine malediction. In the Reformation 'poverty means punishment' observed Foucault,[62] and it is easy to see how he who is cast out and punished by the wrath of God is also cast out and punished by men. All the more so if the poor cannot or will not participate in that great glorification of God which is the end of earthly works.[63] Works have no value *per se*. The total devaluation of the practical world denotes a society in which production is now geared towards accumulation, not towards the use and consumption of goods produced.[64] But it was precisely the absolute worthlessness of worldly activity in comparison with the only aim which had real value — achievement of the state of grace, communion with God — that made man free to increase the glory of God through his earthly life and works which he took as a *sign* of his own eternal well-being. Protestant ideology encapsulates the pessimistic vision of a world engulfed in sin, a divine epiphany in which men sing the praises of the Lord by working, and (some of them) by accumulating and by saving. Luther sees the human situation as a prison, probably a canonical prison given that he is a monk and talks about isolation. On the one hand, has not the state of the priest become the 'priestly nature' of anyone? *Ethics* have taken over religion and in the new religion priesthood is accessible to all. The experience of the ecclesiastical organisation is generalised. Already in Luther we see one of the most important values of the new society — isolation, particularly isolation from the old peasant community and from the ownership of one's own means of production.

If prison is a model of society — and here one is still concerned with metaphor — it will not take many years for the Protestant and above all the Calvinist view of society to create a model of the prison of the future in the shape of the workhouse. A couple of centuries later, in an age and region full of promise for the development of capitalism and its spirit — the English ex-colonies of North America at the beginning of the nineteenth century — the Quaker colonists of Pennsylvania rigorously interpreted Luther's words in their *cellular prisons*, the form finally discovered of bourgeois punishment. The whole secret of the workhouse and the *Rasp-huis* lay, right from the very start, in the way they applied bourgeois *ideals* [65] of life and society to the preparation of people, particularly poor people, proletarians, so that they would accept an order and discipline which would render them docile instruments of exploitation. The eighteenth-century houses of correction were filled with poor people, young people and prostitutes; it was a question of those social categories which had to be educated or re-educated for a well-mannered and laborious life in bourgeois society. They were not simply there to learn, they were there to be convinced; from its inception, it was imperative for capitalism to substitute for the old religious ideology new values and new means of gaining submission. The sword could not be wielded against the multitude indefinitely and there was always the very real fear that the lower classes would find a new solidarity, a new identity, which would enable them to break out of their isolation. Having proclaimed that the isolation of man was the will of God, Luther adds: 'If he rebels against this *and combines with others* and breaks out and takes the sword, then before God he deserves condemnation and death'.[66] Not only did Luther define the actual penal practices of his day (if 'prison' is for everyone, it is just that the poor, guilty only of so being, should end up in prison whilst the rebellious should hang — effectively this is what happened), but he opposed the movement his own words had helped to inspire — the peasant revolt. As the peasant leader correctly put it, this was revolt of the dispossessed against the many-sided process described above, which Marx refers to as 'primitive accumulation'. Such collective rebellion assumed a *political* significance going far beyond the dangers of the immediate responses of theft or banditry. Müntzer was fully aware of this. Referring to Luther, he stated:

> . . . he says in his book on trading that one can with certainty count the princes among the thieves and robbers. But at the same time he conceals the real origin of all robbery . . . For see, our lords and princes are the basis of all profiteering, theft and robbery; they make all creatures their property. The fish in the water, the birds of the air, the plants on the earth must all be theirs (Isaiah 5). Concerning this they spread God's commandment among the poor and say that God has commanded that you shall not steal, but it does them no good. So they turn the poor peasant, the artisan and all living things into exploiters and evil-doers.[67]

But for Luther such rebellion is the worst thing of all. Marcuse remarks, citing Luther:

> The robber and murderer leave the head that can punish them intact and thus give punishment its chance; *but rebellion 'attacks punishment itself'* and thereby not just disparate portions of the existing order, but this order itself.[68]

Throughout the period of absolute monarchy the crime of *lèse-majesté*, which regularly carried the death penalty, constantly increased; for these offenders there was no real possibility of 'correction'. Teaching by dint of flogging and work could only be fruitful as long as rebellion against the dominant social relations was expressed in terms of simply not conforming, however serious this might be in itself (though this depended, on the other hand, on the current need for labour). But if rebellion is directed — even in mystified, unclear forms — against the social relations themselves, against *authority*, clearly nothing can be done. He who rebels against discipline as such rather than against some particular application thereof is not open to *correction*: he deserves death.

The type of workhouse built in Amsterdam was copied in many European towns, paticularly throughout the German-speaking regions.[69] The generalisation of the Dutch initiative was no chance happening. Workhouses appeared wherever there was a notable development of mercantile capitalism: in the Hanseatic League houses of correction (or *Zuchthause*) were established at Lubeck and Bremen (1613), at Hamburg (1622), Danzig (1630). Switzerland was another area in which they developed a few years after the Dutch initiative: at Bern (1614), at Basle (1616), and at Fribourg (1617).

376

The *Rasp-huis* was visited a number of times by people sent by the various cities that were later to set up similar institutions.[70] Again, the fact that these different regions were linked together by the same connective tissue of economy and religion, especially Calvinism, was undoubtedly a factor of some weight favouring the spread of the workhouse. The various institutions had similar features. Generally they housed beggars, the idle, vagabonds, prostitutes, thieves, petty offenders, young criminals, or juvenile offenders and the insane. Here as well, work for the men mainly consisted of making sawdust for dyeing while the women, who were usually prostitutes or vagabonds, had to spin. The immediate success of these institutions was due above all to their profitability. In the case of Amsterdam, for example, where the institution was protected by monopoly, profits were described as exceptional. These institutions generally had two purposes: on the one hand, they were purely disciplinary, which, as we have already underlined, is what gives them the element of continuity; on the other hand, a scarcity of labour in the first half of the seventeenth century emphasised the need to give some vocational training to the inmates (a fact which frequently led the municipalities responsible for these houses into conflict with local guilds). [71]

As the institutions developed over time, those convicted of more serious crimes and sentenced to longer terms were admitted in increasing numbers. Thus, in the long run, imprisonment came to replace other forms of punishment. For some time, there was no rigid classification or separation of the various human and juridical categories. As Rusche and Kirchheimer note, it is possible to formulate a distinction between the *Zuchthaus*, which was meant to be a true and proper prison, and the *Arbeitshaus*, which was meant for the poor, the vagabonds and those imprisoned by police measures, but it was a formal difference of no effective consequence.[72] On the whole, however, it was during the seventeenth and eighteenth centuries that, little by little, there came into existence an institution of a kind which the Enlightenment and subsequent nineteenth-century reform were to bring to fruition in the form of the modern-day prison. Thus, write Rusche and Kirchheimer, 'The early form of the modern prison was bound up with the manufacturing houses of correction'.[73] The workhouse was, at its inception, undeniably a part of the Protestant, and above all Calvinist, heritage and it is significant that a Dutch pamphlet dated 1612, polemicising against Catholicism, holds the miracles of the church saints up to ridicule by contrasting them with the miracles actually performed in the workhouse by St Raspinus, St Ponus and St Labour in reforming vagabonds and criminals.[74]

But confinement soon became general in Catholic countries as well, particularly in France. We have already seen how, in the middle of the sixteenth century, an *Hôpital* came to be set up in Lyons; however this remained a rather isolated case. It was only in 1656 that the *Hôpital Général* was set up in Paris and then spread throughout the French kingdom by the edict of 1676.[75] But the time-lag between the French- and German-speaking regions was not the only factor which distinguished them. Poverty in Paris had reached a remarkably high level and the *hôpital* — which was a regrouping of existing institutions — was oriented more towards the provision of social welfare. In this way, it differed from the corrective and productive bias of workhouses and the *Zuchthaus*. The French admitted large numbers of widows and orphans to their institutions. Their population was vast and heterogenous.[76] Although the importance of work was also strongly emphasised, the Paris *hôpital* seems to have made a heavy financial loss within ten years of its birth.[77] Rusche and Kirchheimer insist that religious differences were of no real relevance to the spread of these institutions. In fact their own evidence shows that the economic situation of France was somewhat different to that of Holland or the Hanseatic League; and because of this it was difficult for both the workhouse and, above all, the new vision of life appropriate to capitalism, to take full root. This was even more obvious when it came to the other Catholic countries.[78]

Despite the fact that *hôpitaux* were the result of a royal initiative, they owed their extension throughout France to the energetic activity of the Jesuit priests, Chauraud, Dunod and Guevarre.[79] In a booklet dated 1639, Guevarre clearly and simply justified confining both the 'good' and 'evil' poor on grounds familiar in Protestant and Catholic workhouses alike: the *good* deserved confinement, which would assist them and make work opportunities available to them; the *evil* would be justly deprived of liberty and punished by having to work. In this way, Guevarre, like Solomon, resolved the contradiction — though it was not recognised as such at the time — between workhouses for the poor and houses of correction for vagabonds and criminals. Both institutions served the same purpose because the real crime was poverty and both had the aim of inculcating a discipline which was perceived as punishment. As Foucault observed:

> Confinement thus came to be doubly justified, in an undissociable equivocation, in the name of good and in the name of punishment. It simultaneously recompensed and punished according to the moral value of those the confinement was imposed upon. Until the end of the classical age, the use of confinement was to be a prisoner of this equivocation; the peculiar reversibility of confinement enabled it to change meaning according to the merit it was accorded to those it was applied to. [80]

In the course of the seventeenth and eighteenth centuries, a marked sensitivity to the concrete aims of punishment pervaded the Catholic world. Reviewing the use of prison punishments made by canonical courts in a work written at the end of the seventeenth century and published posthumously in 1724, the French Benedictine Father Mabillon formulated a series of considerations which anticipated by some decades a number of typical Enlightenment assertions on the penal question. Mabillon was one of the first to put forward the new idea that punishment should be proportionate to the gravity of the offence and to the bodily and spiritual strength of the offender, and to raise the problem of reintegration into the community. [81]

Later developments with regard to English institutions

In the age of mercantile capitalism, young national monarchies sought to prop up the development of capital, which still lacked confidence and security and needed protection and privilege. Workhouses were a typical result. The rising capitalist mode of production needed 'the power of the state, the concentrated and organised force of society'[82] not only 'to "regulate" wages . . . to lengthen the working-day and to keep the labourer himself in the normal degree of dependence',[83] but also in the relations between states and — in a more and more obvious way — when it came to the colonies.[84] However:

> The advance of capitalist production develops a working class which by education, tradition, habit, looks upon the conditions of that mode of production as self-evident laws of Nature. The organisation of the capitalist process of production, once fully developed, breaks down all resistance. The constant generation of a relative surplus-population keeps the law of supply and demand of labour, and therefore keeps wages, in a rut that corresponds with the wants of capital. The dull compulsion of economic relations completes the subjection of the labourer to the capitalist. Direct force, outside economic conditions, is of course still used, but only exceptionally. In the ordinary run of things, the labourer can be left to the 'natural laws of production' i.e. to his dependence on capital, a dependence springing from, and guaranteed in perpetuity by, the conditions of production themselves. [85]

Marx's analytical model of the origins of capital provides us with a synthesis of the essential development of class relations between the seventeenth century and the first half of the nineteenth century.

The next phase in the history of English houses of correction fits into this background. The scarcity of labour throughout the seventeenth and a good part of the eighteenth centuries posed a serious problem for capital which feared a rise in the level of wages above all else.[86] However, the problem was not nearly as serious as it had been in the first years of the seventeenth century. This was due both to renewed population growth and to the continuing rise in the expulsion of the English peasantry from the land and in the expropriation of their property. None the less, it is significant that continued demands were made for the use of forced labour,[87] since it took the capitalist mode of production quite some time to smash residual resistance on the part of a proletariat which retained traces of the old mode of production.

The more the expropriation of the peasantry advances, the less possibility it has of defending itself. It is only the growth of the market that gradually destroys the peasant subsistence economy.[88] In this context, it is hardly surprising that the Elizabethan Poor Laws suffered a major onslaught which continued until 1834 when, shortly after the formal assumption of power by the bourgeoisie, the demands made time and time again were incorporated into the New Poor Law. As is commonly agreed, the various provisions of the Old Poor Law, dating from 1572 to 1601, effectively transformed a system of private charity into a system of public charity; they imposed an obligation on the local community to furnish work for the able-bodied poor. However, the sections of this legislation seeking to provide relief outweighed those which dealt with the provision of work. Critics voiced the unanimous opinion that the provision of a system of relief tended to reduce the availability of labour and thus kept wages at an unnecessarily high level.

> This mischief of high wages to handicraftsmen is occasioned by reason of the idleness of so vast a number of people in England as these are: so that those that are industrious and will work make men pay what they please for their wages: but set the poor at work and then these men will be forced to lower their rates.[89]

379

A chorus of voices was therefore raised in unanimous praise of the benefits to be had from the wide and fairly exclusive use of workhouses.[90] The first result of this was the introduction of the Workhouse or General Act of 1722–3 which permitted groups of parishioners to build workhouses designed to receive anyone requesting some form of assistance.[91] But, as Marshall observes, the provisions of the Old Poor Laws were powerless in the face of structural unemployment.[92] Sufficient capital could not be raised to find work for all the poor and fewer houses of correction were actually built than originally envisaged by the Old Poor Laws.[93] As a contemporary text reports, those still condemned as idlers and vagabonds to flogging or banishment openly cursed the magistrates for their inability to provide them with jobs.[94] All this occurred, as we have already mentioned, during a period marked by the relative scarcity of labour. It is only with great difficulty that one can distinguish the development of true and proper houses of correction from the workhouse or poorhouse. As we have already made clear, no such distinction was made under the Old Poor Law which assigned the ordinary unemployed worker, the vagabond, the thief, etc. to the houses of correction to be built in every parish. This system worked for a time but gradually it broke down. Work in the houses of correction became scarce. Once again vagabonds were whipped or branded rather than being placed in confinement. None the less, the existence of houses of correction did increase the predisposition towards punishment by detention which gradually embraced the old custodial gaol. Although it was only in 1865 that the Prison Act formally eliminated the difference between gaol and Bridewell, it was already possible in 1720 to condemn petty criminals to either institution on purely discretionary grounds. The line formally dividing the workhouse (meant solely for the poor) from the *penal* institution, the Bridewell, as a section thereof (or vice versa) in the same building, was frequently blurred.[95]

Despite continual pressure and repeated efforts to 'set the poor to work' during this period, the overwhelming affinity between houses of correction and the old custodial gaols resulted in a reversion to late medieval methods at least as far as the internal regime of custodial gaols was concerned.[96] Work disappeared completely. There was a return to the dreaded practice of private gain for the warder; all former classifications or ways of differentiating between inmates, however crude they may have been, now disappeared. The female sections of prisons became brothels directed by the gaolers; thus the situation arose which was later to prompt the work and writings of so many reformers in the second half of the eighteenth century. Its most sinister aspect was the scourge of gaol fever which carried off about one fifth of the inmates every year. It spared neither judges, gaolers, witnesses nor the whole apparatus connected in some way or other with prisons. In this period, then even if there was a consolidation of, rather than any change in, the historic trend towards replacing the old forms of corporal and capital punishment with forms of detention, the latter was becoming increasingly pointless and painful for the inmates.

We can trace the roots of this progressive degeneration to the great transformations of the second half of the eighteenth century. The exceptional acceleration in the tempo of economic development — the industrial revolution[97] — shook traditional social equilibrium in England. A revival in population growth coupled with the introduction of machinery and the passage from manufacture to a true and proper *factory system* simultaneously produced a golden age for young capitalism and the darkest age in the history of the proletariat. The remarkably accelerated rate at which capital penetrated into the countryside and the consequent expulsion from it of the peasantry, particularly as a result of the bills for enclosures of commons,[98] helped to throw an unprecedented supply of labour on the market. From about 1760 to 1815 workers had to endure yet another round of wage cuts. The phenomena of urbanism, pauperism and 'criminality' grew to proportions hitherto unknown. The 'dull compulsion of economic relations' replaced statutory violence. It was the age of liberalism: capital could now stand on its own two feet and proudly proclaim itself confident, self-sufficient and scornful of the system of privilege, inequality and authority to which it owed its development in centuries gone by. However this phase did not last very long. Soon, 'direct force outside economic conditions' had to be invoked against the workers' first attempts to organise themselves. The implications of the French Revolution were already clear. The new Napoleonic state was very much stronger, very much more centralised and efficient than that of the *ancien régime*. From the outset, liberalism meant that capital was *free from the state*, that the state was a thing on its own — as the young Marx was to write some decades later [99] — and that the state must render its services to *Monsieur le Capital* — a fact that was made very clear in relation to welfare and prison matters. 'Crime, revolt and incendiarism' are necessitated and spontaneous responses of the poorest section of the proletariat.[100]

The first response to the great rise in pauperism, which was due, among other things, to a rise in the price of corn, was made with the revised provisions of the Old Poor Law. Between 1760 and 1818, the poor-rate tax increased six times to keep up with the growth of pauperism. A series of instruments used earlier now became more widespread: the deterrent workhouse, the roundsman system, the allowance in aid of wages.[101] Under these new circumstances and in the light of an increasingly costly relief system, the criticisms regularly raised in previous centuries grew to a climax. After 1815, it was particularly the allowance in aid of wages or Speenhamland system — that is, a payment given to the poor according to the current price of bread (in fact, a way of avoiding having to pay a minimum wage) — which aroused the fiercest criticism. The traditional and recurrent criticisms that such assistance would encourage indolence and refusal to work and would thereby maintain high wage levels was reinforced by the Malthusian vision of population growth — the extreme form of economic *liberalism*. Relief permitted the survival and reproduction of a surplus population which was both useless in itself and actively harmful to economic development. This was the basic view of the Commission of Inquiry of 1832–4, the product of whose labours was the New Poor Law.[102]

> Convinced with Malthus and the rest of the adherents of free competition that it is best to let each take care of himself they would have preferred to abolish the Poor Law altogether. Since, however, they had neither the courage nor the authority to do this, they proposed a Poor Law constructed in harmony with the doctrine of Malthus, which is yet more barbarous than that of *laissez-faire* because it interferes actively in cases where the latter is passive.[103]

What then was the solution adopted and championed by Nicholls and other reformers? The ideal workhouse had been defined as a house of terror [104] as early as 1770 — though this way of looking at the workhouse had existed earlier. The solution that the English bourgoisie hit upon shortly after its definitive accession to power was that of the deterrent workhouse, that is, the substitution of all forms of outdoor relief by confinement and forced labour. But what was the aim of this measure and in what sense did the reformers see the workhouse as a deterrent? Living and working conditions in workhouses were to be such as to discourage all but the most desperate from entering them. In this respect the words of the commissioners are very revealing:

> Into such a house none will enter voluntarily; work, confinement and discipline, will deter the indolent and vicious; and nothing but extreme necessity will induce any to accept the comfort which must be obtained by the surrender of their free agency and the sacrifice of their accustomed habits and gratifications.[105]

Once more, then, the aim of the workhouses was to make the poor accept any conditions imposed by an employer. [106] Life in the workhouse had to be less bearable in every way (particularly, of course, when it came to living standards) than the life of the lowest stratum of free workers.[107] Thus workhouse detention was to have an effect on the market — not so much because one sector of production enjoyed forcibly reduced labour costs (which had happened before) but rather, because the institution openly terrorised the worker into keeping away from its doors at all costs. The law sought to give a directly political content to formal control over the wage-earning proletariat, coming as it did after the French Revolution and the first struggles of the English workers. Sir George Nicholls, the principal architect of the New Poor Law, regarded the poor as 'potential Jacobins', 'ready to prey on the property of their richer neighbours'.[108] Engels very clearly described life in the workhouse which was so similar to prison in every detail that the poor renamed them 'poor-law bastilles'.[109] Not only did the workhouse ensure a standard of living frequently lower than that of prison, it also imposed a similar series of limitations on individual liberty. Among other things — and this is particularly significant — the work was usually pointless, having no real importance, being designed more for the needs of discipline and training than for profitability.[110] In brief, as Disraeli was to declare, the reform of 1834 'announced to the whole world that in England poverty is a crime'. [111]

I have dwelt at length on the question of relief not only because it can be seen to be directly linked with the rise of the modern prison — indeed the two are confused with each other — but above all because throughout the industrial revolution, this link clearly persisted over and above the variety and scope of the institutions. Throughout the preceding period, an apparent contradiction had been observed in the development of a policy of assistance. This was being challenged more and more by the demand for workhouses, together with the withdrawal of work from prisons, which were very much in decline — at least in the case of houses of correction — not so much in terms of their numbers, which continued to rise, as in the significant worsening of their internal conditions. However, as we have said, this contradiction is only apparent. Not only did the workhouse and the prison share a common destiny but both were also involved in a significant change of direction during the industrial revolution.

The same outlook which stimulated appeals for workhouses and which played a prominent part in the new Poor Law of 1834 can be encountered in the evolution of prisons during this period. The growth of pauperism during the age of industrial revolution was coupled with a growth in crime and rebellion. [112] The cry 'bread or blood' spread through the English industrial districts. It was not only the continental aristocracy but also the English bourgeoisie whose slumbers were disturbed by the spectre of Jacobinism. However, the only way in which the impoverished masses managed to express their opposition at this stage was through individual crime and violence.[113] In the general climate of post-napoleonic restoration, it was hardly surprising, therefore, to hear voices raised in favour of a return to the gallows and so on. The attack on the Enlightenment's so-called philanthropic attitude towards criminality and prison — for example, as it was represented in England through Howard[114] — became a leitmotiv of the reaction against the French Revolution. However, this reaction did not bring about a return to pre-prison punitive forms. Instead it made prison itself more rigid and punitive. On the other hand, in by-passing Enlightenment notions of prison reform based on rationalisation and the introduction of greater decency and dignity, it established some continuity with the events of the preceding century. The root cause here, as has already been seen, lies in an extraordinary increase in the supply of labour which made the old formula for convict labour totally obsolete. It was superseded by an age in which the workhouse and to an even greater extent the prison were distinguished by intimidation and terror. Prison labour was not rejected *a priori*, nor did it cease; it was simply that its punitive and disciplinary aspect became more important than its economic role. This was also because (as a report pointed out at the time) with the introduction of machines, the level of capital investment in all forms of production had risen so much that prison labour could not be carried on without serious risk of loss.[115] On the other hand, the plentiful supply of free labour meant that forced labour no longer functioned as any kind of regulator on external wages as it had done in the age of mercantilism. This made it acceptable to express sympathy with the free workers' protests that convict labour was unfair competition.[116] In any event, even where the provision of work for the poor was supposed to be the sole aim of workhouses, labour was typically intimidatory and useless. In addition, it is useful to take account of the dimensions of the phenomena of pauperism and poorhouses as against those of prison. According to the Webbs' estimate, around 12 to 13 per cent of the English population was being assisted by parishes in 1820 (that is, under the old Poor Law system).[117] In 1845, out of a total of 1,470 970 being assisted, it was estimated that some 215 325 English citizens were being confined as a result of the new Poor Law.[118] In 1782, Howard's findings had shown that a total of 4439 people were being detained in English prisons (of whom about half were debtors). [119] By 1869, the number of registered inmates was 8899.[120] Considering that the real figure may have been appreciably higher in view of what was happening between 1820 and 1840, then, taking the figures as a guide, the imbalance between the size of the problem of poverty and what we can call its criminal emergence is immediately apparent. [121] One can easily understand, therefore, how hardly any attention came to be paid to prisons, in socio-economic terms, compared with the energy expended on the whole problem of pauperism. On the other hand, however, prisons now acquired a *symbolic, ideological* connotation.

In the proposals advanced by Jeremy Bentham, a major representative of the ascendant English bourgeoisie, prison has reached its intermediate stage: the productivist and rehabilitative aims of its earlier days — aims which were revived during the Enlightenment — began to be overtaken by pure control and deterrence. As in any transitional period, the whole question of prisons became a political football. As theorists adjusted their ideas and proposals, intellectual camps were formed now on one position, now on another. Bentham's *Panopticon* [122] was a naive attempt to combine a system of intensified punishment and control with productive efficiency which was never put into practice but which already showed signs of the tendency to favour the first aspect in the years to come. The *Panopticon* is at one and the same time an architechtonic concept and the embodiment of its own ideology:

> The formal principle upon which the Panopticon is based consisted of two multi-floored coaxial cylindrical containers, each having opposing and complementary functions: the circular crowns in correspondence to the floors of the outer cylinder, were placed between six radials in cellular units completely opened out towards the central space and lit by the outer perimeter; this section was allotted to those to be controlled. The inner coaxial cylinder, concealed by thin, opaque partitions placed along the length of the perimeter was for the warders — very few, it was specified — who, without any chance of being seen, could have exercised tight and constant control at every point of the outer cylinder by means of well placed peep-holes; nothing could have escaped their scrutiny. [123]

Life in the 'rudimentary cell' was connected with the introduction in Bentham's first project (1787) of the idea of permanent solitary confinement but in his *Postscript* four years later, the cells were enlarged so that the number of inmates could be increased to four.[124] Without any doubt, however, the 'inspection principle', that is, the possibility of keeping every inmate under constant surveillance (or of making the inmates believe that this was so) with the use of few men, was the essential element in the project. If solitary confinement (which later disappeared) and inspection were the two features the *Panopticon* had in common with modern penitentiaries based on cells, contemporaneously emerging in the United States,[125] then what remains uniquely Benthamite is the prominence given to productivity.[126] Bentham is staunchly utilitarian on this point: 'I would do the whole by *contract*.'[127] Work should not have any punitive dimension but should be administered on purely capitalist criteria: ' I must confess I know of no test of reformation so plain or so sure as the improved quantity and value of their work.' [128] Even with regard to work, the essence of the penalty resides in the privation of liberty, conceived above all, in the form of the privation of the freedom of contract: there is a monopoly of employment to which the inmate is subject, a very convenient situation for the contractor: 'confinement, which is his punishment, preventing his carrying the work to another market subjects him to a monopoly; which the contractor, his master, like any other monopolist, makes, of course, as much of as he can.[129] But punishment by isolation on the one hand and by simple privation of liberty on the other, which still co-exist here, are to become increasingly incompatible. Bentham's architectonic project suits his foremost concerns — control, custody and intimidation — but certainly not the introduction of productive work in prison. Not at a time when the use of a vastly increasingly number of machines was based more and more on co-operation between workers. Perhaps Bentham's later plan to house four inmates in each cell is related to this. It certainly suggests why Bentham's project was not applied in practice despite the fact that in the first years of the nineteenth century the prevailing pressure for reform centred around his appeal for the productive use of prisons.

But there is another element that needs highlighting in Bentham's project — and it is perhaps the most significant one for the epoch and its ideology. The following appears on the frontispiece of the volume in which the *Panopticon* was outlined:

> 'PANOPTICON' or, the inspection-house: containing the idea of a new principle of construction applicable to any sort of establishment, in which persons of any description are to be kept under inspection; and in particular to penitentiary-houses, prisons, houses of industry, work-houses, poor-houses, manufactories, mad-houses, lazarettos, hospitals and schools.

In the opening passages of this work, Bentham repeats that this idea is applicable:

> Without exception, to all establishments whatsoever, in which, within a space not too large to be covered or commanded by buildings, a number of persons are meant to be kept under inspection. No matter how different, or even opposite the purpose: whether it be that of *punishing the incorrigible, guarding the insane, reforming the vicious, confirming the suspected, employing the idle, maintaining the helpless, caring the sick, instructing the willing* in any branch of industry, or *training the rising race* in the path of education: in a word, whether it be applied to the purposes of *perpetual prisoners* in the room of death, or *prisoners for confinement* before trial, or penitentiary-houses, or *houses of correction*, or *work-houses*, or *manufactories*, or *mad-houses*, or *hospitals,* or *schools.* [130]

With particular diligence Bentham now sets about dealing with the application of his project to the model prison in which 'the objects of safe custody, confinement, solitude, forced labour, and instruction were all of them to be kept in view.'[131] One cannot sufficiently emphasise the interchangeable character of the various segregated institutions recently created by bourgeois society when Bentham wrote these pages. Over and above their specific functions, one overall aim united them: control over a rising proletariat. The bourgeois state assigns to all of them a directing role in the various moments of the formation, production and reproduction of the factory proletariat: for society they are essential instruments of social control, the aim of which is to secure for capital a workforce which by virtue of its moral attitude, physical health, intellectual capacity, orderliness, discipline, obedience, etc., will readily adapt to the whole regime of factory life and produce the maximum possible amount of surplus labour. But it is the *inspection principle*, more than any other feature of these institutions, that guarantees the observance of discipline. The *panopticon*'s ability to control its subjects at any time and in any place within its walls, is, to put it crudely — and bourgeois theories in this period *were* crude, that is, they were simple, clear and (almost) uncontested — an extension of the *master's eye*. We can see this quite literally in the contemporary organisation of factory work from which Bentham patently drew a utopia of control for the various segregated institutions.

At this stage, co-operation could not be secured by the automatic workings of the productive process; [132] given machinery from the pre-history of modern technology, labour had to be forcibly organised by the physical authority of the capitalist (or that of his overseer) who co-ordinated the smooth running of the production process with his eye, his voice and his command.

In this respect, it is useful to trace the history of capitalism from its origins in the process of primitive accumulation to the analysis of the essence of capital in its classic eighteenth-century form in the first volume of *Capital* (Part VIII back to III). At this point Marx arrives at an explanation of what lies at the very heart of his theory, the production of surplus value, or rather, the *process of capital valorisation*.[133] At the end of Part II, Marx invites us to follow his analysis of the problem he has posed of that extraordinary exchange of equivalents between capital and labour which has the property of *creating value*, beyond the *sphere of circulation* in the 'secret laboratory of production'. [134] Here the 'secret of the production of surplus-value' is unveiled. [135] As we desert this 'sphere', Marx describes it as follows:

> The sphere of circulation or rather the exchange of commodities within the limits of which moves the purchase and sale of labour power, is in reality a veritable Eden of the natural rights of man. There reigns only Liberty, Equality, Property, and Bentham.[136]

This is not by any means just an exercise in irony. Before this remark, Marx explains how the sale of labour-power respects the general principle of the exchange of equivalents: labour-power is effectively 'paid for at its price'. [137] At this stage there is no question of exploitation. Up to this point, the juridical deception of the contract and the illusion that people freely dispose of their commodities exchanging them at equal values has yet to be revealed. However, the enigma arises from the fact that even by paying for what he buys at its price, the capitalist ends up with a greater value than he had at the beginning: he possesses what he has paid for plus a *surplus value*. Thus, the enigma must reside in the peculiar nature of the commodity he buys, in labour-power. [138] The use-value of this commodity clearly no longer belongs to the seller, the worker, but to the capitalist who has bought it. And it is the peculiar nature of this commodity that the consumption of its use-value *produces value*. [139] But this is only true if the use of labour is such as to produce in the working day a greater value than the capitalist originally advanced. If this is to occur, it depends not only on the amount of time during which the labour power is employed but also on the capitalist's capacity to obtain from the workforce an *average* hourly yield that does not fall short of his expectations, that is, it depends on his ability to bend his labour force to his will and his intelligence (as is in any case his contractual right; but labour-power, just as it possesses the peculiar characteristic of producing value, is also marked by another opposing and complementary peculiarity: its tendency not to let itself be consumed). If this is true, therefore, and it is true that the extraction of surplus value is a question of life and death which decides the very existence of capital as such; then, *de facto, authority in the process of production, authority in the factory,* which is the power of the capitalist to do as he likes with the commodity he has bought in exactly the same way as any other buyer, is a question of life and death.[140] The history of the relationship between capital and labour, history *tout court*, which is the history of class struggle,[141] becomes then the history of capitalistic relations inside the factory, the history of the authority of capital in the factory and correspondingly the history of the *discipline* of the worker and of everything which serves to create, maintain or subvert such authority. It is precisely the irreducible class character of this particular commodity which means it cannot be handed to capital on a plate without a series of complementary treatments which precede, accompany and follow its induction into the productive process. This is the specific task, invented by the bourgeois capitalist class and cited by Bentham, of the segregated institutions, institutions which can be defined as ancillary to the factory in the proper sense. They have the same relationship with the world of production as civil and political equality has with the sphere of circulation, as Marx observes above. The sphere of circulation, of the exchange of equivalents, is the realm of liberty and equality, the realm of the *declaration of rights*; the sphere of production is the realm of exploitation, or accumulation and therefore of authority, of the factory and of other segregated institutions.

Departing from this point, one can comprehend the content of that *religion of capital* [142] which is the dominant ideology in these years, particularly inside the segregated institutions. The great merit of Michel Foucault's recent book [143] is that it places the relationship between *technique* and the *ideology* of control back on its feet, demonstrating how ideology (obedience and discipline) does not come to determine the *practical* reason, the morality, but how on the contrary this is produced by specific techniques of control over the body (in military art, school, ateliers, etc.).[144] However, what is presented to us as the 'political economy of the body' is 'political economy' *tout court*; it is already locked in the concept of labour-power. It should be sufficient to recall the writings of Marx on manufacture already cited or perhaps we should even return to his early work in the *Manuscripts of 1844*.[145] This bourgeois *construction* of the body in the school, the barracks, the prison and the family remains completely incomprehensible (except in terms of an ineffable moment of the history of the spirit) unless we start from the capitalistic management of the labour process (and *at this moment* in the history of capitalism). This had to set itself the task of structuring the body as a machine inside the productive machine as a whole, that is, we must understand that the organisation of work does not treat the body as something extraneous, it *steps through* the body into the muscles and into the head, reorganising simultaneously with the productive process that fundamental part of itself constituted by the labour-power of the body.

In sum, in this age the *machine* constitutes a compound invention in which there resides a dead, inorganic, fixed element and a live, organic variable one. On the whole, therefore, the physical sciences and moral (later social) sciences, sciences of nature and human sciences are placed in an integrated relationship with the technique of formation, of exploitation and of 're-education' of fixed capital ('machinery' in fact) and labour-power (the body, man, the spirit, etc.). The history of segregated institutions and of their prevailing ideology can be reconstructed from capital's fundamental need to extend its command: The history of their ancillary nature can be traced to the factory, which is no more than the extension of the capitalistic organisation of labour above and beyond the factory, the *hegemony* which capital exercises on the whole of social relations. This hegemony should not in any way be understood in terms of an analogy between the factory and the outside world even if it appears as such at first sight; rather, it forms a continuum which pervades every aspect of personal life, commanding remodelling (or creating) social institutions in which the process of formation occurs. As Foucault observes with reference to Bentham,[146] prison is the experimental laboratory of the whole design; the 'Panoptic machine' has the task of producing a type of human being which will constitute the fundamental articulation of the productive mechanism.

Once again, it is not a question of institutions which serve the capitalist organisation of labour but a question of this very organisation as such which, from the family to the school, from the hospital to the prison and so on, organises an essential component of itself, that part of capital from which it is possible to extract surplus value. These institutions, their formative practices, the ideologies and theories prevailing within them, can only be understood in the light of capital's essential need to reproduce itself as it passes through various social moments, thereby producing a new society.

The contradictions at the root of Bentham's hypothesis became more and more obvious in the first decade of the nineteenth century and later on after the 1815 Restoration. In the first years of the nineteenth century, the refusal of reformers to embrace the idea of solitary confinement clearly revealed the impossibility of coupling moral reform and intimidation with productive efficiency and reform by means of labour. Howard's basic orientation on reform prevailed in the laws of 1810 and later on in Peel's Gaol Act of 1823.[147] The idea of group classification, segregation of the sexes, nightly cell isolation and daily communal work, the abolition of private profit for warders, of corporal punishment and the ending of some of the worst abuses of the preceding period were all realisations of the contributions which had been made to the struggle for prison reform by Enlightenment figures from Howard and Bentham to Sir Samuel Romilly and Elizabeth Fry. But the movement in favour of reform was bound to clash increasingly with a reaction in favour of repression which arose out of the socio-economic situation created by the industrial revolution. The fear of Jacobinism, the extreme growth of pauperism and criminality accompanying an immense industrial reserve army and an extremely low standard of living for the proletariat, the appearance of forms of crime which had an unmistakeable *class* content even if they were not yet *political*, made the demands for a return to the good old days of terror and harsh methods grow ever more numerous. [148] The full force of the contradiction between the bourgeoisie and the proletariat, which for some centuries had been apparent on a secondary level (compared with the contradiction that existed between the aristocracy and bourgeoisie), now moved into the centre of the stage. This growth of reaction over the question of crime coincided with a Europe-wide dispute on the Philadelphian *separate* system and the Auburn *silent* system.[149] The first system which, given the different set of social circumstances,[150] had had little success in the United States, was regarded increasingly favourably in Europe as it exactly suited the need for a punitive and deterrent prison without 'useful' labour which was already taking shape in Europe and especially in England. Work in the system of isolation in cells retains only the repetitive, fatiguing, monotonous aspects of work outside. In brief it is still punitive but completely useless. The tread-wheel or crank were simple structures which could be installed in a cell and whose real purpose, despite the appearance of being instruments of labour, was torment and torture. In the period 1840–65 the principle of terror and with it those of cellular isolation and useless work triumphed in England.[151]

Establishment of modern prison practice in continental Europe between the Enlightenment and the first half of the nineteenth century

John Howard, appointed sheriff of Bedford in 1773, took an active interest in prison conditions throughout his county. Indeed he was to dedicate the remainder of his life to the question of prison reform, for which purpose between 1770-80 he travelled extensively throughout Britain and Europe. His account provides us with the fullest survey we have of the way prisons were developing in the latter part of the eighteenth century. [152]

If as we have seen, the English prisons were in serious decay, things were different in the German-speaking areas of Europe which had become the natural breeding-ground of houses of correction. Throughout the seventeenth and eighteenth centuries, houses of correction and workhouses had also flourished in countries not mentioned here but above all, in Germany. In particular this widespread growth took place at the same time as a decline in the usage of old punitive forms consistent with capital or corporal punishment and frequently coincided with the general economic, political and cultural awakening of the Enlightenment (some of the institutions Howard visited were in fact of recent construction). Thus Rusche and Kirchheimer's thesis, according to which there was an overall decay in prisons during this period, should be treated with a certain amount of caution.[153] To be precise, by decay these authors do not mean that there was a reduction in the use of *detentive* punishment or, therefore, in the growth of institutions designed for this purpose, that is, houses of correction (as opposed to the old custodial gaols which Howard frequently found to be semi-deserted). What they are referring to is the deterioration in their internal regimes in which economic functions — and indirectly rehabilitation — were increasingly abandoned in favour of punitive and repressive aims. They attribute this new course to the social consequences of the industrial revolution which through the creation of an enormous reserve army of unemployed throughout Europe, made prison labour (underpaid labour) redundant and the need for open intimidation and socio-political control, if anything, more urgent than ever. If, as Rusche and Kirchheimer contend, the process of decline is linked with the industrial revolution, then we should hardly be surprised to find that most of the evidence supporting their view comes from England. In the same way, it is no surprise that Howard could only discover sporadic signs of deterioration in a more backward country such as Germany, or that the process did not become really general until the influence of the French Revolution and of the English industrial progress was felt in the first years of the nineteenth century and, above all, after the 1815 Restoration.

Howard reserved his highest praise for the Dutch prisons, [154] most of which were still *Rasp-* or *Spin-huis* with a distinctly higher criminal population than had been the case in the seventeenth century. The internal organisation of these institutions was still quite similar to their earlier form. Most of the practical work consisted of rasping wood for dyes; however, as Sellin points out,[155] the daily workload had been reduced by a third and the prisoners fashioned small objects in their spare time to sell to visitors.

About sixty workhouses existed throughout Germany[156] at the end of the eighteenth century. Howard visited many of them:[157] Osnabrück, Bremen, Hanover, Brunswick and Hamburg. The actual gaols housing debtors and those awaiting trial or execution were usually in an horrendous condition: old, unhygienic, often with secret underground floors packed with instruments of torture. However, their population was sparse and many were actually empty. On the other hand, the houses of correction and workhouses were more highly populated; here the men worked on wood (following the Dutch model) whilst the old, the young and women did spinning. There was a great confusion of petty criminals locked up with beggars, vagabonds and those merely suffering from poverty. Often, the only distinction between them was the fact that they were prohibited from mixing or trading with each other. Workhouses thrived in Hamburg in particular, which was a highly-developed city rich in trade: when Howard made his later visits, the Hamburg authorities were preparing a scheme based on workhouses to employ the city's numerous poor.[158] The introduction of the scheme had remarkable effect and Hamburg proudly proclaimed that begging had disappeared from its streets. But then ten years later, in 1801, the administration fell into heavy debt. The appearance of spinning machines had reduced the competitiveness of the old methods of production. In these circumstances the rapid propagation, primarily of the technological results of the English industrial revolution, effectively made itself felt even when it came to forced labour in Germany. The importation of English machinery and French revolutionary ideas prompted a return to methods of prison control based on terror, which was to characterise the major part of the nineteenth century, long before it produced any great changes in the labour market (though the introduction of machines, among other things, did swell the ranks of the unemployed).

Howard visited other workhouses: in Copenhagen, Stockholm (founded in 1750), Petrograd (still under construction at the time of his visit), in Poland (where, however, there was no work), Berlin (founded in 1758), Spandau, Vienna, in Switzerland, Monaco and Nuremberg (the German and Swiss ones were generally much older). There were numerous houses of correction in Austrian Flanders (Belgium), the most famous of which was the *Maison de Force* at Ghent. This was completely rebuilt in 1775, under Maria Theresa, on the foundations of an old house of 1627. [159]

The *Maison de Force* in particular must have had a great impact. It was one of the first great prison establishments built in the form of an eight-pointed star. The building was divided into sections, each corresponding to a different classification. Whilst criminals had separate cells and were subject to nightly separation, the women and vagabonds slept in dormitories. Textile manufacturing was carried out in large communal areas. However, Howard's enthusiasm for its order, moderation and hygiene waned during his last visit in 1783:

> I found here a great alteration for the worse; the flourishing and useful manufactory destroyed; and the looms and utensils all sold, in consequence of the Emperor's too hasty attention to a petition from a few interested persons — that which ought to be the leading view in all such houses is now lost in this house.[160]

Even the food had deteriorated and the small wage earned by each inmate had been reduced to little or nothing. The 'few interested persons' were probably producers competing with the institution; they were in fact the source of most attacks on prison labour. For as long as the development of industry depended on the mercantilist system of privilege and monopoly, the authorities could easily get the better of opposition from competing producers, as we have seen in seventeenth-century Holland. But as capitalism grew and imposed the new doctrine of *laissez-faire*, forms of enterprise outside the laws of the free market, such as those making use of forced labour, began to meet with successful opposition. As a result, prison work either tended to disappear or to become totally unproductive with purely disciplinary and deterrent aims. Opponents could now embroider their attack on convict labour with the very convenient excuse that in a situation of extensive unemployment from which *they* prospered, this kind of work endangered the livelihood of the free unemployed labourer. As a matter of fact, the first working-class organisations increasingly adopted a similarly hostile stance towards convict labour.

There were hardly any examples of this sort of institution in Portugal[161] or Spain. [162] In France, the system was seen right from the start much more as a means of suppressing mendicity rather than as a way of providing work.[163] The late economic development of the *ancien régime* weighed heavily upon France. But the abysmal functioning of the *hôpitaux* was primarily attributed to the idleness of the residents, despite all the efforts of the Constituent Assembly's Committee on Mendicity. [164] Howard found thousands of inmates of every kind in the various *hôpitaux généraux*: debtors, criminals (awaiting sentence), the poor, prostitutes, the insane and those suffering from venereal diseases. Continual revolts broke out and torture was widely used. Many died of frostbite during the bitter winters. There was hardly any work.[165] Howard concluded his analysis of Parisian prisons with a description of the Bastille. He was obliged to rely on second-hand information here since he was rudely refused permission to make a personal inspection of the building. [166]

Looking at Howard's account, it is important to realise that the relationship between prison labour and the standard of living of inmates is more than casual. It would he wrong to establish a strict correlation between work and a rehabilitation attitude on the one hand, or between the non-existence of work and a deterrent attitude on the other. These attitudes have been in constant interaction since the institution's earliest days, a fact that is readily apparent from the conception of the *punitive* character of prison labour (though it should be remembered that capitalist ethics also apply this conception to 'free' labour). Nevertheless, it is true that the very conditions of prison life (the level of hygiene, the possibilities of communication and solidarity between inmates, the standard of food, the possibility of earning small personal allowances, etc.) vary according to how far the internal organisation is part of a framework based on productive or unproductive work. Obviously, in the former case, whoever is in charge is presented with the twofold task of exploiting the labour force as rationally as possible while ensuring their daily reproduction (which is more than simply a question of physical subsistence). This produces a situation in which the standard of living of inmates must be inferior to that of employed workers in the outside world (in accordance with the *less eligibility* principle), although it may well be superior to that of someone who is unemployed outside and may, paradoxically, imply a 'material improvement' for the *lumpenproletariat*. This explains why tough methods are revived and the internal conditions of institutions become most harsh when unemployment rises — as tended to happen in the whole of Europe during the first half of the last century. In general, at least in the period examined up to this point, one can see that the inmates' strength and their living and working conditions tended to keep one step behind that of the proletariat as a whole. As a matter of fact, if this did not happen, prisons would lose all their deterrent power as far as the ruling classes are concerned. At times of great poverty and social change, it is not unusual for the most dispossessed sections of society to rise up in protest in a context in which even prison living standards are superior to those they must endure outside. In his description of conditions in poorhouses resulting from new legislation, Marx observes that prison rations were better than those received by the poor.[167] This is because prisons (which had less social impact in any case on account of their sparse population) were part of the reform movement of the previous century — which from the Restoration onwards was to be derisively termed as Enlightenment philanthropy — while the new English workhouse of 1834 conformed to the objectives laid down by the bourgeoisie. A few years later, the English institution, like those in Europe, took a sharp turn away from the principle of productive work towards a drastic tightening up of its deterrent role.

In the climate of heated ideological debate during the second half of the eighteenth century, a discussion on pauperism, crime and its remedies developed in France. In 1777 the *Gazette de Berne* held a competition to find 'a complete and detailed plan for criminal legislation'. The future revolutionary leader, Dr Jean-Paul Marat, took part with his *Plan de législation criminelle*, published at Neuchatel in 1780. [168] Having dealt with social order and laws in the first part, entitled *fundamental principles for good legislation*, Marat dealt with the *obligation to submit to the law*. [169] Let us take a close look at Marat's argument in order to appreciate fully the consciousness and sensitivity shown by this epoch towards the whole problem.

Marat based his whole argument on an analysis of the concrete situation to which law related. Having noted how 'wealth quickly accumulates in the bosoms of a restricted number of families', producing as a result, 'a multitude of needy persons who will leave their offspring in poverty', [170] he continues:

> Here is why they must die of hunger: the earth has become other people's property and they have no chance of getting anything for themselves. Now, since this disadvantage excludes them from society, are they obliged to respect its laws? Definitely not. If society abandons them they return to a state of nature. So when they forcefully vindicate the rights they have lost with the sole aim of improving their lot, any authority which stands in their way is tyrannical and the judge who condemns them to death is nothing but a vile murderer. If it is true that society must oblige them to respect the established order for the sake of its own self-preservation, it is also true that society must before all else, shelter them from temptation born of need. Society must therefore assure them of adequate means of subsistence and of the chance of suitable clothing, guaranteeing moreover to give them the best possible protection, to look after them in time of

illness and old-age: they cannot renounce their natural rights until society has made available to them a way of life that is preferable to the state of nature. Society has no right therefore to punish those who violate its laws without having made shift in this way to fulfil its obligations towards all its members. [171]

Marat then goes on to examine these principles in relation to a particular crime: theft. But 'any theft presupposes property rights' [172] and, having challenged the various contemporary theories on the origins of such rights, Marat hands over to 'someone unfortunate enough to find himself before the judges':

> Am I guilty'? That's not the point. The real point is that I've done nothing I shouldn't have done. The first right of man is to keep body and soul together and you know yourselves that there's no more important right than that; he who has no way of keeping himself alive other than by stealing is only exercising his rights. You accuse me of disturbing law and order. But how do you expect me to care about your precious law and order when it only reduces me to such misery? It doesn't surprise me at all that you go around preaching that everyone should obey the law — it's the law that allows you to rule over so many unfortunate people. You tell us we've got to work. Easier said than done. What sort of chance did I have? Reduced to poverty through the injustice of a powerful neighbour, in vain I sought the refuge of a peasant's cottage: I was torn away from the plough by a cruel illness which consumes me and made me a burden to my master. There was nothing left for me to do but beg for my bread: but even this pathetic expedient failed me . . . your turning me away made me desperate, having nothing and driven by hunger I took advantage of the darkness of the night to snatch the alms your hard hearts had denied me from a passer-by. It's because I've used my natural rights that you've condemned me. [173]

So what is the answer? The authorisation of theft and anarchy? Certainly not!

> Evil doing is warned against; but what is done to remedy it? Beggars are classed as vagabonds and put in prisons. This is not good politics: I will not discuss whether the government has the right to deprive them of their liberty in this way but I will merely observe that the houses of detention in which they are locked up can only be maintained at public expense, and that the spirit of idleness which they nourish rather than remedying the poverty of the individual, can only raise the general level of poverty. Very well then, what is the remedy? Here it is. Don't keep the poor in idleness, give them work, make it possible for them to satisfy their wants through labour. They must be given a trade, they must be treated as free men. This means that numerous public workshops must be opened for the use of the poor. [174]

During the deep-seated economic crisis which preceded the great revolution, this problematic imposed itself on everyone who lived in France. In town and country alike, the endless 'reserve army' of unemployed were forced to beg, thieve and turn to vagrancy or in the last resort to banditry, if they were to avoid starvation. [175] The revolt of the poor against the process Marx describes as 'primitive accumulation' worked its way through the countryside without pause. By the second half of the eighteenth century, the collective rights, which had always greatly assisted the poor peasants, had been severely eroded by the great property owners and government supported tenants.[176]

> At the end of the *ancien régime*, people everywhere were searching for land; the poor took over the common land, overran forest, open country and the borders of marshland; they complained about the privileged classes who used bailiffs and foremen to farm their land; they demanded the sale or even the free distribution of the King's estates and sometimes of the clergy's property too; there was a very strong movement against the existence of the great estates, for their division into small lots would have provided work for many families. [177]

As a result, 'at least one tenth of the rural population did nothing but beg from one year to another'.[178] The local communities were not always hostile to vagabonds; in certain 'pamphlets of complaint', protests were made against the confinement of vagabonds in houses of detention. The arguments were probably similar to those of Marat. Bands of unemployed beggars and vagabonds roamed town and country; the greater their numbers, the greater the poverty and as their numbers grew so did their sense of desperation: beggars gravitated towards brigandage. Even if those not paying the requested alms did not take the lead from an Arquebus, they still ran the risk of finding their crops dug over, their cattle mutilated or their houses burned down. [179] It was quite clear from the fact that 'when the almshouses were full, the doors were opened' [180] that they were quite inadequate. In fact, objections were raised because of the contamination that resulted from allowing the poor to mix with real criminals. Lefebvre states that this was not the least cause of the 'great fear' pervading France when revolution was imminent in 1789.

The revolutionary penal code of 25 September 1791 crowned the intense agitation for reform of the preceding half-century with the introduction of the principle of legality both in relation to crime and punishment and with the declaration that detention should reign supreme over any other punitive form. At the same time it was emphasised that *hôpitaux* and prisons must be made into places where society would be truly defended on the basis of labour.[181] The idea that punishment should no longer be arbitrary but should be proportional to the gravity of the crime, as laid down in an explicit legal code, played an important role in the struggle of a now confident and developed bourgeoisie against the old state forms (though this approach to penal practice had been formulated as much as two centuries earlier). As the Russian, E. B. Pashukanis, very acutely observed in 1924:

> Deprivation of freedom, for a period stipulated in the court sentence, is the specific form in which modern, that is to say bourgeois-capitalist, criminal law embodies the principle of recompense. This form is unconsciously yet deeply linked with the conception of man in the abstract, and abstract human labour measurable in time . . . For it to be

possible for the idea to emerge that one could make recompense for an offence with a piece of abstract freedom determined in advance, it was necessary for all concrete forms of social wealth to be reduced to the most abstract and simple form, to human labour measured in time . . . Industrial capitalism, the declaration of human rights, the political economy of Ricardo, the system of imprisonment for a stipulated term are phenomena peculiar to one and the same historical epoch. [182]

The notion of proportionality in relation to punishment had already assumed this significance for a writer representing the summit of bourgeois consciousness in its 'classic' period — Hegel.[183] The refusal to use corporal and capital punishment, the notion that a specific crime must correspond to a *quantum* of punishment and that internal prison conditions must be 'humane' therefore began with the practice established in workhouses under the direction of public authorities and merchants. To this the revolutionary impulse of the eighteenth-century bourgeoisie added its struggle for the establishment of a legal code. The origin of this struggle lay not in the confrontation between the bourgeoisie and the proletariat but in the confrontation between the bourgeoisie and the absolute state. Nevertheless, it is important to understand that it was no accident that such principles were to become an increasingly strong weapon in the hands of the proletariat. Enlightenment thought of the second half of the eighteenth century explains and summarises this development. The spread of houses of correction throughout Europe was by no means the only reason why such thought was not simply confined to a declaration of principles. Nor is it at all the case that reformers and politicians were the only ones who saw the connection between penal reform and workhouses; in those works dedicated to law, discussion was not limited merely to principles of natural law but for example it was made very clear that there were connections between poverty, unemployment and the widely varying forms of delinquency.

On the other hand, Hegel and Pashukanis were to express in the most theoretically rigorous terms the formalisation of criminal law according to revolutionary principles: the concept of *labour* represents the necessary welding of the institution's content to its legal form. To calculate, to *measure* a punishment in terms of labour-value by units of time is possible only when the punishment is filled with this significance, when one labours or one is trained to labour (to wage labour, capitalistic labour) .This is also true if one does not work in prison: time (measured, broken up and regulated time) is one of the great discoveries of this period in relation to other ancillary institutions such as the school. [184] Even if the time spent in prison does not reproduce the value of the injury (the basis of retaliatory punishment as Hegel observes), the propaedeutic, ancillary nature of the institution is precisely such as to exact retribution through the very fact of having to serve time, calculable time, measured time, that 'empty form' which is never a mere ideology but which gnaws away at the body and mind of the individual to be reformed, and which shapes him according to *utilisable* parameters for the process of exploitation.

The content of the punishment (the 'execution') is thus linked to its juridical form in the same way as authority in the factory ensures that exploitation can assume the character of a contract. After all, is it not *value* which determines, in Hegel's view, as much the equality between the two sides of the bargain in contractual exchange as that between the two sides of retribution, crime and punishment?[185] Again, it is not a question of analogy, but an expression of the two mutually essential moments in the capitalist structure: circulation and production. Once more, the realm of law (the circulation of goods), the great pride of the revolutionary bourgeoisie in the sphere of law, is intrinsically linked to the relationship of exploitation, that is, the authority and violence which reigns in production (in the factory, in the prison). Such bourgeois conquests, therefore, have much more to do with the consolidation of class hegemony over the social structure as a whole and therefore objectively against the proletariat *as such*, than with bourgeois defence against the absolute state. In any case, in so far as the latter adopts such principles itself, it is increasingly in bourgeois hands.

These are therefore genuine bourgeois-revolutionary conquests in the sense that they revolutionise old methods of handling punitive problems by the application of the new criteria of capitalist relations of production (as workers destined to find themselves behind bars — 'dangerous classes' — will very quickly come to appreciate). And, in fact, whilst the revolutionary bourgeoisie found that a sentence served by working was a concretisation of its conception of life based on labour-value measured in terms of time, the lower classes, in their turn protagonists of the Great Revolution that shook Europe, viewed prisons in a totally different light. The destruction of the Bastille was no isolated fact; although it is true that it was a specific type of prison, that is a fortress for political prisoners, it is not without some irony that the English workhouses of 1834 were, as we have seen, immediately renamed 'poor-law bastilles'. From then on, attacks on prisons and the liberation of prisoners were a constant feature of every uprising and popular insurrection. Although assaults on prisons usually had the aim of releasing 'political' prisoners or at least popular leaders and brigands, etc., to whom the masses felt some kind of affinity, things did not stop there; guided by an acute class instinct, they also unlocked the cells of ordinary thieves, vagabonds and so on without any moralism.

After some delay, the more backward regions of Europe were also affected by the growth of an immeasurably large industrial reserve army, with a concomitant growth in pauperism and criminality. Indeed after the revolution and Jacobinism, whilst working-class organisation was still in its infancy, class war was largely fought out on the terrain of criminality, the violent individual solution. This period was fraught with massive unemployment, extreme poverty and disorganisation of the masses; real wages plummeted to what was possibly an all-time low in the history of capitalism; the masses were driven into begging, stealing and, in some circumstances, violence, banditry and primitive forms of class struggle, for example, incendiarism and machine-breaking. In the face of this phenomenon, the creation of capital itself, its bourgeois political agents no longer had to rely on forced labour in order to drive down free labourers' wages, nor did they have to worry about training and returning the forced labourers to factory work. Prison remained the definitive and increasingly dominant acquisition of bourgeois punitive practice, but its function throughout Europe — at least while the circumstances described above prevailed (until just after the middle of the century) — increasingly acquired a bias towards terror and direct social control; the principle of discipline *tout court* prevailed over that of *productive* factory discipline.

In the more advanced countries the reactionary turn of the 1815 Restoration brought about an alliance between the victorious bourgeoisie and what remained of the old absolutist order together with its theoretical and practical remnants. This turn was an expression of anti-liberal resistance on the one hand, and a growing anti-working-class stance on the other. From the Restoration onwards, the emergence of an incipient political potential among the lower classes made it impossible to divorce the question of crime and prison in particular from the more general class struggle. What had been an unconscious relationship between the new classes of capitalism during its formative period now emerged as a conscious relationship of *political* hostility. During the first decades of the last century, various European governments demonstrated a mounting concern over the question of prison reform as a result of the 'terrible rise in recidivity'.[186] Foreign observers were sent out to other countries, particularly the United States.[187]

It is no accident that statistical research into criminality began in this period and revealed a particularly rapid rise in crimes against property in England and France.[188] A slow but continuous movement in favour of greater severity in penal doctrines and practices began with the Napoleonic Code of 1810 and joined in the attack on revolutionary *philanthropy*.[189] The French code essentially envisaged three types of sanction: capital punishment; forced labour; and the house of correction. The death penalty, however, was not the exceptional measure it had tended to be in earlier revolutionary legislation but was applied to practically all crimes threatening state security, counterfeiting, larceny and arson; in this way, it struck at every kind of subversion which had immediate political–military repercussions and at the two crimes common to the urban and country masses. For the less serious crimes of these classes — vagrancy, mendicancy, rebellion not constituting a serious threat to state security, the offences of striking and of association, etc. — the use of the house of correction was envisaged, of a short, sharp punishment, and above all, one that centred on compulsory labour; in this way, the practice we have seen being used from the foundation of the very first workhouses or houses of correction was formalised. The refinement of legal technique; the ever more complete incorporation in penal law of fundamental civil rights; both went hand in hand with the strengthening and stiffening of repression in other codes as well, such as the Bavarian Code of 1813, which was the work of Anselm Feuerbach. [190]

As we have already seen, one of the main aims to be achieved by coerced labour since prisons first began was the levelling down of wages outside. This could only partially be achieved, however, by means of an economic mechanism pure and simple, that is, by placing unfree labour at the disposal of certain branches of production (if for no other reason than the scarcity of those kinds of labour). It was due, more than anything, to the terror struck in those refusing to work, either at all or in particularly bad conditions, by the idea of prison as their unavoidable fate. Then according to the less eligibility principle, freedom and outside work must always be preferable to confinement. In the period of mounting unemployment and pauperism now being examined, the only possible way of intimidating people who had no chance of finding work anyway was politically, in the sense of deterring the unemployed, the vagabond, etc. from turning to crime, begging and so on, in the attempt to keep alive. But the risks at stake for the poor and the unemployed in these first decades of the nineteenth century were precisely those of survival or of starving to death with their families, and not just of haggling over the *conditions* of exploitation. It was extremely difficult for prison to intimidate them in the light of this, as it only had to provide the bare minimum necessary for subsistence to be preferable to freedom.

Thus, in this period, protests against the work of reform carried out in the late eighteenth century multiplied. Whilst it was conceded that reforms contained some merit, objections were raised as to the excessive improvement of prison conditions. It was said that too much attention had been paid to the *material* aspect and too little to the *spiritual* aspect of detention.[191] That prisoners should enjoy a standard of living similar to that of any free 'artisan', whose own standard was in any case frequently below the minimum level of subsistence, was held to be an impossible state of affairs.[192] As a result, prisoners became ill and died of starvation; Malthusianism was being taken towards its logical conclusion — genocide of the proletariat. [193]

It was in this climate that the reformers now turned their attention towards the American scene. By the end of its first century, the Quaker state of Pennsylvania had already established a prison regime based on solitary confinement: this typically Calvinist system was entirely founded upon the *spiritual* work ethic (just what they were looking for in Europe!) and had no place for productive work. Production, by contrast, was at the basis of the Auburn *silent* system which envisaged solitary confinement at night and silent collective labour during the day.[194] In the new and rapidly growing states of North America, this system soon gained ground as a result of the great shortage of labour that had arisen, in contrast to Europe.[195]

At this point in the history of the Old World, the debate on prison reform fused with a discussion on the merits of these two systems, cross-fertilising each system into a number of possibilities which generated new solutions.

Though some taking part in the debate propounded what was by now a different ideology, they carried on in their activity the tradition of Enlightenment *philosophes*: as scholars representing the widest range of human sciences, they frequently wrote essays, articles and travelogues. Though these projects for reform dealt with different matters, they all had in common the overall organisation, in its multifaceted complexity, of nascent bourgeois civilisation and especially of its state. They were often personally involved in legislative or administrative activity and their interest in the prison question, as it came to be known, was never casual but was always with an eye to the possibilities of practical application. Carlo Ilarione Petitti di Roreto from Piedmont was typical of this breed. In his work of 1840, *Della condizione attuale delle carceri e dei mezzi di migliorarla* (The present condition of prison and ways of improving it), [196] he provides an extensive survey on the state of reform in the nations of Europe at the time and the accompanying theoretical discussion.[197]

Both positions presupposed that it was necessary to avoid the corruption of contact between the various categories of prisoners. Such corruption was said to form the basis of what was considered to be the most worrying phenomenon in the prison question, the rise in recidivism. The supporters of the Auburn system, who were however, in the minority, [198] denounced the remarkable rise in cases of insanity and suicide found in prisons conducted on the Philadelphian model of solitary confinement. At the same time, the supporters of the Philadelphian system made use of the Quaker theory of the great moral effectiveness of meditation and of the comfort offered by sound and reliable visitors, who were allowed for despite the system's rigidity.[199] They further accused the silent system of being very difficult to put into practice and of giving the warders too much scope for the excessive use of violence in the attempt to ensure adherence to the rules. The marked lack of interest shown by European culture on the question of convict labour showed itself in the fact that the fundamental difference between the two systems — the one facilitating the installation of real productive work, the other not — was usually missed or at least was not seen for what it was. For the treasuries of various states, however, the consideration that the Philadelphian system with its costly requirement of cellular buildings would involve great expenditure was much more important. This was later the reason why a number of states which had declared themselves in favour of this solution in principle did not put it in practice.

The system of solitary confinement was the final outcome of a series of international prison conferences, the first one of which took place in Frankfurt. The reasons for this were precisely those stated at the start: the lack of interest in forced labour (provided for under the Auburn-system) when labour was abundant; a preference for the use of terror, never openly admitted but embodied in the choice of the 'Philadelphian System': an awareness of the horror inspired in the potential offender by the prospect of spending a five, ten or twenty-year sentence in solitary confinement — often relieved only by some form of 'work' so pointless and repetitive that it would really amount to physical torture. Again, for the complex reasons we have tried to explain, the serious decline in prison conditions was thus accompanied by an ever more limited use of work. Moreover, the use of work was also impeded by technical considerations: in an age which gave birth to the real modern factory, with its expensive and cumbersome machinery, with the first development of a more structured organisation of labour, only a very single-minded policy bent on transforming prison into factory through capital investment, etc., could have sustained efficient use of convict labour.

On the other hand, it was not only the reservations of reactionaries that discouraged this kind of prison regime. The popular masses themselves were very conscious of the menace convict labour represented in competition with free labour, especially in a situation of widespread unemployment. For many years, the working-class movement thus became one of the principle obstacles to prison labour. In the United States, for example, perhaps the only country which had had significant experience of convict labour, its continual decline from the end of the last century up to 1940 was above all due to the hostility of a strong and organised workers' movement. Even in a situation closer to that under examination — the 1848 Revolution in Paris — one of the first victories of the popular masses was the abolition of work in-prisons, promptly restored after their defeat.[200] However, it is interesting that the fundamental social struggle of the 1848 Revolution was around the demand for 'the right to work'. This led to the opening of the *Ateliers Nationales* along the lines proposed by Considérant and Fourier. Even if the consciousness of the time probably did not make a link between the two problems, it seems to me that there is a direct connection from the workers' point of view between the fight for the right of everyone to work and the fight against convict labour. Free labour must be available to all without the economic and political blackmail of the house of correction! The views of the Parisian Proletariat were to be echoed by Marx many years later in his comments on a demand relating to convict labour in the German Social Democratic Party's Gotha Programme.[201] Marx wrote that prisoners should neither be deprived of 'productive labour' nor be treated 'like animals' from fear of their competition. However, the organised working class's attitude vis-à-vis prison work belongs to a history which begins where we finish. Towards the middle of the last century, prison came of age and was able to take its place in line with the other bourgeois social institutions of capitalism. Its further history is above all the history of a *crisis* which, like the history of the organised working class, already belongs to a different sort of capitalist society.

Notes

1. K. Marx, *Capital*, vol. I (London: Lawrence and Wishart, 1977) p. 668; see the whole of Part VIII.

2. M. Dobb, *Studies in the Development of Capitalism* (London, 1963. Cf. particularly chs 4, 5 and 6: 'The Rise of Industrial Capital', 'Capital Accumulation and Mercantilism' and above all, 'Growth of the Proletariat'.

3. Dobb, ibid., p. 224 Cf. Marx, *Capital*, vol. I, ch. XXVII, pp. 671 ff.

4. For a discussion on this thesis see R. Hilton (ed.), *The Transition from Feudalism to Capitalism. A Symposium* (New York, 1954).

5. Dobb, *Studies in the Development of Capitalism*, p. 42.

6. Marx, *Capital*, vol. I, ch. XVIII, p. 678.

7. Sir Thomas More, *The 'Utopia' and The History of Edward V, with Roper's Life*. Edited, with Intro. by M. Adams, London, n.d., pp. 89-90.

8. Marx, *Capital*, vol. I, ch. XVIII, p. 686.

9. More, *'Utopia'*, p. 98: W. J. Chambliss, 'A Sociological Analysis of the Law of Vagrancy', *Social Problems*, vol . 12, no. 1 (Summer 1964) p. 67.

10. More, *'Utopia'*, pp. 92 ff.

11. F. Piven and R. A. Cloward, *Regulating the Poor* (London, 1972) p. 15.

12. A. van der Slice, 'Elizabethan Houses of Correction', *Journal of the American Institute of Criminal Law and Criminology*, vol. XXVII (1936-7) p. 44; A. J. Copeland, 'Bridewell Royal Hospital', *Past and Present* (1888); Max Grünhut, *Penal Reform* (Oxford, 1948) p. 15; S. and B. Webb, *English Prisons Under Local Government* (London, 1963) p. 12.

13. Grünhut, *Penal Reform*, pp. 15, 16 and van der Slice, *Elizabethan Houses of Correction*, p. 51.

14. F. M. Eden, *The State of the Poor* (London, 1928) p. 16; G. Rusche and O. Kirchheimer, *Punishment and Social Structure* (New York, 1968) p. 41; Piven and Cloward, *Regulating the Poor*, pp. 15, 16; Grünhut, *Penal Reform*, p. 16; van der Slice, *Elizabethan Houses of Correction*, p. 55.

15. Eden, *The State of the Poor*, p. 16.

16. Van der Slice, *Elizabethan Houses of Correction*, p. 54.

17. See Eden, *The State of the Poor*, p. 17; S. and B. Webb, *English Prisons Under Local Government*, p. 13; Rusche and Kirchheimer, *Punishment and Social Structure*, p. 51; van der Slice, *Elizabethan Houses of Correction*, p. 55; Grünhut, *Penal Reform,* p. 16.

18. Eden, *The State of the Poor*, p. 17.

19. Ibid., p. 19.

20. See Piven and Cloward, *Regulating the Poor*, p. 37; also Marx, *Capital*, vol. I, chs. XXVI-XXIX, pp. 686-96; and Dobb, *Studies in the Development of Capitalism*, pp. 231 ff.

21. Details here and in subsequent passages on the demographic situation are drawn from A. Bellettini, 'La popolazione italiana dall'inizio della era volgare ai giorni nostri. Valutazioni e tendenze', in *Storia d'Italia*, vol. V, I (Torino, 1973) p. 489. This essay relates the Italian demographic situation to that of Europe in general.

22. Dobb, *Studies in the Development of Capitalism*, pp. 237 ff.

23. See above, p. 13.

24. Piven and Cloward, *Regulating the Poor*, p. 6.

25. Marx defines Holland as 'the head capitalistic nation of the 17th century', *Capital*, vol. I, ch. XXXI, p. 704.

26. T. Sellin, *Pioneering in Penology* (Philadelphia, 1944) p. 20; Grünhut, *Penal Reform*, p. 17; R. von Hippel, 'Beiträge zur Geschichte der Freiheitsstrafe', *Zeitschrift für die gesamte Strafrechtswissenschaft*, Vol. XVIII (1898) p. 648.

27. See Sellin, *Pioneering in Penology*, pp. 1, 2.

28. Cf. Rusche and Kirchheimer, *Punishment and Social Structure*, p. 42 and Bellettini, *La popolazione*.

29. See Rusche and Kirchheimer, *Punishment and Social Structure*, p. 42.

30. Marx, *Capital*, vol. I, Part VIII, p. 686 ff. and Part III, ch. X: *The Working Day*, pp. 222 ff.

31. See above, p. 13.

32. Piven and Cloward have especially emphasised this, for example in the first chapter of *Regulating the Poor*.

33. I have already cited Sellin; cf. von Hippel, 'Beiträge zur Geschichte', pp. 437 ff. A. Hallema has contributed widely to this theme: A. Hallema, *In em om de Gevangenis, Van vroeger Dagen in Nederland en Nederlandsch-Indie* ('s Gravenhage, 1936) pp. 174-6. Most historical research on penology refers to Dutch workhouses. In Italian see: C. I. Petitti di Roreto, 'Della condizione attuale delle carceri e dei mezzi di migliorarla (1840)' in *Opere scelte* (Torino, 1969) p. 369. M. Beltrani-Scalia, *Sul governo e sulla riforma delle carceri in Italia* (Torino, 1867) p. 393.

34. See Sellin, *Pioneering in Penology*, pp. 23, 24. All the following information on the Rasp-huis is drawn from Sellin.

35. Ibid., p. 26.

36. It was calculated that in the city of Amsterdam, with a population of 100 000, at the time of the opening of the institution there were about 3500 'juvenile delinquents' (ibid., p. 41).

37. Dobb, *Studies in the Development of Capitalism*, pp. 193 ff.

38. See Sellin, *Pioneering in Penology*, pp. 29, 30.

39. For a theoretical discussion on this theme see Dobb, *Studies in the Development of Capitalism*, pp. 281 ff.

40. Marx, *Capital*, vol. 1, p. 331.

41. Ibid., pp. 346, 347.

42. Sellin, *Pioneering in Penology*, p. 59.

43. Ibid., p. 63.

44. Cf. pp. 23 ff.

45. Marx, *Capital*, vol. I, p. 340.

46. See pp. 33 ff.

47. See Sellin, *Pioneering in Penology*, p. 68.

48. See Dobb, *Studies in the Development of Capitalism*, pp. 151 ff.

49. Ibid.

50. Ibid., p. 158. On the 'Ciompi' see V. Rutenberg, *Popolo e movimenti popolari nell'Italia del '300 e '400* (Bologna, 1971) pp. 157-329.

51. See Dobb, *Studies in the Development of Capitalism*, pp. 235 ff. and bibl.

52. Referred to in Rusche and Kirchheimer, *Punishment and Social Structure*, p. 36; Piven and Cloward, *Regulating the Poor*, p. 9; Grünhut, *Penal Reform*, p. 14.

53. In Piven and Cloward, *Regulating the Poor*, p. 9.

54. Ibid., p. 11. Specifically on Lyon, also see: J. P. Gutton, *La Société et les pauvres. L'exemple de la généralite de Lyon, 1534-1789* (Paris, 1971); N. Z. Davis, 'Poor Relief, Humanism and Heresy: The Case of Lyon', in *Studies in Medieval and Renaissance History* (1968) p. 217; R. Gascon, 'Immigration et croissance au XVIe siècle: l'exemple de Lyon (1529-1563)', *Annales* (1970) p. 988.

55. On this specific theme cf. Rusche and Kirchheimer, *Punishment and Social Structure*, pp. 33-52; more generally, see: J. B. Kraus, *Scholastik, Puritanismus und Kapitalismus* (München, 1930); P. C. Gordon Walker, 'Capitalism and the Reformation', *Economic History Review*, vol. VIII (1937) p. 18 and, of course, M. Weber, *Protestant Ethic and the Spirit of Capitalism* (London, 1976), int. A. Giddens.

56. See pp. 33 ff. In the same way, the influence of methodism grew in Great Britain during the industrial revolution: see E. P. Thompson, *The Making of the English Working Class* (Harmondsworth: Penguin Books, 1968) pp. 385 ff. It is no accident that Marx refers to 'the methodist cell system' in *The Holy Family* (Moscow, 1956), though, as we will see, this system was originally more Quaker than Methodist. On this theme, cf. D. Melossi, *The Penal Question in 'Capital', Crime and Social Justice*, no. 5 (1976) pp. 26-33.

57. K. Marx, *A Contribution to the Critique of Hegel's 'Philosophy of Right'*, ed. O'Malley (Cambridge U.P., 1977) p. 138.

58. Cited by H. Marcuse in his 'Study on Authority', *Studies in Critical Philosophy* (London, 1972) p. 65.

59. Marcuse puts this forward in the above study (p. 49 ff.) It is enough simply to mention the fact that it is this family structure which lay at the basis of Freudian theory. A theory, that

is to say, which rose to prominence in this century as the bourgeois consciousness of the crisis in this particular *form* of the family. But see below, note 133.

60. See below, pp. 67 ff.

61. Marcuse, *Study on Authority*, pp. 56 ff.

62. M. Foucault, *Storia della follia* (Milan, 1963) pp. 91, 92. Eng. Trans: *Madness and Civilisation. A History of Insanity in The Age of Reason* (London, 1965).

63. M. Weber, *The Protestant Ethic and the Spirit of Capitalism*, pp. 159 ff.

64. That is to say, as Marx explains with magnificent clarity, this devaluation of the *significance* of works as such as against their value in the eyes of the deity, as a *sign*, exactly corresponds to a society in which works do not imply production for immediate consumption (as in peasant society) but for the market, for exchange (i.e. the difference between *use-value* and *exchange-value*): *work* has value not for what it is but for what it can obtain (*accumulation* or *grace* — it makes no great difference to the *religion of capital*).

65. 'An ideal house of terror', see below, n. 104.

66. *Selected Writings*, vol. III, p. 466, quoted in Marcuse *Study on Authority*, p. 65. My emphasis.

67. Quoted in Marcuse, *Study on Authority*, p. 64n. It is symptomatic that the social strata to which Müntzer refers as the victims of the predatory princes are 'the poor peasant, the artisan', i.e. precisely those who bore the main brunt first of expropriation, then of proletarianisation. On the peasant revolts in Germany, see Engels's classic, *The Peasant War in Germany* (London: Lawrence & Wishart, 1969).

68. Marcuse, *Study on Authority*, p. 65. This conception is essentially at the basis of Hegelian penal theory.

69. Cf. Rusche and Kirchheimer, *Punishment and Social Structure*, p. 44, von Hippel, *Beitrage zur Geschichte der Freiheitsstrafe*, pp. 429 ff.

70. As in von Hippel, 'Beiträge zur Geschichte', p. 648.

71. See Rusche and Kirchheimer, *Punishment and Social Structure*, p. 44.

72. Ibid., pp. 63 ff.

73. Ibid., pp. 65.

74. Ibid., p. 51, n. 139. Von Hippel's 'Beiträge zur Geschichte' contains a full summary of this booklet in German.

75. See Foucault, *Storia della follia* (Madness and Civilisation) p. 82.

76. See Rusche and Kirchheimer, *Punishment and Social Structure*, p. 43; Foucault, *Storia della follia*, pp. 126 ff.

77. See Rusche and Kirchheimer, *Punishment and Social Structure*, pp. 45, 48.

78. See the section in this chapter on the establishment of modern prison practice in continental Europe, and Chapter 2, which deals with Italy. Rusche and Kirchheimer conclude: 'the fact that both the old and new religious doctrines collaborated in the mutual development of the new institution goes to prove that purely ideological viewpoints took second place to economic motives as driving forces in the whole movement.' p. 52 (*Punishment and Social Structure*).

79. Ibid., p. 43; Foucault, *Storia della follia*, p. 85 and pp. 95 ff.

80. Foucault, *Storia della follia*, pp. 98-9.

81. See Rusche and Kirchheimer, *Punishment and Social Structure*, p. 69 ff; Jean Mabillon, 'Reflexion sur les prisons des ordres religioux' in *Ouvrages Posthumes de D. Jean Mabillon et de D. Thierri Ruinart...* (Paris, 1724) pp. 321-35, edited in English in T. Sellin, 'Dom Jean Mabillon — A Prison Reformer of the Seventeenth Century, *Journal of American Institute of Criminal Law and Criminology*, vol. XVII (1926-7) pp. 581-602.

82. Marx, *Capital*, vol. I, p. 694.

83. Ibid., p. 702 and pp. 716 ff.

84. Ibid., p. 702.

85. Ibid., p. 694.

86. See Dobb, *Studies in the Development of Capitalism*, pp. 226 ff.

87. Ibid.

88. Ibid., p. 225.

89. Cited in T. E. Gregory, 'The Economics of Employment in England, 1660-1713', *Economica*, vol I (1921) p. 44. For a survey of various views on this see R. Bendix, *Work and Authority in Industry* (New York–London, 1956) pp. 60 ff; also interesting is D. Defoe's 'Giving Alms No Charity', in *A Select Collection of Scarce and Valuable Economic Tracts* (London, 1859) p. 40; Bendix is very important in relation to the whole of English social policy from the sixteenth century to the nineteenth century (Bendix, first part, Ch. II).

90. See Eden, *The State of the Poor*, pp. 25, 34, 35.

91. See J. D. Marshall, *The Old Poor Law 1799-1834* (London, 1968) p. 14.

92. Ibid., p. 15.

93. See Eden, *The State of the Poor*, pp. 25 ff.

94. Ibid., p. 27.

95. See S. and B. Webb, *English Prisons Under Local Government*, pp. 1517; L. W. Fox, *The Modern English Prison* (1934) p. 3; Grünhut, *Penal Reform*, p. 17.

96. On the following see S. and B. Webb, *English Prisons Under Local Government*, pp. 18 ff.

97. See Dobb, *Studies in the Development of Capitalism*, pp. 256 ff.

98. See above, n. 6.

99. See 'Debates on the Law on Thefts of Wood' in K. Marx and F. Engels *Collected Works* (London: Lawrence & Wishart, 1975) vol. I, pp. 224-63. See also P. Linebaugh, 'Karl Marx. The Theft of Wood and Working Class Composition: A Contribution to the Current Debate', *Crime and Social Justice*, vol. 6 (Fall-Winter 1976) p. 5.

100. See Piven and Cloward, *Regulating the Poor*, p. 29, cf. Thompson, *The Making of the English Working Class*, pp. 59 ff.

101. In relation to these, see Marshall, *The Old Poor Law*. On the Poor Laws in a broader economic and ideological context, see K. Polanyi's *The Great Transformation* (Boston, 1957).

102. For an elaboration on the new poor laws, see Marshall, *The Old Poor Law*, p. 17; Piven and Cloward, *Regulating the Poor*, pp. 33, 34; Rusche and Kirchheimer, *Punishment and Social Structure*, p. 94; F. Engels, *Conditions of the English Working Class in 1844*.

103. Engels, ibid., p. 312.

104. See Marx, *Capital*, vol. I, p. 263.

105. Piven and Cloward, *Regulating the Poor*, pp. 33, 34.

106. Ibid.

107. Ibid., p. 35. This came out of the so-called 'less eligibility' principle.

108. In Marshall, *The Old Poor Law*, p. 30. For the relationship between what nowadays we would define as 'political criminality' and 'common criminality' and which then took on various forms, primitive and barely different form of class struggle in Britain of the industrial revolution, see Thompson, *The Making of the English Working Class*, pp. 61 ff.

109. See Engels, *Conditions of the English Working Class in 1844*, p. 287.

110. Ibid., p. 288.

111. Piven and Cloward, *Regulating the Poor*, p. 35.

112. See Rusche and Kirchheimer, *Punishment and Social Structure*, pp. 95 ff.

113. See ibid., pp. 96, 97 for an account of the rapid rise in the crime rate in England especially from 1810 onwards. It is no accident that the themes of pauperism, alcoholism, prostitution and crime continually crop up in the young Engels's work cited above. The actual situation before Engels, was one in which *mass criminal* activity had barely been superseded by class struggle. This is summed up in Engels' exclamation: 'And he among the "surplus" who has courage and passion enough openly to resist society, to reply with declared war upon the bourgeoisie to the disguised war which the bourgeoisie wages upon him, goes forth to rob, plunder, murder, and burn!' (p. 87) He then describes how the British working class passed through crime, revolt and Luddism to political struggle as a result of winning the right to organise (pp. 214, 215). It is not inappropriate to note, *en passant*, that Marx's well-known judgements of the *lumpenproletariat*, which sparked off a famous politico-philological *querelle* (see *Il Manifesto*, 16 and 23 Jan and 6 Feb 1972) were all delivered, like those presented by Engels, within a particular socio-political context from which they derive their own special validity. It was the particular task of the socialist movement in the last century to transform, willy-nilly, criminal behaviour into mass *political* activity while such behaviour remained characteristic of a section of the working class: the *lumpenproletariat*, to be precise, which was often used in an anti-working-class way. It was quite obvious that with such a political perspective Marx and Engels would denounce the *lumpen* elements. It should also be stressed that the question of the lumpenproletariat as a question of class analysis has not the slightest connection with those of violence and illegality as forms of political struggle. On this point see M. Foucault, *Surveiller et Punir* (Paris, 1975) pp. 261 ff.

114. See J. Howard, *Prisons and Lazarettos, I: The State of The Prisons in England and Wales* (Montclair, New Jersey, 1973) particularly: 'Proposed Improvements in the Structure and Management of Prisons', p. 19.

115. See Rusche and Kirchheimer, *Punishment and Social Structure*, p. 110.

116. Ibid., p. 111.

117. In Marshall, *The Old Poor Law, 1795-1834*, p. 33. The basic text on this problematic in the industrial revolution period is (regarding English history) the work of S. and B. Webb, *English Poor Law History*, vols VII, VIII and IX of their *English Local Government* (London, 1929).

118. See Piven and Cloward, *Regulating the Poor*, p. 35.

119. See Howard, *Prisons and Lazarettos*, p. 492.

120. From the official *Prison Report* by the Home Office for that year.

121. We should also remember that in the transition from one social situation to another, the same results can be achieved with other means, for example other segregated institutions, transportations, etc..

122. See J. Bentham, *Panopticon*, in *The Works of Jeremy Bentham*, vol. IV (New York, 1962) p. 37.

123. See V. Comoli Mandracci, *Il carcere per la società del Sette-Ottocento* (Turin, 1974) pp. 36, 37. Also R. Evans, 'Bentham's Panopticon. An Incident in the Social History of Architecture', *Architectural Association Quarterly*, vol. 3, no. 2 (April/July 1971).

124. See *Postscript* in Bentham, *Panopticon*, pp. 71 ff.

125. Cf. M. Pavarini's essay in the second part of this book.

126. See Bentham, *Panopticon*, p. 47 ff.

127. Ibid., p. 47.

128. Ibid., p. 50.

129. Ibid., p. 54.

130. Ibid., p. 40.

131. Ibid.

132. On the concept of co-operation see Marx, *Capital*, vol. I, pp. 305 ff.

133. See ibid., pp. 181 ff. The thesis set out below is more widely developed in D. Melossi, *The Penal Question in 'Capital'*; D. Melossi, 'Institutions of Social Control and the Capitalist Organization of Work', in NDC/CSE (eds) *Capitalism and the Rule of Law* (London: Hutchinson, 1979) pp. 90-9; D. Melossi, 'Strategies of Social Control in Capitalism: a Comment on Recent Work', *Contemporary Crises* (forthcoming). Particularly the last two essays seek to understand this process from the standpoint of changes in social control as capitalism has developed. It should be stressed that here, on the contrary, the discussion specifically centres on the period of the prison system's maturity, i.e. 'classical' capitalism of the nineteenth century. It is from this starting point (and that of the first volume of *Capital*) that I write here.

134. Marx, *Capital*, vol. I, p. 172.

135. Ibid.

136. Ibid.

137. Ibid.

138. Ibid.

139. Ibid.

140. Marx clearly demonstrates how the principle of authority is incorporated into the capitalist process of production itself in the chapter on co-operation: By the co-operation of numerous wage-labourers, the sway of capital develops into a requisite for carrying on the labour-process itself, into a real requisite of production. That a capitalist should command on the field of production, is now as indispensible as that a general should command on the field of battle': in *Capital*, vol. I, p. 313. Also pp. 305 ff.

141. See K. Marx and F. Engels, *The Manifesto of the Communist Party*.

142. See the section above on the genesis and development of prisons in other European countries.

143. *Surveiller et punir*, already cited. We were able to see Foucault's book only after our own work here had been completed. M. Foucault's book is a brilliant discourse on prison rather than a history of the same. It is thus of little use here if only for its extreme Franco-centrism (every twist and turn is modulated on French history — if this leaves the philosophical discussion relatively unharmed, it is, as I think I have shown, quite misleading from a historical perspective). But I repeat, it seems to me that Foucault's aims (and that which is of most interest in his work) are other than 'historical'. For a debate on this, cf. *La Questione Criminale*, vol. 11, no. 2/3 (1976).

144. See V. Cotesta, 'Michel Foucault: dall 'archeologia del sapere alla genealogia del potere', *La Questione Criminale*, vol. 2, no. 2/3 (1976).

145. On man's estrangement from his body, on the reduction of man to worker, on the whole thematic of the senses and *needs* (pp. 322 ff.) in K. Marx, 'Economic and Philosophic Manuscripts 1844', in *Early Writings*, Intro. L. Colletti (Harmondsworth: Penguin, 1977).

146. See Foucault, *Surveiller et punir*, pp. 197 ff. And as we have seen in Bentham, *Panopticon*.

147. Fox, *The Modern English Prison*, pp. 6, 7; G. C. Marino, *La formazione dello spirito borghese in Italia* (Firenze, 1974) pp. 353-5.

148. See Rusche and Kirchheimer, *Punishment and Social Structure*, pp. 95 ff.

149. See pp. 47 ff.

150. Cf. Pavarini's essay, below.

151. Cf. Fox, *The Modern English Prison*, pp. 14 ff; Rusche and Kirchheimer, *Punishment and Social Structure*, pp. 132 ff.

152. The complete title of Howard's first volume cited here is: *The State of the Prisons in England and Wales, with Preliminary Observations, and an Account of some Foreign Prisons and Hospitals*.

153. Cf. Rusche and Kirchheimer, *Punishment and Social Structure*, ch. VI, pp. 84 ff.

154. See Howard, *The State of the Prisons*, pp. 44 ff.

155. See Sellin, *Pioneering in Penology*, p. 59.

156. See Grünhut, *Penal Reform*, pp. 19 ff.

157. See Howard, *The State of the Prisons*, pp. 66 ff.

158. See Rusche and Kirchheimer, *Punishment and Social Structure*, p. 91.

159. See Howard, *The State of the Prisons*, pp. 145 ff. which includes a reproduction of the plan of the *Maison de Force*; Grünhut, *Penal Reform*, p. 22; L. Stroobant, 'Le Rasphuis de Gand, Recherches sur la repression du vagabondage et sur le système pénitentiaire établi en

Flandre au XVIIe et au XVIIIe siécle', *Annales de la Soc. d'Histoire et d'Archéologie de Gand*, vol. III (1900) pp. 191-307. It was due to the work of the Count Hippolyte Vilain that the new building was made possible. He espoused his programme in an essay which Howard also cites: *Mémoire sur les moyens de corriger les malfaiteurs et les fainéants a leur propre avantage et de les rendre utiles à l'Etat* (Ghent, 1775). The prison at Ghent was generally considered to be the fundamental starting point for the development of the modern prison; it is cited in practically all historic studies on this subject.

160. Howard, *The State of the Prisons*, p. 148

161. Ibid., p. 150.

162. Ibid., p. 153. For Italy cf. pp. 63 fl.

163. See Foucault, *Storia della follia*, pp. 109 ff.

164. Ibid., p. 110; Rusche and Kirchheimer, *Punishment and Social Structure*, p. 91.

165. See Howard, *The State of the Prisons*, pp. 165 ff. For an analysis of the various human types locked up in the Parisian hospitals, see Foucault, *Storia della follia*, pp. 126, 127.

166. See Howard, *The State of the Prisons*, p. 174.

167. See Marx, Capital, vol. I.

168. See J. P. Marat, *Disegno di legislazione criminale* (Milano, 1971). Refer to the preface by M. A. Cattaneo and the scholarly introduction by M. A. Aimo for further material on this work.

169. Ibid., pp. 71 ff.

170. Ibid., p. 72.

171. Ibid., pp. 72- 3.

172. Ibid., p. 73.

173. Ibid., pp. 74- 5.

174. Ibid., p. 78.

175. Cf. G. Lefebvre, *The Great Fear of 1789, Rural Panic in Revolutionary France* (London, 1973). There is extensive material in French on this subject. I will limit myself to citing the following: C. Paultre, *De la répression de la mendicité et du vagabondage en France sous l'Ancien Régime* (Paris: 1906); L. Lallemand, *Histoire de la Charité, t. IV, Les temps modernes*, (Paris: 1910 and 1912); 'Crimes et criminalité en France sous l'Ancien Régime, XVIIe-XVIIIe siécles', *Cahier des Annales*, vol. 33 (Paris, 1971); A. Vexliard, *Introduction à la sociologie du vagabondage* (Paris, 1956).

176. See Lefebvre, *The Great Fear*, pp. 10, 11.

177. Ibid., p. 14.

178. Ibid., p. 14.

179. Ibid., p. 17. Brigandage in Italy is more specifically dealt with later in Chapter 2.

180. G. Lefebvre, *The Great Fear*, p. 21.

181. Cf. Rusche and Kirchheimer, *Punishment and Social Structure*, pp.81-2, 91-2; Foucault, *Storia della follia*, p. 110.

182. E. B. Pashukanis, *Law and Marxism: A General Theory*, ed. C. Arthur (London, 1978).

183. In para. 101 of his *Philosophy of Right*, trans. S.W. Dyde (London 1896), Hegel states in relation to the *lex taliones*: 'This identity, involved in the very nature of the case, is not literal equality, but equality in the inherent nature of the injury, namely, its value.' And: 'Value as the inner identity of things specifically different, has already been made use of in connection with contract, and occurs again in the civil prosecution of crime. By it the imagination is transferred from the direct attributes of the object to its universal nature' (pp. 98, 99, 100).

The young Marx was to develop this concept in an article on the law against thefts of wood. 'Proceedings of the Sixth Rhine Province Assembly. Third Article. Debates on the Law on Thefts of Wood,' in K. Marx and F. Engels, *Collected Works* (London, 1975) vol. I, pp. 224-63. The scope of our research does not permit any discussion of penal theory. It is, however, necessary to mention the profound contradiction which permeates the Hegelian doctrine of retribution. This doctrine is, on the one hand, a philosophical expression of the bourgeoisie's increasing harshness on the question of crime once in power: the rejection of Enlightenment utilitarianism derives, above all, from the need to assert the general and universal validity of order and respect for law. Equally, it is, in Hegel's own words, an identification of the criminal as a "rational being" (see para. 100 of the *Philosophy of Right*) and it is no coincidence that Marx shapes his particular view of the penal question through a discussion of the Hegelian Theory: see Bottomore and Rebel (eds.), *Karl Marx. Selected Writings in Sociology and Social Philosophy* (London, 1956) pp. 228-70 ('Capital Punishment,' from an article in the *New York Daily Tribune*). On the function of the Hegelian theory in this respect see Rusche and Kirchheimer, *Punishment and Social Structure*, p. 101.

184. Cf. Foucault's brilliant discussion in *Surveiller et punir*, pp. 158 ff. on the new mode of controlling time 'par découpe segmentaire, par sériation, par synthése et totalisation.' On a more general discussion than is dealt with here in this relation, see pp. 222 ff.

185. See above, note 183.

186. These words are from Petitti di Roreto, *Della condizione attuale delle carceri*, p. 372.

187. Probably the best known reports came from G. de Beaumont and A. de Tocqueville, *On the Penitentiary System in the United States and its Application in France* (Southern Illinois University Press, 1964). In Petitti's book cited above, these reports are fully documented (pp. 372-3). Also see M. Pavarini's essay below.

188. See Rusche and Kirchheimer, *Punishment and Social Structure*, pp. 96-7.

189. Ibid., pp. 98, 99. In the nineteenth century this came to be a common point from which eighteenth-century social policy was attacked.

190. Ibid., pp. 99-100.

191. See Petitti, *Della condizione attuale delle carceri*, pp. 374-5 and 469.

192. See Rusche and Kirchheimer, *Punishment and Social Structure*, pp. 106-7.

193. See information recorded in Rusche and Kirchheimer, p. 109.

194. See ibid., ch. VIII, p. 127; ch. III of Petitti's study is entirely dedicated to the various systems and contains a full bibliography.

195. See Rusche and Kirchheimer, p. 130.

196. See note 33 above.

197. See Petitti, *Della condizione*, p. 374 ff.

198. Petitti lists the following as being amongst the supporters of this system: 'Messrs Lucas, Mittermaier, Béranger, Madam Fry, Aubanel, Leone Faucher and Grellet Wammy and himself', p. 450.

199. The following supported solitary confinement: 'Moreau-Cristophe, Aylies, Demetz, Blouet, Julius, Crawford, Russel and Ducpetiaux' (p. 452). The people cited here and in note 198 above are amongst the main artificers, both in practical and theoretical terms, of European social policy during the first half of the last century.

The connection between isolation, the penal or *spiritual* conception of punishment, as it was called, and madness, is thus synthesised by Marx in *The Holy Family*: '. . . correctly describes the conditions to which isolation from the outer world reduces a man. For him who sees a *mere idea* in the *perceptible world*, *mere idea*, on the other hand, becomes a *perceptible being*. The figments of his brain assume corporeal form. A world of perceptible, sensible ghosts is begotten within his mind. That is the mystery of all pious visions and at the same time it is the general form of insanity' (Marx and Engels, *The Holy Family*, pp. 244-5).

200. See Rusche and Kirchheimer, pp. 94-5.

201. Marx comments: 'Kleinliche Forderung in einem allgemeinen Arbeiterprogramm. Jedenfalls musste man klar aussprechen, dass man aus Konkurrenzneid die gemeinen Verbrecher nicht wie Vieh behandelt wissen und ihnen namentlich ihr einziges Besserungsmittel, produktive Arbeit, nicht abschneiden will. Das war doch das Geringste, was man von Sozialisten erwarten durfte' (K. Marx, *Kritik des Gothaer Programms*, in MEW, Band 19 (Berlin, 1962) p. 32). Translations are often a little ambiguous. The sense, however, is:

'A petty demand in a general workers' programme. Anyway, it should have been made quite clear that there is no desire to treat run-of-the-mill criminals like animals through fear of competition and especially not to cut them off from their only means of improvement, productive labour. This was surely the least one might have expected from socialists.'

On the positions of the French workers' movement on this subject at the beginning of the last century, see also Foucault, *Surveiller et punir*, pp. 291 ff.

19.

The Trend-Setter
Nils Christie

Whom one loveth, one chasteneth

There are few countries so pleasant to visit as the USA. As a Norwegian, I feel close to home, often better than at home. We often say that there are as many Norwegians in the USA as there are in Norway. They made a good deal by leaving the old country, materially, and maybe also socially. The warm atmosphere in many encounters, the care for new neighbours, the fascination of the variations within the large cities.

These words are being written in an attempt to counteract some completely wrong interpretations of what now follows. I am intending to do the impossible. I am trying to say that I am fundamentally fond of a country and its people, that I feel close to it, also by national heritage. But at the same time, I will claim that there is something extraordinarily alarming in the social fabric of the USA. And precisely because I feel so close, feel the country as so much of myself, it is increasingly difficult to keep quiet and not express my concern.

Most difficult of all is to meet colleagues from the USA. American criminology rules much of the world, their theories on crime and crime control exert an enormous influence. American criminologists are kind and conscientious people, kind to visitors, conscientious in their standards of scientific activity. Their standards become our standards and their solutions tend to be copied abroad.

Maybe these are the reasons why I think of Germany, from the 1920's and later. Germany, that country of culture and insight, that country of science, that country of rational thoughts and romantic hearts. Norway has always been more oriented towards England and the USA than towards Continental Europe. Oceans were better for transport than mountain roads. But respect for Germany was high. Their legal writers were held in high esteem, as well as their general policy of law and order. Scholars went there. Authorities in police and prosecution went there. They were the influential model, maybe for a little too long.

Today we go to America.

The great confinement

When Michel Foucault (1967) wrote his book on Madness and Civilisation, he included a chapter on the "great Confinement". He had France in mind. He described the efforts to keep the deviant classes and categories under control. Hospitals were built, old leprosy-institutions were converted for the purpose, and Paris became a safe city for the bourgeoisie. Foucault also gives figures for the achievements. At the peak, one per cent of the population was institutionalised. And Foucault gives reasons for this great confinement:

Nils Christie: 'The Trend-Setter' from *CRIME CONTROL AS INDUSTRY* (Routledge, 1991), pp. 79-92.

Before having the medical meaning we give it, or that at least we like to suppose it has, confinement was required by something quite different from any concern with curing the sick. What made it necessary was an imperative of labor...From the beginning, the institution set itself the task of preventing "mendicancy and idleness as the source of all disorders." In fact, this was the last of the great measures that had been taken since the Renaissance to put an end to unemployment or at least to begging.

(pp. 46-47)

As we have already demonstrated in [Section 3.4] on *Global Trends,* the prison population for the whole of the USA will soon be half-way towards Foucault's core example of the great confinement. And the U.S. figures apply to the country as a whole, including states and districts with low figures, while Foucault's figures are for Paris alone and therefore much too large for France as a whole. And the U.S. figures include no mental institutions.

The figures are also showing an explosive growth.

In June 1983, *Correctional Magazine* had this to say about the growth in the prison population of the USA:

"Fantastic ... enormous ... terrifying," were the words chosen by Norval Morris of the University of Chicago Law school to describe last year's increase in the U.S. prison population.

"It's an astonishing increase," says Alfred Blumstein of Carnegie-Mellon University in Pittsburgh.

"I am genuinely surprised; that's stunning growth," says Franklin Zimring, director of the Center for Studies in Criminal Justice at the University of Chicago.

"It's even worse than what I had expected," says Kenneth Carlson of Abt Associates in Cambridge, Mass. "It becomes more and more frightening."

This is what these experts said about the growth in the prison population up until 1983. I was also frightened, and put the article aside to write about it. But the figures and the comments were soon to be outdated. Since 1983, in less than ten years, the figures for the number of prisoners have almost doubled.

A more detailed picture of formal control in the USA is presented in Table 1. It shows, first, figures for the three major types of prisons in the USA; Federal prisons, State prisons and Jails. Federal and State institutions are where the more severe sentences are served. As we can see from the table, the bulk of the prisoners are in Federal and State institutions, while roughly one third of the inmates serve in Jail. But this does not necessarily mean that they only serve short sentences. Due to lack of space in Federal and State prisons, the Jails have been forced to receive prisoners that formally belong to the Federal and State Systems. Further down, the Table includes figures for the population on probation and parole.

Table 1   Population under formal control, USA 1990/1991*

			Cumulative
Federal prisons	1991	71 608	71 608
State prisons	1991	751 806	823 414
Jails	1991	429 305	1 252 719
Total prison population 1-3		1 252 719	
Per 100 000 of population			504
On probation	1990	2 670 234	3 922 953
On parole	1990	531 407	4 454 360
Total population under control of penal law:			4 454 360
Per 100 000 of population			1 794

* Bureau of Justice Statistics, Prisoners in 1991 (NCJ-134729). Jail figures are estimates. Probation and Parole figures are from 1990.

The general impression given by the Table is the hugeness of the figures. With a total prison population of more than 1.2 million inmates, the USA is now up to 504 per 100,000 inhabitants in prisons and jails. If we then add probation and parole, we find close to 4.5 million under some sort of legal control. 4.5 million, that means 1,794 per 100,000 inhabitants.

To get an impression of the growth leading up to these figures, we can use the period from 1989 to 1990 where the increase was 8.6 per cent. That meant 58,808 new prisoners in State and Federal institutions. According to Bureau Director Steven B. Dillingham *(Corrections Digest* May 1991, p.1), this equals a need for about 1,100 new prison beds — that is what they use as their counting unit in the USA — every week. The increase in jails was 5.5 per cent, or 21,230 prisoners, which probably meant that the need for new prison "beds" increased to 1,400 or 1,500 each week.

In this perspective, the great confinement of Foucault's ancient Paris is not so great any more. More than 1.2 million prisoners. It is such a large number that it is difficult to grasp. It is more than the population of Prague, and also more than the total population of Copenhagen. If we also include all those on probation or parole in the USA, we exceed the total population of Norway.

It could, of course, be argued that probation and parole are just formalities without content, or only relatively mild forms of control. This may be true in some areas, but not everywhere, as documented in the [next chapter].

Also seen in a larger historical perspective, the increase in the prison population has been quite extraordinary. Diagram 1 (from Austin and McVey 1989, p.2) shows the development from 1850 to 1989. As we see from the diagram, the US development is characterized by three big increases; first from 1850 to 1870, then from 1920 to 1940, and lastly from 1970 and until recently. In the first two periods, the increase came to a stop after twenty years, but this time the growth just continues. Austin and McVey have also made a five year projection of the prison population. They expect an increase of 65 per cent up to 1994. That seems to be an under-estimate (conversation with James Austin).

Diagram 1   Prisoners in USA from 1850 to 1990 per 100.000

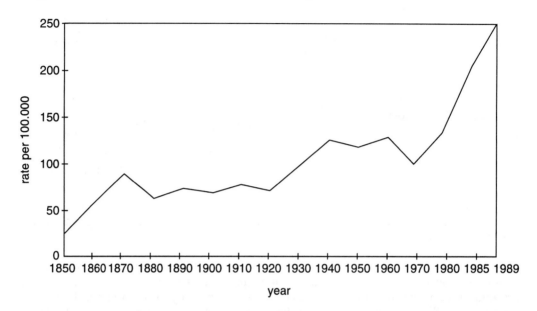

Those who have arrived in Federal or State institutions will mostly stay for a very long time. The average stay for those released in 1990 was close to 24 months. But not all are released. 11,759 inmates were serving what the Americans call "natural life sentences". It is difficult to see what is natural in their conditions. Behind the formulation is a decision to keep them in prison for ever. In addition there were 44,451 serving "ordinary" and life sentences. 105,881 were serving sentences of 20 years or more. 2,424 were waiting for execution *(The Corrections Year-book, 1991).* The living conditions for those waiting for execution have been descrid by Stimson (1991). He ought to know. He is "senior associate in an architectural/engineering/planning firm specializing in quality designed environments for criminal justice facilities". In an article entitled "A Better Design for Safer Detention on Death Row", he describes a design for death row where inmates will have no visual contact with one another, and where they will not be able to communicate. The only people with whom inmates will have contact will be the correctional officers walking the floor. These officers will become familiar with each inmate's behaviour patterns, says Mr. Stimson, and they "will be able to detect anything out of the ordinary." — whatever that might be.

From state to state

But these United States are not very similar to each other when it comes to punishment. This can be seen from Table and Diagram 2. The major impression is one of extreme variation between the states. While North Dakota, Minnesota and West Virginia are at the very bottom with figures well below one hundred per 100,000 inhabitants, Idaho is over 200, New York is over 300 per 100,000, Oklahoma exceeds the 400 figure, Nevada is close to the 500 level, and the Capital itself, the District of Columbia, leads the nation with the unbelievable figure of 1,168 prisoners sentenced to one year or more per 100,000 resident population. This figure is probably unfair to the capital. Since it is a small geographical area, many come to Washington from districts in the vicinity, are arrested and sentenced there, and count in their statistics.

Diagram 2 Prison figures per 100.000 inhabitants 1991 in US. Sentenced to more than 1 year in Federal and State Institutions)

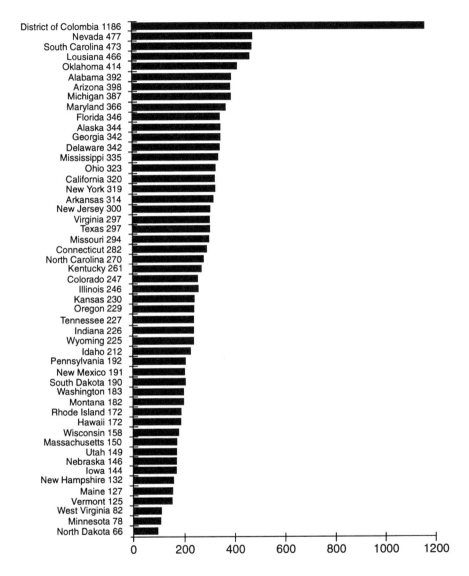

Source: Bureau of Justice Statistics: Prisoners in 1991.

But evaluating these variations, we have to keep in mind that in all these figures we have only included the more severe sentences of more than one year, and also only those served in Federal and State prisons. This means that more than 460,000 prisoners, or 37 percent, are left out of the Table. North Dakota has 68 prisoners per

415

100,000 inhabitants in the table. If we estimate the omission also here to be about 37 percent — probably a rather dubious procedure — North Dakota would reach 93 prisoners per 100,000. This means that North Dakota keeps within the West European level of incarceration. But Minnesota and West Virginia already exceed the level of England and Wales with 108 and 112 respectively if we add the 37 per cent, and from then on, all contact with West European standards is gone. Lousiana, Nevada and South Carolina would with such an estimate each end up with more than 600 prisoners per 100,000 inhabitants. Since females are so rare in prison, this means that at least one percent of the male population in these states are in prison at any time.

States of prisons

Of all the beautiful states, California is probably number one. Here is sun, here is leisure, here is Berkeley and Stanford and the heaven of academic life, here is business and expansion and work, here is the dream-factory of the world: Hollywood.

And here are also some of the more famous prisons in the United States. Alcatraz is gone, but San Quentin remains with a fame stretching far beyond the USA. And here is Folsom with 7,000 prisoners, 500 among them probably never to be released. And in these years, new structures are being added to the great Californian tradition.

California has 101,808 prisoners in Federal and State institutions. Based on those sentenced for one year or more, they have 320 for every 100,000 inhabitants. If we add an estimated 37 per cent for short-termers and those in jails, we end up with 438 prisoners per 100,000 for 1991. But California favours growth and vivacity, and plans for 800 per 100,000 at the turn of the century. And they do not stop at planning, they build. One of the prisons under construction was described like this in the *Los Angeles Times* on May 1, 1990:

> Pelican Bay is entirely automated and designed so that inmates have virtually no face-to-face contact with guards or other inmates. For $22^1/_2$ hours a day, inmates are confined to their windowless cells, built of solid blocks of concrete and stainless steel so that they won't have access to materials they could fashion into weapons. They don't in prison industries; they don't have access to recreation; they don't mingle with other inmates. They aren't even allowed to smoke because matches are considered a security risk.
>
> Inmates eat all meals in their cells and leave only for brief showers and 90 minutes of daily exercise. They shower alone and exercise alone in miniature yards of barren patches of cement enclosed by 20 feet high cement walls covered with metal screens. The doors to their cells are opened and closed electronically by a guard in a control booth.
> . . .
> There are virtually no bars in the facility; the cell doors are made of perforated sheets of stainless steel with slots for food trays. Nor are there guards with keys on their belts walking the tiers. Instead, the guards are locked away in glass-enclosed control booths and communicate with prisoners through a speaker system.
> . . . The SHU (Secure Housing Unit) has its own infirmary; its own law library (where prisoners are kept in secure rooms and slipped law books

through slots); and its own room for parole hearings. Inmates can spend years without stepping outside the Unit.

California's Governor George Deukmejian dedicated the new prison on June 14, 1990. According to *Corrections Digest* (June 27,1990 p. 9) he stated:

"California now possesses a state-of-the-art prison that will serve as a model for the rest of the nation. .... Pelican Bay symbolises our philosophy that the best way to reduce crime is to put convicted criminals behind bars." The Governor also noted that the annual cost of keeping a convicted felon in prison is $ 20,000 compared with the $430,000 that it costs society when a career criminal is at work on the street.

But California is not alone. The *Sunday Oklahoma* of February 24, 1991 has this to report from that state:

Inmates housed in the "high-max" security unit will live 23 hours a day in their cells, with the other hour spent in a small concrete recreation area with 200-foot walls. The space is topped by a metal grate. Theoretically, an inmate could move into the new cellhouse and never again set foot outdoors. The unit's first residents will be the 114 men on death row. The cellhouse also contains a new execution chamber.

The organization Human Rights Watch has investigated prison conditions in the USA. This study is a parallel study to the one by Helsinki Watch on prison conditions in the Soviet Union. In a detailed report (1992) Human Rights Watch describes trends towards total isolation in the U.S. prisons. They call the trend "Marionization". A federal prison with that name implemented a series of extraordinary security measures in 1983, and 36 states have followed suit in creating their own super maximum security institutions called "Maxi-Maxi" in prison jargon.

The confinement in "maxi-maxis" is administered by prison officials without independent supervision and leads to a situation in which inmates may in fact be sentenced twice: once by the court, to a certain period of imprisonment; and the second time by the prison administration, to particularly harsh conditions.

The conditions at Marion are much harsher than in any other federal prison, including confinement of inmates for up to 23 hours a day to their cells and denial of any contact visits (p. 4).

State prisons have the same arrangements. From Florida, this is reported:

A particularly glaring example is the windowless Q-Wing of the Florida State Prison at Starke, from which inmates never go outside and where some prisoners have been held as long as seven years.(p. 4)

. . .

Such a placement is open-ended, and may last, we were informed, for as long as 15 years. The inmate is allowed three showers and two hours of outdoor exercise a week as the only time outside the cell. He can buy a limited number of goods from the canteen and check out one book a week

417

from the library (if he is not on the Library Suspension List, another disciplinary measure at Starke). Inmates under close management can also be deprived of all exercise outside the cell and not allowed outdoors for years at a time. The Florida rules claim that "Close Management is not disciplinary in nature and inmates in close management are not being punished" (p. 44).

Disciplinary confinement is even more serious, meant for prisoners who commit an infraction within the prison. In addition to the restrictions associated with close management, these inmates are not allowed any reading material except legal materials. But life can turn even worse. This prison has a Q-Wing for those who commit further infractions while already in one of the categories described above. Cells here are 6 feet 11 inches by 8 feet 7 inches, with a cement bunk, a toilet and a sink. There is no window and no furniture. The door is of metal. The heat in the cell was stifling, according to the Human Rights Watch (p. 45.)

But the US is a land of contrast. The extreme isolation is the one type of evil. But the extreme contrast to isolation also has its costs. The Human Rights Watch also describes these conditions (pp. 19 and 20):

> Jails are supposed to hold inmates for briefer periods than prisons, and that fact is reflected in the physical structure of most institutions. They often have very limited recreation facilities, house inmates in windowless cells, and provide little or no privacy to the detainees.

> For example, the Criminal Justice Centre in Nashville, Tennessee was built in 1982 with a capacity for about 300 inmates. At the time of our visit in 1990, it held more than 800 inmates and we were told that at some point recently it had held 1,100. For over six months, a staff member told us, the facility's gym was used to house several hundred pre-trial detainees. They had two bathrooms and two showers at the gym. At the time of the greatest overcrowding, additional space in the underground tunnel leading to the courthouse was used to house 200 inmates. There were no showers and no bathrooms in that area.

> ... on Rikers Island in New York City, out of 1,516 inmates at the time of our visit about 300 were housed in cells (mostly segregation) while the rest lived in dormitories and on the decks of converted ferry boats anchored to the shore of the island. Each dormitory housed up to 57 inmates ...

> In the Sybil Brand jail in Los Angeles, women slept in dormitories holding between 130-156 people. The dorms were crowded and offered no personal privacy.

The complaints from these prisoners were strikingly similar to those we have quoted earlier from Russians prisoners [Chapter 5.6]:

> Dormitories were designed for 50, yet held about 90 inmates at the time of our visit. Inmates complained to us about the crowded conditions and about not being able to choose a roommate. A severely overweight woman

418

(she told us her weight was 280 pounds) said that when she and her roommate were both in the cubicle, they literally could not move (p. 34)

One inmate ... described his cell (in another prison): "Peeling paint on walls, leaking plumbing, broken glass in windows, dim lighting, roaches, rats/mice, ants, mosquitoes, moldy pillows and mattress, covered with filth, which have no plastic covers, unbearable heat in the summer, intense cold in winter."

But the USA is also in other ways a country of contrasts. Again, according to the Human Rights Watch (p. 61)

Among institutions visited by Human Rights Watch, only the Bedford Hills facility allowed inmates who gave birth during incarceration to keep their babies in prison. Under a New York state law, female inmates are allowed to keep their babies for one year.

In addition to accommodations for babies, Bedford Hills, a facility where 75 percent of the inmates are mothers, has arrangements to help them maintain contacts with older children. In the summer, the facility runs week long programs for inmates' children who are housed with local families and spend the day with their mothers on the premises. They play with their mothers in a large, toy-filled visiting room, and may also participate in a number of organized activities. In addition, they can also use a playground outside. Year-round, according to the warden, there are bus rides once a month from New York City and Albany, arranged so that children can visit their mothers without having to be accompanied by other relatives.

The crime explanation

The conventional explanation of growth in prison rates is to see it as a reflection of growth in crime. The criminal starts it all, and society has to react. This is the re-active thinking. As we already commented in [Chapter 3.5], this thinking did not hold up for Europe. And it fares no better in the USA:

The prison population has doubled during the last ten years. But here is what the Bureau of Justice Statistics tells (National Update January 1992, p. 5) about the number of victims in that period:

Victimization rates continue a downward trend that began a decade ago.

There were approximately 34.4 million personal and household crimes in 1990, compared with 41.4 million in 1981.

From 1973 to 1990, the rate of personal crimes (rape, robbery, assault, personal theft) fell by 24.5% and the rate for household crimes (burglary, household theft, motor vehicle theft) fell by 26.1%.

Because the NCVS (The National Crime Victimization Survey) counts only crimes for which the victim can be interviewed, homicides are not counted. Their exclusion does not substantially alter the overall estimates.

The number of victims has gone down. Furthermore, and again in sharp contrast to folk-beliefs on crime in the USA, the number of serious offences reported to the police also shows a slight decrease. The FBI statistics on serious offences started at 5.1 million in 1980 and ended at 4.8 million in 1989. But the severity of the sanctions for these crimes has increased. In 1980, 196 offenders were sentenced to prison for every 1,000 arrests for serious crimes. In 1990 the number of imprisonments for such crimes had increased to 332, according to the Bureau of Justice Statistics on Prisoners in 1990.

Mauer (1991, p. 7) has these comments:

> While there is little question that the United States has a high rate of crime, there is much evidence that the increase in the number of people behind bars in recent years is a consequence of harsher criminal justice policies of the past decade, rather than a direct consequence of rising crime.

Austin and Irvin (1990, p. 1) say:

> National statistics show that the majority (65 per cent) of offenders are sentenced to prison for property, drug and public disorder crimes. A significant number (15 per cent) of all admissions have not been convicted of any crime but are returned to prison for violating their parole "conditions" (e.g. curfew violations, failure to particpate in a program, evidence of drug use, etc.)

From their own research — a study based on a random intake to prisons in three states — they also conclude that the vast majority of inmates are sentenced for petty crimes that involve little danger to public safety, or significant economic loss to victims.

The explosion in the number of prisoners in the USA cannot be explained as "Caused by crime". We have to look for other explanations.

20.   Crime Control as a Product
Nils Christie

The crime control market

From the folklore, we know that everything is bigger in the USA than everywhere else. Nonetheless, to a foreigner it is a moving experience to get in one's hand the official publication of the American Correctional Association. The title is *Corrections Today*, a magazine with glossy pages, in colour and perfect print, containing a quantity of advertisements which is probably a considerable source of income to the Association.

In the issue for June 1991, there were 111 advertisements. Three major categories were represented:

1. Building of prisons, entire prisons, or parts of prisons. There were sixteen such ads. You phone and we build. Six months after your call, the prison is ready. Besteel is one of those. In a full page ad we are told:

> Albany County Jail and Penitentiary. 64 bed dormitory style Jail . . . Completed in 6 months.

Bell Construction also has a full page under the title:

> The Pros on Cons.
>
> For more than 20 years we've been building. Building a reputation. Building a client list, and building correctional facilities. That's all we do, we build. And we do it well. Twenty-five correctional facilities worth §300 millions have given us the experience, and now our clients call us the "pros".
>
> Are you building or renovating a correctional facility? Are you interested in a design-built facility at a guaranteed price? If you're interested in finding out more about our experience, call Don Estes, senior vice president at . . .

Some authorities may be in need of a site for their prisons. The Bibby Line group has a solution according to the ancient tradition of the ship of fools:

> Maritime Correctional Facilities.
>
> Times change . . . Bibby OFFERS alternatives to land-based facilities. Bibby DELIVERS:
>
> — Crisis relief within 90-120 days
>
> — Up to 650 beds within 9-12 months.

Nils Christie: 'Crime Control as a Product' from *CRIME CONTROL AS INDUSTRY* (Routledge, 1991), pp. 93-125.

2. Equipment for prisons. In this area, the June issue contained 43 ads of all sorts. Among them were three for telephones particularly suitable for prisons, twenty for electronic surveillance systems of all sorts, three for weapons and seven for other security equipment.

Phones that enforce

is a whole page ad by USWEST Communication:

This phone only does what *you* want it to do. It controls how long callers talk. It bars them from reaching certain numbers. It can monitor and record all phone activity, as directed . . . Keep inmate telephone privileges firmly under your control. . .

Or:

Designed for Criminal Justice Professionals: Drug Abuse? Yes or no in 3 minutes . . . Rapid results leave no time for alibis ... ONTRAK allows no time for excuses and gives you complete control of the testing situation.

"PRISON BAND"

Identify inmates with a heavy duty waterproof wristband. Two locking metal snaps insure a non-transferable heavy duty no-stretch identification system. No special tools are needed to close our metal snaps. Both write on surface and insert card systems are available. SECUR-BAND, the answer for inmate identification.

The issue of *Corrections Today* for June carried an enormous amount of advertisements, but that issue was soon to be dwarfed. In July the number of pages increased from 160 to 256. Ordinary ads increased from 111 to 130. Partly they were of the same types as in June, like the one for tear gas:

The TG Guard system, now installed in major prisons, is a strategic arrangement of tear gas dispensers installed at the ceiling level. These dispensers can be fired from a remote-control console by protected personnel. The firing can be in a chosen pattern and with various levels of concentration to force the inmates to evacuate an area in a route which you determine.

If tear gas is not sufficient, Point Blank Body Armour is available:

Some inmates would *love* to stab, slash, pound, punch and burn you. But they won't get past your S.T.A.R. Special Tactical Anti-Riot vest.

In addition to the usual ads, the July issue also contained sixty yellow pages called:

Buyer's Guide of Correctional Products and Services.

Here were listed 269 companies, with a specification of their products, from A — Access Control system, via P, — Portable Jail Cells, down to X for X-ray and security screening equipment. The list shows the latest in electronics, but also firms with traditions, like the:

Human Restraint Company

> Finest quality leather restraints. Manufactured in USA since 1876. Call or
> write for a free brochure.

This official publication of the American Correctional Association does not only
contain paid advertisements. It also carries articles, squeezed in between the ads. But
several of the articles are written by employees of the very same firms which advertise
in the journal. The July issue has an article by Ostroski and Rohn, both from Precision
Dynamics Corporation, a manufacturer of identification systems. Here is what they tell
us from Los Angeles, which has, in their own words, the largest single detention
facility "in the free world." In this extraordinary place they have trusted inmate
identification wristbands for almost 14 years. But Georgia has a more sophisticated
system:

> the crowded DeKalb County Jail near Atlanta, Ga., houses more than
> 1,200 inmates. In the winter of 1989, officials there decided to begin using
> bar code wristbands that employ the same basic technology as bar codes
> used in clothing stores and supermarkets.
> . . .
> To create a rehabilitative atmosphere — and still maintain a high security
> level — jail officials installed a laser-scanning and portable data-collection
> system to identify and monitor the inmates.
>
> By using hand-held laser units to scan the wristbands, deputies enter data
> into a small computer. This method of gathering information eliminates
> the paperwork involved in monitoring inmate movements.
> . . .
> Technology is now being developed to allow inmate photos to appear on
> the same wristband as the bar-coded informations...Inmates can't switch
> bands, which prevents erroneous releases. (pp. 142-145)

Two pictures illustrate the article. Both show black arms — nothing more — with
wristbands controlled by white arms in one picture, and by the whole of a white person
in the second picture. It is probably not possible to get much closer than that to
humans being handled as commodities, based on a technology so well known from the
supermarkets.

3. The running of prisons also plays a prominent part, with twenty ads in the June
issue:

> When morale's on the line with every meal, count on us . . . Service
> America is working behind bars all across the country, with a solid record
> of good behavior . . . If feeding a captive audience is part of your job, talk
> to the food service specialists who know how to do justice. Call..

Another condition for peace is efficient weapons. Efficient firms provide non-lethal as
well as lethal weapons. Among the non-lethal:

> Cap-Stun II
> Used by the FBI and 1100 Law Enforcement agencies
> Never a law suit involving Cap-Stun in 14 years of use
> Proven effective against Drug Abusers and Psychotics
> Consumer models available for friends and loved ones

Among the 111 advertisements in June, there were also a few for ordinary products for ordinary people, not particularly relevant to the prison markets.

The July issue also contains two other extraordinary items. The one consists of several pages of thanks to the sponsors of the banquet to be held at the 121st Congress of Correction in Minneapolis August 1991. From telephone-companies to manufacturers of bullet-proof glass, they pay, and the prison officers celebrate. An additional attractive feature of the stay in Minneapolis is that you can leave that town "in a beautiful, sporty, brand-spanking-new 1991 Dodge Daytona ES fully equipped with every imaginable accessory!" The only condition is that you visit the Exhibit Hall where the industry shows its products, and leave proof that you have been there. When you are registered in the Hall, you are automatically a participant in the lottery for the car.

*

One personal note, on the adaptability of man: On my first reading of *Corrections Today,* I was close to not trusting my own eyes. The image of the prisoners that emerged through the ads was close to unbelievable. So was the frank exposure of the relationship between the correctional establishment and the industrial interests. Medical journals are of course similar, and pharmaceutical firms excel in their briberies of doctors through sponsorship of their congresses, seminars, trips to Hawaii with spouses included and all that. The American Correctional Association is of another kind. It is the organization with the mandate to administer the ultimate power of society. It is an organization for the delivery of pain, here sponsored by those who make the tools.

But then, to continue my personal note; the next shock came some weeks later, when I re-read the journals. Now the ads no longer had quite the same punch. I saw advertisements for gas dispensers in the ceiling of prisons without immediately connecting the picture or the text to old images of extermination camps, and I read without great excitement about inmates who would love to stab, slash, pound, punch and burn me and other readers. I had got accustomed to it, domesticated to a highly peculiar perspective on fellow beings, and I had also acquired new (reduced) minimum standards for what sort of surroundings some people can decide that other people have to live in.

The money push

It must be obvious by now, so I shall be brief: Prison means money. Big money. Big in building, big in providing equipment. And big in running. This is so, regardless of private or public ownership. In all western systems, private firms are involved in some way or other.

Even the relatively small Federal prison system of the USA comes up with enormous figures. For 1992, the system is requesting more than $ 2.1 billion. This is a 24 per cent increase over last year *(The Washingotn Post,* April 25 1991). According to Knepper and Lilly (1991):

> As prison populations exploded, punishment became big business. If the prison population continues to grow at the 1980s rate, it will cost at least $ 100 million per week just for construction of new facilities. In 1990, total capital and operational expenditures by county, state and federal correctional systems were estimated to be more than $ 25 billion.

Health care and food service are two of the fastest growing sectors in the booming corrections industry, say Knepper and Lilly. In June, the Campbell Soup Company reported that the nation's prison system was the fastest growing food service market. But the biggest profits are made in construction and finance (p. 5):

> The average cost of a U.S.prison bed in 1991–1992 is $ 53,100, up from $ 42,000 in 1987–1988. Not surprisingly, more than a hundred firms specialize in prison architecture alone, and these firms now receive between $ 4 billion and $ 6 billion in prison construction business a year.

Feeley (1991, pp. 1-2) describes some of it like this:

> As of October 1988, more than 25 for-profit companies, many backed by venture capital, were competing for rights to build, own, and operate jails and prisons throughout the United States (Private Vendors in Corrections 1988). Privatization in juvenile correction has grown at an even faster pace. During the past thirty years, placements in private programs (e.g. training centers, residential treatment and counseling programs, foster care, and diversion programs) in lieu of state-run facilities have become quite common, and currently in the United States a substantial portion of all juveniles under court supervision are in the custody of privately operated programs. And in recent years jails, prisons, and juvenile facilities have also turned to private vendors to supply a host of services, including food, health, counselling, vocational training, education . . . .

Furthermore, in recent years the private sector has also radically altered the ways correctional facilities are financed and built. Private lease-purchase arrangements are increasingly replacing government-issued bonds.

Private money is into it all. But the most clear-cut case can of course be found in the private prison itself. Let us turn to that.

Private prisons

Even capital punishment is sometimes administered by private contractors in the United States today.

I find the sentence in a major book on private prisons (Logan 1990, p. 59). There is just this one sentence on capital punishment, squeezed in between examples of all other tasks administered by private agents. So, for the rest we are free to use our imaginations. And I wonder: private contractors for capital punishment — who are they in modern times, and how do they operate? Do they advertise their service? Is it a private, personally-owned firm, or is it registered on the stock exchange as Pain-Delivery Ltd. Limited liability, — limited to what? And what about the equipment needed, chairs, needles, the poison? Do they provide it themselves, or sub-contract? And the training of the staff — do they use the available know-how? Joseph Ingle (personal communication, but see also his book of 1990) has described the phenomenon of the left-leg man — he who, in a team of six, specializes in fastening the strap around the left leg, this in contrast to the right-legger. Six specialists, reducing the man to die to six parts of a thing.

Why react like this to killing by private contractors? Those to be executed are certainly sentenced by ordinary courts. It all follows basic rules, and officials of the state will certainly see to it that everything is done as decided by that state. The whole execution may actually be better performed than if the state had fumbled with it. The last meal may be better prepared, the psychiatrists and priest may be top performers in their professions, far beyond the reach of ordinary state budgets, and the killing itself may take place without the embarrassing aborted attempts sometimes reported from the state service. Those to be killed would probably appreciate the private quality.

This is the basic line of reasoning in the book by Logan, the only difference being that he writes about the private prison, not the private execution. His conclusion regarding private prisons is clear. All the state is doing, private enterprise can do better, or equally well:

> Arguments against private prisons vary in soundness and plausibility, but in no area have I found any potential problem with private prisons that is not at least matched by an identical or a closely corresponding problem among prisons that are run by the government . . . Because they raise no problems that are both unique and insurmountable, private prisons should be allowed to compete (and cooperate) with government agencies so that we can discover how best to run prisons that are safe, secure, humane, efficient, and just (p. 5).

I remain unconvinced, and slightly upset. Why is it that what is so clear to Logan is so utterly unclear to me? His well-ordered book contains a whole chapter on the propriety of private prisons (pp. 49-75). And he finds it proper:

> Our elected leaders exercise very little direct power; rather, they issue instructions and directives that are carried out by subordinates . . . However, it is false to assume that the integrity of a chain of civil servants is necessarily superior to a contractual chain.

Behind this reasoning is John Locke, and particularly Robert Nozick in his earlier writings (e.g. 1974). They lead Logan to this statement (p. 52):

> In the classical liberal (or in modern terms, libertarian) tradition on which the American system of government is founded, all rights are individual, not collective. The state is artificial and has no authority, legitimate power, or rights of its own other than those transferred to it by individuals.

With this perspective, I can understand Logan's private killing and wish for the privatization of pain delivery in general. But it is at the same time an arrangement which can easily develop into a monster, a monster with a soft surface. Robert P. Weiss (1989, p. 38) describes that surface:

> private prison companies . . . have dispensed with paramilitary uniforms and ranking; martial vocabulary and regiment, which have characterized the penal profession since the inception of the penitentiary, are no longer employed. Prison companies still want to create the illusion of legitimate authority, but a business-like image is projected instead of a pseudo-official one. At CCA-run facilities, for example, prisoners are not referred to as 'inmates', instead they are called 'residents', and guards are referred to as 'resident supervisors'. Dressed in camel-coloured sweaters that bear a discreet company insignia, private guards are represented as what one might call 'corporate security technicians'.

Logan's state is a contractual one. Private persons elect a representative. The representative hires a firm to deliver punishments. If the firm is bad, a new one is hired. The private guard represents his firm. There is nothing more to represent, the state is an artifact. But this means that the guard is under diminished control.

In the opposite case, where the state exists, the prison officer is my man. I would hold a hand on his key, or on the switch for the electric chair. He could be a bad officer. And I could be bad. Together we made for a bad system, so well known from the history of punishments. But I would have known I was a responsible part of the arrangement. Chances would also be great that some people in the system were not only bad. They would more easily be personally mobilized. The guard was their guard, their responsibility, not an employee of a branch of General Motors, or Volvo for that matter. The communal character of punishments evaporates in the proposals for private prisons. Since the modern private prison is so much an American invention, it is tempting to ask if they have forgotten their old teacher Charles Horton Cooley (1864-1929) who so clearly saw community as the bed of individuality.

Far back in time, we used to used to mock — fondly — civil servants as persons with two pots of ink on their desks, one for official and the other for private letters. Those days are gone, but not completely. This can be seen if civil servants are found guilty of some kinds of offences, presenting bills for the same air-travel twice, or whatever. Such abuses are mostly seen as more serious matters than if ordinary, private persons commit them. The civil servant represents more than himself, she or he represents the community, that is me. The servant of the state is thus under greater responsibility and control than those who only serve the private firm. This brings us back to the question of honour. If I live under "communal conditions", politicians are a part of me. But so are those given the task and symbolic quality of being state servants with the mandate to carry out essential functions. Their failure is my shame, their success and decency my pride.

Perhaps this view is more foreign to a reader in the USA where private interests and the contractual state have a stronger hold, than to a European, where the state has existed, forever. Dahrendorf (1985) describes those unbelievable days of Berlin in 1945, the interval between two regimes, when the nazi-state collapsed and the USSR took over. Some days without state power, and then back to normal conditions where a state, just a different one, was in command. Perhaps Flemming Balvig (in comments to my manuscript) is right when he says that Europeans to a larger extent regard both national states and national cultures as something that has always existed, something given, while this for Americans, to a somewhat larger extent, is something created by them as individuals. Logan's contractual states may be in harmony with the American self-understanding. But these differences are far from clear-cut. Jessica Mitford ends her book like this (1974, p. 297):

> Those of us on the outside do not like to think of wardens and guards as our surrogates. Yet they are, and they are intimately locked in a deadly embrace with their human captives behind the prison walls. By extension so are we.

> A terrible double meaning is thus imparted to the original question of human ethics: Am I my brother's keeper?

Maybe respect for the civil servant is on the decline on both sides of the Atlantic. Historically, the civil servant was the King's man, civil only in contrast to a military servant. With reduced Royal power, he became — in theory — the servant of the state. In that capacity, this servant has a potentiality for tuning in to the whole set of values in a particular society, values expressed by politicians, by the public in general, or by all sorts of experts. But with the immense growth in the state-administrations of modern nations, another danger becomes imminent; civil servants may end up as servants to their own group, to civil servants in general. The history of the apparatchiks in the former USSR is the prime example of such a development.

Private police

A similar line of reasoning as the one on private prisons can be formulated regarding private police. This is what Rosenthal and Hoogenboom do in a report to the Council of Europe (1990, p. 39):

> Imagine that private policemen were to handle matters more efficiently and more effectively than governmental police forces. Imagine, to take it a step further, that private policemen were also to treat people equally and according to each and every standard of equity. Then, in spite of the satisfactory fulfillment of all those extrinsic conditions, this would not be sufficient evidence in favour of private policing. In a continental setting, people may feel better about the state doing the job — irrespective of the relative quality of its performance.

But developments in most industrialized nations reveal no sensitivity to this problem. On the contrary, there is a definite trend towards large expansion in the sector of private policing. The types of private prisons discussed above are still of minor importance compared to the public ones. Even in the USA, their share of the punishment market probably does not exceed some 10-12 per cent, but private security is expanding, both in the USA and in Europe. In a report from the National Institute of Justice in Washington, Cunningham et al. (1991, pp. 1-5) report:

Private security is now clearly the Nation's primary protective resource, outspending public law enforcement by 73 percent and employing $2^1/_2$ times the workforce, according to a new National Institute of Justice (NIJ) study of the private security industry. Currently, annual spending for private security is $ 52 billion, and private security agencies employ 1.5 million persons. Public law enforcement spends $ 30 billion a year and has a workforce of approximately 600,000.

Nine categories are identified as part of the private security industry:

Proprietary (in-house) security.
Guard and patrol services.
Alarm services.
Private investigations.
Armoured car services.
Manufacturers of security equipment.
Locksmiths.
Security consultants and engineers.
"Other", which includes categories such as guard dogs, drug testing, forensic analysis, and honesty testing.

Diagram 1 Private Security and Law Enforcement Employment

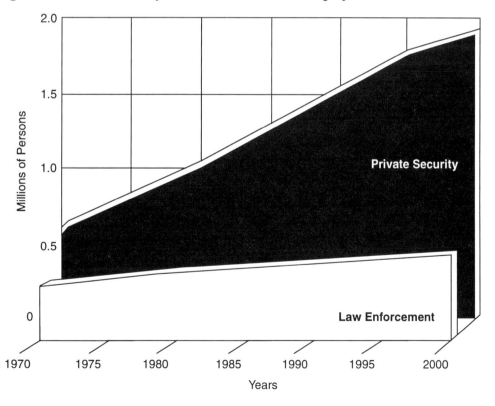

Diagram 2 Private Security and Law Enforcement Spending

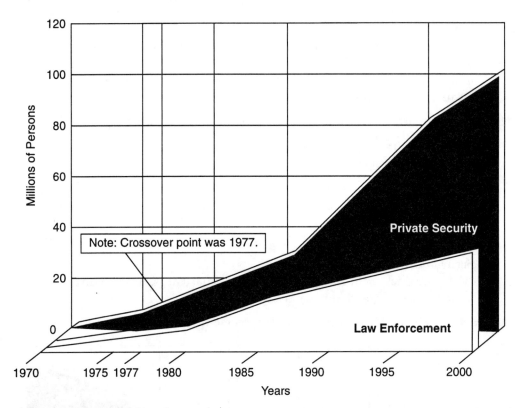

Note: Crossover point was 1977.

Diagrams 1 and 2 are both taken from the report. The first shows the number of persons estimated to work for private security compared to those working for the public one. The second shows spending in billions of dollars. The "Crossover point" at 1977 means that 1977 was the year where more money was used on private than on public security. And in the words of the authors:

> While public expenditures for law enforcement will reach $44 billion by the year 2000, they will be dwarfed by private security expenditures, which will reach $104 billion. The average annual rate of growth in private security will be 8 percent, or double that of public law enforcement.

This growth does not take place in splendid isolation from the ordinary police. Earlier, there were few collaborative efforts between police and private security groups, but this has changed:

> In the 1980's however, the International Association of Chiefs of Police, the National Sheriffs' Association, and the American Society for Industrial Security began joint meetings to foster better cooperation between the public and private sectors. In 1986, with funding from the National Institute of Justice, these organizations set up the Joint Council

430

of Law Enforcement and Private Security Associations. A number of local and regional groups also set up cooperative programs involving the police and private security.

Great Britain shows the same development. And it has come to stay. South (1988, p. 97) writes:

> in foreseeable future circumstances it is unlikely, to say the least, that the private security sector is going to go away. It has been a buoyant and 'recession resistant' industry in most major Western economies since, at least, the 1960s, and all indications suggest that it will continue to grow.

France is in the same situation. Ocqueteau (1990, p. 57) describes how private operators have overtaken or are overtaking state bodies in the United States and Canada.

> ... that is not yet the case for the European mainland. And yet it has been estimated that in France, the country thought to have the highest police complement per inhabitant in Europe, there are three private operators for every five members of the state police force.

This development raises severe problems. But the similarity to the prison arena is not total, as revealed in the stimulating writings of Shearing and Stenning (e.g. 1987), and also in an important article by Phillipe Robert (1989). They begin by considering three major points. First, police have of course evolved from being private to becoming the public instrument for the state. Thus, private police is nothing new. Secondly, with the development of materially rich, large-scale societies, the ordinary police have no chance whatsoever of clearing up more than a tiny fragment of all problems brought before them. This is bound to press forward alternative solutions. And here comes their third point: Private police are, under normal circumstances, also forced to behave as private persons or organizations tend to do. They do not have the penal apparatus at their disposal. They are therefore not particularly oriented towards punishment:

> ... the logic of private security systems is blatantly managerial, concerned with risk management, reducing investment at the least possible cost. Repression is far from being a priority: it is counterproductive to the firm's aims, as well as expensive, since it usually involves the use of public agencies. Prevention, rationalization and compromise are therefore given top priority. (Robert, p. 111).

This, again, opens for possibilities of more civil solutions to conflict where otherwise penal law would be seen as the only — and badly — functioning alternative.

Private police are dependent on having the public police available — as a last resort. But it decreases the authority of the private agency to have to turn to the public one. And it is a dangerous strategy. The efficiency of the private one is dependent on a belief in the public that the ordinary police would give the private agency full support if asked to. Maybe they would not.

While private prisons increase the capacity for incarceration, private police might lead to reduced use of imprisonment. In this perspective, recent developments are not that unattractive. In the opinion of Shearing and Stenning, the contemporary private police are evidence of the re-emergence of private authorities who sometimes effectively challenge the state's claimed monopoly over the definition of order (1987, p. 13):

> . . . what is now known about private policing provides compelling evidence . . . that what we are witnessing through the growth of private policing is not merely a reshuffling of responsibility for policing public order but the emergence of privately defined orders, policed by privately employed agents, that are in some cases inconsistent with, or even in conflict with, the public order proclaimed by the state.

But the possible gain of getting control away from the domain of penal law — the dream-situation for the abolitionist thinkers — has to be balanced against the two major defects of the private police; their class bias and their potentialities for abuse in situations of severe political conflicts.

The class bias has two sides. Least problematic is the obvious fact that upper-class people will be easily able to buy themselves out of embarrassing situations. This is so also within the ordinary penal system. It is close to obvious that all formal systems of control concentrate attention on strata of the population at a safe distance from the power-holders. Exceptional cases of powerful figures brought before the courts are just that: exceptional. A much more problematic effect of private police is that they leave lower class areas and interests unprotected. This is the central message from The New Realists in Great Britain — with Young and Matthews (1992), Young (1989) and Lea and Young (1984) as some of the major exponents. These are completely right when they say that the labour class, and those below, are particularly menaced by ordinary theft, violence and vandalism. A private police, caring for those able and willing to pay, might reduce the interest among the upper classes in having a good, public police, and thus leave the other classes and the inner cities in an even worse situation.

In addition comes the problem of the control of the controllers. How to prevent the private police from becoming a power even more difficult to control than the recent public police? How to control that the public police will not hire, formally or informally, some of the private ones to do what the public police are not supposed to do? How to prevent State power from getting some much wanted help from private groups not hampered by all those soft-handed judges and lawyers?

If the Gestapo or the KGB had been branches of a private firm, hired by dictators, they might have been equally efficient, and ugly in their methods, but would not to the same extent have intimidated their state régimes. When parts of the crime control system belong to the state, there is at least some hope that those parts will be destroyed when the state is destroyed. Hope, but no certainty, as recent developments in several East European states indicate. But if they are private, they are even more protected when the régime falls. Then they belong to a type of organization where both transnational and national interests see to it that they are allowed to continue. The Gestapo and the SS troops were eliminated after the Second World War, but the firms that provided the equipment for the camps and received the prisoners as slave labourers are very much alive in Germany today. So are the Universities that received research material from the camps.

The private push

The essential features of modernity in crime control are illustrated in the privatization movement, and particularly in the re-invention of the private prison. This type of prison is not — in volume of prisoners — the dominant type anywhere in the industrialized world. But it is on its way in, particularly in the United States, but also with spiritual offspring in several European countries. And it is of importance, since it typifies recent trends.

The private prison does not represent a continuation of the old idea of galley slaves and workhouses. The model is municipal care for the poor. Auctions were often arranged. Those who had the lowest bid got the goods — the care of the poor. Possibilities for profit in running poor houses is a debated topic. But with the large-scale arrangements now growing up, no doubt remains. Here it is a question of big money. And, most importantly, with this amount of interplay with private profit interests, even up to the level of private prisons, we are building an important growth factor into the system.

The general debate on "privatization" of prisons, and also of police, has to a large extent been focused on the ethics of it; should private companies be given the right to apply this amount of force, or the debate has been on the economy; will private companies be able to run it more cheaply than the state. But equally important is an awareness of the expansive drive created in a system based on privatization. The central question is, as stated by Feeley (1990, p. 2) *to what extent privatization does expand and transform the state's capacity to punish.*

Logan's (1990) view is that privatization will not necessarily lead to increased capacity in prisons:

> On the whole, however, businesses succeed not by stimulating spurious demand, but by accurately anticipating both the nature and the level of real demand (p. 159).

And how then do you decide what the "real demand" is?

> prison flow should respond to the crime rate, which is largely beyond the control of the state; therefore, prison capacity must be flexible (p. 170).

Right now, there is — according to Logan — a genuine unmet demand for imprisonment (p. 161). And this is worse than oversupply:

> If both oversupply and undersupply can lead to injustice, we should, in principle, err on the side of oversupply, although this is not likely to happen for some time to come (pp. 151-152).

He is so right, particularly based on his own data two pages further on:

> Those who said that the courts were not harsh enough rose steadily from 48.9 percent in 1965 to 84.9 per cent in 1978 . . . from 1980 to 1986, between 82 and 86 percent of Americans advocated stiffer penalties for lawbreakers.

With a view on crime as an unlimited natural resource for the crime control industry, we see the dangers in this type of reasoning. The economic interests of the industry,

433

with confirmation from Logan, will all the time be on the side of oversupply, both of police and of prison capacity. This establishes an extraordinarily strong force for expansion of the system.

In addition comes the fact that privatization makes it simple both to build and to run prisons. Advocates of private prisons are in trouble here. It is difficult both to argue for the speed, flexibility and economic advantages of privately run prisons, and at the same time claim that these advantages will not lead to an oversupply. Logan describes the advantages (p. 79):

> Private companies have demonstrated repeatedly that they can locate, finance, design, and construct prisons more rapidly than the government can. Corrections Corporation of America reports its construction costs to be about 80 per cent of what the government pays for construction. CCA notes that it can build not only faster, thereby saving inflation costs, but also at a lower immediate cost, since construction contractors charge the government more.

Private financing also makes for a simpler life for government, since it does not need to ask the voters for permission to build new prisons. In Logan's words, "... it avoids the cost of a referendum" (p. 79). It also makes it simpler to run the prisons since strikes by employees can more easily be prevented:

> Since a strike or other disruption would allow the government to terminate a contract, unemployment as the result of a strike will be a credible threat to private officers. In contrast, such threats do not often deter strikes in the public sector.

As a help, also to the public sector, Logan suggests:

> to couple legislation requiring that all correctional officers — public and private — be certified, with legislation providing for automatic decertification of officers who participate in a strike.

With private prisons as the extreme example, but also with the economic/industrial establishment as providers of services to prisons run by the public, a highly efficient growth factor is built into the system. Just as illustrated in *Corrections Today*: Interested sellers line up, their tools for the efficient delivery of suffering are displayed, and the prospective buyers are bribed to come and see. When the government is also given help both to avoid their voters and to prevent strikes among the staff, highly efficient mechanisms for expansion are created.

An additional growth factor is the "mental adaptation" created by the many forecasts within the area. As stated in written comments from Flemming Balvig to my manuscript:

> forecasts are a tool of management. It removes the shock in the development. It can not be otherwise. 200,000 prisoners in California in year 2000? This we have known for long. And maybe we end at 190,000 — so, the conditions have not turned out quite as bad as predicted.

Thus the interest becomes focused on the accuracy of the forecasts, not on the horror in the development, not on how to prevent forecasts from coming true.

The technological push

The extraordinary growth in the prison figures for California from 1980 to 1990 has been close to a mystery. Those years were affluent years in California. Frank Zimring (1991, p. 22) has a diagram for the period showing the rate of unemployment moving dramatically downwards, while the rate of imprisonment ascends straight to heaven. Sheldon Messinger also has confusing data. He can show that time served in prison up to first release has gone down steadily the last ten to fifteen years. For a while, the median for males was more than 36 months, but in recent years it has dropped to close to 12 months. This should lead to half-empty prisons in California. But it has not, and Messinger has an explanation: Stays in prison are shorter, but stays outside prison are also a sort of prison, at least for those on early release. Prisoners are released on probation. And probation has changed its character. Diagram 3 is from Messinger (1991, p. 43), and shows the development from 1975 to 1987. What is illustrated here is that release from prison is only a temporary release. In Messinger's words:

> ... release, increasingly, is not the end of the story. Until the first quarter of the 20th century, a first-release from prison was for most prisoners almost certainly the last — on their current conviction, at least: prisoners were discharged from sentence at the prison gate. Next, for the majority of prisoners, first-release from prison served as a gateway to a period of parole-supervision. Even then, however, until the relatively recent past, the first-release from prison was the last under the current conviction: most were discharged at the end of the parole period. Currently, this is not the case; return to prison has become not a rarity but the most common experience for prisoners. Sentences of imprisonment are being served on the installment plan.

And why is that so?

For two reasons. First, probation in Calilornia was in danger of losing ground — and jobs. To survive, probation officers had to choose sides, — between being social workers without jobs, or crime-controllers with both jobs and guns. They chose the latter alternative in a move which illustrates so much of what Stan Cohen (1985) has discussed as role-blurring. Smith (1991 p. 114) describes the development:

> In the late '70s there was a shift in California's parole's role from rehabilitation and service to control and enforcement. This was driven by changes in public attitudes and in the law defining the role of prison and parole to be punitive rather than rehabilitative. Further, there was a serious attempt to statutorily abolish parole. It became clear that if parole was to survive, it would have to take a more aggressive approach.

So, probation officers got their guns. Again according to Smith (p. 124):

> We selected the Smith & Wesson Model 64 .38-calibre revolver. It is relatively lightweight, stainless steel, with a two inch barrel. It carries six rounds and is easy to conceal under the clothes agents normally wear. We chose ammunition that had the maximum stopping power without fragmenting.

Diagram 3   Returns to Prison Within Two Years. By Years of Parole

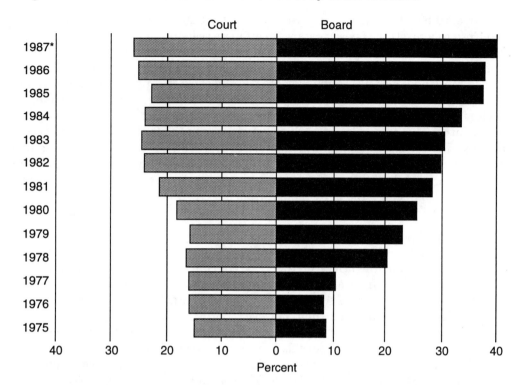

Florida is doing the same. Their Department of Corrections has announced that probation and parole officers will be authorized to wear firearms beginning July 1 (*Correctional Digest,* January 8, p. 10, 1992).

The other reason for the great increase in return to prisons, is that science and technology came to the assistance of the probation workers. Again according to Messinger (p. 36):

> something like 400,000 drug tests were done last year on parolees here. I
> think that's one heck of a lot of urine that has to be taken.

What has happened is that early release is being followed by tight control, and now that the technology is there, it is eagerly used. At intervals, released prisoners are forced to pee. They belong to the segment of the population where drug use is part of the life-style. Before, while probation was still social work, they might have received mild warnings, and hopefully some help to survive. Now a technique exists for control, and back to prison they go. It is a beautiful example of management of the dangerous classes. Now it is not necessarily the original crime which brings them back to prison. It is something in their life-style. Control of drugs means control of the lower classes.

In addition to those returned to prison because of drug use under parole, come those sentenced directly for drug offences. Together these two categories make up a majority of the prison population. In 1986 they were 30 per cent, in 1988 35 per cent, and in

1991 53 per cent of the prison population. In 1995, according to federal prison director Michael J. Quinian, drug offenders in federal prisons will account for 69 per cent of the prison population (*The Washington Post*, April 1991). Austin (1991) documents much the same development at the state level in Florida. But this trend is also, as documented in [Chapter 5.5], clearly visible in European welfare states. Everywhere in modern states, drugs become the major form of deviance used as a key to the control of those at the bottom of society. With a little help from the drug-testing industry, these possibilities are close to unlimited.

The only weak link in the system is the lack of prison capacity. But here, too, industry offers a helping hand. The electronically governed home prison has recently taken a giant stride.

The principles in this type of home prison have long been known, and applied. The prisoner gets an electronic device around his wrist or ankle. The bracelet is connected to the telephone. If the home-prisoner leaves the house, the connection to the telephone is broken, and an alarm sounds in the police or probation headquarters. There is a blossoming market for this device, particularly in the USA, but also abroad. Singapore recently bought equipment worth $ 7 millions in one single transaction (Lacotte 1991).

But the system has one weakness: one cannot know, exactly, what the prisoners do at home. They are, of course, not allowed to touch liquor at home — in their prisons. Maybe they do.

Mitsubishi has solved this problem and brought law and order into American home prisons. In a full-page ad in *Corrections Today* of June 1991, we are shown a whole control package. It contains the usual electronic bracelet, but in addition there is a telephone combined with a television transmitter and a device for testing the blood alcohol level. Soon, I feel sure, televized urinating will also be added. Here is an excerpt of what Mitsubishi describes:

> To meet the growing needs in home detention, a monitoring system must be versatile, reliable, and capable of checking alcohol usage. The risk is too high to settle for less.
>
> . . .
>
> The system automatically calls the client (up to 4 at a time), requests some action (in any language), and records the picture with time, date, and name (providing hard evidence).
>
> . . .
>
> When it comes to Breath Alcohol Testing (BAT), only MEMS provides remote, unassisted, positive visual proof of a client's blood alcohol level and his identity. And, it's all done automatically from the computer base station.

Raw-material for control

Prison, then, solves several problems in highly industrialized countries. It softens the dissonance in welfare states, between the idea of care for the unemployed and the idea that the pleasure of consumption should be a result of production. It also brings parts of the idle population under direct control, and creates new tasks for the industry and its owners. In this last perspective, prisoners acquire a new and important role. They become raw material for control. It is an ingenious device. Welfare cheques provided money which could be used for questionable purposes. To prevent that, welfare was sometimes given in goods, or as requisitions to buy specified necessities. But some recipients would still cheat, and exchange the healthy products for drugs or drinks. Prisons solve this problem. The material standards in some modern prisons are incredibly high. But the consumption is under complete control, an ultimate solution to the ancient problem of industrialization. The potentially dangerous population is taken away and placed under complete control as raw material for parts of the very same industrial complex which made them superfluous and idle outside the walls. Raw material for control, or, if you like, captive consumers of the services of the control industry.

It would have been even more ideal if these prisoners combined being raw material for control with efficient production. Then they would have provided both work for the guards, and commodities for society in general. But this combination seems extraordinarily difficult to get going in industrialized societies of the Western type. *Business Weekly* reports that some 5,000 U.S. inmates are working for private industry. 5,000, — out of 1.2 million. Prisoners are important for the economy of the U.S., but that is for what they need for keep and food, not for what they produce.[1]

The great American tradition

Penal development in the USA has changed dramatically in the last ten years. But seen in the perspective of centuries, nothing is really new. On the contrary, it was the period after World War II which constituted the exception. Now the United States is actually moving back to normal, only with more strength to do so. Two key terms characterize the situation: Privatization and Slavery.

Privatization is nothing new. It was with privatization it all started, first in England and later in the USA. Prosecution was private, the police were private, local prisons were private — run by alehouse-keepers. Most importantly, transportation was a result of private initiative and business instincts. The result was that some 50,000 convicts were shipped across the Atlantic. In the words of Feeley (1991 p. 3):

> Shortly after the first colonists arrived in Virginia in 1607, they were followed by a handful of convicted felons transported there as a condition of pardon to be sold into servitude. Thus was set into motion a new penal system, a system that operated successfully for nearly 250 years . . .
>
> . . . transportation to the New World was a marriage of efficiency and effectiveness. Most of its costs were borne by profit-seeking merchants selling their human cargo and by planters who purchased it. It was effective in that it sanctioned thousands of offenders who otherwise would have gone unpunished.
>
> . . . transportation was an innovation promoted by mercantile interests which was only reluctantly embraced by public officials as they slowly came to appreciate its cost effectiveness.

. . . The policy of transportation multiplied the state's penal capacity and at low cost to the government. It expanded the reach and efficacy of the criminal sanction without the need for a centralized bureaucracy.

And the tradition of privatization was directly converted into prison area. When transportation came to an end, some of the surplus ships were placed in San Francisco Bay. Maritime Correctional Facilities as advertised by the Bibby Line group have a long history. In the San Francisco Bay they housed convicts while they built the prison at San Quentin. The many famous early prisons built in the United States of America were also dependent on money from the private contractors who used convict labour. Several large prisons were leased to private contractors.

> The size of the prison population was determined not by the amount of crime or the need for social control or the efficiency of the police, but by the desire to make crime pay — for government and private employees.

It is Novak (1982) who says this, here quoted by Ericson, McMahon and Evans (1987, p. 358) in an article with the telling title "Punishing for profit". And they add that;

> The Mississippi prison system celebrated the fact that it turned a profit every year until the Second World War. It was only in the late 1920s and into the 1930s that legislation extinguished the convict lease system, apparently in response to pressure from rural manufacturers and labor unions who could not stand the competition, especially with the coming of the Depression

Even the central idea of how prisons ought to be shaped was formulated by persons who wanted to create prisons for profit. It is well-known that Jeremy Bentham designed the Panopticon, the building which so to speak symbolizes total control. 'Panopticon' means total view. Bentham's invention is built as a huge shell in a circle with a tall tower in the middle. In the external circle are the cells. They have windows facing both in and out. In the tower in the middle are the guards. From their position they can see through every cell and observe everything without being seen themselves. It provided for maximum surveillance at a minimum cost. Jeremy Bentham also planned tubes so the sounds from each cell could be monitored.

Bentham designed and developed plans for private contractors to run his institution. What is more, according to Feeley (1991, pp. 4-5), Bentham "campaigned tirelessly to obtain this contract for himself, believing that it would make him a wealthy man ... From the early 1780s until the early 1800s, he was obsessed with this idea. He invested thousands of pounds of his own money in efforts to acquire a site and to develop a prototype of the Panopticon."

He lost his investment. But his basic design became influential, both architectually and economically.

Feeley's conclusion from the history of privatization is that:

> . . . when the state is faced with demands it cannot meet, entrepreneurs can and do help develop a response, ultimately enlarging the state's capacities. As with transportation, early private prison contractors

responded to a widely-felt crisis, developed innovative solutions and quickly implemented them. That their inventions were modified or absorbed by the state does not indicate failure but success.

The other part of the great American tradition came from the import of **slaves** from Africa. No official record was kept of the slave trade. Gunnar Myrdal (1962, pp. 118-119) estimates that it is likely that the total number of slaves imported into the United States before 1860 was under a million. Federal law prohibited the slave trade in 1808. At that time, between 3 and 400,000 had arrived. But more slaves were added through annexations of territory, and most of all by smuggling slaves into the country. A good many of the Negro slaves who were liberated after the Civil War were African-born. Today there are 15 million black males in the USA.

Close to half of the prison population in the USA is black. Marc Mauer has in two reports (1991 and 1992) calculated the figures for black male inmates, and moreover compared them with the situation in South Africa. We give his figures in our Table 1. Half a million black males are now in prison or jail. This means that 3,400 per 100,000 — or 3.4 per cent — of the male black population are in prison just now. How extreme this is, internationally, can be seen when it is compared with South Africa, where 681 per 100,000 black males — or 0.7 per cent — are incarcerated.

Table 1   Black Male Rates of Incarcerations in USA and South Africa 1989 and 1990

	United States	South Africa
Black Male Population 1989	14,625,000	15,050,642
Black Male Inmates 1989	454,724	109,739
Rate of Incarceration per 100,000 1989	3,109	729
Black Male Inmates 1990	499,871	107,202
Rate of Incarceration per 100,000 1990	3,370	681

From Mauer, Table 2.

With 3.4 per cent in prison, one and a half times as many are probably on probation or parole, which means that between seven and eight per cent of black males are under some sort of legal constraint.

Again, this is a conservative estimate. Blumstein (1991, p. 53) has this to say:

> . . . if you focus on the highest risk group — black males in their '20s — the incarceration rate is about 4,200, or about 4.2 percent of the group. That means that almost one of every 20 black males in his '20s is in a state or federal prison today. Adding the local jails, which comprise another 50 percent, we are up to 6.3 percent, which is the fraction of black males in their '20s in the United States who are in either a state or federal prison or a local jail. When you recognize that prison represents about one-sixth of the total number of people under control of the criminal justice system

(including probation and parole), you can then multiply the prior number (the 4.2 percent) by six and that comes to about 25 percent.

25 per cent, that means every fourth black man in his '20s. But this is for the country as a whole. If we also concentrated on youth in the inner cities, it is highly probable that we, according to Blumstein's estimates, would have to conclude that considerably more than this quarter of the black male population was under the control of the criminal justice system at any time.

With all this in mind, it is easy to understand that Marc Mauer (1991, p. 9) formulates one of his sub-titles in his report like this:

AFRICAN-AMERICAN MALES: AN ENDANGERED SPECIES?

And Mauer continues:

> African-American males, who are disproportionately low-income, face a variety of problems, including: the social and economic decline of our inner cities and diminished opportunities for young people; the continuing failure of our schools, health care systems, and other institutional supports to prepare young Black males to occupy legitimate roles in society; continuing poverty and a distribution of wealth which has resulted in even greater disparity between the rich and the poor over the past twenty years.

And this over-representation of blacks is steadily increasing. Austin and McVey (1989, p. 5) point to the war against drugs as one important explanation:

> Drug enforcement has been narrowly focused on crack, the drug of choice among the underclass, which is also disproportionately Black and Hispanic. Consequently, the proportion of offenders sentenced to prison who are non-white is escalating.

Mauer points to the same:

> From 1984 to 1988, the Black community's percentage of all drug arrests nationally increased from 30 percent to 38 per cent. In Michigan, drug arrests overall have doubled since 1985, while drug arrests of Blacks have tripled. With a "war on drugs" primarily waged through the criminal justice system and disproportionally targeting inner-city users, the end result is an increasing number of prisoners and an ever larger share of Black inmates.

Florida is probably the most extreme among states in this regard. In 1982/1983, there were 299 felony drug cases brought against male juveniles in Florida. There were 54 cases against black juveniles. In 1985, the numbers for whites was 336, while the blacks had now — with the figure 371 — passed the whites. But then, in 1989/90, the numbers of blacks had increased to 3415, while whites were lagging far behind with only 526.[2] The architect behind this growth, Governor Marinez, lost the election for a new period as Governor, but has instead become the drug-czar for the whole country.

441

It does not seem unreasonable to think that the combination of being black and poor is a handicap at the court-level as well, although this is debated (cf. the discussion between Wilbanks and Mann 1987). Personally, I have never been able to forget the results in a little study by Wolfgang, Kelly and Nolde as far back as 1962. They compared prisoners admitted to death row. According to all probability, black people came into this queue with greater ease — that means for somewhat less good reasons — than white people. As a result, one might have expected that a relatively smaller quota of black people would eventually be executed after having gone through the various appeal procedures. But the results were the opposite. Relatively more blacks than whites were killed. Mauer's last report (1991, pp. 11-12) gives several examples of general mechanisms working in the disfavour of blacks in the legal process.

But let me add: European prisons have also darkened. And if poverty had colour, they would have darkened even more. There is no reason for European chauvinism *vis à vis* the USA. Both class and race are reflected in the figures on black prisoners from the USA. And both in Australia and in Canada there exists extreme over-representation of ethnic minority groups in prison.

The standard setter

There are no "natural limits" in the perception of what is a large prison population. With the growth in the USA, standards of size change. In a world so influenced by what happens in the USA, this may have an impact all over the industrialized world. Maybe we are unduly lenient in Europe, since the USA seems to thrive with ten times as many prisoners? Ideas of privatization have also crossed the Atlantic. Sir Edward Gardner (1989) was the chairman of the Parliamentary All Party Select Committee on Home Affairs. He took the Committee to the USA, and had this to say on his return:

> . . . all of us, who went over to America to look at these new establishments, wondered if we were wasting our time; in my diary I wrote that this was a proposition that looked more absurd than real. But as members of the Committee went around these institutions in places like Memphis, Panama and Nashville, I can only tell you that we began radically to change our minds. We were astonished by what we saw — the quality of the management and the success of the whole idea of private prisons.

Sir Edward actually changed his views to the extent that he — when he gave his lecture at the Institute for the Study and Treatment of Delinquency — had become the Chairman of the private firm "Contract Prisons PLC".

And he is not alone. Taylor and Peace (1989) make a plea for using this opportunity for reform. The crucial question, they say, is not whether a prison is run for profit, but whether acceptable and relevant standards are applied. Among these, they specify that no private contract should be for a period in excess of five years, after which competitive tender would recur. Furthermore, the private prisons should not be allowed to receive only the easy ones — no-one serving less than 18 months would be eligible. And most important; a conviction-free period after release will be a tacit objective and will form the basis of part of the payment. They argue (p. 192) that if prison privatization takes place as an unthinking copy of North American practice, the situation in the U.K. will probably become worse. And they conclude:

> In short, the potential advantages which prisons offer are specific to a narrow range of possible schemes. Our advocacy of such schemes is therefore a high-risk strategy. If all the right elements are not in place, . . . we will have opened our gates to a particularly unpleasant Trojan Horse.

It is difficult to disagree.

But this perspective of U.S. influence on the rest of the world may be too narrow. It is not only a question of whether what happens in the USA today will happen in the UK and Canada tomorrow. According to Lilly and Knepper (1991), privatization is not a one-way flow of penal policies from the US to the UK:

> . . . the relationship between the two nations is not based on the transfer of correctional policy so much as it is on the joint ownership of corporations . . .[3]

> The relation between the UK and the US involves corporations joining forces to market corrections products and services in both countries. Rather than implementing only US correctional policies in the UK, some British companies have purchased a stake in the US corrections market. Whether or not private prisons appear on wide scale in the UK, its firms will continue to profit from punishments in the US, the largest corrections market.

Some final comments on the industrial drive: If the level and form of control in society is shaped by features of the social organization, it may well be that these general features will manifest themselves everywhere. The total number of prisoners in Europe has also increased during the last years. Diagram 4 illustrates what has happened. And the Netherlands itself has increased its prison population. As described in Chapter 4, the solutions in countries with a low level of prisoners are under strong pressures these days. Particularly important are the developments in drug policy — again with the USA as trend-setter. Of importance also are recent trends in the mass-media. With crime as major content, it is not easy to hold the old line. In addition come two other factors; *the capacity* for modern industrial society to insitutionalize large segments of the population, and also that such a solution *would be in harmony with important other trends in these nations.*

Diagram 4 Developments in the number of prisoners in Council of Europe member States since 1970 excluding Austria, Iceland, the Netherlands, Switzerland and Turkey

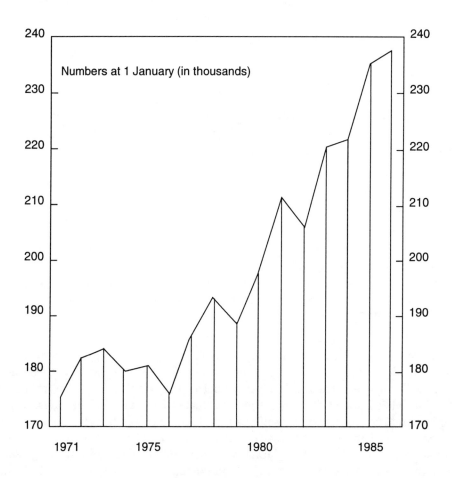

Numbers at 1 January (in thousands)

Notes

1. But in China, the article in *Business Weekly* made large headlines. "The national television news and most major newspapers, all run by the communist government, gave prominent coverage to an account about American-style prison labour published in the Feb. 17 issue of *Business Week* . . . The Chinese reports carried the strong suggestion that the U.S. Government, which accuses China of exporting prisoner-made goods to the United States in violation of U.S. law, should practice what it preaches or change the sermon." *Correctional Digest*, February 19, p .10, 1992.

2. From Florida Supreme Court Racial and Ethnic Bias Commission, 1991.

3. Consider the electronic monitoring market. Electronic monitoring of offenders has generated significant commercial interest. In 1987, three American vendors — BI Incorporated, Correctional Services Incorporated and Digital Products — controlled the market in electronic tagging devices. Since then, two US vendors have combined with

British companies to produce and market an improved device. . . . And in 1989 Corrections Services, Inc., again expanded its international business connections with Japanese-based Mitsubishi; in 1990 C.S.I. further expanded its international business dealings with an agreement with Electron Dart, Ltd. in Tel Aviv, Israel. (Lilly and Knepper, pp. 15-16).

21. Public Imprisonment by Private Means: The Re-emergence of Private Prisons and Jails in the United States, the United Kingdom, and Australia

Douglas C. McDonald

Although privately operated imprisonment facilities were commonplace in previous centuries in England and the United States (Holdsworth 1922-4: 397; Crew 1933: 50; McKelvey 1977: 197-216; Feeley 1991), by the twentieth century, governments had assumed responsibility for nearly all imprisonment and most other criminal justices functions. Indeed, the principle of public responsibility for the administration of justice — and especially for imprisonment — has become so well established that imprisonment is seen by many as an intrinsic function of government (American Bar Association 1989: 3; DiIulio 1990: 172-7; Robbins 1988: 44; Howard League for Penal Reform 1990: 3). Beginning in the mid-1980s, however, a debate emerged in the United States, Britain, and in some other English-speaking countries over the propriety of governments contracting with private firms to operate and even own prisons, jails, and other places of imprisonment. This has gone beyond talk, for governments in the United States, Britain, and Australia are now contracting with private, for-profit firms to operate penal facilities of various types, and a private imprisonment industry has emerged (or, taking a longer historical view, re-emerged).

This essay surveys developments in the United States, Britain, and Australia, the only countries that have so far moved to delegate operations of imprisonment facilities to private entities. The first section provides a thumbnail sketch of developments in these countries since the early 1980s, followed with a discussion of why private imprisonment emerged during this period. Some of the principal issues raised by private imprisonment, including some of the important research questions, are identified and discussed briefly.

The rediscovery of private imprisonment in the United States

The contemporary movement to expand private authority over the administration of penal and detention facilities owes its origins to independent developments on both sides of the Atlantic, although there has been considerable cross-fertilization. Whereas in Britain, the earliest proposals came from policy reformers — for example, the Adam Smith Institute (1984) and McConville and Williams (1985) — the stimulus in the United States came largely from business entrepreneurs who were promoting their own ventures. Policy reformers later developed a more elaborate rationale for opening government to business interests (e.g., President's Commission on Privatization 1988; Stewart 1986; Logan 1990).

Douglas C. McDonald: 'Public Imprisonment by Private Means' from the *BRITISH JOURNAL OF CRIMINOLOGY* (1994), Vol. 34, Special Issue, pp. 28-48. Reprinted by permission of Oxford University Press.

One of the principal seedbeds for the current wave of private imprisonment firms in the United States was the network of detention centres under the authority of the US Immigration and Nationalization Service (INS). Beginning in 1979, the INS began contracting with private firms to detain illegal immigrants pending hearings or deportation. By the end of 1988, the number of private detention facilities had grown to seven, and they held about 800 of the approximately 2,700 aliens in INS custody (McDonald 1990*a*: 92). This was an important market for the emerging private imprisonment firms, giving several of the now significant players their early starts. This included the Corrections Corporation of America (CCA), a Tennessee-based firm that incorporated in 1983 and opened its first detention centre in Houston, Texas the following year, and has since grown into one of the dominant forces in the field. CCA has recently expanded its operations into Britain and Australia through subsidiaries (Corrections Corporation of America 1992; Corrections Corporation of Australia 1992). Another of the large enterprises, Wackenhut, Inc., an established private security firm, entered the private prison business by winning the contract to build and operate a detention facility for the INS in Denver, Colorado (McDonald 1990*a*: 94). There were other smaller entrepreneurs who won some of the early INS contracts and gained attention — e.g., Ted Nissen's Behavioral Systems Southwest — but fell behind when more heavily capitalized firms emerged (Press 1990).

Government officials in the INS 'went private' chiefly because contractors were able to create new detention facilities much more quickly than could the federal government. (Government procurement procedures required long lead times.) Indeed, Wackenhut was able to construct and open a 150-bed facility at breakneck speed: 90 days from the contract's signing. Conveniently, the cost of acquiring this new capacity could be paid for out of the government's operating funds — through per diem reimbursements — rather than requiring the allocation of capital funds for facility construction, which could be a bureaucratically cumbersome process (McDonald 1990*a*).

In addition to the INS detention centres, the private imprisonment industry also established early sites with various low-security facilities, and in the less visible regions of the adult and juvenile penal systems. For example, the federal government's Bureau of Prisons had been contracting with private firms since the late 1960s to operate community treatment centres, halfway houses to which federal prisoners were transferred prior to being paroled (Bronick 1989: 12- 14) .

These developments provoked little controversy or even notice. That changed, however, in late 1985 and 1986. Private firms began taking over or building facilities that were closer to the core of the adult penal system, which had previously been the nearly exclusive preserve of government. In the closing months of 1985, CCA contracted with the Bay County (Florida) government to operate its jail. A similar contract was signed in August of 1986 with the Santa Fe, New Mexico county government. In January 1986, US Corrections Corp. opened a 350-bed prison (the Marian Adjustment Center) in St Mary's, Kentucky, and contracted with the state's Department of Corrections to hold sentenced prisoners (Press 1990).

What brought the issue to public attention and ignited a public policy debate, however, were two incidents. One was CCA's audacious offer to take over the entire state of Tennessee's troubled prison system, with a 99-year lease from the state, for which it would pay $250 million. CCA would then house the state's convicted prisoners at a negotiated per diem rate and would guarantee that the system would meet standards set by a federal court judge, who had earlier found the entire system to be in violation of the US Constitution because of inadequate conditions of confinement. The state ultimately turned down the offer after several months of consideration, but the matter became a national news story (Corrections Corporation of America 1985: Tolchin 1985a, 1985b; Press 1990).

The second signal event was the opening of a small privately operated facility, called the 268 Center, by one Philip E. Tack, in rural Cowansville, Pennsylvania. Tack arranged with the District of Columbia authorities to transfer 55 inmates from the District's jails to relieve overcrowding there, but the townspeople were not pleased. Among other things, the inmates were all black, the townspeople all white. Local residents organized themselves and patrolled the streets with shotguns, fearing escapes. This caught the attention of a prison reform group that got the state legislature to declare a moratorium on privately-operated prisons (Joint State Government Commission 1987; Press 1990; Bivens 1986).

In the train of these events, private imprisonment emerged as one of the most salient issues in correctional circles. The National Institute of Justice convened a conference and circulated reports of the proceedings (Peterson 1988), and Congress held hearings (US House of Representatives 1986). Most of the organized bodies in the criminal justice arena took a stand on the issue. The American Federation of State, County, and Municipal Workers and the National Sheriffs' Association opposed contracting for operations; the American Correctional Association gave it guarded support (US House of Representatives 1986), and the American Bar Association asked for a moratorium pending further study (1986), and upon further study, argued that delegating operating authority to private entities posed grave constitutional and policy problems (1989).

The issue remained in the public eye for a few years, prompting a spate of articles, books, and reports (e.g., Robbins 1988; Logan 1990, 1991; Logan and McGriff 1989; Logan and Rausch 1985; Feeley 1991; Keating undated; Mullen 1985; Mullen et al. 1984; National Criminal Justice Statistics Association 1987; Legislative Research Council 1986; McDonald 1990b; Tolchin 1985a, 1985b, 1985c; Urban Institute 1989; Bowman et al. 1992; also see Immarigeon 1987). By the turn of the decade, however, the debate had died down. There had neither been a rush to privatize correctional facilities, nor had the nascent industry been stopped dead in its tracks. Instead, the industry continued to grow slowly, and new facilities were opened, including major maximum security prisons (four in Texas, for example). The large firms have also broadened their reach into other markets — the United Kingdom and Australia.

By the end of 1990, there existed 44 secure adult facilities operated by private firms in the United States, some of these facilities owned by their operators, holding approximately 15,000 inmates (McDonald 1992). This represented only a small fraction of the approximately 4,900 prisons and jails in this country (American Correctional Association 1991), and they held slightly less than 2 per cent of all inmates under custody at that point (McDonald 1992).

Parallel to these developments was another form of privatization: the construction of privately-owned facilities that were leased to governments for direct government operation. This first emerged in Colorado, where an investment banking firm put together a lease-purchase deal for a county government that wanted to build a new jail. A private corporation was formed to build the new jail, and investors bought 'certificates of participation' — what amounted to corporate bonds. The jail was then leased to the county, and the lease payments were used to repay investors (McDonald 1990c). Similar arrangements were developed for prison and jail construction in other places (Chaiken and Mennemeier 1987).

These emerged largely because of constraints on public officials' ability to authorize capital expenditures for new prisons, and have been used to finance other types of public purchases (Leonard 1986, 1990). In the United States, most state governments build prisons by issuing bonds purchased by investors, but must first obtain the approval of voters to incur these debt obligations. Spurred by a tax revolt that spread across the United States in the late 1970s and early 1980s, citizens were voting down these bonding proposals, even though they were demanding at the same time that more criminals be imprisoned in the hopes of making their communities safer. Public officials saw the 'creative financing' techniques such as lease-purchase arrangements as a convenient way out of this dilemma, as a rent payment could be paid out of government operating budgets. How many facilities were built through lease-purchase arrangements is difficult to determine, for lack of a central accounting system in the US's fragmented federal system.

Developments in Britain

Although proposals for privately operated prisons first surfaced in 1984 and 1985, advanced by the Adam Smith Institute (1984) and two academics, McConville and Williams (1985), the Government had already been contracting for immigrant detention services for a decade and a half (Green undated; Rutherford 1990). In July 1970, the Home Office contracted with Securicor Ltd, a private security firm, to administer detention centres at the four principal airports, as well as various escort services associated with them. By the mid-1980s, when the contemporary debate over privately operated prisons began, the largest facility used by the Immigration Service, a detention centre at Harmondsworth, was privately administered. This and a small number of other private detention centres held a substantial proportion of all detained immigrants — nearly half, according to one survey conducted in April 1988 (Joint Council for the Welfare of Immigrants 1988: 13, quoted in Green undated: 4). In January 1989, Securicor lost the contract for these centres to Group 4 Total Security, the operating arm of Group 4 Securitas International, a subsidiary of a large Swedish firm, Securitas International. The parent firm has operating companies in approximately sixteen different countries (Green undated: 4).

It appears that current developments to contract out for prisons began not as a considered extension of this experience with immigrant detention centres (indeed, this experience has been little studied) but resulted from separate initiatives. In 1986, when attention to private prisons was high in the United States, the Home Affairs Committee of the House of Commons, which exercises parliamentary oversight of the

450

prison system, decided to examine private prisons and jails in the United States as part of its broader inquiry into the state of prisons and jails in England and Wales (Rutherford 1990). On that trip, the chair of the committee, Sir Edward Gardiner, became an enthusiastic proponent of privatization, and the short report that resulted from this visit recommended that the Home Office should, as an experiment, permit private firms to tender for the construction and management of custodial institutions. The committee also recommended that priority be given to contracting out the remand centres 'because it is there that the most overcrowding in the prison system is concentrated' (Home Affairs Committee 1987).

This was followed by two reports, one by Peter Young of the Adam Smith Institute, who argued that the 'monopolistic provision' of imprisonment services should be broken to encourage an increase in the supply of beds, improvements in quality, and cost reductions. Young recommended that five existing prisons be privatized as an experiment and that one new private remand prison in London be built (1987: 2). In the same year, Maxwell Taylor and Ken Pease (1987), two liberal academics, wrote a paper supporting privatization because it could serve as a 'springboard for the development of a truly rehabilitative programme'. This could be done by building incentives into the contracts. As *The Independent* declared, this support by the liberal wing of the penal reform lobby 'gave crucial new authority to the campaign' (5 March 1987).

On 30 March 1988, the Government announced that it intended to publish a discussion document (a 'Green Paper') on private sector involvement in the remand system, and that private management consultants would be engaged to consider the details (Gill 1992: 1). The paper was published the following July (HMSO 1988) and the consultants appointed. Their report, published in March of the following year (Deloitte, Haskins, and Sells 1989), offered a number of specific recommendations. It recommended issuing contracts to private firms to design, construct, and operate remand centres, and to turn existing remand centres over to the private sector. It also recommended issuing between four and ten separate contracts for court and escort duties, each corresponding to geographical districts to be designated. (These tasks include escorting prisoners to and from court, guarding prisoners at court, and providing court security.) This separation between remand centre and escort duties was recommended as a means of increasing the efficiency of staff and managers that would result from concentrating specially trained employees on their principal missions, rather than requiring (or permitting) them to do both. This report was followed by the Government, in July 1990, issuing another discussion paper that adopted most of the consultants' recommendations, inviting comment (Home Office 1990).

The consultants indicated that they were not able to conduct a precise cost-effectiveness analysis of their proposal, but declared that 'our analysis of this information indicates a reasonable prospect of improvements in cost-effectiveness outweighing the additional costs that contracting would cause in contract administration and in monitoring' (Deloitte, Haskins, and Sells 1989: p. iii). They suggested that savings in the remand centres could be generated by expanding the use of clerical services, instituting more flexible work practices, greater use of improved technology, and higher ratios of inmates to staff than currently prevail.

In December 1991, the Government announced its intentions to proceed with contracting out the court escort services, beginning with one newly defined district that would include East Midlands and Humberside. Tenders were received from six firms and a contract was signed in 1993 with Group 4. Service was planned to commence in April 1993 (Gill 1992: 9).

Although the consultants recommended contracting with private firms for the design, construction, and operation of new remand centres, the prison population took 'one of its inexplicable nosedives, such that the urgent need for new places to be built receded' (Gill 1992: 3). The Government decided instead to contract out a new prison that was under construction in the North East of England, the 320-bed Wolds remand prison, in North Humberside. Enabling legislation was needed for this, which was obtained in the Criminal Justice Act 1991. This Act provided the power to contract out the management of new prisons for unsentenced inmates, but was extended once in July 1992 to encompass sentenced prisoners and again in February 1993 to enable contracting out of *existing* prisons. A five-year contract for operating The Wolds remand prison was signed in November 1991, with the Group 4 Remand Services Ltd (Gill 1992: 5).

The second prison to be contracted out was a new one at Blakenhurst, a 650-bed local prison for sentenced and unsentenced prisoners. This contract was awarded in 1992 to UK Detention Services, a consortium of the Corrections Corporation of America and British construction firms John Mowlem and Sir Robert McAlpine (Ford 1992: Corrections Corporation of America 1992). Private operations were scheduled to commence in April 1993 (Clarke 1992).

A frontier of sorts is being crossed in a more recent development: the 'market testing' of the Prison Services' administration of the Manchester prison ('Strangeways'). This prison, originally opened in 1868 as Salford Prison, was the site of a prisoner uprising in April 1990 that lasted nearly a month and left most of the interior destroyed. A refurbishing job was undertaken, and the government invited tenders in October 1992 from private firms to operate the prison. The plan was to make a contracting decision in April 1993, with private operation commencing the following September. Bidders were told to assume that they should anticipate providing the capacity to hold 866 prisoners, but that another 134 cells could be authorized for occupancy, raising the total to 1,000 (Home Office 1992: 13-15).

In contrast to The Wolds and Blakenhurst competitions, the Prison Service was permitted to submit a bid for the Strangeways contract. One apparent purpose of this market testing was to force the Prison Service to reconsider (and perhaps to renegotiate) the labour practices prevailing in its facilities. Kenneth Clarke, at that time the Home Secretary, wrote that 'Market testing will, I believe, cause the prison service to examine its own performance in the light of competitive pressure and encourage the spread of those reforms across public sector prisons much more quickly than would otherwise have been the case' (Clarke 1992). In a briefing paper issued in November 1992 by the Prison Service, the bidding team stated that 'Our aim will be to put forward a winning bid which takes full advantage of the flexibilities available — with the agreement of staff and unions.' However, 'A bid sticking to every detail of a central agreement [between management and labour] dating from 1987 is unlikely to beat the competition . . . Any agreements that hinder the chances of constructing an effective bid will have to be reconsidered in consultation with the unions' (HM Prison Service 1992: 2).

In mid-July of 1993, Derek Lewis, the Director General of the Prison Service announced that the 'in-house bid team' — the Prison Service itself — had won the competition to manage the prison. 'Seven tenders were submitted and there was a very strong field from which to choose', he stated. 'It is quite clear that the spur of competition has generated bids which represent levels of performance and value for money that we have not previously seen in the public or private sector . . . It was a strong and imaginative bid, which offered the best overall value for money' (HM Prison Service 1993a). In the absence of a contract, the Government drew up a service agreement for a five-year period, during which time the team would receive £79 million to fund the prison's operation.

In the wake of this decision, in September 1993, the Government announced that it would further stimulate the development of a private correctional industry by seeking contracts for a number of other prisons. 'Our aim is to create a private sector able to provide sustained competition, said Michael Howard, the Home Secretary. '[The] private sector must be large enough to provide sustained competition and involve several private sector companies — a genuinely mixed economy' (HM Prison Service 1993b). The strategy for accomplishing this will be to contract, during the 'initial phase', with private firms for the management of about 10 per cent of the prisons in England and Wales (12 prisons in total). Moreover, contracts will be issued for the design, construction, and perhaps even the financing of new prisons. The specific prisons to be 'market tested' are to be chosen by the Prison Board, and priority will be given to those that have most room for improvement.

It is possible that contracting out will advance further in Britain than in the United States, in large part because of the Government's broader commitment to rolling back the public agencies' domain. Unlike the United States, a single national government has authority over prisons and jails, permitting a more rapid implementation of changed policy. In the United States, the growth of the private prison industry is slowed by the existence of separate governments (and, therefore, markets) in 3,400 counties, and 50 states, in addition to the federal government. Conversely, a change in administration in Britain might bring a rapid halt to developments there, whereas the march of the private prison industry in the United States is less likely to be affected by the defeat of a conservative administration at the federal level.

Australia

A 1988 report to the Queensland Corrective Services Commission that provided a blueprint for correctional reform in Queensland called for the development of one prison operated and managed by the private sector under contract to the commission (Kennedy 1988). This, the report argued, would create a competitive market for correctional institutions in Australia and Queensland, speeding reform of the prison system. The commission accepted the recommendation and invited tenders to manage and operate the Borallon Correctional Centre, a new 240-bed facility near Brisbane.

The contract was awarded in November 1989 to the Corrections Corporation of Australia, a newly-formed consortium made up of the Corrections Corporation of America, Wormald Security, and John Holland Constructions. Private operations began in January 1990, under a three-year contract that had an option for renewal for another two years. By the end of the first year, the prisoner population was predominantly a medium security one (Macionis 1992: 9).

A second privately-operated prison resulted from the breakdown of negotiations between the commission and the labour union representing staff to be employed at the newly constructed 380-bed Remand and Reception (Arthur Gorrie) Centre at Brisbane. When no agreement could be reached regarding work rules and procedures, the commission informed the Government in October 1991 that it intended to call for tenders for the private sector operation of this facility. This came to pass shortly, and in March 1992, a contract was awarded to Australasian Contract Management (ACM), a consortium of Wackenhut Security and ADT, an Australian-based security company, and the centre went operational in June 1992. This facility is a critical piece of the Queensland correctional system, as it is the main reception centre for the state's 11 facilities; all the initial assessment and classification of prisoners is conducted there (Macionis 1992: 3-4).

The Junee prison in New South Wales, scheduled for opening in March 1993, was the third facility to be contracted out. This 600-bed prison was designed and constructed by ACM, to be operated by that firm for an initial period of five years, with options for renewing a three-year term (Harding 1992: 1). Observing these developments, Harding wrote that 'the momentum seems inexorably to be increasing. Indeed the Wacol contract [for the Queensland Remand and Reception Center] could mean that, for cash-strapped governments, the ideological walls will now come tumbling down. The question is thus not whether privatization will occur; but rather to what extent, in relation to what sorts of institutions and which types of prisoner . . . and above all whether it will improve the overall imprisonment system' (Harding 1992: 1).

Why contract for prison and jail operations?

It is interesting that the development of privately operated prisons has emerged in a few English-speaking countries. Part of this results from language barriers, making it difficult for American firms to penetrate markets where English is not spoken widely (such as France, where the Mitterand Government held discussions with officials of the Corrections Corporation of America in the 1980s).

Rolling back the state

A deeper explanation, however, is found in the ideological orientation of the governments in power at the time of the nascent industry's development. In Britain, the United States, and Queensland, conservative governments held sway. In the former two countries, these governments launched a concerted attack on the institutional structures and ideology of the welfare state. Certainly the most aggressive programme of cutting back the public sector has been in Britain, following Thatcher's election in 1979, which has continued under John Major's administration. This movement of privatization and contracting out for operations in government-owned facilities has been extensive, cutting across a wide variety of services. In the United States, the movement has been less aggressive, largely because the federal government (which was under divided Republican and Democratic control) holds relatively few assets that can be privatized. Nonetheless, the public landscape was combed in the United States in search of targets for privatization of assets or contracting, and prisons were sighted by those advocating broader private sector involvement in the delivery of public services (e.g. President's Commission on Privatization 1988).

Rising prisoner populations

Another contributing factor to these developments was the increasing demand for prison and jail beds, at least in the United States and in Britain. Between 1973 and 1990 in the United States, the numbers of prisoners under custody at any one time grew nearly fourfold (Bureau of Justice Statistics 1991). At the same time, the federal courts were finding a large number of imprisonment facilities — and even entire state prison systems — to be in violation of the Constitution's prohibition of 'cruel and unusual punishment', largely because of overcrowding and inadequate conditions of confinement. By mid-1991, 40 states were operating prisons found by the courts to have unconstitutional conditions (Bernat 1991). The result of both was strong pressure on governments at all levels to acquire new imprisonment facilities, either by constructing new ones or converting buildings once dedicated to other uses.

Similar pressures were being felt in Britain. During the 1980s, prison populations were rising because of the increasing proportions of convicted persons receiving custodial sentences, the imposition of longer prison sentences, and some lengthening of delays in bringing people to trial. Between 1980 and 1987, the growth of the prisoner population was twice that of the increase in capacity, so that by the end of 1987, a capacity shortfall of about 5,800 beds existed. The government responded by increasing expenditures for prison services substantially: a 72 per cent increase between 1980 and 1987, and a prison building programme projected a 53 per cent increase in capacity between 1980 and 1995. Despite this higher level of expenditure, about 40 per cent of all prisoners in 1986-7 were being held in overcrowded facilities, mostly in remand facilities. Remand prisoners were also backed up into police cells; during 1987, police cells held an average of 530 such prisoners (Rutherford 1990: 44-6).

Speedy expansion of capacity

In the United States, the private sector had a special advantage over government that was appealing to public managers: lengthy procurement procedures could be evaded by issuing contracts with private firms. Moreover, public managers did not have to risk having requests to increase public debt for prison construction turned down at the ballot box, because payments for contracted imprisonment facilities could be made with funds from accounts for operations rather than capital accounts. Because these constitutional constraints do not exist in Britain, the private firms were not so advantaged there.

Lower costs

Certainly an important stimulus to contracting has been the belief — or hope — that contracting will be less costly than direct governmental provision. In the United

States, leaders of the private firms have proclaimcd this to be a fact. In Britain, this quest for more cost-effective (or, at least, less costly) imprisonment services appears to be a main reason for turning to the private sector (Clarke 1992), although data on private firms' costs are not public because the Government has agreed to consider this information proprietary and confidential. In Australia, one of the principal reasons that the Queensland Corrective Commission resorted to contracting was that it was unable to obtain agreements from the staff regarding work procedures and, therefore, costs (Macionis 1992). Whether private contracting is, in fact, less costly and more cost-effective remains an open question, as discussed below.

Increased managerial control

Although some have argued that contracting with independent private firms weakens the ability of government managers to control the provision of public services (e.g., DiIulio 1990; AFSME 1984), some government officials who have turned to contractors report that they have done so to *increase* control and better ensure performance. In the United States, the need to increase governmental control was a significant factor in some of the earliest contracts. For example, the Bay County (Florida) commissioners turned to contractors because they were unable to gain assurances from the jail administrator (the sheriff) that the conditions of confinement would be improved. They then contracted with CCA and obliged it to meet certain specified standards by a fixed date (McDonald 1990c: Press 1990). Santa Fe (New Mexico) county commissioners also turned to CCA because they were unable to control the costs of a newly constructed jail (Press 1990). Jails in the United States pose a special case because they are typically under the authority of sheriffs, who are independently elected and do not serve at the pleasure of county commissioners or executives. However, even where political control of prisons is not so fragmented, as in the case of England, the need for gaining stronger managerial control over prisons and prison systems is given as a reason for contracting (Gill 1993; Clarke 1992).

The belief that privatization offers enhanced control over public services appears to be based on several different dynamics of contracting. First, the pressure to compete forces a reconsideration and change of work rules that have been built up in the public sector. Inefficient practices will be more difficult to support if one's employment is at risk. Secondly, contracting forces government agencies to establish specific and written performance standards and goals, something that is done less frequently in direct public provision of services. Thirdly, private firms are exposed to more risk for failing to meet these standards, at least compared to public employees who have expansive rights and protections against dismissal. Fourthly, some have argued (e.g., O'Hare *et al.* 1990) that contracting permits managers to focus attention on the quality of output (including services), rather than on the myriad processes by which outputs are produced.

Finally, in instances where higher-level political or managerial authority is unable to control by command the performance of subordinates, turning to contractors may result in higher levels of compliance with policy and performance objectives. For example, in Massachusetts during the early 1970s, a reform-oriented manager was appointed to run the state's correctional services for youth, but failed to get the entrenched and tradition-bound employees of the agency to change their practices. Nearly overnight, he closed the large closed training schools and contracted with a number of smaller private organizations to care for the youths. Although this event has usually been understood as a crucial event in the 'deinstitutionalization' movement, undertaken to supplant a custodial culture with one that gave higher priority to juvenile rehabilitation, contracting was the tool for accomplishing the reform objective (Coates *et al.* 1978).

This finds an echo in Australia, where contracting has just begun. The Queensland Corrective Commission announced its aim of creating a 'more rehabilitative' environment in its correctional centres. 'In order to achieve this, custodial staff would need to adopt a much different approach to their work than that of the traditional stony face guard on a fixed post . . . [It] has been difficult to bring about the type of cultural change required. Private sector involvement has provided an opportunity to establish centres where staff could be recruited with skills and attitudes commensurate with today's philosophy and direction' (Macionis 1992: 7).

The main issues and research questions

Contracting for imprisonment services raises a number of issues, both normative and empirical. Resolution of the normative questions, posed as either legal or policy issues, turns on choosing values and principles that are to govern practice. Other questions, empirical in nature, can be resolved by observation and, if needed, systematic research.

Is contracting proper?

Probably the central normative issue concerns the proper responsibility of government for imprisonment. In the United States, this has been framed in part as a question of constitutionality: Does government's contracting with private entities for imprisonment conform to the general principles established in the US Constitution? One committee of the American Bar Association has argued that it probably does not: 'there can be no doubt that an attempt to delegate total operational responsibility for a prison or jail would raise grave questions of constitutionality under both the federal Constitution and the constitutions of the fifty states' (American Bar Association 1989). No direct constitutional challenges to private prisons have been brought to the courts, however. Nor are there realistic hopes for such challenges. Since *Carter* v. *Carter Coal Company* (1936), the courts have upheld the federal government's delegation of broad powers to private actors. Delegation by state and local governments has also not been seen to pose federal constitutional issues since the 1920s (Lawrence 1986). Private bail bondsmen's powers to arrest and detain those for whom they have posted bond has been consistently upheld *(Corpus Juris Secundum* undated), as have the detention powers of private security firms (Shearing and Stenning 1981). To be sure, laws in some states regarding private delegation are inconsistent and confusing, so that several legislatures seeking to support privately operated correctional facilities have passed laws explicitly granting these powers.

That private prisons have not been declared unconstitutional does not resolve the question whether delegation of administrative authority over imprisonment is proper and desirable, however. Some have argued that imprisonment is 'intrinsically governmental in nature (Robbins 1988), but this ignores the historical record. Others argue that governments should retain full and direct control over the administration of criminal justice because not to do so weakens the social compact in a pluralistic society (DiIulio 1990). The contrary view is that what matters most is not the legal status of the service provider — whether public or private employee — but the quality of the service, and whether the service conforms to established standards and law (Logan 1990; McDonald 1990c).

What are the consequences of contracting?

Beyond the question of propriety lie a number of empirical questions. What are the consequences of delegating imprisonment authority to private entities? Are privately operated facilities more efficient (by some measure to be specified) and less costly? If a cost difference is found, from what does it result? Is market provision of imprisonment services inherently more cost-efficient than direct government provision? If there is no inherent superiority, under what conditions are privately operated facilities more efficient or less costly? Are there inherent pressures or incentives for private firms to deliver higher or lower quality services? What are the consequences for inmates of delegating imprisonment administration to private firms? Are prisoners cared for and are their rights safeguarded better or worse than in public facilities? Will public policies be adversely affected by the existence of an organized private imprisonment industry?

Unfortunately, many of these questions have not been studied. Many developments are too recent to have been subjected to systematic evaluation. However, parallel experiences that could be studied profitably have been largely overlooked. For example, much could be learned by studying the private sector's involvement in holding delinquent juveniles and other children in trouble. In both Britain and the United States, the institutions for wayward youths were developed largely by the voluntary charitable organizations in the nineteenth century. Although governments in both countries assumed direct control over many parts of the system (more so in Britain than in the United States), there continue to this day two tracks: privately provided and publicly provided juvenile correctional services (McDonald 1992; Lerman 1982; Rutherford 1990). In the United States, the private sector has grown substantially in recent years; by 1989, 67 per cent of all juvenile correctional facilities were privately operated, and held 42 per cent of all children in custody that year (McDonald 1992). These institutions have been little studied, especially for the purpose of assessing the benefits and costs of public and private management. The same is apparently true in Britain. Rutherford writes that even though the British system for 'youth in trouble' is publicly funded, it remains largely hidden from public view, little information about it is collected systematically, and the number of children being held in it is not even known. (Rutherford 1990: 55-6).

Is private imprisonment less costly?

On this important question, advocates and critics have advanced a number of claims. Proponents of contracting argue that government is inherently inefficient (or, in the less absolute version, tends toward inefficiency), relative to private firms (e.g., President's Commission on Privatization 1988). Some see this as the result of government's 'monopolistic' provision of services, devoid of competition, reinforced by the public manager giving higher value to the expanding power rather than controlling costs or delivering cost-effective services (Stewart 1986; Young 1987). Others argue that the costs are lower and efficiency greater because managers in private facilities have more freedom to manage effectively — that is, without countervailing labour organizations and constraints of negotiated work rules (Tolchin 1985a). Critics argue that contracting is more expensive because the cost to government of contracting and monitoring contracts outweighs any savings that may result (e.g. Keating undated).

Donahue (1990) argues that the technical means of producing the service of imprisonment (consisting largely of people guarding other people) are not susceptible to significant improvements in productivity, so that there is little room for a private firm's cutting costs except by reducing services. The limited labour-saving technologies that do exist (e.g., greater use of electronic monitoring and communications systems) are available to government as well as to private correctional organizations.

Few systematic studies comparing the costs of public and private facilities have been done. These include studies of the privately contracted Ocheechobee School for Boys in Florida (Brown et al. 1985), public and private juvenile facilities in the United States (Donahue 1990), a privately operated Hamilton County facility jail in Tennessee (Logan and McGriff 1989), publicly and privately operated detention facilities for illegal immigrants in the United States (McDonald 1990a), public and private facilities in Massachusetts and Kentucky (Urban Institute 1989), and the privately operated Borallon centre in Brisbane (Macionis 1992: 22-3).

In the United Kingdom, independent assessments of the relative costs and cost-effectiveness of private imprisonment will be especially difficult because, as mentioned above, financial information is considered proprietary and is kept secret by the government and the firms.

As discussed more fully elsewhere (McDonald 1990a, 1992), the findings of several of the published studies of costs are of questionable validity because of inconsistencies and shortcomings in the accounting methodologies employed. Public and private accounting systems are quite different, and the costs that these differing systems identify are not always comparable. For example, public accounts often treat capital expenditures inconsistently, which confuses the estimation of operating costs. Whereas private firms typically include in their operating costs the depreciated value of the physical assets employed, governments rarely know the value of their standing assets, and cannot estimate a comparable cost of capital. Moreover, private accounting procedures are designed for the purpose of cost analysis, whereas public accounting systems are designed to control expenditures of appropriated public funds and to identify unwarranted expenditures, including fraud. Using public accounts to estimate costs of public services is difficult because the costs of a discrete service such as imprisonment are often borne by different agencies or government accounts (departments of utilities, health, transportation, employee retirement benefits, etc.). Using expenditures by the correctional agency alone may consequently underrepresent the true cost. Costs measured on a per inmate basis are also misleading if facilities differ in their utilization rates, suggesting that crowded facilities appear less costly to operate than less crowded ones — which may affect the public/private comparison (McDonald 1980, 1989; Wayson and Funke 1989: Clear, Harris, and Record, 1982). Because so few of the studies have conducted a rigorous and comparable accounting of both public and private costs, it is premature to conclude that we know much about the relative cost advantages of privately-operated facilities.

Further experience with private imprisonment services and systematic studies of those experiences will probably show that there is no inherent superiority of contracting, in terms of cost-effectiveness, but that certain privately operated facilities may be more cost-effective than the available public alternatives. The comparative advantage that a private firm will have probably depends upon the conditions found in the public agency that would operate the facility in the absence of contracting. For example, some jails run in the United States by incompetent and independently elected sheriffs may be operated more cost-effectively by contracted firms, but one cannot assume that this will be true for all jails. Where inefficient work rules or practices prevail in publicly-operated facilities, and where the constraints on eliminating them are powerful, private firms may have a distinct advantage, especially if they employ unorganized labour. (This advantage may diminish if employees of private firms organize, however.)

Do profit-seeking firms provide poorer services?

A frequent argument is that the principal incentives operating in profit-seeking private firms work to keep costs at a minimum, which is most readily accomplished by diminishing services or the quality of those services (American Bar Association 1986: 4). However, at least in the early stages of contracting, there appear to be certain disincentives to diminish services: if performance falls below agreed-upon standards in those 'showcase' facilities, firms risk losing contracts and clients. Some managers also argue that cutting services creates morale problems among both inmates and staffs and makes facilities more difficult to manage (Rees 1987). For whatever reason, studies of facilities operated by private firms in recent years have generally reported finding good conditions and services, relative to the public facilities (Logan 1991; Urban Institute 1989; Green undated).

Are prisoners' rights diminished or jeopardized?

One obvious worry is that prisoners' rights and welfare will be sacrificed if they conflict with the pursuit of private profit. Even if private firms agree to respect established rights, it is feared the exercise of these rights will be curtailed. Because prisons are so hidden from public view, the likelihood of detecting such violations is low, and prisoners are relatively powerless to bring attention to their grievances. (This is not unique to private prisons, however, for the actions of public officials managing prisons are kept from public view with nearly equal ease.)

Although these concerns are real, private imprisonment is not likely to be a reprise of the nineteenth century private prisons and jails, at least in the United States. The principle is well established that what matters with respect to supporting prisoners' various rights are the actions of the prison officials, and whether they conform to the existing law and standards, and not the name on the officials' shoulder patch.

Moreover, the courts have stepped in and established prisoners' rights, have set standards for prisons and prison officials to meet, and in some instances have hired private individuals ('special masters') to monitor the prison administration's compliance with court orders. To increase further the monitoring of conditions and the operators' compliance with law and standards, several institutional arrangements recommend themselves. These include establishing independent ombudsmen in the private prisons, grievance procedures — including independent grievance and disciplinary boards, and putting full-time government monitors in the private facilities. Procedures for protecting prisoners' rights can also be written into the contract, so that failure to uphold them can be termed a violation of the contract.

Has a 'penal-industrial complex' captured policy making?

Some observers have argued that the emergence of private imprisonment firms is hastening the development of an unhealthy alliance of private/public interests resembling the military-industrial complex. Schoen (1985) warns that private operators, whose business opportunities derive from the shortfall of cell space relative to demand, may provide influential support for 'get tough' sentencing policies that heighten the demand for prisons and jails. Lilly and Knepper (1992) note further that the real money in the corrections industry is being made not by private prison operators but by firms that supply goods and services to corrections agencies, and conclude that 'the corrections-commercial complex operates without public scrutiny and exercises enormous influence over corrections policy'. Moreover, observing that these firms are increasingly marketing their wares outside the United States, they see a 'correctional-policy imperialism' at work, whereby 'First World nations' are finding 'another means to increase their control over the future of punishment in Third World nations'.

Using the terms 'imperialism', 'subgovernments, and 'military-industrial complexes', Lilly and Knepper paint a picture in which public correctional and penal policy making is distorted — and even captured — by private interests. However, this is a misreading of public–private dynamics in the United States, at least — the only country I know well. There is no evidence that private firms have had any influence over the key decisions that have created the booming prisoner populations. Sentencing laws began to get tougher in the early 1970s for a number of reasons, including a turn away from civil commitment of drug abusers toward one that relied on tough criminal sanctions, growing public fears of crime, and the discovery by political leaders that being tough on crime was an effective strategy for getting elected. Moreover, a key strategy among Republican Party leaders seeking to attract conservative Democratic voters into the Republican tent was to focus attention on social and cultural issues rather than economic ones. Coming on the heels of widespread turmoil in the United States — with the civil rights and black power movements, student unrest, and a popular uprising against the Government's war in Vietnam — calls for 'law and order' became very effective political tools. Contemporary penal policy in the United States was thus forged in the course of a political and policy battle, in which self-interested private correctional interests have played no significant role.

To be sure, businesses have made money from this growing industry, as they have from all large-scale, capital-intensive government programmes. Governments themselves do

461

not manufacture goods, and many businesses have emerged to provide needed services. There has also been a movement of personnel between private firms and public correctional policy making positions (e.g., Sir Edward Gardiner left Parliament to join a private imprisonment firm), but this does not in and of itself indicate that *sentencing* policy is being distorted by private interests. Where private firms are more likely to affect government decision making is in the choice of public or private provision of correctional services. Private firms have been aggressive in lobbying governments to convert at least some of their public operations to privately contracted ones. Where governments have to be careful is to avoid becoming too dependent upon private provision. Strategies to minimize thc risks of this include government retaining ownership of existing correctional facilities, and contracting only for management of new ones — because firms that establish themselves with physical assets in a particular jurisdiction may develop an unbeatable edge over potential competitors in future contract competitions.

The challenges to public administration

The likely outcome of current developments is that correctional systems will probably not be wholly public or wholly private, and that public imprisonment responsibilities will be delivered by differing mixes of private firms and public agencies. At least in the United Kingdom and the United States, interest in introducing market mechanisms such as contracting into more command-oriented public administration will probably survive changes in governing parties. The issue of whether imprisonment operations should be delegated to private contractors will certainly remain controversial, however, because the intersection between state power and individual liberty is felt most sharply in prisons, jails, and other detention centres. Not surprisingly, views about private imprisonment services are most closely linked to deeper political values, which makes it difficult to resolve the public policy debate about contracting. However, knowing more about the actual experiences and consequences of contracting will go a long way toward identifying the most desirable combinations of public and private responsibilities and interests.

There are, I think, three principal challenges to public policy that are posed by private imprisonment firms, all of which deserve the attention of the research community. The first is to devise procedures to assure that prisoners' rights and welfare are protected (which is, of course, a challenge in publicly-operated prisons and jails as well). This is not a difficult task, and there are well-developed models to follow. Learning about the effectiveness of these models in privately operated prisons should be a high priority for research.

The second challenge is to prevent governments' dependence upon private firms, and especially upon entrenched suppliers. Ideally, one might accomplish this by governments creating conditions that engender competition among firms rather than monopolistic dominance by a few giants. (Privatization does not necessarily create a competitive environment.) Precisely how this can be done is difficult to prescribe, as the future shape of a mature private imprisonment industry is not yet known. Current experience offers a relatively wide array of cases to learn from, which are characterized by varying combinations of large and small jurisdictions, centralized and decentralized (or fragmented) correctional systems, differences in scope of contracts (including whether facilities are owned or only operated by contractors), and different contracting arrangements.

The third challenge is to protect the integrity of government procurement processes — one that is faced in nearly all areas of public administration. To the extent that new knowledge needs to be developed here, looking beyond corrections to those other areas of administration is likely to be profitable.

* Douglas C. McDonald, Ph.D., is a senior social scientist in the Law and Public Policy Area of Abt Associates Inc., a policy research organization based in Cambridge, Massachusetts. He conducts research and writes on criminal sentencing, immediate sanctions, corrections policy and financing, privatization, and drug abuse policy and treatment.

References

Adam Smith Institute (1984) *The Omega Justice Report.* London: Adam Smith Institute.

American Bar Association (1986) *Report to the House of Delegates,* unpublished document. Chicago: American Bar Association.

—— (1989) *Report to the House of Delegates,* unpublished document dated February 13. Chicago: American Bar Association.

American Correctional Association (1991) *Directory.* Laurel, MD: American Correctional Association.

American Federation of State, County, and Municipal Employees (AFSME) AFL-CIO (1984) *Passing the Bucks: The Contracting Out of Public Services.* American Federation of State, County and Municipal Employees, AFL-CIO.

Bernat, B. (1991) American Civil Liberties Union, National Prison Project. Personal communication with author, 27 September.

Bivens, T. (1986) 'Can Prisons for Profit Work?', *Philadelphia Inquirer Magazine,* 3 August.

Bowman, G.W., Hakim, S., and Seidenstat, P., eds (1992) *Privatizing the United States Justice System: Police, Adjudication, and Corrections Services from the Private Sector.* Jefferson, NC: McFarland and Company.

Bronick, M.J. (1989) 'The Federal Bureau of Prisons' Experience with Privatization', unpublished paper. Washington, DC: US Bureau of Prisons.

Brown, A., Gerard, R., Howard, R., Kennedy, W., Levinson, R., Sell, C., Skelton, P., and Quay, H. (1985) *Private Sector Operation of a Correctional Institution: A Study of the Jack and Ruth Eckerd Youth Development Center, Okeechobee, Florida.* Washington, DC: National Institute of Corrections.

Bureau of Justice Statistics (1991) *Prisoners in 1990.* Washington, DC: US Department of Justice, Bureau of Justice Statistics.

Carter v. Carter Coal Company (1936) 298 US 238.

Chaiken, J., and Mennemeyer, S. (1987) *Lease-Purchase Financing of Prison and Jail Construction.* Washington, DC: National Institute of Justice.

Clarke, K. (1992) 'Prisoners with Private Means', *The Independent,* 22 December.

Clear, T., Harris, P., and Record A. (1982) 'Managing the Cost of Corrections', *The Prison Journal,* 62.

Coates, R. B., Miller. A. D., and Ohlin, L. E. (1978) *Diversity in a Youth Correctional System: Handling Delinquents in Massachusetts*. Cambridge, MA: Ballinger Publishing Company.

Corpus Juris Secundum (undated) vol. 8, section 87. St Paul, MN: West Publishing Company.

Corrections Corporation of America (1985) *Proposal for State of Tennessee*. Nashville, TN: Corrections Corporation of America.

—— (1992) 'CCA Wins First British Prison Contract,' press release, 8 December. Nashville, TN: Corrections Corporation of America.

Corrections Corporation of Australia (1992) *Borallon Correctional Centre*. Ipswich, Queensland: Corrections Corporation of Australia.

Crew, A. (1933) *London Prisons of Today and Yesterday*. London: I. Nicholson and Waston.

Deloitte, Haskins and Sells (1989) 'A Report to the Home Office on the Practicality of Private Sector Involvement in the Remand System', unpublished document.

DiIulio, J.J. (1990) 'The Duty to Govern: A Critical Perspective on the Private Management of Prisons and Jails', in D. C. McDonald, ed., *Private Prisons and the Public Interest*. New Brunswick, NJ: Rutgers University Press.

Donahue, J. D. (1990) *The Privatization Decision*. New York: Basic Books.

Feeley, M. M. (1991) 'Privatization of Prisons in Historical Perspective'. In W. Gormley, ed., *Privatization and its Alternatives*. Madison, WI: University of Wisconsin Press.

Ford, R. (1992) 'Private Prison Firms Start Brain Drain from Public Sector', *The Times*, 24 December.

Gill, L. F. (1992) 'Private Sector Involvement in the Prison System of England and Wales', unpublished paper delivered at Australian Institute of Criminology Conference, Wellington, New Zealand, 30 Nov.-2 Dec. 1992.

—— (1993) Home Office Remand Contracts Units. Private communication with author on 4 January.

Green, P. (undated) *Private Sector Involvement in the Immigrant Detention Centres*. London: The Howard League for Penal Reform.

Harding, R. (1992) 'Private Prisons in Australia', *Trends and Issues in Crime and Criminology*. Canberra: Australian Institute of Criminology.

HM Prison Service (1992) *Briefing* 54, 10 November.

—— (1993a) 'In House Team to Run Manchester Prison', News release, 15 July.

—— (1993b) 'Michael Howard Unveils Plan for More Private Sector Involvement in the Prison Service', News release, 2 September.

HMSO (1988) *Private Sector Involvement in the Remand System*. Cm. 434.

Holdsworth, W. S. (1992-4) *A History of English Law*, vol. 4, 3rd edn. London: Cambridge University Press.

Home Affairs Committee (1987) *Contract Provision of Prisons, Fourth Report of the Home Affairs Committee*. HC 291.

Home Office (1990) 'Court Escorts, Custody and Security: A Discussion Paper'. London: Home Office.

—— (1992) 'Tender Documents for the Operating Contract of HM Prison Manchester', *Schedule 2: Outline Brief*. London: Home Office.

Howard League for Penal Reform (1990) 'Private Sector Involvement in the Remand System: The Howard League Response to the Discussion Paper "Court Escorts, Custody and Security" '. London: The Howard League for Penal Reform.

Hughes, R. (1987). *The Fatal Shore*. New York: Alfred A. Knopf.

Immarigeon, R. (1987) Privatizing Adult Imprisonment in the US: A Bibliography', *Criminal Justice Abstracts,* vol. 19, pp. 136—9.

Joint Council for the Welfare of Immigrants (1988) *Annual Report 1988*.

Joint State Government Commission (1987) 'Report of the Private Prison Task Force'. Harrisburg, PA: General Assembly of the Commonwealth of Pennsylvania.

Keating, M. J. (undated) *Seeking Profit in Punishment: The Private Management of Correctional Institutions*. Washington, DC: American Federation of State, County and Municipal Employees.

Kennedy, J. J. (1988) *Final Report of the Commission of Review into Corrective Services in Queensland*. Brisbane: State Government Printer.

Lawrence, D. (1986). 'Private Exercise of Governmental Power', *Indiana Law Journal,* 61: 649

Legislative Research Council, Commonwealth of Massachusetts (1986) *Prisons for Profit*. Boston: Legislative Research Council, Commonwealth of Massachusetts.

Leonard, H. B. (1986) *Checks Unbalanced: The Quiet Side of Public Spending*. New York: Basic Books.

—— (1990) 'Private Time: The Political Economy of Private Prison Finance', in D. McDonald, ed., *Private Prisons and the Public Interest*. New Brunswick, NJ: Rutgers University Press.

Lerman, P. (1982) *Deinstitutionalization and the Welfare State*. New Brunswick, NJ: Rutgers University Press.

Lilly, J. R., and Knepper, P. (1992) 'An International Perspective on the Privatisation of Corrections', *The Howard Journal,* 31/3: 174-91.

Logan, C. H. (1990) *Private Prisons: Cons and Pros*. New York: Oxford University Press.

—— (1991) *Well Kept: Comparing Quality of Confinement in a Public and a Private Prison*. Washington, DC: Report to the National Institute of Justice.

Logan, C. H., and McGriff, B. W. (1989) 'Comparing Costs of Public and Private Prisons: A Case Study', *NIJ Reports,* 216: 2-8.

Logan, C. H. and Rausch, S. (1985) 'Punish and Profit: The Emergence of Private Enterprise Prisons', *Justice Quarterly* 2: 303-18.

Macionis, S. (1992) 'Contract Management in Corrections: The Queensland Experience', unpublished paper written for a conference, 'The Private Sector and Community Involvement in the Criminal Justice System', in Wellington, New Zealand, 30 Nov.–2 Dec. 1992.

McConville, S., and Williams, J. E. H. (1985) *Crime and Punishment: A Radical Rethink*. London: Tawney Society.

McDonald, D. C. (1980) *The Price of Punishment: Public Spending for Corrections in New York*. Boulder, CO: Westview Press.

—— (1989) *The Cost of Corrections: In Search of the Bottom Line*. Washington, DC: US Department of Justice, National Institute of Corrections.

—— (1990a) 'The Costs of Operating Public and Private Correctional Facilities', in D.C. McDonald, ed., *Private Prisons and the Public Interest*. New Brunswick, NJ: Rutgers University Press.

—— (1990b) ed., *Private Prisons and the Public Interest*. New Brunswick, NJ: Rutgers University Press.

—— (1990c) 'When Government Fails: Going Private as a Last Resort', in D.C. McDonald, ed., *Private Prisons and the Public Interest*. New Brunswick, NJ: Rutgers University Press.

—— (1992) 'Private Penal Institutions: Moving the Boundary of Government Authority in Corrections', in M. Tonry, ed., *Crime and Justice: An Annual Review of Research*. Chicago: University of Chicago Press.

McKelvey, B. (1977) *American Prisons: A History of Good Intentions*. Montclair, NJ: Patterson Smith.

Miller, A. D., Ohlin, L. E., and Coates, R. B. (1977) *A Theory of Social Reform: Correctional Change Processes in Two States*. Cambridge: Ballinger Publishing Company.

Mullen, J. (1985) 'Correction and the Private Sector', *Privatization Review* 1: 12.

Mullen, J., Chabotar, K., and Carrow, D. (1984) *The Privatization of Corrections*. Washington, DC: National Institute of Justice.

National Institute of Justice (1987) *Contracting for the Operation of Prisons and Jails*. Washington DC: US Department of Justice.

National Criminal Justice Statistics Association (1987) *Private Sector Involvement in Financing and Managing Correctional Facilities*. Washington, DC: National Criminal Justice Statistics Association.

O'Hare, M., Leone, R., and Zeagans, M. (1990) 'The Privatization of Imprisonment: A Managerial Perspective', in D. C. McDonald, ed., *Private Prisons and the Public Interest*. New Brunswick, NJ: Rutgers University Press.

Peterson, J. (1988) *Corrections and the Private Sector: A National Forum,* proceedings of a conference. Washington, DC: National Institute of Justice.

President's Commission on Privatization (1988) *Privatization: Toward More Effective Government*. Washington, DC: The White House.

Press, A. (1990) 'The Good, the Bad, and the Ugly: Private Prisons in the 1980s', in D.C. McDonald, ed., *Private Prisons and the Public Interest*. New Brunswick, NJ: Rutgers University Press.

Rees, J. (1987) private communication with author. (Mr Rees was the chief manager of the Correctional Corporation of America's staff at the Santa Fe County jail.)

Robbins, I. P. (1988) *The Legal Dimensions of Private Incarceration*. Washington, DC: American Bar Association.

Rutherford, A. (1990) 'British Penal Policy and the Idea of Prison Privatization', in D. C. McDonald, ed., *Private Prisons and the Public Interest*. New Brunswick, NJ: Rutgers University Press.

Schearing, C. D., and Stenning, P. C. (1981) 'Modern Private Security: Its Growth and Implications'. *Crime and Justice: An Annual Review*. Chicago: University of Chicago Press.

Schoen, K. (1985) 'Private Prison Operators', *The New York Times,* 28 March.

Stewart, J. K. (1986) 'Costly Prisons: Should the Public Monopoly Be Ended?', in P. B. McGuigan and J. S. Pascale, eds, *Crime and Punishment in Modern America*. Washington, DC: The Institute for Government and Politics of the Free Congress Research and Education Foundation, pp. 365-88.

Taylor, M., and Pease. K. (1987) Unpublished document, later published in R. Matthews, *Privatizing Criminal Justice*. London: Sage.

Tolchin, M. (1985a) 'Prisons for Profit: Nashville's CCA Claims Operations Aid Government'. *The Tennessean*, 24 Feb.

—— (1985b) 'Private Concern Makes Offer to Run Tennessee's Prisons', *New York Times*, 13 Sept.

—— (1985c) 'Experts Foresee Adverse Effects from Private Control of Prisons', *New York Times*, 17 Sept.

US House of Representatives (1986) *Privatization of Corrections: Hearings Before the Subcommittee on Courts, Civil Liberties, and the Administration of Justice of the Committee of the Judiciary, House of Representatives, Ninety-Ninth Congress, First and Second Sessions on Privatization of Corrections, November 13, 1985 and March 18, 1986*. Washington, DC: US Government Printing Office.

Urban Institute (1989) *Comparison of Privately and Publicly Operated Corrections Facility in Kentucky and Massachusetts*. Washington, DC: Report to the National Institute of Justice.

Wayson, B. L., and Funke, G. S. (1989) *What Price Justice? A Handbook for the Analysis of Criminal Justice Costs*. Washington, DC: US Department of Justice, National Institute of Justice.

Young, P. (1987) *The Prison Cell*. London: The Adam Smith Institute.

22.   Visions of Order
Stanley Cohen

Any topic of interest in the social sciences has a peculiarly amorphous quality. It looks distinct, tangible, separate — empirically or conceptually — but the closer you examine it, the more it merges into its surrounding space. So it is with crime control. A matter of restricted scope, the subject of the parochial discipline of criminology, starts dissolving into much wider issues: political ideologies, the crisis in welfare liberalism, the nature of professional power, conceptions of human nature. This chapter embraces such dissolution: the deconstruction of crime control as a separate subject. We move into spaces which are not just amorphous, but imagined and imaginary.

The dystopian assumption

The beginning and the end of the nineteenth century marked two of the more utopian moments in crime-control history. At the beginning were those Great Transformations with which this book started. The founders of the penitentiary system in America and Europe were confident that they could devise a solution to the crime problem, a solution that would result in a better society. Rothman describes well this spirit of optimism, the explicit utopian thinking which informed the design of the asylums. And at the end of the century came the positivist 'revolution' in criminology. Whether it was genuinely innovatory or merely an elaborate justification of existing policy, the new 'science' of criminology took its message from the more general faith in scientific progress. Science and technology (and not just a belief in doing good) could solve social problems and create a new social order.

While these agendas are set by political and economic contingencies, the very idea that a social problem is solvable needs an appropriate belief system. Some beliefs are favourable and others unfavourable to planned intervention.[1] Those nineteenth-century moments of crime control contained favourable beliefs about two constants in the human predicament: human nature and the social order. The crime problem had always presented many awkward cognitive impediments to intervention: original sin, Calvinist ideas of predisposition, social Darwinism and the fatalism even within early biological versions of criminological positivism ('crime as destiny'). But once these beliefs could be neutralized, by-passed or forgotten, the way was open. If only the right combination of benevolence and technology could be found, even the worst of people could be changed and a better social order created.

We have already encountered some of the many twentieth-century assaults on these beliefs: pessimism about changing human nature, scepticism about organized benevolence, disenchantment with progress, distrust of technology, a willingness to settle for limited horizons. This was and is the new 'realism' of crime control. I want now to retrace these beliefs and counter-beliefs, and locate them in the wider context of utopian and dystopian visions. This is not in order to indulge in cheap futurology

Stanley Cohen: 'Visions of Order' from *VISIONS OF SOCIAL CONTROL* (Cambridge: Polity Press, 1984), pp. 197-235. Reprinted by permission of Basil Blackwell Ltd.

but rather to show how social-control ideology is deeply embedded in these more general predictions, fantasies, visions and expectations.

By the time that criminological positivism was establishing itself, the social sciences as a whole had taken it for granted that an analysis of the past and the present could be directed towards visualizing the future. As Kumar notes in his excellent guide to the sociology of industrial society: 'when sociology arrived in Europe early in the nineteenth century, it marked a strand of thinking about man and society that was increasingly directed towards the future.'[2] This strand became dominant as sociologists came to dwell on the Great Transformation which was to become their subject matter — the new social order of industrialism.

Not all this thinking, of course, was optimistic. We know Weber's forebodings about rationalization and bureaucracy, Marx's apocalyptic vision of what had to happen before the new social order could emerge. But an influential stream of these thinkers, represented by Comte, St Simon and the other 'prophets of progress', presented a much less complicated vision of the coming into being of the new social order. Social change was progressive; science and technology would usher in a new era; disease, misery and crime were capable of being vanquished.

With the obvious (though complicated) exception of Marx, few of these nineteenth-century social thinkers expressed themselves in the classic utopian form. Unlike in Plato's *Republic* or the original utopia of Thomas More, they were not constructing ideal societies. Theirs were not visions of what should be, but what is likely to be. And here, while never being quite as complacent as the literary and technological utopianists of their era, they were deeply influenced by the more general cultural optimism about science and technology.[3]

After the First World War, however, even this cautious optimism was to disappear. A bleaker, even apocalyptic world view became dominant. Ominous, irrational forces were at work which made human nature and social order far less amenable to change than had been thought. This was the 'sense of ending'. Moral and material progress were not the same; scientific advances would not necessarily bring happiness. All this is now seen as characteristic of the twentieth-century world view: cynicism, disillusionment, pessimism. This is the 'cheap wasteland philosophy' about which Saul Bellow's heroes muse so often.

In the social sciences, all those grand visions of progress and evolution were buried. Preoccupations became grandly abstract or minutely empirical. Within the limited fields that became known variously as social disorganization, social pathology, social problems and criminology, a degree of optimism remained. But it was only the degree needed to give credibility to the business of intervention. The evils of the big city, the disintegration of primary social control, the loss of community, the impersonality of technology — all such problems must get worse. Intervention could work, indeed it was desperately needed, but this was a rescue operation. The point was to save, treat or prevent the casualties of the machine. The social-problems industry remained the most optimistic part of the social sciences, but it was the optimism of the crusader, the muckraker, the lifesaver, and not the prophet of a new social order.

470

In the 1950s there was some sort of recovery. Industrialism seemed more resilient, and the new theorists of the 'managerial revolution', 'convergence' and the 'end of ideology' began to imply that the structural problems of industrialism were working themselves out.[4] A new note of complacency appeared which was not destined to last very long. By the 1960s the dark side of industrialism was rediscovered. It was not just the 'return' of ideology in the demands of Blacks and other ethnic minorities, gays and other groups labelled deviant, and the women's movement for a different place in the system, but a radical disenchantment with industrial progress itself. For many such groups, for the counter-culture and the new left, and then for the ecology movement, dystopia was already on the way. Most of all, the danger came from the strong state; the quest for 'community' was an anti-statist form of utopian thinking. The machine itself had to be destroyed before it destroyed us. This, as I showed in [chapter 4], was the basis of the destructuring rhetoric. The old apparatus, with its bureaucracies, institutions, professionals (words which now acquired wholly negative meanings), had to be dismantled or by-passed.

In the face of this apparent disintegration of the consensus, theorists started constructing a new vision and a new ideology. 'Post-industrial society' was now on its way. This was claimed to be a transformation which would eventually produce societies as different from the classic industrial society of Marx, Weber and Durkheim as theirs was in turn from early agrarian, pre-capitalist formations. But as Kumar points out, neither the radical harbingers of Future Shock, the Third Wave, the Greening of America nor their more sober academic successors have shown just where this qualitative leap is taking place.

For, despite the pretensions of post-industrial theorists, the future which the real social world of 1984 indicates looks more like an extension of the processes begun in the early nineteenth century. Nothing very new needs to be added to that package of concepts — formalization, rationalization, centralization, bureaucratization, professionalization — through which we understood the coming of industrial society. Not a new social order, but more of the same.

This, of course, was the burden of my account of the fate of those radical destructuring movements. For what is true of the social sciences and society in general, is no less true for criminology and crime (and its control). The general literatures on futurology and post-industrial society however, are remarkably silent about crime and its control, while students of crime rarely articulate more than a vague sense that things are getting worse.

Only one criminologist, Sykes, has formulated this sense more exactly.[5] Conventional crime, he plausibly argues, is likely to continue increasing. Virtually every single causal indicator — economy, ecology, family, education, values, immigration, population, community — points to increasing rates of crime and delinquency.[6] His scenario is familiar enough: middle-class flight to the suburbs; decaying inner-city slums; unskilled and isolated minority groups; chronic unemployment; zero economic growth; disintegration of social ties; alienation and despair; abandonment of welfare ideologies; and so, more homicide, assault, robbery, larceny, rape. At the same time, all sorts of other changes — in technology, property relationships, corporate organization,

471

political legitimacy — are likely to increase the amount of 'unconventional crime': white-collar crime, political crime, official lawlessness and political corruption.

So much for crime. As for its control, beyond the assumption that current policy has arrived at a turning point and that some sort of crisis is ahead, Sykes presents a choice between pessimistic and modestly optimistic alternatives:

> It is possible to envision a society marked by increasing violence and attacks on private property, by intolerance of any deviation from an obsessive morality, and by far reaching police surveillance coupled with a loss of civil liberties in a totalitarian social order. It is also possible (though admittedly more difficult in this disenchanted era) to envision a society with widespread acceptance of and conformity to the criminal law, a modest view of the proper reach of the State, and methods of law enforcement that are just, humane and effective.[7]

A linear projection from current control trends suggests changes much more incremental and ambiguous. The assumptions which Wilkins noted more than a decade ago still apply.[8] First, most criminal-justice planning will continue to seek solutions by means of more of the same. Second, the public will continue with the mistaken and confused belief that because we do not like crime, what we do about it will decrease it. The results of these assumptions will be a total breakdown of the criminal-justice system (somewhere before the year 2000 Wilkins predicts), together with increasing pressure for more and more control. The resultant forms of control will be less noteworthy for their effects on crime than their intrusive side-effects on ordinary citizens: a retreat into fortress living; streets abandoned to outlaws; inconvenience and erosion of civil liberty as a result of continual security checks and surveillance systems. We have already seen this prediction from several theoretical directions: for traditional law-and-order policies based on doing something to individual offenders, 'the game is almost up'. The next technology is the use of cybernetic planning at the level of systems and environments in order to make the initial *act* more difficult. The by-products might be unpleasant, but the old punitive technology will soon be extinct.

Apart from these more imaginative excesses — crises, system breakdown, desolation, totalitarianism — most crime-control predictions are only modestly pessimistic. An optimistic, utopian element in crime-control thinking has always to be maintained: the countervision of order, regulation and security which will replace the imminent threat of breakdown and chaos. This vision appeared in the early penitentiary movement, in the idealistic excesses of scientific positivism, in the Continental social-defence school and today, in the bland technicist criminology peddled by international agencies to the Third World.[9] The visions of chaos dominate; all that can be hoped for is a holding operation. Genuine utopianism only remains on the extreme right with its visions of environmental manipulation, psychotechnology or genetic planning and the extreme left, with its prospect of a 'crime-free' society with the dissolution of capitalism. The dominant tone is the realist right: 'I argue for a sober view of man and his institutions that would permit reasonable things to be accomplished, foolish things abandoned and utopian things forgotten.'[10]

What, though, can be learnt from the much richer world of literary, philosophical and political utopias? This literature has been well chronicled,[11] and so too has the expression of the utopian form in science fiction and its eventual displacement by anti-utopian and dystopian visions.[12] The transitional figure is usually seen as H. G. Wells, the changes in his own long career bridging the nineteenth-century utopias of Samuel Butler, William Morris, Edward Bellamy and Jules Verne with the darker visions of the twentieth century. After Wells, no more traditional utopias were created; they were to come, if anywhere, from architects and planners.

The key literary works of twentieth-century dystopianism have passed into popular consciousness. In each case — unlike in sociologies of the future — social control is a central theme. And in each case there is a similar desolate vision of oppression, rigidity, stifling conformity. In Zamyatin's *We* (published in 1924) people are imprisoned in glass-walled cities and controlled as rigorously as the weather. In Huxley's *Brave New World* (1932), genetic control produces grades of humans designed to function according to predetermined levels of intelligence; science makes life undemandingly pleasant through mind-altering drugs; the very few rebels are banished to a distant island. And then — most resonant of all, of course — came Orwell's *Nineteen Eighty-Four,* a society built around total control, with the proles segregated and the middle class subject to surveillance and thought control. But the element in *Nineteen Eighty-Four* which is so crucial to our theme is that power is an end in itself. This sharply distinguishes it from *We, Brave New World* and virtually the whole utopian tradition where, whatever we might think of the results, the state is benevolent and justifies its policies in the name of the general social good.

By the early fifties, in any event, variants on the dystopian theme had become standard in 'genre' science fiction as well as more respectable literary forms. In a typical example, Vonnegut's *Player Piano* (published in 1952), society is dominated by super-intelligent machines, materially prosperous, but regimented and spiritually empty. The vision became familiar: total social control with the hackneyed plot of the lone individual who somehow escapes conditioning, sees through all the lies and tries to escape. There is no hope of a collective political solution. In science fiction all that changes is the nature of the society's central obsession: nuclear disaster, overcrowding, pollution, crime. The enemies are no longer the old BEM's (Bug Eyed Monsters) from outer space — the symbols, some commentators argue, of communists in the Cold War — but are now within the society.

These 'visions of hell' in science fiction deserve genuine attention from students of social control.[13] They are not predictions of the future in the formal sense. True predictions are more linear: for example, as unemployment increases, so will crime increase. Science-fiction predictions are more imaginary. They involve speculation, guesswork, intuitive leaps. They predict futures rather than one future and allow you to imagine the extremes which might result if a particular value choice is followed through. Linear variables — like population or productivity, the type wisely used in criminology — are merely the flats and props, the background on which the visions are projected.

473

Science fiction is not a world which allows for easy systematization. A sense of these visions is best conveyed through a few random examples.

(1) Current illegalities (all forms of drug use, all sexual relationships) are decriminalized, but new problems and shortages (food, population growth, space, pollution) create new illegal markets and new crimes (hoarding, living in rooms too large); an exaggeration of current values also creates new crimes: 'conscious male chauvinism' becomes a punishable offence; old crimes like witchcraft reappear (in 2183),

(2) Current systems and ideologies of criminal justice break down completely, producing solutions such as: judging machines — analog computers which replace all human discretion; furies — robots who pursue and kill detected offenders; automatic on-the-spot justice by which offenders are tried, sentenced and punished within a few minutes after the offence; bounty hunters: vigilantes who are paid cash rewards for killing anyone carrying out an armed robbery.

(3) New forms of punishment are devised or old ones revived: public executions are staged (in one story, there are mass 'Public Hatings' where the concentrated psychic energy of 70,000 minds burns the flesh off the offender's bones); offenders are implanted with telemachines (in one story, mobile prisons in the form of a three-walled halo which encases the offender and relentlessly accompanies him; if he stops moving the fourth wall joins itself and he is permanently sealed to death in a cube of impenetrable plastic); exile and banishment are also revived (as in Robert Silverberg's famous *Hawksbill Station,* where political deviants are banished back into time, condemned to eternal exile in a penal colony a billion years up the time line, somewhere in the early Paleozoic age).

The question is not whether these things could 'really' happen. As with Orwell's *Nineteen Eighty-Four,* or any species of utopian or anti-utopian thinking, these visions help clarify our values and preferences. Every form of social control, actual or idealized, embodies a moral vision of what should be. As my early chapters made clear, the system's sense of the future is not at all restricted to technical possibilities such as thought control, electronic surveillance or psychotechnology. I am talking about ideological rather than mechanical visions.

Take, for example, the idea that the perfect form of social control should avoid the cost, the physical segregation and the counter-productivity of the closed institution, but still entail moral judgement (stigma) and some real loss to the offender (justice). This is just the solution worked out in Silverberg's haunting story, *To See the Invisible Man.*[14] The prescribed punishment (for coldness) is to be pronounced invisible for a year or other fixed period. A luminous brand is placed on the forehead, no one is allowed to touch the offender, to speak to him, nor, after the first glance, to even look at him. The penalty for contact is to be sentenced to invisibility yourself. A perfect form of community control.

Exaggeration, fantasy, distortion, paranoia, panic mongering. . . No doubt. We must, however, understand these fictions, not to make predictions, but to confront the plaintive refrain which has run through the real stories of social control: 'that's not what we had in mind at all.' Perhaps not; perhaps good intentions do go fatefully wrong. But what is clear, is that many ideas which might seem repulsive to the liberal mind, were those embodied in classic *utopias*, not dystopias or anti-utopias.

In More's utopia, people are under constant observation by neighbours and magistrates. Society is governed by a set of rigid social controls; some deviations are punished by slavery; private political discussion is punished by death. In Bellamy's new society there is an inspectorate alert to any deviations. And so it goes on through virtually all the classic utopian literature: security, well-being, peace and, in socialist versions, equality. But, at the same time, there is suppression of individuality, stifling conformity, rigidity, smugness and complacency. This, of course, was the very combination satirized in the anti-utopias of Zamyatin, Huxley and Vonnegut.

This was not a vision which disturbed Bentham when he published his utopian panopticon plans in 1791 nor was it to worry Skinner's *Walden Two* of 1948. Here was perfect social control: an observed, synchronized society. Liberalism, as we well know, could absorb Bentham and it can even find Skinner appealing — the prospect of a world where people will naturally behave well, without punishment.[15] But we must now ground these visions, not in reality but in another and more specific set of visions — the city of the future. Here, dreams merge most visibly into nightmares, utopias into dystopias. Here too, we will glimpse the possibilities which my next and final chapter presents as real policy choices.

The city as metaphor

Some time in the nineteenth century, the city began to be seen as a special, unique form of social life.[16] Before that, it appeared dominantly as a metaphor or paradigm, a model of society itself. Both these images survive. Alongside our concepts for understanding the uniqueness of the city (the business of all those special disciplines such as urban sociology, urban planning and urban geography), we are haunted by the old idea that the city stands for something. Today, invariably, it stands for disorder, chaos and breakdown. It is assumed that, unless we make radical changes (create a new *kind* of place? start again?), the city of the present — the iconography of violence, crime, insecurity, pollution, traffic congestion, over-crowding — is the society of the future. On the city streets lie the sharpest mirrors of dystopian imagery.

Cities, then, have never been just places, 'almost as soon as they were invented, they spawned a phantom version of themselves; an imaginative doppelganger that lived an independent life in the imagination of the human species at large. In other words, they stood for something.'[17] In the ancient world and then again with the re-emergence of city life in the later middle ages, the city tended to be conceived as a metaphor of order. The patterning of the city, its spatial arrangements, hierarchies, functional specifics, served as a mirror image of what the wider social reality could and should be like. The metaphor of the orderly city was so powerful that it could even serve as a mnemonic.[18] In Plato and Aristotle, then in the Heavenly City of St Augustine, the ordered city was a system for holding chaos at bay. The primordial city of these first utopias was a

475

glimpse of eternal order, heaven on earth. The City of God became a symbolic representation of the universe itself. Here was the scheme of divine order: the temple and the palace at the centre.

As Mumford notes in his astute reading of the utopian literature, this picture was not entirely imaginary. It was an 'after image', an idealized form of the actual ancient city where divine order was embodied in every ritual and practice.[19] The ancient city was not simply the 'utopia' of later versions, but the most impressive and enduring of all utopias, actually embodying and even surpassing the ideal prescriptions of later fantasies.

But alongside the metaphor of order, the city was also used to construct metaphors and maps of hell. There were now secular infernos of crime and punishment, cities where vice and virtue would be stratified. In the City of the Wicked, all evil men were expected to form their own social order, and divine infernos were constructed to look like cities. With the Industrial Revolution, these metaphors gave way to reality and a darker, more complicated image emerged of the city as a problem, a form of evil in itself. This was the point at which social thinkers began constructing their now-familiar picture of urban life: impersonality, segmentalization, market rationality, degradation and anomie. From then onwards, the critique of the metropolis and the quest for community became central to sociological thought.

This was also the point at which the famous literary and political utopias of the nineteenth century were created by Bellamy, Fourier, Owen, Morris, Wells. As Mumford notes, there are close similarities between these visions and the more authoritarian utopias of the ancient and medieval cities. In both cases, we find 'isolation, stratification, fixation, regimentation, standardization, militarization'. And both visions merge into twentieth-century dystopias: 'one suddenly realizes that the distance between the positive ideal and the negative one was never so great as the advocates or admirers of utopia had professed.'[20] Again, the visions were not entirely imaginary; they drew on 'phantom versions' of previous realities.

But whatever the complex relationship between imagination, reality and after-image, the city could never again be used as a symbol of order. From every conceivable direction — anarchist, Marxist, liberal, humanist, conservative — intellectuals mounted their anti-urban attack. The metaphor of order could not be sustained nor (easily) could the tradition of thought that saw the city as the seat of civilization, the repository of grace and progress. Everything that was inhumane and degrading about the emergent industrial order (or capitalism) was to be found in the city. If there was order, it was an artificial, regimented, dehumanizing order. This was contrasted with the natural, organic order of the rual community and even its charming disorder: the irregular winding village lane, the casual conversations and family intimacies which took precedence over the market and the cash nexus. This was the alienation produced by the wrong sort of order. But the dominant vision was the anomie which resulted from too little order: the chaos and degradation of Hogarth, Dore, Dickens, Hugo, those unforgettable images of the areas of misery inhabited by the lumpen, the misfits, the Children of the Jago.

At the more theoretical level, of course, the vision was more complicated. Classical sociological thought contained a deep ambivalence about the city. Marx and Durkheim saw the possibilities for a new form of humanization, a different basis for social solidarity. Then, most notably, came Simmel's vision of the special kind of freedom that results in response to city conditions. The person could free his spirit (who I am) from his acts (what I usually do). This new freedom could be attained precisely because of the anonymity criticized in the anti-urban bias of intellectuals. Within the interstices of the metropolis, the 'I' could transcend mere routine.

But this is to anticipate a much later vision of the city. And, as we have so often seen, social-control thinking is never particularly sensitive to ambivalence. Such nuances would never have been picked up in the two major strands of nineteenth-century crime-control ideology: first, the notion that planning, regulation and classification could keep chaos at bay; second, the idealization of community, the vision of perfect social control in the paradise lost. Sometimes one theme dominated, sometimes the other. Eventually they became combined, symbiotically dependent on each other, in the powerful notion that the anomie and disorder caused by the replacement of natural and effective social control (community) by unnatural and ineffective social control (city, mass society) could be solved by the state. The state would have to compensate for the loss of community.

Before the great industrial cities had created their metaphors, planners and visionaries had, of course, already come together in the project with which this book opened: the closed institution as the answer to the impending problem of social control. Here would be constructed a simulated version, a working model, of what the good society should look like. This indeed was the City of the Wicked, but its order, discipline and hierarchy, its rows, tiers, lines, ceremonies of bell ringing and counting, could point us towards the good city. The perceived problem might have been (in the various versions I examined in chapter 1) an inchoate sense of disorder, a need to reinforce emerging class hierarchies and inculcate habits of work, a reproduction of a general disciplinary mode, but the result was the same.

Whether the planners of the penitentiary were influenced by earlier utopian visions, none of these historians tell us. Foucault, with a characteristic leap of imagination, conjures up the influence of two quite different after-images.[21] The first was the control over *leprosy*. The rituals of exile, banishment and exclusion, the marking and stigmatizing of the leper left behind the models for the Great Incarcerations. This was the political vision of the purified community. The second was control over the *plague*. The projects of surveillance, planning and record keeping that sorted out the contamination, confusions and fear by distributing everyone into fixed spaces and rigid compartments, left behind the models of examination, classification and discipline. This was the political vision of the disciplined society.

These two projects 'came together' (mysteriously) in the nineteenth century. The prison is a space of exclusion, but it also is a space within which people are observed, partitioned, subject to timetables and disciplines. To all historians of the prison and asylum — whether or not they accept Foucault's fanciful archaeology — here was a form of 'moral architecture' — buildings designed not as ostentatious signs of wealth and power, not as fortresses for defence, but for the 'fabrication of virtue'[22] If this was not clear enough in the prisons that were actually built, it was obvious in Bentham's fantasy of the panopticon. This was power and order in its pure utopian form — the 'simple idea' of using architecture to solve problems of morality, health, education and productivity.

Foucault's next imaginative leap, as we have seen, was to visualize 'panopticism' as a generalized principle, extended and dispersed throughout the social network. He fantasized the 'punitive city', as the utopia of the earlier judicial reformers: 'at the crossroads, in the gardens, at the side of roads being repaired or bridges built, in workshops open to all, in the depths of mines that may be visited, will be hundreds of tiny theatres of punishment.'[23] But this fantasy was never realized. Instead (again, mysteriously) came the disciplinary society, the carceral network in which power somehow 'circulated' through small-scale regional panopticons.

Again, there is no need to accept every baroque twist of Foucault's theory, to understand how the nineteenth-century city became the site for these larger visions of social order to be worked out, or to note how Bentham's vision in particular — hierarchy, surveillance, classification — carried an 'imaginary intensity which has persisted for 200 years'.[24] Other observers of the city, such as Marx and Engels, saw the problem of control in much more conventionally political terms. Following their line of thought, Hobsbawm, for example, has examined how the structure of cities might have affected the course of urban riots and insurrections, and what effect the fear of such movements might have had on urban structure.[25] The obvious questions to be asked were: How easily can the poor be mobilized, and suppressed? How vulnerable are centres of authority? Where are barracks and police stations located? What are optimal patterns of transportation? The most famous example of planning for control was, of course, the re-building of Paris and Vienna after the 1848 revolutions to take into account the needs for counter-insurgency: the wide, straight boulevards, for instance, along which artillery could fire and troops advance.

But, as Hobshawn notes, this type of planning was never a dominant policy and in many cities did not occur at all. The powerful had no interest in politicizing the problem of social order, and the Victorian city became the site for a quite different set of plans and visions. The slums emerged not just as a solution (penal colonies to which the poor, the inadequate and the wicked could be sent) but as a problem: places where wickedness was being created. Historians have described how the slums of Victorian England became 'the mental landscape within which the middle class could recognise and articulate their own anxieties about urban existence'.[26] The solutions drew on the images of public health: cesspools of human misery, sewers of vice, cleaning up, germs and infections, isolation and segregation.[27]

For Foucault, the city was not a place for other metaphors, but was to provide a powerful spatial metaphor itself. Here could be observed the new dispersed discourse of power actually spreading itself out, passing through finer and finer channels. He continually uses the spatial metaphors of 'geopolitics' to describe the dispersal of discipline: city, archipelago, maps, streets, topology, vectors, landscapes.[28]

But however we view the emerging control systems — as responses to the dangerous classes, as attempts to recreate community, as exercises in the micro-physics of power or merely as part of the rationalization of the state — they could never leave behind any utopian after-images. Quite the contrary. As Mumford eloquently shows, here, already, is the real dystopia.[29] The dark shadow of the good city is the 'collective human machine': the dehumanized routine and suppression of autonomy, first imposed by the despotic monarch and the army, is now the 'invisible machine' of the modern technocratic state. Well before Foucault (and more clearly and simply), Mumford described how the utopian ideal of total control from above and absolute obedience below had never passed out of existence, but was reassembled in a different form after kingship by divine right was defeated. He also stressed that the new machine must be seen not in terms of its visible parts but the minute, intangible assembly of science, knowledge and administration. The new invisible machine is no longer an agent for creating heaven on earth, the holy city, but itself becomes the utopia which is worshipped and enlarged indefinitely.

It was just this horror of the invisible machine which was to produce the radical destructuring movements, the romantic impulses, the anti-industrial visions of the 1960s. So invisible was the machine, that its most benign parts (therapy, social work, humanitarianism) hid its most repressive operations. Here was Illich's foreboding of industrial nemesis: divine retribution for tampering with nature. The machine had to be exposed and taken apart. But alongside this vision of alienation (too much control), there lies, as in the nineteenth century, the more powerful vision of anomie (too little control). The fear is that the machine is breaking down by itself, and that 'outside', in the chaos of urban life, in the desolate city streets abandoned to the predators, lies the ultimate horror — chaos, disorder, entropy.

But this is to run ahead of the story. We must move from metaphors of the nineteenth-century city to the visions and plans of twentieth-century crime control.

Planning for order

An archaeology of twentieth-century control ideologies would reveal the same combination of elements found in the previous century: after-images of the past, metaphors of the present and visions of the future.

The Progressive Era inherited the resonant images of cleansing and salvation. The city, like the sewers, had to be cleansed of undesirable elements. At the same time, the weak, the young, the defective and the vulnerable had to be saved, both from the city itself and from the hard edge of the control system. The Chicago School allowed for a more ambivalent vision. As Matza explains, they assumed pathology (and this eventually guided their preferred policies) but simultaneously provided evidence for diversity.[30] They drew from Simmel and their own journalistic feel for the city some sense of the urban potential for freedom and tolerance. Park (like Simmel) visualized a freedom not of identity, but of behaviour, not transcendental searching for self-hood but space to be an innovator, a deviant.

It was just this vision which was to give Goffman his only optimistic edge: the extraordinary human ability to create an identity in the cracks, the interstices of the system. And it was this vision that inspired the libertarians, labelling theorists and non-interventionists of the sixties to construct their visions of cultures of civility: areas of the city where deviance could become diversity, where people could do their thing without interference by the machine.[31]

To their radical critics, these cultures of civility were merely 'ghettoes of freedom', yet further evidence of repressive tolerance. In any event, it was the 'pathology' and not the 'diversity' of the Chicago School which was to influence social-control policy. Their dominant vision was the traditional one: deviance as the product of disorganization, a breakdown of social control, a fragmentation of the social bond. Within their complex moral geography of the city — those unforgettable concentric circles — the solution for the areas of disorganization was to restore community control.

This was solid liberal social reformism, not utopianism. To the same extent that the Chicagoans were not interested in macro-social theory, they also did not attempt to construct visions of the good society. This has remained true of all modern strands of crime-control planning. Despite the obviously moral nature of the problem of crime, only a handful of criminologists have even tried to connect their plans, policies and preferences to some over-arching moral vision.[32] There was little utopian thinking, as we saw, in the general intellectual culture, so most criminologists settled for the realistic amelioration of a bleak future. Even good intentions go wrong, so let's settle for caution, realism, scepticism and, at the extreme, even nihilism.

Only in some sectors of urban planning and architecture, did some remnants of classic utopianism stay alive. Here, in the blueprints of Frank Lloyd Wright and Le Corbusier, was a more ambitious vision of the future: the good city in the ideal society.[33] These writings are extraordinarily resonant to the student of social control. On the one hand, is the theme of the city as unnatural and immoral, the plans to remould it to resemble a village; on the other (especially in Le Corbusier) the idealized vision of machinery and mass production, the tower blocks in parks, the roads leading through parks to the Radiant City.

Le Corbusier is especially interesting. To his hostile critics, constructions like *Unite d'Habitation* exemplify perfectly the tendency for the anti-industrial motive (the return to community, the harmony of daily life and home, the cosmic harmony of man with nature) to create, paradoxically, the most artificial of environments.[34] This is very similar to the critique of ersatz community control, and Le Corbusier's admirers tell a classic tale of good intentions gone wrong. Gardiner notes that none of his cities were actually built (they got no further than drawing models); his imitators copied his outlines but not his underlying principles; his original vision never intended an epidemic of concrete towers surrounded by black asphalt and car parks.[35] Le Corbusier wanted order, but he also wanted space, easy communication, air, sunlight, grass and trees.

On the city streets, however, these visions of the good life must have looked as remote as the visions of the well-ordered asylum looked to its average inmates. From the end of the 1950s onwards, and with relentless momentum ever since, the cities became the arena for the 'crisis'. Architects and planners, urban renewers and developers, politicians and big business, capitalism itself were all to blame for the decline in the city. As metaphor and social fact, the city became identified with crime, racialism, poverty, unemployment, discrimination, violence and insecurity. The city was a mnemonic not for order, but for the separate parts of a collective cultural nightmare:

- middle-class (meaning, in the USA, largely white) exodus to the suburbs;

- outward migration of shops, offices, factories;

- a live central business district but, just beyond, a dead space: houses abandoned, store fronts boarded up;

- whole blocks decayed, taken over by freaks, junkies, drop outs, winos, derelicts of all sorts;

- the inner city as a whole occupied by minority groups, the poor, the disadvantaged, the stigmatized;

- a few remaining middle-class fortresses, their occupants dodging the muggers and predators on the streets;

- blackboard jungle schools, scenes of violence, disorder and drug abuse;

- a physical landscape devastated by vandalism, graffiti and neglect.

I am not concerned with the factual basis of this scenario. The point is that over the last few decades it became so familiar, even so banal a part of popular consciousness, that it was difficult to even think of the future in any other terms.[36] My interest here is in the kind of counter-planning this vision evoked. In Britain where, of course, the full urban-crisis scenario took longer to establish, the period leading up to the radical conservatism of the Thatcher governments saw no drastic changes in social policy. The hard end remained hard while the soft end (welfare, care, social work) increased in more or less incremental fashion. The conservatism of the late seventies sharpened this bifurcatory line and inverted its priorities: law-and-order politics became dominant and welfare resources began to be drained.

In the USA, at the beginning of the sixties, liberal social planning entered a moment of optimism not again repeated in the subsequent twenty years. The hope that the Great Society could be built stimulated that famous series of reform programmes: War on Poverty, Urban Renewal, Mobilization for Youth. In addition to their conventional liberal reform ideology, these programmes contained many of the same radical elements as their destructuring counterparts: visions of decentralization, citizen participation, self-help. And they also contained conservative, social-control elements: placating, tokenism, informing, co-option, keeping trouble-makers off the streets. Today's judgements about the balance between these various elements and about ultimate matters of 'success' and 'failure' resolve themselves into familiar lines: reforms never tried properly, good intentions gone wrong, success, but in terms of regulation.

However we resolve this debate, it is clear that the actual (or putative) failure of these programmes to deal with crime on the streets or to confront the urban-crisis scenario, allowed older visions of order to become dominant. The subsequent liberal retreat from doing good meant little opposition to this dominance. Even at the time that liberal and radical alternatives were being suggested or implemented at the periphery (the soft end), the centre remained informed by the older vision. Official policy documents, for example, routinely invoked the urban-crisis scenario: the middle class locked in fortified high-rise cells or guarded compounds; slums as areas of terror completely out of police control; armed guards patrolling all public facilities. They used this as a warning of what might happen without 'effective public action'.[37]

What 'effective public action' meant, was a depolitized version of those momentary nineteenth-century visions: reconstructing the city to meet the needs of social control. The spatial metaphors were simple and appealing: clean up the streets, the Safe Streets Acts, defensible space, residential security. This was just the move which futurists of crime control now regard as the way ahead: from older law-and-order responses directed at the individual offender, to dealing with systems, spaces, opportunities and environments. The idea was to manipulate the external environment to prevent the initial infraction. Concurrent liberal thinking could only offer programmes which were negative and abolitionist: decarceration, diversion, decreasing the intensity of intervention. Here was 'effective public action', something positive: continue with the older hard-edge policies directed at the individual offender (deterrence, incapacitation, just deserts) and, in the meantime, develop a technology of primary prevention. The attraction of preventive social control, moreover, was that at last there was the prospect of helping the potential victim.

The message became even more convincing when the safe-streets and target-hardening elements could be supplemented by invoking the rhetoric of community. For, after all, fortress living, closed-circuit television surveillance, armed guards patrolling schools, libraries and play grounds were simultaneously 'solutions' but also the very *problems* in the urban nightmares which were being constructed. The ideology of community offered something more palatable: citizen involvement in law enforcement, community policing, neighbourhood crime-prevention teams, block watches and whistle blowers.

The CPED movement (Crime Prevention Through Environmental Design) became the perfect combination of these trends. A dispassionate history of this movement remains to be written, but from its succeeding enthusiasts,[38] we can pick up its main appeal: urban environments can be designed or redesigned to reduce the opportunities for crime (or the fear of crime), but without resorting to the building of fortresses and the resulting deterioration of urban life. This is not just law enforcement and punishment and not just armed guards and big-brother surveillance, but the 'restoration' of informal social control and a way of helping ordinary citizens 'regain' control and take responsibility for their immediate environment.

Gardner sets out the three main conceptual models behind the CPED movements, all of them influenced by the dreadful realization that while the medieval fortress town has been a place of safe retreat against the external enemy, the enemy was now within the gates.[39]

1) The notion of the *urban village:* originating in the Chicago School's model of urban disorganization and breakdown, and then revised in Jane Jacobs' eloquent picture of *The Death and Life of Great American Cities* (published in 1961), the stress is on recreating the

social spaces for mutual recognition, surveillance ('the eyes on the street'), good neighbourliness, intimacy and communal responsibility. It assumes that a certain cultural homogeneity exists, or that this can be recreated.

(2) The ambivalent model of the *urban fortress:* reliance on technology, physical security and technical isolation from a hostile environment.

(3) The notion of *defensible space,* associated with the extremely influential work of Oscar Newman.[40]

It is here in the third model, that the social and the physical are combined: the ideal of the urban village comes together with the conscious planning of the physical environment in order to reduce crime and vandalism. Buildings, public-housing projects or estates and whole neighbourhoods are designed to allow for intensive monitoring and control by residents ('natural surveillance'); purely public areas are reduced or, at least, clear perceptual barriers created between communal, semi-public and private spaces; recognizable zones and hierarchies of interest are created by design and planning. The stress is on territoriality; proprietal interest and felt responsibility. More recently, Newman has extended his notion of defensible space to the wider ideal of a 'community of interests': the use of quota systems, allocations and housing subsidies to group people by common interest and life-style.

Current CPED thinking highlights one or other of these elements, combines them or tries to transcend them. But there is a common vision: territorial control, defensible space, close surveillance and, above all, the need to incorporate crime-control considerations into urban planning and design. Current evaluations of actual CPED programmes suggest only the most modest of gains in reducing crime rates.[41] But let us leave aside the question of effectiveness and concentrate on the vision.

There was undoubtedly a radical, humanistic edge to the movement. Note Newman's stress on matters of ownership, control and power; the support of local community against big-business interests, the question of the sheer unpleasantness of an environment conducive to crime. But there is a sense in which this vision of order is quite opposite to the premises of humanistic, utopian town planning. It is true that Jane Jacobs (and her predecessors) emphasized community cohesion, a sense of territory, mutual responsibility and a network of informal controls. In her often quoted words: 'the first thing to understand is that public peace . . . of cities is not kept primarily by the police . . . It is kept primarily by an intricate, almost unconscious network of voluntary controls and standards among the people themselves . . . and enforced by the people.'[42] But just because of this emphasis, humanists opposed the division of the city into specialized districts along functional lines. They argued, romantically perhaps, for diversity and tolerance, not conformity, for street activity and bustle, not just 'watching eyes'.

In practice, however, town planning — even of such humanistic utopian projects as the Garden City and the New Town — became a vision of order, a reaction to the dominant urban metaphors of disease, cancer, decaying blight, slum, apocalypse and death. As Jencks suggests, all this crisis-talk, the cancer metaphor, the 'eschatological and hysterical terms' in which urban problems were discussed, often exacerbated the deteriorating situation they were meant to cure. There was a 'metaphorical revenge', and the counter images of cleanliness and cosiness led planners to design 'salubrious and sterile' solutions, which were then condemned just as harshly.[43]

These contrasting visions — purity and order as opposed to a certain disorder and chaos — are captured in Sennet's critique of city life.[44] I will do no more than paraphrase this. The search for community, he argues, is indeed a response to real psychic needs — for relatedness, intimacy, warmth, sharing, and fraternity, the possibility of creating somewhere in the city a life different from the impersonal machine. But this need stems from the specifically adolescent search for a purified identity: an attempt to steel oneself in advance against the unknown, the pain of uncertainty. Everything can be solved by 'planning': building a self-image (and a city to match it) which filters out all threats of the unknown, and wards off any sense of dissonance.

The myth is created of the purified community. But, for Sennet, these are 'pseudo' communities, with 'counterfeit' feelings. Their only sense of relatedness comes from feeling the same, from trying to exclude the others who are different (in terms of class, race or moral status). Their intolerance of ambiguity gives an exaggerated sense of threat and disorder. All this is quite different from the 'real' urban communities of decades ago, with their variety, complexity and chaos, their tolerance of disorder. Sennet describes the aim of city planning now as the simplification of social life, a hunger for total pre-planning to prevent anything unexpected: 'the essence of the purification mechanism is a fear of losing control.'[45] This is revealed by the flight to the suburbs, away from the richness of city life to the sanitized community with its intense private family and its rigid separation of social life (home, school, shopping centre).

Sennet's own preference is for a 'new anarchism', a new kind of urban confusion and tolerance for diversity and disorder. He constructs a genuine utopian vision, precisely opposite to that of the planners, crime controllers and environmental designers. Cities should be made *more* disorderly; there should be contact without sameness; we should actually look for and create places with a high level of tension and unease; people should be made to confront each other through various forms of non-violent contact; centralized social-control bodies, pre-planning and zoning should all be removed. A chapter on 'ordinary lives in disorder' presents a blueprint of what it might be to grow up in this sort of disordered urban milieu. This would be true growing up: abandoning the adolescent need for order and embracing the chaotic structure of human experience which can only be found in the dense, uncontrollable environment of the city.

Here, and in his later related writings,[46] Sennet, of course, is working out a broader critique of American society. The thesis is that social trouble comes not from the *decline* of the family, of privacy, of the small tribal unit. The problem is the *increased* intimacy and intensity of these forms, the consequent pressure on them and the corresponding decline of a meaningful public life. For him, the good life lay somewhere in the bustling streets and cafes of Europe in another century, in the anonymity of a true public space, in a world before the cults of intimacy, sincerity, authenticity and 'destructive *Gemeinschaft'* .

This is not utopian anti-modernism, not a glance back to the same mythic past which inspired the rhetoric of community control, but it is nonetheless a glance back to the past. Once again, reality conjures up different images, and the future conjures up different after-images.

Now it is time to go back again to the real world of crime control, this time to find the overall maps on to which these visions and plans are projected.

Maps and territories

Let us go along with the standard assumption that crime, delinquency and allied social problems will continue to increase or at least stay much the same. Let us assume that no foreseeable innovations and permutations in existing control systems will radically 'solve' these problems. And let us also assume that the city, as image and reality, will be the territory where these futures will be most visible. Given these assumptions, it does not seem likely that much of the destructuring impulse will survive. That is to say, notions such as tolerating disorder, dismantling the machine and disestablishing the establishment will look even more quixotic than they do today. The response to real or perceived breakdown is to call for more regulation, order and control. Only anarchists, we are told, can be in favour of chaos. So, do more (which means more of the same) rather than less.

But how will these forms of social control be deployed in social space? At the end of [chapter 2] I described two opposed forms of deployment: the older patterns of exclusion, stigma and segregation, and the 'new' counter-ideologies of integration and absorption. This difference is captured (a little more vividly) in Levi-Strauss's binary opposition between *vomiting out and swallowing up* as modes of deviancy control:

> If we studied societies from the outside, it would be tempting to distinguish two contrasting types: those which practise cannibalism — that is, which regard the absorption of certain individuals possessing dangerous powers as the only means of neutralising those powers and even of turning them to advantage — and those which, like our own society, adopt what might be called the practice of *anthropemy* (from the Greek *emein,* to vomit); faced with the same problem the latter type of society has chosen the opposite solution, which consists of ejecting dangerous individuals from the social body and keeping them temporaily or permanently in isolation, away from all contact with their fellows, in establishments especially intended for this purpose.[47]

Let me convert this physiological metaphor into a spatial one. The vomiting-out mode stands for the possibility of separation, segregation, isolation, banishment, confinement. I will call this simply *exclusion:* temporarily or permanently, deviants are driven beyond social boundaries or separated out into their own designated spaces. The swallowing-up mode stands for the possibility of incorporation, integration or assimilation. This is *inclusion:* deviants are retained, as long as possible within conventional social boundaries and institutions, there to be absorbed. Modes of coping with unruliness in the classroom may serve as a crude illustration of these alternatives. Exclusion leads to measures such as expulsion; separate classes, schools, or units for designated troublemakers; special diagnostic labels such as 'hyperactivity' with treatments such as drugs. Inclusion leads to measures such as unobstructive techniques of assuring internal obedience; preventive conditioning by systems of reward and punishment aimed at all; deliberate extension of the boundaries of tolerance.

These are not, of course, total and exclusive alternatives and, anthropologists notwithstanding, whole cultures cannot easily be divided into inclusionary and exclusionary types. Most societies employ both modes of control, constantly oscillating between one and the other. Moreover, as I have consistently shown, reforms motivated by the inclusionary impulse often end up being exclusionary. This might happen when the decision about *whom* to include calls for an act of formal classification, which then immediately results in another form of separation. It is also by no means obvious that exclusion must be the more intensive and less tolerant mode. We might separate a group only to ignore it completely, while inclusion might entail massive efforts to achieve normative or psychic change. These are some of the social policy dilemmas which I raise in the [next chapter]. Here I want to project these abstractions onto a recognizable map of the future city.

The map is not the territory any more than the menu is the meal. But we need these maps for visualizing, knowing and planning. The elaborate classifications which early prison managers constructed within their institutions were 'atlases of 'vice', cities of the wicked in which every type of depravity was carefully separated out. At the end of the nineteenth century, phrenologists constructed maps of the head, plotting actual areas of good and evil.[48] Their social-reform counterparts were preoccupied with streets and sewers, plotting out like Mayhew, the domains and contours of poverty, despair and pathology. The Chicago School produced those famous moral maps of the city: concentric zones on to which grids of crime, delinquency, suicide and other forms of social disorganization were projected. Ecological analysis continued in criminology, and today's urban geographers, town planners and statisticians are all too busy with their maps of target areas, defensible spaces, high-crime zones, robbery-trip routes and spatial patterns of offenders. And in everyday perception and journalistic cliché, we give moral meanings to the territories of slum, downtown, safe streets, public park, suburb. This is how the word 'ghetto' is used. (It shows how language changes — nowhere in the modern world have there been ghettos of the type in which European Jews were forced to live.)

All these linguistic and metaphorical exercises share the common positivist obsession to differentiate and classify. This master impulse is obviously more compatible with the exclusionary mode, but let us see how these alternative spatial metaphors might work themselves out in the city.

Inclusion

Foucault's 'punitive city' contained one part of the inclusive vision: social control was not concentrated and centralized, but dispersed throughout the social body. But in another way, this was not inclusion at all. The punishments were to take place in

486

visible, open 'theatres' and therefore (presumably) would have been obtrusive and stigmatizing. In the control system actually created there was also 'dispersal' — but this was in the shadow of the great exclusionary institution of the prison and, moreover, each form of dispersal was simultaneously a way of classifying people, placing them into separate spaces.

A much more genuine, radical and 'purer' vision of inclusion lay behind the destructuring movements of the sixties. Every one of the messages was directed against exclusion and (if only by implication) in favour of inclusion: formal structures should be made less formal; central systems should be decentralized or dispersed; the professional power to exclude should be weakened; segregation in closed institutions should give way to integration in the open community; the visible and the stigmatizing should be rendered invisible and normal; the master institutions should not exclude their deviants but absorb them; the boundaries of control should blur or disappear into their surrounding space.

Forget, for the moment, the empirical results of the reforms inspired by the inclusionary message. This chapter deals with visions, not reality. We have to try to imagine, rather, how exactly the new inclusionary social order would deal with its deviants. Families, schools, work-places, neighbourhood blocks: would these all become 'tiny theatres' of social control, unobtrusively processing their 'own' deviants? Would formal agencies still remain, taking on a more limited role with more serious offenders, but in an 'inclusive' way?

Let us imagine the latter possibility in the city. Streets, blocks and neighbourhoods are not bounded institutions like families, schools or factories: a solution is needed to the problem of control without exclusion. We already know what such solutions look like: discreet surveillance, data banks, crime prevention through environmental design, community policing, secret agents, informers and decoys, defensible space. These systems constitute 'social control' primarily in the sense of observation, opportunity reduction, primary prevention and detection. Unless the system is totally successful, matters of adjudication, punishment and deployment still remain. And it was of course *total* success which the behaviourist utopias promised. The current system of preventive control reassembles much of the panopticon vision: visibility (you know about the TV screens and data banks); unverifiability (you do not know when you are being watched or checked); anonymity (it does not matter who is operating the system — it could be a computer); and the absence of force (you should want to be good).

But despite these facile similarities, it is quite obvious that nothing like this vision of total 'inclusive' surveillance has been assembled or even envisaged, nor is it likely to be. What is striking, though, is that the radical, 'humanist' edge of the inclusionary movement offered no alternative to these forms of control through surveillance. Again, what would inclusionary, integrative, or absorbing families, schools, neighbourhood or factories actually look like? It was, in fact, assumed from all sides that the preventive system would not and could not be a total success. The problem of what to do with the individual offender still remained.

Here, the solutions of the community-control movement were little more than permutations of the traditional model of probation: counselling, service, treatment, reporting, observation — but trying to be more unobtrusive and invisible (as with the boy by the lake) and to blur the boundaries of control. Tracking, befriending, shadowing and even house arrest are just more imaginative variants of the same model.

The genuine futurists of crime control went only a little further. A widely quoted plan for 'restraint in the community', for example, would put on one side 'suspendees' (those threatened with a sentence, but otherwise ignored) and on the other, 'isolates' (the serious offenders who are humanely segregated).[49] This leaves 'restrainees': each is assigned to his own private field officer who has the sole function of reporting to the police when the restrainee is observed committing an offence. The restrainer has no direct contact with his target, indeed the restrainee does not even know his identity. This random element is close to the panopticon principle: the restrainee will always be in a state of uncertainty, not knowing what risks he runs. He is allowed to live freely, but if convicted of a new offence, then the next level of punishment will be unequivocally imposed.

Invisible community restraint could also be achieved — more cheaply and effectively, its proponents maintain — by the more sophisticated method of 'technological incapacitation'. The use of radio telemetry devices (externally worn or implanted and linked to a location-monitoring system which would limit the offender to designated areas) has been explicitly justified on inclusionary grounds. The offender's normal productive activity would not be inhibited (he goes to school, works, supports his family, pays taxes). There is no visible or identifiable stigma. The punishment is not permanent or disabling and there is no segregation, isolation or special institutions. Here is a newspaper account of a somewhat primitive version of the technology:

Bleeper Could Cut Jail Numbers

An association has been set up in Britain to study the possibility of giving some criminals an alternative to jail by fitting them with an electronic device that emits a regular signal and enables their movements to be tracked by computer.

The Offender's Tag Association, launched by Mr Tom Stacey, a publisher and prison visitor, has the backing of Mr Carl den Brinker, the technical director of a leading electronics company, and the Rev Peter Timms, a former governor of Maidstone Prison.

A similar idea, which may be launched this week as a pilot scheme in Albuquerque, New Mexico, has caused controversy among lawyers and penal reformers in the United States.

Supporters say it would ease prison over-crowding, but opponents have declared that it will bring 1984 to Albuquerque a year early.

Mr Stacey said last week that there were important differences between his idea and the American version, which plans to make lesser offenders serve their time under a form of 'house arrest'.

He favours a scheme which would alert the authorities whenever an offender leaves a specified area. The signal would then be received in another zone.

Offenders would wear a 'bracelet' containing a tiny transmitter, giving out an inaudible electronically coded signal to provide an instant 'fix' on his whereabouts.

Mr Stacey believes that such a system would enable less serious offenders to continue living in the community, while meeting society's legitimate demands for protection.

He said that the system would have to be run by the police. Other members of the association, however, said it could be under the control of the probation service.

The idea has become technically feasible since the Government gave the go-ahead for the construction of a national network of cellular radio. A feasibility study carried out at Kent University showed that although technically possible, such a scheme would be prohibitively expensive.

A single channel allocated nationally on the cellular radio waveband would enable a theoretical maximum of 500 offenders to be monitored in each 'cell,' which covers a one-mile radius.

Four mini-computers would suffice for the whole of London, and in the early stages each offender's transmitter would cost between £700 and £1,000.

According to Mr Stacey, the idea could 'revolutionise the treatment of a large swathe of offenders in urban areas.' He added 'The advantages for the prison system are that it would reduce decisively the pressure on prison space and also on attitudes throughout the penal system.

In the United States Judge Jack Love has made himself a guinea pig for a similar idea by wearing an 'electronic leash' for the past three weeks.

A steel fetter that contains a miniaturised radio transmitter is riveted around his right ankle. Every 90 seconds it beeps a tell-tale report on the judge's whereabouts to a police computer in Albuquerque.

The judge is wearing the 5 oz gadget wherever he goes — in court, in his car, in the shower, in bed. It fits over his sock and his high western boot. 'Most time I just don't know it's there,' he said last week.

Starting this week, if the New Mexico Supreme Court approves, Judge Low will begin a 90-day pilot programme with up to 25 offenders on probation. Their movements would be monitored by the so-called 'snoop bracelet.'

The bracelet is riveted on by four steel bolts. But couldn't a wearer remove it with ease? 'Sure', said Judge Love. 'But the whole psychology of it is that he won't want to. This is the liberty card keeping him out of jail. The people who wear it, drunk drivers and so on, are going to be the people most frightened of going to jail.[50]

Leaving entirely aside questions about technical feasibility or moral desirability, note that such solutions are directed at an extremely limited part of the inclusionary vision: 'keeping people out of jail'. Even here, although the offender is neither banished nor as visibly stigmatized as a leper, he is surely every bit as classified as the actual or potential plague victim. In fact, systems such as Intensive Intermediate Treatment could come from Defoe's image of the 'plague city'[51]: regular reports to the supervising social worker, attendance for debriefing/decontamination sessions at the centre (for cognitive retraining, behaviour modification, improving self-concept), presence at an attendance centre to avoid sites of infection and contagion like the Saturday afternoon football game, night restriction or curfews, tracking for the rest of the time.

But however strange the after-images of some of its individual results, the point is that the inclusionary vision has never really been assembled as a whole. And, given its component parts (Gemeinschaft iconography, environmental design, restraint in the community), this is hardly a simple project. Even the most imaginative of science-fiction writers have not contemplated anything like it.[52]

To assemble the version of inclusion which emerged from the community-control movement, I will take the strategies and agencies described in [chapter 2], and project them only slightly into the future. (Outsiders to this world might need reminding that these are all real programmes.) This would be the composite picture:

> Mr and Mrs Citizen, their son Joe and daughter Linda, leave their suburban home after breakfast, saying goodbye to Ron, a 15-year-old pre-delinquent who is living with them under the LAK (Look After a Kid) scheme. Ron will later take a bus downtown to the Community Correctional Centre, where he is to be given two hours of Vocational Guidance and later tested on the Interpersonal Maturity Level scale. Mr C. drops Joe off at the School Problems Evaluation Centre from where Joe will walk to school. In his class are five children who are bussed from a local Community Home, four from a Pre-Release Facility and three who, like Ron, live with families in the neighbourhood. Linda gets off next — at the GUIDE Centre (Girls Unit for Intensive Daytime Education) where she works as a Behavioural Contract Mediator. They drive past a Threequarter-way House, a Rape-Crisis Centre and then a Drug-Addict Cottage, where Mrs C. waves to a group of boys working in the garden. She knows them from some volunteer work she does in RODEO (Reduction of Delinquency Through Expansion of Opportunities). She gets off at a building which houses the Special Parole Unit, where she is in charge of a 5-year evaluation research project on the use of the HIM (Hill Interaction Matrix) in matching group treatment to client. Mr C. finally arrives at work, but will spend his lunch hour driving around the car again as this is his duty week on patrol with TIPS (Turn in a Pusher). On the way he picks up some camping equipment for the ACTION weekend hike

(Accepting Challenge Through Interaction with Others and Nature) on
which he is going with Ron, Linda and five other PINS (Persons In Need
of Supervision) . . .

Clearly, a lot of inclusionary *work* is going on here, and perhaps the anthropologist would see this as 'swallowing up'.

Exclusion

Compared with the inclusionary mode — which appeared so prominently in recent progressive social-control talk — the exclusionary mode yields by far the more integrated set of plans and visions. It is undoubtedly easier to understand, it has a firmer historical and institutional base and it is psychologically more resonant and satisfying.

The final 'exclusion' of the death penalty aside, this mode of control was represented in pre-modern societies by such sanctions as banishment and physical stigmatization. Banishment offered total removal of the deviant while those sanctions which marked the offender permanently — branding on the forehead, cutting off thieves' hands or liars' tongues — were self-confirming forms of separation. These people could never be absorbed and could survive only by marginal activities. Whole sections of early cities contained these deviants, bound together by their stigma.

There is no need to chronicle here again the transition to the modes of exclusionary control so characteristic of the industrial age: the route through transportation and penal servitude, the retention of capital punishment and then the prison and the whole apparatus of modern corrections. The impulse to classify, separate, segregate and exclude constitutes the very heart of the system. But even if we step outside the formal apparatus — into the wider space of the city — the exclusionary ideal has retained its traditional resonance.

The resulting map, however, would yield neither the punitive city, nor the disciplinary society's invisible micro-systems of power, nor its contemporary equivalent, the 'integrated community-control continuum' in which the Citizen family were so busy. Instead, there would be the purified city — a landscape rigidly and visibly divided not in terms of its physical characteristics (rivers, bridges, streets) or social uses (shops, homes, schools, offices) but its moral attributes. There would be an exact geographical form to match degree of attributed stigma with intensity of social control.

When the Chicago School drew their maps, they implied a 'natural' patterning of social disorganization and consequent deviance, a shake up or drift inherent in the growth of the city which would produce that form. Later students of urban life, politics, and planning saw this process in more political terms: not natural ecological growth, but planned political outcomes. Starting not with problems of social control, but questions about race relations, social class, power or the fiscal crises, this literature contained powerful exclusionary images. There is the notion, for example, of the city as 'internal colony' exploited by centres of power elsewhere and descended on by suburbanites for work, entertainment and essential services. Let me list a few other of the images more relevant to the control question.

Sternlieb gives us 'the city as sandbox'.[53] The inner-city fears not exploitation (as in the colonial model) but indifference and abandonment. The city loses its jobs, its other economic functions, its role as a staging point for new immigrants, and becomes like a sandbox in which adults park their troublesome children. There the children can play, more or less undisturbed in their own territory. Government programmes — social, educational, welfare and health agencies — take the form of toys thrown to children. These have the symbolic functions of placebos — ways of placating the inhabitants (the poor, the racial minorities) who are left to play as the jobs, professions and services drift away to the suburbs.

Long gives us 'the city as reservation'.[54] The old inner cities, sites now of unemployment and underemployment, poor public services, chaotic and ineffective schools, justify their existence by finding a new role 'as an Indian reservation for the poor, the deviant, the unwanted and for those who make a business or career of managing them for the rest of society'. The choice for urban politicians is between accepting this model of the Indian reservation of inmates and keepers, economically dependent on transfer payments from the outside society in return for custodial services, or moving towards 'colonial emancipation', self-help and the development of a viable local economy. Organized central interests, as well as those of the local bureaucrats, keepers, professionals and the natives themselves, will be inclined to perpetuate the reservation model.

Then Hill, after reconsidering these visions created at the beginning of the seventies, gives us the 'pariah city'.[55] The political economies of the ageing central cities, he argues, already contain elements of the sandbox and the reservation: they are places for the economically disenfranchised labour force; many traditional jobs are absorbed by low-paid workers in and from the Third World; government funds (food stamps, housing, security and health payments) subsidize professional keepers or local slum landlords and merchants; containment and care becoming lucrative private businesses; a growing municipal bureaucracy is sustained by the plight of the poor; despair and apathy are rife. Hill questions some of this imagery. For him, the pariah city is not exactly an isolated reservation in the desert but the core of a complex system of economic institutions, mass media, transportation and politics. Even if the city stagnates, this nerve centre remains. The dominant tendency, he argues, is the state capitalist city, with its corporate management, technology and efficient capital accumulation.

But whatever the theoretical questionings,[56] the dominant image remains: the move to the suburbs; the old urban centres deserted and left to the socially marginal; a high degree of separation and exclusion within the city. All this sounds familiar to critics of decarceration. This is precisely their scenario for 'community care and treatment': decayed zones of the inner city inhabited by the old, confused and ill dumped from their institutions and 'left to rot in broken-down welfare hotels or exploited in private nursing homes; psychotics wandering the streets 'locked in or locked out' of dilapidated boarding houses, barely able to cash their welfare checks, the prey of street criminals and a source of nuisance and alarm to local residents too poor to leave; an increasing ecological separation into 'deviant ghettos', 'sewers of human misery', garbage dumps for 'social junk' lost in the interstices of the city.[57]

492

All this might be termed exclusion through 'zones of neglect'. Our map would also have to show certain 'free zones' in which various forms of deviance or illegality (notably, the classic 'crimes without victims' — gambling, prostitution, drugs, pornography) would be tolerated or conveniently overlooked. This might be exclusion in the name of a vague liberal tolerance or, as Sykes suggests, the deliberate creation of 'combat zones' which can be kept under surveillance, thus allowing some degree of control over what cannot be entirely suppressed.[58] The standard model is the legal segregation of strip bars, X-movies, massage parlours and so on.

It is difficult to conceive of hermetic separation and exclusion, if only for the simple reason that the physical and the social do not coincide (even to the extent that they might have done in those maps of the Victorian city). And cultural or political differences will produce patterns unlike that of the central sandbox, reservation or pariah inner city. In Britain, for example, it has long been noted that the apparently 'clean' housing estate beyond the green belt and away from the inner-city slum may be the dumping ground for problem families and a source of crime. Or urban renewal may leave uneven pockets of poverty dotted throughout the city. Particular estates or high-rise blocks may become segregated versions of what their utopian planners might originally have visualized as forms of inclusion.

In addition, changes might occur through patterns of class struggle and accommodation.[59] Unlike in the medieval city, with its clear hierarchies, the poor might not accept what is being done for them (though a typical reaction — vandalizing and devastating their surroundings — might only increase their segregation). And the planners, lacking the homogeneous vision of their autocratic Victorian class, might be open to ideas other than continual segregation. Still, even in Britain, where the reservation scenario has not been established, radical visionaries see separation:

> a distinct compartmentalization of the city, area by area. There is a hostile city centre, defended like a medieval keep by an urban motorway either looking like a moat, or fearsome battlements — the inhabitants gone. The horrific vision of a city forsaken by any life, with traffic circulating unendingly round its ring road . . . Surrounding this there are a series of enclosed camps, hemmed in by the arteries which once gave them life. People only enter and leave by controlled exit points to go to work . . . Then a further series of scattered encampments cluster the outer ring road, in the same state of isolation: workers commute to the city centre from outer suburbs, others travel out to the ring road factories. They never meet.[60]

If such radical criticism (and popular consciousness) tend towards exclusionary images of the city, this is even more apparent in science fiction. The overwhelming sense from these visions is a total separation and enclosure.[61] The forces of chaos, darkness and entropy — represented by crime, pollution, traffic congestion, or overpopulation — move inexorably closer and they have to be contained by barriers and enclosures. In one vision, the city regains its medieval role as fortress: the white middle classes occupy enclaves and sanctuaries in the inner city, undesirables and racial minorities are banished to reservations beyond the border. In the opposite vision — more dominant and corresponding more closely to what urban sociologists claim is already happening — the reservations are in the inner city and the white, the middle classes or the powerful have fled to sanitized suburbs beyond the city boundaries.

Writers like Barry Malzberg and Robert Silverberg have, obsessively, produced permutations on these themes. Malzberg describes a Manhattan totally populated by a violent, malevolent and degraded class, the 'lumpen': one-tenth are there by choice, the rest as a penalty, or a result of idiocy, incompetence or a relationship with someone in these categories. Everyone else is 'outside'.[62] In Silverberg's 'Black is Beautiful', Blacks occupy a domed inner city and whites are commuters or come as tourists on helicopter buses to see how Blacks are managing their affairs.[63] It is like a city with an invisible wall. Silverberg and many others have also worked out a vision of lateral rather than horizontal separation. In *The World Inside,* people live in Urban Monads ('Urbmons'), thousand-floor buildings stratified into cities of different levels of status and intellectual ability.[64]

There is no shortage, then, of general visions of exclusion which correspond to dominant patterns of crime control. This correspondence might already be happening in movements such as CPED and defensible space. As Newman himself warned 10 years ago, the 'neat and workable' solution of letting urban core areas deteriorate, then putting a fence of police around them is 'done, though not talked about'. It might 'just happen' and become institutionalized. 'Remember that if all of us here are looking for solutions to crime problems, then this is one of the neatest simplest, most effective — even though it is morally unacceptable — ways. There is a real danger that we will fall into the trap of accepting it when things become desperate.'[65]

Conclusion: domains of control

I have given but a sample of the images and visions yielded by those two contrasting modes of control. First, there is *inclusion,* with its metaphors of penetration, integration and absorption, its apparatus of bleepers, screens and trackers, its utopia of the invisibly controlling city. Then there is *exclusion,* with its metaphors of banishment, isolation and separation, its apparatus of walls, reservations and barriers, its utopia of the visibly purified city.

As I will show in the [next chapter], these images point to very real policy choices. But when put into practice, the contrasts cannot always be sustained. The two visions merge, with exclusion tending to dominate. Thus, the creation of forms of control informed by the inclusionary vision — those 'wider and different nets' — leads to new modes of separation. At the heart of the inclusive system administered by Mr and Mrs Citizen were tests, diagnostic devices, screening systems, labels and categories. Inclusionary principles such as tolerance and non-intervention can also find their expression in the rigid ecological separation of deviants. And the decentralization impulse — an attack on the exclusionary powers of professionals, bureaucracies and the central state itself — might result in repressively localistic, parochial and xenophobic institutions.[66] Starved of resources — because the shut-off valve on what flows into the neighbourhood or school is somewhere else — these institutions deteriorate and become themselves controlled through exclusion.

To understand these apparent paradoxes or unintended consequences, we must return to the same deposits of power discussed earlier. In particular, those questions about community and state become important — and both inclusion and exclusion reveal similar contradictions. Let me give some examples.

(1) The trouble with inclusion is that it is only utopian when it is explicitly anti-statist. Inclusion, self-help and community are all inconsistent — as the anarchist tradition correctly shows — with state regulation and ownership. Thus, when the principle of inclusion is taken over by the state, the result looks appalling — the perfectly functioning totalitarian society. If the inclusive community apart from the state looks like pure utopia, the inclusive state is pure dystopia.

(2) This is complicated by the question of ownership — the 'commodification of space' as Marx saw it. The public exclusionary mode (deportation, imprisonment) is very different from the private exclusionary mode. To the extent that state intervention is being replaced by market mechanisms, new forms of private exclusion develop ('privatization'). With erosion of support for public institutions (school, welfare, police) and a decline of public services (whether garbage collection or health), the private sector not only offers replacement services (like private security) but 'commodifies' its own space. The pure market allows for increasing ecological separation based on lifestyles, age, special needs, degrees of deviance: buildings blocks, neighbourhoods, even whole 'villages' (like Century City) which resemble medieval gated towns.

(3) To borrow Marxist terminology again, there is the 'fetishization of space'. Ever since the nineteenth-century ideal of moral architecture, reformers have exaggerated the extent to which social problems can be solved merely by reordering physical space. This is true whether the visions are inclusionary or exclusionary: the culture of diversity or the pariah city. This is to by-pass the central debate in urban sociology: the city as ecological, a system in itself, versus the city as political, merely a site for practices worked out elsewhere. These are the terms in which movements like neighbourhood justice or CPED need to be analysed.

(4) Then a final example of a paradox inherent in the inclusionary vision — a structural paradox which is not just a question of faulty implementation. When matters such as boundary blurring, integration and community control take place, the result is that more people get involved in the 'control problem'. In order to weaken, by-pass or replace the formal apparatus, more rather than less attention has to be given to the deviance question. In order to include rather than exclude, a set of judgements have to be made which 'normalizes' intervention in a greater range of human life. The result

is not just more controllers (whether professionals or ordinary citizens) but also an extension of these methods to wider and wider populations. The price paid by ordinary people is to become either active participants or passive receivers in the business of social control.

It is difficult to know just how far this process of indefinite 'inclusion' might go. The type of theoretical problems I listed and (more important) all sorts of 'external' contingencies — political, economic, demographic — make any predictions extremely hazardous. But, as a conclusion to this chapter, let me try.

If we superimpose the newer 'inclusionary' controls onto the more traditional forms of exclusion (notably incarceration) and their counterparts in the city (reservations, sandboxes, or whatever), we arrive at the likeliest future of social control. It is a future of decisive and deepening bifurcation: on the soft side there is indefinite inclusion, on the hard side, rigid exclusion.

By 'soft', I mean mental health, the new growth therapies, middle-class 'thought crime', the tutelage of family life, the minor delinquent infractions. Here, inclusive control will be extended in two ways:

(1) there is the enterprise of inner space: new therapies, professions, specialities, movements and cults will continue to expand, taking in the unreached, the healthy neurotic, the potentially deviant and the ordinary citizen. More domains of inner life will be penetrated in the same way as stages of the biological lifespan have been medicalized (life from birth to death as a series of risk periods, each calling for professional observation, check–ups, tutelage, supervision and intervention) or psychologized (by being turned into a series of growth periods, life crises, identity transitions or 'passages').[67] The aim is to discourage anything from being casual — leisure, family, child rearing, sexuality. The cults of efficiency and happiness will offer themselves everywhere: posture, reflexes, orgasm, diet, breathing, dreams, relationships, psychic plumbing, child rearing. The end-point of this 'triumph of the therapeutic' is a 'colonization of the subjective' and a gradual coalescence of the therapeutic with mass culture itself.[68]

(2) Then there is the enterprise of social space. There will be an extension of those types of inclusionary work in which the Citizen family were involved: dispersed, invisible, integrative, and relatively non-stigmatizing. Schools, families, neighbourhoods, youth organizations and work-places will increasingly be exploited as sites for this type of control. More importantly, this sort of enterprise will become diagnostic, predictive and preventive. Urban environments and situations will become sites for behaviour control.

These later forms of intervention (CPED, target hardening, innovations in surveillance techniques, proactive policing) will of course, be more directed at hard rather than soft forms of deviance. But, at the hard end, exclusionary methods will continue to dominate. For one thing, it is virtually impossible even to visualize a society in which the invasion of subjective space and the preventive surveillance of social space can be so total and successful as to prevent all deviance. At their purest, these forms of inclusion work because they are voluntary or simply because they are not recognized to be social control. But they require a back-up sanction: if you do not take the initiative yourself or if we do not spot you in advance, this is what might happen to you.[69]

There are other far more important functions to exclusionary control, however, than this purely instrumental back up. The bifurcatory principle itself — which, in the absence of evidence to the contrary I take to be a cultural universal — demands sorting out, separation and segregation. It is obvious that the inclusionary mode neither fulfils these symbolic functions nor answers the instrumental demand for a solution to hard-end crime.

At the symbolic level, social control must fulfil the functions of creating scapegoats, clarifying moral boundaries and reinforcing social solidarity. The primeval form of scapegoating directs aggression towards individuals not responsible for the group's frustration (which may be caused by external threat or internal discord). In the ancient Hebraic ritual, the high priest puts his hand on the goat, confesses injustices and sins, then the animal is driven out into the wilderness. This is to leave people feeling purified and solidified. These functions remain when societies move towards putting blame not on the community or its arbitrary 'representative' but on certain individuals who are then *properly* caused to suffer.

It is quite clear that neither the psychological functions of scapegoating (cleansing, reminding the righteous of their purity),[70] nor the classic social functions described by Durkheim (boundary maintenance, rule clarification, social solidarity) can be served by inclusionary control. Indeed, by not developing an alternative conception of stigma, by trying to abolish or downgrade all elements of ceremonial status degradation,[71] and by persisting in labelling-theory's touching faith that deviants are not, after all, very different from non-deviants, inclusionary controls are ill-equipped to foster social integration. The rituals of blaming are difficult to sustain: they lose their moral edge. Exclusionary control is symbolically much richer: stigma and status degradation are sharper, deviants are clearly seen as different from non-deviants and, above all, there is the promise that they will be vaporized, thrown down the chute or filed away, and not just keep coming back to be 'reintegrated'.

The purely instrumental, rather than symbolic, advantages of exclusion are even more obvious. Inclusion simply does not offer any solution to 'crime on the streets'. It is increasingly likely that bifurcatory separation will take more and more rigid forms and that those selected for the hard end — career criminals, dangerous offenders, recidivists, psychopaths, incorrigibles or whatever — will be subject to more and more punitive forms of exclusion. The rigid application of just deserts, long sentences in tougher prisons, selective incapacitation and a greater use of the death penalty, can be expected. We have noted the predictions: most projected economic, political and technological changes will lead to an increase in serious crimes to which society is vulnerable and a political ideology which will insist on a rigid bifurcatory and punitive agenda in order to command legitimacy.

In symbolic and instrumental terms, then, we can expect a future trade-off. As payment for voluntarily submitting to psychic help, for cooperating in all sorts of inclusionary projects and for tolerating a certain amount of inconvenience, the ordinary citizen will want to be reassured that the state means business. If I buy all the self-help books, become the foster parent of a troublesome child, spend my evenings patrolling my block, tolerate the crazy old ladies mumbling on the buses and let myself be frisked at airports, then I want to be sure that the exclusionary lines are properly and firmly drawn.

Leaving aside crime control in the formal sense, exclusion also fits better the realities, images, desired states and projected futures of the city. The utopian vision has always been homogeneity, conformity, stratification and separation. The point of exclusion is to create purified domains inhabited by just the right groups: not too old and not too young, not too blemished or disabled, not troublesome or noisy, not too poor, not with the wrong-coloured skin. This was the vision which Sennet criticized: unable to face up to diversity, the city tries to purge any form of unpleasantness. The 'innocent' scapegoat, the justly punished offender, the members of high-risk groups are all candidates for exclusion.

So, we arrive at a vision not too far from Orwell's. Middle-class thought crime is subject to inclusionary controls; when these fail and the party members present a political threat, then 'down the chute'. Working-class deviant behaviour is segregated away and contained; if the proles become threatening, they can be 'subjected like animals by a few simple rules'.

There is another resonant set of control images from twentieth-century fiction. This is Burroughs' vision of the soft machine, with its refined techniques of inclusionary control, blurring imperceptibly into the terrifying finality of the hard machine. There are pushers, agents, informers and charlatan doctors; there are the reconditioning centres, and the methods of autonomic obedience processing; there is Dr Shafer, the Lobotomy Kid, trying to produce the Complete All American De-Anxietized Man. All these agencies are *senders* (a key word for Burroughs). They are sending messages and this, in cybernetic terms, is the meaning of social control: 'nothing but the sending of messages which effectively change the behaviour of the recipients'.[72]

This type of language is important. It removes from 'control' its everyday connotations — dominate, manipulate, use as an instrument, impose one's will, govern another's movements — and allows the word to be used as if it were 'value free'. As Skinner explains: 'what is needed is more "intentional" control, not less, and this is an important engineering problem.'[73]

There is never the fear of too much control, but of too much chaos. If we feel we are losing control, we must try to take control. The senders start feedback loops which can never end; like drug addicts, they satisfy needs only to stimulate them further. Thus, 'control can never work . . . it can never be a means to anything but more control . . . like junk.'[74]

Notes

1. One of the few social-problems texts that examines the role of belief systems in justifying intervention is Richard Henshel, *Reacting to Social Problems*, (Ontario: Longman Canada, 1976).

2. Krishan Kumar, *Prophecy and Progress: The Sociology of Industrial and Post Industrial Society*, (Harmondsworth Penguin, 1978), p. 14.

3. On the themes of optimism and pessimism in sociology, see more generally, Lewis Killian, 'Optimism and Pessimism in Sociological Analysis', *American Sociologist*, V (1971), pp. 281-6.

4. For a guide to this literature and that of post-industrialism, see again Kumar, 'Prophecy and Progress'. The enjoyable standard criticism of the 'sunshine boys' of sociology, was Dusky Lee Smith, 'The Sunshine Boys: Toward a Sociology of Happiness, *The Activist*, 14 (Spring 1964), pp. 166-77.

5. Gresham Sykes, *The Future of Crime*, (National Institute of Mental Health. Washington DC: US Government Printing Office, 1980).

6. There is, however, one variable — changing age-structure — which could reduce the level of crime. For some years, American criminologists have predicted that with ageing of the baby-boom cohort, crime rates would decline. For the past three years, this has already been happening and is likely to continue for at least the next decade, the usual 'other things being equal'.

7. Sykes, *The Future of Crime*, p. 7.

8. Leslie T. Wilkins, 'Crime in the World of 1990', *Futures*, (September 1970), pp. 203-14 and 'Crime and Criminal Justice at the Turn of the Century', *Annals*, 208 (July 1973), pp. 13-20.

9. Stanley Cohen, 'Western Crime Control Models in the Third World: Benign or Malignant?', in S. Spitzer and R. Simon (eds), *Research in Law, Deviance and Social Control*, (Connecticut: JAI Press, 1982), vol. 4.

10. James Q Wilson, *Thinking About Crime*, (New York: Random House, 1975), pp. 222-3.

11. Most notably in the Manuels' massive recent volume: Frank G. and Fritzie P. Manuel, *Utopian Thought in the Western World*, (Oxford: Basil Blackwell, 1979).

12. See, for example, Mark R. Hillegas, *The Future as Nightmare: H. G. Wells and the Anti Utopians*, (New York: Oxford University Press, 1967); Fred Polak, *The Image of Future*, (Amsterdam; Elsevier, 1973), Chad Walsh, *From Utopias to Nightmare*, (New York: Harper and Row, 1962). For some interesting general comparisons between utopian and science fiction forms see Raymond Williams, 'Utopia and science fiction', in P. Parrinder (ed.), *Science Fiction: A Critical Guide*, (London: Longman, 1979). I use 'utopia' and 'dystopia' throughout this chapter in the rather loose and non-technical sense of visions of good places and bad places.

13. The uninitiated might try the following anthologies: Hans Santesson (ed.), *Crime Prevention in the Thirtieth Century*, (New York: Walker Publishing Co., 1969) and Joseph D. Olander and Martin Harry Greenberg (eds), *Criminal Justice Through Science Fiction*, (New York: New Viewpoints, 1977). Major science-fiction writers who have given explicit attention to deviance and social control include Theodore Sturgeon, Robert Silverberg, Alfred Bester, John Brunner and Ray Bradbury. Outside the genre, Antony Burgess's *A Clockwork Orange* is probably the best known. My subsequent examples all appear in these sources.

14. First published in 1962 and reprinted in *The Best of Robert Silverberg*, (London: Futura Publications, 1978). This collection also contains *Hawksbill Station*.

15. For these, and quite opposite, views on Skinner's utopia see Harvey Wheeler (ed.), *Beyond The Punitive Society*, (London: Wildwood House, 1973).

16. I have drawn, in this section, upon Richard Sennett's useful collection *Classical Essays on the Culture of Cities*, (New Jersey: Prentice Hall, 1969).

17. Jonathan Miller, 'Introduction to Metaphoropolis', *Architectural Design*, 38 (December 1968), p. 570. See also in same issue, D. P. Walker, 'Poneropolis', pp. 581-96.

18. Francis Yates, 'Architecture and the Art of Memory', *Architectural Design*, 38 (December 1968), pp. 573-8.

19. Lewis Mumford, 'Utopia, the City and the Machine', in Frank F. Manuel (ed.), *Utopias and Utopian Thought*, (London: Souvenir Press, 1973), p. 151.

20. *Ibid.*, p. 9.

21. Michel Foucault, *Discipline and Punish: The Birth of the Prison*, (London: Allen Lane, 1977), pp. 195-200.

22. Robin Evans, *The Fabrication of Virtue: English Prison Architecture, 1750-1840*, (Cambridge: Cambridge University Press, 1982).

23. Foucault, *Discipline and Punish*, p. 113.

24. *Ibid.*, p. 205.

25. Eric Hobsbawn, 'Cities and Insurrections', *Architectural Design*, 38 (December 1968), pp. 579-88.

26. Gareth Stedman–Jones, *Outcast London*, (London: Oxford University Press, 1971), p. 151.

27. See Geoffrey Pearson, *The Deviant Imagination*, (London: Macmillan, 1975), pp. 149-76 for an analysis of this type of nineteenth-century social-control imagery.

28. Besides *Discipline and Punish* itself, see also the interview with Foucault, 'Questions on Geography', in C. Gordon (ed.), *Power/Knowledge: Selected Interviews and Other Writings By Michel Foucault, 1972—1979*, (Brighton: Harvester Press, 1980), pp. 63-77.

29. Mumford, 'Utopia, the City and the Machine', pp. 17-22.

30. David Matza, *Becoming Deviant*, (Englewood Cliffs NJ: Prentice Hall, 1969); see especially pp. 45-9 on 'The Chicago Dilemma'. Matza's exegesis of the Chicago School and functionalism is essential to understand the theoretical basis of deviance and Controltalk.

31. Howard S. Becker (ed.), *Culture and Civility in San Francisco*, (Chicago: Aldine, 1971).

32. The most important exceptions in criminology are Nils Christie's vision of a 'pain-reduced' society (which I discuss in chapter 7) and the Marxist vision of a 'crime-free' society. In general political thinking, the anarchist tradition has been the only one consistently interested in linking crime control to visions of the good society. On the pragmatics of his tradition, see Colin Ward, *Anarchy in Action*, (London: Allen and Unwin, 1973) for a much too idealistic account, see L. Tift and D. Sullivan, *The Struggle to be Human: Crime, Criminology and Anarchism*, (Orkney: Cienfuegos Press, 1980).

33. For an introductory collection of visions of the future city by planners and social scientists, see Andrew Blowers *et al.* (eds), *The Future of Cities*, (London: Hutchinson, 1974).

34. Jencks deals with these criticisms and paradoxes in terms of the 'multi-valence' of Le Corbusier's work. See Charles Jencks, *Modern Movements in Architecture*, (Harmondsworth: Penguin, 1973), pp. 14-19, 24-26 and chapter 4.

35. Stephen Gardiner, *Le Corbusier*, (London: Fontana, 1974), especially pp. 111-20.

36. Two good collections of such science-fiction visions produced in the sixties and seventies, are Roger Elwood (ed.), *Future City*, (New York: Pocket Books, 1974), and Ralph Clem *et al.* (eds), *The City 2000 A.D: Urban Life Through Science Fiction*, (Greenwich: Fawcett, 1976).

37. *To Establish Justice, to Ensure Domestic Tranquility. Final Report of the National Commission on the Causes and Prevention of Violence* (Washington DC: US Government Printing Office, 1969), p. 46.

38. For example, Shlomo Angel, *Discouraging Crime Through City Planning*, (Berkeley: Institute of Urban and Regional Development, 1968); Richard A. Gardner, *Design for Safe Neighbourhoods: The Environmental Security Planning and Design Process*, (Washington DC: LEAA, September 1978); and Clarence R. Jeffrey, *Crime Prevention Through Environmental Design*, (California: Sage, 1977). The actual results of CPED projects are usefully reviewed in Charles A. Murray, 'The Physical Environment and the Community Control of Crime', in James Q Wilson (ed.), *Crime and Public Policy*, (San Francisco: ICS Press, 1983), pp. 107-24.

39. Gardner, *Design for Safe Neighbourhoods*, pp. 11-17.

40. Oscar Newman, *Defensible Space: Crime Prevention through Urban Design*, (New York: Macmillan, 1972), *Architectural Design For Crime Prevention*, (Washington DC: US Government Printing Office, 1973), *Design Guidelines For Creating Defensible Space*, (Washington DC: LEAA, 1975) and *Community of Interest*, (New York: Anchor Press, 1980).

41. Murray, 'The Physical Environment and the Community Control of Crime'.

42. Jane Jacobs, *The Death and Life of Great American Cities*, (New York: Vintage Books, 1961).

43. Jencks, *Modern Movements in Architecture*, pp. 245 and 299-303.

44. Richard Sennet, *The Uses of Disorder: Personal Identity and City Life*, (New York: Alfred Knopf, 1970).

45. *Ibid.*, p. 98.

46. Richard Sennet, 'Destructive Gemeinschaft', in N. Birnbaum (ed.), *Beyond The Crisis*, (New York: Oxford University Press, 1977), pp. 171-97, and *The Fall of Public Man*, (London: Oxford University Press, 1978). Note also the complementary argument in Lasch's writing on the family.

47. Claude Levi-Strauss, *Tristes Tropiques*, (Harmondsworth: Penguin, 1977) p. 508.

48. Valenstein nicely describes contemporary visions of thought control as 'modern phrenology based on the belief that the brain is organized into neat functional compartments that conform to our social needs'. See Elliot Valenstein, *Brain Control: A Critical Evaluation of Brain Stimulation and Psychosurgery*, (New York: John Wiley, 1976), pp. 350-1.

49. Judith Wilks and Robert Martinson, 'Is the Treatment of Criminal Offenders Really Necessary?', *Federal Probation*, 40, 1 (March 1976), pp. 3-9.

50. Hugo Davenport and William Scobie, 'Bleeper Could Cut Jail Numbers', *The Observer*, 10 April 1983. On the original Albuquerque experiment, see 'Wearing A Jail Cell Around Your Ankle', *Newsweek*, 21 March 1983.

51. I am grateful to Barbara Hudson for drawing my attention to this comparison.

52. Note, though, Alfred Bester's solution in *The Demolished Man*: the control system overall is exclusionary, but experts trained in extra-sensory perception ('espers') can detect (and therefore prevent) any hint of deviant thoughts or intentions in another person's mind. See Alfred Bester, *The Demolished Man*, (Harmondsworth: Penguin, 1966).

53. George Sternlieb, 'The City as Sandbox', *The Public Interest*, 25 (Fall 1971), pp. 14-21.

54. Norton E. Long, 'The City as Reservation', *The Public Interest*, 25 (Fall 1971), pp. 22-38.

55. Richard Child Hill, 'Fiscal Collapse and Political Struggle in Decaying Central Cities in the United States', in W. K. Tabb and L. Sawers (eds), *Marxism and the Metropolis: New Perspectives in Urban Political Economy*, (New York: Oxford University Press, 1979), pp. 213-40.

56. For a recent summary, see Roger Friedland, *Power and Crisis in the City*, (London: Macmillan, 1982).

57. Andrew Scull, *Decarceration: Community Treatment and the Deviant*, (Englewood Cliffs NJ: Prentice Hall, 1977), pp. 1-2.

58. Sykes, *The Future of Crime*, p. 18.

59. James Finlayson, *Urban Devastation: The Planning of Incarceration*, (Solidarity Pamphlet, no date).

60. *Ibid.*, p. 21.

61. For examples, see Elwood (ed.) *Future City*, and Clem (ed.), *The City, 2000 AD*.

62. Barry Malzberg, *The Destruction of the Temple*, (London: New English Library, 1975). Part of this story appears also as 'City Lights, City Nights' under Malzberg's pen name, K. M. O'Donnell, in Elwood (ed.), *Future City*.

63. Robert Silverberg, 'Black is Beautiful', in Clem (ed.), *The City, 2000 AD*.

64. Robert Silverberg, *The World Outside*, (London: Granada, 1978).

65. Oscar Newman, 'Defensible Space', in *Policy Development Seminar on Architecture, Design and Criminal Justice*, (Washington DC: LEAA, 1975), p. 52. Note Newman's alternative: 'dispersing the ghettoes' — moving 'the core of the crime problem' into other areas by mixing in a quota of 20-30 per cent of low-income families.

66. William Ryan, *Blaming the Victim*, (New York: Random House, 1976), pp. 336.

67. Ivan Illich, *Limits to Medicine*, (Harmondsworth: Penguin, 1977), pp. 85-96.

68. Joel Kovol, 'Therapy in Late Capitalism', *Telos*, 30 (Winter 1976-77), pp. 73-92.

69. In the Urbmon of 2381 when your threshold for 'thwarting acceptance' begins to dip, you turn yourself in to 'consolers' or 'blessmen', moral engineers who help you adjust to reality. You must do this before things get really uncontrollable, which leads to countersocial behaviour — which means 'down the chute': Silverberg, *The World Inside*.

70. See Russel Eisenman, 'Scapegoating as Social Control', *Journal of Psychology*, 61 (1965), pp. 203-9.

71. See Harold Garfinkel, 'Conditions of Successful Degradation Ceremonies', *American Journal of Sociology*, LXI (March 1956), pp. 420-24.

72. This type of cybernetic language is used by Tony Tanner to describe how Burroughs (and similar modern writers) deal with the fear of entropy and chaos. See Tony Tanner, *City of Words: American Fiction 1950-1970* (London: Jonathan Cape, 1971), especially chapters 5 and 6.

73. B. F. Skinner, *Beyond Freedom and Dignity*, (London: Jonathan Cape, 1972), p. 177.

74. William Burroughs, *The Naked Lunch*, (London: Calder, 1959), p. 164.

364
Soc

The sociology of
crime and deviance.

DATE			